The New York Times

Guide to

New York City

2003

The New York Times
New York, New York

Please send all comments to:
The New York Times Guide to New York City
122 E. 42nd St., 14th Floor
New York, NY 10168

Published by:
The New York Times
229 W. 43rd St.
New York, NY 10036

ISBN 1-930881-06-1
First Printing 2002
10 9 8 7 6 5 4 3 2 1

For the *New York Times*: Mitchel Levitas, Editorial Director, Book Development;
Thomas K. Carley, President, News Services Division; Nancy Lee, Director of Business
Development.

Correspondents for the *Times*: Randy Archibold, James Barron, Ben Brantley, Barbara Cros-
sette, David W. Dunlap, Leslie Eaton, Grace Glueck, Abby Goodnough, Laurel Graeber,
Clyde Haberman, Anemona Hartocollis, Amanda Hesser, Stephen Holden, Bernard Holland,
Leslie Kaufman, Randy Kennedy, Michael Kimmelman, Anna Kisselgoff, Douglas Martin,
Herbert Muschamp, Robin Pogrebin, Frank Prial, Rita Reif, Tracie Rozhon, Susan Sachs,
Roberta Smith, Jennifer Steinhauer, Anthony Tommasini, Amy Waldman, Claire Wilson.

Maps: Charles Blow, Natasha Perkel

Prepared by Elizabeth Publishing: *General Editor:* John W. Wright.
Senior Editors and Writers: Alice Finer, Alan Joyce, Cheryl Farr Leas, Lisa Renaud.
Writers: Kurt Hettler, Jerold Kappes, Gloria Levitas, Elda Rotor.

Design and Production: G&H SOHO, Inc., Hoboken, N.J.: Jim Harris, Gerry Burstein,
Mary Jo Rhodes, Christina Viera, Kathie Kounouklos.

Cover Design: Barbara Chilenskas, Bishop Books

Distributed by St. Martin's Press

Table of Contents

PHOTOS

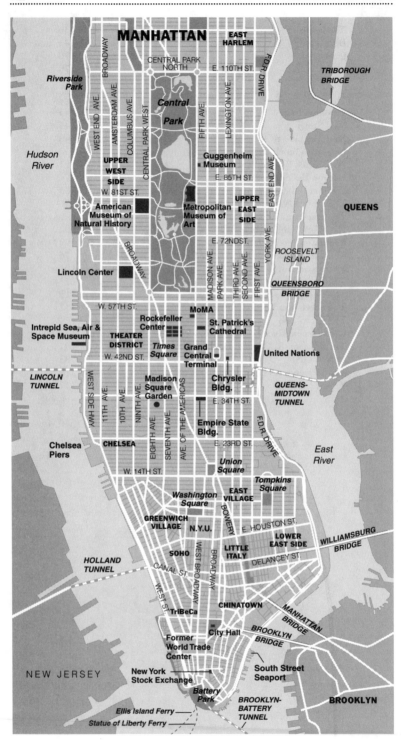

Manhattan Highlights

Visiting New York

GETTING THERE
By Car

It's not a great idea to bring a car into Manhattan: traffic is horrendous; street parking is tough to find; and garages charge astronomical fees. If you really must drive to Manhattan, plan to put your car in a garage and keep it there until you're ready to leave. Call your hotel beforehand to inquire about parking fees; private garages may be cheaper.

Directions from the South and West: From the New Jersey Turnpike (I-95) to Midtown Manhattan, take exit 16E to the Lincoln Tunnel, which will bring you to 42nd St. and Ninth Ave. To get downtown, go to exit 15W and take the Holland Tunnel, which will leave you on or near Canal St. You can also use exit 13 and take the Goethals Bridge onto the Staten Island Expressway, which goes to the Verrazano Bridge. From here, follow the signs to the Shore Parkway to the Gowanus Expressway to the Brooklyn Battery Tunnel, which will bring you downtown.

Directions from the West: I-80 is the major highway leading to the George Washington Bridge, which will take you onto the Cross Bronx Expressway unless you exit almost immediately. For the east side of Manhattan, look for the exit to the Harlem River Drive (this leads to the FDR Drive). For the west side, take the Henry Hudson Parkway or Riverside Drive (south).

Directions from the North: The New York State Thruway (I-87) becomes the Major Deegan Expressway as you enter the Bronx. If you wish to go to Manhattan's west side, exit at the Cross Bronx Expressway (west) and quickly exit at the Henry Hudson Parkway (south); this turns into West Street (usually called the West Side Highway). If you want the east side of Manhattan, stay on 87, go past Yankee Stadium to the Third Ave. Bridge, or a little farther to the Triborough Bridge. Both lead to the FDR Drive.

Directions from New England: Take I-95 to the Bruckner Expressway (I-278) to the Triborough Bridge to the FDR Drive (for the east side); for the west side take the Bruckner to the Cross Bronx Expressway (west) to the Henry Hudson Parkway.

By Train or Bus

Major Terminals

Grand Central Terminal
42nd St. at Park Ave.
www.grandcentralterminal.com
Schedules: (212) 532-4900

Penn Station
32nd St. at Seventh Ave.

Port Authority Bus Terminal
Between Eighth and Ninth Aves., 40th to 42nd St.
Schedules: (212) 564-8484

Rail Lines

Amtrak
www.amtrak.com
Arrivals and departures at Penn Station
Major areas served: In addition to service from Florida and nationwide, there
are frequent trains from Washington, D.C. and Boston—including the new
high-speed (extra fare) Acela.
Phone: (800) 872-7245

Long Island Rail Road (LIRR)
www.mta.nyc.ny.us/lirr
Arrivals and departures at Manhattan's Penn Station, Jamaica Center Station
in Queens and Brooklyn's Flatbush Avenue Station
Major areas served: Points throughout Long Island
Phone: (718) 217-LIRR (5477), (718) 558-3022 (TTY), (516) 822-LIRR
(5477) or (516) 231-LIRR (5477)

Metro North
www.mta.nyc.ny.us/mnr
Arrivals and departures at Grand Central Terminal and 125th Street Station (all
lines); Fordham (Fordham Rd. at Webster Ave.—New Haven and Harlem lines
only); other stations in the Bronx serve individual lines.
Major areas served: Westchester, Putnam and Dutchess Counties in New York
State; Fairfield and New Haven Counties in Connecticut with connections to
the rest of the state.
Phone: (212) 532-4900), (800) METRO-INFO, (800) 724-3322 (TTY)

New Jersey Transit
www.njtransit.state.nj.us
Arrivals and departures at Penn Station
Major areas served: Points throughout New Jersey, including Atlantic City;
Philadelphia
Phone: (800) 626-7433, (973) 762-5100

Bus Lines

Greyhound
www.greyhound.com
Arrivals and departures at Port Authority (Eighth Ave. at W. 42nd St.) and Queens Village (219–17 Hillside Ave.)
Major areas served: United States (points throughout the country); Canada; Mexico
Phone: (800) 231-2222

Peter Pan Trailways
www.peterpan-bus.com
Arrivals and departures at Port Authority (Eighth Ave. at W. 42nd St.)
Major areas served: Points between Boston and Washington, D.C., including all of New England.
Phone: (800) 343-9999

Regional Buses
Arrivals and departures at Port Authority (Eighth Ave. at W. 42nd St.)
Phone: (212) 564-8484

New Jersey Transit
www.njtransit.state.nj.us
Arrivals and departures at Port Authority (Eighth Ave. at W. 42nd St.) and George Washington Bridge Bus Station (at 179th St., between Broadway and Ft. Washington Ave.)
Major areas served: Points throughout New Jersey, including Atlantic City and the Jersey Shore; Philadelphia; Wilmington, Delaware and Washington, D.C.
Phone: (800) 626-7433, (973) 762-5100

MTA Long Island
www.mta.nyc.ny.us/libus
Arrivals and departures at Flushing (Main St. and Roosevelt Ave.) and Jamaica Center, 179th St. (at Hillside Ave., Jamaica)
Major areas served: Points in Nassau and Suffolk Counties, including Jones Beach, Roosevelt Field and Walt Whitman Mall.
Note: Free transfer with MetroCard
Phone: (516) 766-6722, (516) 228-4000 (Paratransit)

Hampton Jitney
www.hamptonjitney.com
Arrivals and departures at 86th St. (between Lexington and Third Aves); 69th St. (at Lexington Ave.); 59th St. (at Lexington Ave); and 40th St. (between Lexington and Third Aves.)
Major areas served: Points between Manhattan and Montauk, including the Hamptons.
Phone: (800) 936-0440, (516) 283-4600

By Plane

New York City has three major airports: John F. Kennedy International Airport in Queens (about an hour's drive from Midtown), La Guardia Airport in Queens (about a half hour drive from Midtown), and Newark International Airport in New Jersey (about a 45-minute drive from Midtown). Information about the airports, including ground transportation options, is available at *www.panynj.gov*.

Almost every major carrier serves at least one of these airports; many serve two or all three New York airports, so it's worth your while to compare fares. (At present, the nation's two most popular discount airlines, Southwest and Jet-Blue, have not made inroads at all three airports. JetBlue has limited flights in and out of JFK; Southwest has service only into MacArthur Airport on Long Island.)

Getting into the City from the Airports

By Taxi

Once you arrive, the easiest option is to hop into a cab. Each airport has a taxi stand with uniformed dispatchers, and lines tend to move quickly. Fares do not include tolls and tips. From La Guardia to Midtown, expect to pay $18–$25. From JFK, there's a flat fare of $35 from the airport to anywhere in Manhattan (the flat-fare structure does not apply when going from Manhattan back to JFK). From Newark, you cannot get a New York yellow cab; the dispatcher will give you a written slip with the fare based on your destination. It'll usually run $32 to $40.

By Car Service

Private car and limousine services offer door-to-door service from the airports to your destination. They are slightly more expensive than taxis, and service can be uneven, but they allow you to avoid taxi-stand lines. Since they operate with flat fares, you don't have to worry that your taxi meter is ticking ever upward in rush-hour traffic. (Taxis always make sense from JFK, which has a flat-fare structure for yellow cabs.) Call 24 hours in advance, and choose from indoor pickup (more expensive, since you have to pay for parking) or curbside pickup (you'll call the service as soon as you land, then wait for about 10 minutes for your car). You can usually pay by credit card when you reserve. You can also reserve pickup at your door when you're ready to return to the airport.

Among the major car services are Allstate (212-333-3333), Carmel (212-666-6666), Legends (888-LEGENDS) and Tel-Aviv (212-777-7777).

By Airtrain from Newark

From Newark International Airport, you can take a cheap and efficient new service called the **Airtrain** (*www.airtrainnewark.com*) to get into Manhattan. Take the Airtrain Newark from the terminal to the new Rail Link station, where you can connect to New Jersey Transit rail service to Penn Station. Service runs every five to seven minutes; the fare is $11.55. Travel time is 20 minutes.

By Van or Shuttle Bus

Super Shuttle (800-BLUE-VAN or 212-258-3826; *www.supershuttle.com*) offers service from all three airports, dropping you off at the door of your destination. Vans run every 15 to 30 minutes around the clock and do not require reservations; just go to the ground-transportation desk or use the courtesy phone in the baggage claim area. When you're ready to return to the airport, you do need to make a reservation a day or two in advance. Fares run $13–$22 per person, depending on the airport and your destination.

New York Airport Service (718-875-8200; *www.nyairportservice.com*) provides van service every half hour from JFK and La Guardia to Grand Central, the Port Authority, Penn Station and select Midtown hotels. The fare is $10 from La Guardia to Manhattan ($12 for specific hotel drop-off), $13 from JFK to Manhattan ($15 for hotel drop-off).

Olympia Airport Express (877-894-9155 or 212-964-6233; *www.olympiabus.com*) provides frequent motorcoach service from Newark Airport to Manhattan (stopping at Penn Station, the Port Authority and Grand Central). The fare from the airport to Manhattan is $11 to $14.50, depending on your destination (discounts are available for seniors and disabled passengers). For an extra $5, you can transfer at Grand Central to a Midtown shuttle van, which serves select hotels.

If you use a van or bus service for your return trip to the airport, be sure to allow lots of time before your departure in case traffic is bad.

By Public Transportation

Public transportation options from the New York–area airports are poor; they all involve lengthy travel time and multiple transfers. The only option worth recommending is available from JFK (and even this one is a 90-minute hassle, only for those with time to spare and an extremely tight budget). From the JFK terminal, take a free shuttle bus (which says "Long-Term Parking") to the Howard Beach station. From here, you can get the A subway train to Manhattan. For more information call the M.T.A. at (718) 330-1234.

VISITOR INFORMATION

New York has lots of resources to help you find your way and plan your time. There are two visitor information centers in Midtown West. Both have bus and subway maps, and much more.

Before you leave home, contact the **New York Convention & Visitors Bureau** at (800) NYC-VISIT or (212) 397-8222 (*www.nycvisit.com)* to order the bureau's Official NYC Visitor Kit. It includes a pocket-size guide to New

York, a fold-out map, a newsletter about upcoming events and brochures from various New York attractions. It's $9.95 for rush delivery, $5.95 for non-rush or free for the city guide only. To speak to a travel specialist with specific questions, call (212) 484-1222.

New York Today, *The New York Times'* online service (*www.nytoday.com*), offers a wealth of information about New York City events, arts and entertainment, restaurants, shopping, sports, news, weather, traffic conditions and special events. The site is updated daily, giving users access to the latest information. Features of the site include the **Around Town** section, with overviews, attractions and current events listings for specific neighborhoods in all five boroughs; comprehensive, searchable databases of *New York Times* restaurant, hotel and movie reviews; and *newyork.urbanbaby.com,* with helpful information on living in or visiting New York with children. **Note:** Visitors with some brands of hand-held computers can also download **Vindigo** (*www.vindigo.com*), which gives users access to descriptions and walking directions for thousands of restaurants, bars and stores, plus current movie listings and showtimes, all drawn from New York Today's online database.

The Times Square Visitors Center
1560 Broadway (between 46th and 47th Sts.) (212) 869-1890. The center has an information desk where help is available in five languages. You'll also find racks and racks of brochures and discount coupons; an MTA booth selling MetroCards and offering maps and information; a row of computer terminals where you can spend 10 free minutes on the Internet; an out-of-town newspaper stand; a New York City souvenir shop; a full-price theater ticket desk; a sightseeing desk selling Circle Line cruises and Gray Line bus tours; ATMs and currency exchange machines; and clean bathrooms. The center is open daily from 8 A.M. to 8 P.M.

New York City & Co.
810 Seventh Ave. (between 52nd and 53rd Sts.) (212) 484-1222 or (800) 692-8474. This center, operated by the New York Convention and Visitors Bureau, has an information desk with a multilingual staff. Touch-screen terminals offer information on events and attractions (you can also use them to buy tickets to attractions, saving yourself a wait on line). You'll also find racks of brochures, an ATM, a MetroCard machine, a one-hour photo developer and discount coupons.

GETTING AROUND

Subways and buses are run by the **Metropolitan Transportation Authority (MTA),** which has a 24-hour Travel Information Center offering directions by telephone at (718) 330-1234. The Web site, *www.mta.nyc.ny.us,* has extensive information, including maps and service updates. Subway stations and cars have subway maps, too; some buses have bus maps.

Useful Web Sites

www.nyc.gov
Official New York City Web site

www.mta.nyc.ny.us
Official site of the Metropolitan Transit Authority, with info on subways,
buses, MetroCards and trips out of town

www.nycvisit.com
Web site of the New York City Convention and Visitors Bureau

www.aaccessmaps.com/show/map/us/ny/nyc_area_hwy
www.cmap.nypirg.org/webmaps/MyGovernmentNYC.htm
For detailed local maps

www.nytoday.com	*www.newyork.citysearch.com*
www.timeoutny.com	*www.metronewyork.com*
www.villagevoice.com	*www.newyorker.com*

For arts and entertainment, restaurant reviews, shopping, sports, news,
weather, info on city activities and events, and more.

There are three modes of transportation to get you around the city—not
counting your own two feet, which is really the best way to go.

1. Subways are usually the fastest way to get you where you're going, which is
why they're the preferred mode of transit for New Yorkers themselves. The subway is relatively safe, but you should always be alert to what is going on around
you. There's a massive crush of people during morning and evening rush hours,
but trains run frequently. A $1.50 fare will take you to the far ends of the city,
although there are rumblings that a fare increase is in the works. (*See section*
"MetroCards" *in this chapter for best fare deals.*)

2. Buses are much, much slower than subways, but they have advantages.
There are no stairs to climb and no sweltering underground platforms in summer. They also offer many more alternatives for going crosstown than the subway. Buses also allow you to take in the street scene as you go. As with subways,
the fare is $1.50.

3. Taxis are convenient, and they're better than buses at weaving through traffic. (Don't even try to take a cab in Midtown during rush hour or right before
theater curtains rise.) There are taxi stands at the airports, at major hotels, and
at Penn Station, Grand Central Terminal and the Port Authority Bus Terminal.
Otherwise, taxis cruise the streets, looking for customers. See the section on
taxis below for further tips.

Yellow cabs are regulated by the city, which makes them a safer bet than unmarked gypsy cabs. The gypsies usually charge lower fares, but may fleece the unsuspecting. Only yellow cabs can legally pick up passengers on the street.

There are also dozens of Limousine services (*see section* "Limousine and Car Services" *in this chapter*), which are usually more expensive than yellow cabs. You must call ahead to schedule service.

The Subway System

The New York subway system may be one of the oldest in the world, but it is also one of the most efficient. It runs 24 hours a day, 365 days a year and covers every area of the city except Staten Island. There are over 722 miles of track and 469 stations.

While it's true that parts of the subway are run down, and the screeching noise from older trains can cause jangled nerves, one look at the traffic jams in Midtown and at the bridges and tunnels will tell you why millions of New Yorkers ride the subway every day.

Manhattan
West Side: served by the A, B, C, D, 1, 2, 3 and 9 trains. The A, 2 and 3 are express lines. The C, 1 and 9 are local trains, which stop more frequently. E, F and V lines run local north–south service south of 50th St., then head east for crosstown stops on 53rd. The N and R run north–south below 57th St., then head east for crosstown stops on 60th St.

See the Note below about service changes.

East Side: served by the 4, 5 and 6 trains. Trains run along Lexington Ave. north of 42nd St., and along Park Ave. to the south. The 4 and 5 are express trains; the 6 is local. They all have interchanges with the E, F, N, R, the 42nd St. Shuttle (S) and the 7 line.

Bronx:
Served by the B, D, 1, 2, 4, 5, 6 and 9 trains.

Brooklyn:
Served by the A, C, F, G, M, Q, R, W, 2, 3, 4 and 5 trains.

Queens:
Served by the E, F, G, J, M, N, R, V, W, Z and 7 trains.

Notes: Because of construction, the B and D lines have been replaced by the Q and W lines, which make express stops in Manhattan along the N/R Broadway line to 57th Street. The B and D resume their normal routes from 34th uptown.

Since September 11, 2001, 9 service has been suspended; the 3 stops at 14th Street; and the 1 goes out to Brooklyn. But the 1, 2, 3 and 9 lines are scheduled to return to their normal routes; *www.mta.nyc.ny.us* will have the latest news.

Some Advice from the Natives About Subways

Subways are safe, but **be alert,** especially when you're packed tight on a crowded train. **Beware of pickpockets,** a crafty lot. Keep your hands on your purse and your wallet; don't leave valuables near the top of a backpack slung behind you. Don't wear flashy jewelry. At night, **don't ride in the last car,** which tends to be the emptiest and riskiest. If you're nervous, seek out the middle car, where the operator is positioned to open and close the doors. (In fact, subways run less frequently late at night, so it's best to take a cab when it's late.)

Take note of posted signs that tell you if trains will not be running or be re-routed (often on the weekends) because of construction. Loudspeaker announcements are almost always unintelligible. **Don't hesitate to ask someone for directions**—you'll be amazed at how New Yorkers like to show off their knowledge of the subway system.

The Metropolitan Transportation Authority has a 24-hour Travel Information Center, which you can call at (718) 330-1234, but it is not always completely informed about weekend service. It can, however, give directions. The MTA also posts weekly service notices on its Web site, *www.mta.nyc.ny.us.*

The Bus System

Very important: you **must** have a token, a MetroCard or $1.50 in coins when you board. The driver does not handle money. You pay your fare with coins or a token, or by dipping a MetroCard in the fare box. If you are paying cash and do not have the right coins, maybe you can find someone on the bus who can make change for your paper money or pay for you with his MetroCard and take your cash—if not, you'll have to get off.

City bus lines run the length and breadth of Manhattan. They are especially useful for getting across town (east–west). All routes within Manhattan begin with the letter M. Many of the crosstown routes have the same number as the street on which they cross. Traffic on the principal crosstown streets runs in both directions; all the rest are one-way. As a general rule, even-numbered streets are one-way from west to east, and odd-numbered streets run east to west.

Here are the crosstown routes:

M-8 runs on 8th and 9th Sts. from Avenue D and 10th St. to Christopher St.
M-14 operates on 14th St.
M-16 and **M-34** operate on 34th St.
M-23 operates on 23rd St.
M-27 and **M-50** operate on 49th St.; the **27** goes to Penn Station.
M-31 crosses 57th St., then up Madison Ave. and across E. 72nd St.

M-42 operates on 42nd St.

M-66 operates on E. 67th St. westbound and crosses Central Park at 66th St.; eastbound it operates on W. 65th St. until it crosses Central Park, then continues on E. 68th St.

M-72 operates on W. 72nd St. and E. 72nd St., crossing Central Park at 65th St. eastbound and 66th St. westbound.

M-79 operates on E. 79th St. east of Central Park and W. 81st St. west of the park.

M-86 operates on 86th St. and crosses Central Park on that street.

M-96 operates on 96th St. and crosses Central Park on that street.

M-106 operates on 106th St. east of Central Park, and 96th St. west of the park.

M-100, M-101 and **Bx-15** operate on 125th St.

M-116 runs across 116th St. to Manhattan Ave., then down to W. 106th St.

MetroCards

MetroCards are the smart way to pay your subway or bus fare. You can buy them in subway stations and at 3,000 other locations—newsstands, restaurants, hotels, pharmacies and wherever an orange-and-blue MetroCard sign is posted. Most subway stations have automated vending machines that will allow you to pay by credit or debit card.

A $4 the **"Funpass"** MetroCard permits unlimited rides on buses and subways for one day; they're a great deal if you'll be doing heavy sightseeing. Funpasses may be purchased from machines in subway stations—not from token clerks—and at both of the tourist information centers mentioned earlier in this chapter.

A $17 **weekly MetroCard** permits unlimited rides during the seven days after you first use it. A $63 **monthly card** permits unlimited rides for 30 days after the first use. Otherwise, you can **pay per ride** and put any value on the card that you choose (minimum of $3, or two rides). If you buy one for $15 (10 rides), you automatically get an 11th ride free. The readers on the turnstiles will tell you how much value you have left.

The use of a MetroCard is usually simple: just swipe it through the slot at a subway turnstile or dip it into a bus fare box. But sometimes a turnstile will tell you to swipe the card again . . . and again . . . and again. The key is to place the card all the way down in the slot, hold it firmly and run it all the way through quickly and smoothly. If all else fails, go to the token clerk, who should then let you through the "special entry" turnstile.

Transfers: A MetroCard permits transfers between subways and buses and vice versa, and between buses and buses, so long as you do not transfer to the same route you started on. After you use your card at the start of a trip, you have two hours to transfer to another route, not necessarily connecting with the first leg of your trip, at no extra charge. (The card "knows" when your two hours has expired.) Note: When you pay a bus fare with cash or a token the fare box will give you a transfer for another bus ride within two hours. It will not work for the subway.

Taxis

A taxi's roof light will tell you if it is available. Look for cabs with the center section lit. They are empty, looking for customers. If the center section is off and the two ends are lit, they say "OFF DUTY" and the driver is not interested in you. If the entire light is off, don't bother with frantic waving—the cab has a passenger. Unlike some other cities, cabs with passengers do not stop to pick up more. (Hailing taxis in the rain is maximum frustration. Consider some other way to go.) Taxis cannot pick up more than four passengers.

Hailing a cab: Just stick your arm out and all the way up, and don't be shy. Yell "taxi" if necessary—no one in New York will look strangely at you for yelling. Get off the sidewalk if there is a lot of traffic or if parked cars will prevent taxis from seeing you. Be watchful of cars and trucks swerving into the lane where you may be standing. Don't jump ahead of other passengers who were trying to hail a cab before you arrived.

Rules and Traditions: First of all, you should always remember that a New York taxi driver is *required* by law to take you anywhere within the city—even to the far ends of Brooklyn or Staten Island—as well as to Newark Airport and Westchester or Nassau Counties. Cabs are required to pick you up if you have a seeing-eye dog or are in a collapsible wheelchair. While some drivers have less-than-adequate English skills, most New Yorkers will tell you that they are far more courteous and respectful than drivers of earlier periods. Unfortunately, like their predecessors, the long hours and low pay often lead to aggressive and reckless driving, so:

- Buckle your seat belt.
- Tell the driver to slow down if you become fearful. Don't be afraid to insist that the driver refrain from using a cell phone.
- Take a fare receipt from the cab driver when you get out. It gives the trip number and the taxi's official medallion number—information you need if you want to make a complaint or trace something you may have left in the cab. It also shows the 24-hour consumer hotline, (212) NYC-TAXI.

Fares: Yellow cab fares start with an initial charge of $2. The fare rises by 30 cents for every 1/5 mile traveled, and by 20 cents for every 90 seconds in stopped or slow traffic. From 8 P.M. to 6 A.M., there is a surcharge of 50 cents per trip. The metered fare does not include a tip; add 10 to 15 percent.

Limousine and Car Services

There are dozens of limousine and car services, from long white Lincolns equipped with bars and TVs to regular sedans. They often cost more than taxis, but will come when you want them. You must call for them in advance. Among the major companies are **Tel Aviv** (212-777-7777), **Carmel** (212-666-6666), **Sabra** (212-777-7171) and **Allstate** (212-333-3333).

Tips on Tipping

Many visitors—as well as many long-time residents—are unclear on who should be tipped and how much. Below are some general guidelines. Visit *www.nyc.gov/consumers* for more information.

Restaurants: Tip the waiter 15 to 20 percent of the total bill before tax, according to quality of service. (Note: an easy way to calculate a reasonable tip in New York City is to double the 8.5 percent tax.) In more upscale restaurants that have a sommelier or wine steward, tip 8 to 10 percent of the cost of wine (cost of wine is subtracted from the bill when calculating the server's tip).

Some restaurants automatically add a gratuity for large parties (usually 15 to 20 percent for parties of eight or more). Customers should be informed in advance, but some restaurants are less forthcoming than others. Don't be shy about asking about this policy when dining with larger groups.

Hotels: *Shuttle bus driver:* $1. *Bellhop:* $2 per bag. *Maid:* $2 per person per night. *Room service:* 10 to 15 percent of the bill. *Bellman:* $2 for each visit to the room. *Parking attendant:* $2 or more.

Taxis: Compared with many other cities, New York's taxi charges are not out of line. We urge visitors to tip generously if the ride is satisfactory; drivers depend on tips to raise their pay to a decent level. Some rules of thumb: never tip less than $1. Tip $2 when the fare is over $6, $3 if over $10. For trips to the airports, tip $6 to $10, more if the driver helps with your luggage.

Beauty Salons: A beautician, barber or manicurist should receive anywhere from 10 to 20 percent of the cost of the service, depending on how long it takes and how labor-intensive. Never tip less than $2.

Exploring New York

New York reveals itself in fascinating ways to those visitors who take the time to walk its streets. No other American city is more inviting to explore on foot, more geared to the pedestrian rather than the car.

Only by walking can you begin to sense New York's trademark energy and drive, its swirl of cultures and its layers of history. You'll learn much more about New York by strolling its streets than you will from the top of a tour bus.

Because there is so much to see, you'll want to read this chapter carefully as you plan an intinerary. It's also a good idea to consult the chapter on **The Arts,** which has complete listings for all the top art museums, galleries and performing-arts institutions.

Street Smarts

Most first-time visitors have never experienced the hazardous traffic conditions found in New York. Cars, trucks, buses and aggressive bicycle messengers all compete for a favored place on the road; people on foot are seen as just another impediment to their halting progress through the city.

The traditional pedestrian's right of way is, as Shakespeare says, "more honored in the breach than the observance." So walk defensively: Assume that a taxi will run a red light, or a truck or van will turn rapidly into the crosswalk so he doesn't have to wait for all the pedestrians to cross.

You'll notice almost immediately that New Yorkers pay no attention whatsoever to "Walk" "Don't Walk" signs (it's that New York state of mind, the part that asks: why trust a sign? I have eyes!). But if you're new here, you should obey the signs for a few days, until you get the hang of crossing when it's safe.

Don't stand in the middle of the sidewalk while you are talking, studying a map or looking up at a tall building. Always step back toward the buildings. New Yorkers are an impatient lot, and they will shove right past you.

Crime Safety

New York's crime rate has shown a few disconcerting signs of inching upward again in this recent economic downturn, but nevertheless, the city is much safer now than it was in the 1980's and early 1990's. In terms of crime statistics, this is one of the safest big cities in America. Still, it's always smart to err on the side of caution. Here are some common-sense rules:

- Avoid desolate areas at night. Subways run infrequently late at night, and platforms may be a little creepy, so take a cab home after a late night out.
- Don't walk in Central Park at night unless there is a major event or you've attended a play at the Delacorte Theater.
- Keep your money in an inconspicuous place. Women should grasp their pocketbooks or wear them across the body; men should be sure a wad of

money is not bulging conspicuously in their pants pocket. Be conscious of keeping backpacks and purse zippers closed and within your view; bury your valuables at the very bottom of large bags, so pickpockets can't get at them without your noticing.

- Don't wear valuable necklaces that can be ripped off with ease.

Public Bathrooms

New York City is notorious for its lack of public bathrooms. Although there are always plans in the works to improve the situation, it hasn't happened yet. Here are a few places where you can find relief as you stroll around the city:

- Department stores
- Hotel lobbies
- Bryant Park (behind the Public Library on the 42nd St. side)
- Mid-Manhattan Library (across Fifth Ave. from the Public Library)
- Donnell Library (across 53rd St. from the currently closed Museum of Modern Art Midtown location)
- Grand Central Terminal
- Pennsylvania Station
- Port Authority Bus Terminal (well, don't expect it to pass the white glove test)
- Central Park Boathouse
- Coffee bars
- Barnes & Noble branches
- Visitor centers (Broadway between 46th and 47th Sts.; Seventh Ave. between 52nd and 53rd Sts.)

Finding Your Way

New York City is made up of five boroughs and stretches for 10 to 20 miles in several directions. If you can spend more than a few days in New York, by all means take the time to visit such wonderful places as the Bronx Zoo (especially if you've got kids in tow) or the Brooklyn Museum of Art. These are world-famous institutions and shouldn't be dismissed just by reason of location. You'll find complete descriptions of outer-borough highlights at the end of this chapter.

But the focal point for most leisure visitors is the island borough of Manhattan. As the accompanying maps make clear, Manhattan—or "the city," as many natives call it—is one of the easiest places in the world to visit. The island is only 13 1/2 miles long and 2 1/3 miles wide at the center (not even a mile at the southern tip). Here's a brief guide to its layout:

Avenues: run north to south. North is synonymous with "uptown"; south is "downtown." The higher the number in a building's street address, the further uptown it will be.

Streets: run east to west on the grid above 14th Street.

East Side-West Side: The dividing line is Fifth Avenue. All addresses on the east side of Fifth begin at 1 East; on the west side of Fifth they begin at 1 West. The higher the number in the address, the further east or west the location will be from Fifth Avenue (for example, 200 West 50th St. is farther west than 100 West 50th St.)

Streets are for the most part numbered consecutively and laid out in a grid. From 8th Street north to 181 Street (and beyond), you will always know where you are relative to, say, 42nd Street. South of 8th Street, in Manhattan's oldest neighborhoods, the streets have names and are not laid out according to any logical master plan. You'll need to a good map to navigate these areas.

Many (but not all) *avenues* (again, these run north–south) are also numbered. Starting at the East River, the East Side avenues, in order, are York, First, Second, Third, Lexington, Park, Madison and Fifth. After Fifth Avenue, which divides East Side from West Side, the West Side avenues are the Avenue of the Americas (more commonly referred to as Sixth Ave.), Seventh, Broadway (which cuts diagonally across the city, forming squares where it intersects with other avenues; it eventually crosses over to the East Side), Eighth, Ninth, 10th, 11th and 12th Avenues. Uptown (above Midtown, on the Upper West Side), the West Side avenues assume new names (Eighth Avenue becomes Central Park West; Ninth becomes Columbus Avenue; 10th becomes Amsterdam; 11th becomes West End Avenue; and 12th becomes Riverside Drive).

NEW YORK'S
TOP 25 ATTRACTIONS

American Museum of Natural History
Brooklyn Bridge
Bronx Zoo
Brooklyn Botanic Garden
Cathedral of St. John the Divine
Central Park
Chrysler Building
Ellis Island
Empire State Building
Grand Central Terminal
Guggenheim Museum
Lincoln Center
Metropolitan Museum of Art
Museum of Modern Art (currently MoMA QNS)
New York Botanical Garden (Bronx)
New York Public Library
Radio City Music Hall
Rockefeller Center
St. Patrick's Cathedral
Staten Island Ferry
Statue of Liberty

Times Square
United Nations
Whitney Museum of American Art
Yankee Stadium

SUGGESTED WALKING TOURS

Each of these walks can easily serve as a day's sightseeing itinerary. They link together many of Manhattan's top attractions, while offering you plenty of opportunity to go with the flow of New York's street life—shopping and noticing wonderful architectural details as you go.

Lower Manhattan

Lower Manhattan was the birthplace of New York City. It was first settled in the 17th century, when the Dutch founded the colony of Nieuw Amsterdam on the site of today's Financial District. It boasts a spectacular array of architecture, dense canyons of neo-classic temples and soaring skyscrapers.

Tragedy forever marked this neighborhood, of course, on September 11, 2001. Our walk will take in many historic streets where life carries on just as before, but we'll also stop at the site of the fallen towers, where so many visitors feel compelled to pay their respects in person.

Those of you with a surfeit of time and energy should start out by taking the A or C train to High Street in Brooklyn and hoofing it back into Manhattan. There's no more beautiful walk in New York than the stroll along the wooden pedestrian path of the **Brooklyn Bridge,** where the skyline views are still magnificent, if sadly changed now. The Brooklyn Bridge remains a marvel of engineering. Its soaring Gothic support towers stand tall as a monument to modern New York's ingenuity and ambition.

If the 30-minute bridge crossing has left you hungry, you can turn right (north) once you've arrived in Manhattan. You're on the edge of **Chinatown,** which offers a huge array of dining options. You can also turn south toward **South Street Seaport,** which offers everything from an authentic British pub to sit-down seafood meals.

Those of you without the energy to walk the Brooklyn Bridge, can join in at at the foot of **City Hall Park.** Branching to your right is Park Row, where Greeley, Pulitzer, Hearst, Ochs and other newspaper titans held forth for most of the 19th and some of the 20th century. No. 41 was the original *New York Times* building, now part of Pace University.

City Hall itself, housing the offices of the mayor and the city council, is an elegant Georgian and French Renaissance-style marble building built in 1803. It presides over the northern edge of elegantly manicured City Hall Park. On the northern edge of the park stands **Tweed Courthouse,** a magnificent structure built in the 1870's by "Boss" Tweed, who pilfered public construction funds on a massive scale (his plasterwork contractor was paid over $45,000 for a single day's work!). Stroll across the park, admiring its lovely gardens, until you emerge on Broadway.

On Broadway at Park Place, Cass Gilbert's opulent **Woolworth Building** rises in Gothic splendor, complete with gargoyles, spires, lacy stonework and flying buttresses. The structure reigned for a while as the tallest building in the world when it opened in 1913. Be sure to peek inside the sumptuous lobby, with its vaulted ceiling of blue and gold mosaics; don't miss the architect's jest, a whimsical carving of Woolworth counting his nickels and dimes.

Continue south on Broadway. Just past Vesey Street, you'll see historic **St. Paul's Chapel,** New York's only intact pre-Revolutionary church. George Washington worshiped here on the day of his inauguration in 1789, and continued to attend during the months when New York was the capital. His pew is to the right as you enter. More recently, St. Paul's served as a place of rest and refuge for the rescue workers of Ground Zero. For months after the attacks, the fences along the churchyard were covered with makeshift memorials and tributes left by visitors from all over the world.

Now you've arrived at **Ground Zero** itself, the site of the fallen Twin Towers. There is not much left to see—it's a vast construction pit now—but the emptiness speaks volumes. As of this writing, there are viewing platforms at Liberty Street. You can also wander around the perimeter of the site, along Broadway and Vesey, Liberty and West Streets, noticing the protective sheeting that hangs like widow's veils over the damaged buildings that still stand nearby. The streets immediately surrounding the Trade Center have become an odd mixture of sincere grief and tourism; some people come to say a prayer or lay flowers, while vendors sell tacky Ground Zero baseball caps.

Head back to Church Street and take it south for a few blocks to Wall Street, where you'll turn left. At the corner of Broadway and Wall Street stands **Trinity Church.** The first Trinity Church was the tallest structure in the city when it was built in 1697, but it was destroyed in the great fire that leveled much of downtown New York in 1776. A map inside the church, behind the last pews on the left, shows where Alexander Hamilton, Robert Fulton and others are buried in the church's historic graveyard.

Directly across Broadway at 1 Wall Street is the **Bank of New York** with an eye-popping Art Deco lobby of red and gold mosaic.

Wall Street itself is a surprisingly narrow little lane, but it's lined with appropriately powerful neoclassical towers. The **New York Stock Exchange** is located at 20 Broad St., between Wall Street and Exchange Place. Once open for tours, the Exchange has been guarded and cordoned off since the 9/11 attacks (it may reopen to tours during the lifetime of this edition). Nevertheless, the exterior of this 1903 Beaux Arts temple is pretty impressive, with massive Corinthian columns and an allegorical pediment sculpture titled *Integrity Protecting the Works of Man* (insert your own Worldcom joke here).

Diagonally across from the Exchange stands **Federal Hall National Memorial.** George Washington was sworn in as the first president of the United States on the steps of an earlier building on this site in 1789. Also at Federal Hall,

John Peter Zenger was acquitted of seditious libel in 1735, giving birth to the concept of freedom of the press. Exhibits inside illuminate the role of Lower Manhattan in the nation's early history.

Make your way back to Broadway and start heading south. This is the famous **"Canyon of Heroes,"** the setting for celebratory ticker-tape parades, which have been held throughout the past century to honor war heroes, astronauts and victorious Yankee squads. At no. 28 stands the **Museum of American Financial History,** worth a quick stop if Stock Exchange tours have not resumed when you visit.

At the end of Broadway is a tiny green space, **Bowling Green Park,** which claims to be the very spot where Peter Minuit purchased Manhattan Island from a band of Indians for $24, in the very first New York real estate swindle on record. In colonial times, the park featured a gilded equestrian statue of King George III, but it was toppled by a mob in 1776 when the colonies were in revolt. Here you'll also see the famous "Charging Bull" statue, a symbol of Wall Street optimism (you might want to take your picture with it if you're feeling good about your portfolio).

Below Bowling Green Park is a gorgeous 1907 Beaux Arts building designed by Cass Gilbert. Once the U.S. Customs House, it now houses the **National Museum of the American Indian,** a branch of the Smithsonian. The enormous sculptures out front were the work of Daniel Chester French; they represent Asia, America, Europe and Africa.

No. 1 Broadway is the building with blue awnings across the street. One entrance says "Cabin Class," and the other "First Class." Now a Citibank branch, this was where travelers of an earlier day booked passage on the United States Lines. The bank has preserved the hall as it was, a grand space befitting a great steamship company.

Now continue south into leafy **Battery Park,** the perfect place to relax and enjoy the breezes and the views, which extend out to the **Statue of Liberty,** holding her torch over New York Harbor. You can catch a ferry here if you'd like to sail out to the statue or to Ellis Island, which features riveting exhibits on the immigrant experience.

You can also opt to rest your weary feet by enjoying a picnic in the park, before mustering up the energy to visit the moving **Museum of Jewish Heritage—A Living Memorial to the Holocaust.** It stands just north of Battery Place, where the park meets the southern edge of the upscale but sterile residential neighborhood known as Battery Park City.

Greenwich Village

Greenwich Village long ago earned a reputation as a magnet for bohemians and intellectuals. Generations of artists and writers—Henry James and Edgar Allan Poe, Jackson Pollack and e.e. cummings—gave the neighborhood its freewheeling identity, and radical thinkers from Upton Sinclair to John Reed have held forth in smoky Village cafes.

But it's been many years since starving artists were able to afford these rents. While the neighborhood does retain a definite live-and-let-live, left-of-center vibe, it's gone upscale these days. The really cutting-edge art scene has long since fled to Chelsea, the East Village, Brooklyn and Queens.

Nevertheless, the Village remains one of New York's most appealing neighborhoods, and an especially lovely place to stroll. Leafy streets, lined with Federal-style town houses and ivy-covered brownstones, meander at will, defying the symmetrical street grid pattern that brings order to the world above 14th Street. (Bring along a good map so you'll be able to wander without getting hopelessly lost.) Neighborhood residents remain loyal to the local organic bakery and the corner produce market. Funky craft stores, artsy boutiques and sidewalk cafes refuse to give way to Pottery Barns and Starbucks. It's a neighborhood on a very human scale, with small delights around every corner.

Start your stroll by taking the A, C or E train to Eighth Avenue and 14th Street, the Village's northern border. Head south along Eighth Avenue until you reach **Bleecker Street,** branching off toward your left. Now stroll along Bleecker, which will give you a good snapshot of the neighborhood. The three blocks between Bank Street and Charles Street offer terrific shopping, with a good concentration of antiques dealers, plus funky and affordable purses, jewelry, candles, cigars and more. You'll pass the chic **Marc Jacobs** boutique; **Les Pierre Antiques,** for upscale French Country pieces; **Kim's Music and Video, Rebel Rebel** and **Bleecker Bob's** for a great selection of used CDs; **Details,** for fun, colorful housewares and gifts; and **Condomania,** which sells a wider variety of condoms than you're likely to need during your stay in New York.

Bleecker intersects with **Christopher Street,** where you can veer off for more shopping. This is the heart of New York's gay community—the Gay Liberation Movement was born here during the famed Stonewall Rebellion of 1969—so many shops cater to a gay and lesbian clientele.

One block beyond Christopher is **Grove Street,** where you'll turn right. Walk one more block to the intersection of Grove and Bedford. At the corner of Bedford and Grove stands a picturesque **wood-frame house;** sections of it date back to the early 19th century. Nearby, notice the house at **102 Bedford St.** with an odd chalet-style curved cornice. The very antithesis of gritty radical bohemia, Walt Disney himself, once lived here. Continue along Grove Street, and peek into the charming **private courtyard** between nos. 10 and 12 Grove St.

Now head a few steps south of Grove Street on Bedford Street. At no. 86 is the unheralded entrance to **Chumley's** (purposefully made unobtrusive to throw off the cops back in Prohibition days). This is one of New York's classic bars—definitely take a peek inside, as long as you can find the way in (take the steps right into the seemingly private courtyard, and don't be shy about asking for the bar's location if you can't find it). Chumley's has been a writer's hangout for decades, attracting patrons like Calvin Trillin, John Steinbeck, John Dos Passos, Allen Ginsberg and many, many more. Pull up a chair near the fireplace and have a pint.

Grove Street dead-ends into Hudson Street near historic **St. Luke in the Fields** church, founded by Clement ("Twas the Night Before Christmas") Moore in 1822. Take Hudson Street one block south to **Barrow Street** and turn right. It's a splendid stroll along Barrow, which is lined with Federal-style and Italianate brownstones. Take Barrow for a couple of blocks to Washington Street, then turn left; take Washington one block to **Morton Street,** and turn left again. Morton is one of the most picturesque streets in the Village, lined with postcard-perfect brownstones.

Take Morton back two blocks to Hudson Street, make a right, then a left onto **St. Luke's Place,** which is lined with gingko trees and stately mid-19th-century Italianate town houses. At no. 6 is a gorgeous home once occupied by flamboyant New York mayor Jimmy Walker, a hard-partying public servant who was eventually forced to resign in disgrace. The brownstone at no. 10 was used for exterior shots of the Huxtable home in *The Cosby Show*. Theodore Dreiser, Marianne Moore and Sherwood Anderson all called this block home at one time or another.

Take St. Luke's back to Bedford Street and turn left. Just before you get to Commerce Street, be sure to notice **75 1/2 Bedford St.,** which a plaque proclaims to be the narrowest house in the Village (at 9 1/2 feet wide, it probably is). Edna St. Vincent Millay once lived here; later tenants included Cary Grant and John Barrymore.

Retrace your steps back south to Morton Street, and take Morton up to its terminus at Bleecker Street. Cross Bleecker and stroll along Cornelia Street. Cornelia ends at West 4th Street, which you'll take, heading east across Sixth Avenue. One block past Sixth Avenue is Macdougal Street, where you'll see the legendary **Provincetown Playhouse,** managed by Eugene O'Neill in the 1920's and site of the premieres for many of his plays. Bette Davis made her stage debut here. (If you need a break at this point, make a detour south along Macdougal to the corner of Bleecker Street, where you can snag an outdoor table at the atmospheric **Café Figaro** for a cappucino pick-me-up.)

At Macdougal and West 4th, you're at the southwest corner of **Washington Square Park.** It's not really much of a park at all, but rather the neighborhood's version of a town square. A triumphal arch designed by Stanford White presides over the park so majestically that you'd never guess this was once a lowly potter's field; in the early 19th century, felons met the hangman's noose on this spot as public executions were carried out at the Hanging Elm near Macdougal Street.

Despite Washington Square's seedy history, this area become a haven for the monied classes inhabiting the rarified world of Henry James and Edith Wharton. Stroll up the western edge of the park, and make a right onto **Washington Square North.** You can almost picture carriages arriving by the glow of gaslights for an elegant dinner party in this row of elegant and formal Greek Revival town houses, most of which date back to the 1830's.

At the northeast corner of the square, head north for one block along University Place. Turn left into **Washington Mews,** a charming cobblestone street lined with vine-covered two-story 19th-century buildings. These adorable houses are mostly converted stables and carriage houses, originally built to serve the wealthy residents of Washington Square North. They're typical of the surprises hidden around every corner of this wonderful, historic neighborhood.

Midtown

Midtown is the heart of Manhattan, packed with architectural landmarks, the city's most popular retail shopping and several of its top museums. This tour is a good overview for first-time visitors, since it takes in many of New York's top attractions.

Start your tour by taking the B, D, F, N, Q, R, V, 1, 2 or 3 train to 34th Street. You have just been deposited at the gates of **Macy's,** the world's largest department store. It is worth seeing if you've never been before, but don't expect a civilized Harrods-style shopping experience. Especially in the holiday season, Macy's is migraine-inducing, with less-than-helpful service.

Head east along 34th Street, toward the **Empire State Building,** which soars skyward from the corner of 34th and Fifth. Completed in 1931, it is 102 stories of pure romance and Art Deco splendor. Visitors can take the elevators up to the 86th- and 102nd-floor observatories, where the views are marvelous.

Turn left and head north up Fifth Avenue, pausing to shop as you like. There's a **Yankees Clubhouse** store between 36th and 37th Streets; **Lord & Taylor,** an understated classic of a New York department store, stands at 39th Street. Just across the street is the former **Tiffany Building** (409 Fifth Ave.), designed in 1906 by Stanford White, who based it on a 16th-century Venetian palazzo.

At 42nd Street, you'll reach the magnificent main branch of the **New York Public Library,** a 1911 Beaux Arts temple with rows of Corinthian columns. Two vigilant stone lions (dubbed Patience and Fortitude by Mayor Fiorello La Guardia) stand sentry at the entrance.

Take a detour east along 42nd Street for a look at **Grand Central Terminal,** Manhattan's famously bustling train station, which combines subways, underground shopping concourses, a food court and 48 sets of railroad tracks into one smoothly functioning beehive of activity. Enter at 42nd Street and Vanderbilt Avenue. Walk down the entrance ramp, where you'll see the entrance to the main concourse. Take a look inside—it's a breathtaking space, with sweeping staircases and a vaulted ceiling soaring overhead, dotted with the constellations. Retrace your steps to the ramp on which you just entered; here you'll see some food counters for a quick bite, or you can take an escalator down to the food court, which offers an enormously varied selection. (But don't sit here if it's a nice day—we're headed off to a terrific picnic spot in just a minute.) Behind the escalator is a New York Transit Museum store, selling unique souvenirs of your visit to the city.

Now exit Grand Central, and backtrack along 42nd Street. When you reach Fifth Avenue, cross to the south side of 42nd Street, pausing for a moment in the crosswalk to look up and catch a perfect view of the gleaming spire of the **Chrysler Building,** another of New York's Art Deco masterpieces.

Keep heading west, past the library, to **Bryant Park,** a lovely green oasis in the heart of Midtown. Grab a chair and join the festive crowds of neighbor-hood workers who come here for their lunch breaks every day. (If you didn't already buy lunch at Grand Central, there are several places in Bryant Park itself to pick up a casual bite.)

After your lunch, continue up Fifth Avenue. Stretching from 48th to 50th Streets between Fifth and Sixth Avenues is **Rockefeller Center,** a magnificent complex of towering skyscrapers. Enter between 49th and 50th Streets, past Channel Gardens (and a branch of the Metropolitan Museum of Art gift shop) to the main plaza, which everyone recognizes as the home of the giant Rock Center Christmas tree and its petite skating rink, tucked under the golden statue of Prometheus. Dominating the plaza is the soaring Art Deco GE Build-ing; make sure to stop inside and marvel at its beautiful lobby, adorned with murals by José-Maria Sert. NBC's television studios are nearby (including the streetside set used for the *Today* show). If you continue across to Sixth Avenue, you'll see **Radio City Music Hall,** recently restored to all its original deco splendor.

Return to Fifth Avenue. On the east side of Fifth, between 49th and 50th, stand the chic confines of **Saks Fifth Avenue.** Across 50th Street rise the twin Gothic spires of **St. Patrick's Cathedral,** seat of the Archdiocese of New York. It's worth a peek inside to see the interior, where Zelda and F. Scott Fitzgerald were married, and where funeral services were held for Bobby Kennedy.

Continuing uptown, there's no shortage of shopping. At 51st Street, bar-gain hunters will love **H&M,** for sexy, trendy sportswear at jaw-droppingly low prices, and **Sephora,** a stunning cosmetics emporium with offerings at all price levels.

Architecture buffs may want to detour east along 53rd Street to see **Lever House** and Mies van der Rohe's **Seagram Building,** two prime examples of the sleek, stark International style. At 55th and Madison (one block east of Fifth) is Philip Johnson's pink granite **Sony Building,** with Chippendale-style orna-mentation atop the roof. Inside is the interactive **Wonder Lab** (free admis-sion), which offers the chance to try out the latest gee-whiz electronic gadgets from Sony.

Continue north on Fifth to 57th Street. This is one of the toniest intersec-tions in New York, home to blue-chip **galleries,** a **Prada** boutique, **Bergdorf Goodman** and the legendary **Tiffany's** (worth a browse even if you can't afford its pricey baubles, always packaged in a blue box with a signature white rib-bon).

At 59th Street, the **Plaza,** probably the world's most famous hotel, sits like a giant wedding cake. Eloise had the run of the place in Kay Thompson's beloved children's books, and it's been featured in movies from *North by North-west* to *Home Alone 2*. Eddie Murphy tied the knot here, and more recently, Michael Douglas wed Catherine Zeta-Jones in an intimate little ceremony for

700 of their closest show-biz friends. The Oak Room bar is a plush, clubby place to sink into a comfortable chair and have a drink.

Now your inner child wants you to take yourself across Fifth from the Plaza to **F.A.O. Schwarz.** It's a toy store extraordinaire, a veritable wonderland of fun stuff.

The tour will leave you at the corner of **Central Park.** This is one of the park's loveliest sections, near the zoo and Wollman Rink. Buy a hot dog from one of the street vendors and stake out your own bench.

The Upper West Side

The Upper West Side is one of Manhattan's most prosperous neighborhoods, but it lacks the stuffiness and sterility of the Upper East Side, that enclave of the super-rich just across the park. Instead, this is home to bankers, lawyers, media types, rumpled intellectuals, yuppies pushing strollers and out-of-work actors walking their dogs. It's a livable, convenient neighborhood, with a tiny dash of hip and a decidedly liberal bent (hence its nickname, the People's Republic of the Upper West Side).

Once upon a time, when most of Manhattan was concentrated way downtown, this was considered the country—rural farmland that was much too remote for development. Obviously, development did come, originally led by grand apartment buildings, many of which stand to this day. The neighborhood declined in the mid-20th century, as thousands of poor Hispanic immigrants settled here; these were the gang-ridden mean streets depicted in *West Side Story*. But gentrification began in the late 1960's, spurred by the construction of **Lincoln Center.** Patches of the neighborhood remained mired in poverty and crime well into the 1980's, but after a couple of stock-market booms, the entire West Side has now been thoroughly gentrified, with skyrocketing apartment prices. Residents bemoan the ever-widening presence of big-chain mega-stores (you can't throw a rock without hitting a Starbucks these days), but a few mom-and-pop stalwarts remain. This is a good walk if you'd like to see how New Yorkers really live outside the bustle of Midtown.

Start by taking the 1 or 9 train to the 86th Street station, and heading south down Broadway. If you've got kids in tow, you'll want to stop at the **Children's Museum of Manhattan,** on 83rd Street between Broadway and Amsterdam. The hands-on exhibits are so engaging that they make learning painless.

Continuing south down Broadway, you'll pass a few of the retail landmarks that define the neighborhood. Between 83rd and 82nd Streets is a **Barnes & Noble** superstore. West Siders railed against its presence (as West Siders are wont to do) when it arrived in the early 1990's, eventually crushing the independent Shakespeare & Co. a block south, but it has won over locals with its massive selection and frequent appearances by high-profile authors. At 80th Street stands a West Side icon, **Zabar's.** This is one of the city's top gourmet stores, with a dizzying selection of cheeses, breads, prepared foods, salads and much more. You may want to pick up a few items now, for a picnic in Central Park later on the tour—and while you're at it, maybe you should nosh on a fresh-from-the-oven bagel from **H&H,** just across 80th Street.

Farther south, the massive **Apthorp** apartment building dominates an entire city block between 79th and 78th Streets. Take a peek inside the iron gates to envy the residents' private courtyard.

At 74th Street, you'll see **Fairway,** another West Side institution, and the best place in town to buy fabulous produce at bargain prices. This is another good place to assemble your picnic.

A block farther south stands the grand **Ansonia Hotel,** a wedding-cake confection taking up an entire block between 74th and 73rd Streets. Originally opened in 1904 as a luxury residential hotel, the Ansonia offered its tenants a grand ballroom, a swimming pool, a theater and a system that sent messages swooshing in pneumatic tubes from room to room. Live seals splashed in the fountain, and W. E. D. Stokes, the architect, kept a pet bear and chickens in the roof garden. Celebrities from Enrico Caruso to Babe Ruth have lived here, and the Chicago White Sox conspired here to throw the 1919 World Series.

Cross over to the east side of Broadway. Between 74th and 73rd Streets is the monumental **Apple Bank for Savings,** with a heavy limestone facade and intricate ironwork doors. Continue down to 72nd Street, where you might want to stop in at **Gray's Papaya** for the "recession special" (a hot dog and a papaya drink for $1.95). Take 72nd Street east, where you'll spot a branch of **Krispy Kreme** on the north side of the street (double-dare you to resist if the "Hot Doughnuts Now" sign is lit).

Now turn left on Columbus and wander uptown for several blocks, stopping at any boutique that catches your fancy. As you approach 77th Street, you'll see the grounds of the **American Museum of Natural History.** This is one of New York's top attractions, with a world-class collection of dinosaurs. Stop in if you have time, or continue up the Columbus Avenue side, and take the path through the museum lawn, passing the **New York Times time capsule** (established at the turn of the millenium and designed by Santiago Calatrava) at 79th Street. The path curves around the building at 81st Street. Up ahead you'll see the glorious **Rose Center for Earth and Space.** Even if you don't have time for the riveting Harrison Ford–narrated Space Show, you can admire the building, a stunning glass cube enclosing a glowing white globe.

At the corner of 81st Street and Central Park West rise the three cupola-topped towers of the **Beresford,** another grand apartment building. Jerry Seinfeld has a multimillion-dollar duplex here, and is currently building a private garage on 83rd Street with space for his collection of 20 Porsches—so he need not ever have a George Costanza–style meltdown over finding a parking spot.

Turn right down Central Park West, heading past the equestrian statue of Teddy Roosevelt outside the Natural History Museum. Below 77th Street, you'll pass the **New-York Historical Society,** a manageably sized museum with fascinating exhibits of the world's most unmanageable city.

Between 75th and 74th Streets stands the **San Remo,** another landmark apartment building designed by Emery Roth, architect of the Beresford. In the depths of the Depression, the projects fared poorly, and the two buildings were sold together for the total sum of $25,000 (a fee that would not buy you a broom closet in the San Remo today).

At Central Park West and 72nd Street stands the brooding fortress-like hulk of the **Dakota** (so named because the developer's friends told him the site was so far north that it might as well be in Dakota territory). Though it's been home to an illustrious group of tenants over the years—Lauren Bacall, Boris Karloff, Judy Garland, Leonard Bernstein, William Inge and many more—the Dakota will forever be associated with John Lennon, who was tragically gunned down outside its gates on 72nd Street. John's widow, Yoko Ono, still lives here.

It's only appropriate, after visiting the Dakota, to make a pilgrimage into Central Park across the way. Just inside the 72nd Street entrance is **Strawberry Fields,** a beautifully landscaped area dedicated to Lennon's memory. It's one of the loveliest, most tranquil spots in the park, and a perfect place to spread out your picnic and end your tour.

The Upper East Side

The Upper East Side is synonymous with old money; this is the land of blue-bloods and blue-haired ladies. That generalization doesn't hold true throughout the neighborhood, of course—the farther east you go from Central Park, the more affordable and down-to-earth things become. But for our purposes, we'll stay close to the park and take a look at the lifestyles of the rich and famous, the mansions of titans such as Vanderbilt, Carnegie and Whitney. Many of their homes are now museums, schools, charitable organizations or embassies; others have been subdivided into some of the most expensive apartments in the world.

Start by taking the 4, 5 or 6 train to 86th Street. Walk west along 86th Street till you reach Fifth Avenue. The giant **brick-and-limestone mansion** at the southeast corner was built in 1914, and was later purchased by Mrs. Cornelius Vanderbilt in 1944. The founder of the Vanderbilt fortune, Commodore Cornelius Vanderbilt, was a notorious tightwad, but he left a bundle for generations of his descendants to build impressive homes.

Turn left and head down Fifth Avenue, toward the apartment building at no. 1040 that was the **home of Jackie Onassis.** Jackie loved living in the city, since New Yorkers take pride in playing it cool around celebrities; by blending into the scenery, she achieved a small measure of privacy here. Jackie O. was often spotted jogging around the Central Park reservoir nearby.

Continue strolling down Fifth, past the Metropolitan Museum of Art. At the southeast corner of 82nd Street stands the **former mansion of Benjamin Duke.** Born to a tobacco farming family in North Carolina, Duke and his younger brother, James, were founders of the American Tobacco Company and the principal benefactors of a little college that became Duke University. The Benjamin Dukes bought their place from a developer who built it on spec in 1901. They later sold it to his brother, James, who lived there until he built his own nearby. Members of the Duke family and their relatives, the Biddles, lived in the Benjamin Duke house until recently.

The French Gothic palace on the southeast corner of 79th Street, property of several millionaires at different times, belongs now to the **Ukrainian Institute of America.** The onetime home of financier Payne Whitney (given to him as a wedding present by a doting uncle) between 78th and 79th Streets now serves as the French Embassy's cultural offices.

James Duke's place, modeled on a chateau in Bordeaux, rose on the northeast corner of 78th Street in 1912. A leading critic calls it "one of the most magnificent mansions in New York." Duke's widow and their daughter, Doris Duke, lived there until the late 1950's when they gave it to New York University. It is now **NYU's Graduate School of Art History.**

At 75th Street on the northeast corner, the **Commonwealth Fund** occupies the home of Edward Harkness, son of one of John D. Rockefeller's original partners in the Standard Oil Company. Edward Harkness built most of the undergraduate dorms at Harvard and Yale. The Commonwealth Fund, founded by his mother, devotes Harkness millions to health and medical research.

At 75th Street, you might take a detour east to Madison Avenue and the **Whitney Museum of American Art.** Even if you don't have the time for a full-fledged museum visit, this is a great place to rest and refuel; Sarabeth's at the Whitney stands head and shoulders above your average museum cafeteria. This stretch of Madison Avenue is also prime **gallery-hopping** territory.

On East 73rd Street between Fifth and Madison stands the house **Joseph Pulitzer** built—no. 11, the one with lots of columns—now subdivided by 13 less affluent tenants. Despite the luxury of this home, Pulitzer, German-born publisher of the *New York World* and the *St. Louis Post-Dispatch,* barely lived here, due to his extreme sensitivity to sound (a special soundproof room constructed here apparently didn't satisfy him).

Continuing down Fifth Avenue, you'll reach the mansion of coke and steel tycoon Henry Clay Frick, which stretches from 70th Street to 71st Street and encompasses a lovely courtyard and pool. Frick, once chairman of Carnegie Steel, was an avid collector of art, especially of the Italian Renaissance. The mansion was designed by the same architects who designed the New York Public Library, and planned from the start as both home and gallery. Frick left the house and the art to the city, and the **Frick Collection** is one of the real jewels of New York City's art scene.

Turn onto **East 70th Street** and stroll away from the park for a few blocks, continuing all the way to Lexington Avenue. This is one of the most elegant streets in Manhattan, lined with a row of stunningly beautiful town houses.

At the northeast corner of Park Avenue and 70th Street is the **Asia Society,** founded by John D. Rockefeller in 1956 to foster better relations between America and Asia through culture and the arts. Its galleries are worth a look.

Walk south and look for **680 Park Ave.,** at the north corner of 68th Street. Designed by McKim, Mead & White, this neo-Federal town house was built for banker Percy Rivington Payne. It later became the Soviet Mission to the United Nations; Nikita Khrushchev stayed here while visiting the U.N.

Continue down to 66th Street, and turn right, heading back toward Central Park. At 3 East 66th St. was the **home of Ulysses S. Grant** from 1881 to 1885. Forced into bankruptcy after a scandal-ridden presidency and ravaged by cancer, Grant retired here to concentrate on penning his memoirs. After his death, his autobiography met with great critical acclaim and earned a tidy sum for his family.

The **Roosevelts' twin town house** is worth a final two-block walk from Fifth Avenue to no. 47–49 East 65th Street. It has just one front door. Inside the vestibule were separate entrances to FDR's domineering mother's quarters on the left, and her son's on the right. (Small wonder that Eleanor didn't like it.) The Roosevelts lived there in 1920–21 when FDR was convalescing from polio and stayed there whenever they were in the city. The house is now a student center for Hunter College, which is nearby on Park Avenue.

At Fifth Avenue and 61st Street stands **the Pierre,** one of Manhattan's poshest hotels and a member of the Four Seasons chain. Amid lavish trompe l'oeil murals, you can indulge in the pricey pleasure of afternoon tea in the Rotunda Lounge. The Café Pierre bar is an elegant spot for a cocktail.

GUIDED SIGHTSEEING TOURS

Boat, bus and other vehicular tours tend to have reasonably regular schedules, but some seasonal change can occur. Schedules, prices and meeting places for most of the walking tours listed here can vary wildly throughout the year, so call or check each company's Web site well in advance to avoid surprises.

Walking Tours

Adventure on a Shoestring (212) 265-2663. This group offers well-regarded and affordable 90-minute tours of New York's most interesting neighborhoods. Most outings focus on areas in lower Manhattan, but tours of Astoria, Hoboken and Roosevelt Island are also available. Tours include chats with members of the community when possible, and some walks are followed by lunch at local ethnic restaurants. Price: $5 (meals not included).

Big Apple Greeter (212) 669-2896 *www.bigapplegreeter.org.* This terrific non-profit organization matches visitors with knowledgeable and enthusiastic volunteers, who take pride in introducing their guests to New York's hidden secrets. You must call in advance to make a reservation, which gets you a very personal 2- to 4-hour tour in any of the five boroughs, designed just for yourself, your family or a small group of friends. It's a fantastic bargain, and a memorable way to get an insider's view of the city. **Price:** Free.

Big Onion Walking Tours (212) 439-1090 *www.bigonion.com.* Big Onion offers two-hour tours every weekend and holiday. Themes range from neighborhood tours and in-depth historical and ethnic surveys to special holiday and eating tours. All guides hold advanced degrees in American history, and are wonderful fonts of fun facts about New York. No reservations are required, although you should call ahead on the day of the tour to confirm the schedule; just meet at the designated starting point and bring cash. **Price:** $12 adults; $10 students and seniors; special tours $14–$18.

Central Park Conservancy (212) 360-2727 *www.centralparknyc.org*. The Central Park Conservancy sponsors one-hour tours that explore the history, ecology, design and simple beauty of Central Park. Routes vary, and some tours require registration. **Price:** Free.

Harlem Spirituals Gospel and Jazz Tours (212) 391-0900 *www.harlemspirituals.com*. Despite the name, Harlem Spirituals offers tours in every New York borough. But the Harlem tours are the real draw here, featuring everything from a Sunday gospel service to Saturday-night soul food and jazz tours. Tours leave from the company's Midtown offices and include transportation to Harlem. **Prices:** $30–$95 adults; $22.50–$95 children. Prices vary with the tour option you pick, and the food or entertainment that's included.

Joyce Gold History Tours (212) 242-5762 *www.nyctours.com*. All of these highly recommended two- to three-hour tours are conducted by Joyce Gold herself. An instructor of history at NYU and author of several walking guides to New York City, Ms. Gold boasts an extensive list of neighborhood tours heavy on history, with titles like "East Village—Culture and Counter-Culture" and "The New Meat Market—Butchers, Bakers and Art Scene Makers." No reservations are needed. **Price:** $12.

Municipal Art Society Tours (212) 935-3960 *www.mas.org*. The MAS program "Discover New York" sponsors a diverse selection of year-round tours of New York's neighborhoods, history and culture. Some special tours, like "Cast in Iron: Manhole and Chute Covers" have companion lectures and slide shows. Some tours require reservations, so call ahead. **Prices:** Weekdays $12, or $10 for students and seniors. Weekends $15, or $12 seniors and students.

New York City Cultural Walking Tours (212) 979-2388 *www.nycwalk.com*. Alfred Pommer has been researching and conducting a wide array of tours for over 15 years. Featured walks include multi-ethnic heritage tours, as well as staples like the "Bohemian Walking Tour of Greenwich Village" and the unusual "Gargoyles in Manhattan." There is a different tour each month, March through December. **Prices:** Varies, but usually around $20.

New York Talks and Walks (888) 377-4455 *www.newyorktalksandwalks.com*. Dr. Philip Schoenberg offers a multitude of seasonal, ethnic and historical tours, including the "Hidden Treasures of Chinatown" and the "Jewish Gangster Tour." Reservations are not required, but call ahead to confirm the schedule. **Prices:** Most tours $12–$15.

92nd Street Y Tours (212) 415-5599 *www.92ndsty.org/tours/tours.asp*. There are dozens of walks to choose from here, covering the art, architecture, crafts, music, dance, Jewish history and culture of each destination. In addition to neighborhood walking tours, look for specialty offerings, such as bike tours, "Inside Woodlawn Cemetary," "Chinatown's Herb Markets," "A Private Peek into the World of Fashion" and much more. **Prices:** $20–$35.

Radical Walking Tours (718) 492-0069 *www.he.net/~radtours*. These tours are led by historian Bruce Kayton. Walks explore significant sites in New York's history of political activism, with an emphasis on topics like civil rights, labor history and gay and lesbian liberation. No reservation required. **Price:** $10.

Savory Sojourns (212) 691-7314 *www.savorysojourns.com*. These tours can be expensive, but for your money you get a five- to six-hour eating tour of one of the city's neighborhoods, complete with market stops, cooking demonstrations, kitchen tours of acclaimed restaurants, food, beer and wine. This company is run by Addie Tomei (Marisa's mom). Reserve well in advance. **Prices:** $70–$155, including food.

Urban Explorations (718) 721-5254. Patricia Olmstead's operation covers many neighborhoods and themes, including trips through gay and lesbian Greenwich Village, tours of private artists' lofts, visits to hidden gardens and stops at feminist landmarks. **Prices:** $12; $10 students, seniors and repeat customers.

Wall Street Walking Tour (212) 606-4064 *www.downtownny.com*. Every Thursday and Saturday, the Downtown Alliance sponsors a free walking tour of Lower Manhattan. Meet on the steps of the U.S. Customs House, at Bowling Green. Reservations are required for groups, but not individuals. **Price:** Free.

Wildman Steve Brill's Food and Ecology Tours (914) 835-2153 *www.wildmanstevebrill.com*. Steve Brill, once arrested for eating dandelions in Central Park, now offers four-hour tours of city parks teaching identification and applications of a variety of wild plants. Walkers are encouraged to bring bags and containers to carry home wild herbs, mushrooms and berries. Reserve 24 hours in advance. **Prices:** $10 adults; $5 children.

Bus Tours

On Location Tours (212) 239-1124 *www.sceneontv.com*. This company's Manhattan bus tour shuttles visitors to sites used as exterior settings for a number of TV shows, including the *Friends* apartment building and the *NYPD Blue* precinct house. A New Jersey *Sopranos* tour ($30) comes complete with cannoli; the *Sex and the City* tour ($30) features stops for cocktails and shoe-shopping. Reserve in advance. **Prices:** $20 adults; $10 children 10 and under.

Gray Line (212) 397-2600 *www.graylinenewyork.com*. Hop-on, hop-off tours of Manhattan, the boroughs and beyond. The "Total New York" tour includes a two-day bus ticket and free admission to the Statue of Liberty, plus the Empire State Building observation deck; there's also a Harlem Gospel tour. **Prices:** $26–$75 adults, from $16 children ages 5–11.

Kramer's Reality Tour (800) KRAMERS or (212) 268-5525 *www.kennykramer.com*. Kenny Kramer, the real-life inspiration for the most annoying character on *Seinfeld*, hosts overpriced three-hour "multi-media" tours of the Seinfeld universe every Saturday at noon. See locations like the "Soup Nazi" shop, Joe's Produce Store and Monk's Restaurant, and feast on the "Real Kramer's Original Famous Pizza." Reservations are required. **Price:** $37.50.

Cruises

Circle Line (212) 563-3200 *www.circleline.com*. Tours leave from Pier 83 at the west end of 42nd St. and Pier 16 at the South Street Seaport. The three-hour "Full Island" cruise draws the biggest crowds, but you'll see just as many major sights on the shorter cruises. Stick with the one-hour "Liberty Cruise," the Beast speedboat ride (great for kids!) or one of the themed trips. **Prices:** $16–$24 adults; $11–$20 seniors; $7–$12 children ages 12 and under.

New York Waterways (800) 533-3779 *www.nywaterway.com*. Tours depart from Pier 78 at the west end of 38th St. and Pier 17 at the South Street Seaport. This is the Circle Line's biggest competitor, offering a similar variety of cruises on their new, clean boats. Besides the standard harbor cruises, they also run special baseball cruises to Yankees and Mets games and a number of cruises to destinations up the Hudson. **Prices:** Harbor Cruises $19–$24 adults; $9–$12 children. Other cruises $10–$66.

Spirit Cruises (212) 727-2789 *www.spiritcruises.com*. Another catch-all cruise operator, offering a variety of packages that take in the major sites of New York's harbor and rivers, combined with decent entertainment and so-so food. Tours depart from Chelsea Piers on the Hudson at W. 23rd St. (A more upscale competitor is **World Yacht;** 212-630-8100; *www.worldyacht.com*.) **Prices:** $28–$78, depending on day and time of cruise.

Other Transportation

(See also chapter **Sports & Recreation***, section* "Biking.")

Crypt Keeper Tours (888) EXHUMED or (212) 679-9777 *www.cryptkeepertours.com*. Visit sites of famous people's deaths (including John Lennon, Sid Vicious, Jackie Onassis, Andy Warhol and Typhoid Mary) in a vintage hearse. Reservations are required. **Price:** $45.

Liberty Helicopter Tours (212) 967-4550 *www.libertyhelicopters.com*. These are expensive and brief tours, but they do offer a unique perspective on the city. Trips tend to range from five to 20 minutes and take in most of the major sights, from the Statue of Liberty to Central Park. Reserve in advance. **Prices:** $55–$180.

NEW YORK CITY
SEASONAL EVENTS

Winter

The Nutcracker New York State Theater at Lincoln Center (212) 870-5570 *www.nycballet.com*. The New York City Ballet performs this holiday classic each year with students from the School of American Ballet.   *November-December*

Christmas Spectacular Radio City Music Hall, 1260 Sixth Ave. (at 50th St.) (212) 247-4777 *www.radiocity.com*. The Radio City Christmas Spectacular features the famed Rockettes in Santa hats, high-kicking alongside larger-than-life Nutcracker soldiers.   *November-early January*

Christmas Window Displays Along Fifth Avenue in Midtown, marvel at the intricate winter scenes in department store windows. (Lord & Taylor, Saks Fifth Avenue and Barney's are the most popular). Check out the Cartier building wrapped for Christmas in an enormous red bow and the doormen at FAO Schwarz dressed as wooden soldiers.   *December*

Christmas Tree Lighting Ceremony Rockefeller Center (212) 632-4000. One of the tallest Christmas trees in the country is mounted in Rockefeller Center, where it is strung with five miles of lights and lit by a celebrity in a nationally televised ceremony that includes an ice-skating show and other entertainment.   *Early December*

Messiah Sing-Along Avery Fisher Hall, Lincoln Center (212) 333-5333 *www.lincolncenter.org*. The National Chorale Counsel organizes this sing-along of Handel's "Messiah" led by 20 conductors with an audience of up to 3,000, including four trained soloists to rescue the arias. No experience is necessary and lyrics sheets are provided. Amateurs, professionals, even high school choirs participate.   *Mid-late December*

New Year's Eve Ball Drop Times Square (212) 768-1560. *www.timessquare-bid.org*. It's not officially the New Year until the ball drops over Times Square. The new and improved ball is now adorned with a stunning 12,000 rhinestones and 180 75-watt bulbs. Arrive early, since the area is packed with revelers hours before midnight.

New Year's Eve Fireworks Central Park. Spectators gather at Tavern on the Green and other spots throughout the park for views of the annual fireworks display. Festivities begin at 11:30 P.M.

New York National Boat Show Jacob K. Javits Convention Center, 655 W. 34th St. (at 11th Ave.) (212) 216-2000 *www.javitscenter.com*. Enormous crowds show up each year to see 400 of the world's leading manufacturers show off the latest power-boats—from small craft to yachts—and marine accessories. Seminars on fishing and boating are also offered.   *Nine days in early January*

Winter Antiques Show Seventh Regiment Armory, Park Ave. (at 67th St.)
(718) 292-7392 *www.winterantiquesshow.com*. The city's premier antiques fair—
featuring collections ranging from ancient to Art Nouveau—is also a benefit for
East Side House Settlement.   *Mid-late January*

Outsider Art Fair The Puck Building, 295 Lafayette St. (at Houston St.)
(212) 777-5218 *www.sanfordsmith.com*. This three-day event draws an international crowd of dealers, collectors and art aficionados. Thirty-five dealers
exhibit self-taught, visionary and art brut pieces to crowds in the thousands. It's
a good place for celebrity sightings and the occasional star-studded seminar.
                                                          Late January

Chinese New Year For information, call the Chinese Cultural Center at (212)
373-1800. Celebrate the year of the sheep in 2003 in Chinatown, on and around
Mott Street. Five days of celebrating culminate in a colorful procession of lions
and dragons made from wood and silk that wind their way through the narrow
and festively decorated streets. Fireworks were banned in 1997, which has taken
some of the bang out of the festivities, but the colors, lights, dancing and food
still make it quite an experience.   *Begins first full moon after January 21*

Westminster Kennel Club Dog Show Madison Square Garden, Seventh
Ave. (at 33rd St.) (212) 465-6741. *www.westminsterkennelclub.org*. The nation's
most prestigious dog show features 3,000 pampered pooches that are pared down
to seven finalists and then a single winner of "Best in Show." About 30,000
spectators show up for the two-day event.   *Mid-February*

The Art Show Seventh Regiment Armory, Park Ave. (at 67th St.)
(212) 766-9200 *www.artdealers.org*. Sponsored by the Art Dealers Association
of America, this is New York's foremost art fair. Seventy of the nation's leading
galleries gather to exhibit works that span five centuries from 17th-century masters to contemporary artists in a range of media that includes painting, drawing,
print, sculpture, photography and video.   *Mid-late February*

Spring

International Cat Show Madison Square Garden, Seventh Ave. (at 33rd
St.) (212) 465-6741. Hundreds of fabulous felines representing 40 breeds
compete for the Best of Show award with all the composure for which cats are
famous. After, you can shop for cat accessories at the cat supermarket or listen
to lectures on topics like cat acupuncture, massage and feline aerobics. *March*

Manhattan Antiques and Collectibles Triple Pier Expo 12th Ave.
(between 48th and 51st Sts.) (212) 255-0020 *www.antiqnet.com/stella*. Nine
hundred dealers take over Piers 88, 90 and 92 along the Hudson River to sell
everything from posters, toys, textiles, fashions and furniture to silver, porcelain,
fine china, paintings, jewelry and glassware. The selection is particularly strong
in mid-century modern collectibles and Americana.
        One weekend in mid-March; again for two weekends in mid-November

St. Patrick's Day Parade Fifth Ave. (from 44th to 86th St.) (212) 484-1222.
(212) 484-1222. In one of the city's oldest annual events, 150,000 Irish
Americans and other revelers draped in green join the festivities along Fifth
Avenue (starting at 11 A.M.) and fill the city's bars well into the night. You
can find green beer, green bagels and virtually everything in the shape of
shamrock, as New York goes Hibernian for a day. For best views of the parade,
line up early.   *March 17*

International Asian Art Fair Seventh Regiment Armory, Park Ave. (at 67th
St.) (212) 642-8572 *www.haughton.com*. Top dealers from around the world
gather at the Armory to sell art from Southeast Asia and the Middle and Far
East. The art, sculpture, ceramics and textiles typify the talent and skills of Eastern Artists over the centuries. Fourteen thousand people come to browse and
buy items that range anywhere from $200 to hundreds of thousands of dollars.
Late March

New Directors/New Films (212) 875-5610 *www.filmlinc.com*. This film festival, sponsored by MoMA and the Film Society of Lincoln Center, features works
by emerging, overlooked and new directors. Such notables as Wim Wenders,
Spike Lee and Steven Spielberg have screened films in past years. Since MoMA's
Midtown location is currently under renovaton, check the Web site for locations
of this year's screenings.   *Late March-early April*

Ringling Bros. and Barnum & Bailey Circus Madison Square Garden, Seventh Avenue (at 33rd St.) Seventh Avenue (at 33rd Street) (212) 465-6741
www.ringling.com. Kicking off its New York run each spring, the circus's lions,
tigers and bears (and elephants) parade along 34th Street to Madison Square
Garden at midnight on the night before the first performance. The spectacular
procession of animals is a great way to get a free peek at "The Greatest Show on
Earth."   *Late March-early May*

Whitney Biennial Whitney Museum of American Art, 945 Madison Ave. (at
75th St.) (212) 570-3600 *www.whitney.org*. Every two years since 1932, the
Whitney has presented an exhibition of what it regards as the most influential
contemporary American art, often highlighting works by innovative and vanguard artists. The Biennial will be held next in 2004.   *Late March-early June*

Easter Parade Fifth Avenue (44th-57th Sts.) (212) 484-1222. In a tradition
dating back to the Civil War era, the Easter Parade draws crowds of bonneted
spectators sporting everything from the classic bowler to the more extravagant
flowering bonnets. The best perch is the platform at St. Patrick's Cathedral, if
you can get near it.   *Easter Sunday*

New York International Auto Show Jacob K. Javits Convention Center,
655 W. 34th St. (at 11th Ave.) (800) 282-3336 *www.autoshowny.com*. North
America's first and largest auto show features hundreds of the newest cars and
concepts as well as classics from automotive history.   *Mid-April*

New York Antiquarian Book Fair Seventh Regiment Armory, Park Ave. (at 67th St.) (212) 777-5218 *www.sanfordsmith.com*. About 180 international book dealers offer rare books, manuscripts, autographs, fine bindings, maps, modern firsts, illustrated books, children's books and more. Admission to the show is $15.   *Mid-April*

Macy's Flower Show 34th St. (at Broadway) (at Broadway) (212) 494-2922 *www.macys.com*. With the arrival of spring, Macy's becomes a botanical paradise, displaying over 30,000 varieties of flowers, plants and trees from around the world.   *Late March-early April*

The Cherry Blossom Festival Brooklyn Botanic Garden (718) 622-4433 *www.bbg.org*. To celebrate the blooming of the Garden's 200 cherry trees, this festival features classical Japanese dance performances accompanied by bamboo flutes and taiko drums. There is storytelling, as well as lessons in calligraphy, flower arranging, oriental brush painting, block painting and origami. Check the Web site for an update of the blossom status.   *Late April or early May*

TriBeCa Film Festival Venues throughout the neighborhood *www.tribecafilm-festival.org*. This brand-new film festival, the brainchild of Robert De Niro and producer Jane Rosenthal, made a splashy debut in 2002 by premiering *Star Wars Episode II* and drawing a flock of celebrities. The festival was launched to help revitalize Downtown New York after the 9/11 attacks, and it was so successful that it's sure to be a major event in years to come. Buy tickets well in advance on the festival's Web site.   *May*

Bike New York: The Great Five Boro Bike Tour (212) 932-BIKE *www.bike-newyork.org*. America's largest bicycling event draws 30,000 riders who traverse 42 miles (68k) and five boroughs. The tour starts in Battery Park with a sendoff by the mayor and ends with a ride across the Verrazano-Narrows Bridge to Staten Island. A post-ride festival and picnic given by sponsors features food, concessions and activities.   *Early May*

Ninth Avenue International Food Festival Ninth Ave. (37th-57th St.) (212) 581-7217. Hundreds of stalls are set up along Ninth Avenue for two days to serve every type of ethic food you can imagine—from Thai to Italian. Live music keeps things festive, and vendors sell plants, crafts and T-shirts while over a million people sample the gamut of New York's ethnic cuisines.   *Mid-May*

Bird Watching in Central Park Central Park (212) 427-4040 *www.nyc-parks.org*. With 275 species sighted at last count, Central Park is one of the 14 best bird watching places in North America. From parrots to bald eagles to the red-tailed hawks that nest along Fifth Avenue, all manner of birds show up for springtime in the park. Many of the more exotic species arrive en route from southern states, Mexico and even the tropical rain forests.   *May-June*

Fleet Week U.S.S. *Intrepid* Sea, Air and Space Museum (46th St. at 12th Ave.) (212) 245-0072 *www.uss-intrepid.com*. Fifteen to 20 battleships, aircraft carriers and other ships from the U.S. Navy and Coast Guard as well as foreign fleets sail up the Hudson, past the Statue of Liberty, and dock at Pier 86, where 10,000 uniformed personnel disembark so curious New Yorkers can explore their vessels for free. During the week there are also parachute drops and air displays that are sure to impress the kids.   *Late May*

Washington Square Outdoor Art Exhibition Washington Square Park (212) 982-6255. For nearly 70 years, the 20 blocks in and around the park have been transformed into an arts and crafts fairground on Memorial Day and continuing for the three following weekends. Around 600 exhibitors participate each day of the fair from noon until sundown.   *Starts Memorial Day*

Summer

Lower East Side Festival of the Arts Theater for the New City, 155 First Ave. (at 10th St.) (212) 245-1109. This annual three-day cabaret-style festival featuring more than 20 theatrical troupes celebrates the culture of the Lower East Side.
Early June

Metropolitan Opera Parks Concerts Various parks throughout the five boroughs (212) 362-6000 *www.metopera.org*. Each year the Met presents free performances of two operas in Central Park and other locations throughout the city. Bring a picnic and grab a patch of grass early if you want to get a good view.
June

Bryant Park Free Summer Season Sixth Ave. (at 42nd St.) (212) 922-9393. Lunchtime concerts and performances are a favorite of Midtown workers throughout the summer. The free classic movies under the stars on Monday evenings have become a beloved New York tradition. Bring a blanket and a picnic and arrive early for some prime lawn space.   *June-August*

Celebrate Brooklyn! Performing Arts Festival Prospect Park Bandshell, 9th St. (at Prospect Park West), Park Slope (718) 855-7882 *www.bkny.net/celebrate*. Some 25 free outdoor performances in music, dance, film and theater are offered for nine weeks in Prospect Park. The city's longest-running free performing arts festival attracts top-notch acts from around the country and the world. Check the Web site for a schedule of events.   *June-August*

Central Park SummerStage Rumsey Playfield, Central Park (at 72nd St.) (212) 360-2777 *www.summerstage.com*. Since its founding in 1986, Summer-Stage has presented over 500 free weekend afternoon concerts and performances for over 5 million people. Everyone from the latest pop stars to up-and-coming artists have graced the stage; the 2002 season featured an array of world music acts, plus headliners like Lucinda Williams, the B-52s, the Tom Tom Club and John Mayer. Occasional benefit shows charge admission to help fund the program.   *June-August*

Puerto Rican Day Parade Fifth Avenue (44th to 86th Sts.) (718) 401-0404. With sizzling music, colorful floats and an enthusiastic crowd, this is one of New York's most festive parades.   *Second Sunday in June*

Belmont Stakes Belmont Race Track, Elmont, Long Island (516) 488-6000 *www.nyracing.com/belmont*. The final leg of the Triple Crown is a major event on the horse-racing circuit.   *Sunday in early June*

Toyota Comedy Festival Various venues throughout the city. *www.toyotacomedy.com*. Thirty venues host over a hundred big-name comedy acts; 2002 brought Bill Cosby, Lewis Black, Steven Wright, Dave Attell, Jon Stewart and many more.   *Early-mid June*

Museum Mile Festival Various locations (212) 606-2296 *www.museummilefestival.org*. For one day in June, you can get into nine of the city's major museums for free, enjoying live entertainment along Fifth Avenue (82nd-104th Sts.) as you stroll from one to the other.   *Second Tuesday in June*

JVC Jazz Festival (212) 501-1390 *www.festivalproductions.net/jvc/ny*. From small clubs to Carnegie Hall and Lincoln Center, world-class jazz musicians and lesser-known artists take to New York's stages for performances and jam sessions.   *Mid- to late June*

Mermaid Parade Boardwalk at Coney Island (W. 10th-16th St.) (718) 372-5159 *www.coneyisland.com*. To kick off the summer, hundreds of mermaids, as well as mermen, merchildren and other sea creatures march down the boardwalk in a colorful display. Elaborate floats and outlandish costumes make this one of the city's most unique parades.   *Saturday after summer solstice*

Lesbian and Gay Pride Week and March Fifth Ave. (from Columbus Circle to Christopher St.) (212) 807-7433. Thousands take to the streets to celebrate the birth of the gay liberation movement in the world's largest gay pride parade. A week of events surrounds the flamboyant parade, including an outdoor dance party at the West Side Piers, a film festival, club events throughout the city and many other activities.   *Late June*

Restaurant Week *www.restaurantweek.com*. A prix-fixe lunch at over 100 of the city's top restaurants is only $20.03 for a week in June. Check the Web site for a list of participants; as soon as they're announced in mid- to late May, reserve immediately—places fill up fast. Some restaurants continue the deal throughout the summer.   *Late June*

Midsummer Night Swing Lincoln Center Plaza (212) 875-5766 *www.lincolncenter.org*. Nothing can quite compare to dancing under the stars with Lincoln Center's famed fountain as a backdrop. Top dance bands play everything from swing to salsa. Dance lessons, which are included in the price of admission, begin at 6:30 P.M. and the featured band goes on at 8 P.M. The dance floor can get awfully crowded, so you might just listen in for free on the edges of the plaza.   *Late June-late July*

Lincoln Center Festival Lincoln Center (212) 875-5928 *www.lincolncenter.org*. This festival showcases dance, theater, music and opera in and around Lincoln Center's several venues, with performances by the Center's regular companies and other artists from around the world. The festival also offers special symposia about and inspired by the festival's performances.   *July*

New York Shakespeare Festival Delacorte Theater, Central Park (at 81st St.) (212) 539-8750 *www.publictheater.org*. Sponsored by the Joseph Papp Public Theater, this is New York's quintessential summer event. Celebrity performers often headline these free outdoor performances; the 2002 season featured Julia Stiles, Jimmy Smits and Kristen Johnston in *Twelfth Night*. Available at the Public Theater and the Delacorte Theater starting at 1 P.M. on the day of the performance, tickets can be difficult to come by.   *July-August*

Macy's Fourth of July Fireworks Spectacular Over the East River (212) 484-1222 *www.macys.com*. The FDR Drive is closed to traffic for a few hours so pedestrians can get a better look at the lavish 30-minute display launched from two points on the East River beginning at 9 P.M.   *July 4*

New York Philharmonic Concerts in the Parks Various locations (212) 875-5656. The Philharmonic presents free evening concerts in parks throughout the city.   *Late July-early August*

Mostly Mozart Avery Fisher Hall, Lincoln Center (212) 875-5030 *www.lincolncenter.org*. The Mostly Mozart Festival Orchestra—along with world-class soloists and guest performers—presents around 30 concerts in a four-week period each summer.   *Late July-late August*

Harlem Week Throughout Harlem (212) 484-1222 *www.harlemweek.com*. The Taste of Harlem food festival, the Black Film Festival and a lively street fair along Fifth Avenue (125th-135th St.) are highlights, along with open houses, block parties, outdoor concerts and special events at area jazz clubs.   *August*

Hong Kong Dragon Boat Festival The Lake at Flushing Meadows-Corona Park, Queens (718) 539-8974 *www.hkdbf-ny.org*. More than 80 teams from across the U.S. and Canada race traditional 39-foot boats decorated like Chinese dragons in a spectacular display. Admission is free.   *Mid-August*

Lincoln Center Out-of-Doors Lincoln Center (212) 875-5108 *www.lincolncenter.org*. Everything from classical music and dancing to children's puppet shows is featured in this series of free performances on the plazas of Lincoln Center.   *August-September*

U.S. Open Tennis Championships USTA National Tennis Center, Flushing Meadows, Queens (718) 760-6200 or (888) OPEN-TIX *www.usopen.org*. This Grand Slam event is the premier U.S. tournament on the tour. Fans can pay top dollar for a seat at the showcased matches, or purchase grounds admission, which entitles them to wander from one early-round match to another; prices go up and the tournament progresses. Buy tickets well in advance; they go on sale in June.   *Late August-Labor Day*

Wigstock Pier 54 (12th-13th Sts. on the Hudson) (800) 494-8497 or (212) 439-5139 *www.wigstock.nu*. With up to 10,000 bewigged spectators and around

60 performers, this drag festival may be the city's most colorful. Tickets run
about $25.   *Labor Day weekend*

West Indian Day Carnival Eastern Parkway (Utica Ave.-Grand Army Plaza),
Brooklyn (212) 484-1222, (718) 625-1515. A crowd of nearly 2 million revelers
turns out to celebrate Caribbean culture in New York's biggest and most energetic parade. The parade of extravagant costumes and colorful floats caps a
weekend of festivities beginning Friday evening with reggae, salsa and calypso
at the Brooklyn Museum.   *Labor Day*

Autumn

Broadway on Broadway 43rd and Broadway (212) 768-1560
www.timessquarebid.org. For a couple of hours each year, Broadway is accessible
to everyone. On a stage erected in the middle of Times Square, a free concert of
highlights from the season's biggest shows features big stars and splashy production numbers.   *Mid-September*

Feast of San Gennaro Mulberry St. (Houston-Worth Sts.) (212) 764-6330
www.san gennaro.org. Since 1926, Little Italy's main drag, Mulberry Street, has
been transformed into a fairground for 11 days each September. Three million
people turn out each year for food, fun and music at this festival honoring the
patron saint of Naples.   *Mid-September*

Atlantic Antic Atlantic Ave. (Flatbush Ave.–East River) (718) 875-8993
www.atlanticave.org. With music, food, arts and crafts, a children's circus and
over 450 vendors, the Antic is one of Brooklyn's largest street fairs, drawing
nearly 1 million people each year.   *Last Sunday in September*

New York Film Festival Lincoln Center (212) 875-5601 *www.filmlinc.com*.
Approximately 20 independent, foreign and big-studio films are screened in a
two-week run at Lincoln Center. Held annually since 1965, the festival has pre-
miered films by directors such as Martin Scorsese, Jean-Luc Godard and Robert
Altman.   *Late September-early October*

Columbus Day Parade Fifth Ave. (44th-86th Sts.) (212) 484-1222. Columbus may have landed far from New York on a Spanish ship, but he was born in
Italy. That's enough for the city's Italian-Americans, who are front and center
for this parade up Fifth Avenue.   *Columbus Day, second Monday in October*

Halloween Parade Sixth Ave. (from Spring St. to 23rd St. or Union Square)
(212) 475-3333, ext. 4044 *www.halloween-nyc.com*. Over 25,000 participants
take to the streets of Greenwich Village for the most famous Halloween parade
in the country. Join the crowd of elaborately costumed revelers or have nearly
as much fun watching from the sidelines.   *October 31*

BAM Next Wave Festival Brooklyn Academy of Music (718) 636-4100
www.bam.org. BAM showcases experimental works by both established and
lesser-known contemporary artists from around the world in music, theater and
dance.   *October-December*

New York City Marathon Starts Staten Island side of the Verrazano-Narrows Bridge (212) 860-4455 *www.nycmarathon.org*. This 26.2-mile race, one of the most prestigious in the world, finishes in Central Park as a crowd cheers on the 35,000 participants each year. Spectators line the streets handing out drinks all along the course, which hits each of the five boroughs. The 2002 event will be held on November 3. *Last Sunday in October or first Sunday in November*

Big Apple Circus Damrosch Park, Lincoln Center (212) 268-2500 *www.bigapplecircus.org*. With its local roots, intimate one-ring big top and kid-friendly mission, the Big Apple Circus has staked out its own ground between the glitz of the Ringling Brothers circus and the adults-only artistry of the Cirque du Soleil. *November-January*

Macy's Parade Central Park West (at 77th St.) to Macy's (Broadway and 34th St.) (212) 494-2922 *www.macys.com*. From 9 A.M. to noon on Thanksgiving, a procession of floats and huge cartoon character balloons marches down to Macy's in this children's favorite. Catch the inflating of the balloons the night before at Central Park West and 77th Street (6–11 P.M.). *Thanksgiving Day.*

MANHATTAN NEIGHBORHOODS
Lower Manhattan

On September 11, 2001, the world watched in horror as two hijacked commercial airplanes destroyed the **World Trade Center,** killing almost 3,000 innocent victims (a number that includes hundreds of fallen rescue workers). In addition to the Twin Towers, five other World Trade Center buildings were destroyed, and more than a dozen other buildings sustained serious damage.

Almost a year later, much of Lower Manhattan shows no lasting effects of the attack—stockbrokers in suits and ties charge through the Financial District, cellphones in hand, just as they did before. In the streets immediately surrounding the World Trade Center, though, it's a different story. It's no longer a beehive of frantic emergency activity; the rubble has been cleared, and the rescue workers have gone home. The Trade Center site itself was cleared of all debris months ahead of schedule; it now sits silently, as the Lower Manhattan Development Corporation struggles to reach a consensus about what sort of memorial and new construction might rise here.

Across West Street (West Side Highway), the **World Financial Center** remains, and after a few months of exile, many of its corporate tenants returned. The beautiful Winter Garden was heavily damaged, but as of this writing workers are attempting to complete its restoration in time to observe the first anniversary of the attacks.

Although a number of major corporations have left Downtown and thousands of jobs have been lost, many businesses have reopened. Retailers (including the beloved discounter Century 21) are trying valiantly to make a go of it, despite the loss of foot traffic. Residents have returned to their homes and attempted to regain some semblance of normalcy; those who did leave

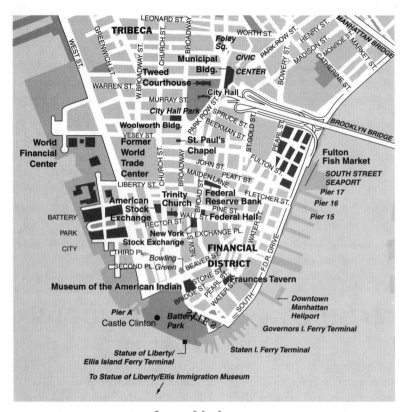

Lower Manhattan

have been largely replaced by new tenants eager to participate in the neighborhood's revitalization.

Local subway lines were severely damaged, but the MTA acted swiftly to restore service. The 1/9 line was most heavily affected; the Cortlandt St., Rector St. and South Ferry stations are all still closed as of this writing, though they are likely to reopen by the time you visit. Officials promise a heavy emphasis on improving the transportation infrastructure as part of the effort to restore the neighborhood; already, several new ferry routes from Brooklyn and New Jersey have picked up the slack from the demolished PATH station.

It's perfectly safe to visit this neighborhood, which boasts an incredible treasure trove of historic sites and architectural attractions. In fact, visitors can't seem to stay away from Ground Zero itself. Compelled to bear witness to history and pay their respects in person, millions have made pilgrimages to the site. In the early months, they stared in horror at the enormity of the ruins. Now there's little more to see than an empty pit, with the surrounding buildings sheathed in protective netting, but still they come.

Lower Manhattan has adjusted uneasily to this surreal influx of tourism. Many visitors are sincere and respectful, but victims' family members and neighborhood residents have frequently been jolted by the sight of vendors hawking crass souvenirs and tourists snapping smiling photos as if they were in Disneyland.

Viewing platforms have been erected at Liberty Street to accommodate those who wish to pay their respects. The platforms are temporary, and they may or may not be in place when you visit; there's also talk of erecting a new glass partition around the edges of the site to allow for viewing. (212-484-1222, *www.nycvisit.com* or *www.downtownny.com*, for the latest logistical information. Tickets are no longer required.)

In Battery Park stands a **temporary memorial,** the damaged bronze sphere that once stood on the World Trade Center plaza between the Twin Towers. After visiting Ground Zero, it's often a healing and meditative experience to wander along the waterfront, where you can gaze out toward the Statue of Liberty, still standing sentinel over New York Harbor.

Subway: 1, 2, 3, 9 to Chambers St. or Park Pl.; E to World Trade Center; N, R to Rector St. or Whitehall St.; 4, 5 to Wall St. or Bowling Green. Subway access may change (service should be restored on the 1, 2, 3, 9 lines soon); check *www.mta.nyc.ny.us* for updates.

HIGHLIGHTS OF THE NEIGHBORHOOD

Battery Park Bordered by Battery Place and State St. at the southern tip of Manhattan. Wedged below the concrete canyons of the Financial District, windswept Battery Park is a lovely greenspace at the tip of Manhattan, offering sweeping vistas out to New York Harbor. From here, a paved recreation path extends up the entire West Side of Manhattan, serving up gorgeous water views to joggers, bikers and in-line skaters. Built entirely on landfill, Battery Park is filled with historic landmarks, including **Castle Clinton National Monument** (212-344-7220), a circular fort designed in 1811 to protect against British invasion. Castle Clinton, now the setting for outdoor concerts in summer, is the place to **buy tickets for boat trips to Ellis Island and the Statue of Liberty** *(see box)*. Battery Park is also the departure point for the **Staten Island Ferry** *(see listing below)*. Within the park stands Fritz Koenig's damaged bronze sphere, created as a symbol of world peace and once placed on the plaza between the Twin Towers. Recovered from the World Trade Center site, it is damaged but still intact, and it was placed here on the six-month anniversary of the attacks as a **temporary memorial to the victims of 9/11. Subway:** N, R to Whitehall St.; 4, 5 to Bowling Green; 1, 9 to South Ferry.

Bowling Green Broadway and Whitehall Sts. This petite green triangle was Manhattan's first park, once used as a cattle market and later as a bowling lawn. A statue of King George III stood in the park until 1776, when an angry mob toppled it, railing against oppressive British rule. (The statue's remains were then melted down and turned into ammunition.) One statue that has survived here is the famous **"Charging Bull,"** a symbol of Wall Street optimism (although there's always the possibility that a mob of angry investors might demolish that one, too). At the south end is the elegant U.S. Customs House, which houses the **National Museum of the American Indian** (*see listing below*). A farmers' market operates here daily. **Subway:** N, R to Whitehall St.; 4, 5 to Bowling Green; 1, 9 to South Ferry.

Brooklyn Bridge Manhattan entrance: Park Row at Centre St. Brooklyn entrance: Washington St. at Adams St. One of the grandest and most potent symbols of New York City since the day it opened in 1883, the Brooklyn Bridge still provides probably the best free tourist activity in the whole city— walking across it toward the Manhattan skyline.

To start on the Brooklyn side, climb the three flights of stairs on Washington Street. (The closest subway stop is the High Street station on the A line). You will be following in the steps of President Chester A. Arthur, who led the first group of pedestrians across. And you will thank John A. Roebling, who designed the bridge in 1867 and put the elevated walkway in the center, above other traffic, so that pedestrians could "enjoy the beautiful views and the pure air."

From end to end, it is more than a mile—6,016 feet. The portion over the East River soars 135 feet above mean high water.

But long before you thread through the massive keyholes of the bridge's Gothic-arched towers (at the time they were built, the towers were taller than anything on either shore, besides the Trinity Church spire), you will easily understand why the bridge has loomed so large in the nation's imagination.

Over the years, it has loomed indeed. It has been painted by everyone from George Bellows to Georgia O'Keeffe. Its glories have been sung in poetry and prose by thousands, including Hart Crane, the poet who asked: "How could mere toil align thy choiring strings!"   —*Randy Kennedy*

City Hall/City Hall Park Broadway and Chambers St. (212) 788-6865. Topped by a cupola that once offered commanding views of the countryside, **City Hall** is now dwarfed by office towers. An amalgamation of French Renaissance and Federal design, completed between 1802 and 1812, it houses the offices of the mayor and the City Council. The steps outside are the setting for official receptions in which the mayor bestows the key to the city on winning teams and visiting dignitaries. The interior has a remarkable pair of cantilevered stairs under a central rotunda.

City Hall presides over the lovely green lawns of **City Hall Park.** Among the sights in and around the park are an entrance ramp to the **Brooklyn Bridge** pedestrian walkway, the **Woolworth Building** and the **Municipal Building** (*see separate listings for each of these attractions*).

The Italianate **Tweed Courthouse,** just north of City Hall, was the old New York County Courthouse. It's a stunningly beautiful building—but then again it should be, since William "Boss" Tweed ran up the construction bill from the budgeted $250,000 to $14 million in one of the biggest swindles in city history.

Across Chambers Street from the Tweed Courthouse stands the grandiose **Surrogates Court Hall of Records.** It boasts a sumptuous lobby with murals and an arched mosaic ceiling with an Egyptian motif. Whether or not citizens'

Brooklyn Bridge

records merited such splendor is another matter altogether, but the building itself is definitely worth a visit.

From here, take Elk Street up toward Duane Street, where you'll find the **African Burial Ground.** Some 20,000 African Americans were laid to rest here during the 18th century. The site was uncovered in 1991 during construction of the Federal office tower across the street.

Farther north along Centre Street are today's active court buildings. At 40 Centre Street is the **United States Courthouse,** a mid-1930's Classical Revival skyscraper topped with a golden pyramid. The **New York County Courthouse** moved to its current location at 60 Centre Street in 1927. This hexagonal, Roman classical building is a frequent backdrop for *Law & Order* and countless other television shows and films.
Subway: J, M, Z to Chambers St.; 4, 5, 6 to Brooklyn Bridge–City Hall; N, R to City Hall; 2, 3 to Park Place.

Federal Hall National Memorial 26 Wall St. at Nassau St. (212) 825-6888 *www.nps.gov/feha.* Wall Street's version of the Parthenon, Federal Hall stands on the site of George Washington's inauguration as the nation's first president in 1789; a dignified statue of Washington towers over the front steps. It was also here that publisher John Peter Zenger stood trial in 1735 for seditious libel; his acquittal was the basis for the concept of freedom of the press. One of the finest Greek Revival buildings in the city, this former U.S. Customs House and early Federal Reserve branch was designed in 1834 and built in 1842. Behind its portico of severe Doric columns and five-foot walls, the building houses a museum of constitutional history. **Admission:** Free. **Hours:** Mon.–Fri. 9 A.M.–5 P.M. **Subway:** J, M, Z to Broad St.; 2, 3, 4, 5 to Wall St.

Federal Reserve Bank 33 Liberty Place (between Nassau and William Sts.) (212) 720-6130 *www.fednewyork.org/nycinfo.html* Five stories below Liberty Street, the Federal Reserve's New York branch houses a substantial share of the world's gold reserves. The bank offers tours of the underground vaults, which store approximately $100 billion worth of gold ingots for some 60 countries. A government bank for banks, the Federal Reserve regulates U.S. currency, supervises commercial banks and has considerable impact on the economy through its influence on the money supply and interest rates. Its rusticated limestone building is reminiscent of a Florentine Renaissance palazzo. Reserve in advance for free hour-long tours, offered five times daily on weekdays only. There's also a new exhibit, created in collaboration with the American Numismatic Society, on "The History of Money"; admission is free, and hours are Mon.–Fri. 10 A.M. –4 P.M. **Subway:** J, M, Z to Broad St.; 2, 3, 4, 5 to Wall St.

Fraunces Tavern Museum 54 Pearl St. (at Broad St.) (212) 425-1778 *www.frauncestavernmuseum.org*. The 18th-century Fraunces Tavern, now a small museum of American history, has been substantially rebuilt since it served as a watering hole George Washington and the Sons of Liberty. The Long Room, where Washington made his farewell address to his Revolutionary War officers, is one of the several period rooms where displays are located. The museum offers tours, lectures and performances coordinated with current exhibitions, as well as special events on Washington's Birthday and Independence Day. After an extensive renovation, the restaurant at Fraunces Tavern (call 212-968-1776 for reservations) reopened in 2001; dining here or stopping by for a drink is a great way to soak in the historic atmosphere. **Admission:** $3 adults; $2 students and seniors; free for children under 6. **Hours:** Mon.–Fri. 10 A.M.–4:45 P.M. **Subway:** N, R to Whitehall St.; 2, 3 to Wall St.; 4, 5 to Bowling Green; J, M, Z to Broad St.

Irish Hunger Memorial Vesey St. and North End Ave. (in Battery Park City). Completed in July 2002, the Irish Hunger Memorial commemorates the great Irish famine of 1845–52. Designed by sculptor Brian Tolle, it brings to fruition efforts dating back several decades to build a memorial to the famine in New York, where so many Irish immigrated to escape its reach.

The memorial is a startlingly realistic quarter-acre replication of an Irish hillside, complete with fallow potato furrows, stone walls, indigenous grasses and wildflowers and a real abandoned Irish fieldstone cottage. The 96-by-170-foot

Ruby Washington/The New York Times

Wall Street

field rests on a giant concrete slab that is raised up and tilted on a huge wedge-shape base. It slopes upward from street level to a height of 25 feet. A packed dirt path winds up the slope, culminating in a hilltop with sweeping views of Ellis Island and the Statue of Liberty.

The field is a walk-in relic of a distant time and place tenderly inserted into the modern world almost as if it were an offering. From its inception, the memorial was also intended to be a reminder of world hunger. The plinth is lined with glass-covered bands of text that mingle terse facts about the Irish famine with similarly disturbing statistics about world hunger today, along with quotations from Irish poetry and songs. It shows instances of suffering, prejudice and mismanagement so specific that they can't help but reverberate into our own time.

Located two blocks from Ground Zero, the Irish Hunger Memorial is likely to be embraced by many as a symbol of the hundreds of firefighters, police officers, rescue personnel and office workers of Irish descent who died in the World Trade Center attack. The memorial has arrived at a time when Americans have a deeper understanding of tragedy and grief, of fate's capriciousness and of the complexities of power. It commemorates human failure, human loss and human perseverance in a war fought with land, food and political might at the cost of at least one million lives. —*Roberta Smith*

Municipal Building 1 Centre St. (at Chambers St.). Roughly a decade after the merger of the five boroughs in 1898, the city held a competition for an office building to house various city agencies under one roof. The resulting Beaux-Arts skyscraper—designed by McKim, Mead & White and completed in 1914—stands guard over the approach to the Brooklyn Bridge. The building's entrance, which incorporates a Roman triumphal arch, boldly straddles Cham-

The Statue of Liberty & Ellis Island

These days, nothing more inspiring than the baggage claim area at John F. Kennedy International Airport greets most visitors and immigrants to the United States. But a century ago, the exhilarating sight of the Statue of Liberty towering over the entrance to New York Harbor signaled to shiploads of travelers, both the bedraggled and the bejeweled, that they had reached the shores of a new land.

At Ellis Island, only paperwork was processed for first-class and second-class passengers; the passengers themselves were inspected on their ships and dispatched directly to Manhattan. But each day saw up to 5,000 poor and working-class immigrants, fresh from a two-week ocean voyage in steerage, herded inside and inspected for disease, deformities and destitution.

Inspired by the colossal monuments of Egypt and an outsized 19th-century French fascination with American egalitarian ideals, the Statue of Liberty still has the power to take your breath away, just as it thrilled the 12 million immigrants who passed it on their way to Ellis Island in the first decades of the 20th century.

Resolute and stern, the massive female figure, 151 feet high from her toes to the top of her torch of freedom, rests on a 150-foot-high pedestal at the tip of a tiny landscaped island in New York Bay. Gardens around the base offer a sumptuous view of the skyscrapers of Lower Manhattan.

The idea for a grand statue to celebrate friendship between France and the United States originated in 1865 around the Parisian dinner table of Edouard de Laboulaye, a scholar of the American Constitution. (A great-grandson of de Laboulaye spearheaded fundraising in France for restoration of the statue 100 years after it opened). Alexis de Tocqueville, another admirer of American democracy, is said to have been a guest at the dinner. So was the sculptor who would design the statue, Frédéric-Auguste Bartholdi.

A highlight for many visitors is the 354-step climb up a narrow, twisting staircase to the statue's crown, where glimpses of the New York and New Jersey coasts are visible on clear days through smallish Plexiglas windows. Because of overheated conditions in the stairwell, only passengers on the first two morning ferries are allowed in the crown in summer.

But there is a better view from the skinny outdoor walkway around the base of the statue. It can be reached by an elevator, or up four flights of steps. Inside the pedestal, an informative museum shows the evolution of Bartholdi's vision of what the statue should look like, the engineering used to keep it stable in the tricky harbor winds, and the lasting impressions it made on generations of immigrants. A delightful collection of old Statue of Liberty kitsch, as opposed to the new collection in the gift shop downstairs, concludes the exhibit, demonstrating the monument's enduring role as both icon and huckster.

(**Important note:** As of this writing, visitors cannot enter the Statue, including its pedestal, crown or museum, due to tightened security. This policy is subject to change, so check the Web site for the latest updates before visiting. The view from the grounds alone is still worth making the trip.)

At Ellis Island, renovations of the long-abandoned site have recreated the processing center as it looked in the first decades of the 20th century. Even if you do not trace your roots to an ancestor who arrived in the United States through Ellis Island—and these days, fewer than 40 percent of Americans do—you may well feel a kinship with the 12 million anxious immigrants who shuffled through the echoing halls of this red-brick way station between 1892 and 1954 on their way to a new life in a new land. All through the impressively restored building, there are bigger-than-life sepia photos of the evocative faces that passed through Ellis Island to become symbols of the American experience. Among them: a young boy in a jauntily angled embroidered cap, his lips pursed as if he is trying to suppress a grin of pure exultation. Two Dutch brothers, each with a processing number pinned to his shirt and each with a determined gaze already directed far beyond New York Harbor. A pair of dignified young black women coming from Guadeloupe in 1911, both in ankle-length lace-trimmed dresses and tiny hats shaped like a handful of rose petals.

The main processing center is the only part of the original compound that i open to the public. Displays on its three floors use film, photos, turn-of-the-last-century posters and the voices of reminiscing immigrants to show a broader story of immigration. You hear immigrants tell their stories of adjustment, discrimination, poverty and success. You learn about the nativist movements that feared immigrants; a 1902 political cartoon shows them as the personification of "filth" and "disease." And you see how popular culture was enriched by immigrants—as in the old song, "Hello Wisconsin, Won't You Find My Yonnie Yonson?"

The long-awaited Family History Center opened in 2001, where visitors can look up the immigration records of anyone who arrived by way of Ellis Island up to 1924.

—*Susan Sachs*

Information, (212) 363-3200, or (212) 269-5755 for ferry and ticket info. *www.nps.gov/stli* and *www.nps.gov/elis*.

Hours: Daily 9 A.M.–5 P.M. (last ferry departs Manhattan at 3:30 P.M.), with extended summer hours. **Admission:** Free. Round-trip ferry tickets (with stops at both sights) $8 adults, $6 seniors, $3 children under 17. Ferry departs from Manhattan's Battery Park; buy tickets in the park at Castle Clinton.

James Estrin/The New York Times

Statue of Liberty

bers Street. Best known as the place where thousands of couples get married every year, the Municipal Building is coincidentally crowned by a round, colon-naded tower that resembles a wedding cake. Instead of two colossal newlyweds, however, the top of the building houses a monumental gilt sculpture called *Civic Flame*. **Subway:** J, M, Z to Chambers St.; 4, 5, 6 to Brooklyn Bridge/City Hall.

Museum of American Financial History 28 Broadway (near Bowling Green) (212) 908-4110 *www.financialhistory.org*. The small Smithsonian affiliate, housed in the site of Alexander Hamilton's law office and the former headquarters of John D. Rockefeller's Standard Oil Company, focuses on the history of money. Displays include photos of history Wall Street scenes, interactive financial news terminals, actual ticker tape from the crash of 1929 and much more. The museum also sponsors weekly neighborhood walking tours; call ahead to confirm the schedule and check prices. **Admission:** $2. **Hours:** Tue.–Sat. 10 A.M.–4 P.M. **Subway:** N, R to Whitehall St.; 4, 5 to Bowling Green; 1, 9 to South Ferry.

Museum of Jewish Heritage—A Living Memorial to the Holocaust 18 First Pl., Battery Park City (at West St.) (212) 509-6130 *www.mjhnyc.org*. This museum on the water's edge, beautifully designed by award-winning architect Kevin Roche, organizes its displays around three themes: Jewish Life a Century Ago, The War Against the Jews and Jewish Renewal. With thousands of photographs, displays, artifacts and documentary films, the museum uses personal stories to place 20th-century Jewish history and the Holocaust in context. **Admission:** $7 adults; $5 students and seniors; children under 5 free. Hours: Sun.–Wed. 10 A.M.–5:45 P.M.; Thu. 10 A.M.–8 P.M.; Fri. 10 A.M.–5 P.M. **Subway:** N, R to Whitehall; 4, 5 to Bowling Green; J, M, Z to Wall St.; 1, 2 to Wall St.

National Museum of the American Indian, George Gustav Heye Center 1 Bowling Green (between Whitehall and State Sts.) (212) 514-3700 *www.si.edu/nmai*. This branch of the Smithsonian is located in the former U.S. Customs House, a spectacular domed Beaux-Arts landmark designed by Cass Gilbert at the foot of Broadway. The collection of artifacts housed here spans more than 10,000 years of history, representing virtually all tribes of the continental United States, Canada, Hawaii and Central and South America. **Admission:** Free. **Hours:** Daily 10 A.M.–5 P.M. (closes at 8 P.M. on Thu.). **Subway:** N, R to Whitehall St.; 4, 5 to Bowling Green; 1, 9 to South Ferry.

New York City Police Museum 100 Old Slip (at the East River, between Water and South Sts.) (212) 480-3100 *www.nycpolicemuseum.org*. This museum moved in early 2002 to the headquarters of the city's first police precinct. With interactive exhibits, computer simulations, vintage uniforms, weapons and antique badges, the museum presents a multifaceted view of the rigorous, clearly dangerous, at times political and often tedious life of a police officer. **Admission:** $5; $3 seniors; $2 children ages 6–18. **Hours:** Tue.–Sat. 10 A.M.–5 P.M. **Subway:** 2, 3 to Wall St.

New York Stock Exchange 20 Broad St. (between Wall and Exchange Sts.) (212) 656-5165 *www.nyse.com*. On a good day—a day when the stock market is soaring—you can almost smell the money in the air outside the New York Stock Exchange. If you go inside, you can see it being made (or lost).

The Exchange, its security tightened after 9/11, was closed to visitors as of

Fred R. Conrad/The New York Times

New York Stock Exchange

this writing, but there are tenative plans to reopen for tours late in 2002 (call ahead or check the Web site for new visiting hours and ticket procedures). If tours follow their old format, you'll be admitted to the third-floor "Interactive Education Center," which is full of rather silly propaganda, plus a lively video clip that helps to explain exactly what it happening on the floor of the Exchange. From the glassed-in visitors' gallery, you can gaze at the main trading floor. The effect is rather like watching a really fancy ant farm. Hundreds of strangely dressed people bustle about, bark at each other, gab on phones, peer at computer screens and drop little bits of paper all over the floor. Most of them are brokers carrying big buy and sell orders to the specialists, auctioneers of a sort. Each specialist handles trading in several stocks.   —*Leslie Eaton*
Subway: J, M, Z to Broad St.; 2,3, 4, 5 to Wall St.

St. Paul's Chapel 211 Broadway (between Fulton and Vesey Sts.) (212) 602-0800, or (212) 602-0747 for concert info *www.saintpaulschapel.org*. New York City's oldest church building, St. Paul's served uptown parishioners of Trinity Church as the colonial city expanded northward, and is still considered a satellite of Trinity. Completed in 1766, the church is a New York brownstone version of London's St. Martin-in-the-Fields, a marble Georgian church that greatly influenced American ecclesiastic architecture. George Washington worshiped here on the day of his inauguration and during the 18 months New York was the nation's capital. The leafy graveyard behind the church preserves a parcel of the 18th-century countryside. Despite its proximity to the World Trade Center, the chapel miraculously survived the 9/11 terrorist attacks unscathed, and in the months of recovery and cleanup, it served as a place of refuge to the rescue and construction workers. In conjunction with Trinity Church, St. Paul's offers a well-attended lunchtime concert series. **Subway:** 2, to Park Place; N, R to Cortlandt St.

Shrine of St. Elizabeth Ann Seton 7 State St. (between Whitehall and Pearl Sts.) (212) 269-6865. This 1793 Federal-style building is dedicated to Elizabeth Ann Seton, the first American-born Catholic saint. Seton, who founded the American Sisters of Charity, the first order of nuns in the U.S., lived here from 1801 to 1803. The building is one of the few surviving mansions in Lower Manhattan. The adjoining church was built at the same time.

Skyscraper Museum 2 West St. (in Battery Park City) (212) 968-1961. *www.skyscraper.org.* This collection illuminating the history of the skyscraper has been moving from venue to venue, but it will move into its new permanent home (in a Skidmore, Owings & Merrill tower that also houses the Ritz-Carlton) in late 2002. It will contain a permanent exhibit on the evolution of New York's incredible skyline, plus a series of changing exhibits. Confirm the admission price and open hours before you go. **Subway:** 4,5 to Bowling Green; 1 to Rector St. or South Ferry.

South Street Seaport Encompassing 11 blocks at Water and South Sts. (Visitors Center at 12 Fulton St.) (212) 748-8600 or (212) SEA-PORT *www.southstreetseaport.com* or *www.southstseaport.org.* For hundreds years, South Street Seaport was a thriving commercial dockland of warehouses and markets, the nation's busiest port, with a bustling traffic of China clippers, schooners, ferries and fishing boats. Barges floated down from the Erie Canal bearing cargo from middle America. This busy East River port became obsolete in the late 19th century, however, as bigger ships powered by steam docked at new and larger piers on the Hudson River.

When restoration of the area began in the 1960's, a jewel of a neighborhood was restored to evoke a great age in New York's maritime history. There were cobbled streets free of traffic and piers open to the wind and water. But alas, the redevelopment has ultimately turned the Seaport into a theme-park shopping mall, especially at **Pier 17,** where tourists pack bland restaurants and shop in chain retailers just like those back home. Still, it's a pleasant place to spend a sunny day (even Pier 17 offers wonderful water views from its outdoor decks), and there are frequent festivals, concerts and cultural events, many of them free. You can also visit the Lower Manhattan **TKTS booth,** at the corner of John and Front Streets; here you can pick up same-day discounted tickets for a Broadway or Off-Broadway show.

But there's history to be found here, if you're willing to look for it. At the Water Street entrance to the Seaport is the **Titanic Memorial Lighthouse,** built in 1913 to commemorate the sinking of this unsinkable ship. On Fulton Street between South and Front Streets is **Schermerhorn Row,** a series of early 19th-century Georgian- and Federal-style buildings once used as warehouses by leading merchants. Right on Schermerhorn Row is the **Visitors Center,** which displays paintings, prints, ship models and changing exhibitions.

Moored nearby are a handful of historic ships, including the *Peking,* one of the largest sailing vessels ever built when it was launched in 1911 (visitors can climb aboard and go below decks to explore).

Subway: 2, 3, 4, 5, J, Z, M to Fulton St.

Staten Island Ferry southeast end of Battery Park (718) 815-2628 *www.ci.nyc.ny.us/html/dot.* Historically, there have been few better bargains in New York than a ride on the Staten Island Ferry. For decades, it cost only a nickel. That changed in the mid-1970's, when the first of several fare increases took effect, inching the price up eventually to $.50 for the round trip between Battery Park in Manhattan (a short walk from the N/R stop at Whitehall or the 4/5 station at Bowling Green) and St. George, Staten Island. But these days a ferry ride is absolutely the best deal in town. It costs nothing, part of a new system of free mass-transit transfers.

The ferry is a lifeline to the city for many Staten Islanders; some 30,000 people ride it each midweek day. But it also provides as romantic a journey as the city can offer. The ferry operates 24 hours a day—every 15 minutes during rush hours, every 30 minutes the rest of the day and evening, and once an hour at night. To truly appreciate the grandeur of New York, ride the ferry at sunrise, starting with the 25-minute trip from Manhattan to Staten Island and then reversing the journey on the next boat back. At dawn, the first rays of the sun strike the glass towers of Lower Manhattan, while off to the left, the Statue of Liberty's torch still burns bright in the vanishing darkness.   —*Clyde Haberman*

Trinity Church and Museum Broadway (at Wall St.) (212) 602-0800 of (212) 602-0747 for concert info *www.trinitywallstreet.org.* At the foot of Wall Street stands Trinity Church, once the tallest structure in Manhattan. The first Episcopal church in New York, the parish was chartered in 1697 (two earlier churches on this site were destroyed by fire). The Gothic-style church on the site now was built in 1846 by Richard Upjohn, complete with flying buttresses, vaulted ceilings and doors modeled after Ghiberti's Gates of Paradise in Florence. Many prominent New Yorkers, including Alexander Hamilton, Robert Fulton and William Bradford, are buried in the graveyard next to the church. During the summer months, office workers on their lunch breaks take to the benches here, enjoying the sun in this rare downtown patch of open space. The church features a small museum, and offers a free tour daily at 2 P.M. Trinity also hosts an acclaimed lunchtime concert series of chamber and orchestral music. **Subway:** 4,5 to Wall St.

Woolworth Building 233 Broadway (at Park Place, opposite City Hall Park). View this dramatic structure from a distance far enough to take in the Gothic flourishes of intricately carved buttresses capped by a summit that sits like a medieval castle 792 feet above lower Broadway. The building is truly from another era, when corporate barons like F.W. Woolworth, of five-and-dime fame, battled for skyscraper supremacy. Designed by the celebrated architect

Cass Gilbert, the Woolworth Building was the tallest skyscraper until the Chrysler Building (and countless others subsequently) conquered it in 1930. It remains a standout among the more contemporary glass-and-steel boxes of the nearby financial district. Somewhere inside are a swimming pool and a store-room of Gothic ornaments to replace the ones adorning the exterior. The only area open for casual visitors is the lobby, a sight itself to behold, with its murals and marble splendor. Peer up into the vaulted ceilings of tiled mosaics, and check out the carved figures under the crossbeams (that's Cass Gilbert holding a model of the building, and Frank Woolworth counting nickels and dimes). **Subway:** 2, 3 to Park Place; N, R to City Hall.   —*Randy Archibold*

World Financial Center and Winter Garden 1 World Financial Center (between Albany and Liberty Sts.) (212) 945-0505 *www.worldfinancialcenter.com*. Built on landfill along the Hudson River, this commercial development includes shops, restaurants, gallery space, a yacht har-bor and the Winter Garden performance space. A sleek, modern complex (one wag called it "Dallas without the parking"), the World Financial Center was damaged in the attacks of 9/11, but has been repaired and reopened to corporate tenants. The Winter Garden, a spectacular glass-vaulted public space, complete with a monumental arced staircase and 40-foot-tall palm trees, was ravaged. It is undergoing extensive restoration (workers are replacing 2,000 glass panes in the arched ceiling, half of the grand staircase, much of the marble flooring and all 16 of the towering palms) and as of this writing, it is poised to reopen. Outside, a promenade circles the yacht harbor, and the proximity of the water reminds visitors and residents alike that they are indeed on an island. **Subway:** 1, N, R to Cortlandt St.

Highly Recommended Neighborhood Restaurants
*(See chapter **Restaurants** for reviews.)*

Bayard's	☆☆	$$$	NEW AMERICAN
Delmonico's	☆	$$$	ITALIAN/NEW AMERICAN
Les Halles Downtown	☆	$$$	FRENCH

Chinatown

Geography, New York style: China shares a border with Italy, and has for more than a century. The boundary is fluid, to be sure, and Chinatown's expansion in recent years across the traditional demarcation line of Canal Street has whittled Little Italy down to Tiny Italy. The area has Vietnamese, Cambodian and His-panic communities, too, and some traces of a once-vibrant Jewish culture. But since 1965, the Chinese population has exploded; this is now the largest Chi-nese community in the Western Hemisphere and one of the most densely popu-lated sections of the city.

In this self-sufficient community, with its large population of non-English speakers, many residents never leave the neighborhood (many of them toil in sweatshops, manufacturing clothing). On narrow streets, fishmongers and greengrocers spill onto the sidewalks. Exotic shops offer teas and Chinese herbs. In late January or early February, the **Chinese New Year** is marked by a raucous street festival (former mayor Giuliani took some of the sizzle out of the celebration when he banned firecrackers).

To the outsider searching for the perfect egg roll, Chinatown may seem changeless. Yet along with the infusion of Hong Kong capital has come a shift in the economic center from Mott Street to **the Bowery** and **East Broadway,** while the traditional dominance of immigrants from China's Guangdong Province is being ceded to those from Fujian.

There are an estimated 300 restaurants in the area focusing on any of several Chinese cuisines. After dinner or dim sum, try the **Chinatown Ice Cream Factory** (65 Bayard St. between Mott and Elizabeth Sts.) for a scoop of green-tea ice cream. The **Pearl River Mart** at Canal Street and Broadway carries a huge selection of Chinese imports—dishes, traditional costumes and decorations, housewares and food. Along with smaller import shops, most Chinatown streets (particularly **Canal Street**) are lined with little storefronts and sidewalk stands selling everything from cheap electronics and batteries to Rolex knockoffs and discount luggage.

Just south of the Manhattan Bridge entrance (at Bowery and Canal St.) past Confucius Plaza, one of the area's newer housing developments, is **Chatham Square.** Here the Kimlau Arch honors Chinese soldiers killed in American wars. Where Catherine Street meets East Broadway is the **Republic National Bank,** the quintessential Chinatown building designed with the flourishes of a pagoda.

Subway: J, M, N, Q, R, W, Z, 6 to Canal St.; F to East Broadway.

HIGHLIGHTS OF THE NEIGHBORHOOD

Columbus Park Mulberry St. at Bayard St. This mostly concrete plaza in the heart of Chinatown seems like a lush oasis when you enter it from some of the narrowest and most congested streets in the city. The park's benches and stone chess tables are usually occupied, from dawn to dusk, by elderly Chinese women and men playing cards and mah-jongg. The park is located on the site of the Mulberry Bend, an infamous tenement slum of the 1800's, terrorized by gangs like the Plug Uglies and the Dead Rabbits. The buildings were torn down at the urging of the reformer Jacob Riis, who wrote a scathing report on the area's disgraceful condition. Now, as he dreamed, the neighborhood has a safe and welcoming place to play and congregate.

Museum of the Chinese in the Americas 70 Mulberry St. (at Bayard St.) (212) 619-4785 *www.moca-nyc.org.* This institution is dedicated to preserving and interpreting the history of the Chinese people in the Western hemisphere. Located on the second floor of a century-old school building in the heart of Chinatown, it offers educational and community programs and facilities for

research on Chinese/Asian American studies. **Admission:** $3; $2 students and
seniors; free for children under age 12. **Hours:** Tue.–Sat. noon–5 P.M.

Recommended Inexpensive Neighborhood Restaurants
(See chapter **Restaurants** *for reviews.)*

Evergreen Shanghai	CHINESE
Goody's	CHINESE
Joe's Shanghai	CHINESE
New York Noodle Town	CHINESE
New Green Bo	CHINESE
Nha Trang	VIETNAMESE

The Lower East Side

The Lower East Side remains a tapestry of cultures and a celebration of New
York's diversity. Since the mid-19th century it has been the gateway to America
for countless generations of immigrants. Waves of families from Eastern Europe,
Italy, Ireland, Germany, and more recently China, Puerto Rico and the Dominican Republic, have passed through here. For many decades, it was a landscape
of poverty; Lower East Side tenements were the first stop in America for new
immigrants struggling to make a living in factories and sweatshops.

As recently as the 1980's, this was a crime-ridden area with drug dealers on
every corner. But in the last two decades, the forces of gentrification have
brought amazing change to the neighborhood. The Lower East Side has become
a hangout for hipsters, a thriving center for art, fashion and nightlife. This is
where old New York meets cutting-edge chic, and the result is a fascinating,
edgy neighborhood with an abundance of raw energy. It's still grungy, still rough
around the edges—nothing has been totally sanitized here. The current Lower
East Side story is a mix of the old, the new and the resurrected.

In the storefronts on blocks like **Essex Street** (between Canal and Grand
Sts.), the Lower East Side of the past and present converge. Asian-owned electronics stores abut old Jewish businesses. Signs in Yiddish alternate with signs in
Chinese along this stretch; locals pack **Kossar's Bagelry** for some of the best
bagels in the city, as others settle down for a Sichuan lunch a few doors away.

To the north, **Delancey Street** bisects the area, beyond which residents are
largely Hispanic, with a strong showing of younger newcomers. This thorough-
fare offers mostly discount goods and cheap knock-offs, and an occasional
shaved-ice snow cone vendor. **Ratner's,** a Delancey Street relic, has been serving Jewish dairy food since 1905—only now it's a fraction of its former size,
closed six days a week and shares a building with **Lansky Lounge,** an old
speakeasy turned swanky supper club for hipsters. (The building is currently up
for sale, leaving its future unsure.)

Rivington Street, one block north of Delancey, is dotted with Puerto Rican
and Dominican businesses and is home to **ABC No Rio,** one of several area
cultural centers. It's also home to **Schapiro's Kosher Wines,** the last function-

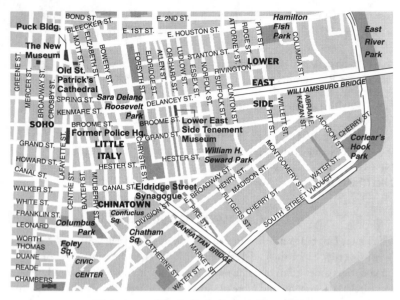

Chinatown/Little Italy/Lower East Side

ing winery in the city, family-run since 1899, and **Streit's Matzos,** one of the premier suppliers of matzo and other Jewish staples for over 75 years.

    Clinton Street, especially between Stanton and Rivington Streets, is lined with an interesting assortment of restaurants. The Lower East Side was once considered to out-of-the-way for a serious restaurant, until celebrity chef Wylie Dufresne became a neighborhood pioneer with his acclaimed 71 Clinton Fresh Food (he has since left the kitchen there, but maintains a presence on Clinton Street with his own restaurant). The dining scene has never looked back since.

    Just west of Rivington is the **Orchard Street Bargain District** (*see chapter* **Shopping**), where peddlers with pushcarts once crowded the streets. Shoppers still come to the area for discount leather goods, luggage and clothing.

    Orchard and Ludlow Streets are home to some of the most hottest boutiques and a slew of chic bars and lounges (*see chapter* **Nightlife**). A few paces away are some of the Lower East Side's classic eateries. **Katz's Delicatessen,** an area artifact and originator of the World War II slogan, "Send a salami to your boy in the Army," still carves pastrami and corned beef by hand. (It's a hoot to see this classic deli invaded by pierced and tattooed club kids in the wee hours.) The kitschy Borscht Belt party atmosphere of **Sammy's Roumanian,** the enormous garlic-rubbed beef tenderloins and the bowls of schmaltz (rendered chicken fat) on every table are a nostalgic paean to the days before cholesterol consciousness. A new resident of 87 Orchard St. is **Guss' Pickles,** which was a fixture on Essex Street for more than 90 years. Stop in and buy a few pickles from their massive barrels (the neighborhood once supported about 80 pickle shops!). Also don't miss **Russ and Daughters** for smoked fish and other deli specialties and **Yonah Shimmel,** supplying noshers with knishes since 1910. Next door is the lyrical brick facade of **Landmark's Sunshine Cinema,** a modern art-film multiplex with stadium-style seating, recently opened in what was a century ago a showplace for Yiddish vaudeville and films.

Subway: F to Delancey St.; F, V to Second Ave.; J, M, Z to Essex St.

HIGHLIGHTS OF THE NEIGHBORHOOD

ABC No Rio 156 Rivington St. (between Clinton and Suffolk Sts.) (212) 254-3697. This cultural center has sponsored punk rock concerts, political discussions, film showings and poetry readings as well as art exhibitions.

Eldridge Street Synagogue 12 Eldridge St. (between Canal and Division Sts.) (212) 219-0888. Even in a state of disrepair, the Eldridge Street Synagogue's intricate carved facade and stained-glass windows stand out amid the tenements. Built in the late 1800's by immigrants from Eastern Europe, it was the first large-scale Orthodox synagogue in New York. It is being restored under the stewardship of the Eldridge Street Project, which offers tours of the building, lectures, and educational programs including rugelach baking lessons and genealogy workshops.

Henry Street Settlement—Abrons Arts Center 466 Grand St. (at Pitt St.) (212) 598-0400. In its century or so of existence, the Henry Street Settlement has presented a multitude of cultural and community-related activities—including opera, music, dance, theater, talks and workshops. The hub of the Settlement, which occupies a row of handsome Greek Revival town houses, is the Abrons Arts Center. Most performances take place in the 350-seat Harry De Jur Playhouse, a national historic landmark. There is also a smaller theater, a recital hall, an outdoor amphitheater, classrooms, studios and art galleries.

Lower East Side Tenement Museum 90 Orchard St. (at Broome St.) (212) 431-0233 *www.tenement.org*. If a museum is meant to teach us who we are and where we've come from, then a glimpse into this dingy time capsule may be more meaningful than a visit to the Louvre or the Met. Thousands of new arrivals, hailing from 25 different nations, found their first home in America at 97 Orchard St., a five-story tenement that illuminates the story of the great waves of immigration of the late 19th and early 20th centuries. Several apartments have been faithfully restored to their exact lived-in condition, and tour guides recount the real-life stories of the families who occupied them in fascinating detail.

The only way to see the museum is by joining an hour-long guided tour; there are two main options, both of them fascinating. On weekends, you can also choose the 45-minute **Confino Family Apartment tour,** an interactive living history program in which kids can touch artifacts, try on period clothes and dance to the music on the wind-up victrola. The museum also sponsors neighborhood walking tours on many weekends.

Each apartment tour is limited to 15 visitors, so buy your tickets in advance through Ticketweb at (800) 965-4827 or *www.ticketweb.com*. **Admission:** $9 adults; $7 students and seniors. Confino Apartment $8 adults, $6 seniors and students. **Hours:** Visitor Center daily 11 A.M.–5:30 P.M. Tenement tours depart every 40 minutes Tue.–Fri. 1– 4 P.M.; Sat.–Sun every half-hour 11 A.M.–4:45 P.M. Confino Apartment tour Sat.–Sun hourly noon–3 P.M.

Schapiro's Wine Company 126 Rivington St. (between Essex and Norfolk Sts.) (212) 674-4404 *www.schapiro-wine.com*. The grapes are grown upstate, where much of the wine is now fermented and bottled, but some is still produced in ancient barrels on the premises. On Sundays from 11 A.M. to 5 P.M., Norman Schapiro, a real old-time character, offers free tours of the winery and tastes of his wines, ranging from the treacly sweet to the dry.

Williamsburg Bridge Delancey St. and the East River. The Williamsburg Bridge was born of a dare. Could Leffert Lefferts Buck, the city's chief engineer, build a bridge that was longer than the Brooklyn Bridge in half the time and with less money? He could and he did. When it opened in 1903, the Williamsburg was the world's longest suspension bridge at 7,308 feet, with a main span of 1,600 feet (five feet more than the Brooklyn Bridge, thank you very much). At a cost of $24,188,090, it came in $906,487 under its rival. And it was built in seven years; the Brooklyn took 13.

Selected Restaurants and Food Shops

Guss' Pickles
87 Orchard St. (near the Lower East Side Tenement Museum)

Katz's Delicatessen
205 E. Houston St. (at Ludlow St.)   (212) 254-2246

Kossar's Bagelry
39 Essex St. (between Hester and Grand Sts.)   (212) 387-9940

Ratner's
138 Delancey St. (between Norfolk and Suffolk Sts.)   (212) 677-5588

Russ and Daughters
179 E. Houston St. (between Orchard and Allen Sts.)   (212) 475-4880

Sammy's Roumanian
157 Chrystie St. (between Delancey and Houston Sts.)   (212) 673-0330

Streit's Matzos
150 Rivington St. (at Suffolk St.)   (212) 475-7000

Yonah Shimmel Knishes
175 E. Houston St. (between Eldridge and Forsythe Sts.)   (212) 477-2858

Highly Recommended Neighborhood Restaurants
(See chapter **Restaurants** *for reviews.)*

aKa Café	$25 & Under	FUSION
Alias	$25 & Under	NEW AMERICAN
71 Clinton Fresh Food	☆☆ $ $	BISTRO/NEW AMERICAN

Little Italy/Nolita

Historically, Little Italy was a family neighborhood, home to several waves of immigrants who settled in its five- and six-story tenement buildings. Some of them moved up and out, but others turned into the gray-haired grandmothers who still sit out on the stoops in pleasant weather.

The Italians moved in during the 1850's. In the first half of the 20th century, nearly everyone was of Italian descent. Since the late 1960's, when the United States opened its doors to Chinese immigrants, Chinatown has been creeping northward, crossing over its traditional Canal Street boundary. Although many Italian restaurants and stores remain, much of Little Italy proper—the blocks between Canal and Kenmare Streets—has the feel of Chinatown.

Mulberry Street is the real Italian heart of the neighborhood. It's lined with dozens of Italian restaurants and sidewalk cafes serving such specialties as coal-oven pizza and chocolate cannoli. **Ferrara** (195 Grand St.) has been producing traditional Italian desserts for 110 years. Try **Puglia** (189 Hester St.) for a unique, family-style dining experience. **Mare Chiaro** (176 1/2 Mulberry St.), with its Sinatra photos and authentic feel, is the place to go for a drink *(see chapter* **Nightlife***)*. For a taste of the area's Mafia past, go to the former site of **Umberto's Clam House** (149 Mulberry St.) where mobster Joey Gallo was gunned down in 1972. A couple of blocks north was the **Ravenite Social Club** (247 Mulberry St.), now a boutique, which served as the late John Gotti's unofficial headquarters until he was arrested there in 1990.

The big annual event is the **Feast of San Gennaro,** which starts the Thursday after Labor Day. For 10 days, several streets are closed to traffic, and the neighborhood becomes one giant colorful street festival, with rides, music and lots of food.

Old St. Patrick's Cathedral on Prince Street (at Mulberry St.) was founded by Irish immigrants in 1809. The cathedral became a parish church in 1879 when it was eclipsed by the new St. Patrick's Cathedral on Fifth Avenue. The old church was the childhood parish of Martin Scorsese and served as a backdrop for several movies, including two in Francis Ford Coppola's *Godfather* trilogy.

Nolita (which stands for **No**rth of **L**ittle **Ita**ly) is the extension of Little Italy north to Houston Street. A young crowd of artists, professionals and hipsters has recasting this neighborhood in the decidedly upscale mold of nearby SoHo. A host of sophisticated boutiques (many of them selling pricey shoes and handbags), galleries, cafes and nightclubs have sprouted in once-vacant storefronts *(see also chapters* **Shopping** *and* **Nightlife***)*. The heart of the action here is along **Elizabeth Street,** especially between Houston and Spring Streets.

Subway: F, S, V to Broadway–Laffayette St.; N, R to Prince St.; 6 to Spring St.

Recommended Inexpensive Restaurants

Lombardi's	PIZZA
Funky Broome	CHINESE

TriBeCa

TriBeCa can look and feel rather desolate. There is little activity on the streets, compared with SoHo and other trendy downtown neighborhoods. It's hard to tell which of the many cast-iron loft buildings have apartments tucked inside and which are commercial spaces. But that impression is misleading, for there's an interesting array of galleries, retail stores and acclaimed restaurants mixed in with the residential buildings that occupy this patch of Lower Manhattan (bounded to the north by Canal Street, to the east by Broadway, to the south by Chambers Street and to the west by the Hudson River).

TriBeCa was a bustling commercial and manufacturing center in the 19th century. Since the neighborhood was near the river and several shipping piers, wealthy merchants built warehouses there to hold agricultural goods, including spices, nuts and coffee. Factories and warehouses dominated the neighborhood well into the 20th century, but most were abandoned by 1970. That's when artists began trickling in, transforming space in many empty lofts into studios, galleries and living quarters.

Savvy real estate developers came up with the name TriBeCa, from Triangle Below Canal Street. By the early 80's, the neighborhood was drawing invest-ment bankers who liked its proximity to Wall Street, celebrities who liked its relative privacy, and anyone else who could afford the vast loft apartments whose values were shooting up.

A well-known landmark is the **Odeon,** the sleek and cavernous restaurant that played a leading role in *Bright Lights, Big City,* Jay McInerny's novel about the hedonistic nightlife of young New Yorkers in the 80's. TriBeCa is also home to a handful of hip restaurants owned by Robert De Niro and Drew Nieporent, including **Nobu,** for creative, adventurous Japanese cuisine; and **TriBeCa Grill,** a bustling spot offering contemporary American food and great stargazing.

Miramax has its headquarters here, as does neighborhood resident Robert De Niro, who opened the **TriBeCa Film Center** at 375 Greenwich St. TriBeCa was hard hit by the terrorist attacks of September 11, so De Niro created the **TriBeCa Film Festival** to welcome the world back to Downtown and publicize the creative spirit and resilience of the neighborhood.

Reade Street between Broadway and Church has some fine examples of the marble and cast-iron buildings that the neighborhood is known for, as does **Duane Street** between Church and West Broadway. Franklin, White and Walker Streets are also good places to check out the local architecture.
Subway: A, C, 1, 2, 3, 9 to Chambers St.; A, C, E, 1, 9 to Canal St.; 1, 9 to Franklin St.

Highly Recommended Neighborhood Restaurants
*(See chapter **Restaurants** for reviews.)*

Bouley	☆☆☆☆	$ $ $ $	FRENCH
Chanterelle	☆☆☆	$ $ $ $	FRENCH
Danube	☆☆☆	$ $ $ $	EAST EUROPEAN/GERMAN

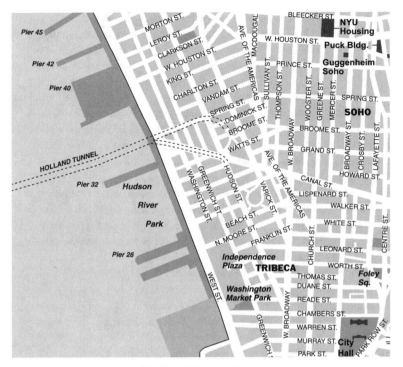

TriBeCa/SoHo

F.illi Ponte	☆☆	$ $ $ $	ITALIAN
Layla	☆☆	$ $ $	MIDDLE EASTERN
Next Door Nobu	☆☆☆	$ $ $ $	JAPANESE
Nobu	☆☆☆	$ $ $ $	JAPANESE
Odeon	☆☆	$ $	BISTRO/NEW AMERICAN
Salaam Bombay	☆☆	$ $	INDIAN
Tribeca Grill	☆☆	$ $ $	NEW AMERICAN

SoHo

Art and commerce coexist in SoHo (for South of Houston St.) more fiercely, perhaps, than anywhere else in New York City, yet still haven't driven each other out. (Artists who can't afford million-dollar lofts are a different matter.) There is impromptu art, like the fetchingly arranged baskets of unbelievably yellow tomatoes at **Dean & DeLuca** (*see chapter* **Shopping**) or the plumage of an elegant woman stepping down restaurant row on West Broadway. And then there is the more institutional art: the **200-odd galleries** that have colonized the neighborhood since four prominent uptown dealers, Leo Castelli, Ileana Sonnabend, John Weber and Andre Emmerick settled in the big loft building at 420 West Broadway in 1971 (*see section* "Galleries" *in chapter* **The Arts**).

The arrival of the big-four dealers signalled the transformation of a once-gritty warehouse neighborhood populated, often illegally, by penniless artists.

Today it's a chic scene, with limousines idling outside stores where a deceptively minimalist esthetic—lots of space, little merchandise—telegraphs old-money taste to new-money patrons. Many working artists have moved on to Chelsea.

Mr. Castelli, who used to put artists on a payroll whether they produced or not, introduced Andy Warhol's Campbell's Soup cans to SoHo. The neighborhood went on to nurture the wiggly post-graffiti art of Keith Haring and Jean Michel Basquiat. Mary Boone, a Castelli protégée who promoted Julian Schnabel and David Salle, has since moved her gallery north of 58th Street, where she was arrested for handing out nine-millimeter cartridges to visitors the way coffee shops offer mints. (She might've gotten away with it downtown.)

In SoHo, almost nothing lacks elegant style, from the ornate brackets at upscale hardware store **Anthropologie** (375 West Broadway), to the handmade note papers at **Kate's Paperie** (561 Broadway), to the french fries with lemony mayonnaise at **Balthazar** (80 Spring St.). Trendy clothing and accessory designers like **Anna Sui** (113 Greene St.), **kate spade** (454 Broome St.) and **Agnes B.** (79 Greene St.) also have shops here.

Cheap rents are a thing of the past SoHo these days, gone with the sweatshops that once occupied the 26 blocks of the historic cast-iron district (once called Hell's Hundred Acres, because of the frequent fires fueled by cloth and chemicals). Since Jill Clayburgh became a painter and drank at the **Spring Street Bar** (corner of Spring and Mulberry Sts.) in Paul Mazursky's 1978 movie, *An Unmarried Woman*, the anonymous artist homesteaders have been replaced at various times by celebrity denizens like Maus cartoonist Art Spiegelman, sculptor Claes Oldenburg, art critic Robert Hughes, actor Willem Dafoe, monologuist Spalding Gray and New York's favorite celebrity couple, Matthew Broderick and Sarah Jessica Parker.

Would they, let alone the original artists, have discovered SoHo without its architecture? From the magical **Puck Building** (295 Lafayette St.), with its gilded homage to *A Midsummer Night's Dream* on East Houston, to the **Haughwout Building** (488–492 Broadway), to the **Marble House** (southern edge of Mercer and Canal), the area is filled with distinctive buildings. The most famous, of course, are the post–Civil War cast-iron buildings, their Italianate elegance belying their seminal role as the grandfather of prefab architecture, the Sears catalog of building design, with owners choosing a Doric capital from column A and a Corinthian from column B. The bottle-glass sidewalks once allowed sunlight to illuminate the storage vaults below. Some streets are still paved with Belgian brick (not cobblestone) brought over as ship's ballast.

On Sullivan Street there are still some remnants of the Italian population that once called this area home. **Joe's Dairy** (156 Sullivan Street) and **Pino's Prime Meats** (149 Sullivan Street) are classics.

For children, a cast-iron tour can be almost as much fun as the **New York City Fire Museum**, with its collection of old firefighting equipment. Just buy a pack of cheap magnets; they'll help you tell the authentic cast-iron facades from the ringers.   *—Anemona Hartocollis*

Subway: F, S, V to Broadway–Lafayette St.; N, R to Prince St.; C, E, 6 to Spring St. or Bleecker St.

HIGHLIGHTS OF THE NEIGHBORHOOD

(*For the* **Drawing Center,** *the* **New Museum of Contemporary Art** *and coverage of the gallery scene, see chapter* **The Arts.** *For the* **Children's Museum of the Arts,** *see chapter* **New York for Children.**)

New York City Fire Museum 278 Spring St. (between Hudson and Varick Sts.) (212) 691-1303 *www.nycfiremuseum.org*. Located in a 1904 firehouse, the New York City Fire Museum traces the history of New York's Bravest from the 1600's to the present. The permanent collection includes a horse-drawn fire-fighting carriage and an exhibit on the "bucket brigade." An exhibit of photographs records the nation's most serious fires, including New York's Triangle Shirtwaist fire of 1911 and the Chicago fire of 1871. Expect changing exhibits relating to the destruction of the World Trade Center, in which 343 firemen were lost. Real firefighters are often on hand to share stories and fire-safety tips. This is a good place to buy authorized FDNY logo gear. **Admission:** $4 adults; $2 seniors and students; $1 children under age 12. **Hours:** Tue.–Sat. 10 A.M.–5 P.M., Sun 10 A.M.–4 P.M.

Highly Recommended Neighborhood Restaurants

(*See chapter* **Restaurants** *for reviews.*)

Balthazar	☆ ☆	$ $	BISTRO/FRENCH
Fiamma Osteria	☆ ☆ ☆	$ $ $	ITALIAN
Honmura An	☆ ☆ ☆	$ $ $	JAPANESE/NOODLES

Recommended Inexpensive Restaurants

Jean Claude	BISTRO/FRENCH
Pão	PORTUGUESE
Soho Steak	BISTRO/STEAK

NoHo

It's easy to forget that NoHo, wedged between the West Village, the East Village and SoHo, is a neighborhood in its own right (New Yorkers have been known to debate whether or not it even exists). But while it shares many qualities with its better-known neighbors, NoHo—which stretches from Houston Street to Astor Place, and from Mercer Street to the Bowery—has its own quirky history.

Some of the city's glitziest families, including the Astors and the Vanderbilts, were drawn to the neighborhood in the 1830's. They lived in the Greek Revival town houses known collectively as **Colonnade Row** (Lafayette St. between Astor Pl. and Great Jones St.). Only four of the nine mansions remain, and although the city has designated them landmarks, they are in shabby shape.

One of the old mansions houses the **Astor Place Theater** (434 Lafayette St.) where the ever-popular performance troupe called Blue Man Group has been putting on a wacky show involving Twinkies, paint and marshmallows since 1991. But NoHo's most venerable performance venue is the **Joseph Papp Public Theater** (425 Lafayette St.). The big old Italian Renaissance-style building origi-nally belonged to John Jacob Astor, the city's first multimillionaire and one of

NoHo's most famous residents. He donated the building to the city in 1854, and it became New York's first free public library. The building was set to be demolished in the 1960's, but at the last minute it was renovated and reopened by Joseph Papp, founder of the New York Shakespeare Festival. There are six theaters inside, and altogether they seat more than 2,500 people. *Hair* and *A Chorus Line* opened there, and the theater now stages about 25 productions a year.

The city designated much of NoHo a historic district in 1999, after a three-year crusade by residents to preserve the largely intact rows of 19th-century loft buildings scattered throughout the neighborhood. The buildings, with facades of marble, cast iron, limestone and terra cotta, once housed retail stores topped by manufacturing spaces or warehouses.

Artists began moving into the area in the early 1970's, trickling north from SoHo in search of cheaper rents. They adopted the name NoHo—for North of Houston—and in 1976 got the city to rezone the neighborhood similarly to SoHo, allowing artists to live and work in the same space.

NoHo has no park, school or library, but trendy bars and restaurants abound. One popular dinner spot is the **Time Café** (380 Lafayette St.), an 1888 building designed by Henry J. Hardenburgh, architect of the Plaza Hotel and the Dakota apartment house on Central Park West. In the basement is **Fez,** a neo-Moroccan lounge with Persian rugs, plenty of couches and performances that range from folk music to poetry readings.

—Abby Goodnough

Subway: F, S, V to Broadway–Lafayette St.; 6 to Bleecker St.

HIGHLIGHTS OF THE NEIGHBORHOOD

Merchant's House Museum 29 E. 4th St. (between Lafayette St. and Bowery) (212) 777-1089 *www.merchantshouse.com*. If you get a charge out of browsing through the pages of *Architectural Digest*, you'll enjoy this small museum, housed in a Greek Revival town house. It provides a historically accurate glimpse of the lifestyle of an affluent 19th-century family, with original furnishings and exhibitions related to the period. Lectures and readings are held throughout the year. **Admission:** $5 adults; $3 students and seniors; free for children under 12. **Hours:** Thu.–Mon. 1–5 P.M., plus guided tours Sat.–Sun. on the half hour.

The East Village

The East Village has always been a place for bold statements. It was here, at **Cooper Union,** in what is now the city's oldest auditorium, that Abraham Lincoln delivered the fiery anti-slavery speech that helped him win the Republican nomination in 1860. It was on St. Marks Place that Leon Trotsky started talking about revolution before joining one in Russia. And it was in the smoky music clubs around the Bowery, most notably **CBGB** (*see chapter* **Nightlife**), many decades later, that punk rock got its deafening start.

These days, skyrocketing rents and new $12-a-drink bars have arrived. But the East Village—stretching from the East River to the Bowery, and from 14th

East Village/Lower East Side

Street to Houston Street—has not lost the rough edges it acquired back in the early 1960's, when radicals, musicians, artists and hippes flocked here, having been priced out of Greenwich Village. Stroll, for example, past the **Hell's Angels'** headquarters on East 3rd Street. Most of the members are middle-aged now, but the plaque near the door still offers this youthful advice: "When in doubt, knock 'em out." Or get a mug of beer at **McSorley's** (E. 7th St. near Third Ave.), which looks as if no one has mopped the floor since the first mugs were filled there in 1854 (or 1862, depending on whose version of New York bar history you believe).

There are also still a few traces left of the neighborhood's multi-ethnic past. Beginning after World War II, the East Village became the center of the city's Ukrainian community, as immigrants fleeing Soviet oppression joined others who had settled in the neighborhood around the turn of thelast century. On Second Avenue you can still spot old men reading *Svoboda,* the Ukrainian-American newspaper. You can also grab a blintz or a bowl of borscht at **Veselka,** an honest-to-goodness Ukrainian diner at the corner of 9th Street.

Practically all evidence has disappeared of the days when a stretch of Second Avenue was known as the Jewish Rialto, the Broadway of Yiddish theater. But a quick side trip on East 10th Street takes you to the **Russian and Turkish Baths,** a cavernous, tiled throwback to a time when the neighborhood was filled with "shvitzes," Yiddish slang for sweat or steambath. For $20, there's an endless supply of steam and for a little more, a vigorous oak-leaf scrub is available, designed to draw out the body's toxins.

Little India (E. 6th St. between First and Second Aves.) offers a cluster of cramped Indian restaurants with nearly identical menus and décor. These are

great places to stop for a cheap tasty meal. For dessert, grab a cannoli at
Veniero's (342 E. 11th St.) or **De Roberti's** (176 First Ave.) around the corner.
These turn-of-the-century shops are two of the city's oldest Italian pasticcerias.

The best example of the East Village's bohemian credentials can be found on
St. Marks Place, which—despite the presence a Gap and a Subway sandwich
shop—still manages to attract nightly crowds of the heavily pierced and the col-
orfully coifed to its used-record stores, bars and cafes. The street is not, however,
quite as scrappy as it used to be: If you decide you would like a tattoo, there are
places to get one while you sip a cappuccino.

St. Marks dead-ends at another of the neighborhood's raucous landmarks,
Tompkins Square Park, where riots erupted back in 1988 when the police
moved in impose a curfew. Three years later, the police cleared out homeless
people and self-styled anarchists and closed the park for extensive renovations
and clean-up. Today, the loudest place in the park is usually near the chess
tables, where speed players shout to throw off their opponents' concentration.

The easternmost part of the East Village, from Avenues A to Avenue D, was
known until only a decade ago mostly for its abundance of drug dealers and
crime. But this area—called **Alphabet City**—has been undoubtedly the most
changed by the neighborhood's rapid gentrification. On the same corner where
heroin sales were once the main commercial activity, upscale bakeries are doing
a brisk business in blackberry scones. Buildings once called tenements now offer
$1,500-a-month, closet-sized studios with superfast Internet connections. So
what about all the radicals, musicians and artists who came to the neighborhood in search of lower rents? They're searching elsewhere.

—*Randy Kennedy*

Subway: F to Second Ave. or Broadway–Lafayette St.; 6 to Astor Pl. or
Bleecker St.; N, R to 8th St.; L, N, Q, R, W, 4, 5, 6 to Union Sq.

HIGHLIGHTS OF THE NEIGHBORHOOD

Cooper Union 30 Cooper Square, E. 8th St. and Fourth Ave. (212) 254-6300
www.cooper.edu. Housed in the city's first steel-frame building, Cooper Union
was New York's first free nonsectarian college, founded in 1859 by Peter
Cooper, the industrialist who built the first U.S. locomotive. Cooper wanted to
offer students the technical education that he himself had never received and to
create a center for open discussion. The school's Great Hall is just that. Inaugu-
rated in 1859 by Mark Twain, it served as the site for Lincoln's "right makes
might" speech in 1860. Today you can still attend lectures and concerts there.
In the triangle south of the building is a statue of Peter Cooper by Augustus
Saint-Gaudens. The gallery features exhibitions of fine art, architecture and
graphic design. Very competetive, the school offers a college degree in engineering, architecture and the graphic arts—and tuition is still free.

Grace Church 802 Broadway (at 10th St.) (212) 254-2000. This Gothic-style
Episcopalian church, built in 1846, was designed by James Renwick, who later
achieved fame as the architect of St. Patrick's Cathedral. Later in the century, a

marble spire was added to the white limestone church, as were several adjacent Gothic Revival buildings.

Nuyorican Poets Cafe 236 E. 3rd St. (between Aves. B and C) (212) 505-8183 *www.nuyorican.org.* Since the 1970's, the Nuyorican Poets Cafe has been in the vanguard of the neighborhood's alternative culture. A product of the black and Latino liberation movements, the cafe spawned the spoken-word poetry slams popularized by MTV in the early 1990's. The slams, contests in which the audience judges poets in game show fashion, still take place in the high-ceilinged space, as do featured reader nights, Latin big-band music blowouts and occasional theater productions and film screenings.

Russian and Turkish Baths 268 E. 10th St. (between First Ave. and Ave. A) (212) 473-8806 *www.russianturkishbaths.com.* There is nothing particularly remote or serene about these baths, housed in a timeworn tenement. But a visit there offers a voyage to an era when the neighborhood bustled with peddlers and Yiddish-speaking immigrants. Before the arrival of sushi and $10 martinis, a dozen or so public bathhouses were basic amenities for people deprived of indoor plumbing. Today, only the 10th Street Baths remain. Aside from the steep $22 admission charge and a juice bar—which still serves pierogen and pickled herring—little seems to have changed at what regulars still call "the shvitz," a temple to the art of sweating. And most of the clientele is refreshingly oblivious to the latest fitness fads.

St. Marks Church in the Bowery 131 E. 10th St. (between Second and Third Aves.) (212) 674-6377 *www.saintmarkschurch.org.* Tilted on a true east-west axis, this Episcopal church sits on land that was the farm of New Amsterdam's Governor Peter Stuyvesant. A Federal-style fieldstone building completed in 1799, the city's second-oldest church (after St. Paul's Chapel) was later outfitted with a Greek Revival steeple and a cast-iron portico. Following a devastating fire in 1978, the interior was restructured into a versatile open space that functions as a venue for the performing arts as well as religious services. In addition to its ongoing Poetry Project, the progressive East Village church hosts an outdoor pop music series. Stuyvesant and his wife are buried under the church.

Ukrainian Museum 203 Second Ave. (between 12th and 13th Sts.) (212) 228-0110 *www.ukrainianmuseum.org.* The East Village is home to a small but thriving Ukrainian population. The Ukrainian Museum houses permanent and changing exhibitions of folk art, fine art, photos, documents, coins, stamps, textiles, costumes, Easter eggs and rare books. The museum is in the process of raising funds to move into a larger facility on East 6th Street. **Admission:** $3 adults; $2 students and seniors. **Hours:** Wed.–Sun. 1–5 P.M. **Subway:** L, N, Q, R, W, 4, 5, 6 to 14th St./Union Sq.

Highly Recommended Neighborhood Restaurants
*(See chapter **Restaurants** for reviews.)*

Bambou	☆☆	$ $ $	CARIBBEAN
Tappo	☆	$ $ $	MEDITERRANEAN

Recommended Inexpensive Restaurants

Acquario	MEDITERRANEAN
Boca Chica	LATIN AMERICAN
Cyclo	VIETNAMESE
Euzkadi	BASQUE
First	NEW AMERICAN
Flor's Kitchen	LATIN AMERICAN
Frank	ITALIAN
Holy Basil	THAI
Lavagna	MEDITERRANEAN
Le Tableau	MEDITERRANEAN
Moustache	MIDDLE EASTERN
National Cafe	CUBAN/LATIN AMERICAN
Soba-Ya	JAPANESE/NOODLES
Xunta	SPANISH/TAPAS

Greenwich Village

Back in the earliest days of New York City, the Village was full of rolling farm-land and winding country lanes. Wealthy New Yorkers would arrive for short holidays, seeking to escape the congestion of Lower Manhattan. But the Village evolved into something decidedly less bucolic and serene. For generations, this was where radicals, writers, artists and intellectuals lived the bohemian life, starving for the sake of their art in tiny garrets and debating politics and philos-ophy in smoky cafes. This was where to find Dylan Thomas hoisting a few pints, Eugene O'Neill scribbling away at his latest play or John Reed furiously denouncing the bourgeois.

Throughout the 1960's, the Village was a hotbed of counterculture. Beatnik poets and bongo drummers held forth in nightclubs, experimental theater flour-ished and druggy musicians abounded. After a police raid of the **Stonewall Inn** (an incarnation still stands on Christopher Street), a group of gay men, tired of being harassed and closeted, staged an uprising that ignited the gay liberation movement. To this day, the Village is a stronghold of gay and lesbian culture.

The neighborhood has become too expensive to be considered truly bohemian anymore (it's home to Gwenyth Paltrow and a bevy of celebrities), but it's still got a funky charm and an anything-goes sensibility. Parking yourself at an outdoor cafe for a couple of hours of people watching (perhaps at **Café Reggio,** at 119 Macdougal St., or **Cafe Borgia,** 185 Bleecker St., where Allen Ginsberg and Jack Kerouac staged wild poetry readings back in the 60's) is end-lessly entertaining—street life in the Village is always unpredictable, always flamboyant.

The shady, tree-lined streets of the Village are populated with lovely brown-stones and town houses, not with towering high-rises. It's one of the most intriguing shopping areas in the city; on the same block, you can find high-priced antiques and used records, sleek designer fashions and vintage clothing, the latest kitchen gadgets and temporary tattoos. A handful of landmark clubs

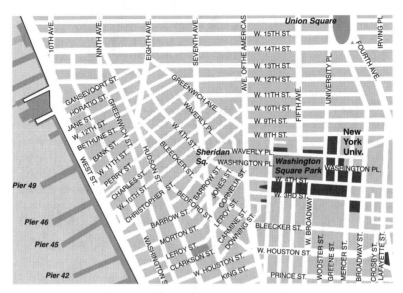

GreenwichVillage/West Village

with steep cover charges maintain the Village's longtime reputation as a hotbed
of great jazz; today they're outnumbered by clubs featuring rock, blues and alternative sounds. Add into this mix a huge array of restaurants, neighborhood pubs
and sleek cocktail lounges, and you've got a rollicking nightlife scene.

It's also fun to stroll to the far western reaches of the Village (near Chelsea),
where a whole new community has taken shape in the old **Meatpacking District.** Where workmen once hauled sides of beef through these desolate streets
near the Hudson River, supermodels now hop from bar to bar, downing $12
Cosmopolitans. An enormous concentration of galleries, bistros, dance clubs,
antiques dealers and designer boutiques has sprouted up just in the last few
years, as entrepreneurs have snapped up grimy warehouses and transformed
them into hipster hangouts through chic post-industrial design. It's a white-hot
area, a sizzling scene on weekend nights.

Subway: A, C, E, F to W. 4th St.–Washington Sq.; A, C, E, F, V, 1, 2, 3, 9 to
14th St.; 1, 9 to Christopher St.

HIGHLIGHTS OF THE NEIGHBORHOOD

Church of St. Luke in the Fields 487 Hudson St. (between Grove and
Christopher Sts.) (212) 924-0562 *www.stlukeinthefields.org.* "'Twas the night before
Christmas," the opening line of Clement Clarke Moore's famous Yuletide poem,
has special meaning for parishioners at this enchanting Federal-style landmark
church. Moore was a founding warden of the church, which was built in 1822 as a
satellite of Trinity Church. Strolling through the delightful gardens behind St.
Luke in the Fields adds to the sense of being in a remote village. In 1981, a devastating fire (the second in the church's history) destroyed the structure, and it was

restored to capture its original simplicity. The church is extremely active in neighborhood life and maintains a high musical profile. The St. Luke's Chamber Ensemble was born here, and the West Village Chorale regularly performs.

Church of the Ascension Fifth Ave. and 10th St. (212) 254-8620 *www.ascensionnyc.org,* Richard Upjohn's legacy to New York City includes several wonderful churches, among them the Church of the Ascension. Completed in 1841, the church was the first built on Fifth Avenue, which was then an unpaved track ending in a wooden fence at 23rd Street. A Gothic Revival-style brownstone structure, the church relates closely to Upjohn's earlier (and better-known) Trinity Church in Lower Manhattan. The beautiful interior is famous for its John LaFarge mural and stained-glass windows, and exquisite marble statuary by Louis Saint-Gaudens. The extraordinary Voices of Ascension, a professional choir and orchestra, presents some of the finest choral concerts in town.

Forbes Magazine Galleries Fifth Ave. at 12th St. (212) 620-2200. Malcolm Forbes, millionaire publisher, collected glamorous friends, bejeweled Fabergé eggs, toy soldiers, toy boats, old Monopoly games, autographs and presidential papers. Except for the glamorous friends, it's all here, tastefully exhibited on the ground floor of the Forbes magazine building. **Admission:** Free. **Hours:** Tue.–Wed. and Fri.–Sat. 10 A.M.–4 P.M.

New York Public Library—Jefferson Market Library 425 Sixth Ave. (between Ninth and 10th Sts.) (212) 243-4334. You can't miss this eyeful of bright red stone and ornate pinnacles, towers, carvings and stained-glass windows, all topped off with a clock tower that still keeps perfect time. These days it houses a branch of the New York Public Library, but it was originally built in 1877 as a courthouse, on the site of a public meat-and-produce market. The courthouse was part of a complex including a firehouse and a jail, which stood in the area now occupied by a lush community garden.

New York University Information Center, 40 Washington Sq. South (at Wooster St.) (212) 998-4636 *www.nyu.edu.* Sometimes it seems as if everywhere you turn in Greenwich Village, you see a violet flag on a building telling you that you are looking at another part of New York University's sprawl. Washington Square Park is the de facto center of the campus, surrounded by university offices, student centers, dorms and libraries. Founded in 1831, NYU hosts some 17,000 undergraduate and 18,000 graduate students, and boasts the nation's largest open-stack library. The university sponsors performances at several of its auditoriums, including the Loewe Auditorium, the NYU Theater and the Loeb Student Center.

75 1/2 Bedford Street (at Commerce St.). Only 9.5 feet wide and dating from 1893, this house is said to be the narrowest in the city. Edna St. Vincent Millay, Margaret Mead, William Steig and Cary Grant all lived in this tiny place at one time or another. Around the corner at 38 Commerce Street you can also visit the **Cherry Lane Theater,** opened by Millay and friends in 1924 in an old barn and still in operation.

Washington Mews Fifth Ave., between Washington Sq. North and E. 8th St. This private street of two-story houses in Greenwich Village once functioned as stables and service quarters for the residents of the Greek Revival row houses along Washington Square North. These 19th-century structures were converted into private residences during the early 1900's, and were leased to New York University in 1949. Today, some of the buildings contain NYU offices, but this cobblestone street maintains its quiet charm.

Washington Square Park W. 4th St. (at Macdougal St.) (212) 387-7676. Washington Square Park brings together downtown's diverse population. Musicians jam near the central fountain as skateboarders jump park benches. Students from nearby NYU lounge or shoot films, gay and straight singles swap canine tales as their dogs frolic and children swing in the fenced playground. The southwestern corner is also the proving ground for the city's most serious chess players. The park's identifying landmark is Stanford White's large marble arch, constructed in 1895 to commemorate George Washington's inauguration. In the early part of the 20th century, the artists Marcel Duchamp and John Sloan climbed onto the arch to declare the secession of the neighborhood from the United States. A generation earlier, Henry James named a novel for the square. But as a public gathering place, the park also has its dark history, having served in the early 19th century as a graveyard and the site of public hangings. You would be excused for thinking it's haunted, as the gallows tree remains standing and many of the graves were left undisturbed when the park was established in 1827.

Washington Square Park

Highly Recommended Neighborhood Restaurants
(*See chapter* **Restaurants** *for reviews.*)

Babbo	☆☆☆	$$$$	ITALIAN
Blue Hill	☆☆	$$$	FRENCH
Gotham Bar and Grill	☆☆☆	$$$$	NEW AMERICAN
Jarnac	☆	$$$	FRENCH
Surya	☆☆	$$	INDIAN
Washington Park	☆☆	$$$	NEW AMERICAN

Recommended Inexpensive Restaurants

Bar Pitti	ITALIAN
Cookies and Couscous	MOROCCAN
Do Hwa	KOREAN
Good	LATIN AMERICAN
Grange Hall	AMERICAN
Le Gigot	FRENCH
Little Basil	THAI
Marumi	JAPANESE/SUSHI
Mexicana Mama	MEXICAN
Moustache	MIDDLE EASTERN
Paradou	FRENCH/SANDWICHES
Pearl Oyster Bar	SEAFOOD
Pepe Verde	ITALIAN

The Flatiron District/Union Square/Gramercy Park

The neighborhoods that make up the broad swath of Manhattan between Sixth Avenue and the East River, from 14th to 27th Streets, contain some of the best preserved historic districts and landmarks in the city, as well as a host of chic spots for shopping, dining and nightlife. The area is dotted with little emerald oases—five parks whose importance far exceeds their acreage.

Madison Square (Fifth Ave. and 23rd St.) was once home to a depot of the New York and Harlem Rail Road and two earlier incarnations of Madison Square Garden. It offers a front-row view of two quintessential New York buildings: the **Flatiron Building** (175 Fifth Ave.) and the **Metropolitan Life Insurance Building** (1 Madison Ave.), whose 1909 tower with its four-faced clock and lantern is still intact despite substantial renovations. Also in the area are the exquisite **Appellate Division Courthouse** (27 Madison Ave.), the headquarters of the **New York Life Insurance Company** since 1928 (51 Madison Ave.). The Flatiron District earned the nickname "Silicon Alley" in the heyday of the dot-com firms once based here, but few of the companies have survived.

Union Square (14th-17th St. and Broadway) was once a rallying place for

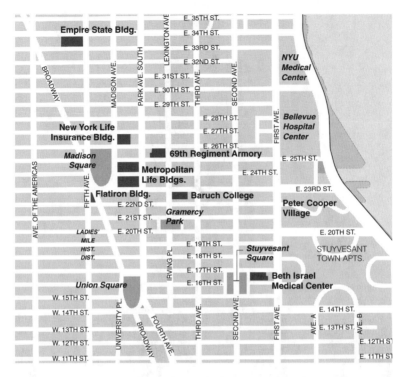

Flatiron/Union Square/ Gramercy Park

the Labor movement, but it got its name as the union of the Bloomingdale Road (now Broadway) and the Bowery Road (now Fourth Ave.). By turns the province of aristocrats, anarchists and addicts, it has in recent decades felt more like a village green, thanks to the wonderful farmers' market established there in 1977 *(see section* "Food Markets" *in chapter* **Shopping***)* and to a major renovation that was completed in 1992. In the decade that has followed, an array of trendy restaurants has sprung up along the edges of the square, along with a Barnes & Noble superstore and a Virgin Megastore. After the 9/11 attacks, Union Square was a magnet for New Yorkers, who gathered here to mourn as a community.

Between Madison Square and Union Square from Broadway to Sixth Avenue is **Ladies' Mile,** the post–Civil War shopping district that was the former home of Lord & Taylor (901 Broadway) and B. Altman & Co. (615–629 Sixth Ave.) until department stores began to migrate uptown in the early decades of the 20th century. The buildings that once housed the dry-goods emporiums of the Gilded Age have been restored to retail life as home furnishing stores, like **ABC Carpet and Home** on Broadway and **Bed, Bath & Beyond** on Sixth Avenue. This area is a hotbed for upscale restaurants; Park Avenue South, in particular, is a veritable Restaurant Row.

Gramercy Park (Lexington Ave. and 21st St.), a fenced and locked enclave (only those lucky residents who live directly on its perimeter are given keys),

The Flatiron Building

remains one of the most genteel squares in urban America, as it has been since 1831. One of the city's earliest high-rise apartment buildings stands on the park's southeast corner, while several town houses with ornate wrought iron porches endure on the western side. At 15 Gramercy Park South stands the elegant head-quarters of the **National Arts Club** (212-477-2389; *www.nationalartsclub.org*), which promotes American art by awarding prizes and scholarships. The club's headquarters is a Gramercy Park brownstone, which Calvert Vaux (Frederick

Law Olmsted's partner in the design of Central Park) renovated in a Victorian Gothic style for Gov. Samuel J. Tilden.

Nearby is the **69th Regiment Armory** (68 Lexington Ave.), which hosted the celebrated 1913 "Armory Show" that introduced America to modern art and continues to host various arts and antiques shows. Also in the area are several prominent nightspots, like Irving Plaza *(see chapter* **Nightlife***)*.

Subway: L, N, R, Q, W, 4, 5, 6 to Union Sq.; N, R, 6 to 23rd St. or 28th St.

HIGHLIGHTS OF THE NEIGHBORHOOD

Center for Jewish History 15 W. 16th St. (between Fifth and Sixth Aves.) (212) 294-8301 *www.cjh.org.* Newly opened in 2000, the Center for Jewish History is an enormous complex dedicated to exploring Jewish history, art, culture and literature. Its main exhibition space, the Yeshiva University Museum, features a variety of displays, including a sculpture garden and a collection of Judaica confiscated by the Nazis. Additional resources include a Reading Room, a geneaology institute, national archives of the Jewish people in America, and scholarly research institutes. There's also an auditorium that features a wide variety of films, lectures and performances. **Admission:** Yeshiva University Museum: $6 adults; $4 students and seniors; free to other facilities. **Hours:** Yeshiva University Museum: Sun. and Tue.–Wed. 11 A.M.–5 P.M.; Thu. 11 A.M.–8 P.M.; Reading Room and Geneaology Institute, Mon.–Thu. 9:30 A.M.–4:30 P.M. Other galleries: Mon.–Thu. 9 A.M.–5 P.M.; Fri. 9 A.M.–4 P.M. **Subway:** F, L, N, R, V, 1, 2, 3, 4, 5, 6, 9 to 14th St.

Flatiron Building 175 Fifth Ave. (at 23rd St.). Originally known as the Fuller Building, the Flatiron Building took its nickname from its shape—an odd triangular design devised to fit on this peculiar plot of land (it's only 6 feet across at its narrowest end). The architect, Daniel H. Burnham, designed this early skyscraper, built in 1902, by overlaying an Italian Renaissance terra-cotta facade on a modern steel frame. The tall, wedge-shaped office building looks like a ship sailing uptown. Today the revitalized surrounding Flatiron District has taken on the building's name.

School of Visual Arts Museum 209 E. 23rd St. (between Third and Fourth Aves.) (212) 592-2144 *www.schoolofvisualarts.edu.* The School of Visual Arts trains students as professional graphic and fine artists. Its museum features changing exhibitions by students and established artists; in the past, it has featured works by Willem de Kooning, Keith Haring and Roy Liechtenstein. Most of the work is contemporary, but shows span an array of mediums including illustration, fine art, sculpture, animation and photography. The school hosts film, music and lecture events throughout the year, and there are three additional on-campus galleries for student exhibits.

Theodore Roosevelt Birthplace 28 E. 20th St. (between Park Ave. South and Broadway) (212) 260-1616 *www.nps.gov/thrb.* This brownstone, which includes period rooms restored to their appearance from 1865 and 1872, is a reconstruction of the four-story house where Theodore Roosevelt was born and lived until he was 14. During much of his childhood, Roosevelt was confined to the house with a variety of illnesses, including chronic asthma. There are 250,000 objects in the permanent collection, including T.R.'s christening gown and the stuffed Teddy bears that take his name. The site, which can only be seen on a guided tour, boasts the largest collection of the president's memorabilia anywhere. Displays from the permanent collection change regularly, and the museum hosts concerts and lectures throughout the year. **Admission:** $3 adults; free for children under 17. **Hours:** Mon.–Fri. 9 A.M.–5 P.M. Tours leave hourly, with the last tour at 4 P.M.

Highly Recommended Neighborhood Restaurants
(*See chapter* **Restaurants** *for reviews.*)

Blue Water Grill	☆	$ $	SEAFOOD
Campagna	☆ ☆	$ $ $	ITALIAN
Eleven Madison Park	☆ ☆	$ $ $	NEW AMERICAN
Gramercy Tavern	☆ ☆ ☆	$ $ $ $	NEW AMERICAN
I Trulli	☆ ☆	$ $ $	ITALIAN
Mesa Grill	☆ ☆	$ $ $ $	SOUTHWESTERN
Patria	☆ ☆ ☆	$ $ $	LATIN AMERICAN
Tabla	☆ ☆ ☆	$ $ $ $	PAN ASIAN
Veritas	☆ ☆ ☆	$ $ $ $	NEW AMERICAN

Recommended Inexpensive Restaurants

Chat 'n Chew	NEW AMERICAN
Mavalli Palace	INDIAN/VEGETARIAN

Chelsea

The formerly gritty neighborhood of Chelsea is better known these days for up-and-coming **art galleries** (some 170 in all), a vibrant gay and lesbian community and a sprawling riverside sports complex. The galleries are mostly concentrated in the 20's between Tenth and Eleventh Avenues; it's fun to spend a day gallery hopping before strolling down south to the neighboring **Meatpacking District** to drop into one of its trendy bistros, bars or clubs (*see the section on* "Greenwich Village," *earlier in this chapter, as well as chapters* **Restaurants** *and* **Nightlife**).

Chelsea stretches from Sixth Avenue to the Hudson River, roughly between West 14th and West 28th Streets. Its eastern end, along Sixth Avenue, is increasingly dominated by big-box stores like **Bed, Bath & Beyond** and **Old Navy.** For an outdoor shopping alternative, try the weekend flea market at the corner of Sixth Avenue and West 26th Street. It's a fun place to troll for kitschy treasures, although true bargain hunters will scoff at the prices. If you've got a green thumb, make a beeline for the nearby flower district (around 27th St. and Sixth Ave.).

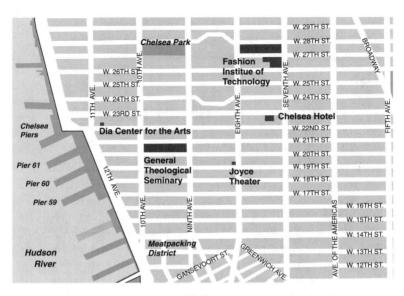

Chelsea

For more breathing room, wander over to the residential cross streets
between Seventh and 10th Avenues, where 19th-century brownstones prolifer-
ate and river breezes often take wanderers by surprise. West 20th, 21st and 22nd
Streets between Eighth and 10th Avenues are especially winsome blocks, perfect for strolling. **Cushman Row** (408–18 W. 20th St., between Ninth and 10th
Aves.) contains some particularly notable Greek Revival row houses (1839–40).
One landmark worth glimpsing is the **General Theological Seminary,** whose
ivy-covered, Gothic-style buildings occupy the block between Ninth and 10th
Avenues, from 20th to 21st Street.

Eighth Avenue in Chelsea is another heavily trafficked retail strip, where
quirky boutiques mix with restaurants whose tables spill onto the sidewalks in
the warmer months. There are also many bars and clubs catering to the area's
large gay community *(see chapter* **Nightlife***)*.

One of Chelsea's most lively thoroughfares is West 23rd Street, whose best-
known landmark is probably the **Chelsea Hotel** (222 W. 23rd St. between Seventh and Eighth Aves.). In the past it was a beloved, if verging on decrepit, way
station for artists, poets and rock musicians—everyone from Eugene O'Neill
and Thomas Wolfe to Lenny Bruce and Sid Vicious have stayed here. Renovations have removed a good deal of the outright seediness, since a crop of new
boutique hotels is providing stiff competition. If you're hungry, grab a choco-
late-frosted doughnut from the **Krispy Kreme** shop down the block.

Fitness fanatics would say that no tour of Chelsea is complete without a stop
at the **Chelsea Piers** sports complex, which occupies four piers on the Hudson
River from 17th to 23rd Street *(see chapter* **Sports & Recreation***)*. There are ice
and roller skating rinks, a health club, a fieldhouse for soccer and other sports,
batting cages, a driving range and a bowling alley.

For those not inclined to exert themselves, Chelsea Piers also has benches on which to loaf an afternoon away, with views across the river to Jersey City and, if you linger long enough, the setting sun.   *—Abby Goodnough*

Subway: C, E, F, V, 1, 9 to 23rd St.

HIGHLIGHTS OF THE NEIGHBORHOOD
(For the **Dia Center for the Arts,** *the* **Center for Jewish History,** *the* **Joyce Theater, The Kitchen** *and coverage of the gallery scene, see chapter* **The Arts.***)*

Fashion Institute of Technology Seventh Ave. and 27th St. (212) 217-5779 *www.fitnyc.suny.edu.* The alma mater of superstars like Calvin Klein and Norma Kamali, the Fashion Institute of Technology (FIT) is the training ground for many of the players, and even more of the workers, in New York's garment industry. The maze of buildings that make up the campus occupies a full block. You'll notice a proliferation of fashion-forward students in the neighborhood sporting their own exotic designs. The museum at FIT (free admission; open Tue.–Fri. noon–8 P.M., Sat. 10 A.M.–5 P.M.) boasts one of the world's largest collections of costumes, textiles and accessories of dress from the 18th to the 20th century, and it presents inventive fashion-related exhibitions. The institute's functional auditorium serves as home base to the Village Light Opera Group.

Highly Recommended Neighborhood Restaurants
(See chapter **Restaurants** *for reviews.)*

Chelsea Bistro & Bar	☆☆	$ $ $	BISTRO/FRENCH
Frank's	☆	$ $ $	STEAKHOUSE
Periyali	☆☆☆	$ $ $	GREEK
The Red Cat	☆	$ $	NEW AMERICAN
The Tonic	☆☆	$ $ $	NEW AMERICAN

Recommended Inexpensive Restaurants

Bright Food Shop	NEW AMERICAN
El Cid	SPANISH
Grand Sichuan	CHINESE
Gus's Figs Bistro & Bar	MEDITERRANEAN
Le Zie 2000	ITALIAN
Royal Siam	THAI

Murray Hill

When the British landed in 1776 near importer Robert Murray's country estate (which stood near where E. 37th St. crosses Park Ave.), Murray's wife and daughters are said to have invited British General Sir William Howe to tea, a respite that diverted Howe's forces long enough to allow George Washington's exhausted American troops to escape to Harlem.

The core of old Murray Hill—which stretches along the middle to upper 30's between Madison and Third Avenues—includes landmarks like the **Pierpont**

Morgan Library and the renovated carriage houses of **Sniffen Court** (150–158 E. 36th St.). Side streets are lined with diplomatic missions, social and cultural clubs and mid-range hotels.

Murray Hill residents have long been wary of commercial development. When Benjamin Altman opened what was among the first luxury department stores on Fifth Avenue and 34th Street in 1906, he disguised it as an Italian palazzo in an effort to allay those fears. The landmark B. Altman & Co. building now houses the Public Library's high-tech **Science, Industry and Business Library** (188 Madison Ave. at 34th St.), the **Graduate Center of the City University of New York** (365 Fifth Ave. at 34th St.) and **Oxford University Press.** The west side of Fifth Avenue bustles with small retail stores, while a number of Asian, Indian and Middle Eastern restaurants line Third Avenue. On the northern edge of Murray Hill is **Tudor City,** completed in 1928, a middle-class "city within a city."

Anchoring the area on the south is the picturesque **Church of the Transfiguration** on 29th Street (between Madison and Fifth Aves.). It earned a place in the hearts of actors in 1870 when the minister at a nearby church refused to bury actor George Holland, and suggested instead "the little church around the corner."

Subway: 6 to 33rd St.; S, 4, 5, 6, 7 to Grand Central.

HIGHLIGHT OF THE NEIGHBORHOOD

The Pierpont Morgan Library (at Madison Ave.) (212) 685-0008 *www.morganlibrary.org.* The world's most powerful financier in his day, J. P. Morgan started collecting medieval and Renaissance manuscripts, rare books and English and American authors' manuscripts in 1890. Within a decade, his collection had grown to such an extent that he needed an entire building to house it. Designed by Charles McKim and completed in 1906, the neoclassical building that houses the library opened to the public in 1924, serving as both a museum and a center for scholarly research. In addition to drawings by Dürer, Blake and Degas, and the country's largest collection of Rembrandt etchings, the Morgan owns 1,300 manuscripts and a working draft of the U.S. Constitution. The library's literary holdings include illuminated manuscripts, three copies of the Gutenberg Bible, letters by Jane Austen, Charles Dickens's manuscript of *A Christmas Carol* and Henry David Thoreau's journals. Musical texts include handwritten works by Bach, Mozart, Schubert and Stravinsky. **Admission:** $8 adults; $6 students and seniors; free for children under 12. **Hours:** Tue.–Thu. 10:30 A.M.–5 P.M., Fri. 10:30 A.M.–8 P.M., Sat. 10:30 A.M.–6 P.M., Sun. noon–6 P.M.

Highly Recommended Neighborhood Restaurants
*(See chapter **Restaurants** for reviews.)*

Asia de Cuba	☆	$ $ $	ASIAN/LATIN
Hangawi	☆ ☆	$ $	KOREAN/VEGETARIAN
Icon	☆ ☆	$ $	NEW AMERICAN

Recommended Inexpensive Restaurants

Da Ciro	ITALIAN
Evergreen Shanghai	CHINESE
Wu Liang Ye	CHINESE

Midtown East

From the European jet setters who browse in the posh boutiques along its affluent avenues, to the diplomatic polyglot that is the **United Nations,** Midtown
East is one of New York City's most cosmopolitan areas and one of its largest
business districts. Its skyscrapers host many corporate headquarters that are
filled each day by commuters who pass through the cavernous Beaux Arts concourse of **Grand Central Terminal.** Park Avenue and other neighborhood thoroughfares are lined with "glass boxes" like **Lever House,** completed in 1952
(390 Park Ave. between 53rd and 54th Sts.); and Art Deco marvels like the
Chrysler Building, the **Waldorf-Astoria Hotel** (Park Ave. at 49th St.), a
favorite stopover for U.S. presidents and other visiting dignitaries, and the
Chanin Building, on the southwest corner of 42nd Street and Lexington
Avenue.

    Saks Fifth Avenue, Henri Bendel and **Takashimaya** are only a few of the
stylish retail landmarks in the area (*see chapter* **Shopping**). Neighborhood
streets and avenues are dotted with grand hotels and cultural institutions like
the **Japan Society** and the **Dahesh Museum** (*see chapter* **The Arts**).

    At rush hour, pedestrians and drivers battle for control of the asphalt. It is
hard to imagine Midtown East ever being the tranquil place it once was when
turtles thrived near the quiet cove from which the **Turtle Bay** area takes its
name. The most serene spots left are the affluent cul-de-sacs of **Beekman and
Sutton Places.**

    Second Avenue between 43rd and 53rd Streets is the commercial hub of
Turtle Bay, lined with shops, businesses and a variety of clubby steakhouses and
elegant restaurants. The **Amish Market,** on 45th Street just off Second
Avenue, stocks a wide variety of produce, cheese and specialty items.

    Turtle Bay's most charming side-street enclave is **Turtle Bay Gardens His-
toric District,** a stretch of 10 town houses on the north side of East 48th Street
and 10 on the south side of East 49th Street between Second and Third
Avenues. Gardens residents have included Katharine Hepburn, Stephen Sond-
heim and E.B. White, who wrote about the neighborhood for *The New Yorker.*

Subway: S, 4, 5, 6, 7 to Grand Central; E, N, R, V, W to Fifth Ave. or Lexington Ave.; 6 to 51st St.; 4, 5, 6 to 59th St.

HIGHLIGHTS OF THE NEIGHBORHOOD

(*For the* **Dahesh Museum,** the **Whitney Museum of American Art—Philip
Morris Branch,** *see chapter* **The Arts.**)

Chrysler Building 405 Lexington Ave. (between 42nd and 43rd Sts.) (212)
682-3070. In late 1929, New Yorkers gawked as the Chrysler Building emerged

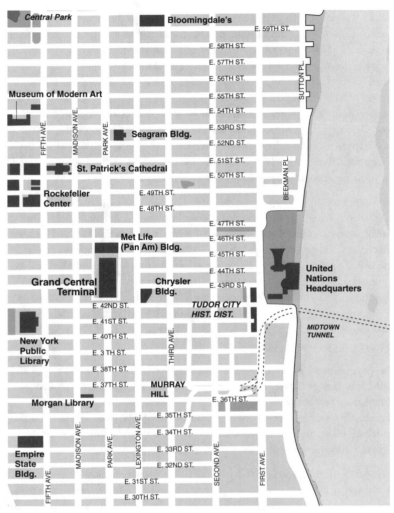

Midtown East/Murray Hill

from its construction scaffolding. The brilliant steel ornaments and spire were unlike anything else in New York, and at 1,046 feet, 4.75 inches high, it was the tallest building in the world.

Kenneth Murchison, an architect and critic of the time, admired the steel crown and "the astonishing plays of light which nature alone can furnish." While other buildings had been put up with distinctive spires, they were all in traditional materials: copper, terra cotta, iron, stone, brick. But on the Chrysler Building, the entire upper section above the 61st floor—and much of the ornamentation below—is gleaming chrome-nickel steel, which reflects sunlight with dazzling brilliance.

From a distance, the Chrysler Building seems like near kin to the Empire State Building, which took away its height record in 1931. But unlike the Empire State, which was proudly hailed by one of its architects as a building where "hand work was done away with," the Chrysler Building is like a giant craft project. The metal is generally soldered or crimped—all by hand—and the thick, wavy solder lines and the irregular bends all betray individual craftsmanship. The broad surfaces of metal, almost all stamped to form on the site, are wavy and bumpy, like giant pieces of hand-finished silver jewelry.

Just as surprising is the section just below the spire. So solid-looking from the outside, this part has no occupants and only intermittent flooring; only a few of the triangular openings have glazing. Inside, the wind rushes through what seems like a high, thin gazebo-shell of steel, at striking variance with the otherwise modernistic solidity of this continually fascinating building.

—Christopher Gray

Citicorp Center 153 E. 53rd St. (between Lexington and Third Aves.). The wedge-shaped spire of Citicorp Center, designed by Hugh Stubbins and Emery Roth, was designed to hold penthouse apartments, but residential zoning was denied. The aluminum and glass tower is headquarters for the Citigroup conglomerate, but it also has commercial, retail, mass-transit and even religious functions. The 915-foot building, supported entirely by four massive pillars, hovers over a sunken plaza that connects a multilayered shopping mall, a subway crossroads and a church. The starkly modernist St. Peter's holds Sunday jazz vespers and weekday concerts.

French Institute and Florence Gould Hall 55 E. 59th St. (between Park and Madison Aves.) (212) 355-6100 *www.fiaf.org*. The French Institute/Alliance Française offers language courses as well as a variety of cultural events with French themes. Florence Gould Hall offers films, concerts and dance, while the smaller Tinker Auditorium holds lectures, receptions and cabaret performances. There's a downtown branch at 95 Wall St. **Subway: 4, 5, 6 to 59th St.**

Grand Central Terminal 42nd St. at Park Ave. *www.grandcentralterminal.com*. On its physical merits alone, Grand Central Terminal is one of New York's great treasures. Its main concourse is an immense, bustling space with a blue-green ceiling painted to resemble a starlit sky. But Grand Central is vastly important also as a historical and political symbol, for it lies at the heart of court decisions affirming the city's right to protect its architectural heritage. Opened in 1913, the Beaux-Arts monument was threatened in the 1960's by developers who planned to demolish the concourse and build office towers all around it. Preservationists took their case to court and to the public, with high-profile assistance from Jacqueline Kennedy Onassis. They won. In 1978, the United States Supreme Court ruled that the city had a right to protect Grand Central—and, by extension, other landmarks—from destruction. After falling into disrepair, the station got an expensive cleanup in the 1990's that restored much of its original grandeur. Above all, Grand Central remains what it has always been: one of the world's busiest train stations, with half a million people passing through it each day.

—Clyde Haberman

Additional notes on Grand Central: Trains serve suburban New York, Connecticut, upstate New York and points west; several subway lines converge here. There's also the **Grand Central Market** for gourmet goods, and an extensive downstairs food court. More formal dining choices include **Michael Jordan's,** for fine steaks and a great view of the twinkling stars in the constellations on the

The Seagram Building

Park Avenue and 20th-Century Architecture

To a surprising number of architects and city-lovers, the so-called Park
Avenue Corridor is the architectural heart of the 20th century. The corridor
is the crystallization of the New York myth, the soaring city of work and
ambition, where the sky is the limit and dreams are fulfilled. It symbolizes
New York's displacement of Paris as the century's most vibrant City of Light.

The corridor contains several individual buildings of distinction from the
1950's to 60's, including the **Seagram Building** (*disscussed in detail below*),
Lever House, 500 Park Avenue and the **Chase Building** (originally the
Union Carbide Building), the last three designed by the New York firm Skidmore, Owings & Merrill, and Philip Johnson's Russell Sage Foundation (originally Asia House). James Ingo Freed's **Park Tower**, completed in 1981, is a
somber late addition to the group, while Frank Lloyd Wright's 1958 **Mer-
cedes-Benz Showroom** (originally Jaguar) offers a quirky footnote to the
ramp of the Guggenheim Museum's rotunda.

But much of the corridor's power lies in the aggregate, in the mix of lesser
buildings with well-known landmarks. At the century's outset, long before the
first curtain wall was actually hung, architects used to dream about the gleaming cities that glass would enable them to build. Here, the dream was realized.

The term International Style was coined by Philip Johnson and Henry
Russell Hitchcock for an exhibition in 1932 at the Museum of Modern Art.
In the postwar decades, the International Style became shorthand for the
steel and glass towers like the Seagram Building, the supreme example of the
genre, designed by Mies van der Rohe and Philip Johnson in 1957–58.

Mies described his own aesthetic as one of "almost nothing," a paring
down of form to the discreet articulation of construction and enclosure.
Walls were reduced to the transparent membrane of the glass curtain wall.
Structure was expressed on the exterior by the application of nonstructural
I-beams. This approach exemplified the architect's belief that less is more. It
enlarged the artistic significance of proportion, scale, quality of materials and
refinement of detail.

Not long ago, it was said that these buildings represented a rejection of
history. In fact, the International Style was grounded in 19th-century histori-
cism: the view that each epoch should produce a distinctive architectural style.

In the early 1960's, the International Style was a symbol of urban sophistication in many Hollywood movies, as accurate a barometer as we have of
popular desires. In *Breakfast at Tiffany's, The Best of Everything* and even several Doris Day comedies, the glass tower epitomized worldly aspiration and
success. In the reflections of the crystal canyon, the world of external reality
merges with the subjective realm of ambition, fantasy and desire.

No design in recent years has given firmer shape to this idea than Christian de Portzamparc's **LVMH Tower** at 19–21 East 57th Street. Described by
Mr. Portzamparc as an homage to the city of glass, the 23-story tower features

a faceted glass skin that unfolds like a crystal flower. While the tower can't possibly be mistaken for an International Style skyscraper, LVMH responds to the context of the mythical New York where modernity took root. And it is the first blossom that this root has sent forth in many years.

Seagram Building and Plaza 375 Park Ave. (between 52nd and 53rd Sts.) (212) 572-7000. For much of the past thousand years, the pendulum of Western architectural taste has swung between two esthetic poles: Gothic and classical, they eventually came to be called. Because it fuses elements of both positions in a supremely elegant whole, the Seagram Building is my choice as the millennium's most important building.

The 38-story Manhattan office tower was designed in 1958 by Ludwig Mies van der Rohe in association with Philip Johnson and is the most refined version of the modern glass skyscraper. It faces Park Avenue across a broad plaza of pink Vermont granite, bordered on either side by reflecting pools and ledges of verd antique marble. The tower itself is a steel-framed structure wrapped in a curtain wall of pink-gray glass. Spandrels, mullions and I-beams, used to modulate the surface of the glass skin, are made of bronze. The walls and elevator banks are lined with travertine.

Mies once defined architecture as the will of an epoch translated into space. For architects of his generation, this meant reckoning with the reality of the industrial age and the transforming power of machine technology. But it also meant overcoming the war of the styles, which had fragmented architecture into battling ideological camps.

In the Seagram Building, the classical elements are more obvious: the symmetry of its massing on the raised plaza; the tripartite division of the tower into base, shaft and capital; the rhythmic regularity of its columns and bays; the antique associations borne by bronze.

The building's Gothicism is subtler. It is evident in the tower's soaring 516 feet, the lightness and transparency of the curtain wall, the vertical emphasis conveyed by the I-beams attached to the glass skin and the cruciform plan of the tall shaft and the lower rear extension. Indeed, the Gothic cathedral was the prelude to the whole of modern glass architecture.

Today we recognize that Gothic and classical represent more than two architectural styles. They stand for two views of the world, neurologists have determined, that correspond to functions located in the left and right sides of the brain. The classical is rational, logical, analytic. The Gothic is intuitive, exploratory, synthetic. In hindsight, we recognize, too, that there's little to be gained by embracing one side at the other's expense. The business of civilization is to hold opposites together. That goal, often reached through conflict, has been rendered here by Mies with a serenity unsurpassed in modern times.

—Herbert Muschamp

stunning sky ceiling, and the landmark **Oyster Bar,** for a wide variety of fresh seafood. The **Municipal Arts Society** (212-935-3960; *www.mas.org*) conducts free tours of the building, departing from the information booth in the main concourse every Wednesday at 12:30 P.M. The **Grand Central Partnership** (212-697-1245) offers its own free tours on Fridays at 12:30 P.M.; meet outside the station in front of the Whitney Museum at Philip Morris.

Japan Society 333 E. 47th St. (between First and Second Aves.) (212) 832-1155 *www.japansociety.org.* The Japan Society's mission is to promote better relations between the U.S. and Japan and to bring New Yorkers a wonderful blend of the traditional and the contemporary in Japanese culture. Events include regular film series and live kabuki theater. Art exhibitions, such as "Early Buddhist Art from Korea and Japan: 6th–9th Centuries" (scheduled for spring 2003), are mounted in elegant galleries. The society also offers language lessons at all levels. **Admission:** $5 adults; $3 students and seniors. **Hours:** Galleries: Tue.–Fri. 11 A.M.–6 P.M.; Sat.–Sun. 11 A.M.–5 P.M. **Subway:** 4, 5, 6 to 42nd St.

MetLife Building 200 Park Ave. (between 43rd and 45th Sts.) (212) 922-9100. Pan Am's former headquarters was the world's largest commercial office building when it was completed in 1963—its mammoth bulk effectively blocking the vista up and down Park Avenue. A team that included Emery Roth and Sons, Pietro Belluschi and Walter Gropius used concrete curtain walls to frame the building's structure. The lobby doubles as a concourse leading to Grand Central. In the 1980's, Metropolitan Life Insurance bought the building from the financially troubled airline, and the MetLife logo supplanted Pan Am's globe as a landmark of Manhattan's skyline.

Chester Higgins, Jr./The New York times

The United Nations

St. Patrick's Cathedral Fifth Ave. (at 50th St.) (212) 753-2261 *www.ny-arch-diocese.org/pastoral*. St. Pat's is the Roman Catholic cathedral for the archdioceses of New York, which covers Manhattan, the Bronx, Staten Island and several upstate counties, and is generally recognized as a center of Catholic life in America. Its design, by James Renwick, was based on the great cathedral in Cologne, Germany. The nave was opened in 1877, almost 20 years after the start of construction; the 330-foot twin spires were completed in 1888. At the time it stood on the northern edge of the city, visible from miles around. Architectural purists deride its mixed forms and the lack of flying buttresses, but it is a grand and elaborate statement nonetheless, surrounded now by city skyscrapers.

A magnificent rose window over the central portal measures 26 feet in diameter. The cathedral's 70 stained-glass windows were crafted in studios in Chartres and Nantes in France, Birmingham, England, and Boston—and not finally completed until the 1930's. The 14 stations of the cross were carved in Holland. The Pietà is three times larger than the Michelangelo masterpiece in St. Peter's in Rome, and there are three organs.

United Nations First Ave. at 42nd St. (212) 963-8687, ext. 1 for tour info. *www.un.org*. Literally in a world of its own, United Nations headquarters and its grounds occupy a strip of international territory on the edge of Manhattan, running between First Avenue and the East River from 42nd to 48th Street. The site was donated to the U.N. in 1946, a year after the organization's birth, by John D. Rockefeller, Jr. Designed by an international team of architects, including Le Corbusier, three connected buildings—the boxy Dag Hammarskjold Library, the glass-walled Secretariat tower and the low-slung General Assembly—dominate the site. Erected between 1947 and 1953, they frame a central fountain crowned with a 21-foot-high bronze sculpture, *Single Form* by Barbara Hepworth, dedicated to the memory of Hammarskjold, the only Secretary General to have been killed in office, on a peace mission to the Congo in 1961. Daily public tours take in the most famous indoor chambers, including the Security Council and General Assembly halls. An eclectic collection of artwork donated by many countries is scattered throughout corridors and lounges. In the basement, shops sell jewelry and handicrafts from around the world, international books for adults and children and souvenirs of the U.N. itself. There are also outdoor attractions, especially when the weather is warm. Visitors stop to see the colorful array of flags from 188 nations flying along First Avenue or to enjoy walking on the riverside promenade and through the quiet formal gardens that form a two-block oasis of serenity north of the 46th Street visitors' entrance. The gardens form a backdrop for several other monumental sculptures dedicated to the ideal of peace among nations.   —*Barbara Crossette*

Additional notes on the U.N.: Visitors can enjoy lunch on weekdays in the Delegates' Dining Room. Call ahead for reservations at (212) 963-7626. Be sure to bring along a photo I.D., dress nicely and be prepared for a security check before the elevator attendant takes you up. Lunch buffets are $22. **Tours:** $8.50 adults; $7 senior citizens; $6 students; $5 children ages 5–14. No children under age 5. **Hours:** Daily 9:30 A.M.–4:45 P.M. (no weekend tours Jan.–Feb.). Tours in English leave approximately every 30 min. Schedules may be limited during special events.

Highly Recommended Neighborhood Restaurants
(See chapter Restaurants for reviews.)

An American Place	☆☆	$ $ $ $	NEW AMERICAN
Bouterin	☆	$ $ $ $	FRENCH
Brasserie	☆☆	$ $ $	BISTRO/FRENCH
Chola	☆☆	$ $	INDIAN
Della Femina	☆	$ $ $ $	NEW AMERICAN
Felidia	☆☆☆	$ $ $ $	NORTHERN ITALIAN
Fifty Seven Fifty Seven	☆☆☆	$ $ $ $	AMERICAN
The Four Seasons	☆☆☆	$ $ $ $	NEW AMERICAN
Guastavino's	☆☆	$ $ $ $	ENGLISH/FRENCH
Heartbeat	☆☆	$ $	NEW AMERICAN
Il Valentino	☆☆	$ $	ITALIAN
Kuruma Zushi	☆☆☆	$ $ $ $	JAPANESE
La Grenouille	☆☆☆	$ $ $ $	FRENCH
Le Cirque 2000	☆☆☆	$ $ $ $	NEW AMERICAN
Le Colonial	☆☆	$ $	VIETNAMESE
Lespinasse	☆☆☆☆	$ $ $ $	FRENCH
Lutéce	☆☆	$ $ $ $	FRENCH
March	☆☆☆	$ $ $ $	NEW AMERICAN
Michael Jordan's	☆☆	$ $ $ $	STEAKHOUSE
Oceana	☆☆☆	$ $ $ $	SEAFOOD
Olica	☆☆☆	$ $ $	FRENCH
Patroon	☆☆☆	$ $ $ $	NEW AMERICAN
Shun Lee Palace	☆☆	$ $ $ $	CHINESE
Smith & Wollensky	☆☆	$ $ $ $	STEAKHOUSE
Solera	☆☆	$ $ $ $	SPANISH
Sono	☆☆	$ $ $ $	JAPANESE/FRENCH
Sushi Yasuda	☆☆☆	$ $ $ $	JAPANESE/SUSHI
Zarela	☆☆	$ $	MEXICAN/TEX-MEX

Recommended Inexpensive Restaurants

Jubilee	FRENCH
Katsu-Hama	JAPANESE
Meltemi	GREEK/SEAFOOD

Midtown West

There is probably more to see and do in Midtown in the West 30's, 40's and 50's than anywhere else in the city—not least the sizzling wattage of the newly booming Times Square. Long touted as "the crossroads of the world," it is fast becoming America's carnival midway. Shaking off its seedy past and ridding itself of porn theaters, this neighborhood has become family-friendly. Amid the

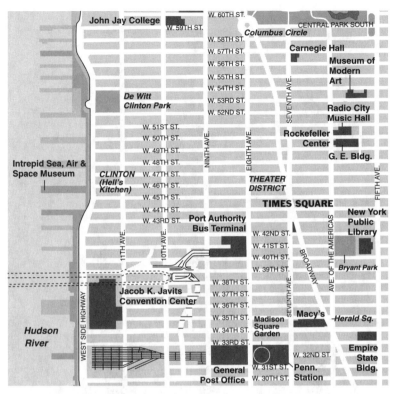

Midtown West

famous swirl of neon signs and the glitz of Broadway theaters, it has sprouted attractions like theme restaurants, high-tech arcades and even a branch of London's silly **Madame Tussaud's Wax Museum.** Everything is supersized, including the massive **Virgin Megastore** and a flagship branch of **Toys R Us.**

But Midtown is also the tonier gleam of **Rockefeller Center,** the breathtaking pinnacle of the **Empire State Building,** the vigilant marble lions guarding the Fifth Avenue entrance to the **New York Public Library.**

If you're a fan of the *Today* show or *Good Morning America*, see them live and full-size through the plate glass of their **street-level studios**—in Rockefeller Center and Times Square, respectively. (For tickets to other TV shows, see the box later in this section.) **MTV** has studios behind glass in Times Square, too, not so easy to view because they are on the second floor; to find them, listen for squealing teeny-boppers. For headier music, there's **Carnegie Hall** on 57th Street (*see chapter* **The Arts**). For a corned beef sandwich that feeds two, there's the **Carnegie Deli** just two blocks away.

Broadway and Seventh Avenue in the 30's have been the main arteries of the **Garment District** for more than 100 years, home to the warehouses and workshops of the fashion industry.

The biggest attraction for most visitors is **Broadway theater.** The epicenter of the Theater District is at Broadway and 42nd Street; dozens of theaters line

The Empire State Building

Broadway and its side streets in the 40's. (*See chapter* **The Arts** *for details on finding out what's playing and how to get tickets.*)

West of the Theater District is a residential neighborhood famed as **Hell's Kitchen,** the rough-and-tumble home of immigrant Irish in the second half of the 19th century—former Senator Daniel Patrick Moynihan grew up there. Greeks, Eastern Europeans, Puerto Ricans and other groups moved in later. The p.c. name for the area now is **Clinton** (for DeWitt, not Bill) and its residents are young professionals, theater people and remnants of the old immigrant groups. **Restaurant Row** (46th St. between Eighth and Ninth Aves.) is a long block of restaurants side-by-side, all packed with theater-goers before curtain time—and half-empty after 8 P.M. A host of affordable ethnic restaurants and bars lines Ninth Avenue, catering to the rapidly growing younger population.

Subway: A, B, C, D, E, F, N, Q, R, S, V, W, 1, 2, 3, 9 to 34th St.; A, B, C, D, E, F, N, Q, R, S, V, W, 1, 2, 3, 7, 9 to 42nd St.; B, D, F, S, V to 47th-50th

St.–Rockefeller Center; N, R, W to 49th St.; 1, 9, C, E, to 50th St.; F, N, R, Q, S, W to 57th St.; A, B, C, D, 1, 9 to 59th St.

HIGHLIGHTS OF THE NEIGHBORHOOD

(For the **American Craft Museum, American Folk Art Museum** *and the* **International Center of Photography,** *see chapter* **The Arts.** *For* **Carnegie Hall** *and full coverage of Broadway theater, see section* "The Performing Arts" *in chapter* **The Arts.** *For* **Madison Square Garden,** *see chapter* **Sports & Recreation.***)*

Bryant Park Sixth Ave. (stretching from 40th to 42nd Sts.) *www.bryant-park.org.* On warm weekdays, Midtown workers descend on Bryant Park to shed ties and high heels for some lunchtime relaxation. They arrange the park's folding chairs to gossip, or stretch out on the luxurious lawn for cat-naps. Regulars play chess near a statue honoring the park's namesake, William Cullen Bryant, longtime editor of the *New York Post* and an early advocate of radical ideas such as abolition and public parks. At the rear of the New York Public Library, there's the lovely **Bryant Park Grill** (212-840-6500), offering upscale bistro food and summertime alfresco dining. Dotting its tree-lined boundaries are statues commemorating literary figures ranging from Goethe to Gertrude Stein, making the park a great place to read a chapter before heading back to the office. Probably the best time to go, though, is Monday nights in the summer, when HBO presents free movie classics on a huge screen.

Empire State Building 350 Fifth Ave. (between 33rd and 34th Sts.) (212) 736-3100 *www.esbnyc.com.* Known as the "Empty State" after it was completed in 1931, the Empire State Building remained half-rented during the Depression. Nevertheless, it is one of New York's great icons. Designed by Shreve, Lamb and Harmon, the Empire State was constructed at breakneck speed on the former site of the original Waldorf-Astoria Hotel. This glorious Art Deco tower won a three-way competition with the Chrysler Building and 40 Wall Street to become the world's tallest skyscraper, a title it kept for more than half a century. After the destruction of the Twin Towers, the Empire State Building is once again the tallest building in the city, and New Yorkers hold it a little more dearly in their hearts. The building's spire, immortalized as King Kong's perch, was designed—but used only once—as a mooring mast for dirigibles; it is flood-lit at night, adding a glamorous note to the skyline. Visitors can ascend the elevators to **observation decks** on the 86th and 102nd floors, where the panoramic views are breathtaking. **Admission:** $9 adults, $7 seniors over age 62, $4 children ages 5–11. Ticket lines can be brutal, but you can avoid them by ordering online, though there's a $2-per-ticket service charge. **Hours:** Observatory daily 9:30 A.M.–midnight. Last elevators ascend at 11:15 P.M.

General Post Office 421 Eighth Ave. (between 32nd and 33rd Sts.) (212) 330-3601. When you're running to get a package postmarked before midnight, the main post office's staircase feels as monumental as it looks. The facility is open 24 hours a day. (Check out the scene on the night of April 15, when late tax filers race to meet the midnight deadline.) Built in 1914 and designed by McKim, Mead and White as a complement to the first Pennsylvania Station—a landmark that was demolished in the 1960's—the Classical Revival building stretches across two city blocks.

The post office's unofficial motto is spelled out above a parade of imposing Corinthian columns: "Neither snow nor rain nor heat nor gloom of night stays these couriers from the swift completion of their appointed rounds." After a campaign by former Senator Daniel Patrick Moynihan, plans are now being developed to turn a large part of the building into a new train station to replace the current, uninspiring incarnation of Penn Station.

Jacob K. Javits Convention Center 655 W. 34th St. (between 11th and 12th Aves.) (212) 216-2000 *www.javitscenter.com*. The convention complex, boasting over 17 acres of floor space, was designed by the architectural firm of I. M. Pei. The New York International Auto Show, held here each April, alone draws more than one million visitors.

Museum of Television and Radio 25 W. 52nd St. (between Fifth and Sixth Aves.) (212) 621-6600 or (212) 621-6800 *www.mtr.org*. Don't expect to find the same kind of displays and exhibits that you'd find in other museums here. The real treasure here is the incredible archive, a collection of thousands of classic TV episodes, commericals and specials. The theaters offer special screenings, but most visitors opt to sign out tapes of their favorite programs, which they can screen at private consoles (you can request up to four shows in one sitting). **Admission:** $6 adults; $4 students and seniors; $3 children under age 13. **Hours:** Tue.–Sun. noon–6 P.M. (until 8 P.M. Thu., Fri. theater programs until 9 P.M.).

New York Public Library Fifth Ave. and 42nd St. (212) 661-7220, or (212) 869-8089 for info on exhibits and events. *www.nypl.org*. One of the world's

Nancy Siesel/The New York Times

New York Public Library

greatest libraries, this two-block-long Beaux-Arts palace of books has long been thought of as the main branch of the New York Public Library system, which includes 85 branches in the Bronx, Manhattan and Staten Island. But the building is actually the biggest of the system's four research libraries, formally known as the Humanities and Social Sciences Library. No books are allowed to leave the building. Its 15 million items, from rare illuminated manuscripts to pulp fiction to Cherokee literature, may be checked out and read in the library.

It is a place where leafing through a book takes on a whole new meaning. The Main Reading Room on the third floor stretches the length of a football field. Beneath its soaring ceiling murals of bright blue skies and clouds, readers can plug in a laptop, peruse a newspaper or just daydream.

Anyone can ask for a book to be fetched from seven floors of stacks underneath the room or two more floors concealed under the lawn of Bryant Park next door. There are about 132 miles of shelves in the stacks, not open to the public. (In order to maintain the proper hush, tourists are encouraged to take scheduled tours of the Reading Room.)

The library came along relatively late in the city's history—it is just 100 years old. A little-known architecture firm, Carrere and Hastings, won a competition to build what was then the largest marble structure ever attempted in the country.

And the famous marble lions? They have stood guard at the Fifth Avenue entrance since the beginning of Mayor Fiorello La Guardia's administration. He dubbed the one to the south Patience and the one to the north—you guessed it—Fortitude. —*Randy Kennedy*

Radio City Music Hall 1260 Ave. of the Americas (at 50th St.) (212) 247-4777 *www.radiocity.com.* Radio City Music Hall is Manhattan's version of a natural wonder. It's our Rainbow Arch, our Old Faithful, our Niagara Falls. After a $70 million restoration in 1999, the great hall's awesome beauty can be seen once again in the genius of its original conception.

Completed in 1932, the Music Hall is a tribute to the Rockefeller family's spirit of culturally progressive enterprise. Like Rockefeller Center, which surrounds it in Midtown, the theater countered the Great Depression with a great infusion of hope in the city's future. Radio City! Live from Radio City!

Always seen as a place for families, the Music Hall opened at a time when family entertainment might include ballet, symphony and opera, along with comedy, popular song, acrobatics and the Rockettes. The vaudeville mix was recognizably of the radio age, when folks gathered round the Bakelite console to hear their favorite shows. The Music Hall gave them tunes and great visuals besides.

Three New York architectural firms are credited with the design of the theater. These firms brought to harmonious realization the unlikely alliance between the patrician Rockefellers and the plebeian Samuel L. Rothafel, known as Roxy, an impresario of movie palaces for the masses.

The building is a triumph of processional design. Its most dramatic aspect is an expanded version of an effect common in theater architecture: the disarming contrast between a small-scale exterior and an interior of epic proportions. The entrance and ticket lobby are lodged on the ground floor of an office tower that gives little sign of the grandiose space inside.

The ticket lobby is in keeping with the scale of the building's exterior, but the box offices anticipate the amplitude within. From here we proceed to a grand ocean liner of a space, the Grand Foyer. Moderne rather than modern, the foyer is one of the world's great Art Deco interiors, its length and height amplified by mirrors of gold-backed glass.

Entering the auditorium, we find ourselves on the deck of the ocean liner, gazing out to sea, precisely the image Roxy Rothafel wanted his architects to capture for his new 6,000-seat show palace. In time the showman's wish was conveyed to the young Edward Durell Stone, a draftsman in one of the three architectural firms responsible for the design. In later life, Stone made his mark with Manhattan buildings like the Museum of Modern Art and the General Motors Building. At age 30, Stone found himself designing the most stupendous arch this side of Rome.

The auditorium's formal power is derived from the plain, unadorned half-circle of the proscenium, and from the projection of that shape from the front to the rear of the house. Like a dome, the design eliminates both walls and ceiling. This is why the auditorium is psychologically so overwhelming. No matter where you sit, you have the sensation of tumbling through the sky. This feeling is heightened by the broad strips of air-conditioning grilles, also used for lighting, that radiate longitudinally from the proscenium. These bands further diminish the orientation that walls and ceiling usually provide. It's a cinematic effect, the architectural equivalent of the simultaneous reverse track and forward zoom in Hitchcock's *Vertigo*.

For design historians, the Music Hall is forever linked to Donald Deskey, responsible for the theater's iconic Art Deco interiors. Plate-glass vanity tables, metal tube chairs, mohair sofas, round mirrors, balustrades, light fixtures, theater seats: these are some of the classic pieces Deskey created for the Hall.

—*Herbert Muschamp*

Rockefeller Center Between 48th and 52nd Sts., Fifth to Seventh Aves. (212) 332-6868 *www.rockefellercenter.com*. This soaring 18-building complex of monumental architecture in the heart of Manhattan includes some of New York's best-known skyscrapers and landmarks, including the Art Deco splendor of **Radio City Music Hall** (*see listing above*). The central sunken plaza is magically transformed into the focal point of the city's holiday festivities each winter, as skaters twirl and glide on the ice of the tiny **Rink at Rockefeller Center** (212-332-7654; *see also chapter* **Sports & Recreation**), under the massive **Rockefeller Center Christmas tree** and the watchful eye of Paul Manship's golden statue of **Prometheus.** In any season, the plaza is an impressive sight, ringed by the flags of all United Nations member countries. The 70-story **G.E. Building** soars overhead; step into its lobby to check out the murals by José Maria Sert. Paul Goldberger once called this

Fred R. Conrad/The New York Times

Radio City Music Hall

space "a setting for a 1930's movie about corporate power, pulsing with the energy of capitalism both real and romantic."

The brainchild of John D. Rockefeller, the complex incorporates office buildings, stores, theaters and open space. NBC's New York studios are scattered throughout the complex; *Saturday Night Live* and *Late Night with Conan O'Brien* are among the shows filmed here *(see the box in this section for details on obtaining tickets)*. Each weekday morning brings crowds who've come to stand outside the glass studios of the *Today* show; in summer, the show sponsors free outdoor concerts each Friday morning.

Rockefeller Center was the largest privately sponsored real estate venture ever undertaken in New York City when construction began in 1929. Originally it was to include a new Metropolitan Opera House, those plans were scrapped after the stock market crash that October. Mr. Rockefeller then reconceived the project as an entirely commercial complex. Rockefeller Center is home to over 100 works of art, all chosen along one theme: "The Progress of Man." One of the most notable pieces, "Atlas" (Lee Laurie, 1937) stands in front of the International Building (630 Fifth Ave.). There are also wonderful facade sculptures, including "News" (Isamu Noguchi, 1940). An impressively dynamic stainless steel relief adorns the **Associated Press Building,** at 50 Rockefeller Plaza, depicting five news reporters.

Times Square Broadway and Seventh Ave., from 42nd to 47th Sts. *www.timessquarebid.org.* New Yorkers insist on calling it the Crossroads of the World. Of course, New Yorkers like to think of their city as the center of the cosmos, so it is hardly surprising that they attach mere global import to the dot on the hometown map where Broadway and 42nd Street collide. For once, however, the New York penchant for overstatement happens to be fact.

Times Square is, without a doubt, the most recognized intersection on the planet, and never is that more true than on **New Year's Eve.** Hundreds of thousands of people jam the square and tens of millions more watch on television as a glittering ball slowly descends, ticking off the final seconds of the dying year (the special ball manufactured to mark the year 2000 was made by Waterford Crystal, covered with 144 strobe lights and 12,000 rhinestones). By now, some

The G.E. Building at Rockefeller Center

are willing to believe that there would not be a new year without this communal gathering in the heart of New York.

It wasn't always like that. At the turn of the last century, the area was a humble place called Long Acre Square. The name was changed in 1904 when *The New York Times* moved there; the cachet of the Times Square name attracted people to the surrounding blocks, and the square became a neighborhood. For decades to come, Times Square would provide the country with some of its most enduring images, from the finger-snap pace of the crowds outside Jack Dempsey's restaurant to the strangers exultantly embracing on VJ Day. All it took was an overhead shot of the neon-bathed square to tell moviegoers that they were entering a world of sophistication.

Decay set in with the Great Depression; by the 1970's, Times Square had become synonymous with sleazy arcades and tawdry sex shows. The menace and sheer creepiness of the place was memorably captured by Martin Scorsese in his 1976 film, *Taxi Driver*. Historic theaters and hotels were sacrificed for office space, the Times moved around the corner and the building's terra-cotta facade was replaced with faceless white marble.

But the 90's brought rebirth, with porno houses giving way to the likes of Disney shows. Some find the new attractions a tad too sanitized, but few truly mourn the passing of the dope dealers and pimps.

Today, there is no better place to people-watch than Times Square. Street performers, gawking tourists and get-out-of-my-way New Yorkers—they are all here, and are easily the most fascinating thing about the place. For show business, there's also no place like Times Square. In the early years of the last century, a big show could earn an average of a million dollars in its first year. By 1999, Broadway was still packing them in, with attendance a record 11.6 million and a box-office take of $588 million, also a record. (*See the "Performing Arts" section in chapter* **The Arts** *for more on Broadway theater, including how to get tickets.*) There are also about 1,500 businesses and organizations here; 21 million square feet of office space and 2.4 million more being built; one-fifth of all New York City hotel rooms; 3.9 million overnight visitors each year, and 26 million day-trippers; more than 251 restaurants, 10 movie theaters and 22 landmarked Broadway theaters. And believe it or not, nearly 27,000 people actually live in the Times Square area; 231,000 folks go to work there every day.

Through the years, Times Square has evolved and is still evolving. Yet it remains the place to gather, whether to watch a televised space shot or protest a war or celebrate triumph over tyranny. It is far more than a neighborhood. It is America's town square. —*Clyde Haberman*

U.S.S. Intrepid Sea-Air-Space Museum Pier 86, 46th St. at 12th Ave. (212) 245-2533 *www.intrepidmuseum.org*. Launched in 1943 and decommissioned in 1974, the *Intrepid* once housed more than 100 aircraft and a crew of over 3,000. This aircraft carrier was deployed in World War II, the Korean and Vietnam Wars and served as a recovery vessel for NASA capsules. There are jets and prop planes on the flight and hangar decks, and exhibits relating to the ship's history and

If You'd Like to Be Part of the Studio Audience . . .

Many TV shows are taped in New York live (and eager) audience. Unfortunately, tickets are tough to get, even if you plan months in advance.

If all else fails, you can always join the crowds outside the **Today** show's glass-walled studio on the southwest corner of 49th Street and Rockefeller Plaza. Tapings are Mon.–Fri. 7–10 A.M.

For more show tapings in the area, call the New York Convention & Visitors Bureau at (212) 484-1222.

The Daily Show With Jon Stewart Taped Mon.–Thu. at 5:45 P.M. at 513 W. 54th St. No one under 18. Call (212) 586-2477 weeks in advance, or stop by Mon.-Thurs. 10:30 A.M.–4 P.M. to ask about cancellations.

Late Night With Conan O'Brien Tapings are Tues.–Fri. at 5:30 P.M. No one under 16 admitted. Arrive at 4:45 P.M. at the 49th Street entrance to 30 Rockefeller Plaza. Reserve months in advance by calling (212) 664-3056. Standby tickets are available at 9 A.M. outside the studio; line up early.

The Late Show with David Letterman Tapings are Mon.–Thu. at 5:30 P.M., and again on Thu. at 5:30 and 8 P.M. No one under 18 admitted. Send a postcard at least 6 to 9 months in advance (two tickets max; one request only, or all will be disregarded), to Late Show Tickets, Ed Sullivan Theater, 1697 Broadway, New York, NY 10019. You can also register at *www.cbs.com/latenight/lateshow* to be notified of tickets that may become available for specific dates in the next 3 months.

Live With Regis and Kelly Tapings are Mon.–Fri. at 9 A.M. at ABC Studios at Columbus Avenue and West 67th Street. No one under 10 admitted. Send your postcard requesting up to four tickets at least a full year in advance to Live! Tickets, Ansonia Station, P.O. Box 230777, New York, NY 10023-0777 (212) 456-3054. Standby tickets are sometimes available; arrive at the studio by 7 A.M.

Saturday Night Live Tapings are Sat. at 11:30 P.M. (arrival time 10 P.M.). No one under 16 is admitted. Unfortunately, tickets are so hot that the lottery system for advance tickets is usually suspended. However, you can try for standby tickets on the day of the taping, which are distributed at 7am outside 30 Rockefeller Plaza, on the 49th Street side of the building (first-come, first-served; one ticket per person). For advance tickets, call (212) 664-3056 as far in advance as possible to determine the current procedure.

The View Mon.–Fri., 11 A.M. No one under 18 admitted. Send ticket requests to The View, Tickets, 320 W. 66th St., New York, NY 10023 or go online at *www.abc.go.com/theview*. Requests should be made four to six months in advance. Standby tickets are available before 10 A.M.

undersea exploration. A flight simulator recreates the feeling of being inside an F-18 fighter during the Gulf War. The open-air flight deck allows access to the navigation bridge and wheelhouse, and close examination of planes, helicopters and gun galleries. The destroyer *Edison* and the submarine *Growler* lie alongside. All three vessels are open to visitors, but the 900-foot *Intrepid*, which occupies an area greater than a Midtown block, is the most impressive. A new interactive exhibit called "All Hands on Deck" allows kids to get a first-person experience of how things work on a real Navy warship. **Admission:** $13 adults; $9 students, seniors and veterans; $6 children ages 6–11; $2 children ages 2–5; children under 2 free. **Hours:** Apr.–Sept. Mon.–Fri. 10 A.M.–5 P.M., Sat.–Sun. 10 A.M.–7 P.M.; Oct.–Mar. Tue.–Sun. 10 A.M.–5 P.M. only. Last admission 1 hr. before closing.

Highly Recommended Neighborhood Restaurants
(See chapter **Restaurants** *for reviews.)*

Aquavit	☆☆☆	$$$$	SCANDINAVIAN
Chez Josephine	☆☆	$$$	BISTRO/FRENCH
Cho Dang Gol	☆☆	$$$	KOREAN
Christer's	☆☆	$$$	SCANDINAVIAN
Churrascaria Plataforma	☆☆	$$$	BRAZILIAN
Estiatorio Milos	☆☆	$$$$	GREEK/SEAFOOD
Firebird	☆☆	$$$	RUSSIAN
Judson Grill	☆☆☆	$$$$	NEW AMERICAN
Kai	☆☆	$$$$	JAPANESE
Kang Suh	☆☆	$$	KOREAN
La Caravelle	☆☆☆	$$$$	FRENCH
La Côte Basque	☆☆☆	$$$$	FRENCH
Le Bernardin	☆☆☆☆	$$$$	FRENCH/SEAFOOD
Molyvos	☆☆	$$$	GREEK
Osteria Del Circo	☆	$$$	ITALIAN
Petrossian	☆☆	$$$$	RUSSIAN
Remi	☆☆	$$$	ITALIAN
San Domenico	☆☆☆	$$$$	ITALIAN
Sea Grill	☆☆	$$$	SEAFOOD
Thalia	☆☆	$$$	NEW AMERICAN
"21" Club	☆☆	$$$$	NEW AMERICAN
Viceversa	☆	$$	ITALIAN

Recommended Inexpensive Restaurants

Carnegie Deli	DELI
Chimichurri Grill	LATIN AMERICAN
Han Bat	KOREAN
Havana NY	LATIN AMERICAN
Los Dos Rancheros	MEXICAN
McHale's	BAR SNACKS/BURGERS
Rinconcito Mexicano	MEXICAN

Topaz Thai   THAI
Wu Liang Ye   CHINESE

The Upper East Side

From the stately homes and manicured flower beds along **Park Avenue** to the
art galleries and pricey boutiques on **Madison Avenue,** the Upper East Side has
all the trappings of power and privilege. Walk along Park or its side streets on a
weekday morning and you're likely to see professional dog walkers being tugged
along in a tangle of pedigree poodles, or uniformed children traipsing off to
Spence, Chapin and other exclusive private schools.

Historically, the Upper East Side has been an old-money enclave, home to
some of the nation's wealthiest corporate titans and robber barons. But the
Upper East Side has a more diverse population than its reputation suggests,
especially on the far eastern side of the neighborhood. On Lexington Avenue,
institutions such as **Bloomingdale's, Hunter College** and the **92nd Street Y**
lure shoppers, students and culture lovers from across the city. Farther east, middle-class families and young professionals who've snagged rent-stabilized apartments fill the high-rise apartments that sprang up after World War II.

This area boasts some of the best-known cultural institutions in the world.
Museum Mile, along Fifth Avenue, is home to the **Metropolitan Museum of
Art,** the **Solomon R. Guggenheim Museum,** the **Jewish Museum,** the
Museum of the City of New York and **El Museo del Barrio.** The Frick and
Carnegie mansions house the **Frick Collection** and the **Cooper-Hewitt
National Design Museum,** respectively (*see chapter* **The Arts** *for full listings of
all these museums*). The mansions are two remnants of Millionaire's Row, where
European-style grand residences overlooking Central Park were built in the
early 1900's by super-rich industrialists competing to outdo each other. Several
institutions dedicated to world societies and cultures are also located here
including the **Asia Society** and the **China Institute in America** (*see section*
"Institutes of World Culture" *in* **The Arts**).

Farther south is the **Seventh Regiment Armory** (Park Ave. and 66th St.),
an 1879 medieval-style building that became the model for armories throughout the country. With its Tiffany interiors and enormous drill room, the armory
hosts frequent art and antiques shows. Also at the southern end of the neighborhood are several private clubs that are housed in historic buildings. Worth
seeing are the **Metropolitan Club** (1–11 E. 60th St.; designed by Stanford
White in the 1890's), the **Knickerbocker Club** (2 E. 62nd St.) and the **Lotos
Club** (5 E. 66th St.).

In **Yorkville** (70th-96th St., east of Lexington Ave.), the Old World flavor
of this once German and Hungarian (also Irish and Czech) enclave is fading.
There are remnants such as **Schaller and Weber** (1654 Second Ave. between
85th and 86th Sts.), which has been selling authentic German sausage and
other specialties since 1937. For the most part, the old groceries and bakeries
have been replaced by a more youthful spirit found in the cafes along Second
and Third Avenues and bars that fill with exuberant drinkers on weekends. Jog-

Fred R. Conrad/The New York Times

Metropolitan Museum of Art

gers and inline-skaters take to the **East River esplanade** and **Carl Schurz Park** outside **Gracie Mansion,** the mayor's official residence.

Across the East River, just minutes away by aerial tram, lies tranquil **Roosevelt Island,** the site of a prison, an almshouse and an insane asylum from the early 1800's through the early 1900's. Today, the island is a mixed-income residential community that offers an escape from Manhattan's frenzy. At East 61st Street and Second Avenue, you can take a quick tram ride over the East River to enjoy wonderful Manhattan skyline views from this tiny island.

Subway: 4 (express), 5 (express) and 6 (local) make stops along Lexington Ave. from 59th St. to 125th St.

HIGHLIGHTS OF THE NEIGHBORHOOD
(*For* **Metropolitan Museum of Art, Guggenheim, Frick Collection, Whitney, Cooper-Hewitt National Design Museum, El Museo del Barrio** *and* **Neue Gallery New York,** *see* "Art Museums and Galleries" *in chapter* **The Arts.**)

Asia Society 725 Park Ave. (between 70th and 71st Sts.) (212) 517-ASIA *www.asiasociety.org.* The Asia Society was founded by John D. Rockefeller III to introduce Americans to the cultures of Asia and the Pacific. Scholarly symposia, films, public programs and publications have long been central to its mission, with an emphasis on the arts. Today its elegant galleries (expanded in a 2001 renovation) feature changing exhibitions for connoisseurs as well as for the general public. **Admission:** $7 adults; $5 students and seniors; free for children under 16; free to everyone Fri. 6–9 P.M. **Hours:** Galleries Tue.–Sun. 11 A.M.–6 P.M. (till 9 P.M. on Fri.). **Subway:** 6 to 68th St.

Carl Schurz Park East End Ave. at 84th St. (212) 360-1311. Named after a newspaper editor and reform politician, Carl Schurz Park is the site of **Gracie Mansion,** the mayor's official residence. (Billionaire Mayor Bloomberg prefers his own plush Upper East Side digs, and has declined the invitation to move in.) Stretching along the East River, the park is also one of the city's quietest. Benches line a relaxing promenade that offers views of tugboats, Hell's Gate Bridge and the Roosevelt Island lighthouse. To the delight of loungers, the brick paths make the park a terrible place for in-line skating. The park has a basketball court and children's playground.

China Institute in America 125 E. 65th St. (between Park and Lexington Aves.) (212) 744-8181 *www.chinainstitute.org.* The China Institute offers classes in Chinese languages, arts and calligraphy; hosts lectures, films and discussions; and stages art shows in its galleries. Courses for children are also available. **Admission:** $3 adults; $2 students and seniors. **Hours:** Galleries Mon.–Sat. 10 A.M.–5 P.M. (till 8 P.M. Tue. and Thu.), Sun. 1–5 P.M. **Subway:** 6 to 68th St.

Goethe-Institut/German Cultural Center 1014 Fifth Ave. (between 82nd and 83rd Sts.) (212) 439-8700. This institute, funded by the German government, promotes German language and culture abroad. The New York center, one of roughly 150 branches in some 60 countries, organizes lectures, art exhibitions and concerts of contemporary classical music. Occupying a Beaux-Arts limestone town house, the institute also collaborates with other organizations around the city in presenting film series and music performances. The organization operates a lending and reference library at its Fifth Avenue headquarters, and offers language courses through NYU's Deutsches Haus. **Subway:** 4, 5, 6 to 86th St.

Jewish Museum 1109 Fifth Ave. (at 92nd St.) (212) 423-3200 *www.thejewishmuseum.org.* Located on Museum Mile in a Gothic chateau built in 1908, the Jewish Museum is dedicated to exploring Jewish identity, from artworks by Marc Chagall to video archives preserving the Jewish comedy of television's golden age. The two-floor permanent exhibit is the intriguing "Culture and Continuity: The Jewish Journey," which explores 4,000 years of history through archeological treasures, ceremonial objects, art and interactive media. The museum has shown work by individual artists such as Camille Pisarro and Lasar Segall, and mounts thematic exhibitions, such as 2002's controversial "Mirroring Evil: Nazi Imagery/Recent Art." The museum also hosts film screenings, lectures, panel discussions, concerts and family programs. **Admission:** $8 adults; $5.50 students and seniors; children under 12 free; Thu. 5–8 P.M., pay what you wish. **Hours:** Sun. 10 A. M.–5:45 P.M.; Mon.–Wed. 11 A.M.–5:45 P.M.; Thu. 11 A.M.–8 P.M.; Fri. 11 A.M.–3 P.M. Closed Sat. **Subway:** 6 to 96th St; 4, 5, 6 to 86th St.

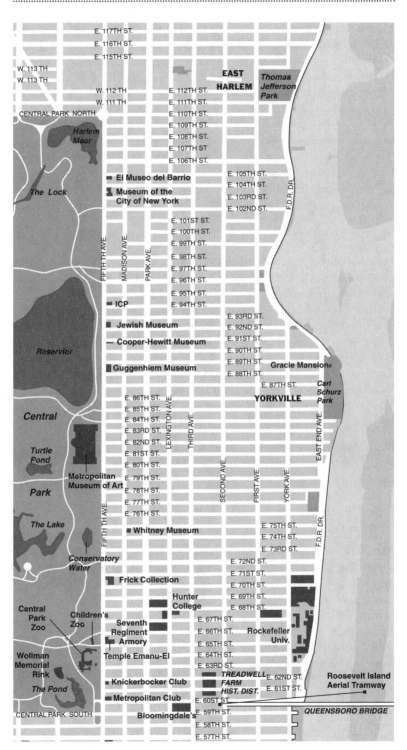

Upper East Side

Mount Vernon Hotel Museum and Garden 421 E. 61st St. (between First and York Aves.) (212) 838-6878. This small museum sits within earshot of the FDR Drive and in the shadow the Queensboro Bridge, so it's hard to imagine that people once flocked here for a peaceful escape from the hustle and bustle of downtown. But after an hour or so wandering through the museum's nine richly appointed period rooms and relaxing on a stone bench in the 18th-century-style gardens, it seems more plausible. In the 1830's, wealthy New Yorkers would retreat to what was then called the Mount Vernon Hotel for the weekend. The Federal-style structure, built in 1799, is the only remaining building of its kind in Manhattan. Abigail Adams Smith, daughter of President John Adams, originally commissioned it as part of a planned 23-acre estate modeled after Mount Vernon, though her project was never completed. **Admission:** $4 adults; $3 students and seniors; free for children under 12. **Hours:** Tue.–Sun. 11 A.M.–4 P.M.

Museum of the City of New York 1220 Fifth Ave. (between 103rd and 104th Sts.) (212) 534-1672 *www.mcny.org*. Created in 1923 to collect and preserve the history of the city, the museum's intimate galleries are filled with a rich trove of artifacts from the 19th and 20th centuries, including period rooms, furniture, silver, theater costumes, prints, photographs and rare manuscripts. Its collections trace the development of the modern city and its people, from the skating ponds portrayed in Currier & Ives prints to the skyscrapers photographed by Berenice Abbott. Visitors can count on exhibits about the history of Broadway theater and American decorative arts. Kids will be drawn to the historic fire pumps and a gallery of toys and dolls. **Admission:** $7 adults; $4 students, children and seniors. **Hours:** Wed.–Sat. 10 A.M.–5 P.M.; Sun. noon–5 P.M.

New York Society Library 53 E. 79th St. (between Madison and Park Aves.) (212) 288-6900 *www.nysoclib.org*. The Society Library is the city's oldest library, dating from 1754. It is a membership library with nearly 200,000 volumes. (Annual family membership is $150.) Nonmembers can use the ground floor for reference or reading without charge; it's a wonderful old-fashioned reading room filled with Audubon sketches.

Temple Emanu-El 1 E. 65th St. (at Fifth Ave.) (212) 744-1400 *www.emanuelnyc.org*. Temple Emanu-El is home to what is said to be the largest Jewish congregation in the world. The impressive limestone Moorish-Romanesque structure was completed in 1929 on the site of an Astor mansion. In size and beauty it rivals some of Europe's cathedrals. The sanctuary, which seats 2,500, has an extraordinary bronze ark in the shape of a Torah and is decorated with marvelous mosaics by Hildreth Meiere. The temple regularly hosts concerts and lectures. **Hours:** Open to visitors daily 10 A.M.–5 P.M. Services held Sun.–Thu. at 5:30 P.M., Fri at 5:15 P.M., Sat. at 10:30 A.M. Free tours after Sat. services.

Highly Recommended Neighborhood Restaurants

*(See chapter **Restaurants** for reviews.)*

Atlantic Grill	☆	$ $	SEAFOOD
Café Boulud	☆ ☆ ☆	$ $ $ $	FRENCH
Cafe Sabarsky	☆ ☆	$ $	AUSTRO-HUNGARIAN
Centolire	☆ ☆	$ $ $	ITALIAN
Circus	☆ ☆	$ $ $	BRAZILIAN
Commissary	☆	$ $ $	NEW AMERICAN
Daniel	☆ ☆ ☆ ☆	$ $ $ $	FRENCH
Etats-Unis	☆ ☆	$ $ $	NEW AMERICAN
Jo Jo	☆ ☆ ☆	$ $ $	FRENCH
Little Dove	☆ ☆	$ $ $	NEW AMERICAN
Maya	☆ ☆	$ $ $	MEXICAN/TEX-MEX
92	☆	$ $	NEW AMERICAN
Paola's	☆ ☆	$ $	ITALIAN
Payard Pâtisserie	☆ ☆	$ $ $	BISTRO/FRENCH
Red Bar Restaurant	☆	$ $ $	american/BISTRO

Recommended Inexpensive Restaurants

Bandol	FRENCH
Bistro Le Steak	BISTRO/STEAK
Congee Village	CHINESE
La Fonda Boricua	LATIN AMERICAN
Luca	ITALIAN
Pig Heaven	CHINESE
The Sultan	TURKISH
Taco Taco	MEXICAN/TEX-MEX
Uskudar	TURKISH

The Upper West Side

How to explain the Upper West Side? It has **Columbus Circle** at one end and **Columbia University** at the other. In between is a rectangle four miles long and one mile wide that is unlike any other neighborhood in the United States. The 10023, 10024 and 10025 zip codes are three of the most liberal districts in the country. But the rectangle is really a place of contrasts. It is a place of rich and poor, sometimes on the same block, of ethnic and religious variety, of churches and synagogues, and of culture that ranges from **Lincoln Center** to small neighborhood stages.

The Upper West Side was farmland until well after the Civil War—the city, such as it was, covered only the lower third of the island of Manhattan. Before the proud apartment buildings began marching up Central Park West, Central Park's 843 acres were penciled off as a big green rectangle— "the grand-daddy of all American landscaped parks," an American Institute of Architects guide called it. But Frederick Law Olmsted, principal designer of the park, did not want New Yorkers to think of the park as architecture. "What we want to gain is tranquility and rest to the mind," he said. The park is full of places where one can gain both. (*See section* "Central Park" *later in this chapter.*)

From there, you can see **the Dakota,** an apartment building so spacious that Leonard Bernstein had no trouble fitting two grand pianos into his living room. The Dakota was also home to John Lennon, who was brutally murdered just outside the archway that leads to the building's elegant courtyard. His widow, Yoko Ono, still lives in the Dakota, only a short walk from **Strawberry Fields,** an area inside the park honoring his memory.

Up Central Park West, past the twin-towered **San Remo** apartments, are the museums. The **New-York Historical Society** has kept the hyphen that the rest of the city dropped more than a century ago. Next door is the **American Museum of Natural History.** The oldest section of the museum was designed by Calvert Vaux, Olmsted's collaborator on the design of the park just across the street. The museum's newest addition is the sleek glass box that encloses the Hayden Planetarium in the **Rose Center for Earth and Space.** Three blocks west is Broadway; the stretch between 74th and 80th Streets is a food shopper's paradise, with markets like **Fairway, Citarella** and **Zabar's.**

Three stops beyond 96th Street on the No. 1 local is **Columbia University.** The campus was laid out by Charles Follen McKim, a partner in McKim, Mead & White, the legendary firm that satisfied the city's lust for carefully proportioned neoclassical creations at the beginning of the 20th century. The newest building on the Columbia campus is an $85 million student center, a gleaming glass box that opened in 1999, completing McKim's master plan.

—*James Barron*

Subway: 1 (local), 2 (express), 3 (express), 9 (local) make stops along Broadway from 59th St. to 96th St. (1, 9 continue uptown on the West Side); B, C make stops along Central Park West. Subway access may change over the lifetime of this edition (as of this writing, there was no 9 train, and the 2 was local, but normal service should be restored soon); check *www.mta.nyc.ny.us* for updates.

HIGHLIGHTS OF THE NEIGHBORHOOD

(*See chapter* **The Arts** *for information on* **Lincoln Center,** *the* **Miriam and Ira D. Wallach Art Gallery** *and the* **Nicholas Roerich Museum.**)

American Museum of Natural History Central Park West and 79th St. (212) 769-5100 *www.amnh.org.* Holden Caulfield reported in *The Catcher in the Rye* that he loved this huge, hushed museum because "everything always stayed right where it was."

But over the last several years, the Natural History Museum—the largest of its kind in the world, with about three-quarters of a million square feet of public exhibition space—has actually moved a lot of things around. There's a high-tech **IMAX theater** offering a rotating selection of features on a giant screen. The world-famous dinosaur halls were expanded and spruced up in the late

1990's, and the fossils themselves were rearranged to conform with new anthropological research. The towering Tyrannosaurus Rex was completely reshaped into a low stalking pose with its tail in the air. The Barosaurus, probably the first thing you will see when you walk in, still towers; at five stories, it is the world's tallest free-standing dinosaur exhibit.

In 2000, the museum opened the **Rose Center for Earth and Space,** which encloses the rebuilt Hayden Planetarium, now the most technologically advanced planetarium in the world. The Rose Center includes a recreation of the birth of the universe in the Big Bang Theater, and a dazzling variety of exhibits relating to Mother Earth and outer space (*see full listing below*).

But if you get tired of flash, the museum still has many reliable standbys to remind you of its origins. There's Akeley Hall, with its silent herds of stuffed elephants; the famous Star of India sapphire, the world's largest; and the 15.5-ton meteorite in the main Hall of the Universe.

In summer 2003, the museum will unveil a $25 million renovation of its Hall of Ocean Life. Its beloved 94-foot model blue whale will be suspended in a fully immersive marine environment with video projections, interactive computer stations and new ocean dioramas. —*Randy Kennedy*

Admission: $10 adults; $7.50 students and seniors; $6 children ages 2–12. Museum admission plus IMAX movie, $15 adults, $11 students and seniors, $9 children ages 2–12. Museum admission plus Space Show at Rose Center, $19 adults, $14 seniors and students, $11.50 children ages 2–12. **Hours:** Daily 10 A.M.–5:45 P.M.

The Ansonia 2109 Broadway (between 73rd and 74th Sts.) The thick, soundproof walls of the Ansonia have long harbored musicians. Enrico Caruso and Igor Stravinsky once lived upstairs in the Beaux-Arts apartment building, which dates from 1904, and Bette Midler launched her career singing downstairs in the Continental Baths, a gay spa that doubled as a cabaret in the 1970's. In more recent years, the building has been the site of fierce battles between the landlord and rent-regulated tenants, some of whom operate music rehearsal studios in their apartments. A confection of balconies, turrets and dormer windows, the restored 17-story facade gives its block of upper Broadway the look of a Parisian boulevard exaggerated on a New York scale.

Cathedral Church of St. John the Divine 1047 Amsterdam Ave. (212) 316-7540, or (212) 932-7347 for tour info. *www.stjohndivine.org.* The clerics at the Cathedral Church of St. John the Divine like to call it a medieval cathedral for New York City, not just in architectural style but in spirit and commitment. The cathedral is the seat of the Episcopal Diocese of New York; its bishop once said it combines all the life and struggle of the city. Peacocks strut across the bucolic 13-acre grounds, delighting the children who chase after them for tail feathers. Artists in residence haunt the basement vaults, rehearsing their pieces, then perform them in the eclectic splendor of the Gothic, Romanesque and Byzantine sanctuary. The cathedral tends to New York's forgotten homeless, and holds memorial services for many of the city's most

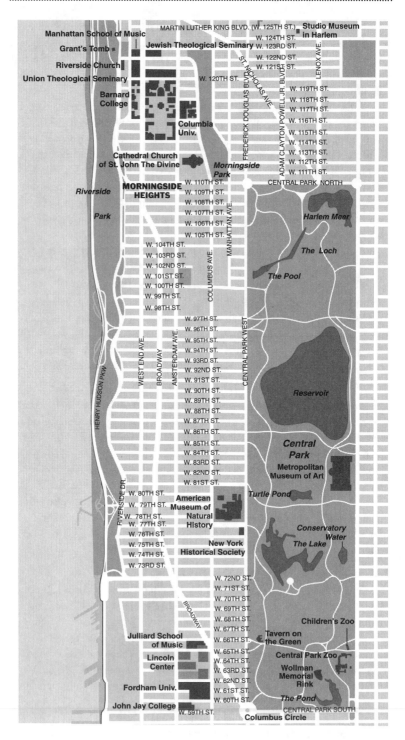

MARTIN LUTHER KING BLVD. (W. 125TH ST.)
W. 124TH ST.
W. 123RD ST.
W. 122ND ST.
W. 121ST ST.
W. 120TH ST.
W. 119TH ST.
W. 118TH ST.
W. 117TH ST.
W. 116TH ST.
W. 115TH ST.
W. 114TH ST.
W. 113TH ST.
W. 112TH ST.
W. 111TH ST.
CENTRAL PARK NORTH
W. 110TH ST.
W. 109TH ST.
W. 108TH ST.
W. 107TH ST.
W. 106TH ST.
W. 105TH ST.
W. 104TH ST.
W. 103RD ST.
W. 102ND ST.
W. 101ST ST.
W. 100TH ST.
W. 99TH ST.
W. 98TH ST.
W. 97TH ST.
W. 96TH ST.
W. 95TH ST.
W. 94TH ST.
W. 93RD ST.
W. 92ND ST.
W. 91ST ST.
W. 90TH ST.
W. 89TH ST.
W. 88TH ST.
W. 87TH ST.
W. 86TH ST.
W. 85TH ST.
W. 84TH ST.
W. 83RD ST.
W. 82ND ST.
W. 81ST ST.
W. 80TH ST.
W. 79TH ST.
W. 78TH ST.
W. 77TH ST.
W. 76TH ST.
W. 75TH ST.
W. 74TH ST.
W. 73RD ST.
W. 72ND ST.
W. 71ST ST.
W. 70TH ST.
W. 69TH ST.
W. 68TH ST.
W. 67TH ST.
W. 66TH ST.
W. 65TH ST.
W. 64TH ST.
W. 63RD ST.
W. 62ND ST.
W. 61ST ST.
W. 60TH ST.
W. 59TH ST.
CENTRAL PARK SOUTH

Manhattan School of Music
Grant's Tomb
Riverside Church
Union Theological Seminary
Jewish Theological Seminary
Studio Museum in Harlem
Barnard College
Columbia Univ.
Cathedral Church of St. John The Divine
Morningside Park
MORNINGSIDE HEIGHTS
Riverside Park

ST. NICHOLAS AVE.
FREDERICK DOUGLAS BLVD.
ADAM CLAYTON POWELL JR. BLVD.
LENOX AVE.
MANHATTAN AVE.
COLUMBUS AVE.
WEST END AVE.
BROADWAY
AMSTERDAM AVE.
CENTRAL PARK WEST
HENRY HUDSON PKWY.
RIVERSIDE DR.

Harlem Meer
The Loch
The Pool
Reservoir
Central Park
Metropolitan Museum of Art
Turtle Pond
Conservatory Water
The Lake
American Museum of Natural History
New York Historical Society
Children's Zoo
Tavern on the Green
Central Park Zoo
Wollman Memorial Rink
The Pond
Julliard School of Music
Lincoln Center
Fordham Univ.
John Jay College
Columbus Circle

Upper West Side/Morningside Heights

famous citizens. About the only time you might see an elephant on Amsterdam Avenue is early fall, when St. John's clergy bless animals large and small in honor of St. Francis.

Neighborhood residents have affectionately nicknamed the cathedral, with its soaring Gothic arches, two luminous rose windows and carved stone figures, St. John the Unfinished. When its cornerstone was laid in 1892, on the site of a former orphan asylum, it was envisioned as a great acropolis on a hill, the rocky schist of upper Manhattan. Indeed, it is second in size only to St. Peter's Basilica in Rome, with more floor area than Notre Dame and Chartres combined, and still growing, mainly upward. Construction ceased during the iron and steel shortages of World War II. During the civil rights struggles of the late 1960's, the Diocese hesitated to lavish money on a building in an area filled with poverty, and dedicated itself to good works instead. Work has slowly resumed.

On the vertiginous vertical tour, you can peer down from the crossway more than 100 feet above the floor—the real excitement of the cathedral for visiting schoolchildren. A guided tour through the interior helps uncover details from the whimsical (the prayer bay dedicated to sports) to the sobering (the bay dedicated to the healing arts, now dominated by a memorial to those who have suffered and died from AIDS). Among the profusion of icons, both sacred and mundane, are an ostrich egg, a symbol of meditation, donated by P.L. Travers, the author of Mary Poppins, and a prominently displayed pair of menorahs donated by Adolph Ochs, former publisher of *The New York Times*. The bronze lights in front were salvaged from the demolished Penn Station. The bronze doors were fabricated in Paris by Ferdinand Barbedienne, who also cast the Statue of Liberty. Emerging miraculously unscathed (except for damage to its gift shop) from a frightening fire in December 2001, St. John's is truly, as its founders hoped, a house of prayer for all nations.   —*Anemona Hartocollis*

Admission (suggested): $2; tour $3; vertical tour $10. **Hours:** Mon.–Sat. 7 A.M.–6 P.M., Sun 7 A.M.–8 P.M. Tours offered Tue.–Sat. at 11 A.M., Sun at 1 P.M. Check the Web site for schedule of services.

Columbia University 116th St. and Broadway (212) 854-1754 *www.columbia.edu.* Built on the site of a former insane asylum, Columbia University's main campus represents one of the most balanced expressions of Beaux-Arts urban design in America. Chartered as King's College before the American Revolution, New York's Ivy League university moved from Madison Avenue and 49th Street to Morningside Heights at the turn of the last century. McKim, Mead & White designed a symmetrical quadrangle of Italian Renaissance-style buildings around the classical Low Library, whose monumental stone staircase has become a favorite warm-weather hangout for students. As Columbia expanded into a major research university, it overflowed its original four-block plan, creating tensions with the surrounding community. A stage for beatniks in the 1950's and student protests during the Vietnam War, Columbia has in recent years become a quieter place, both politically and culturally. Despite gentrification moving up the Upper West Side, the university's neighborhood—with its academic bookstores and antiquated coffee shops—maintains a certain detachment from the rest of the city. *(See chapter* **The Arts** *for Columbia University's* **Miriam and Ira Wallach Art Gallery.***)*

The Dakota 1 W. 72nd St. (at Central Park West) Located far uptown amid largely vacant lots when it was completed in 1884, the Dakota was so named because the developer's friends told him it was as remote as the Dakota Territory. An early luxury building in an era when rich New Yorkers had only just begun to move from town houses into apartments, the Dakota came equipped with steam-pumped elevators and ceilings that soar as high as 15 feet. In addition to John Lennon, who was fatally shot here in 1980, the building has housed a flock of arts and entertainment figures, including Leonard Bernstein and Lauren Bacall, and provided the setting for *Rosemary's Baby*. During the building's recent restoration, the mute yellow brick lost its brown patina. With its steeply gabled roof and massive structures—features that Henry J. Hardenbergh, the architect, deployed in his later design for the Plaza Hotel—the Dakota stands like a fortress guarding the 72nd Street entrance to Central Park.

Grant's Tomb Riverside Dr. at 122nd St. (212) 666-1640 *www.nps.gov/gegr*. Quick! Who's buried in Grant's Tomb? Don't groan at the old joke. It is asked only because most people give the wrong answer, or at least an incomplete one.

Of course, the tomb contains the remains of Ulysses S. Grant, the great Civil War general and perhaps not-so-great 18th president. But many are unaware that next to him, in a matching sarcophagus of red granite, lies his wife, Julia Dent Grant. Grant, who died in 1885, had wanted to be buried at West Point, but his wife would not have been allowed to join him there. Thus he became the only president buried in New York City, in a neoclassical granite monument overlooking the Hudson.

For decades after its dedication in 1897, the tomb was among the most celebrated buildings in the country. Time dimmed its popularity. Over the years, the memorial deteriorated into a graffiti-scarred drug hangout, until finally in the 1990's the National Park Service gave it a much deserved face-lift.

Visitors are few. That is good news for anyone interested in a tranquil refuge, embodying Grant's epitaph, chiseled above the entrance: "Let us have peace."
—*Clyde Haberman*

Morningside Park Morningside Ave. (at 110th St.) (212) 360-1311. Morningside Park was built in 1887 atop the cliffs just to the east of the site, now occupied by Barnard College, where the Battle of Harlem Heights was fought in 1776. (A later battle over Columbia University's plans to build a gym in the park led to the student demonstrations and takeover of the campus in 1968.) The thin 31-acre park, which lies between Harlem and the Columbia campus, includes a concourse at the top of a tall stone wall built along Morningside Drive. The promontories on the concourse offer commanding views of spirited basketball and handball games in the courts below.

New-York Historical Society 2 W. 77th St. (at Central Park West) (212) 873-3400 *www.nyhistory.org*. New York City's oldest museum in continuous operation, the society is an important institution for the study and preservation of the city's history and culture. The society's art collection includes landscape paintings by major artists from the Hudson River School, 135 Tiffany lamps and one of the largest collections of miniature portraits in the country. The building also houses a highly regarded print collection with thousands of photographs, architectural drawings and ephemera (available by appointment only) and a research library with over two million manuscripts, 10,000 maps, and hundreds of photographs, prints and other materials. Temporary exhibits cover a wide range of topics, including the aftermath of September 11. **Admission:** $5 adults; $3 students and seniors; free for children 12 and under. **Hours:** Tue.–Sun. 10 A.M.–5 P.M.

Riverside Church Riverside Drive and 120th St. (Claremont Ave. and 121st St.) (212) 870-6700 *www.theriversidechurchny.org.* Built in 1930 and modeled after the cathedral in Chartres, France, this mammoth Gothic-style church bordering **Riverside Park** has magnificent stonework and stained-glass windows. The church's nearly 400-foot tower has an observation deck affording spectacular views of the city and the Palisades across the Hudson. At $1 to ascend, it's a true bargain. Aside from vistas of the landscape, there are unique views inside of the peregrine falcons that have taken up residence, as well as a close-up look at the innards of the famous carillon, a gift of the Rockefeller family. (It has 74 bells—one weighing 20 tons—making it the world's largest.) You can hear it played every Sunday at 3 P.M. And though 120th Street is not on the maps of most theatergoers, the resident Melting Pot Theater is worth a visit. It seats about 270, has great sightlines, an ample stage and first-rate lighting and sound systems. The theater focuses on plays and musicals generally geared toward a family audience.

Rose Center for Earth and Space 79th St. and Central Park West (212) 769-5100 *www.amnh.org/rose.* The $210 million Rose Center for Earth and Space opened in February 2000, offering visitors a virtual journey through time, space and the mysteries of the cosmos. The 333,500-square-foot, seven-floor facility includes the new Hayden Planetarium, the Cullman Hall of the Universe and the Gottesman Hall of Planet Earth. The Hayden Planetarium contains the Space Theater and the Big Bang Theater, featuring narrated visual and audio effects simulating how the universe began. The Cullman Hall of the Universe is a 7,000-square-foot permanent exhibition hall on the bottom level of the Rose Center, divided into four zones that illustrate the processes that led to the creation of the planets, stars, galaxies and universe.

The domed Space Theater offers synthetic views of the cosmos far more detailed than the most elaborate Hollywood productions. With the help of a supercomputer, a state-of-the-art Zeiss star projector, an advanced laser system, a gigantic database and, of course, the hemispheric Space Theater itself, the builders have created a marvelous celestial playhouse. The **Space Theater show,** "The Search for Life: Are We Alone?," narrated by Harrison Ford, is a spectacular virtual ride through the universe.

The sky show occupies the upper half of the center's 87-foot diameter sphere; the lower half is devoted to a very brief light and sound show depicting the Big Bang. Between the upper and lower levels of the Rose Center is a spiral walkway with a splendid gallery of 220 astronomical photographs.

The spiral ramp itself is one of many devices incorporated in the Rose Center to impart a sense of scale—in particular, an appreciation of the staggering dimensions of the universe. The length of the walkway, nearly 100 yards, represents a span of about 13 billion years, at the end of which is a single hair, the thickness of which represents the duration of human history. Some of the most interesting photographs along the walkway show the results of gravitational lensing, an effect not explained until we reach a little enclosure called the Black Hole Theater on the lowest level of the center, which gives viewers the flavor of relativity theory, of the genius of Einstein and of the bizarre distortions enormous masses cause in nearby space-time.

Admission: Entrance (with no Space Show) is included with admission to the American Museum of Natural History (*see listing above*), which is $10 adults; $7.50 seniors and students; $6 children ages 12 and under. Admission to the museum and the Rose Center, plus the Space Show, $19 adults; $14 seniors and students; $11.50 children ages 12 and under. You can purchase advance tickets to the Space Show online or at (212) 769-5200. **Hours:** Sat.–Thu. 10 A.M.–5:45 P.M.; Fri. 10 A.M.–8:45 P.M. Space shows run throughout the day.

Highly Recommended Neighborhood Restaurants
(*See chapter* **Restaurants** *for reviews.*)

Calle Ocho	☆	$ $	PAN-LATIN
Gabriel's	☆ ☆	$ $ $	ITALIAN
Jean Georges	☆ ☆ ☆ ☆	$ $ $ $	NEW AMERICAN
Ouest	☆ ☆	$ $ $	NEW AMERICAN
Picholine	☆ ☆ ☆	$ $ $ $	MEDITERRANEAN/ FRENCH
Ruby Foo's	☆ ☆	$ $	PAN-ASIAN

Recommended Inexpensive Restaurants

Alouette	BISTRO/FRENCH
Avenue	BISTRO/FRENCH
Gabriela's	MEXICAN
Gennaro	ITALIAN/MEDITERRANEAN
Isola	ITALIAN
Josie's	NEW AMERICAN
Luzia's	PORTUGUESE
Max SoHa	AMERICAN/ITALIAN
Metsovo	GREEK
Mughlai	INDIAN
Turkuaz	TURKISH/MIDDLE EASTERN

The Rose Center for Earth and Space

Harlem

The Harlem Renaissance of the 1920's brought the world the likes of
Langston Hughes, Countee Cullen, Dorothy West and Zora Neale Hurston.
The Harlem renaissance now underway is bringing the community the likes of
the Gap, Starbucks and . . . Bill Clinton. It is an economic blooming as sure
as the literary one of generations ago. And visitors will find plenty to satisfy
their interest in both.

Harlem emerged in the 18th century as an upper Manhattan getaway for
wealthy downtowners, who gave way to a succession of immigrants—Jews,
Irish and, in the early 1900's, blacks, who turned it into the capital of black
America. Its exact boundaries are disputed; geography and emotion don't
always mix. But Harlem's history and legend indisputably resonate today, particularly among black Americans. In its heydey in the 1920's and 30's, jazz and
blues luminaries such as Ella Fitzgerald and Duke Ellington played long into
the night at places like the Savoy and Cotton Club, now long gone. Langston
Hughes gave poetry readings at the Harlem YMCA, one of the early cultural
centers, and 125th Street bustled with the energy of any village main street.

Eventually, with the flight of the middle class and the scourge of drugs and
crime, Harlem slid into a decay from which it is only now emerging. The middle and upper classes are moving back into its elegant brownstones and newer
housing, and the neighborhood once again is growing into a popular tourist
destination. The decision by Mr. Clinton to locate his post-presidential offices

on the 14th floor of 55 West 125th St. was seen by many in the community as an affirmation of Harlem's rebirth.

Popular new restaurants such as **Bayou, Jimmy's Uptown, Sugar Shack** and **Amy Ruth's** are drawing a racially mixed clientele, joining legendary mainstays like **Charles' Southern Style Kitchen,** offering what many consider the best soul food in the city. The **Lenox Lounge,** more than a half-century old and recently renovated, offers jazz, along with more intimate settings like **St. Nick's Pub** (*see chapter* **Nightlife**).

All the change suits many residents just fine, but it has irked others who scoff at the rising rents and worry that gentrification will diminish Harlem's status as the capital of black America.

The most popular destination remains **125th Street,** the thriving main shopping strip. The **Apollo Theater** is the 86-year-old showplace where Billie Holiday, Aretha Franklin, Count Basie, Lauryn Hill and many others graced the stage—and many more got the "hook" for disappointing feisty audiences. A weekly television variety program, *Showtime at the Apollo,* is produced there.

Famous places such as the Audubon Ballroom, where Malcolm X was assassinated in 1965, have disappeared. But many cultural and historic spots remain. **The Schomburg Center for Research on Black Culture, the Studio Museum in Harlem** (*see chapter* **The Arts**) and the **National Black Theater** (212-722-3800) all have deep roots in the community and offer frequent exhibitions and shows that testify to the importance of black culture.

New development on 125th Street includes a 285,000-square-foot shopping mall called **Harlem U.S.A.,** a nine-screen cinema, Old Navy, a branch of the New York Sports Club and the **Hue-Man Experience Bookstore and Cafe,** the largest African-American-owned bookstore in the country.

The new development has not reached much into nearby East Harlem, though **El Museo del Barrio,** on Fifth Avenue at 104th Street (*see chapter* **The Arts**), is worth the trek for a look at the Hispanic culture that defines East Harlem.   —*Randy Archibold*

Subway: A, B, C, D, 2, 3 to 125th St.; B, C, 2, 3 to 135th St.; A, B, C, D, 3 to 145th St.

HIGHLIGHTS OF THE NEIGHBORHOOD
(*For the* **Studio Museum in Harlem,** *see chapter* **The Arts.**)

Abyssinian Baptist Church 132 Odell Clark Place (W. 138th St., between Adam Clayton Powell and Malcolm X Blvds.) (212) 862-7474 *www.abyssinian.org.* The Abysinnian Baptist Church has become such a popular attraction that it has had to turn away tourists on Easter. Known for its rousing gospel choir, this 1923 Gothic church was home for many years to rousing sermons by Adam Clayton Powell, the charismatic preacher and congressman. A memorial room displays artifacts from his life. Visit during Sunday services (at 9 A.M. and 11 A.M.) if you can, and afterward head over for a soul food lunch at Sylvia's nearby. (The church asks that if you attend services, you stay for the entire one-an-a-half- to two-hour duration, and refrain from taking photos or video.)

Hamilton Grange National Memorial 287 Convent Ave. (between. 141st and 142nd Sts.) (212) 283-5154 *www.nps.gov/hagr*. Alexander Hamilton—George Washington's aide during the Revolutionary War, then a member of Congress, co-author of the Federalist Papers and first U.S. Secretary of the Treasury—commissioned architect John McComb Jr. to design a Federal-style country home on a sprawling 32-acre estate in upper Manhattan. This house was completed in 1802 and named "The Grange" after the Hamilton family's ancestral home in Scotland, but served as his home for only two years. On July 11, 1804, Hamilton was fatally wounded in a duel with his political rival Aaron Burr. Rangers offer hourly guided tours. **Admission:** Free. **Hours:** Fri.–Sun. 9 A.M.–5 P.M.

The Project 427 W. 126th St. (bet. Morningside and Amsterdam Aves.) (212) 662-8610. This interesting development in the Harlem contemporary art scene was started by the writer Christian Haye in 1999. The Project has assembled an international roster of young artists from Europe, Asia, Africa and the United States. Recent exhibits have included work by Paul Pfeiffer, Tom Gidley and Martín Weber.

Schomburg Center for Research on Black Culture 515 Malcolm X Blvd. (at 135th St.) (212) 491-2200 *www.nypl.org*. The Schomburg Center's holdings are built on the personal collection of Arturo Alfonso Schomburg, a Puerto Rican black scholar and bibliophile who died in Brooklyn in 1938 at the age of 64. Schomburg's materials were added to the Division of Negro Literature, History and Prints of the 135th Street branch of the New York Public Library in 1926. It became a research library of the Public Library system in 1972. The collection has grown to include more than five million items—books, manuscripts, art objects, audio, video and even sheet music—documenting the history and culture of people of African descent throughout the world. Call ahead to make an appointment to view the art and artifacts collection.

Recommended Inexpensive Restaurants
(See chapter **Restaurants** *for reviews.)*

Amy Ruth's	SOUTHERN
Bayou	CAJUN/SOUTHERN
El Fogon	SPANISH
Emily's	SOUTHERN
Sylvia's	SOUTHERN

Washington Heights/Inwood

Dominican immigrants are only the latest arrivals in Washington Heights, an area that has been the first stop for many new Americans. In the early 1900's, the Irish poured into the area, especially to Inwood. In the period around World

War II, a large contingent of German Jews—including a young Henry Kissinger—made a home in the northern section near Fort Tryon Park.

Before the surge of immigration, Washington Heights was a rural retreat where the wealthy had country estates. It was spaciousness that first attracted two major institutions: Columbia-Presbyterian Hospital, which opened in 1928, and Yeshiva University, which came in 1929. Other landmarks include the Cloisters, the Metropolitan Museum of Art's showcase for medieval art, which sits atop a hill in Fort Tryon Park as an oasis of tranquility amid a noisy city. Long gone is the Polo Grounds, the former home of the baseball and football Giants, which overlooked the Harlem River at 157th Street.

At Manhattan Island's northernmost tip, Inwood lies between the Harlem River and Inwood Hill Park, where the borough's last stands of primeval forest remain. This neighborhood's newest arrivals are young professionals seeking affordable apartments in the Art Deco apartment buildings. On the banks of the Harlem River near Broadway, another dream lives on at Baker Field, where Columbia University's football team continues its often quixotic quest for glory.

Subway: A, C, 1, 9 make stops from 168th St.–Washington Heights uptown into Inwood.

HIGHLIGHTS OF THE NEIGHBORHOOD

American Numismatic Society Broadway (at 156th St.) (212) 234-3130 *www.amnumsoc.org*. Filthy lucre looks wholesome and interesting in "The World of Coins," a permanent exhibition chronicling the history of units of exchange, including cowrie shells, beads, paper money and credit cards. Some of the earliest coins ever found are here: crudely shaped knife pieces dating to 1000 B.C., from China. Among the many oddities on view are a bronze coin struck with an unflattering portrait of Cleopatra and a 1,000,000,000,000,000,000,000-pengo bill (Comrade, can you spare a quintillion pengos?) from the inflation-ridden Hungary of 1946. **Admission:** Free. **Hours:** Tue.–Fri. 9 A.M.–4:30 P.M.

The Cloisters Fort Tryon Park (near 190th St.) (212) 923-3700 *www.metmuseum.org*. Set atop a hill in Fort Tryon Park, with stunning views of the Hudson River, the Cloisters houses much of the Metropolitan Museum of Art's extensive collection of medieval art. Surrounded by lovely gardens planted according to horticultural information found in medieval treatises and poetry, the complex encompasses a 12th-century chapter house, five cloisters from medieval monasteries and a Romanesque chapel (which occasionally hosts concerts). The collection features 5,000 works on art from medieval Europe, including rare illuminated manuscripts, stained glass, sculpture and the priceless series of Unicorn Tapestries, woven around 1500. It's a soothing spot for conversation and contemplation. **Admission:** Included in same-day admission to the Met. $10 adults; $5 students and seniors; free for children under 12. **Hours:** Tue.–Sun. 9:30 A.M.–5:15 P.M. (closes at 4:45 P.M. Nov.–Feb.). **Directions:** A to 190th St., then a 10-min. walk along Margaret Corbin Dr. (or take the M4 bus 1 stop from the subway station to the Cloisters).

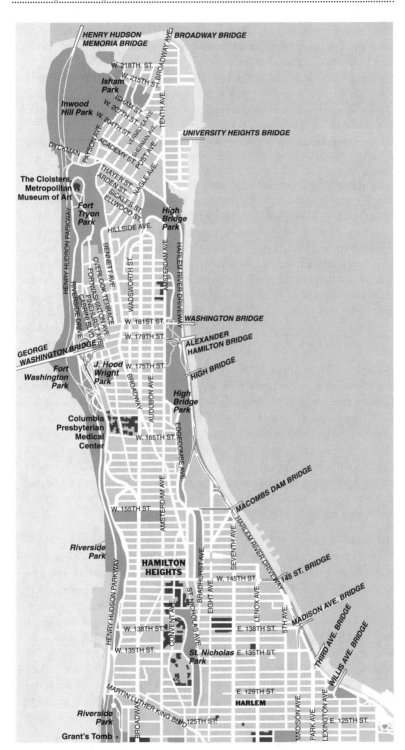

Upper Manhattan

Dyckman Farmhouse 4881 Broadway (at 204th St.) (212) 304-9422
www.dyckman.org. One of the few reminders that Manhattan was once farmland is standing its ground at the northern tip of Manhattan. The existing
Dyckman Farmhouse, with a Dutch-style gambrel roof and field stone walls, was
rebuilt in the 1780's after the original house was destroyed during the Revolutionary War. It once stood amid fields and fruit orchards. The museum features
five period rooms, a reconstructed German military hut and a reproduction of a
kitchen smokehouse. As of this writing, it is closed for restoration, but it should
reopen in September 2002.

Fort Tryon Park 741 Fort Washington Ave. (at 193rd St.) (212) 360-1311.
Best known as the site of the Metropolitan Museum's **Cloisters** *(see separate listing above)*, Fort Tryon Park encompasses Manhattan's highest point, Linden
Terrace, 268 feet above sea level. Surrounded by 66 hilly, wooded acres north of
Washington Heights, the park's promenades offer unsurpassed views of the Hudson River and the Palisades. The site once held Fort Tryon, a Revolutionary
War fort captured by the British and named for William Tryon, the last British
governor of New York. During the 19th century, several large mansions were
built in the area. John D. Rockefeller Jr. hired Frederick Law Olmsted Jr., son of
the designer of Central Park, to turn his estate into a park, which he donated to
the city in 1930. The Cloisters opened there eight years later.

George Washington Bridge Fort Washington Ave. at 178th St. The longest
suspension bridge in the world when it opened in 1931, the George Washington
Bridge remains New York City's only bridge across the Hudson. The bridge's
towers were supposed to be sheathed in granite; as a result of the Depression,
however, the steelwork was left exposed. They are now illuminated at night.
With the postwar rise in automobile traffic, a lower level was added in 1962. Le
Corbusier, the French proponent of modernist architecture, called the steel-
cabled structure the most beautiful bridge in the world. "It is blessed. It is the
only seat of grace in the disordered city," he said. A pedestrian and bike lane is
set off from traffic.

Highbridge Park (212) 691-9510. Highbridge Park, designed in 1888 by
Samuel Parsons Jr. and Calvert Vaux, begins in a thin spit called Coogan's Bluff
that rises abruptly at West 155th Street and Edgecombe Avenue. In the swamps
below, abutting the Harlem River, were the Polo Grounds, once home to the
baseball and football Giants (kids who didn't have the price of admission could
perch on the bluff and see part of the field). The southern zone of the park,
stretching roughly 20 blocks uptown to the grand old High Bridge itself, was
long impassable. But in 1997 the Parks Department began the arduous work of
opening a trail along the route of the buried Croton Aqueduct. Three bridges—
the Washington, the Hamilton and the pedestrian High Bridge—traverse the
midpoint of the park within seven blocks. Rather than being a fatal incursion,
the spans with their warren of access amps lend to this stretch of park beneath
them an extra dimension of drama.

The George Washington Bridge

Hispanic Society of America Broadway at 155th St. (212) 926-2234 *www.hispanicsociety.org*. The Hispanic Society of America, in its atmospheric shabby-genteel Beaux-Arts setting on Audubon Terrace, is filled with fabulous paintings by El Greco, Goya and Velázquez, as well as fine examples of decorative arts, sculpture and textiles. There are some amazing pieces, like a breathtaking 10th-century Hispano-Mooresque ivory box; the only comparable pieces of this kind locally are a few precious examples in the Met's collection. The Society also maintains a 250,000-volume research library (open to the public with photo ID) on all aspects of history and culture in Spain, Portugal, Latin America and the Philippines, as well as an extensive collection of rare books (contact the Society for viewing information). **Admission:** Free. **Hours:** Museum and library Tue.–Sat. 10 A.M.–4:30 P.M.; museum only Sun 1–4 P.M.

Inwood Hill Park Seaman Ave. at 207th St. (212) 304-2381. The most dramatic approach to the park is from the north, along 218th Street, a five-minute walk from the 215th Street subway station on the No. 1 line. You'll come upon a vista unlike any other in Manhattan. To the north, on your right, is the Harlem River on its final leg before joining the Hudson in the swirl of Spuyten Duyvil. The sheer cliff on the far side, threaded at its base by Metro North tracks, defines Marble Hill, its heights studded with ungainly apartment buildings. Straight ahead is a tidal lagoon (bordered by swamp grasses, it is the only accessible salt marsh in Manhattan and a magnet for water birds). Off to the left are low rolling athletic fields where soccer is the favored sport. Straight ahead, Inwood Hill itself juts into Spuyten Duyvil, which is spanned by the Henry Hudson Bridge to the Bronx, its steel gridwork painted bright blue. Beyond that is the low-slung Amtrak bridge, part of the shoreline route to Albany. The final piece of this tableau is the noble New Jersey Palisades, looming up a mile away across the Hudson. Before heading into the forest, stop first at the park's ecology center on the lagoon. You can pick up a map and a schedule of tours (including canoe expeditions) led by urban park rangers year round.

Morris-Jumel Mansion 65 Jumel Terrace (at 160th St. and Edgecombe Ave.) (212) 923-8008 *www.morrisjumel.org.* In the midst of an urban neighborhood scenically situated on a high bluff, a delightful enclave suddenly opens up. In its center is a columned, white, two-story house, all peaks and gables, in a verdant acre-and-a-half setting of greenery. The Georgian-Federal mansion was built in the 1760's as a summer home by Roger Morris, a Tory who left during the Revolution. George Washington made it his headquarters in 1776 as his troops were being driven from the city. During that retreat, he made the troops bite back in the Battle of Harlem Heights, in July 1776, when the British actually gave ground to the Americans. The mansion's name also recognizes a later occupant, Stephen Jumel, a wine merchant whose widow, Eliza, married Aaron Burr in the front parlor in 1833. The mansion's eight rooms are furnished in old-style elegance with 1,000 artifacts dating between 1740 and 1860 (including a fine collection of Chippendale and French and American Empire-style furniture pieces). **Admission:** $3 adults; $2 students and seniors. **Hours:** Wed.–Sun. 10 A.M.–4 P.M.

Trinity Cemetery Amsterdam Ave. (at W. 153rd St.) (212) 368-1600 *www.trinitywallstreet.org/cemetery.html.* Spread across a sloping hillside, Trinity Cemetery was opened in 1843 after a series of epidemics left the congregation's Wall Street churchyard dangerously overcrowded. Many of New York's most prominent citizens ended up on this rocky promontory, which overlooks the Hudson River and the Palisades. As soon as you pass through the tall, wrought-iron gates on West 153rd Street, the roar of Broadway is eclipsed by the cawing of ravens. A century-old canopy of ash and oak trees keeps the grassy knolls and manicured walkways appropriately shady and peaceful. Trinity's monuments are richly varied in material, form and symbolism. Look for broken columns (died in the prime of life), sheaves of wheat (lived to a ripe old age), polished spheres and shrouded urns (symbols of the soul). There are Gothic-style marble mausoleums, towering steles of brownstone and simple slabs that conceal spacious subterranean vaults. Among those buried at Trinity are John Jacob Astor, the fur trader turned real estate tycoon, who was the wealthiest man in the United States on his death in 1848; John James Audubon, the naturalist and former owner of this farmstead; and Clement Clarke Moore, who wrote "A Visit From St. Nicholas."

Recommended Inexpensive Restaurant

El Presidente   CARIBBEAN/PAN-LATIN

Central Park

The miracle of Central Park (*www.centralpark.org* or *www.centralparknyc.org* for information on the park, special events, sports and walking tours) is partly that it exists at all, but even more that it exists smack in the middle of a huge, throbbing city. The very incongruity of its charms—rolling meadows, jagged cliffs, graceful bridges and more than 26,000 trees—takes your breath away.

Central Park almost didn't happen. If the land had not been snapped up by city fathers in the early 1850's, Manhattan would have quickly and inexorably become a single rectilinear street grid. Central Park was America's first major public park to be designed and built, as opposed to simply preserving nature. Frederick Law Olmsted and Calvert Vaux planned each square foot of the 843-acre park to create the effects of nature. A fake waterfowl here. A shrub placed there for almost painterly reasons. The goal was country in the city.

Olmsted and Vaux created an illusion of immense size by curving paths, carefully composed vistas and other landscaping techniques. From no point in the park can you see side to side or end to end. Illusion becomes reality. Not for nothing are the park's founders sometimes called the precursors to Disney.

For the visitor, the best place to get an idea of the designers' intent is to go to the **Ramble,** a 38-acre "wild garden," in the words of Olmsted. The Ramble is located in the middle of the park between 73rd and 79th Streets; except for the underlying bedrock, it's a completely artificial creation. Paths twist and turn through the brush and there are scenic overlooks and rustic log structures. A tumbling stream called the Gill gurgles by.

The Ramble is one of the many great places for **birdwatching** in Central Park, which is a major stop along the Atlantic flyway. More than 275 species, from rare owls to hummingbirds have been spotted there. One of the park's more fascinating curiosities is located at the **Loeb Boathouse,** on the east side of the park between 74th and 75th Streets, where birders record their sightings in a loose-leaf notebook that visitors are welcome to examine or add to. The Boathouse is at the eastern entrance to the Ramble, where volunteers raise wildflowers to attract butterflies. So far 26 species have been spotted.

The Boathouse is on a **20-acre lake,** the largest of seven bodies of water in the park. You can rent rowboats for $10 an hour ($30 deposit); a gondola for $30 an hour (seats six), or bikes ($14 for a tandem, $6 for a children's bike). It is one of the real pleasures of New York City to row in the shimmering duck-filled lake, marveling at the graceful cast-iron **Bow Bridge,** all in the shadow of grand apartment buildings and skyscrapers.

But the best things in Central Park are free. One of the visual delights of the park, **Belvedere Castle,** a Gothic fantasy, contains a nature center where would-be naturalists can borrow backpacks that contain binoculars, a birding guide and other reference material and notepaper. At the **Charles A. Dana Discovery Center,** a beautifully restored nature center on **Harlem Meer** at the northeast corner of the park, 50 bamboo fishing rods are lent out free of charge to fish for (and release) catfish, bluegills and other fish. Bait is also provided, either night crawlers or biscuit dough.

Central Park is a fabulous place for kids. The **zoo** in the southeast corner, with its underwater view of swimming polar bears—and adjacent **children's zoo,** where kids can pet a Vietnamese pot-bellied pig—is worth a leisurely couple of hours. The **carousel** (mid-park at 64th St.) is the fourth generation of its genre—the first was turned by a blind mule and a horse—and whirls at a briskly invigorating pace. Nearby at 66th Street and the East Drive, the statue of **Balto,** the sled dog who took medicine to Nome, Alaska, to squelch a diph-theria epidemic, has been polished by generations of loving, fascinated hands.

But there are also elements clearly for adults, and not just the **Tavern on the Green** restaurant, with its gorgeous garden featuring Japanese lanterns and whimsical topiary shrubs. (You can also sip wine and dine elegantly at the **Park View at the Boathouse**—or, more likely grab a hot dog for $1.50 from any of scores of vendors in the park.) Adults will also be drawn to **the Mall** on the east side between 66th and 69th Streets, where the elegant elm trees and lines of benches feel like Paris, especially in winter.

There is so much else of interest in Central Park: the elegant **Conserva-tory Garden** at Fifth Avenue and 105th Street with its French, Italian and English floral treatments; the **Shakespeare Garden** on the west side between 79th and 80th Streets, composed entirely of plant species mentioned by the Bard, including a red mulberry said to be taken from Shakespeare's mother's garden; and, of course, **Strawberry Fields** on the west side between 71st and 74th Streets, built in memory of John Lennon by Yoko Ono. At its center is a mosaic, impressed with the word "Imagine."

And don't forget the **Naturalist's Walk,** a walk along the park's west side that celebrates biodiversity. Or the **Egyptian Obelisk** (east side at 81st St.), a 71-foot-tall stone needle that dates back to 1500 B.C. Or **the Pond** at the southeastern entrance, where J.D. Salinger's Holden Caulfield watched the ducks.

But the heart and soul of the park are in the large places where people can come together and play ball, picnic and sunbathe—all kinds of people from all kinds of circumstances, exercising the democratic vision of parks so audaciously pioneered by Olmsted and Vaux. There's the **Sheep Meadow** on the west side of the park between 66th and 69th Streets, and the **Great Lawn** in mid-park between 79th and 86th Streets. You can fly kites, throw Frisbees or stare into your lover's eyes. These are the true backyards of New York City.

A last thought, which might well be a visitor's first. The **Central Park Conservancy,** which since 1980 has raised millions to restore and improve the park, runs a visitor's center in what was once **the Dairy,** which originally dispensed glasses of free milk. It is on the East Side at 65th Street. You can get directions, brochures and see exhibits that include a flip map showing how the park was built from the original landforms.   —*Douglas Martin*

Transportation: West side of park: A, B, C, D, 1, 9 to 59th St.-Columbus Circle or any B/C subway stop or M10 bus stop between 59th and 110th Sts. East side of park: N, R, W to Fifth Ave. at 59th St.; any 4, 5, 6 subway or M1, 2, 3, 4 bus stop between 59th and 110th Sts.

PARK ATTRACTIONS

The Arsenal 64th St. and Fifth Ave. Originally built in 1848, the Arsenal is one of only two buildings in Central Park that stood here before the park existed. This imposing structure resembles a medieval castle, with many architectural and artistic touches added over the years inside and out. It's worth visiting for its Depression-era murals and art exhibits focused on New York or Central Park. It also houses Olmsted and Vaux's original "Greensward Plan" for the park. This landmark building is now the headquarters of New York City's Dept. of Parks and Recreation and the Central Park Wildlife Conservation Center.

Arthur Ross Pinetum Mid-park, 84th–86th Sts. This collection of 20 species of pine tree (plus elms and oaks) is the largest collection of evergreens in Central Park. Walking tours of the Pinetum are available starting at nearby Belvedere Castle, including a popular seasonal tour in early December. Bird-watchers also come here to spot owls in the pines, and there is a small playground that finds more use as a quiet picnic spot.

Balto East Drive at 66th St. This is one of the most sought-out sites in the park, and is the only park statue commemorating an animal. Balto was a heroic Siberian husky who braved a blizzard to bring diptheria antitoxin to Nome, Alaska; he was also the subject of a popular animated film. Created by Frederick George Richard Roth in 1925, Balto sports a golden back and snout, the patina and outer layer of bronze rubbed off by fingers, noses and backsides of thousands of worshipful children.

Belvedere Castle Mid-park at 79th St. This impressive Victorian structure, perched atop the highest natural point in the park, was occupied by the U.S. Weather Bureau from 1919 to the early 1960's, then fell into disrepair until the Central Park Conservancy restored and reopened it in 1982. The site now offers good views of the park as well as excellent bird-watching. It also houses the

Henry Luce Nature Observatory, where visitors can explore the plants and animals of the park through interactive exhibits. Also available are backpacks with information and binoculars to help budding scientists study the nearby Ramble or Turtle Pond (available Tue.–Sun. 10 A.M.–5 P.M.).

Bethesda Terrace and Fountain Mid-park at 72nd St. The split-level Terrace, decorated with detailed carvings of plants and animals, is one of the most popular areas of the park, affording gorgeous views of the Mall, the Lake, the Ramble, and all the human activity around the plaza. **Bethesda Fountain** itself, possibly the most-photographed monument in Central Park, commemorates the opening the Croton Aqueduct in 1842. It was the only sculpture called for in the original park plan, and its creator, Emma Stebbins, was the first woman to receive a commission to produce a major piece of public art in the city.

The Carousel 65th St. Transverse and Central Drive. This is one of the largest merry-go-rounds in America, with 58 hard-carved horses and two chariots. Built in 1908 by the firm of Stein and Goldstein, respected carvers from Brooklyn, it was rescued from Coney Island by the Parks Department. Today the quaint building and calliope music draw over 250,000 riders per year. Rides are 90¢. **Hours:** Daily 10:30 A.M.–6 P.M. (closes at 5 P.M. in winter).

Central Park Drive This six-mile road circling the park has a lane set aside for bikers, joggers, and in-line skaters. The best time to use it is when the park is closed to traffic: Monday to Friday 10 A.M. to 3 P.M. and 7 to 10 P.M., and from 7 P.M. Friday to A.M. Monday. Keep alert, since this lane gets heavy use from high-speed athletes on wheels.

Central Park Wildlife Center East Side, 63rd–66th Sts. (212) 861-6030 *www.wcs.org/zoos.* Generations of New Yorkers have grown up with the Central Park Zoo. The oldest zoo in the city began in the 1860's as a menagerie to house animals given to the park, but has since been renovated many times and rechristened as the Central Park Wildlife Conservation Center. Divided into three zones (Arctic, rain forest and temperate), the center features animals in naturalistic settings (though you've got to admit those poor polar bears don't seem happy on sweltering summer days). Its emphasis on public education is evident in the newly remodeled **Tisch Children's Zoo,** in which interactive nature exhibits have replaced kitschy storybook characters. Admission to the children's zoo is included in the general admission price, but make sure you bring along an extra pocketful of quarters for the feed dispensers. Kids love to feed the goats, cows and potbellied pig. Parents will also want to check on sea lion, polar bear and penguin feeding times—all of which provide a fascinating spectacle for kids and adults. The beloved **George Delacorte Musical Clock,** between the Wildlife Center and the Children's Zoo, draws crowds on the hour and half-hour when a menagerie of motorized animals twirl around the clock to nursery-rhyme tunes. **Admission:** $3.50 adults; $1.25 seniors; 50¢ children ages 3–12; children under 3, free. **Hours:** Apr.–Oct. Mon.–Fri. 10 A.M.–5 P.M., Sat.–Sun. 10 A.M.–5:30 P.M. Nov.–Mar. daily 10 A.M.–4:30 P.M.

Charles A. Dana Discovery Center Mid-park at 110th St. Central Park's newest building, on the north shore of Harlem Meer at the top of the park, offers general park information, conducts nature classes, showcases community projects and art, and loans out poles for catch-and-release fishing in the Meer (available Tue.–Sun. 10 A.M.–4 P.M. from Apr.–Oct.). A deck outside the Center looks out over the Meer to the south, and an outdoor plaza, bordered by trees, hosts concerts and special public events throughout the year.

Chess and Checkers House East Side at 65th St. This is the park's largest and most ornate wooden summer house. Playing pieces for the 24 indoor and outdoor tables here can be borrowed from the Dairy, and children's chess lessons are offered by the Central Park Conservancy in the summer.

The Concert Ground Mid-park, 69th-72nd Sts. (212) 360-2756. Music, theater, and dance performances are occasionally held at the neoclassical limestone **Naumberg Bandshell.** Behind the shady Wisteria Pergola to the east of the bandshell, Rumsey Playfield hosts **SummerStage** (*www.summerstage.org*), a series of free summer concerts (everything from rock and folk to world music).

Conservatory Garden East Side, 104th-106th Sts. One of Central Park's best-kept secrets, these six acres of horticultural magnificence are tucked away behind wrought-iron gates that once served as the entrance to the Vanderbilt mansion at Fifth Avenue and 58th Street. This is the only formal garden in the park, with trees, flowers, statues and fountains spread throughout three very different sub-gardens (on Saturdays, you can often see several wedding parties who pile in here for formal photographs). To the north is a French-style garden, with concentric rings of flowers around a central fountain. There are massive displays of tulips in the spring, chrysanthemums in the fall, and white roses in the summer. The central area is done in an Italian style, with a carefully tended central lawn and a simple fountain. The southern portion of the garden was created in an English style, and is perhaps the most popular of the three, due to its statuary fountain featuring characters from *The Secret Garden*.

Conservatory Water East Side, 72nd-75th Sts. The name of this popular pond comes from the conservatory, or greenhouse, that was meant to be built nearby. Most park patrons know it as the boat pond, because of the numerous model ships floating in it on most good days. The **Kerbs Memorial Boathouse,** on the east side of the pond, rents out boats and sells refreshments beside a large patio. In summer, storytellers can often be found near the **statue of Hans Christian Andersen** to the west of the pond; children love to climb on the **Alice in Wonderland** statue to the north.

The Andersen statue is also the best vantage point for one of the park's most remarkable wildlife dramas. For years, a pair of red-tailed hawks have been nesting on the 12th-floor ledge of a building just across from the pond, at Fifth Avenue and 74th Street. One most weekends, hawk watchers bring in telescopes and offer all passersby close-up views of the nest.

The Dairy East Side at 65th St. During 19th-century "milk scandals" and diph-theria outbreaks, this Swiss-Gothic hybrid cottage served as a distribution cen-ter for fresh milk brought in from farms outside New York. It now serves as Cen-tral Park's **Visitor Information Center and Recreation Building.** The Dairy houses exhibits and information about the park, including an excellent flip map documenting the changes wrought on the landscape during park construction, as well as before-and-after photographs of the area. **Hours:** Daily 11 A.M.–5 P.M. (closes 4 P.M. in winter).

Delacorte Theatre Mid-park at 80th St. (SW corner of Great Lawn) (212) 539-8655. For over 30 years, the Delacorte has offered free **Shakespeare in the Park** performances in July and August (212-539-8750 or *www.publictheater.org* for information). With Belvedere Castle looming nearby, the Turtle Pond to the east, and the Great Lawn across a path to the north, a star-studded evening of theater in Central Park can be unforgettable. New Yorkers and tourists line up for hours to get tickets, which are distributed at 1 P.M. the day of the perfor-mance (limit two per person). Tickets are also available from the Joseph Papp Public Theater at 425 Lafayette Street, near Astor Place.

The Great Hill West Side, 103rd-107th Sts. This green field offers picnic tables, a soft-surface walking or jogging path, and, in August, the "Great Jazz on the Great Hill" concert organized by the Central Park Conservancy.

The Great Lawn Mid-park, 79th–86th Sts. Today the Lawn is one of the most popular areas of the park, but until 1934 this was the site of the Croton Reser-voir. When the city's water supply changed, the reservoir became obsolete. It was filled in with rubble from city construction to become the Great Lawn, a pond and two playgrounds. These 13 acres of grass, with eight softball fields, are used for all manner of private and public functions; they look terrific after a massive restoration project in the late 1990's. The Great Lawn has been the site of some of New York's largest outdoor events, including Paul Simon's 1991 con-cert and Pope John Paul II's 1995 Mass (which drew 600,000 and 350,000 peo-ple, respectively); it also plays host to annual summer concerts by the Metropol-itan Opera and the New York Philharmonic. All this use takes its toll, however, so the rules here are strict these days: no dogs, no bicycles, permits required for ball games. It is open only when the Keeper of the Great Lawn feels the lawn can handle public use.

Harlem Meer East Side, 106th–110th Sts. A walking tour of the 11-acre Meer (Dutch for "small sea") takes in an impressive array of plants and wildlife, including some impressive oak, beech and gingko trees. The formerly fenced-off edge of the Meer has been restored to a more natural state, including a small sandy beach near the Charles A. Dana Discovery Center. At the southeast cor-ner of the Meer, follow some steps to the water, where you will find yourself completely surrounded by flowers, with a private view of the water.

The Jacqueline Kennedy Onassis Reservoir Mid-park, 85th–96th Sts. Until 1991, this 106-acre body of water still provided water to parts of Manhat-

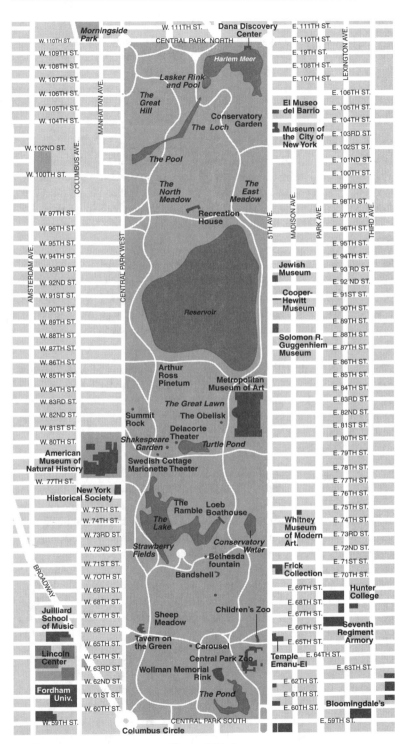

Central Park

tan and the Bronx; now three huge tunnels bring water from upstate New York, but the Reservoir remains a good spot for jogging, bird watching and observing the city skyline. The New York Road Runners Club (which organizes the New York City Marathon) holds weekly races on the 1.58-mile track, which is especially beautiful when the cherry trees bloom in the spring. Also worth a look are three elegant cast-iron pedestrian bridges that span the Bridle Trail, and three Vaux-designed gatehouses containing water-treatment equipment.

The Lake Mid-park, 71st-78th St. After the Reservoir, this is the largest body of water in Central Park. Its meandering shoreline offers many sights and attractions, from the wisteria arbor in the south and **Bow Bridge,** the beautiful span in the center of the Lake, to the ornate Ladies' Pavilion on its northwest shore. Some of these sights may be best viewed from one of the rowboats available for rental at the **Loeb Boathouse** *(see below)*, at the northeastern edge of the Lake.

Lasker Rink and Pool Mid-park, 108th–109th St. (212) 534-7639. Located just below the scenic Harlem Meer, the Lasker Rink is open for ice skating during the winter season ($3 adults, $1.50 children and seniors; $3.50 for skate rental). In summer, this is Central Park's only swimming pool, available at no cost. Swimmers must wear a swimsuit (no denim shorts or t-shirts). Lockers are available, but bring your own lock.

Lawn Sports Center West Side at 69th St. (north of Sheep Meadow). Visitors can play croquet or lawn bowling on two tiny lawns from May 1st to October 1st. The New York Croquet Club (212-369-7949) offers free clinics on Tuesday nights and tournaments on weekends; the New York Lawn Bowling club (212-289-3245) also offers free lessons and regular club games.

Loeb Boathouse East Side, 74th–75th Sts. The original Vaux-designed wooden building burned down long ago, but the current Loeb Boathouse has become a hub of park activity. The restaurant, **Park View at the Boathouse** (212-517-2233), is a romantic, two-star favorite; more casual dining is possible at an outside cafe. Energetic visitors can **rent bicycles** (choose from three-speed, 10-speed or tandems, from $10 to $20 an hour, with a deposit required) and **rowboats** ($10 for the first hour, $30 deposit is required; reservations accepted). Those in search of more relaxation can take a ride in a genuine Venetian **gondola.** Bird watchers come here to enter their sightings in the **Bird Register,** a large notebook stored in the Boathouse. And the Conservancy has installed a small wildflower garden, meant to attract butterflies, to the west of the Boathouse entrance.

The Mall (Literary Walk) Mid-park, 69th–72nd Sts. Four long rows of American elms, often the first park stop for spring warblers, form a cathedral-like canopy over the Mall. This grand promenade is one of only two formal elements remaining from Olmsted and Vaux's original park design (the other is Bethesda Fountain), and it contains many of the park's best-known sculptures. Among them are William Shakespeare, Robert Burns, Victor Herbert, Beethoven and

Christopher Columbus. At the southern end of the walk is a tribute to Frederick Law Olmsted—a memorial flower garden surrounded by American elms.

Merchants' Gate and Maine Monument Southeast park entrance (Columbus Circle). Most of the original entrances to the park were dedicated to different professions, and Olmsted and Vaux insisted on very modest designs for the gates. Over time, however, the city added striking military monuments to the entrances along Central Park South, including this massive pylon commemorating the sinking of the battleship *Maine* in 1898. The monument honors the Americans killed in the Spanish-American War, and was partially funded with pennies and nickels collected from schoolchildren after the war.

Naturalists' Walk West Side, 77th–81st Sts. This landscape was restored with the nearby American Museum of Natural History in mind: a dramatic variety of flowers, plants and trees have been introduced to this area, attracting birds and butterflies and making it a natural destination after exploring the museum's Hall of Biodiversity and other exhibits.

The North Meadow Mid-Park, 97th–102nd Sts. This is the largest grassy space in Central Park, divided only by 12 fields for baseball, softball and soccer. Inside the landmark **North Meadow Recreation Center,** the Conservancy offers a wide range of programs for children, from computer-based education to more physical activities. Any visitor with a photo ID can borrow one of the Center's Field Day kits, containing items like balls, Frisbees and jump ropes.

The Obelisk (Cleopatra's Needle) East Side at 81st St. This 3,500-year-old stone obelisk was erected behind the Metropolitan Museum on January 22, 1881, after being uprooted from the city of Heliopolis, making a tumultuous ocean crossing, and crawling through the streets of Manhattan for four months. It remains the oldest man-made object in the park. Each corner is supported by a massive bronze replica of a sea crab—the originals of which are in the Met's Sackler Wing.

The Pond Southeast corner of the park. Once an area of foul swampland, this is now one of the most attractive parts of Central Park, well shielded from street noise by trees and rocks. The small fenced-in area here is the Hallett Nature Sanctuary—four acres of park left untended, creating a haven for animals (like woodchucks, rabbits and raccoons) and plants (including Black Cherry trees and many wildflowers). An excellent view of the Pond is available from Gapstow Bridge at the northern end of the Pond, or from the Cop Cot (Scottish for "little house on the crest of the hill"), near the Sixth Avenue park entrance.

The Pool West Side, 100th–103rd Sts. This body of water is a romantic place, sheltered by weeping willows and an impressive assortment of other tree species. A small peninsula on the south shore is a good spot for duck feeding or for viewing the Pool's foliage.

The Ramble Mid-park, 73rd–79th Sts. It's hard to believe that this 38-acre sprawl of pathways, streams, cliffs and trees is entirely man-made—meticulously designed by Frederick Law Olmsted and carved out of a natural hillside. This may be the easiest place to get lost in Central Park, so bring along a map. But the opportunity to lose yourself and escape from the crush of city life has also made it one of the most popular destinations in the park, a fact that has in turn led to an ongoing need for restoration. This is also one of the best sites for **bird watching** in the country, ranked among the top 15 by the Audubon Society. Over 200 different species of birds have been seen here; the best time for birding is during spring and fall migration, in April and May and again in September and October.

The Ravine Mid-park, 102nd–106th Sts. Stretching from the southern end of Lasker Rink to the Pool just above West 100th St., the Ravine is a peaceful destination filled with wildflowers, bird-watching trails, and odd and beautiful bridges. One of the most impressive of these is Huddlestone Arch, a careful assemblage of rough boulders fitted together without any mortar or other binding material.

Shakespeare Garden West Side, 79th–80th Sts. Once an extension of the Ramble, this area was dedicated to Shakespeare on the tricentennial of his death in 1916. This meandering, four-acre garden showcases about half of the 200 plants mentioned in the Bard's works, including a mulberry tree said to be grown from a cutting from Shakespeare's mother's garden. Bronze plaques provide the quotations relevant to each plant.

Sheep Meadow Mid-park, 66th–69th Sts. This 15-acre meadow was an actual grazing field for sheep until the 1930's, when the sheep were shipped out and their building became the Tavern on the Green restaurant. In the 1960's and 70's the field suffered severe damage from sporting activities, concerts and hippie be-ins. But since the 1980's, the Park Conservancy has exercised strict control over meadow visitors. On warm summer days, this rolling lawn still attracts thousands of walkers, sunbathers and people-watchers. Radios, team sports and dogs are prohibited, but often show up anyway. Just outside the northern fence is Lilac Walk, lined with 23 varieties of lilac. The Meadow is open mid-April to mid-October, dawn to dusk in fair weather.

Strawberry Fields West Side, 72nd St. The landscaping of this area was made possible by Yoko Ono, who presented it to the city in memory of John Lennon, who was murdered outside the nearby Dakota apartment house in 1980. There is an incredible variety of plants and trees, all donated by countries around the world, forming a "Garden of Peace." The most evocative touch is a gift from the city of Naples, Italy: a mosaic with the word "Imagine" at its center.

Summit Rock West Side, 81st–85th Sts. At 137.5 feet, this is the highest point in Central Park. An ampitheater overlooks the south and east slopes, and a path leads up the southern slope to a beautiful green lawn that affords good views of the park and the Upper West Side. This and adjacent areas of Central Park were home to 5,000 New Yorkers before the city purchased the land and began park construction. At the time, there were nearly a thousand buildings on the land, including factories and churches. Seneca Village occupied this territory in the mid-1800's; this was one of the best-known African-American communities in New York, composed mostly of free black land-owning families.

Swedish Cottage Marionette Theater West Side at 79th St. (212) 988-9093. This replica of a 19th-century Swedish schoolhouse seats 100 children and features central air-conditioning and a state-of-the-art stage. Puppet shows, often classics like Peter Pan or Cinderella, are staged at 10:30 A.M. and noon Tuesday through Friday, 1 P.M. on Saturdays (no Saturday shows in July or August). The season runs from early November through mid-August; advance reservations are required. **Prices:** $6 adults; $5 children.

Turtle Pond Mid-park, 79th–80th Sts. When the old Croton Reservoir was filled in with construction debris in the 1930's, becoming the Great Lawn, the southern end became Belvedere Lake. It quickly attracted a wide range of aquatic life and the site was rechristened in honor of some of its more popular inhabitants in 1987. A 1997 renovation altered the pond's shoreline, added new plants and introduced Turtle Island, a new habitat for the turtles and birds that make their home here. A dock and nature blind offer great views of the pond and its denizens sunning themselves on dead tree trunks.

Wollman Memorial Skating Rink East Side at 62nd St. *www.wollmanskatingrink.com.* The 33,000-square-foot Wollman Rink offers a spacious ice-skating area and an unparalleled view of the Duck Pond framed by landmark buildings like the Plaza Hotel. During the summer months, Rollerblades replace ice skates at Wollman Rink. Rollerblades and safety equipment (state law requires children 14 and under to wear helmets and pads) can be rented for rink use ($6) or for park use ($15 with a $100 deposit). **Admission:** $7.50 adults ($8 on weekends); $3.75 children under 12 and seniors. Skate rental is $3.75.

SPORTS IN CENTRAL PARK
(See also chapter **Sports & Recreation.***)*

Baseball/Softball: The **North Meadow** has baseball diamonds. The **Great Lawn** has seven softball fields; five more are at the **Heckscher Ballfields.** Arsenal West (16 W. 61st St.) is the place to go for permits, or call (212) 408-0226. Permits are expensive, and are usually snatched up well in advance by organized leagues, but you might find a pickup game on the Great Lawn.

Biking: Stick to the roads: park security may confiscate your bike if you ride on walkways or trails. Rental bikes are available near **Loeb Boathouse,** at 74th St. and the East Drive *(see listing above).* The **Central Park Drive** loop is 6 miles; this road is closed to cars 10 A.M.–4 P.M., and then again 7 P.M.–dusk. Even when vehicular traffic is permitted, there is a multi-use lane for runners, bikers and in-line skaters.

Boating: Rowboats and gondolas can be rented at the **Loeb Boathouse** *(see listing above).*

Fishing: The **Dana Discovery Center** *(see listing above)* loans out poles and bait for catch-and-release fishing; fishing in the Lake is permitted, but may become more restricted in the future following the poisoning of some birds.

Horseback Riding: Horse rentals and riding lessons are available at the **Claremont Riding Academy** at 175 W. 89th St.; call (212) 724-5100 for information. The park's bridle path runs around the Reservoir and northern quadrant of the park, and down the west side to 60th St.

Ice Skating: Available November through March at **Wollman** (212-439-6900) and **Lasker** (212-534-7639) rinks *(see listings above for more information)*.

In-line Skating: The park drives are popular with skaters, but some prefer the area at the north end of the Mall and the driveway to the west of the Mall. From April to September, **Wollman Rink** *(see listing above)* is also open for in-line skating.

Running: There are designated running lanes on all park drives, and the entire road is closed to automobile traffic between 10 A.M. and 4 P.M. and after 7 P.M. on weekdays, and from 7 P.M. Friday to 6 A.M. Monday.

Swimming: Swimming is forbidden in all open bodies of water in the park, but Lasker Rink (212-534-7639) becomes a free swimming pool in July and August.

Tennis: The **tennis center** to the northwest of the Reservoir houses 30 courts; permits are required most of the time and are available at the Arsenal. Call (212) 360-8131 for details.

Lonnie Schlein/The New York Times

The Sheep Meadow in Central Park

THE BOROUGHS

THE BRONX

"The Bronx is up" in more ways than one. Geographically, this is the northern-most part of the city and the only borough attached to the U.S. mainland. More important is the Bronx's rise from the ashes of the burning buildings and crime-ridden streets of the 1970's. Renewed vibrancy and pride have come to the borough that was a collection of rural villages in the 1890's, before being annexed into the expanding city. Throughout the early decades of the 20th century, the Bronx was mainly populated by waves of Irish and German immigrants seeking the open, green space of the borough, made accessible by the growth of the subway system. Early Bronxites could watch D.W. Griffith making movies in a local studio, and some spent their summers living in tents on a rocky shoreline, where Robert Moses later hauled in sand for Orchard Beach in the 1930's.

Perhaps best known as the home of the **Bronx Zoo** and **Yankee Stadium**, the Bronx also features the green spaces of the **New York Botanical Garden**, **Van Cortlandt and Pelham Bay Parks**, as well as **Wave Hill** in Riverdale. **City Island** is a virtual New England village.

The Bronx is home to several colleges and universities: **Fordham University** and **Manhattan College; Bronx Community College**, once the uptown campus of NYU, with its Hall of Fame for Great Americans; and **Lehman College**, formerly Hunter College.

Many visitors to the Bronx travel to **Woodlawn Cemetery** to view its grandiose mausoleums and especially the grave of Herman Melville (the man at the gate is happy to tell you where to find it). Those more interested in the living go to **Arthur Avenue** in the Belmont section of the borough. There they find lively food shopping and excellent Italian dining just down the street from the zoo and opposite Fordham University's Rose Hill campus.

How did the Bronx get its name? Yes, the Bronx River flows through the borough, but the name probably goes back to the early Dutch settlers of the city that was originally called New Amsterdam. The first Dutch inhabitants of the area were Dutch farmer Jonas Bronck and his family, who owned a 500-acre farm near what is now Morrisania. According to legend people would say they were going to visit "the Broncks," thereby establishing the use of the definite article in the borough's name, the only one of the five with that distinction.

HIGHLIGHTS OF THE BRONX
(For **Yankee Stadium,** *see chapter* **Sports & Recreation.***)*

Bartow-Pell Mansion Museum 895 Shore Rd. (718) 885-1461. A 150-year-old Federal-style mansion with formal gardens, the Bartow-Pell house is all but hidden in foliage several yards off the heavily traveled road to Orchard Beach. The neo-classical stone mansion has a magnificent Greek Revival interior com-

The Bronx Zoo

Sprawling over 265 acres, with paths winding through lush greenery shaded by canopies of trees, the Bronx Zoo can feel as much like a park as an animal repository. But turn any corner, and you will be reminded exactly where you are. The zoo has more than 7,000 animals, of over 700 species, enough to make any skeptic marvel at nature's prolific creativity. There are the exotic: cassowaries (flightless birds capable of killing a person with their toenails); Mongolian wild horses, completely extinct in the wild; a 24-foot-long reticulated python; black-necked swans. And there are the routine but lovable: massive, placid elephants; vanilla-colored polar bears; docile zebras.

The zoo has contrived all sorts of settings to let nature do its thing, and let you watch. The "World of Darkness," for example, takes you through a darkened building so you can see how nocturnal animals behave—bats spread their wings, a gopher snake resolutely devours a mouse (conveniently delivered by a zoo keeper). And some of the outdoor settings are lovely, such as the steep, grassy hill that is home to gelada baboons and nubian ibex, with their baroquely curled horns.

The zoo brings not just the wild, but the world, to the city. JungleWorld, housed in a 37,000-square-foot building, recreates four Asian habitats. One of them is a mangrove forest, which most of us will never see, stocked with animal inhabitants like bear cats, the black leopard and the Asian small-clawed otter, the world's smallest otter species. The Bengali Express Monorail crosses the Bronx River to take you on a leisurely, photo-friendly journey though Wild Asia. There are antelopes, deer, wild cattle with their white-stockinged feet, Indian rhinoceros—the largest land animal on earth—Asian elephant and the Siberian tiger.

The Bronx Zoo opened in 1899, and has not stopped growing since. The

AP Photo/Kathy Willens

highlight of the zoo, opened in 1999, is the Congo Gorilla Forest. It is 6.5 acres of a green playland, or homeland, for African rain forest animals, with 11 waterfalls, 55 artificial rain forest trees, misting machines and even jungle sounds. The animals range from tiny, scampering colobus monkeys to brilliantly vareigated mandrills to massive, lolling silverbacks. Some of the gorillas, who group around male leaders, are lazy, some bawdy, some familially inclined, but all are fascinating to watch. Only a layer of glass separates the masses from the apes—close enough, it seems, to touch them.

The gorilla exhibit includes a film on their threatened habitats, which is in keeping with the larger mission of the Wildlife Conservation Society: to preserve species and habitats around the world. The conservation message is ubiquitous, and effective. The diversity of species on display generates amazement—but also alarm, given the number that are on the edge of extinction. The zoo's educational mission succeeds as well, managing to teach, for example, about stork breeding habits. The zoo also does its part to promote procreation: more than 300 animals were born there in 1998.

But the best thing about any zoo—and certainly the Bronx Zoo—is serendipity: turning a corner to catch a glimpse of a giraffe's awkward beauty as it nibbles grass from a sun-bathed plain. Making a wrong turn that introduces you to the primeval-looking marabou stork. Looking up as you trudge toward the exit to see a North American brown bear standing atop a boulder.

Throughout, of course, there are ample opportunities to consume food, drink and souvenirs. Be warned that a day at the zoo will not necessarily come cheap, particularly for a family, given the extra charges for the Children's Zoo, the Bengali Express Monorail and the Congo Gorilla exhibit.

The crowds can be overwhelming as well, sometimes giving the zoo the feel of an amusement park. Be prepared, for example, to wait 45 minutes or more for Congo Gorilla Forest on a summer weekend.

But those gripes aside, it is a remarkably pleasant way to spend a day, not least because you get to see New Yorkers in nature themselves—for once, unhurried, and perhaps only mildly more aggressive than many of the animals they are contemplating. —*Amy Waldman*

Fordham Rd. and Bronx River Pkwy. (718) 367-1010 *www.wcs.org/zoos.* **Admission:** $9 adults; $5 seniors and children ages 2–12. Wed. admission free, except during Holiday Lights. Extra admission fees for special exhibits: Congo Gorilla Forest $3; Holiday Lights (evenings, Nov. 26–Jan. 2) $6; Children's Theater $2; Butterfly Zone $2; Bengali Express Monorail, Skyfari Aerial Tramway and Zoo Shuttle $2 each; camel rides $3. **Hours:** Mon.–Fri. 10 A.M.–5 P.M.; Sat.–Sun. and holidays 10 A.M.–5:30 P.M. **Services:** Baby stroller rental; wheelchairs available by reservation at (718) 220-5188. Extensive educational and kids' programs available. **Directions:** By subway, 2 to Pelham Pkwy., then walk west to the Bronxdale entrance. Or take Liberty Lines' BxM11 express bus, which makes various stops on Madison Ave. and will take you directly to the zoo; call (718) 652-8400 for details.

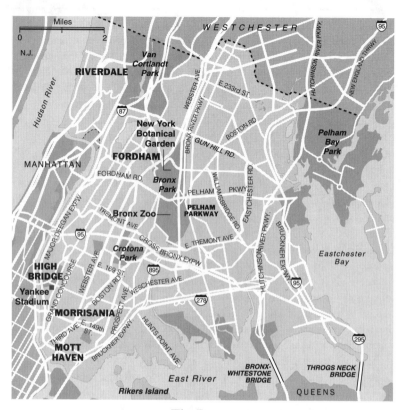

The Bronx

plete with an elegant freestanding elliptical staircase. The 19th-century Empire décor is an example of the finest quality found in New York homes at that time. The house sits on property purchased from the Indians by Thomas Pell in 1654, in a nine-acre setting that preserves with its original surroundings. **Admission:** $2.50 adults; $1.25 seniors and students. **Hours:** Wed., Sat. and Sun. noon-4 P.M.; call in advance for tours. **Subway:** 6 to Pelham Bay Park (about a mile from the station).

Bronx Museum of the Arts 1040 Grand Concourse (at 165th St.) (718) 681-6000. This is the only arts museum in the Bronx that exhibits 20th-century and contemporary art, particularly by Bronx artists or artists related in some way to the borough. Known for its high-quality, well-curated exhibitions, it's one of the many well-kept secrets in the Bronx. The permanent collection includes a strong collection of work by artists of African, Asian and Latin-American ancestry. **Admission:** $3 adults; $2 seniors and students; free for children under 12. **Hours:** Wed. 3–9 P.M., Thu.–Fri. 10 A.M.–5 P.M.; Sat.–Sun. noon–6 P.M. Closed Mon. –Tue. **Subway:** C, D, 4 to 161st St.; D to 167th St.–Grand Concourse.

City Island Just off the northeastern edge of the Bronx, City Island is a year-round virtual village of some 4,000 permanent residents, with one main drag, many boatyards and marinas, several newish condominium colonies and a serious concentration of seafood restaurants (including the ever-popular **Lobster Box,** 718-885-1952). It's a quiet enclave for much of the year, though it's bustling in summer. A mile and a half long and no more than half a mile wide, the island blends the forlorn mystery of a Hopper dreamscape with a cheerful blue-collar brawn and flashes of intriguing wealth. **Le Refuge Inn** on City Island (718-885-2478) is a charming French provincial bed-and-breakfast with an acclaimed restaurant and a series of Sunday string quartet concerts. At the **Boat Livery,** 663 City Island Ave. (718-885-1843), you can rent a small motorboat for the day to explore City Island and nearby High Island. **Directions:** 6 train to Pelham Bay Park, then take the Bx 29 bus.

Edgar Allan Poe Cottage 2640 Grand Concourse (between 192nd and 193rd Sts.) (718) 881-8900. Edgar Allan Poe moved to this cottage in Kingsbridge, the Bronx, from Manhattan in 1846, hoping that the country air would help his wife recover from tuberculosis. For three years, he lived in the tiny house, where he wrote "Annabel Lee." Three period rooms—a kitchen, parlor and bedroom—are filled with furniture from the 1840's, including Poe's own rocking chair and bed plus the bed where his wife died not long after the move. At the museum you can watch a 20-minute film on Poe's life and the house's history. A small gallery houses paintings, photographs and drawings from the 1840's. **Admission:** $2. **Hours:** Sat 10 A.M.–4 P.M., Sun 1–5 P.M. **Subway:** B, D, 4 to Kingsbridge Rd.

Hall of Fame for Great Americans University Ave. at W. 181st St. (718) 289-5162. This landmark institution was founded in 1900 as part of the uptown campus of New York University (now Bronx Community College). The main attraction here is the 630-foot open air Colonnade, honoring Americans who have played a significant role in the nation's history—authors, inventors, statesmen, artists, military leaders and many more. **Admission:** Free. **Hours:** Daily 10 A.M.–5 P.M. **Subway:** 4 to Burnside Ave.

New York Botanical Garden Opposite the Bronx Zoo, Bronx River Pkwy. at Fordham Rd. (718) 817-8700 *www.nybg.org.* This elegant, expansive garden was created in 1891, inspired by the success of the Royal Botanic Garden at Kew, England. The 250-acre garden was planted between 1895 and 1896; the landscape and construction work began in 1899. The lush grounds feature 48 different garden and plant collections, including thousands of shrubs and trees, plus day lilies, herbs, magnolias, roses, tulips, orchids and many more. Fifty acres of virgin forest have been preserved to show New York's original landscape before any settlers arrived. The Bronx River flows through the site, next to a stone mill dating from 1840.

The garden runs hands-on discovery, craft and gardening activities for everyone on weekends. There are special events throughout the year, such as a holiday model train show and the **Everett Children's Adventure Garden,** with attractions like topiary bunnies, outdoor mazes and interactive features. There's also a terrific garden shop, and a cafe and picnic tables.

It's worth the small extra charge to visit the spectacular **Enid A. Haupt Conservatory,** a beautiful Victorian greenhouse featuring rain forest and desert ecosystems and dazzling seasonal displays. That's especially true this year, for through August 2003, the conservatory is hosting **15 sculptures on loan from the Museum of Modern Art.** Among the works displayed here are Rodin's *St. John the Baptist Preaching* and *Monument to Balzac;* Picasso's whimsical *She-Goat;* Henry Moore's *Family Group* and *Reclining Figure II;* and Giacometti's *Tall Figure III.* **Admission:** Grounds only, $3 adults, $2 seniors and students, $1 children ages 2–12. Entry to grounds free all day Wed. and Sat. 10 A.M. –noon. (Separate admission to Conservatory and Children's Adventure Garden. Tram and golf cart tours available at additional fee.) Garden Passport, which includes the Conservatory, the Children's Adventure Garden and a narrated tram tour, $10 adults, $7.50 seniors and students, $4 children ages 2-12. **Hours:** Grounds and Conservatory, Apr. –Oct. Tue.–Sun 10 A.M.–6 P.M., Nov.–Mar. Tue.–Sun. 10 A.M.–4 P.M. Also open Mon. holidays. Children's Adventure Garden open same hours on weekends, more limited on weekdays. **Directions:** Metro North from Grand Central to Botanical Garden.

Van Cortlandt Park Broadway and W. 240th St. (at Birchhall Ave.) (718) 430-1890. Frederick Van Cortlandt's stone mansion, built in 1748 and today the Bronx's oldest building, served as Revolutionary War headquarters for both George Washington and a British general. In the late 19th century, the Van Cortlandt family donated the house and the surrounding 1,146 acres to the city. The park's southern portion houses the **Van Cortlandt House Museum,** a lake, a golf course and playing fields for soccer, cricket, rugby, baseball and hurling. Meanwhile, the northern end of the park remains largely pastoral; along with a nationally renowned cross-country track, it features nature trails that wind through a 100-year-old hardwood forest populated by foxes, raccoons and pheasant. **Subway:** 1, 9 to 242nd St.–Van Cortlandt Park.

Wave Hill 675 W. 252nd St. (at Independence Ave., near Palisade Ave.) (718) 549-3200 *www.wavehill.org.* This was once a private estate, comprised of an 1843 stone mansion (which once hosted Teddy Roosevelt, Mark Twain and Arturo Toscanini) and 28 bucolic acres overlooking the Hudson. Now a center for the arts and environmental studies, Wave Hill is a lovely place to walk along wooded paths or through carefully tended gardens and greenhouses. It's a magical setting for concerts, literary readings and art exhibitions—so lovely that it's a favorite spot for weddings. **Admission:** $4 adults, $2 seniors and students. Free in winter, and on Sat. mornings and Tue. in summer. Hours: Tue.–Sun. 9 A.M.–4:30 P.M. and some Mon. holidays. Extended hours in summer. **Directions:** Metro North from Grand Central to Riverdale, then a 5-block walk.

BROOKLYN

If you're not a native, all you might know about Brooklyn is this: The Brooklyn Bridge is at one end, Coney Island is at the other, and the Dodgers used to play ball somewhere in between. Historically, though, Brooklyn has given more to the world than Jackie Robinson and Nathan's Famous hot dogs—for one thing, it has always nourished all types of artistic voices, from Walt Whitman to Spike Lee. The borough is home to millions who are drawn to New York but find Manhattan life too hectic or too expensive.

The original town of Breuckelen was chartered by the Dutch West India Company in 1646 and incorporated into Kings County in 1683. Despite British occupation during the Revolutionary War, the resident population continued to grow, reaching over 4,500 by 1800. By then, more than 30 percent of the county's residents were of African descent. During the Civil War, Brooklyn found itself at the center of the abolitionist movement in America. The area was home to some of the first black landowners in America, as well as one of the first towns (Weeksville) settled by freed slaves.

At the start of the war, Brooklyn ranked as the third largest city in the U.S., and its dynamic population and proximity to New York had already sparked a major cultural renaissance. In 1855, a Brooklyn resident named Walt Whitman published *Leaves of Grass;* the next decade saw the creation of the Philharmonic Society of Brooklyn, the Brooklyn Academy of Music and the National Association of Baseball Players—the first such centralized organization in the country. In 1867, Olmsted and Vaux completed work on **Prospect Park,** which rivals Central Park in its beauty and the genius of its design and execution. **Eastern Parkway,** another of the duo's designs, opened a year later, becoming the nation's first six-lane parkway.

The second major wave of immigrants began to arrive from eastern and southern Europe around 1880; the increased labor force helped Brooklyn to become the country's fourth largest producer of manufactured goods. In 1883 the magnificent **Brooklyn Bridge** opened a vital link to Manhattan; it was soon followed by an elevated railroad and electric trolley service. Brooklynites fought hard for years to retain the borough's identity and political independence, but in 1898, a close vote finally consolidated Brooklyn into Greater New York City. Brooklyn entered the 20th century as a borough of New York, with a population of over one million.

The **Williamsburg and Manhattan bridges** (as well as the IRT, New York's first subway line) made the Manhattan–Brooklyn commute even easier. The "Great Migration" of African-Americans to Brooklyn began around 1915, adding to the steady influx of European immigrants. By 1930, half of the borough's residents were foreign born, and a substantial percentage remained African-American—but the Depression was tough on these immigrants and poor families from the rural South, and some of Brooklyn's beautiful neighborhoods turned into slums.

Lately, things are looking up. Business is growing again in the downtown Brooklyn area, especially the business district around **Borough Hall** and the

Metrotech Center. The **Brooklyn Academy of Music's Next Wave Festival,** begun in 1983, has consistently drawn cutting-edge artists—as well as crowds from Manhattan. And as Manhattan rents creep skyward, more young professionals are drifting across the river, bringing new life (and money) to old neighborhoods, and making areas like **Brooklyn Heights** and **Park Slope** some of the more desirable addresses in New York. Brooklyn's population of nearly 2.5 million makes it (unofficially, of course) the fourth largest city in the U.S., and it seems poised for many more changes in the century ahead.

The Brooklyn Academy of Music

It's the oldest performing arts center in the United States, yet the Brooklyn Academy of Music (BAM) is synonymous with the avant-garde. The neighborhood around BAM, Fort Greene, is a friendly, multicultural community with quite a few interesting shops and restaurants along Fulton Street.

BAM Opera House The main building houses the main stage, which is the BAM Opera House. Seating 2,109, it hosts programs like the innovative **Next Wave Festival,** bringing the best in new music, dance, opera and theater to New York each fall (festival regulars include Laurie Anderson, Philip Glass and Robert Wilson). Other annual Opera House performers include the Brooklyn Philharmonic and BAM Opera.

BAM Harvey Theater Built in 1904 as a legitimate theater and later used to show movies, the Harvey Theater (once named the Majestic) was abandoned in 1968 and lay dark until its renovation in 1987. But don't be fooled by the term "renovation": The building's shell, with exposed brick, crumbling paint, chipped friezes and exposed ducts, was deliberately left more or less intact. The theater has 900 seats and practically no obstructed views. BAM uses it to stage dance, jazz, theater and opera.

BAM Rose Cinemas Also housed in the main BAM building, the Rose Cinemas shows first-run independent and foreign films in four theaters with good sightlines and good-size screens. One of those screens is devoted exclusively to a program featuring classic American and foreign films, documentaries, retrospectives and special festivals.

BAMcafé A good place for food and drinks before and after BAM performances. The café also hosts BAMcafé Live every Thursday, Friday and Saturday night, featuring a wide range of musical and spoken-word performances (no cover, $10 food and drink minimum).

30 Lafayette Ave. (off Flatbush Ave.), Brooklyn (718) 636-4100 *www.bam.org* Tickets are available at the box office or through TicketMaster. **Subway:** 2, 3, 4, 5, M, N, Q, R, W to Pacific St./Atlantic Ave.

Brooklyn Heights/Cobble Hill/ Carroll Gardens

In 1965, **Brooklyn Heights** was designated the city's first historic district, assuring protection for brick and brownstone row houses on streets that have been little altered since the Civil War. The area is now one of Brooklyn's most desirable (and expensive) residential areas, and remains a popular destination for architecture lovers. Its serene, leafy streets are lined with lovely brownstones and gracious town houses. **Montague Street,** the neighborhood's main commercial drag, is lined with shops, chain stores and restaurants.

Brooklyn Heights has played host to some impressive literary figures over the years, including Walt Whitman, who wrote *Leaves of Grass* while living here. Truman Capote, Arthur Miller and W.H. Auden all lived here for a time, and Thomas Wolfe completed *You Can't Go Home Again* in a house on Montague Terrace. Today, Norman Mailer lives in one of the elegant brownstones on Columbia Heights.

One of the best reasons to visit, however, has to be the **Brooklyn Heights Promenade.** Stretching from Montague to Middagh Street, it offers striking views of the Lower Manhattan skyline and the Brooklyn Bridge. Lined by the lush gardens of picturesque town houses and offering inviting benches, the walkway draw joggers, families and—at night—romancing couples. The view of Manhattan is startling: You're far enough away to take it all in, but close enough that the buildings still loom large. If you lean over the railing a bit, you'll realize that the peaceful esplanade juts over the Brooklyn-Queens Expressway.

The best ending to a visit here is a stroll back across the **Brooklyn Bridge** *(see the section on* Lower Manhattan *earlier in this chapter).* The footpath is accessible from Cadman Plaza Park, and the trip toward Manhattan offers the best views and photo opportunities.

If you want to venture a little deeper into Brooklyn, head south to the quiet neighborhood of **Cobble Hill,** most of which is part of a New York City Historic District. In the 1930's, Thomas Wolfe lived here on Verandah Place. Jenny Jerome, the mother of Winston Churchill, was born on Amity Street in 1854. And Louis Comfort Tiffany in 1917 designed the windows, high altar and other appointments of the **Episcopal Christ Church and Holy Family** at 326 Clinton St., a Greek Revival structure built in 1842.

Restaurants and specialty food shops dot **Atlantic Avenue,** offering Middle Eastern delicacies, particularly from Egypt, Yemen and Morocco. The **Sahadi Importing Company** at no. 187 offers a fascinating selection of dried fruits, spices, olives and much more. Atlantic Avenue is also well known for its antiques stores.

Carroll Gardens, slightly farther south, has long had a strong Italian-American flavor that is still very much in evidence. **Court Street,** the area's commercial district, has a high density of Italian restaurants and pizzerias. The **Carroll Gardens Historic District** contains more than 160 buildings, including houses on President and Carroll Streets between Smith and Hoyt Streets, mostly brownstones erected between 1869 and 1884. **Smith Street** has been experiencing something of a renaissance over the past few years as young professionals and artists have been populating the area. New restaurants, cafes, bars and hip boutiques now line its sidewalks.

Subway: Brooklyn Heights: 2, 3 to Clark St. or Borough Hall; 4, 5 Borough Hall; N, R, to Court St. Cobble Hill: 2, 3, 4, 5 to Nevins St. Carroll Gardens: F to Carroll St. or Bergen St.

HIGHLIGHTS OF THE AREA

Borough Hall Court St. (at Joralemon St.) (718) 875-4047. This historic building won a Municipal Art Society award after its renovation around 1990. The plaza between Borough Hall and the nearby Supreme Court is the site of a large greenmarket on Fridays and Saturdays, and is a popular spot for rollerbladers and local office workers on their lunch breaks. Tours of the building are available on Tuesdays.

Brooklyn Historical Society 128 Pierrepont St. (between Clinton and Montague Sts.) (718) 222-4111 *www.brooklynhistory.org*. Founded in 1863 as the Long Island Historical Society, the society has long housed the world's most extensive collection of Brooklyn artifacts in its landmark building. Its collections range from fine paintings and sculpture to an outstanding collection of ephemera on the late, lamented Brooklyn Dodgers. The landmark building is closed for a major renovation; it will reopen in spring 2003. Until then, the collection is displayed at a temporary location at 45 Main St. The society continues to offer free neighborhood guides, and a series of informative Brooklyn walking tours.

New York Transit Museum Boerum Pl. and Schermerhorn St. (718) 243-3060 *www.mta.info/museum*. This small but fascinating museum, housed in an authentic old subway station, offers a glimpse into New York's past through multimedia exhibits and authentic artifacts. Some of the old turnstiles are made of wood and ask for just five cents; the subway cars include magnificent wooden carriages from the early 1900's, with big windows and narrow wicker benches. And the kids can touch and play with nearly everything—you can even sit in a motorman's seat and operate a signal tower. The museum is currently closed for renovation, but will reopen in 2003.

Plymouth Church of the Pilgrims 75 Hicks St. (near Henry St.) (718) 624-4743. From the pulpit at this historic church, pastor Henry Ward Beecher, one of the 19th century's most passionate abolitionists, delivered thundering sermons denouncing the evils of slavery. (Beecher's sister, Harriet Beecher Stowe, also took up the cause as the author of *Uncle Tom's Cabin*.) The church itself was sometimes referred to as the Grand Central Terminal of the Underground Railroad. Abraham Lincoln once worshipped here. Plymouth Church features windows designed by Louis Comfort Tiffany.

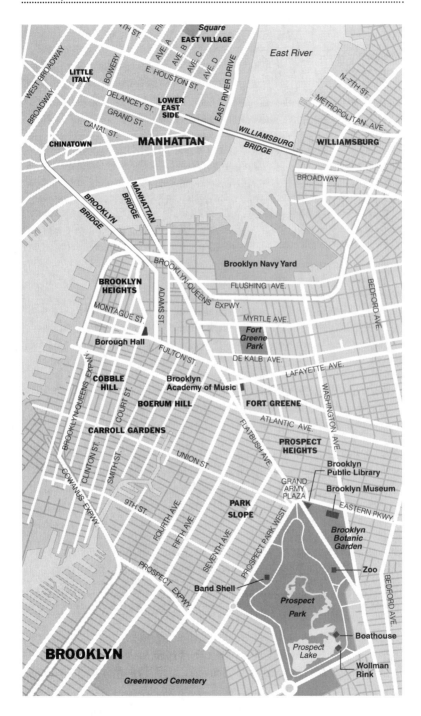

Brooklyn

Park Slope and Vicinity

At the turn of the century, Park Slope was one of the wealthiest neighborhoods in the country. But by the 1920's, mansions were being razed to make room for apartment houses, and brownstones were going out of fashion. By the end of World War II, many buildings had been carved up into low-income rooming houses. Through the 50's, middle-class families fled to the suburbs and urban decay set in. But in the early 60's, a few adventurous pioneers, recognizing a real estate bargain, arrived to renovate and restore fading brownstones and eventually reverse the area's precipitous decline.

Park Slope has been on the rise ever since; today it's known as an enclave for families and young professionals. A stroll down **Eighth Avenue** takes you past some of the finest brownstones in New York; start near Grand Army Plaza at the historic **Montauk Club** (at Eighth Ave. and Lincoln Pl.), and follow Eighth Avenue south, exploring the homes on President Street, Carroll Street and Montgomery Place.

In few other parts of Brooklyn does the past so enrich the present. The **Soldiers' and Sailors' Memorial at Grand Army Plaza,** with its twin Doric columns, grand arch and crowning statue of Victory in her horse-drawn chariot, is modeled after the Arc de Triomphe. Gorgeous **Prospect Park** *(see section below)* on the neighborhood's eastern edge is thronged on weekends. And every Labor Day weekend, the massive **West Indian American Day Parade** rolls along nearby Eastern Parkway, the first six-lane parkway in the world *(see section* "New York City Seasonal Events" *earlier in this chapter.)*

With its handsome brownstone row houses, and thriving Seventh and Fifth Avenue shops and restaurants, Park Slope is one of the city's most vibrant neighborhoods. Its proximity to the park, the **Brooklyn Public Library,** the **Brooklyn Museum** and the **Brooklyn Botanic Garden** adds to its desirability, as does easy subway access to Manhattan. Rents and property values have been climbing ever upward, pushing many of the area's younger and less affluent residents into nearby **Prospect Heights**, a neighborhood that's beginning to blossom.

Residents invariably speak of neighborhood's sense of community. It's a kid-friendly place, where shopkeepers know their customers by name and people stop in the street to chat. The population mix is diverse, with whites, blacks, Hispanics and Asians, and a sizable lesbian and gay community.

Subway: F, Q to Seventh Ave.; 2, 3 to Grand Army Plaza; R to Union or 9th St.

HIGHLIGHTS OF THE AREA

(For the **Brooklyn Children's Museum,** *see chapter* **New York for Children.**)

Brooklyn Botanic Garden 1000 Washington Ave. (at Eastern Parkway) (718) 622-4433 *www.bbg.org*. In this stunningly beautiful and tranquil place, you can forget you're anywhere near a city. The best time to visit the garden is late March through mid-May, when the cherry trees flower in all their glory.

But there's plenty more to see year-round. Wander through the famous collection of bonsai trees or steam yourself in a fern grotto in the Warm Temperate Pavilion. Admire a great reproduction of a Kyoto temple or visit the orchids in the Aquatic House.

In all, more than 12,000 kinds of plants from around the world fill the intricate, multilevel gardens and the interiors of soaring greenhouses in the Steinhardt Conservatory. And you might catch a wedding party spilling out of the glass-and-steel Palm House, the conservatory's Victorian centerpiece.

It's hard to imagine that the whole 52-acre spread was, in the late 1800's, mostly an ash dump. By the mid-1920's, the bonsai collection had already begun and the famous rose garden was being built. In the garden now, you can find a hybrid tea rose named for Audrey Hepburn and another variety called Elizabeth Taylors. In 1955, the Fragrance Garden was built, the first in the country to be designed for the vision-impaired. By the late 1970's, the garden was even granted its own patent—for developing the first yellow magnolia.

—Randy Kennedy

Admission: $3 adults; $1.50 seniors (free for seniors on Fri.); free for children under 16. **Hours:** Grounds Tue.–Fri. 8 A.M.–6 P.M.; Sat.–Sun. 10 A.M.–6 P.M. Closes at 4:30 P.M. Oct.–Mar.

Brooklyn Museum of Art 200 Eastern Parkway (at Washington Ave.) (718) 638-5000 *www.brooklynart.org.* As Brooklyn's population skyrocketed in the 19th century, the Brooklyn Museum grew from a library for apprentices into a full-fledged museum with an encyclopedic scope. Its monumental Beaux-Arts building, designed by McKim, Mead and White in 1893, is just one pavilion of a larger plan that was never completed. Having divested its science and natural history exhibits in the 1930's, the museum now concentrates on the fine arts. It is one of the largest art museums in the country.

From its inception, the museum has sought to serve as more than a repository of high culture. The museum has an impressive track record for presenting blockbuster exhibitions (such as "Monet and the Mediterrenean," "Star Wars: The Magic of Myth," and "Sensation," which famously drew the wrath of then-Mayor Giuliani) and smaller, highly innovative shows (on topics such as the relationship between hip-hop and fashion). From March 7 to June 15, 2003, the museum will feature "The Last Expression: Art from Auschwitz," a series of 200 works retrieved from German archives; each piece was created by a Jew, Gypsy or resistance fighter interned in a Nazi concentration camp.

The museum's more than 1.5 million objects of art exemplify a comprehensive range of cultures—from classical antiquity to Asia to colonial America. The Egyptian art collection, which is housed in ultramodern galleries designed by Arata Isozaki, is one of the finest in the world. (In March 2003, the museum will debut seven newly designed galleries that significantly increase the number of Egyptian pieces on display.) Other highlights include a Gilbert Stuart portrait of George Washington and an array of sculptures by Rodin. There are also 28 period rooms featuring American decorative arts. In addition to its many educational activities, the museum also hosts thematic series of films.

Admission: $6 adults; $3 students and seniors; free for children under 12. **Hours:** Wed.–Fri. 10 A.M.–5 P.M.; Sat.–Sun. 11 A.M.–6 P.M. (open until 11 P.M. first Sat. of each month, with free admission, cash bar and live music from 5 P.M.). Closed Mon.–Tue.

Grand Army Plaza Intersection of Prospect Park West, Flatbush Ave. and Eastern Pkwy. This triumphal arch commemorates the soldiers and sailors who fought for the Union Army during the Civil War (which interrupted the construction of the park). The Arch was designed by John H. Duncan, the designer of Grant's Tomb, and sculpted by Frederick William MacMonnies. Art exhibits and tours are held in the spring and fall (call 718-965-8999 for information on seeing the top of the arch). Nearby Bailey Fountain is the site of the second-largest greenmarket in New York, after Union Square.

Prospect Park

As a destination in itself or as a starting point for exploring Brooklyn's artistic and cultural treasures, Prospect Park (718-965-8951, or 718/965-8999 for events information; *www.prospectpark.org*) is well worth the trip from Manhattan. This 526-acre triangle is considered by many to be the crowning achievement of Olmsted and Vaux, who designed Central Park a decade earlier. It's easy to combine a stroll in the park with a visit to the nearby **Brooklyn Museum of Art, Brooklyn Botanic Garden** and **Brooklyn Public Library,** or an exploration of **Park Slope,** one of Brooklyn's most beautiful neighborhoods, which lies just outside the park across Prospect Park West.

The park itself has many formal attractions, starting with its grand main entrance: the 72-foot-tall **Memorial Arch in Grand Army Plaza** with its bronze sculptures honoring the soldiers and sailors of the Union forces in the Civil War. The park offers **Wollman Rink** for skating and **Lefferts Homestead,** a historic farmhouse with a children's museum. There's **a zoo, a carousel** and many fine examples of architecture from the late 19th and early 20th centuries, such as the whimsical **Oriental Pavilion** and neighboring formal garden. And don't miss the elegant Italian-style **boathouse** with its romantic setting along the **Lullwater,** a fingerlike extension of Prospect Lake, and its view of the graceful arched **Lullwater Bridge,** designed by McKim, Mead & White. At the lake, people feed ducks, fish for striped bass or pedal a boat into one of the many small inlets that make this body of water feel much larger than its 60 acres.

Twenty years ago the park was run-down and somewhat menacing: every building was closed and visitors had dwindled to 1.5 million annually. But with low crime rates, renewed confidence in public safety and numerous restoration projects, the park has undergone a renaissance. Bit by bit, the park has begun once again to serve as an urban oasis for its visitors.

The **Prospect Park Alliance** offers free tours of the park every Saturday and Sunday at 1 P.M. and 3 P.M. (*www.prospectpark.org*, 718-965-6988). The free **Heart of Brooklyn** trolley leaves the Wollman Rink on the hour and makes a complete loop around the park, with stops near the carousel, the zoo, Grand

Army Plaza (at about 15 and 40 minutes past the hour), Brooklyn Museum of Art, Brooklyn Botanic Garden, the Picnic House, Bandshell and other locations on the park's perimeter.

For more information on the park, including its tennis center and skating rink, see chapter **Sports and Recreation.**

Parking: Available at Wollman Rink, Bartel-Pritchard Circle, Litchfield Villa and the Picnic House. **Subway:** 2, 3 to Grand Army Plaza; F, Q to Seventh Ave.

SITES OF INTEREST IN PROSPECT PARK

(For the **zoo,** *see chapter* **New York for Children.***)*

The Boathouse/Audubon Center near the Lincoln Rd. entrance (off Ocean Ave.) (718) 287-3400. A graceful 1905 Beaux Arts structure set on the Lullwater, the Boathouse is a lovely and historic structure. It recently emerged from a major five-year renovation, and has reopened as the first **Audubon Center** in New York City (open Wed. and Thu. afternoons; all day on Fri., weekends and holidays). It offers nature trails, educational programming for all ages, interactive exhibits and electric boat rides on the Lullwater. This is a good place to pick up visitor information and get yourself oriented.

Lefferts Homestead Children's Historic House Museum Flatbush Ave. and Empire Blvd. (in Prospect Park) (718) 789-2822. Peter Lefferts was an affluent farmer, a delegate to the New York State Constitutional Convention in 1788 and head of the largest slaveholding family in Kings County. One of the few surviving Dutch-American farmhouses in Brooklyn, the homestead, which couples Dutch colonial architecture with Federal details, was built in 1783 to replace the earlier family home, destroyed by fire in the Battle of Long Island in 1776. The period rooms reflect daily life in the 1820's, with changing exhibitions detailing the concerns of the day, including slave emancipation and the opening of the Erie Canal. The museum has a strong educational focus, offering tours, sheep shearing, story telling and numerous family events. **Admission:** Free. **Hours:** Thu.–Fri. 1–4 P.M., Sat.–Sun. 1–5 P.M.

Litchfield Villa 95 Prospect Park West (between 4th and 5th Sts.) (718) 965-8951. Built in 1857 by prominent Brooklyn businessman Edwin Litchfield, this building is now the headquarters for City of New York/Parks & Recreation, as well as the office of the Prospect Park Administrator and the Prospect Park Alliance. It offers a dramatic hillside view of Park Slope and is an outstanding example of mid-19th-century romantic Italianate architecture.

The Long Meadow off Prospect Park West, 15th to Union St. This 90-acre expanse of grass stretches nearly a mile down the west side of Prospect Park, and may be the most visited and familiar site in the park. Many of the park's six million annual visitors end up here at some point to play ball, fly kites or just lie on the grass. The Metropolitan Opera also performs in the meadow once each June, and the New York Philharmonic Orchestra plays one evening concert each July, complete with fireworks.

The Music Pagoda Lincoln Rd. and Ocean Blvd. Dating back to 1887 and resembling a Chinese city gate, this is the site of numerous concerts, religious ceremonies, and other activities throughout the year.

Playgrounds The Prospect Park Alliance has directed extensive playground renovations over the last decade, making the park's major play areas safer and more entertaining for kids. There are six playgrounds around the perimeter of the park, including the **Tot Spot** (at the Garfield Pl. entrance), which is designed specifically for the three-and-under set. The **Imagination Playground** (Ocean Ave. entrance) features safe, modern play equipment, as well as a water-spouting dragon and a storytelling area with an array of statues of characters from the books of Brooklyn-born author Ezra Jack Keats. **Harmony Playground** (near the bandshell at Prospect Park West between 9th and 11th Sts.) just emerged from a $1.7 million renovation in 2002; it features whimsical water motifs. In addition to the playgrounds highlighted above, there are renovated playgrounds near the Lincoln Rd., 3rd St. and Vanderbilt St. park entrances.

Prospect Lake Southeast edge of the park. Swimming is prohibited in this 60-acre lake, but it hosts all kinds of other activities throughout the year. Visitors are welcome to fish on a catch-and-release basis, and each July kids 14 and under can compete in the annual Macy's Fishing Contest (same-day registration is available for individuals). **Pedal boats** are also available for rental at the Wollman Center and Rink for $10 per hour (718-282-7789).

Prospect Park Band Shell 9th St. and Prospect Park West (718) 855-7882. This amphitheater on the edge of Park Slope is one of the city's most pleasant venues for a summer afternoon or evening concert, particularly when it is part of the eclectic "Celebrate Brooklyn!" series. The world music concerts—from African to Brazilian to Asian—are some of the best in the city. Readings, children's shows, rock and folk music and occasional opera and classical performances round out the offerings, most of which are free.

Prospect Park Carousel Enter at Empire Blvd. and Flatbush Ave. (718) 965-6512. This is one of only 12 remaining carousels designed by renowned carver Charles Carmel. The carousel, which operates from April through October, features 51 magnificent horses and an assortment of other animals. Rides are 50¢.

ACTIVITIES IN PROSPECT PARK

Baseball: Permits are required to play baseball or softball on the **9th Street ballfields** at the southwest end of the Long Meadow. Call (718) 965-8943 for permits or (718) 965-8969 for more information on playing ball in Prospect Park.

Bicycling: Cycling is permitted only on designated bicycle and runner lanes around the edge of the park. The **Kissena Cycling Club** (718-343-7343) and the **Metropolitan Cycling Association** (718-522-7390) can offer information on bicycle races.

Birding: The **Urban Park Rangers** (718-438-0100) and the **Brooklyn Bird Watchers Club** (718-875-1151) run bird-watching tours in the park. See also the listing above for the **Boathouse,** which is home to a brand-new **Audubon Center** (718-287-3400).

Festivals: Prospect Park festival information is available at (718) 965-8999 and on the sandwich boards at Park entrances. One of the largest festivals is the **Celebrate Brooklyn! Performing Arts Festival,** running annually from June through August at the Band Shell. See *www.bkny.net/celebrate.*

Horseback Riding: Prospect Park's bridle path runs from Park Circle to the end of the Long Meadow. Contact **Kensington Stables** for horse rental information (718-972-4588).

Nature Walks: Park visitors can join the Prospect Park Alliance and the Urban Park Rangers (718-438-0100) from April through November to explore the Prospect Park Ravine, Brooklyn's last remaining forest. Guides and maps for self-guided walking tours are available at the Prospect Park Alliance office in Litchfield Villa and at the Wollman Rink. Nature trails start at the Boathouse's Audubon Center.

Running: Running is permitted only on the 3.35-mile running lane along Park Drive, and on other sidewalks and paved surfaces in the park.

Williamsburg

Over the past several years, Williamsburg's well-established Hasidic, Puerto Rican, Dominican and Polish communities have made way for a newer group of residents—artists and hipsters seeking affordable space close to Manhattan. The neighborhood today is an odd mix of gritty urban decay with an overlay of trendy boutiques, bars and cafes.

In the mid-1800's, Williamsburg was a fashionable resort area, with hotels, clubs and beer gardens near the Brooklyn ferry attracting wealthy industrialists and professionals. The neighborhood's nature changed with the 1903 opening of the **Williamsburg Bridge** and the 1905 inauguration of trolley service over the bridge. Jews and other Eastern European immigrants flooded in from the crowded Lower East Side, followed by various groups of working-class immigrants, including Puerto Ricans seeking jobs in area factories. In 1957, the Brooklyn-Queens Expressway opened, slicing through the area.

As recently as 1990, it was hard to find basic services in Williamsburg, even along the neighborhood's main drag, **Bedford Avenue.** There is still a shortage of banks and ATM machines but the area now abounds with coin laundries and convenience stores. So far, chain stores are nonexistent, but food markets and cheap cafes flourish here. There's also the landmark **Peter Luger Steak House,** still holding forth in its original 1887 location.

In the past decade, Williamsburg has sprouted a cluster of **art galleries,** with the largest concentration on Bedford Avenue and its surrounding side streets, where old-world Polish delicatessens are sandwiched in between galleries, shops, restaurants and bars. A day or night in this part of Williamsburg can include everything from fusion food to avant-garde circus performances.

Subway: L train to Bedford Ave. or Lorimer St.; G to Metropolitan Ave.

HIGHLIGHTS OF THE NEIGHBORHOOD
(For the **Williamsburg Bridge,** *see* "Lower East Side" *earlier in this chapter.)*

McCarren Park Northern end of Bedford Ave. (between N. 12th St. and Leonard Ave.). The park is a spiffier spot these days after undergoing some long-overdue repairs. From spring through fall, this is a great place to take in the local scene: Older Polish couples dance to live polka music; Latino families play fierce games of soccer and volleyball and stage huge festive barbecues; young hipsters sunbathe or play Frisbee; and Hasidic men toss around baseballs.

Metropolitan Pool and Bathhouse 261 Bedford Ave. (718) 965-6576. This historic site was reopened in 1997 after a major renovation. The 1922 building, which includes a 30-by-75-foot swimming pool, two new locker rooms, a community room and a fitness area, was originally designed by Henry Bacon, architect of Washington's Lincoln Memorial.

Art in Williamsburg

Art Moving 166 N. 12th St. (between Berry St. and Bedford Ave.) (718) 302-9314. Art Moving is the accidental gallery of the artist Aaron Namenwirth, who in 1992 moved into a storefront that had been occupied by one of Williamsburg's first galleries. Passersby regularly inquired about the next show, and the previous tenant's mail, including many artists' slides, continued unabated. Finally Mr. Namenwirth began holding sporadic shows of his own, showcasing neighborhood artists.

Galapagos 70 N. 6th St. (between Wythe and Kent Aves.) (718) 782-5188 *www.galapagosartspace.com*. This Williamsburg bar and arts center is hard to find but worth the hunt for its seductive front-entrance reflecting pool, expansive cathedral-like interior (brilliantly spotlit with candles on the walls) and a stark, minimalist bar ringed with tables. Ocularis is Galapagos's screening room, which seats about 100 people and offers regular Sunday films. In addition to movies and art exhibits, look for dance and theater performances in a 125-seat back room. Open after 6 P.M. every night (to 2 A.M. on weeknights, to 4 A.M. on weekends).

Holland Tunnel 61 S. 3rd St. (between Berry St. and Wythe Ave.) (718) 384-5738. One of the quirkiest art spaces in Williamsburg, Holland Tunnel is run by Pauline Lethen, an energetic Dutch woman who sees it partly as a conduit for Dutch art (hence the title). It occupies a small pre-fab gardener's shed set in a pretty little yard behind an old apartment building. Open only on weekend afternoons.

Pierogi 2000 177 N. 9th St. (at Bedford Ave.) (718) 599-2144. Joe Amrhein decided to promote the work of Williamsburg artists by filling a flat file with their drawing portfolios, creating a remarkably efficient and mobile way to let interested parties see the work of hundreds of artists. Mr. Amrhein also mounts ambitious solo shows highlighting neighborhood arts in the gallery space.

Coney Island

A seemingly endless stretch of sand, a boardwalk offering every imaginable variety of fast food, water-squirt games, a roller coaster that defines the term death-defying, a Ferris wheel you can see from miles away at night, carnival music, the world's best hot dog, cheap beer—no wonder Coney Island became the most famous beach in America. If you pay a visit today, however, you'll see an entirely different "Coney" from the one of story and fable. The old bathhouses are crumbling, many buildings are run down and the Boardwalk has lost a lot of luster since the days when crowds jammed the shops or huddled near the now-silent Parachute Jump to marvel at the bravery of the men and women who soared 250 feet into the sky in an open seat.

Nevertheless, it's a fascinating journey to the far reaches of Brooklyn. In summer, crowds still pack the sands and the Boardwalk, and the lighthearted fun in the sun captures the essence of Coney Island's heyday. In the off-season, there's a haunting, evocative quality to the shuttered remnants of New York's most beloved beach escape. The Boardwalk stretches from the community of Brighton Beach through Coney Island to Sea Gate, a strip that has known better and worse days. At the turn of the century, the eastern end was a high-society preserve, with oceanfront luxury hotels, restaurants, theaters and a racetrack. But anti-gambling sentiment closed the track in 1910, and by 1920, all the hotels were gone. To the west around Coney Island, more popular attractions developed, with the great amusement parks of Dreamland, Luna Park and George C. Tilyou's Steeplechase.

The arrival of the subway in 1920 created what was known as "a poor people's paradise"; soon hundreds of thousands of working-class New Yorkers were spending weekends at the beach. Decline set in during the social dislocations of the 1960's. Changing populations and a series of fires in the flimsily built fun parks brought decaying buildings, poverty and crime. In more recent years, Russian and Ukrainian immigrants have established a thriving beachhead in the area.

For decades, Coney Island seemed a ghost of its former self, but now a whole new generation of New Yorkers has discovered the pleasures of a Nathan's hot dog, the thrills of the **Wonder Wheel** and the performing dolphins of the **New York Aquarium** (*see chapter* **New York for Children**). Baseball recently returned to Brooklyn in a gorgeous little field of dreams on Surf Avenue, with a view of the beach and the Boardwalk from the grandstand. The **Cyclones** (*www.brooklyncyclones.com*)**,** a Mets minor-league affiliate, arrived in 2001 to much enthusiasm from Brooklynites, many of whom never recovered from the departure of the Dodgers nearly a half century ago (*see chapter* **Sports & Recreation**). Although a promised Coney Island renaissance has not entirely materialized, the opening of **Keyspan Park** promises further economic growth and an influx of new energy and hope.

After you exit the subway, head straight for Coney Island's legendary **Boardwalk,** which is the hub of all the action. If it's a nice day, bring a beach towel

Cyclone Roller Coaster at Coney Island

and relax on the sands. Otherwise, just stroll along the 2.5 miles of oceanfront, stopping for a circus sideshow, a ride on the Ferris wheel or a bite of saltwater taffy. At West 17th Street, **Steeplechase Pier** allows you to walk 1,000 feet out over the Atlantic as the waves lap beneath you. Here you can gaze out to sea, claim a bench for a picnic or watch the fishermen hook herring.

The Boardwalk also offers a nostalgic bird's-eye view of some of the most evocative remnants of Coney Island's glory days, which faded decades ago. The **Brighton Beach Baths,** a once-posh beach club that opened in 1907, currently remains shuttered. Until it is razed to make way for housing, its swimming pools, playing courts and bandstand are landmarks from long-ago summers. At West 17th Street, the old 250-foot-high **Parachute Jump** looks remarkably intact. Originally a ride at the 1939–40 New York World's Fair, it was moved here in 1941.

The Boardwalk is also the setting for the flamboyant **Mermaid Parade,** held annually on the first Saturday after the summer solstice (*see section* "New York By Season" *earlier in this chapter*). Check out *www.coneyisland.com* for an overview of the neighborhood and its current events.

Subway: F, N, Q, W to Coney Island—Stillwell Ave. (about an hour from Manhattan).

HIGHLIGHTS OF THE NEIGHBORHOOD
(*For the* **New York Aquarium for Wildlife Conservation,**
see chapter **New York for Children.**)

Astroland Amusement Park 1000 Surf Ave. (718) 265-2100 *www.astroland.com*. This small amusement park has been a Coney Island tradition for 40 years. It has a host of thrill rides, including a water flume, bumper cars and a tilt-a-whirl, and more. Kids will like the tamer rides scaled just to their size. But Astroland is best known as the home of the **Cyclone,** a rickety wooden dandy of a roller coaster that's been scaring the living daylights out of its shrieking riders for decades. **Admission:** $14.99 for unlimited rides during a specified period of several hours, or pay per ride at $2–$5 each. Cyclone is $5, with re-rides at $4. **Hours:** Spring and Sept. weekends only, from noon till closing (which depends on crowds and weather). Mid-June to Labor Day daily noon–midnight.

B & B Carousell Surf Ave. at W. 10th St. Its painted steeds were carved around 1920 in the renowned workshop of Marcus Illions, a Polish immigrant who established the fancifully flamboyant Coney Island style of carousel horses. The beautiful Gebruder organ still cranks out classic carousel tunes while the ride is spinning. Unlike many other attractions, the carousel (with its misspelled sign) operates year-round.

Coney Island Museum 1208 Surf Ave. (at W. 12th St.) (718) 372-5159. This small museum is stocked with mementos from the great pay-one-price amusement centers, like Luna Park, Dreamland and Steeplechase, that once ruled the shore. Chief among the antic artifacts are a fun-house mirror, an original wicker Boardwalk Rolling Chair and one of the wooden Steeplechase Horses. The museum has a video loop of rare Coney Island film clips, which includes a bizarre 1904 film of an elephant being electrocuted, a stunt apparently engineered by Thomas Edison to persuade the public that the electric chair would be the most humane form of capital punishment. **Admission:** 99¢. **Hours:** Sat.–Sun. noon–sundown.

Deno's Wonder Wheel Park 1025 Boardwalk (at W. 12th St.) (718) 372-2592 *www.wonderwheel.com*. This amusement park features 25 rides (including the legendary **Wonder Wheel** Ferris wheel, and a slew of kiddie rides), plus two arcades and live entertainment. **Admission:** $15 for unlimited rides, or pay per ride. **Hours:** Apr.–May and Sept.–Oct. weekends only. Memorial Day–Labor Day daily 11 A.M.–midnight.

Flea Market Surf Ave. between W. 8th and W. 10th Sts. Open-front shops and alley stalls under the moving frieze of elevated trains display all sorts of new and used merchandise: kitchen utensils, tools, bric-a-brac, clothing, electronics, videotapes and CDs, a few genuine antiques and a lot of dusty junk. Most of the vendors are Russian immigrants who sometimes feign a language barrier when it suits them, but all bargain handily in English.

Sideshows by the Seashore Surf Ave. and W. 12th St. Step right up, folks! And leave your political correctness behind. This is a traditional 10-in-1 circus sideshow, complete with "human curiosities" like Koko the Killer Clown, The Painproof Rubber Girl and assorted other fire eaters, sword swallowers and snake charmers. The theater, which seats 99 spectators, was originally **Childs' Restaurant,** a magnificent dining palace that featured singing waiters when it opened back in 1923. (In the 1950's and 60's, it was Dave Rosen's Wonderland Circus Sideshow, which featured sideshow legends such as Jojo the Dogfaced Boy.) Performances run continuously on weekends, depending on the crowds and the weather. **Admission:** $5 adults, $3 children under 12.

Recommended Brooklyn Restaurants

Brooklyn Heights

Gage & Tollner $$ SEAFOOD/SOUTHERN
372 Fulton St. (between Adams and Jay Sts.)   (718) 875-5181
Gage & Tollner opened in 1879 and moved to its current downtown Brooklyn location in 1892. It's a wonderfully old-fashioned room. The beautiful old gas-fired lights have been retrofitted and acoustic tiles have been removed, exposing the original vaulted ceiling. The menu has barely changed in a century, with old favorites like soft clam bellies, lobster Newburg, she-crab soup and massive deep-fried "blooming onions." Closed Sun. **Price range:** Entrees $15–$27.

Grimaldi's $$ PIZZA
19 Old Fulton St. (between Front and Water Sts.)   (718) 858-4300
This stellar pizzeria in the shadow of the Brooklyn Bridge makes classic, coal-oven New York pizza. Crusts are thin and crisp in the center, blackened and blistered around the dense and bready edges. The mozzarella is fresh; the tomato sauce is fragrant and homemade. Expect a wait and expect to hear Sinatra playing in the background. **Price range:** Pies $15 and up. Cash only.

River Café   ☆☆ $$$$ NEW AMERICAN
1 Water St. (at the Brooklyn Bridge; between Furman and Old Fulton Sts.)
(718) 522-5200
Is this New York City's most romantic restaurant? With waterside seating, a spectacular view of downtown Manhattan, soft lighting, heaps of flowers and live piano music, it's certainly a contender. Such a view might have made the food irrelevant, but this has been a seminal restaurant in the annals of New American food. The menu is excellent and innovative; brunch is a special pleasure. So too is the dessert made of chocolate and shaped like the Brooklyn Bridge. **Price range:** Prix fixe $70; tasting menu $90.

Carroll Gardens

Banania Café $25 & Under   FRENCH
241 Smith St. (between Butler and Douglass Sts.)   (718) 237-9100
Banania, named for a French children's drink, has an enticing menu of reasonably priced bistro dishes with Asian and Middle Eastern touches. Calamari rings, for example, are dusted with cumin, roasted and served with carrot purée, a happy match of power and pungency. Among main courses, braised lamb shank and moist roasted cod are delicious. **Price range:** Entrees $12–$15. Cash only.

Ferdinando's Focacceria **$25 & Under** ITALIAN
151 Union St. (between Columbia Pl. and Hicks St.) (718) 855-1545
They filmed *Moonstruck* on this street, and you can see why. Ferdinando's is a
throwback to turn-of-the-century Brooklyn, before Ebbets Field had even been
built. The menu offers old Sicilian dishes, like chickpea-flour fritters; vasteddi, a
focaccia made with calf's spleen; and pasta topped with sardines canned by the
owner. Closed Sun. **Price range:** Entrees $10–$13. Cash only.

Patois **$25 & Under** BISTRO/FRENCH
255 Smith St. (between Douglass and Degraw Sts.) (718) 855-1535
This small storefront restaurant offers rich, gutsy bistro fare that can range from
authentically French tripe stew—a mellow, wonderful dish, if not destined for
popularity—to juicy pork chops and satisfying casseroles. Dishes don't always
work, but it's nice that Patois is trying. Closed Mon. Price range: Entrees
$10–$17.

Tuk Tuk **$25 & Under** THAI
204 Smith St. (near Butler St. (718) 222-5598
Tuk Tuk offers the clear, bright and balanced flavors for which Thailand is
known. While the kitchen is aiming for more authentic Thai flavors than the
usual tamed and sweetened New York versions, the narrow, minimalist dining
room, with its long brick wall, handsome hanging lights and bleached wood
floor, fits right into the Smith Street lineup of casually appealing restaurants.
Cash only. **Price range:** Entrees, $6–$16.

Smith Street Kitchen **$25 & Under** SEAFOOD/NEW AMERICAN
174 Smith St. (between Warren and Wycoff Sts.) (718) 858-5359
The small dining room has an inviting lived-in look, service is solicitous without being overfriendly and the restaurant takes its obligations seriously. Perhaps
best of all, Smith Street Kitchen offers excellent value. The menu is small, but
the appetizers include some exceptional selections, like a small tart filled with
sweet lobster and smoky chorizo along with mushrooms, spinach and tomato
confit. The main courses are less consistent, but thick slices of grilled tuna left
rosy in the middle and flavored with sesame oil are excellent, as is sautéed cod.
The pear bread pudding can take its place among the bread pudding elite. **Price
range:** Entrees $15–$22.

Sur **$25 & Under** ARGENTINE
232 Smith St. (between Butler and Douglass Sts.) (718) 875-1716
This brick-walled, candlelit Argentine restaurant is warm and inviting without
any of the usual gaucho clichés. The focus, naturally, is on beef. Try the lean,
almost grassy Argentine sirloin, served with a mound of crisp, salty french fries.
Alternatives to beef include juicy and flavorful roast chicken and several pasta
dishes. For dessert, try the crepes filled with *dulce de leche*, a sublime caramel-
like confection of cream and sugar. **Price range:** Entrees $12–$19.

Cobble Hill/Boerum Hill

Brawta $25 & Under   CARIBBEAN
347 Atlantic Ave. (between Hoyt and Bond Sts.)   (718) 855-5515
Brawta, Jamaican patois for "something extra," offers top-flight Jamaican food
in a relaxed, colorful dining room. Rotis—peppery stews of chicken or mellow
goat rolled up in huge, soft flatbreads—are superb, as is the spicy jerk chicken.
Coco shrimp is an unusual and generous shrimp curry made with coconut milk.
Don't miss the traditional Caribbean beverages, like sweet-and-spicy sorrel and
the thick sea moss, a legendary boon to male virility. For dessert, try the bread
pudding. **Price range:** Entrees $9.50–$18.

Saul $25 & Under   NEW AMERICAN
140 Smith St. (between Dean and Bergen Sts.)   (718) 855-5515
The small menu in this sweet little brick storefront offers strong, clear flavors,
bolstered by background harmonies that augment without overshadowing. The
main courses seem familiar—salmon, chicken, pork loin—but they are beautifully handled and surprisingly good. Desserts are wonderful, like lush baked
alaska with a chocolate cookie crust. **Price range:** Entrees $15–$20.

Fort Greene and vicinity

Cambodian Cuisine $25 & Under   CAMBODIAN
87 S. Elliott Pl. (between Fulton St. and Lafayette Ave.)   (718) 858-3262
A great place to try the exotic flavors of Cambodia, though there's no decor to
speak of and service can be gruff. In the signature dish, chicken *ahmok,* chicken
breast is marinated in coconut milk, lemongrass, galangal and kaffir lime and
steamed until it achieves a soft, pudding-like texture. **Price range:** Entrees
$3.50–$14.95.

Junior's $$ DINER
386 Flatbush Ave. (at DeKalb Ave.)   (718) 852-5257
There's a full menu of meat, fish and pan-ethnic dishes, but the real house specials are the superb cheese blintzes (minus strawberry sauce), hefty egg dishes,
corned beef or tongue sandwiches—and especially that gloriously creamy but
firm cheesecake, best when plain. **Price range:** Entrees $6–$10.

Locanda Vini & Olii $25 & Under   ITALIAN
129 Gates Ave. (between Cambridge Pl. and Grand Ave.)   (718) 622-9202
This mom-and-pop trattoria was a pharmacy for 130 years. The woodwork has
been lovingly restored, and many old features have been left intact. But
Locanda's menu is full of surprising dishes. Superb choices abound among the
pastas, especially the *maltagliati,* fat strands of carrot-colored pasta in a light
ricotta sauce with soft fava beans, diced prosciutto and plenty of sage. Closed
Mon. **Price range:** Entrees $6.75–$18.50.

Park Slope

Al di la $25 & Under   ITALIAN
248 Fifth Ave (at Carroll St.)   (718) 783-4555
The food at Al di la is soulful and gutsy, with profound flavors. This neighborhood restaurant serves on bare wooden tables, but hints at a more sensual attitude with such luxurious touches as velvet drapes and chandeliers. The chef
coaxes deep flavors out of simple dishes, and all the pastas are wonderful. **Price
range:** Entrees $9–$17.

Bistro St. Mark's $25 & Under   BISTRO
76 St. Mark's Ave. (between Flatbush and Sixth Aves.)   (718) 857-8600
Bistro St. Mark's blends so inconspicuously with its surroundings that you might
walk by. But a look at the menu provokes a double take, because this is no simple
bistro fare. Try the glistening mackerel tartar topped with a luscious smidgen of
caviar and dressed in capers and a bracing sauce gribiche, or the moist and delicious skate wing, dusted with ground walnuts. **Price range:** Entrees $14–$19.

Blue Ribbon $$ NEW AMERICAN
280 Fifth Ave. (at First St.)   (718) 840-0404
The Brooklyn outpost of the Blue Ribbon empire feels like many things at once.
It's part saloon, part oyster bar, part bistro and part diner. The extensive menu
hops from raw bar and clam stew to hummus and hamburgers. This is home
cooking, no matter where home happens to be. The staff is exceptional, and the
bar is friendly and comfortable, making this a great place in the area for a drink.
Price range: Entrees $8–$25.

Chip Shop $25 & Under   ENGLISH
383 Fifth Ave. (at 6th St.)   (718) 832-7701
At this small, authentically English fish-and-chips restaurant, much of the food
is honest and forthright, filling and satisfying. With music at high volume, the
pitch is clearly toward a younger crowd, but the yellow dining room is cheerful
and pleasant. The mushy pea fritter is a wonderful dish. You can also try some of
England's greatest pub hits, like fine bangers and mash. For a complete sugar
buzz, try the deep-fried Mars bar. **Price range:** Entrees $6–$11. Cash only.

Coco Roco $25 & Under   LATIN AMERICAN
392 Fifth Ave. (near 6th St.)   (718) 965-3376
This bright, pleasant restaurant offers some of the best Peruvian food in New
York. The menu ranges from tender, delicious ceviches from Peru's coast to
Andean dishes that have been enjoyed since the days of the Incan empire.
Roast chicken is excellent, and desserts like rice pudding and lucuma ice cream,
made with a Peruvian fruit, are wonderful. **Price range:** Entrees $8.95–$16.95.

Cucina ☆ $$ ITALIAN
256 Fifth Ave. (between Garfield Pl. and Carrol St.   (718) 230-0711
In a bid for a second life as newer, more ambitious restaurants opened in the

area, Cucina has taken on a new chef and partner. There is still serious work to do, but Cucina is beginning to feel fresher and more vigorous than it has in a long time. Try the spaghetti frutti di mare. **Price range:** Entrees, $14–$28.

Rose Water $25 & Under   NEW AMERICAN
787 Union St. (between Fifth and Sixth Aves.)   (718) 783-3800
Rose Water's innovative cooking, moderate prices and relaxed ambience would be exciting anywhere. Try a *brik,* a crisp North African turnover filled with ground lamb, caraway and mint and surrounded with a pungent parsley sauce. Rose Water offers fabulously tasty pork chops as well as a thin-sliced rump steak, beautifully flavored with cloves. **Price range:** Entrees $12.50–$16.50.

Prospect Heights

Garden Café $25 & Under   NEW AMERICAN
620 Vanderbilt Ave. (at Prospect Pl.)   (718) 857-8863
This family-run operation near the Brooklyn Academy of Music serves an ever-changing menu of artful American food that is always satisfying. Standards like grilled veal chops and steaks are superb, and the chef occasionally comes up with dishes like jambalaya with Middle Eastern spices. Closed Sun., Mon. **Price range:** Entrees $17.50–$20.

Tom's Restaurant $ DINER
782 Washington Ave. (at Sterling Pl.)   (718) 636-9738
Around the corner from the Brooklyn Museum is Tom's, a 65-year-old Brooklyn institution offering terrific diner fare at ludicrously low prices. With a classic diner menu (they still serve cherry lime rickeys) and the warmest atmosphere (and kitschiest décor) in town, Tom's alone is worth a trip to Prospect Heights. Closes daily at 4 P.M. Closed Sun. **Price range:** Entrees $5 and up.

Williamsburg

Bahia $25 & Under   SALVADORAN
690 Grand St. (near Manhattan Ave.)   (718) 218-9592
Although the extensive menu includes burgers and Buffalo wings, the special-ties are typical Salvadoran dishes like *pupusas,* corn pancakes with small amounts of meats and vegetables stuffed into the center. If you pile a side of coleslaw on the pupusa and eat them together, it's rich, tangy magic. Don't pass up *horchata,* a sweet iced rice drink with cinnamon and cocoa. **Price range:** Entrees $6.50–$15.

Diner $25 & Under   DINER
85 Broadway (at Berry St.)   (718) 486-3077
Diner brings the diner idea up to date, offering the sort of everyday food that appeals to the local artsy crowd. The basics are fine, and other dishes can be superb, like skirt steak, perfectly cooked whole trout, black bean soup and eggs scrambled with grilled trout. The atmosphere is bustling, funky and smoky. **Price range:** Entrees $6.50–$15.

La Brunette $25 & Under   FRENCH/CARIBBEAN
300 N. 6th St.   (718) 384-5800

This small, ambitious French-Caribbean restaurant is located on a corner practically underneath the Brooklyn-Queens Expressway. Inside, La Brunette is certainly inviting. The narrow front room, done up in blond wood with a little bar, seems a little harder-edged than the more comfortable rear room. And the short menu, if not novel, is intriguing, with a combination of Caribbean flavors and French techniques. Price range: Entrees, $11–$13.

Oznot's Dish $25 & Under   MEDITERRANEAN
79 Berry St. (at N. 9th St.)   (718) 599-6596

Oznot's is truly unusual, a veritable flea market of mosaics, mismatched furniture and artwork set on a rickety, uneven wood floor. The blend of Mediterranean food is just as interesting, with dishes like grilled shrimp served over tabbouleh with fennel chutney. Main courses include fish and seafood stew served in a tomato-saffron broth and fennel-dusted tuna with hummus and tapenade. **Price range:** Entrees $10–$18.

Peter Luger   ☆☆☆ $ $ $ $ STEAKHOUSE
178 Broadway (at Driggs Ave.)   (718) 387-7400

Peter Luger serves no lobsters, takes no major credit cards, lacks a great wine list and looks like a simple beer hall. Service, though professional and often humorous, can sometimes be brusque. So why is it packed night and day, seven days a week? Simple: Peter Luger has the best steaks in New York City. The family that runs the restaurant buys fresh shortloins and dry-ages them on the premises. Your mouth will start watering the second that fine aroma wafts across the table. An occasional diner will choose the thick and powerfully delicious lamb chops, or the nicely done salmon. And even side dishes have their moments. But the steak's the thing here, and they serve just one cut: an enormous porterhouse charred to perfection over intense heat. **Price range:** Avg. price for three courses $60. Cash only.

Plan Eat Thailand $25 & Under   THAI
133 N. 7th St. (between Bedford and Berry Sts.)   (718) 599-5758

This unusual, much-applauded Thai restaurant has its ups and downs, but more often than not, it comes through with just-fine sushi and spicy, meticulously prepared Thai dishes like ground pork salad, sautéed bean curd and striped bass with crunchy greens. Huge crowds pack into the post-industrial space, partying with two bars and a DJ. **Price range:** Entrees $4.75–$12.95. Cash only.

Relish $25 & Under   NEW AMERICAN/DINER
225 Wythe Ave. (at N. 3rd St.)   (718) 963-4546

Relish is a sleek diner of gleaming, embossed stainless steel. The chef is clearly at home in the modern vernacular, and his menu is rarely pretentious and often winning. You might raise an eyebrow at ordering foie gras in a diner, but this version is quite good. Among the main courses, juicy, flavorful chicken and fresh waffles are served with a mound of garlic-imbued kale. **Price range:** Entrees $11–$17.

Coney Island

Gargiulo's $$$ ITALIAN
2911 W. 15th St. (between Surf and Mermaid Aves.)   (718) 266-4891
In business since 1907 and at this location since 1928, Gargiulo's is a longtime favorite, especially for subtle, freshly prepared Neapolitan specialties. You won't go wrong with roasted peppers, fried calamari with a delicate tomato sauce dip, baked clams, mussels in tomato broth, all of the southern pastas and lobster oreganato (here called *racanati*). **Price range:** Entrees $8.50–$24.

Nathan's Famous $ FAST FOOD
1310 Surf Ave. (between Stillwell Ave. and W. 16th St.)   (718) 946-2202
Famous indeed is this 1916 original, opened to compete with the long-gone Feltman's, where Charles Feltman, a German immigrant, is believed to have invented the hot dog by slipping a frankfurter into a long heated roll. One of his waiters, Nathan Handwerker, spun off his own version, and the rest is hot-dog history. It is said that these juicy all-beef franks are still made according to the meat and spice recipes developed by Nathan and his wife, Ida.

Totonno Pizzeria $$ PIZZA
1524 Neptune Ave. (between W. 15th and W. 16th Sts.)   (718) 372-8606.
Just three blocks off the Boardwalk, in the heart of what's left of Coney Island's Little Italy, this is a highly touted 74-year-old pizzeria, more interesting for its history than for its pizzas, which can be fine or fair.

Brooklyn Nightlife

Go out in Brooklyn? On the weekend? For New Yorkers in the know, that was once an unbearably tepid proposition. But the Brooklyn-Manhattan power balance is changing. Trendsetters exiled to Brooklyn because of Manhattan's stratospheric rents eventually found themselves loving their new neighborhoods, and a wave of hip new restaurants and bars has followed them. But even as the hot spots multiply, you can also find a wealth of classic Brooklyn hangouts that stick to the basics, offering a good time with affordable drinks and few pretenses.

Brooklyn Heights, Cobble Hill, Boerum Hill & Carroll Gardens

The Bar 280 Smith St. (at Sackett St.) (718) 246-9050. If you look closely, you'll notice details like black-vinyl barstools, red holiday lights, glittery tables and mismatched chairs. But it's just a no-nonsense place to throw back a few cold ones in the company of real people wearing ratty T-shirts and smoking borrowed cigarettes. No supermodels in designer duds here.

Boat 175 Smith St (between Warren and Wyckoff Sts.) (718) 254-0607. This neighborhood joint has a friendly, attentive staff and a laid-back clientele. There's plenty of seating, with cafe-style tables in front, a long wooden bar and the lounge at the rear.

Brooklyn Inn 138 Bergen St. (at Hoyt St.). Believed to have opened in 1868, the Brooklyn Inn is a regal, historic bar where the residents of Boerum Hill still gather over drafts of beer. There is no sign out front, adding to the bar's mystique. The high ceilings, woodwork and stained-glass panels are impressive.

Gowanus Yacht Club 323 Smith St. (at President St.) No phone. The tongue-in-cheek name lends a false air of formality this utterly laid-back atmosphere. The beer garden's décor was clearly a result of two-stop shopping — that which couldn't be found at a thrift store was supplemented with plywood from Home Depot. Cans of Pabst Blue Ribbon and other cheap swill are $2. It's the ultimate local's hangout for the neighborhood's young professionals.

Halcyon 227 Smith St. (between Butler and Douglass Sts.) (718) 260-9299. Halcyon, a hipster cafe/bar, is filled with couches, tables, books, board games, lamps and other retro pieces from the 1950's through the 70's—all for sale. There's also a rear patio and a record store with 6,000 new and used records. Every Saturday night, there's a dance party with a DJ.

Last Exit 136 Atlantic Ave. (between Henry and Clinton Sts.) (718) 222-9198. With its brick walls, red track lighting, vintage couches, art on the walls and a full house of young, laid-back hipster types, you might think you're in the East Village. But the lack of attitude will tell you otherwise.

Pete's Waterfront Ale House 155 Atlantic Ave. (between Clinton and Henry Sts.) (718) 522-3794. Pete's is a classic, amiable neighborhood bar. Neither too divey nor too formal, it's all about decent beer in a nice, well-ventilated space that offers a kid- and dog-friendly environment.

Quench 282 Smith St. (at Sackett St.) (718) 875-1500. Behind its sleek, frosted-glass exterior, Quench—a highlight on the Smith Street scene—exudes an air of unpretentious sophistication. Illuminated orbs hang from the ceiling, while the rich wood floor and bar gives the place a relaxed elegance.

Fort Greene

Alibi 242 DeKalb Ave. (between Vanderbilt and Clermont Aves.) (718) 783-8519. Alibi is a dive bar in the great East Village tradition. This one, though, lives across the East River in Fort Greene. Pratt students pack in, joining a decent-sized crowd.

Frank's Lounge 660 Fulton Street (at S. Elliott Pl.). (718) 625-9339. This old-school lounge is a Fort Greene gem. With Christmas lights, red vinyl seats and three-inch stucco spikes hanging from the ceiling over the bar, Frank's is a kitsch-lover's dream. Events like Movement (every other Wednesday) attract the areas young and hip. Check local listings for DJs and other events both in the lounge and in the loft upstairs.

Park Slope & Prospect Heights

(See also section "Gay & Lesbian" *in chapter* **Nightlife***. For* **South Paw** *see* "Popular Music Venues" *in chapter* **Nightlife***.)*

Freddy's 485 Dean St. (at Sixth Ave.) (718) 622-7035. With a neighborhood feel, cheap drinks and backroom pool table, Freddy's is the ultimate dive. Everyone is welcome here; the crowd is a mix of older regulars, younger locals and everything in between. Look for occasional live music.

The Gate 321 Fifth Ave. (at 3rd St.) (718) 768-4329. The Gate is a textbook example of low-key charm, from the attractive, distressed wood benches and tables to the amiable Irish bartender. This place provides a welcome antidote to the cutesiness of Park Slope.

Great Lakes 284 Fifth Ave. (at 1st St.) (718) 499-3710. On a busy Friday night, Great Lakes seems to have been transplanted straight from Manhattan. It's dimly lit, smoky and filled with well-dressed young professionals chatting about their day, sitting on couches and listening to the jukebox.

Loki 304 Fifth Ave. (at 2nd St.) (718) 965-9600. Dark and cavernous, with something for everyone, Loki's front room is dominated by a long, dark-wood bar lined with candles—the perfect cafe-style ambiance for a quiet after-work read. Loki's middle space is its rumpus room, with a pool table, jukebox and a dart board. And finally, tucked behind a cascade of heavy, red-velvet curtains, is a back room filled with a lavish, haphazard assortment of plush couches.

O'Connor's 39 Fifth Ave. (between Bergen and Dean Sts.) (718) 783-9721. Although O'Connor's might look scary from the outside, it's actually a delightful neighborhood bar where a mix of Park Slope residents socializes with ease. A second-generation Irish bar that was a speakeasy during Prohibition, O'Connor's is beer- and smoke-worn, with rickety old wooden booths.

Williamsburg & Greenpoint

(For **Northsix** *and* **Warsaw***, see* "Popular Music Venues" *in chapter* **Nightlife***.)*

The Abbey 536 Driggs Ave. (between N. 7th and N. 8th Sts.) (718) 599-4400. Seeking a cozy cloister on a chilly night? Take refuge in the monastic intimacy of the Abbey. Exposed brick and a red felt pool table exude warmth, while torch-like wall candles dripping big blobs of wax enhance the medieval feel. Within, talkative, dressed-down twenty-somethings cluster in booths, perch on stools, and circle the pinball machine.

Enid's 560 Manhattan Ave. (at Driggs Ave.) (718) 349-3859. This spot has struck the perfect formula for hipster cachet. Once a raw loft space, Enid's has been transformed into a comfortable SoHo-style living room, complete with amber lighting and just the right hints of a suburban rec room (including plastic-covered couches and the "Revenge from Mars" pinball machine).

Galapagos 70 N. 6th St. (between Wythe and Kent Aves.) (718) 782-5188. The species may be less varied here than on the actual Galapagos Islands—it's packed with Williamsburg and Manhattan creative types, mostly—but the scenery is lush and the competition for mates is no less fierce. Better drown your dating sorrows in drink and take some Miyako sushi down with you. The music is international, but tends toward electronica, intensifying as the night progresses.

Iona 180 Grand St. (between Bedford and Driggs Aves.) (718) 384-5008. Housed in a mid-19th-century Williamsburg building, Iona has all the hallmarks of a classic Irish pub. But unlike the brassier versions of this New York standby, Iona's worn mahogany bar, creaking floors, plank tables, and soft lighting give it what so many of its brethren lack: atmosphere. This lived-in ambiance has made it a favorite for young locals, many of whom shun the trendier, faux-dive bars in the area. Subway: L to Bedford Ave.

Mug's Ale House 125 Bedford Ave. (between N. 10th and N. 11th Sts.) (718) 384-8494. The name of this traditional bar and grill derives from the beer steins strung along the top of wall—they range from a simple glass to a monstrous, elaborate German tankard. Though it has a full bar, Mug's is, of course, all about beer, with over 20 varieties on tap for $3 to $5 a pint.

Pete's Candy Store 709 Lorimer St. (between Frost and Richardson Sts.) (718) 302-3770. As its name suggests, Pete's Candy Store is full of treats. The small, comfortable space is at once eclectic and traditional, a cross between a hip bar and a genuine sweets shop. Its appeal is in the details: tables covered in Japanese newspaper, a menu of various "toasted sandwiches," plastic chickens roosting in a bale of hay in the storefront window.

Sweet Water Tavern 105 N. 6th St. (between Berry and Wythe Sts.) (718) 963-0608. The steamed-up windows on the facade of this longtime Williamsburg joint seem to advertise a wanton world behind the glass. People hang out at the bar, mill around the pool table or crowd into the small back room, where you'll find a jukebox heavy on punk and metal tunes, a pinball machine and a wall full of playfully obnoxious graffiti.

Teddy's 96 Berry St. (at N. 8th St.) (718) 384-9787. Teddy's is a homey tavern, where mouthwatering pub fare, drinks and good spirits are served up nightly. The ornate, dark wood furnishings don't just look old: They once inhabited a brewery that opened this space in the 1890's. Performers appear every other Thursday; on Saturday nights, DJs are featured.

Union Pool 484 Union Ave. (at Meeker Ave.) (718) 609-0484. This joint — a former pool-supply store, hence the name — is a mere two stops on the L from

Manhattan, and feels like it. The crowd is distinctly Williamsburg, with a smat-
tering of rock-a-billy types rubbing elbows with working stiffs and scruffy artists,
while the surroundings are classy and comfortable. An attractive finishing
touch is the bar's retro refrigerator, which displays a wide selection of chilled
bottled beers and picture-perfect whole limes, lemons and oranges.

QUEENS

There's more to Queens than two airports and Archie Bunker. Ethnically
diverse and mostly residential, it is the second most populous borough (over 2
million residents) after Brooklyn, but far and away the largest in terms of geography, occupying one-third of the city's total area. Its neighborhoods are still
identified by the original names they bore as villages before being merged into
New York City in 1898—Flushing, Jamaica, Astoria (named for John Jacob
Astor), Little Neck (where the clams got their name), the Rockaways (with
their gorgeous Atlantic Ocean beaches) and the upper-class enclaves of Forest
Hills and Douglaston. Industry is concentrated in Long Island City, which faces
Manhattan across the East River, and in nearby neighborhoods such as Steinway (where William Steinway once made pianos and his heirs still do) and
Astoria (where Gloria Swanson, Rudolph Valentino and the Marx Brothers
made movies in the Kaufman Astoria studios, still the largest film and TV studios in the East).

Queens was mostly farmland until the Queensboro Bridge linked it to Manhattan in 1909. Today the borough is heavily populated by first- and second-
generation immigrants. There are more than 100,000 Chinese and Koreans in
Flushing. An Indian community thrives in Jackson Heights. There's a heavy
concentration of Greeks in Astoria, Irish in Sunnyside and Latinos in Elmhurst.
To see for yourself, take "the international express"—the No. 7 subway line
from Times Square, once famously derided for the diversity of its ridership by
noted social critic and redneck relief pitcher John Rocker. A 15- to 30-minute
ride from Midtown Manhattan will deposit you at Queens landmarks like Shea
Stadium, the U.S. National Tennis Center and the New York Hall of Science.

Astoria/Long Island City

Although Astoria has long been known as a Greek neighborhood, the area is
extraordinarily diverse, with large numbers of Italians, Brazilians, Indians and
Koreans making this Queens enclave their home. Once written off as just a
wind-swept industrial district along the East River, perhaps worth visiting for its
great Greek diners, it's now becoming known as one of the city's most exciting
destinations for art. Along with the waterfront section of nearby Long Island
City, this part of Queens now a bona fide cultural scene.

P.S. 1 Contemporary Art Center, the **Isamu Noguchi Sculpture Museum,**
the **American Museum of the Moving Image** and the **Socrates Sculpture Park**
are all worth the trip across the river, but Long Island City really hit the big time
as the temporary home of the Museum of Modern Art (until the Midtown loca-

tion is reopened in 2005). **MoMA QNS** (*see the full listing in chapter* **The Arts**) has created an enormous buzz, and has put Long Island City on the map; check the museum's Web site at *www.moma.org* for details.

On weekends, you can hop from one museum to another by taking the new **Queens Artlink** (*www.moma.org/qal*), a free shuttle bus that runs continuously between MoMA QNS, P.S. 1, the Noguchi Museum, the Socrates Sculpture Park and the American Museum of the Moving Image on Saturdays and Sundays from 11:30 A.M. to 5:30 P.M.

HIGHLIGHTS OF THE AREA
(*For* **MoMA QNS,** *see chapter* **The Arts.**)

American Museum of the Moving Image 35th Ave. at 36th St., Astoria (718) 784-0077 *www.ammi.org*. Before Hollywood drew much of the film industry west, Long Island City was the heart of American film production. Now, appropriately, it is the location of this museum devoted to the art, history, technology and social impact of film and television. The exhibits here skillfully demonstrate the science of moving images with demonstrations of film editing, animation, special effects and other processes. There's also a fascinating collection of memoribilia and sets from familiar movies and television shows. The museum also offers screenings of avant-garde films. **Admission:** $8.50 adults; $5.50 students and seniors; $4.50 children ages 5–18; free for children under 5. **Hours:** Tue.–Fri. noon–5 P.M., Sat.–Sun. 11 A.M.–6 P.M. Screenings Sat.–Sun. at 6:30 P.M. Closed Mon. **Subway:** R, V, G to Steinway St.; N, W to Broadway. The Queens Artlink shuttle bus stops here.

Gantry Plaza State Park 49th Ave. on the East River (718) 786-6385 *www.queenswest.com*. The miracle of Gantry Park is that it takes risks in a city that has long been frightened of them. The payoff is spectacular. With the Manhattan skyline as a backdrop and gorgeous light bouncing off the river, the site itself is magnificent. The park takes its name from two giant, hulking structures of blackened iron on the site, which used to lift freight trains onto river barges. The gantries are as powerful as the triumphal arches and classical monuments built by the City Beautiful Movement a century ago. So is the brick power station, with its quartet of de Chirico stacks, that looms nearby. Visitors are greeted by a circular area that encloses a fog fountain, a shallow cauldron of seething mist that in summer cools the air. Beyond is a large, hemispherical plaza for performances.

The plaza connects to two of four piers that project into the river. Each is different in length, shape and furnishings. One has a circular lunch bar, with stools and awning. Another, the Star Gazing Pier, is outfitted with overscaled wooden chaises. On the Fishing Pier, there's a large, free-form table complete with running water, for dressing the catch of the day. But the best thing about the piers is the views they afford of each other and the people using them. Or you can proceed along one of the paths that lead away from the plaza's southern edge. The widest path, paved with stone, defines the water's edge in a series of graceful, serpentine arcs. Along the way, it passes over a bridge that looks down on a small river inlet. From there, you can make your way down almost to the water. A second path, lined with gravel, takes you on an inland ramble, through vegetation and stone blocks clustered in crystalline formations. The blocks echo the Manhattan skyline and partly take the place of benches. The overall effect is of a Cubist rock garden. **Subway:** 7 to Vernon Blvd.   —*Herbert Muschamp*

Isamu Noguchi Garden Museum 32–37 Vernon Blvd. (at 33rd Rd.), Long Island City. (718) 204-7088 *www.noguchi.org*. Noguchi is best known for melding Eastern and Western influences in his stark, beautiful abstract sculptures. He also designed the world-famous Akari lamps, the multishaped paper lanterns that have become a staple of SoHo lofts (these are available in the gift shop, along with books, cards and prints). This museum's permanent Long Island City location is a lovely indoor/outdoor Japanese garden, a marvelous place to find tranquility in this bustling city. However, it's currently undergoing a major renovation that's scheduled for completion in spring 2003. Until then, the museum has a temporary location at 36-01 43rd Ave. (at 36th St.) in Sunnyside. This temporary facility can't accommodate outdoor installations, although the curators have made a wonderful attempt to bring elements of nature into the gallery space. **Admission:** $5 adults; $2.50 students and seniors. Hours: Mon. and Thu.–Fri. 10 A.M.–5 P.M.; Sat.–Sun. 11 A.M.–6 P.M. Closed Tue.–Wed. **Subway:** Temporary location in Sunnyside, 7 to 33rd St.; permanent location in Long Island City, N to Broadway. The Queens Artlink shuttle bus stops here.

Museum for African Art 36–01 43rd Ave. (3rd floor), Long Island City, Queens (212) 966-1313 *www.africanart.org*. Until recently, you were more likely to encounter sub-Saharan African sculpture in an anthropology textbook than in an art museum. Today, African art is considered one of the most inventive art forms of the past two centuries, and the Museum for African Art can take much of the credit for this shift. The museum mounts provocative changing exhibitions on the rich and varied artistic heritage of African art, which include historical surveys in addition to contemporary works. In the fall of 2002, the collection moved to this temporary facility in Queens (in the same building as the Noguchi Museum); it will remain here until its new home on Museum Mile is completed in 2005. The new facility opened with an exhibit featuring 70 ceremonial masks from across the continent; the show will run through Black History Month, February 2003. **Admission:** $5 adults; $2.50 students, seniors and children. **Hours:** Tue.–Fri. 10:30 A.M.–5:30 P.M. (to 8:30 P.M. third Thu. of each month); Sat.–Sun. noon–6 P.M. Closed Mon. **Subway:** 7 to 33rd St./Queens. The Queens Artlink shuttle bus stops here.

P.S. 1 Contemporary Art Center 22–25 Jackson Ave. (at 46th Ave. and 46th Rd.), Long Island City (718) 784-2084 *www.ps1.org*. Across the East River in Long Island City, the P.S. 1 Contemporary Art Center is far from SoHo and Museum Mile. But its outer-borough location is an apt metaphor for the center's focus on marginal artists and art that isn't often exhibited in more traditional museums. P.S. 1 occupies a Romanesque Revival school building, built from 1893 to 1906. Renovated by Frederick Fisher, it features a dramatic front entry, a two-story project space for large-scale exhibitions and a 20,000-square-foot outdoor courtyard that serves as a sculpture garden. An affiliate of MoMA, P.S.1 does not focus on assembling a permanent collection, but rotates many long-term, site-specific installations throughout its 125,000 square feet of gallery space by artists including James Turrell, Pipilotti Rist, Richard Serra, Lucio Pozzi, Julian Schnabel and Richard Artschwager. **Admission:** $5 adults; $2 students and seniors. **Hours:** Thu.–Mon. noon–6 P.M. Closed Tue.–Wed. **Subway:** E, V to 23rd St.–Ely Ave.; 7 to 45th Rd.–Court House Sq.; G to 21st St./Van Alst. or Court Sq. The Queens Artlink shuttle bus stops here.

The Queensboro Bridge (59th Street Bridge). Silhouetted against a darkening sky, this elaborate expanse linking Queens and Manhattan looks like a work of crochet. Walking across on the south side, a look through the lacy structure reveals an incredible panorama of Midtown skyscrapers. From the north walk, you will see river currents rushing over rocks, and get a good close-up view of Roosevelt Island and the little red Roosevelt Island tram that ferries residents to and from Manhattan.

Socrates Sculpture Park Broadway and Vernon Blvd., Long Island City (718) 956-1819 *www.socratessculpturepark.org*. This 4.5-acre jewel on the banks of the East River in Long Island City was once a ship yard, then for 20 years an illegal dump site. Through the efforts of sculptor Mark di Suvero, the site was converted in the mid-1980's to an outdoor sculpture park featuring semi-annual exhibitions of public sculpture in a variety of media. Among the sculptures are subtle and pleasing artistic touches: winding paths, marble benches, and stones carved to resemble a child's letter blocks. In summer, the park hosts music and dance performances, plus screenings of international films—all set against the spectacular backdrop of the Manhattan skyline. **Admission:** Free. **Hours:** Daily 10 A.M.–sunset. **Subway:** N, W to Broadway, then walk 8 blocks toward the East River. The Queens Artlink shuttle bus stops here.

Steinway and Sons Piano Factory 19th Ave. and 38th St. (718) 721-2600. Steinway's 440,000-square-foot factory in Astoria, built in the 1880's, still produces great pianos. A tour of the factory affords a close-up view of some 300 master craftsmen who saw, bend and sand the wood, put on the strings and voice the instruments. Visitors are also allowed to enter the factory's "pounder" room, where a machine tests the integrity of each instrument by banging on all 88 keys at once, 10,000 times. Call ahead before going; tours were not offered in the summer of 2002. **Subway:** N to Ditmars Blvd.

AREA RESTAURANTS

Chips   **$25 & Under**   MEXICAN
42-15 Queens Blvd., Long Island City   (718) 786-1800
The smallest and perhaps the cutest restaurant near MoMA QNS is this Mexi-

can shoebox with hot pink tablecloths, hand-painted chairs, sombrero light fixtures and bright colors everywhere. The shrimp cocktail with avocado and the chicken served with an excellent dark mole sauce are among the high points. **Price range:** $10–$15 per person for lunch.

Christos Hasapo-Taverna $25 & Under   GREEK/STEAK
41–08 23rd Ave. (at 41st St.), Astoria   (718) 726-5195
Meals in this cheerful, handsome Greek steakhouse begin with fresh *tzatziki,* a combination of yogurt, garlic and cucumber, and *tarama,* the wonderful fish roe purée. Appetizer portions are big and easily shared. Richly flavored steaks and chops dominate the menu, and on some nights, more traditional fare, like piglet and baby lamb, is turned on the rotisserie. Best desserts include baklava, a wonderful apple cake and a plate of prunes and figs marinated in sweet wine. **Price range:** Entrees $20–$25.

Churrascaria Girassol $25 & Under   BRAZILIAN
33-18 28th Ave., Astoria   (718) 545-8250
With juicy, salt-edged steaks, rich sauces mellowed with palm oil and the prospect of unlimited meat courses, Girassol is a little bit of paradise for carnivores. The chef and owner, Lilian Fagundes, prepares almost everything from scratch, like an excellent *feijoada,* a richly flavorful black bean stew filling an iron kettle, thick with all manner of pork. **Price range:** Entrees $10–$18.

Dazies $25 & Under   ITALIAN
39-41 Queens Blvd., Long Island City   (718) 786-7013
With its dark wood, dark lighting, piano music and plush linens, this classic Italian restaurant is a favorite with the staff at nearby MoMA QNS. That's not a surprise, given the welcoming, gracious atmosphere, the uncommon competence of the kitchen, the comfortable familiarity of the menu and the credible wine list. This is the closest thing in the neighborhood to an expense-account restaurant. **Price range:** About $30–$40 per person for lunch with appetizer and main course.

Elias Corner $25 & Under   GREEK/SEAFOOD
24–02 31st St. (at 24th Ave.), Astoria   (718) 932-1510
This bright, raucous Greek seafood specialist offers no menus. Regulars know to check the glass display case in front to select the freshest-looking fish. Go in the off hours, before the crowd arrives. Otherwise the wait is interminable and the staff becomes harried. **Price range:** Entrees $13–$17. Cash only.

The New Thompson's Diner $25 and Under   CARIBBEAN
32-44 Queens Blvd. (at 33rd St.), Long Island City   (718) 392-0692
Just below the 33rd Street 7 train stop, close to MoMA QNS, there's nothing fancy about this old-time joint. But an abundance of rice, garlicky red beans and well-roasted pork with crisp skin will run you only about $6. The diner's

fried chicken, marinated in a tomato sauce before being lowered into the frier, is awfully good, too. **Price range:** Less than $10 per person. Cash only.

Tauneung $25 and Under   KOREAN
43-01 Queen Blvd. (near 43rd St.), Long Island City   (718) 706-9205
The barbecue is the reason to visit here. It's a do-it-yourself affair, performed over live coals that are lowered into a cavity in the middle of your table, then covered with a rack. On it you can grill marinated short ribs or other cuts of beef, pork, chicken or shrimp. **Price range:** About $20 if you have barbecue, $10 if you order other dishes.

Tournesol $25 & Under   BISTRO/FRENCH
50-12 Vernon Blvd., Long Island City, Queens   (718) 472-4355
Like a flower poking through the gritty concrete near the mouth of the Queens-Midtown Tunnel, Tournesol, is a spray of brightness on a field of gray. The pleasant dining room, with textured beige walls, a handsome bar and mirrors, works for first dates or family gatherings, while the chef displays a sure hand with Tournesol's small selection of bistro dishes. Cash only. **Price range:** Entrees, $12–$17.

Ubol's Kitchen $25 & Under   THAI
24–42 Steinway St. (near Astoria Blvd.), Astoria   (718) 545-2874
This plain-Jane but authentic Thai restaurant does not stint on its spicing or seasoning. Dishes marked on the menu as hot and spicy can be counted on to be searing, while dishes traditionally rich in fish sauce are suitably pungent. Top dishes include spicy salads and curries. **Price range:** Entrees $6.95–$14.95.

Uncle George's $25 & Under   GREEK
33–19 Broadway, Astoria   (718) 626-0593
A cross between a giant diner that's open 24/7 and a boisterous family restaurant, Uncle George's is an Astoria Greek classic. Portions are big, service is speedy and the menu offers every kind of Greek dish, from great grilled fish to the ubiquitous spanakopita (spinach pie). You won't leave hungry. With bright lights, plastic table covers and seats crowded into every available spot, it's fair to say that the draw isn't the décor. **Price range:** Entrees $6–$14. Cash only.

Water's Edge   ☆☆ $$$$ NEW AMERICAN
44th Dr. at the East River, Long Island City   (718) 482-0033
This is romantic special-occasion dining, with a lovely extra twist. From Manhattan, you reach the Water's Edge by taking a free ferry ride from 34th Street and the East River. The restaurant sits on a barge in the river, offering a magnificent ship captain's view of Midtown. The menu falls squarely in the mainstream, with all the trendy Asian touches and newly familiar ingredients. **Price range:** Prix-fixe dinner $50–$80.

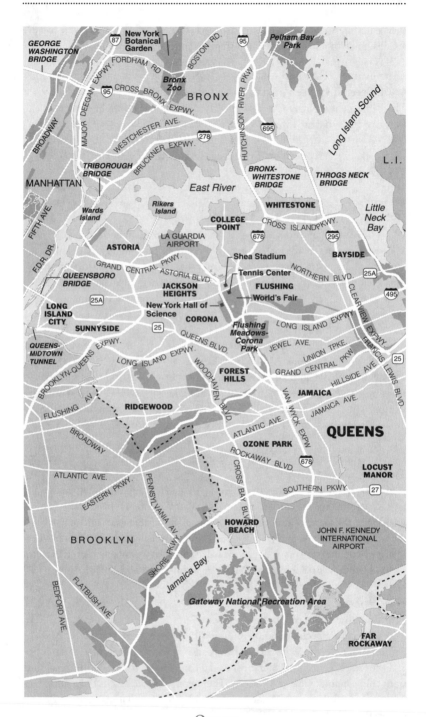

Queens

Flushing Meadows—Corona Park

Immortalized as the "Valley of the Ashes" in F. Scott Fitzgerald's *The Great Gatsby*, these former marshes were filled in long ago and became a park in 1939, when the site hosted the New York World's Fair. (It did so again in 1964.) There's something for everyone at the park: You can catch a Mets game at **Shea Stadium,** or play on the same courts that host the U.S. Open at the **U.S.T.A. National Tennis Center** (*see chapter* **Sports & Recreation**). You can also marvel at the 12-story-high **Unisphere,** visit the **New York Hall of Science** to marvel at the collection of American spacecraft (*see chapter* **New York for Children**) or walk around a scale model of New York at the **Queens Museum**— all of which were first built for the '64 fair.

HIGHLIGHTS OF THE NEIGHBORHOOD

(*For* **Shea Stadium** *and* **USTA National Tennis Center,** *see chapter* **Sports & Recreation.** *For* **New York Hall of Science,** *see chapter* **New York for Children.**)

Bowne House 37–01 Bowne St. (between 37th and 38th Aves.), Flushing (718) 359-0528. One of the city's oldest and most historic homes, this farmhouse was built by John Bowne in 1661. He lived there and used it as New Amsterdam's first indoor Quaker meeting place, in defiance of Governor Peter Stuyvesant's ban on the sect. Nine generations of Bownes lived here while a bustling Flushing neighborhood grew up around them. The house, a fine example of vernacular Dutch-English architecture, features restored rooms that are complete with period furniture and pewterware. **Admission:** $2 adults; $1 children and seniors. **Hours:** Tue. and Sat.–Sun. 2:30–4:30 P.M. **Subway:** 7 to Main St.–Flushing.

Flushing Town Hall 137–35 Northern Blvd. at Linden Pl. (718) 463-7700. This two-story brick Romanesque Revival building served as Flushing's town hall until 1900, when the village was incorporated into New York City. Constructed in 1862 on what are believed to have been the Matinecock Indians' burial grounds, it is a veritable encyclopedia of American history. It served as a militia depot during the Civil War, a forum for speeches by Ulysses S. Grant and Teddy Roosevelt, a performance space for P.T. Barnum and Mark Twain, as well as a traffic court, jail, opera house, ballroom, police precinct and even a dinner theater. The Flushing Council on Culture and the Arts maintains three galleries here with rotating art exhibits; there's also a visitors center and cafe, plus occasional jazz concerts and other cultural events. **Hours:** Mon.–Fri. 10 A.M.–5 P.M., Sat.–Sun. noon–5 P.M. Subway: 7 to Main St.–Flushing.

Louis Armstrong's House 34-56 107th St., Corona (718) 478-8274 *www.satchmo.net.* Louis and his wife, Lucille, lived here from 1943 until they died. The house was built in 1910, and remains today just as Lucille left it when she passed away in 1983. It is currently undergoing restoration in hopes of opening it to the public as a historic home museum and theater in fall 2003. In the meantime, you can visit the **Louis Armstrong Archives** at nearby Queens College, 65-30 Kissena Blvd., in Flushing (call 718-997-3670 to make an appointment before visiting).

Queens Museum of Art New York City Bldg. (111th St. and 49th Ave., next to the Unisphere), Flushing Meadows/Corona Park. (718) 592-9700 *www.queensmuse.org.* If you go to the Queens Museum only to see the Panorama, an immense model of New York City, it would be well worth the trip. Originally built for the 1964 World's Fair, the model replicates in painstaking detail the geography, buildings, bridges and roads of all five boroughs at a scale of 1,200 to 1. The world's largest scale model, it fills a room the size of two basketball courts. The museum is housed in one of the few remaining buildings of the 1939 World's Fair (it was also home to the United Nations General Assembly from 1946 to 1952). In addition to exhibiting contemporary art, the museum has an impressive collection of World's Fair memorabilia, an assortment of Tiffany lamps and a sculpture hall. The museum's satellite exhibition space at **Bulova Corporate Center** in Jackson Heights features a permanent sculpture exhibit as well as rotating shows of work by emerging artists. **Admission:** $5 adults; $2.50 students and seniors; free for children under 5. **Hours:** Tue.–Fri. 10 A.M.–5 P.M.; Sat.–Sun. noon–5 P.M. **Subway:** 7 to 11th St.

AREA RESTAURANTS

East Buffet & Restaurant $25 & Under   CHINESE
42-07 Main St., Flushing   (718) 353-6333
This huge, glossy Chinese eating hall seats 400 people in the buffet hall and 350 in another room for sit-down service. Three islands in the center of the buffet area hold more than 30 dim sum selections, a dozen soups, 40 dishes served cold and another 40 served hot. In the sit-down area, try the extraordinary sticky rice, steamed in bamboo leaves and stuffed, tamale-like, with chopped pork. **Price range:** Dinner $20–$25.

Joe's Shanghai   ☆☆ $ CHINESE
136–21 37th Ave. (near Main St.), Flushing   (718) 539-3838
Joe's signature dish, "steamed buns," is alone worth the trip. The buns are wonderful soup dumplings that hold a lusty blend of pork or crab meat in a richly flavored broth. Among entrees, look for dishes like stewed mussels in black bean sauce; beef shank with bean curd Sichuan style; crabs, steamed and served over sweet sticky rice; tea-smoked duck; and braised pork shoulder in brown sauce. **Price range:** Entrees $9.50 and up. Cash only.

Kabab King Diner $25 & Under   PAKISTANI
73-01 37th Rd., Jackson Heights, Queens   (718) 457-5857
A bright and cluttered Pakistani restaurant, Kabab King looks like a cabby

haunt, with a big steam table and communal tables, where diners eat with plastic utensils from plastic foam plates. But behind the steam table, where assorted curries and stews sit warming, emerge kebabs as moist and succulent as you can imagine, layered in a thick yogurt marinade, well-herbed and intensely spiced. Cash only. Open 24 hours. **Price range:** $7 is the upper limit.

Kazan Turkish Cuisine   **$25 & Under**   TURKISH
95–36 Queens Blvd., Rego Park   (718) 897-1509
Kazan's stone oven produces exceptional pide, soft football-shape loaves of bread dotted with sesame seeds, which are just right with any of the superb cold appetizers. Eggplant is excellent, either charcoal grilled and puréed with garlic or left chunky and served with tomato and garlic. Kazan's short selection of main courses also includes some real winners like *shish yogurtlu*, juicy chunks of tender grilled lamb served over a sauce of yogurt blended with tomatoes. *Kasarli kofte* is another standout, made with chopped lamb blended with mild kasseri cheese, which gives the meat an unusual airiness. **Price range:** Entrees $9–$14.

La Esquina Criolla   **$25 & Under**   SOUTH AMERICAN
94-67 Corona Blvd., Corona   (718) 699-5579
La Esquina Criolla is both meat market and restaurant. While some customers may take home one of the reasonably priced steaks, almost everybody in the throng on a Saturday night is filling up right there. It's hard to imagine a sweeter restaurant, despite a language barrier. And you can't get a better steak value than La Criolla's shell steak. Also good is the beefy skirt steak or the enormous mixed grill plate. Cap it off with an excellent flan topped with creamy *dulce de leche*. **Price range:** Entrees $5.95-$19.95.

Master Grill   **$25 & Under**   BRAZILIAN
34–09 College Point Blvd., Flushing   (718) 762-0300
Possibly the most elaborate Brazilian rodizio in the city: Master Grill feels like an enormous banquet hall, with seating for 1,000 people and a samba band playing full tilt. It's all great fun if you're in the mood. The buffet itself is the size of a small restaurant, where you can fortify yourself with all manner of marinated vegetables, fruit, seafood, pasta, rolls, roasted potatoes and fried plantains. The parade of all-you-can-eat grilled meats, from chicken hearts to six kinds of beef, goes on as long as you can hold out. **Price range:** All you can eat $19.95.

Pachas   **$25 & Under**   LATIN AMERICAN
93–21 37th Ave., Flushing   (718) 397-0729
When a menu offers food from more than one land, the trick is knowing which way to go. Sometimes this is an easy call, but the Colombian-Venezuelan menu at Pachas presents problems. Order from the much bigger Colombian menu. A simple *arepa con queso*, fragrant with corn, is served steaming with a block of dense, salty cheese on top. Even better are the sublime *arepa buche*, a blend of tender tripe, tomato and onion, boiled down to a soulful essence. Pachas has no

liquor license but makes excellent *batidos*, or fruit shakes, in tropical flavors.
Price range: Entrees $6–$13.

Pearson's Texas Barbecue $25 & Under   BARBECUE
71–04 35th Ave., Jackson Heights   (718) 779-7715
The only pit barbecue restaurant in New York City. In the rear, burnished slabs
of pork ribs glisten behind a counter next to piles of plump sausages and chickens turned almost chestnut by smoke. The glory of Pearson's is its brisket,
superb, tender and fully imbued with smoke from the rosy-brown, almost crisp
exterior through to the pink center. **Price range:** Sandwiches $5.95; barbecue
by the pound $5–$15. Cash only.

Penang $$ MALAYSIAN
38–04 Prince St., Flushing   (718) 321-2078
What started as a small Malaysian storefront has turned into an institution serving surprisingly authentic Malaysian flavors. The dish not to miss is the *roti
canai*, a seductive, savory crepe served with coconut milk sauce. **Price range:**
Avg. entree $13.95.

Pio Pio $ PERUVIAN
84–13 Northern Blvd., Jackson Heights   (718) 426-1010
With brick walls, a pressed tin ceiling and big windows, this is an attractive
restaurant and a good place for a date. The menu is brief and the specialty is the
moist and beautifully spiced roast chicken. Tostones are excellent, as are the
pisco cocktails. Ceviche is served only on weekends. **Price range:** Combination
dinner $20 for two people.

Shanghai Tang $25 & Under   CHINESE
135–20 40th Rd., Flushing   (718) 661-4234
This bright, handsome restaurant, one of the best Chinese places in Flushing,
serves many excellent Shanghai specialties. You know you're in for an
unusual meal when you enter and see fish tanks full of lively eels. Service is
unusually friendly and helpful. **Price range:** Entrees $6.95–$14.95 (specials
to $24.95).

Spicy and Tasty $25 & Under   CHINESE
133-43 Roosevelt Ave., Flushing, Queens   (718) 939-7788
Sichuan cooking is known for dishes designated as "ma-la," as in the excellent
ma-la cold noodles, thin noodles in peppery, lively sauce with a mildly sweet
sesame flavor. Try the tea-smoked duck, with its lacquered, rosy skin and moist,
mildly smoky interior, but even better is the tea-smoked pork with leeks. Spicy
and Tasty also offers its share of more challenging dishes, like shredded stomach,
duck feet and pig intestines. Cash only. **Price range:** Entrees, $7–$17.

Other Attractions in Queens

Gateway National Recreation Area (718) 354-4606 *www.nps.gov/gate*. This 26,000-acre recreation area extends through three city boroughs and into northern New Jersey. It encompasses a series of beautiful beaches along the Atlantic shoreline, including popular **Riis Park** (which has parking, restrooms, showers, recreational fields, picnic tables and food vendors). Throughout the preserve, you can explore decomissioned military sites, walk nature trails, enjoy water sports, cycle along bike paths and much much more.

One section of the NRA, the **Jamaica Bay Wildlife Refuge** near Kennedy Airport (718-318-4340), spans an area almost the size of Manhattan and offers a visitors center. Thousands of birds—including geese and ducks—stop here during their migration north and south along the Atlantic flyway. (The best time to visit is in the spring or fall, when birds fill the skies.) Over 300 species of birds and 65 species of butterflies have been found on the 9,000-acre preserve. Diverse habitats include salt marshland, upland fields, woods, ponds and an open expanse of bays and islands. **Admission:** No entrance fees, but Riis Park and Sandy Hook beaches have parking fees. There's a $25 fee for an annual fishing permit. **Subway:** A, S to Broad Channel.

Queens County Farm Museum 73–50 Little Neck Pkwy. at Union Tpke., Floral Park (718) 347-3276 *www.queensfarm.org*. This 47-acre, 200-year-old farm became such an anomaly that the city decided to turn it into a museum. But it's not what you'd expect. To this day it continues as a working farm with planted fields, orchards and livestock. The historic 1770's home features period rooms and changing exhibitions on the history of agriculture. Special events include agricultural and craft fairs, apple festivals and antique car shows, as well as quilting, candle making and other craft demonstrations and courses. A seasonal farmstand sells fresh produce, and a greenhouse offers the chance to buy house and garden plants. **Admission:** Free. **Hours:** Mon.–Fri. 9 A.M.–5 P.M.; Sat.–Sun. 10 A.M.–5 P.M. **Directions:** E, F to Kew Gardens, then take the Q 46 bus to Little Neck Pkwy.

STATEN ISLAND

The reaction to New York City's so-called forgotten borough is usually the same: "Staten Island? You must be kidding." Disdainful Manhattanites dismiss it out of hand. But Staten Island is a wonderful place to explore—and to some, it's so out, it's in. There are great little museums, three centuries of American architecture, historic military sites, extensive gardens and lots of programs for children. Nature lovers can meander through 7,500 acres of lush protected parkland and along miles of uncrowded beaches, or discover wetlands that are ripe for canoeing and communing with herons and cormorants.

Staten Island can seem surprisingly big to first-time visitors, so a car can be an advantage. But even if you don't drive here, the borough is well served by public transportation, starting with the **Staten Island Ferry.** The Staten Island Railroad and many bus routes ply the borough, and there's efficient express bus service from Manhattan (all of these services take MetroCards).

Cycling around the borough is especially fun in nice weather, and both the ferry and the local trains are bike friendly. The City Department of Transportation publishes a free bike map, which can be picked up at the Staten Island Visitors Bureau in either ferry terminal.

The ferry is still the best way to get to Staten Island. Once a bargain at a nickel a ride, it is now absolutely free and as breezy and romantic as ever. Riding one of those big orange boats at sunset on a summer evening is like a mini-cruise and almost as restorative.

Boats leave from South Ferry in Manhattan and dock in St. George, the county seat and transportation hub, which is also home to the borough's newest landmark, the **Richmond County Bank Ballpark,** home to the **Staten Island Yankees** (*www.siyanks.com*), the Bronx Bombers' minor-league affiliate. Since the first ball was thrown out in June 2001, the Baby Bombers have drawn huge crowds, as much for the sport—and the rivalry with the Brooklyn Cyclones—as for the stadium's sweeping views of New York Harbor.

Another new landmark for St. George is the brand-new **National Lighthouse Museum,** which began opening in phases in the summer of 2002. Housed in what was most recently a Coast Guard base adjacent to the ferry terminal, it explores the science and lore of lighthouses.

Another proposal envisions adding a satellite of the **Staten Island Institute of Arts and Sciences** along the leafy new port-side promenade. The institute, the borough's main museum, is just a three-block walk from the ferry terminal. It has a large cache of possessions, from bugs and botanicals to paintings and decorative objects, displayed in regular temporary exhibitions. Look for surprise gems such as paintings by the Staten Island native Jasper Cropsey, or works by Chagall, Warhol, Toulouse-Lautrec, Piranesi or Dürer.

The **Newhouse Center for Contemporary Art,** just a 10- to 15-minute ride west along Richmond Terrace by car, bus or bike, is the main exhibition space at the borough's best-known art and performance site, the 83-acre **Snug Harbor Cultural Center.** Opened 200 years ago as a haven "for aged, decrepit and worn-out sailors"—or Snugs, as the retired seamen were called—Snug Harbor is a collection of 28 buildings in the Greek Revival, Italianate and Beaux-Arts styles, all of which are slowly being spruced up.

There is an 1892 music hall that is just a year younger than Carnegie Hall and a new museum, the Noble Maritime Collection. The museum opened in November 2000 in a three-story 1844 Greek Revival structure, which was renovated almost exclusively with volunteer labor. It focuses on the work of John A. Noble, the Paris-born lithographer, painter and seaman whose favorite subject was wooden sailing vessels.

You could spend a whole day at Snug Harbor, which offers an escape for every taste and age. If nature is what you crave, amble into the **Chinese Scholar's Garden** and you are instantly transported to China's Suzhou province, and maybe to another level of consciousness. The crown jewel of the **Staten Island Botanical Garden,** the Scholar's Garden was created by 40 artisans from China and is the only garden of its kind in the United States. Seasonal changes in light and flora make it an oasis at any time of the year.

The **Jacques Marchais Museum of Tibetan Art,** on Lighthouse Hill in the middle of the island, has a wonderful garden, too, though a bit more intimate. Cyclists and hikers will find climbing the hill a bit daunting, but the surprise of finding a replica of a Himalayan monastery tucked in among the trees soon makes you forget your fatigue. The collection of Tibetan artifacts inside was praised for its authenticity by the Dalai Lama, who visited in 1991.

Youngsters visiting Staten Island probably won't care about the deeper meaning of Moon Gates and mandalas, but they might go for the Botanical Garden's mazes. Through a clutch of screaming peacocks is the **Connie Gretz Secret Garden,** complete with circuitous paths, hedges and a turreted castle. Inspired by Frances Hodgson Burnett's book, it's a good place for the little ones to let loose.

And then there's always the **Carousel-for-All-Children** in Willowbrook Park, about 10 minutes by car. Its 51 old-fashioned wooden animals, hand-carved and hand-painted, revolve on a structure decorated with scenes of Staten Island. (*See chapter* **New York for Children** *for the* Staten Island Children's Museum *and the* Staten Island Zoo.)

A flood of development since the 1964 opening of the **Verrazano-Narrows Bridge** has robbed the island of much of its charm and character. But scattered among new houses and the kinds of elaborate lawn ornaments that make one long for the simpler days of petrified fawns, are some unusual things, both old and new, that add to the borough's appeal.

Doug Schwartz's **rock installation** is one. If you're driving or biking down Hylan Boulevard, stop by the beach at the end of Sharrots Road, at Mount Loretto, a former orphanage where some church scenes in *The Godfather* were filmed. A work in progress for 10 years, the installation is made up of rock circles and towers that are meant to evoke life, death, the sky and taking care of day-to-day affairs, says the artist, who is also the groundhog trainer and tropical forest keeper at the Staten Island Zoo.

On Lighthouse Hill near the Tibetan Museum, the **Crimson Beech,** a 1950's prefab house designed by Frank Lloyd Wright, is regarded as a piece of important mid-20th-century culture.

The same can be said for **Mandolin Brothers,** a bustling little shop-cum-museum close to the zoo, which is one of the world's foremost dealers in new and vintage guitars and other fretted instruments. The shop has been responsible for bringing some unlikely tourists to Staten Island: Joni Mitchell, for one, who immortalized the shop in a song, and George Harrison, who popped in one day unannounced and went on a 40-minute shopping spree.

If you love history, **Historic Richmond Town,** a village of 27 structures, offers not Disney-style reproductions but restorations of actual Staten Island buildings, some local and others moved to the 100-acre site from other island communities. The oldest is the red 17th-century Voorlezer's house, which is the oldest known school in the United States. The collection of 18th-century Dutch Colonial farmhouses and workshops and a 19th-century country church are interesting for their insight into long-ago community and family life. The **County Fair** here, with its pig races and do-wop concerts, is the borough's end-of-summer rendezvous of choice.

At the **Conference House,** 15 minutes or so by bike from the Oakwood train station, you can begin to trace Staten Island's role in international politics. It was here in September 1776, with 32,000 British troops and Hessian mercenaries billeted among the island's 3,000 residents, that Lord Admiral Richard Howe met with Benjamin Franklin, John Adams and Edward Rutledge in a failed attempt to hammer out the finer points of the country's independence. The Conference House is in Tottenville, the end of the train line and Staten Island's southernmost tip. An unusual mix of Victorian houses and cottages, old mansions, odd urban and industrial ruins, beaches and tranquil wooded areas like Blue Heron Pond as well as relatively traffic-free streets, make this whole area a popular cycling destination.

The area also has lots of little green pockets, most of them too dense for cycling but great for hikes. The Urban Park Rangers offer canoeing lessons at **Wolfe's Pond Park,** but those with their own canoe or kayak can discover how unusual the **William T. Davis Wildlife Refuge** is. Part of the 2,800-acre **Green-belt,** a collection of six Staten Island parks and nature preserves, it has a network of navigable creeks whose grasses and banks are a habitat for native wildlife and temporary quarters for many migratory birds. It also provides a bird's-eye view of the old Fresh Kills Landfill.

For those interested in things military, **Battery Weed,** a multitiered fortress, is a short bus or bike ride from the ferry. It is one of the oldest forts in the nation and one of only three examples of its kind ever built. The site, **Fort Wadsworth,** visible from the Verrazano-Narrows Bridge as one crosses from Brooklyn, is the oldest continuously staffed military post in the United States.

The 19th century might be considered Staten Island's Golden Age, when the borough appealed even to international political exiles. The Italian patriot Giuseppe Garibaldi forged the plan for his country's independence in the home of Antonio Meucci, said to be the true inventor of the telephone. At the **Garibaldi-Meucci Museum,** between the ferry and Fort Wadsworth, you can see some of the first telephones and assorted Garibaldi memorabilia, including the red shirt he wore defending Rome against the French in 1849.

In the 19th century, life was madcap for the privileged classes on Staten Island, a playground for families like the Vanderbilts and the Cunards. You can see the busy life of the borough's comfortably wealthy as it was captured on film by one of their own, Alice Austen, at her family's home, now a museum. Austen was one of the first American women to take up photography. Her vine-covered cottage, **Clear Comfort,** serves as a museum of the Victorian lifestyle as well as a photo gallery showing prints by Austen and other photographers. It is a poignant memorial to her and to a forgotten era in the forgotten borough.

—Claire Wilson

Staten Island

Getting There: By **subway and ferry,** take the 1, 9 to South Ferry (service had not been restored as of this writing, but may be back by the time you visit), the 4, 5 to Bowling Green, or the N, R to Whitehall Street. Walk to the ferry terminal, and take the Staten Island Ferry (free) to St. George.

From Manhattan, there are 30 **express buses** (1X, 9X, 10X, for example) that go to various Staten Island destinations. For info, call (718) 330-1234.

By car from Manhattan, take either the Brooklyn Bridge or the Brooklyn Battery Tunnel to Route 278, then head for the Verrazano-Narrows Bridge (toll is $7 from Brooklyn, no toll back to Brooklyn). This takes you to the Staten Island Expressway. From New Jersey, there are three bridges: from the Bayonne Bridge, Route 440 takes you to Route 278; from I-95, the Goethals Bridge takes you to Route 278; from the Outerbridge Crossing, Route 440 takes you to the West Shore Expressway and then to Route 278.

ATTRACTIONS

(For the **Staten Island Ferry,** *see section* "Lower Manhattan" *earlier in this chapter. For the* **Staten Island Children's Museum** *and* **Staten Island Zoo,** *see chapter* **New York for Children.** *For the* **Staten Island Yankees,** *see chapter* **Sports &** **Recreation.** *See the essay above for more details about the sights listed below.)*

Alice Austen House 2 Hylan Blvd., Rosebank (718) 816-4506. **Admission:** $2 adults; free for children under 6. **Hours:** Thu–Sun. noon–5 P.M. **Bus:** S-51.

Carousel-for-All-Children Willowbrook Park, 1 Eaton Pl., Willowbrook (718) 477-0605, (718) 667-2165. **Tickets:** $1 a ride. **Hours:** Daily 11 A.M.–5:45 P.M. **Bus:** S-62 to the park's gate on Victory Blvd.

Conference House waterfront at end of Hylan Blvd., Tottenville (718) 984-2086. **Admission:** $2 adults; $1 seniors and children. **Hours:** Wed.–Sun. 1–4 P.M. Closed Jan.–Feb. **Bus:** S-78 to Craig Ave.

Fort Wadsworth and Battery Weed Bay St. at Hylan Blvd. (718) 354-4500 *www.nps.gov/gate*. Added to the sprawling Gateway National Recreation Area in 1995, Fort Wadsworth was a linchpin to the defense of New York Harbor for nearly two centuries. Park rangers lead walks and tours highlighting both its history and its shoreline environment. **Admission:** Free. **Hours:** Visitor Center (offering exhibits, tours and a short film on the history of New York's harbor defenses) Wed.–Sun. 10 A.M.–5 P.M. **Bus:** S51 to Von Briesen Park.

Garibaldi-Meucci Museum 420 Tompkins Avenue, Rosebank (718) 442-1608. **Admission:** $3. **Hours:** Tue.–Sun. 1–4:30 P.M. **Bus:** S52, S78 or S79.

Historic Richmond Town 441 Clarke Ave., Richmond (718) 351-1611 *www.historicrichmondtown.org*. Staten Island's answer to Colonial Williamsburg is this a living-history complex of 27 buildings set on 100 acres; costumed actors give visitors a glimpse into everyday colonial life. **Admission:** $5 adults; $4 seniors; $3.50 children ages 5–17; free for children under 5. **Hours:** Jun.–Aug., Mon. and Wed.–Sat. 10 A.M.–5 P.M., Sun. 1–5 P.M. Sept.–May, Wed.–Sun 1–5 P.M. **Bus:** S-74 from ferry terminal to Richmond Rd. and St. Patrick's Pl.

Mandolin Brothers 629 Forest Ave., West Brighton (718) 981-3226 *www.mandoweb.com*. **Hours:** Mon.–Sat. 10 A.M.–6 P.M. **Bus:** S-48 to Forest and Pelton Aves.

Jacques Marchais Museum of Tibetan Art 338 Lighthouse Ave., Richmond (718) 987-3500 *www.tibetanmuseum.com*. This hilltop museum is designed to resemble a Himalayan Temple, with art, ritual objects and musical instruments. **Admission:** $5 adults; $3 students and seniors; $2 children under 12. **Hours:** Daily 1–5 P.M.

National Lighthouse Museum 1 Lighthouse Plaza, St. George (718) 556-1681 *www.lighthousemuseum.org*. Tours Wed. and Sat. at 11 A.M. and 1, 2 and 3 P.M.; Sun. at 1, 2 and 3 P.M. Reservations required. **Admission:** $2. **Directions:** Walk from ferry.

Staten Island Institute of Arts and Sciences 75 Stuyvesant Pl., St. George
(718) 727-1135. The oldest cultural organization on Staten Island, the museum
offers interactive children's programs as well as art and natural science exhibits,
including more than 500,000 entomological specimens, 25,000 plant specimens, and shells and archaeological objects. The general collections include
ethnographic art, paintings, sculpture, crafts, prints and drawings, including a
portion of the Kress Collection of the Italian Renaissance. You'll also find historic collections of 19th- and 20th-century American costumes and 18th- to
20th-century American, European and Asian furniture and decorative arts. In
addition, the museum sponsors a smaller exhibit at the ferry terminal. **Admission:** $2.50 adults; $1.50 seniors and children. **Hours:** Mon–Sat. 9 A.M.–5
P.M.; Sun. 1–5 P.M. **Directions:** Walk from ferry.

Snug Harbor Cultural Center 1000 Richmond Terrace, Livingston (718)
448-2500, or (718) 815-SNUG for tickets to events *www.snug-harbor.org*.
Snug Harbor's 26 architecturally impressive buildings are now home to art galleries, performance spaces, cultural and educational institutions, all set on 86
acres of wetlands, woods and botanical gardens. The complex includes the
Newhouse Center for Contemporary Art (admission $2; open Wed.–Fri. and
Sun 11 A.M.–5 P.M., Sat. 11 A.M.–7 P.M.); the **John Noble Maritime Collection** (718-447-6490; admission $3, $2 seniors and students; open Sat.–Sun. 1–5
P.M.); the **Staten Island Botanical Garden** (718-273-8200; *www.sibg.org*;
admission charges and hours for various parts vary), which encompasses the
Chinese Scholar's Garden; and the **Staten Island Children's Museum** (718-
273-2060; admission $5; open Tue.–Sun. noon–5 P.M., with an 11 A.M. open-
ing time in Jul.-Aug.) **Bus:** From the ferry terminal, head to Ramp D and take
the S-40 bus. Snug Harbor is less than 2 miles away.

Verrazano-Narrows Bridge With a main span of 4,260 feet, this is the longest
suspension bridge in the United States and the second longest in the world.
Even so, the Verrazano-Narrows forever plays second fiddle to the Brooklyn
Bridge. It lacks its elder sibling's pedestrian walkway, its close-up views of Manhattan and its rich, romantic history. But there's no denying the Verazzano's
grandeur, with a total length (including the approaches) of over two and a half
miles. Due to seasonal expansion and contraction of the bridge's cables, the
roadway can be 12 feet lower in the summer than in the winter.

The Verrazano-Narrows opened to traffic in 1964. It is the youngest span in
New York, but it is literally and figuratively linked to the past. The name comes
from Giovanni da Verrazano, the first European to sail into New York Harbor,
and the ends of the bridge lie in the historic guardians of the harbor: Brooklyn's
Fort Hamilton and Staten Island's Fort Wadsworth. Today, the bridge is the
only direct link between Brooklyn and Staten Island, and it offers the shortest
route between Long Island and the Middle Atlantic states.

AREA RESTAURANTS

Aesop's Tables 1233 Bay St., Rosebank (718) 720-2005. Among the best, with a garden out back.

Adobe Blues 63 Lafayette Ave., New Brighton (718) 720-2583. Casual Mexican, not far from St. George.

American Grill 420 Forest Ave., West Brighton (718) 442-4742. Good bet for American fare.

Cargo Cafe 120 Bay St., St. George (718) 876-0539. Much better than it looks. Great fries, and a five-minute walk from the ferry.

Denino's Pizzeria Tavern 524 Port Richmond Ave., Port Richmond (718) 442-9401. Thin-crust pizza and a big line to get in. Try the white pizza.

Killmeyer's Old Bavarian Inn 4254 Arthur Kill Rd., Charleston (718) 984-1202. German food, great old bar and a beer garden out back.

Ralph's Ice Cream Store 501 Port Richmond Ave., Port Richmond (718) 273-3675. The authority—in the city, not just the borough—on Italian ice.

The Arts

New York is a cauldron of creativity, the center of the nation's artistic life. Its galleries and stages feature the best and the brightest from all over the world.

Like so many other aspects of New York, the sheer number of artistic possibilities available here can be overwhelming to visitors. If you love painting, you can visit five world-class museums, or go gallery hopping in hopes of discovering new talent. Music lovers might be able to choose from among 10 or more classical music performances on a single evening. And it goes without saying that New York offers the best in American theater—from big, brassy Broadway musicals to experimental dramas.

Whatever your artistic interests, New York won't disappoint you. The only hard part will be choosing your pleasure.

ART MUSEUMS AND GALLERIES

New York City has dozens of museums and hundreds of art galleries. Even for the most committed art lover, it's a dizzying array of choices. First-time visitors might focus on the Metropolitan Museum of Art, which in itself is overwhelming in its scope. The hottest ticket in town is currently MoMA QNS, the temporary location for the Museum of Modern Art; its innovative gallery space and blockbuster shows ensure that it will continue to generate buzz even after the hoopla of its new opening has died down.

If your tastes lean toward contemporary art, make a beeline for the Whitney, the even more cutting-edge New Museum of Contemporary Art or P.S. 1, MoMA's more experimental sibling. Classicists may branch out beyond the Met to explore the Brooklyn Museum of Art, or smaller gems, such as the Frick.

Gallery-goers will find a cluster of blue-chip galleries on the East Side, around 57th Street and Madison Avenue. SoHo made its splash in the art world long ago, and has transformed itself from a daring new outpost of art into a more upscale neighborhood dotted with established, high-toned galleries. Chelsea (especially West Chelsea) boasts the hippest, most dynamic collection of galleries in Manhattan; it has blossomed from a funky frontier into a mature force in the contemporary art world. Harlem, too, has attracted a host of new artists as the neighborhood has gentrified. Out in Brooklyn, Williamsburg is bursting with creativity, with a much younger, lighter focus.

There's something for every taste. So read the listings that follow, see what piques your interest and plan your itinerary (consult the **Exploring New York** chapter to see what other sights are nearby). New York's art world doesn't sit still, so there's always something new to see, even for locals who spend a lifetime trying to take it all in.

Museum Mile

The Met, being the country's, if not the world's, premier art museum, is naturally the locus of art in the city and, particularly, of Museum Mile, the city's catchphrase for a stretch of Fifth Avenue on the Upper East Side of Manhattan that also encompasses the Frick Collection, the Guggenheim Museum, the National Academy of Design, the Jewish Museum, Neue Gallery New York, and several other institutions that encapsulate the artistic diversity of New York.

A visit to the Met should include checking out the European paintings, the Near Eastern and Egyptian rooms, and the Greek and Roman galleries, which include the coffered, skylit, barrel-vaulted gallery beside the Great Hall at the entrance to the museum (one of the city's most splendid public spaces). If you can't bear the inevitable crowds at the special exhibitions and in the Impressionist galleries, you should seek out less trammeled quarters. Examples include the Islamic galleries, with the burbling fountain in the Nur ad-Din Room; the Astor Court; a scholar's garden in the Chinese galleries, where you can approach Zen calm; the rooms of musical instruments, of arms and armor and of American pioneer and Colonial-era furniture, which are so obscure that you almost feel like a pioneer yourself for going to see them.

Another must on Museum Mile, the Frick Collection, is almost everyone's favorite small museum, the finest private collection put together in America, even counting Isabella Stewart Gardner's collection in Boston. The Frick building, a mansion designed in 1913 by Thomas Hastings, the architect of the New York Public Library, is one of the last of the great former private houses on Fifth Avenue. Picture for picture (Bellini, Holbein, Rembrandt, Vermeer, Fragonard, the list goes on), the quality of the collection is unsurpassed in America.

Farther up Museum Mile, tourists ogle Frank Lloyd Wright's spiral Guggenheim often without bothering about the art in it, although the perma-

Major Art Museums

Metropolitan Museum of Art   UPPER EAST SIDE
Fifth Ave. at 82nd St. (212) 535-7710   *www.metmuseum.org*
The Met is a national treasure, one of the world's great museums, ranking right up there with the Louvre. The collection as a whole is simply outstanding. From ancient Greek vases and statuary to canvases by Monet, Jasper Johns and Ellsworth Kelly, its variety is breathtaking.

This magnificent museum boasts more than two million works of art—paintings, sculpture, decorative arts, artifacts from ancient cultures, arms and armor, elegant clothing and musical instruments. There are 53 galleries devoted solely to European painters, and another maze is devoted to Americans.

nent collection, which includes the Justin K. Thannhauser Collection, is, after the Modern's collection, the top overview of art from the first half of the 20th century regularly available in the city.

The Jewish Museum is the best institution of its kind in the country, with not only objects related to the history of Judaism but also a strong exhibition program emphasizing modern and contemporary art.

The Whitney Museum of American Art, a block off Fifth, on Madison Avenue, isn't technically on Museum Mile but should be on the itinerary, too. It has permanent galleries where visitors can see the Hoppers and Calders they expect to find there, and a lively program of changing exhibitions.

The savvy traveler along Museum Mile also makes sure to see the less-heralded stops at the north end of Fifth. One of the best choices is El Museo del Barrio, a museum of the art and culture of Latin America and the city's expanding Latino community. Like the Studio Museum in Harlem, El Museo del Barrio was founded during the late 1960's in a period of upheaval, when artists of many backgrounds clamored for places to show their work. The Museum of Modern Art, with its stress on high European modernism and big-name postwar Americans, wasn't paying them enough attention, they felt, and so they came up with the idea of community-based institutions, the result being a new breadth of collections and exhibitions—and renewed debate, as these young museums themselves turned into established institutions and faced criticism from within their own diversifying communities.

New York, they demonstrated, rejects the status quo, whatever it may be, which is of course the city's virtue. Its museums reflect this fact as well as anything else. To travel along Museum Mile from Frick's mansion to El Museo del Barrio is to see a fraction of what's going on in art, but it's to go a long distance toward understanding the essential nature of a place where culture, like the rest of life, remains a moving target.

—*Michael Kimmelman*

(See the "Washington Heights/Inwood" *section in chapter* **Exploring New York** *for details on* **the Cloisters,** *the Met's showcase for medieval art.)*

NAVIGATING THE MET

Since the collection is far too large to absorb in a single visit, it's smart to draw up a game plan before you plunge in. Unfortunately, for all its grandeur, the Met doesn't make it easy to find your way around. There is a very general floor plan of the whole museum at both information desks as you enter the main lobby (available in several languages in addition to English). If you want a detailed map of where to find Rembrandt, van Gogh or another specific artist, you have to ask. There are two detailed maps for the European paintings and sculpture, none for other collections.

Some galleries are numbered, but many aren't. As you enter a gallery, you may see numbers on your right and on your left; as a general rule, the one on your right is the one you are entering.

Finding the daily tour schedule is another challenge. It is posted on a obscured wall at the southern end of the lobby, to your left as you enter, just before the long corridor of Greek and Roman statuary. The children's gift shop is hidden, too. It's at the top of the main stairway, to the right, but you wouldn't know it until you are at the door. The escalator to the second floor isn't obvious, either; look left as you approach the main stairs.

Best bet: The Met's Web site (**www.metmuseum.org**) is excellent. Things that are hard to find in the museum itself are easy to find online, including daily schedules of tours and gallery talks, the exact location of the painting you're looking for, and everything else you might want to know before you mount the steps on Fifth Avenue.

Once you're at the museum, ask any uniformed guard to help you find your way. They are walking, talking catalogs, and they're happy to help.

Each of the Met's departments is a museum in itself. It would take more than an afternoon to fully explore the holdings of any one section. Wandering through the galleries, you'll stumble onto some wonderful surprises—a living room designed by Frank Lloyd Wright in the American Wing, a detailed scale model of the Parthenon at the street-level entrance to the museum, a tranquil Chinese scholar's garden in the Astor Court on the second floor and, in the music collection nearby, violins made by Nicolo Amati and his student Antonio Stradivari in the 17th century.

You may get more from your visit, however, by picking some objects or areas ahead of time, and searching them out. Or take a "highlights" tour to see what interests you and then go back and give it more time yourself.

Among the many **special exhitions** to look for are: "Richard Avedon: Portraits," running from late September 2002 through early January 2003; the Janice Levin Collection of Impressionist Paintings, scheduled from mid-November 2002 through early February 2003; and "Manet/Velázquez: The French Taste for Spanish Painting," running from March 4 through June 8, 2003.

Main Floor

As you enter the main lobby, the **Egyptian Art** collections and the **Temple of Dendur** are to your right, **Greek and Roman Art** to your left.

At the entrance to the Egyptian section, kids can walk right into a spooky tomb. The Met's own archeological explorations are responsible for more than half of the collection, which extends chronologically through 40 galleries. The Temple of Dendur was a gift from Egypt in recognition of U.S. aid in saving ancient monuments from the rising waters of the Nile behind the Aswan Dam.

The Greek and Roman works encompass a full range of classical art, from jewelry and pottery to sculpture and painting, with prize examples of Greek vases and Roman portrait busts.

Beyond these galleries lie a spacious **cafeteria** and a **restaurant** (which may be moving, so check ahead.)

Straight through the main lobby from the entrance, passing to either side of the main stairway, you will find **Medieval Art** and a large spread of **European Sculpture and Decorative Arts.** This is one of the museum's largest collections. One of its gems is an ornate 15th-century *studiolo*—it means "little study"—with walls of inlaid woodwork that look three-dimensional but are actually flat. There are only two such rooms in the world, this one and another in the ducal palace in Urbino, Italy.

Continuing straight ahead to the back of the museum, don't miss the eclectic **Robert Lehman Collection** of Impressionists and Old Masters, paintings and drawings, and pieces of decorative art. The gallery space, on two floors, is designed to evoke Lehman's own stately home on East 54th Street in Manhattan. Highlights include an "Annunciation" by Botticelli; a Rembrandt sketch of Leonardo's "Last Supper"; a Leonardo sketch of "A Bear Walking"; paintings by Rembrandt, El Greco, Goya, Renoir, Seurat and van Gogh; and some impressive pieces of Renaissance earthenware and Venetian glass.

The southern flank of the first floor houses the **Arts of Africa, Oceania and the Americas** and a series of galleries of **20th-century art.** The third-world collections are based on an entire museum given to the Met by Nelson Rockefeller (the Museum of Primitive Art, which he founded). Highlights include royal decorative art from the Court of Benin in Nigeria, and the world's most comprehensive collection of gold objects from the Americas.

The **20th-century collection,** on two floors in the southwest corner of the building, is where to find Jasper Johns, Picasso, Braque, Modigliani, O'Keeffe and Pollock.

In the northern flank of the first floor is the stunning **Arms and Armor** collection, as well as the **Temple of Dendur.** Another knockout at the same end of the museum is a grand wrap-around panorama of the palace and gardens at Versailles, from the early 1800's. Standing in the center of this large chamber, you can imagine you are there on the palace steps. And while you are at the north end of the building, check out the Met's collection of classic baseball cards, exhibited in the hallway behind Dendur on the way to Versailles.

The Arms and Armor collection is unique among American museums, with elegantly etched armor and weaponry ranging from the fourth century B.C. to the 19th century A.D., and from ancient Egypt and Islam to the Americas. The Japanese pieces are generally regarded as the finest anywhere outside Japan.

The **American Wing,** on two floors, is a magnet for tourists and New Yorkers alike. Everyone will recognize the epic "George Washington Crossing the Delaware," 21 feet wide, painted in Düsseldorf some 75 years after the fact by Emanuel Leutze. Note also the surrounding display of that particular gallery (no. 223). It has been arranged to resemble the museums of a century ago, crammed full of art, with three, four or five paintings hung one above the other.

Elsewhere in this wing are familiar Washington portraits by Gilbert Stuart and Charles Willson Peale, as well as John Singer Sargent's "Madame X," Frederic Church's "Heart of the Andes," Alfred Bierstadt's "Rocky Mountains: Lander's Peak," along with paintings by Winslow Homer, James McNeill Whistler and Mary Cassatt (whose brother, president of the Pennsylvania Railroad, told her she would never amount to anything as a painter), and sculptures by Frederic Remington and John Quincy Adams Ward.

Extraordinary features of the wing include **25 period rooms,** furnished and decorated just as they were in years and centuries past; a renowned collection of **stained glass,** much of it by Louis Comfort Tiffany; and an upstairs "attic" of shelves where the museum displays things it doesn't have room to display out front. There you will see rows of antique chairs, Lincoln busts, crystal goblets and much, much more. This sort of display is especially useful to students and scholars, but made interesting for anyone by its sheer volume.

Second Floor

Straight ahead at the top of the central stairway from the lobby, push through a pair of glass doors and enter the wonderful world of **European Paintings.** This is one of the two collections for which there are detailed maps if you ask for them at the information desk in the lobby. The works here are the Old Masters—starting with three enormous paintings by Tiepolo in the first gallery, past an remarkable diptych of "The Crucifixion" and "The Last Judgment" by Jan van Eyck (the most celebrated painter of 15th-century Europe), to Bruegel, Rubens, El Greco, Raphael, Titian, Tintoretto, Vermeer, Rembrandt, Hals, Gainsborough, Velázquez, Fragonard, Goya and still more. The Met has more Vermeers than any other museum.

These galleries are not to be confused with **Nineteenth-Century European Paintings and Sculpture**—the second collection for which there is a detailed map. Reach this area by turning left at the top of the central stairs and walking through a long gallery hall of etchings and photographs. Don't hurry. The etchings are the works of great artists; they illustrate how an artist sketches out ideas for later paintings—whole scenes, or a torso, or maybe just an elbow or a nose.

In the 19th-century galleries you will find the popular works of the **Impressionists,** but first a large expanse of Rodin's sculptured marbles. Inside are the young Claude Monet's vibrantly colorful "Garden at Sainte-Adresse," daring for its time; a Cézanne still-life once owned by Monet; Edouard Manet's peaceful "Boating"; van Gogh's "Cypresses"; and room after room featuring Bonnard, Degas, Rousseau, Daumier, Toulouse-Lautrec, Renoir and more.

Adjacent to these galleries are, to the west, the second-floor space of the **20th-Century Art** collection, and on the Fifth Avenue side to the east, **Islamic Art** and **Ancient Near Eastern Art.** The long Fifth Avenue side of the second floor proceeds geographically from the Near East at the southern end, through the balcony over the lobby to a half-dozen sectors of **Asian Art—Chinese, Japanese, Korean, South Asian and Southeast Asian**—at the northern end.

The Islamic collection may be the most comprehensive permanent Islamic art installation anywhere. Items of note include miniature paintings and huge 16th- and 17th-century carpets, as well as glass and metalwork from Egypt and Mesopotamia. Ancient and Near Eastern Art spans nearly 9,000 years, from Mesopotamia to the Indian subcontinent. The Asian collections are reputed to be the largest and most comprehensive in the West; they're best known for their

Chinese calligraphy, folding screens and other decorative objects from Japan, sculpture from Southeast Asia and paintings from the Himalayan kingdoms. Here, too, is the restful **Chinese Scholar's Garden** called Astor Court, behind a wall with a round entryway symbolizing a full moon. Enter and sit a few minutes. You will be almost alone.

Close by are the upper floor of the **American Wing** and the **Musical Instruments** collection, where you will find a piano made by the instrument's inventor, Bartolomeo Cristofori; two guitars owned and used by Andres Segovia; and all sorts of rare horns, harps and other music makers from distant lands and other times.

Ground Floor

Entering the museum through the street-level door to the south of the outside steps, or through the parking garage, there is an information desk where you'll pay your admission fee, a splendid model of the Acropolis, and a coat check (where the line moves faster than at the one upstairs in the main lobby). The museum library is down here, too.

The galleries of **The Costume Institute** are also on the ground floor, but they are entered from above, by stairs or an elevator from the main floor in the middle of Egyptian Art. A little hard to find, the institute is a small three-gallery treasure. Fashions dating from the 18th century and to the present are exhibited on mannequins in glass showcases with informative descriptions, and shows are organized around themes and particular designers.

Sculpture Garden

Last but not least, weather permiting, take yourself up to the rooftop **Sculpture Garden,** not only for the sculpture but for an aerial view of Central Park. The **cafe** here is a nice place to take a break.

Admission: $10 adults; $5 students and seniors; children under 12 free with an adult. **Hours:** Fri.–Sat. 9:30 A.M.–9 P.M.; Sun. and Tue.–Thu. 9:30 A.M.– 5:30 P.M. Closed Mon. **Special programs:** Check the museum's online calendar for guided tours, gallery talks, lectures, films, workshops and family activities; most are free with museum admission. The Great Hall Balcony Bar is open Fri. –Sat. evenings, with live music 5–8 P.M. **Subway:** 4, 5, 6 to 86th St.

Solomon R. Guggenheim Museum   UPPER EAST SIDE
1071 Fifth Ave. (at 89th St.) (212) 423-3500   *www.guggenheim.org*

Long before it was completed in 1959, the Guggenheim—the strange round building in a city full of square boxes—was already suffering darts from critics. It was called everything from a washtub to an indigestible hot-cross bun. Robert Moses, the city's irascible master builder, said it looked like an inverted oatmeal dish.

But the museum's creator, Frank Lloyd Wright, called it nothing less than "the liberation of painting by architecture." And on the first Sunday it opened, 10,000 people lined up to get in for 50 cents a head. (Only 6,000 made it; bribes offered to guards did not work.)

The Guggenheim as Architecture

Frank Lloyd Wright's Guggenheim has always been like an explosion on Fifth Avenue. It is strident, it is loud, it defers not a whit to anything around it. It breaks every rule. It is so astonishing as a piece of architecture, of course, that it makes you feel that rules hardly matter. But the very way in which Wright's building breaks the rules of urban design becomes its own rule: the way it clashes with its surroundings is the way the Guggenheim communicates its architectural essence.

It has been a commonplace since this building opened in 1959 to speak of it as inhospitable to paintings, to talk of the long spiral ramp and slanted walls as Wright's way of forcing painting to be subservient to architecture. While this complaint has always been exaggerated—Wright's space can work wonderfully for the display of large Color Field abstractions, Calder mobiles, Pop Art and other postwar works—there is no question that the architecture fights the art a lot of the time. The building usually ends up in the foreground of one's consciousness, no matter what the paintings.

The rush of joy that Wright's great rotunda brings has always been worth its limitations as a gallery. There aren't a lot of cathedrals in New York—never mind that, there isn't a lot of architecture anywhere that is capable of making the heart beat faster, that so fills you with the sense that the making of enclosure can be an act of opening up, a discovery of noble possibilities. It is a wonderful paradox to find, in the act of enclosing, revelation. There is nowhere else in New York where the passion of architecture is more clearly there, set more directly in front of us for all to see and understand.

The north side addition (1992) contains double-height galleries, which give the Guggenheim the ability to display large contemporary canvases for the first time. While the galleries are not ideal display spaces—they are a bit narrow, and the elevator core intrudes partway into them—they are more versatile than anything the museum has had until now. This, then, is the great achievement: the building is now a better museum and a better work of architecture. If the Guggenheim's roles as a museum and as a piece of architecture have always been somewhat at odds, this renovation at least partly resolves them.

—*Paul Goldberger*

Today, after a $24 million renovation and the addition of a controversial 10-story annex in 1992, the landmarked museum, considered by some to be Wright's masterpiece, is celebrating its 40th anniversary. Along with one of the world's largest collections of Vasily Kandinsky, it has works by many major 20th-century artists—Constantin Brancusi, Alexander Calder, Marc Chagall, Robert Delaunay, Paul Klee, Joan Miro and Pablo Picasso. The building itself is, of course, a major attraction. And worth the trip, despite its admission charge, which is one of the highest in the city.

The Solomon R. Guggenheim Museum

Instead of moving from room to room, as in other museums, you take the elevator to the top, 92 feet up, then soak up the art as you descend a gently sloping circular ramp, glancing across the sweeping rotunda at other art lovers winding their way around you.   —*Randy Kennedy*

Admission: $12 adults; $8 students and seniors; children 12 and under free. **Hours:** Fri.–Sat. 9 A.M.–8 P.M.; Sun.–Wed. 9 A.M.–6 P.M. Closed Thu. **Special programs:** Check the Web site for a schedule of guided tours, lectures, films, workshops and family activities. Tours are free, but other programs require a fee and advance registration. **Subway:** 4, 5, 6 to 86th St.

Frick Collection   UPPER EAST SIDE
1 E. 70th St. (between Fifth and Madison Aves.) (212) 288-0700 *www.frick.org*
This stately Upper East Side mansion, completed in 1914, offers a fascinating glimpse into New York's Gilded Age. Each lavishly furnished room has been preserved much as it was during the heyday of its owner, Henry Clay Frick (1849–1919), a railroad and steel baron. Frick amassed an extraordinary personal art collection (not to mention an array of 18th-century French furniture, Chinese porcelain vases and Italian bronzes). Start by viewing the video that's screened every half hour in the Music Room, and consider taking the free audio guide to the permanent collection that's included with your admission fee and available in several languages.

The galleries are intimate and serene; care is taken to offer appropriate lighting and a quiet atmosphere, allowing the art to shine. Highlights of the permanent collection include Bellini's "Saint Francis in Ecstasy," dell Francesca's "St. John the Evangelist," van Eyck's "Virgin With Child, With

Saints and Donor," Vermeer's "Officer and Laughing Girl," Holbein's "Sir Thomas More and Thomas Cromwell," Rembrandt's "Self-Portrait," and Stuart's "George Washington."

Admission: $10 adults; $5 seniors and students. No children under age 10; ages 10–16 must be accompanied by an adult. **Hours:** Tue.–Thu. and Sat. 10 A.M.–6 P.M.; Fri. 10 A.M.–9 P.M.; Sun. 1–6 P.M. Closed Mon. **Special programs:** Frequent free lectures and classical and chamber-music concerts; check the Web site for details. **Subway:** 6 to 68th St.

Whitney Museum of American Art   UPPER EAST SIDE
945 Madison Ave. (at 75th St.) (212) 570-3676   *www.whitney.org*

Founded in 1914 by Gertrude Vanderbilt Whitney—mostly as a response to a rebuff from the Metropolitan Museum, which refused donation of the original 500-work collection—the Whitney opened in 1931 in three adjoining Greenwich Village brownstones. Today its home is a hulking Madison Avenue building designed by Bauhaus icon Marcel Breuer.

The Whitney takes a dynamic and uninhibited approach to 20th-century and contemporary American art; it's a more freewheeling and controversial collection that what you'll find at MoMA. Two entire floors, redesigned since 1998, showcase highlights of the comprehensive permanent collection, which features seminal works by Louise Nevelson, Claes Oldenburg, Reginald Marsh, Jasper Johns and Georgia O'Keeffe—not to mention the entire artistic estate of Edward Hopper. Most visitors are enchanted by Alexander Calder's charming "Calder's Circus," an intricate installation that recreates an entire miniature Big Top performance.

Every two years, the Whitney stages the **Biennial,** a much-hyped and often-controversial exhibition that surveys the cutting edge of contemporary American art (next scheduled for spring 2004).

Sarabeth's at the Whitney is a huge cut above the typical museum cafeteria; it's a lovely place to take a lunch break.

(See "Other Art Museums" *below, for details on the* **Whitney Museum of Art—Philip Morris Branch,** *the museum's small corporate-funded offshoot.)*

Admission: $12 adults; $9.50 students and seniors; members and children under 12 free. Fri. 6–9 P.M., pay as you wish. **Hours:** Tue.–Thu. and Sat. –Sun. 11 A.M.–6 P.M.; Fri. 1–9 P.M. Closed Mon. **Special programs:** Free guided tours daily; check the Web site for lectures, seminars, walking tours, family activities, concerts, films and workshops. **Subway:** 6 to 77th St.

MoMA QNS   QUEENS
33rd St. and Queens Blvd. (212) 708-9400   *www.moma.org*

Let's first be grateful they didn't just shut down until the renovations on West 53rd Street in Manhattan are finished in 2005. Instead, the Museum of Modern Art has moved into a temporary home in Long Island City, in the former Swingline staple factory.

The new facility, cleverly designed by Michael Maltzan, with Scott Newman of Cooper, Robertson & Partners, is not small, although with 25,000 square feet

MoMA QNS

of gallery space, it's smaller than you might imagine for such a great institution. (Expect bedlam for the "Picasso and Matisse" show scheduled to run from February 13 through May 19, 2003.) But overall, it's a relief to find a museum that has become more, not less manageable in size, even if this condition was born of necessity, not principle, during the interim before the Modern reopens on a gigantic scale back in Manhattan.

The lack of windows, the polished gray concrete floors, movable white walls and black-painted ductwork on the ceiling approximate the classic industrial loft aesthetic, an openwork plan with movable partitions that benefits the open-endedness of modern art. The galleries are efficient and airless, like the inside of a storage center, which is exactly what this building is. On the other hand, there is something touching and apt about seeing priceless Cézannes, Seurats and Braques in a makeshift, unadorned setting: they look fresh and by contrast seem to pop off the walls. The galleries will do for a few years, and there's plenty to mull over in them now, starting with the films and videos flickering on the walls around the lobby, a decorative distraction that brightens the elegantly complicated choreography of the serpentine ramps.

The paintings collection, obviously truncated in more limited space, has enough of the museum's favorites (Picasso's "Demioselles d' Avignon," Cézanne's "Male Bather") to placate traditionalists, but what's interesting is that the tilt of the display seems more toward the recent past than it was on 53rd Street. The byproduct of the reduced galleries and their open layout is a fortuitous telescoping of art across the last century, so that you now see, in the same space, Mondrian, Ellsworth Kelly, Blinky Palermo, Matisse and Pollack.

—*Michael Kimmelman*

Art in the Outer Boroughs

Most Manhattanites are convinced that their island borough is the center of the universe, artistically speaking (and in every other way, too, but that's another story). But despite Manhattan's dominance, there's a flourishing cultural life in the outer boroughs. Outer-borough attractions are covered in detail in the **Exploring New York** chapter, but a number of highlights deserve special mention here.

The big news on the museum scene this year is MoMA's temporary move from Midtown Manhattan to Long Island City, Queens. Actually, Queens has been quietly evolving for years as a locale for artists and museums, of which the Modern's arrival is only the latest sign. MoMA's relocation places the main museum in closer proximity to its more cutting-edge affiliate, **P.S. 1** (*www.ps1.org*), located at 22-25 Jackson Ave., Long Island City. P.S. 1 is devoted solely to contemporary arts, with frequently changing exhibits and an acclaimed studio program. Also worth a visit on a nice day is the funky **Socrates Sculpture Park** (*www.socratessculpturepark.org*), where an array of large-scale outdoor sculpture enjoys an East River setting at Broadway and Vernon Boulevard.

Long Island City is also home to the **Isamu Noguchi Garden Museum** (*www.noguchi.org*), which displays a wonderful collection of works from this acclaimed Japanese-American sculptor. A renovation of its permanent site in Long Island City began in February 2002; while that location is closed, there's a temporary exhibition space at 36-01 43rd Avenue in nearby Sunnyside, Queens. Housed in the same Sunnyside building is the temporary home of the **Museum of African Art** (*www.africanart.org*), which will reside in Queens until its new home on Manhattan's Museum Mile is completed in 2005.

In Astoria, Queens, exhibits at the **American Museum of the Moving Image** (*www.ammi.org*) offer a fascinating glimpse into the art of filmmaking—supplemented, of course, by frequent screenings, lectures and panel discussions.

Note: MoMA has always had an exceptionally strong collection of international films, Hollywood movies, TV documentaries and video art. While the Midtown location is being renovated, MoMA will run its film and media exhibitions in the **Gramercy Theatre** on East 23rd Street (212-777-4900) beginning in October 2002. Admission prices are the same as those at MoMA QNS (though visitors will receive free admission with a MoMA Qns ticket stub from the previous seven calendar days, and vice versa).

Admission: $12 adults; $8.50 students and seniors; children under age 16 accompanied by an adult free. Fri. 4–7:45 P.M. pay as you wish. **Hours:** Sat.–Mon. and Thu. 10 A.M.–5 P.M.; Fri. 10 A.M.–7:45 P.M. Closed Tue.–Wed. **Subway:** 7 local train to 33rd St./Queens. (*See the box* "Art in the

On weekends, you can visit all of the museums mentioned above by taking advantage of the brand-new **Queens Artlink** (*www.moma.org/qal*), a free shuttle bus that runs continuously between MoMA QNS, P.S. 1, the Noguchi Museum, the Socrates Sculpture Park and the American Museum of the Moving Image on Saturdays and Sundays from 11:30 A.M. to 5:30 P.M.

In Flushing Meadows/Corona Park, the **Queens Museum of Art** (*www.queensmuse.org*) boasts a wide array of holdings, including a fascinating scale model of New York City created for the 1939 World's Fair and a large collection of Tiffany glass.

Brooklyn also boasts a thriving arts scene. **Williamsburg** is bursting with galleries and art installations, with a focus on edgy young artists. A stroll along Bedford Avenue, the neighborhood's main drag, will give you a good snapshot of Williamsburg's personality.

The **Brooklyn Museum of Art** (*www.brooklynmuseum.org*) is an outstanding museum, well worth a trip from Manhattan. Its temporary exhibitions are often blockbusters, and its permanent collection is wide-ranging, encompassing ancient Egyptian artifacts, European and American painting and sculpture, extensive Asian and African galleries, and dozens of period rooms displaying the decorative arts.

The prestigious **Brooklyn Academy of Music** (*www.bam.org*) is the oldest performing arts center in the nation; its inventive programming draws huge crowds and has given its neighborhood, Fort Greene, an interesting, funky personality.

Up in the Bronx, art lovers may want to check out the **New York Botanical Garden** (*www.nybg.org*). Until August 2003, 15 masterpieces from MoMA's sculpture collection are on display in a specially designed setting within the courtyard of the garden's magnificent Victorian glasshouse. Innovative plantings, elegant reflecting pools and towering evergreens provide a gorgeous setting for sculpture by Rodin, Picasso and Henry Moore.

Outer Boroughs" *for details on MoMA's* **P.S. 1** *affiliate and other Long Island City attractions, plus the new* **Artlink** *shuttle bus. See also the* "Queens" *section in chapter* **Exploring New York** *for further details and nearby dining choices.)*

Other Art Museums

(For other types of museums and historic houses, many containing collections of art, see chapter **Exploring New York**. *Also see section* "Institutes of World Culture," *at the end of this chapter.)*

American Craft Museum MIDTOWN WEST 40 W. 53rd St. (between Fifth and Sixth Aves.) (212) 956-3535 *www.americancraftmuseum.org*. This institution is dedicated to exhibiting and supporting contemporary crafts. A visit here will dispel the notion that crafts aren't truly an art form—you'll see no macaroni necklaces on the museum's three floors of exhibition space. Instead, the work ranges from utilitarian objects with a strong aesthetic focus to sculptural pieces with a barely conceivable utility. The exhibits tend to be carefully designed and thematic, exploring a single craft, material or artist. Don't miss the lovely gift shop. The museum will eventually move to a new home at 2 Columbus Circle. **Admission:** $8 adults; $5 seniors and students; children under 12 free. Thu. 6–8 P.M., pay as you wish. **Hours:** Fri.–Wed. 10 A.M.–6 P.M.; Thu. 10 A.M.–8 P.M. **Subway:** E, V to Fifth Ave.; N, R to 49th St.

American Folk Art Museum MIDTOWN WEST 45 W. 53rd St. (between Fifth and Sixth Aves.) (212) 265-1040 *www.folkartmuseum.org*. This small gem of a museum is worth a visit not only for its fascinating look at the American folk-art tradition, but also for its stunning gallery space—a brand-new, state-of-the-art facility that won glowing reviews for architects Tod Williams and Billie Tsien. This wonderful building finally gives the museum a presence in the city's cultural scene that had long eluded it. The collection offers a glimpse into America's shared national experiences and the diversity of its heritage, with items such as weathervanes, textiles, flags, quilts, sculpture, 18th- and 19th-century portraits and more. The museum also mounts provocative shows of "outsider art," or "untrained art." Don't miss the wonderful gift shop. **Admission:** $9 adults; $5 students and seniors; children under 12 free; free for everyone Fri. 6–8 P.M. **Hours:** Tue.–Sun. 10 A.M.–6 P.M.; Fri. 10 A.M.–8 P.M. Closed Mon. **Subway:** E, V to Fifth Ave.; B, D, F, Q, V to 47th–50th Sts./Rockefeller Center. The museum has an annex, the **Eva and Morris Feld Gallery,** in its old location at 2 Lincoln Square, across from Lincoln Center; admission is free.

The Cloisters WASHINTON HEIGHTS/INWOOD Fort Tryon Park (212)923-3700 *www.metmuseum.org*. Perched on a cliff overlooking the Hudson in the northernmost reaches of Manhattan, this is the Metropolitan Museum's satellite branch, an extraordinary collection of art and architecture from medieval Europe. *(See full listing in* "Washington Heights/Inwood" *section of chapter* **Exploring New York***.)*

Cooper-Hewitt National Design Museum UPPER EAST SIDE 2 E. 91st St. (at Fifth Ave.) (212) 849-8300 *www.si.edu/ndm/*. Peter Cooper would have been proud. The small museum he envisioned more than 100 years ago to support Cooper Union's instruction in the applied arts developed into what is now the country's best place to view and study design. In 1897 Sarah, Eleanor and Amy Hewitt, Cooper's granddaughters, opened a museum modeled after Paris's Musée des Arts Décoratifs in the Cooper Union Building. The museum has amassed a collection encompassing objects as diverse as radiators, gloves and 18th-century French furniture, all of them showcasing the beauty and utility of fine design. Part of the Smithsonian Institution since 1969, it later moved to Andrew Carnegie's Fifth Avenue mansion. Recent shows have focused on everything from Alexander Calder's designs for everyday objects to architects' plans for doghouses. From November 2002 to February 2003, look for an exhibit titled

"New Hotels for Global Nomads." **Admission:** $8 adults; $5 students and seniors; children under 12 free; Tue. 5–9 P.M. free for everyone. **Hours:** Tue. 10 A.M.–9 P.M.; Wed.–Sat. 10 A.M.–5 P.M.; Sun. noon–5 P.M. Closed Mon. **Subway:** 4, 5, 6 to 86th St. or 96th St.

Dahesh Museum MIDTOWN EAST 601 Fifth Ave. (between 48th and 49th Sts.) (212) 759-0606 *www.daheshmuseum.org.* The Dahesh Museum's mission is collecting, preserving, exhibiting and interpreting 19th- and 20th-century European academic art. Modern art was founded in opposition to academic art, which was subsequently dismissed for over a century. As the word "academic" became derogatory, once-influential artists and teachers like William-Adolphe Bouguereau, Jean-Léon Gérome and Alexandre Cabanel were derided as reactionaries. More recent scholarship has taken a less ideological view. Drawing from its own collection as well as others, the Dahesh allows the most popular art of its time to be seen on its own terms. **Admission:** Free. **Hours:** Tue.–Sat. 11 A.M.–6 P.M. Closed Sun.–Mon. **Subway:** B, D, F, S, V to 47th-50th St.–Rockefeller Center; 6 to 51st St.

Dia Center for the Arts CHELSEA 545 and 548 W. 22nd St. (between 10th and 11th Aves.) (212) 989-5566 *www.diacenter.org.* The Dia Center was a pioneer on the art world's latest frontier, West Chelsea. It provides exhibition space for large-scale works—particularly earth works and Minimalist sculpture—that conventional museums have trouble accommodating. In addition to long-term installations, including Walter De Maria's "Earth Room" and "Broken Kilometer," this 40,000-square-foot renovated warehouse also focuses on single-artist exhibitions that last anywhere from a few months to several years. Dia operates a space across the street from the main building, which also hosts installations. The center is also one of Chelsea's best hangouts, including a rooftop coffee bar overlooking the Hudson River—especially nice at sunset. The permanent collection includes works by Joseph Beuys, John Chamberlain, Walter De Maria, Dan Flavin, Donald Judd, Imi Knoebel, Blinky Palermo, Fred Sandback, Cy Twombly and Andy Warhol. **Admission:** $6 adults; $3 students and seniors; children under 10 free. **Hours:** Wed.–Sun. noon–6 P.M. Closed Mon.–Tue. **Special programs:** Check the Web site for lectures, poetry readings, music performances and more. **Subway:** C, E, 1, 9 to 23rd St.

Drawing Center SOHO 35 Wooster St. (between Broome and Grand Sts.) (212) 219-2166 *www.drawingcenter.org.* This small nonprofit museum is dedicated to drawings, loosely defined as original works on paper. Past exhibits have included wall drawings, monoprints and computer-generated drawings. In addition to its four or five annual group shows, usually featuring emerging artists, the center mounts historical and special exhibitions, such as the working drawings of Ellsworth Kelly. Across the street is the Drawing Room, an annex dedicated to site-specific projects by individual artists. The gallery sponsors the "Line Reading" series, which features prominent authors exploring the relationship between literature and the visual arts; there are also children's programs, lectures and performances. **Admission:** Free. **Hours:** Tue.–Fri. 10 A.M.–6 P.M.; Sat. 11 A.M.–6 P.M. **Subway:** J, M, N, Q, R, W, Z, 1, 6, 9 to Canal St.

El Museo del Barrio UPPER EAST SIDE 1230 Fifth Ave. (at 104th St.) (212) 831-7272 *www.elmuseo.org*. Located in Central Park's Heckscher Building, El Museo was founded by a group of Puerto Rican educators, artists and activists in 1969 to serve the Puerto Rican community in nearby Spanish Harlem. Its mission has since expanded in response to the growth of New York's Latino population—particularly the Mexican, Central and South American, and Caribbean communities. The collection ranges from pre-Columbian artifacts to contemporary videos to a splendid installation of Puerto Rican religious figures called *santos*. **Admission:** $5 adults; $3 students and seniors; children under 12 free. **Hours:** Wed.–Sun. 11 A.M.–5 P.M. **Subway:** 6 to 103rd St.

International Center of Photography MIDTOWN WEST 1114 Sixth Ave. (at 43rd St.) (212) 857-0000 *www.icp.org*. Established in 1974 on Museum Mile, the ICP relocated to Midtown in 2000. These sleek new galleries offer expanded exhibit space for the ICP's permanent collection and frequently changing temporary exhibitions. The museum's scope encompasses everything from fashion photography to photojournalism, including the complete works of Robert Capa, the founder's brother. In addition to hosting lectures, films and gallery tours, ICP also offers an extensive roster of continuing-education courses. **Admission:** $9 adults; $6 seniors and students. **Hours:** Tue.–Thu. 10 A.M.–5 P.M.; Fri. 10 A.M.–8 P.M.; Sat.–Sun. 10 A.M.–6 P.M. Closed Mon. **Subway:** B, D, F, V to 42nd St.

Miriam and Ira D. Wallach Art Gallery UPPER WEST SIDE Columbia University, Schermerhorn Hall (between Broadway and Amsterdam Ave.) (212) 854-7288 *www.columbia.edu/cu/wallach*. This facility serves Columbia as a resource for teaching and study, and a public exhibition space. As its curators are often graduate students and faculty from the art history department, the gallery's exhibitions tend to be well researched and often have titles that require two sentences and a colon. They are nevertheless treasure troves, presenting issues, methods and art not often seen elsewhere. **Admission:** Free. **Hours:** Wed.–Sat. 1–5 P.M. **Subway:** 1, 9 to 116th St.

National Academy of Design UPPER EAST SIDE 1083 Fifth Ave. (between 89th and 90th Sts.) (212) 369-4880 *www.nationalacademy.org*. Occupying a grand Beaux Arts town house on Museum Mile, this institution aims to uphold the academic tradition by sponsoring a fine arts school and a professional organization for artists. The museum here, in addition to hosting the nation's oldest juried show and rotating temporary exhibits, has a large permanent collection of 19th- and 20th-century American art. Its holdings range from the landscapes of the Hudson River School to masterworks of Fauvism, abstraction and magic-realism. **Admission:** $8 adults; $4.50 students and seniors. **Hours:** Wed.–Thu. noon–5 P.M., Fri.–Sun 11 A.M.–6 P.M. Closed Mon.–Tue. **Subway:** 4, 5, 6 to 86th St.

Neue Gallery New York UPPER EAST SIDE 1048 Fifth Ave. (at 86th St.) (212) 628-6200 *www.neuegallery.org.* In late 2001, this brand-new facility opened its doors on Museum Mile. Focusing on the art of Germany and Austria, the collection of painting, sculpture and decorative arts features works by Gustav Klimt, Max Beckmann, Erich Heckel and others. Special programming includes chamber music, cabaret performances, lectures and film. The museum's Café Sabarsky is a lovely spot to indulge in a traditional Viennese pastry. **Admission:** $10 adults; $7 students and seniors. No children under age 12; ages 12–16 must be accompanied by an adult. **Hours:** Sat.–Mon. 11 A.M.–6 P.M., Fri. 11 A.M.–9 P.M. Closed Tue.–Thu. **Subway:** 4, 5, 6 to 86th St.

New Museum of Contemporary Art SOHO 583 Broadway (between Prince and Houston Sts.) (212) 219-1222 *www.newmuseum.org.* The New Museum lives on the cutting edge of the art world; it's built a reputation for controversial exhibitions, edgy programs and a mixed critical reception. The focus is global, with works in a wide range of media, and the curation is provocative. The museum hosts a variety of panel discussions, film screenings and lectures. The Zenith Media Lounge (free admission) is dedicated to experimental video and digital art. **Admission:** $6 adults; children 18 and under free; free for everyone Thu. 6–8 P.M. **Hours:** Tue.–Wed. and Fri.–Sun. noon–6 P.M.; Thu. noon–8 P.M. Closed Mon. **Subway:** F, S, V to Broadway–Lafayette St.; C, E, N, R to Prince St.; 6 to Spring St. or Bleecker St.

Nicholas Roerich Museum UPPER WEST SIDE 319 W. 107th St. (between Broadway and Riverside Dr.) (212) 864-7752 *www.roerich.org.* Nicholas Roerich, the Russian-American star of this one-man museum, was a true Renaissance man, involved in a vast range of artistic, philosophical and spiritual pursuits. He worked with Stravinsky to design sets and costumes, studied Russian archaeology, wrote, painted and traveled extensively. The museum features a permanent collection of Roerich's works and personal memorabilia, including numerous paintings inspired by his interest in Buddhism and the Tibetan highlands. **Hours:** Tues.–Sun. 2–5 P.M. **Subway:** 1, 9 to 110th St.

Studio Museum in Harlem 144 W. 125th St. (between Lenox Ave. and Adam Clayton Powell Blvd.) (212) 864-4500 *www.studiomuseuminharlem.org.* Dedicated to African-American art, as well as work from Africa and throughout the diaspora, the Studio Museum was organized in 1967. The permanent collection includes works by Romare Bearden, Elizabeth Catlett, Jacob Lawrence and Norman Lewis, and the James Van Der Zee photographic archives; there's also a changing array of thematic and single-artist shows. The museum has undergone an extensive renovation in the last couple of years, adding a new gallery space, an auditorium, workshop space, a reading room and a cafe. **Admission:** $5 adults; $3 students and seniors; $1 children under 12; free first Sat. each month. **Hours:** Sun. and Wed.–Fri. noon–6 P.M.; Sat. 10 A.M.–6 P.M. Closed Mon.–Tue. **Subway:** 2, 3 to 125th St.

Whitney Museum of American Art—Philip Morris Branch MIDTOWN EAST 120 Park Ave. (at 42nd St.) (917) 663-2453. Philip Morris's headquarters

building across the street from Grand Central Terminal houses a Midtown exhibition space for the Whitney Museum. The Sculpture Court accommodates
large sculptures that the museum cannot, while the gallery primarily shows contemporary painting and smaller sculptures. **Admission:** Free. **Hours:** Gallery
Mon–Fri. 11 A.M.–6 P.M.; Thu. until 7:30 P.M. Sculpture Court Mon.–Sat.
7:30 A.M.–9:30 P.M.; Sun. 11 A.M.–7 P.M. **Subway:** 4, 5, 6, 7, S to 42nd St.

Art Galleries

There are probably more art galleries with active exhibition schedules in New
York than anywhere else—far too many to list them all here. But the names and
brief descriptions of the dealers below represent a hearty sampling. From paintings to ceramics, from photography and film to Conceptual art, from small decorative objects to massive installations, their exhibitions make up an art menu
unequalled in range and variety.

The criteria for the listed galleries are that they hold regular exhibitions and
they are open to the public during normal viewing hours (generally from 10
A.M. to 6 P.M. five days a week, closed Sundays and Mondays). But it is always
wise to call first, check *The New York Times* on Friday for art listings, or visit
"Art and Museums" on *www.nytoday.com.*

Other resources for gallery-goers include the "Cue" section of *New York* magazine (also available at *www.nymetro.com*); *The New Yorker's* "Goings on about
Town" section (*www.newyorker.com*); and sites such as *www.galleryguide.org.*

SoHo

ACE Gallery 275 Hudson St. (at Dominick St.) (212) 255-5599. The menu in
this large arena is Abstract Expressionist, Pop, Minimal and Conceptual art
from 1960 to the present, along with established and emerging U.S. and international art going back to 1980. The exhibition schedule is full of surprises,
from a huge suite of wall paintings by the Minimalist Sol LeWitt to an all-out
show of creations by the fashion designer Issey Miyake. Behind it all is a sharp
contemporary sensibility.

Howard Greenberg 120 Wooster St., 2nd Fl. (between Prince and Spring Sts.)
(212) 334-0010. With one of the biggest inventories in the trade, this gallery
focuses on classic 20th-century European and American photography. It handles the estates of such icons as Ruth Orkin, Roman Vishniac, James Van Der
Zee, Andre Kertesz and Ralph Eugene Meatyard, and represents well-known
contemporaries like William Klein, Sarah Moon, Bill Owens, Ralph Gibson,
Gordon Parks and Mary Ellen Mark. Theme shows have dealt with American
car culture, the New York subway and civil rights, among other topics.

Nolan/Eckman 560 Broadway (at Prince St.) (212) 925-6190. This small, intimate and easy gallery specializes in works on paper by contemporary American
and German artists. Shows range from the outrageous, no-holds-barred polemics
of the cartoony Peter Saul to the less scandalous musings of German stars like
Gerhard Richter, Martin Kippenberger and Sigmar Polke.

Phyllis Kind Gallery 136 Greene St. (between Prince and Houston Sts.) (212) 925-1200. The quirky, the odd and the offbeat are to be found at this SoHo gallery, whose offerings run from far-out folk art like the garrulous paintings of the preacher Howard Finster to the wacky renderings of Chicago School painters like Jim Nutt. The gallery's lively Chicago sensibility reveals its start in the Second City.

Chelsea

Barbara Gladstone Gallery 515 W. 24th St. (between 10th and 11th Aves.) (212) 206-9300. An émigré from SoHo (where it opened in the early 1980's) to Chelsea, this gallery represents all areas of the visual arts, with the emphasis on Conceptual, installation, video and photographic work. The rhapsodic filmmaker Matthew Barney is one of its stars, along with the painters Anish Kapoor and Lari Pittman, the photographers Richard Prince and Shirin Neshat, the German installation artist Gregor Schneider and the Italian Conceptual artists Mario and Marisa Merz.

Cheim and Read 521 W. 23rd St. (between 10th and 11th Aves.) (212) 242-7727. One of the most wide-ranging galleries in Chelsea, this spacious ground-floor showcase handles a variety of contemporary painters, sculptors, photographers, video and installation artists of different generations. The gallery emphasizes art with strong psychological themes, like that of the sculptor Louise Bourgeois, as well as work devoted to the language of painting, like the abstractions of Richmond Burton. Other high-profile artists represented by the gallery are the painters Joan Mitchell, Louise Fishman, Pat Steir and Juan Uslé; the sculptor Lynda Benglis; the photographers William Eggleston, Robert Mapplethorpe, Adam Fuss and Jack Pierson; and the installation artist Jenny Holzer.

Feigen Contemporary 535 W. 20th St. (between 10th and 11th Aves.) (212) 929-0500. The newest branch of the veteran Richard L. Feigen Gallery, which in its uptown headquarters focuses on Old Masters, Feigen Contemporary moved from Chicago to Chelsea in 1997. It represents emerging, mid-career and established contemporary artists, ranging from James Rosenquist and the estate of Ray Johnson to the young video artist Jeremy Blake.

Leslie Tonkonow Artworks + Projects 535 W. 22nd St. (between 10th and 11th Aves.) (212) 255-8450. The roster of this young gallery emphasizes photographers from all over the world, among them the Korean Nikki S. Lee, the Japanese Tokihiro Sato and the American team of Robbins and Becher. But a recent move into larger quarters allows the showing of other kinds of visual artists, too, such as the sculptors Beverly Semmes and Robert Watts. The dealer's eye for lively talent makes the gallery a cool stop on the Chelsea trail.

Matthew Marks Gallery 523 W. 24th St. and 522 W. 22nd St. (between 10th and 11th Aves.) (212) 243-0200. It takes not one but two spacious galleries in Chelsea to display the work of the 20-odd artists on Matthew Marks's superstar roster, ranging from the English figure painter Lucian Freud and the estate of the Abstract Expressionist Willem deKooning to the very contemporary abstract painter Terry Winters and the much-admired but widely differing photographers Nan Goldin and Andreas Gursky.

MetroPictures 519 W. 24th St. (between 10th and 11th Aves.) (212) 206-7100. Receptive to the new and far-out, this gallery, which opened in SoHo in 1980 but now occupies a vast Chelsea space, carries on with a group of contemporaries that have become more established over the years. They include the painter, sculptor and filmmaker Robert Longon, the video installation artist Tony Oursler and the photographer Cindy Sherman.

Paula Cooper 534 W. 21st St. (between 10th and 11th Aves.) (212) 255-1105. Founded in 1968, this gallery was one of the very first to open in SoHo, establishing early on an agenda focused on (but not limited to) Conceptual and Minimalist sculpture. Sol LeWitt, Carl Andre, Donald Judd, Robert Grosvenor and Dan Flavin were among early exhibitors, but the gallery also has different breeds of artists in its stable, among them the painters Jennifer Bartlett and Michael Hurson, the sculptors Jonathan Borofsky and Jackie Winsor and the photographer Peter Campus.

Sonnabend Gallery 536 W. 22nd St. (between 10th and 11th Aves.) (212) 627-1018. Noted for introducing 60's proto Pop pioneers like Rauschenberg and Johns to Europe, Illeana Sonnabend came to New York in 1970 and has assembled a stable of internationally known contemporary European and American painters, sculptors, photographers and installation artists. Some of its current stars are the English conceptualists Gilbert and George, kitsch-loving sculptor Jeff Koons, assemblagists Ashley Bickerton and Haim Steinbach from the East Village "Neo-Geo" movement of the mid-1980's, German photographers Bernd and Hilla Becher and site sculptors Anne and Patrick Poirier.

Yancey-Richardson 535 W. 22nd St. (between 10th and 11th Aves.) (212) 343-1225. Focusing on contemporary and vintage 20th-century photography, this small gallery is known for excellent shows of the work of individual photographers, among them the Czech Josef Sudek, the Brazilians Sebastiao Selgado and Mario Cravo Netto, along with U.S. lensmen Julius Shulman, Lynn Geesaman, Andrew Moore and the Depression era's Marian Post Wolcott.

Midtown and Uptown

Barry Friedman, Ltd. 32 E. 67th St. (between Park and Madison Aves.) (212) 794-8950. European decorative arts of the 20th century dominate this sumptuous town house, including French furniture and objects of the 1930's and 40's, Wiener Werkstatte and Bauhaus productions and avant-garde paintings from the 20's and 30's, works on paper, sculpture and contemporary vintage photography. The gallery is also moving into the field of contemporary decorative arts with shows of studio glass, art furniture, ceramics and wood objects by artists from all over the world. A keenly discriminating taste prevails.

C & M Arts 45 E. 78th St. (between Park and Madison Aves.) (212) 861-0020. Distinguished presentations of European and American masters—from Impressionists through Matisse, Picasso, deKooning, Jackson Pollock and Joseph Cornell—are at home in this discriminating gallery, quartered in what was once a luxurious town house. The gallery, opened in 1992, does relatively few shows, but high standards prevail.

Edwynn Houk 745 Fifth Ave. (at 57th St.) (212) 750-7070. Specializing in masters of 20th-century photography, with an emphasis on the 1920's and 30's as well as the work of contemporary Americans, this elegantly understated gallery has a cavernous space in which to show them. It represents the estates of Brassai and Dorothea Lange, among others, and is the exclusive representative for such American contemporaries as Elliott Erwitt, Sally Mann, Lynn Davis and Andrea Modica.

Gagosian 980 Madison Ave. (at 76th St.) (212) 744-2313; 555 W. 24th St. (between 10th and 11th Sts.) (212) 741-1111. Big-name contemporaries as well as the works of Pop artists light up the big spaces of this two-location gallery. Large-scale installations by Richard Serra, Mark di Suvero, Damien Hirst and others appear in the huge Chelsea branch; the Madison Avenue gallery handles more conventional-size works. The sculptors Maya Lin and Elyn Zimmerman and the painters Ed Ruscha, Annette Messager, James Rosenquist and David Salle are also on the roster.

Galerie St. Etienne 24 W. 57th St. (between Fifth and Sixth Aves.) (212) 245-6734. Austrian and German Expressionism from the turn of the last century through the 1920's are the house specialties at this gallery, along with the work of American folk artists. Founded in 1939 by Dr. Otto Kallir, St. Etienne was the first to show Grandma Moses. The gallery introduced major Expressionists like Gustav Klimt, Oskar Kokoschka and Egon Schiele to the United States, and deals with other Austrian and German modernists, including Kaethe Kollwitz, Lovis Corinth and Paula Modersohn-Becker. Its stable of classic American folk painters includes John Kane, Morris Hirshfield and Horace Pippin.

Garth Clark 24 W. 57th St. (between Fifth and Sixth Aves.) (212) 246-2205. This small but serious showcase for 20th-century ceramics handles a mix of artists spanning the century. Some come from the ceramics world, like George Ohr, Beatrice Wood and Ron Nagle; others, better known as painters or sculptors, have turned their hands to ceramics, among them Lucio Fontana, Sir Anthony Caro, Joan Miró and Louise Nevelson.

Hirschl & Adler; Hirschl & Adler Modern 21 E. 70th St. (at Madison Ave.) (212) 535-8810. American and European paintings, watercolors, drawings and sculpture from the 18th through the early 20th century are the province of this active gallery, along with American prints of all periods and American decorative arts from 1810 to 1910. Established in 1952, it occupies a handsome landmark town house that is also home to a contemporary arm that deals with European and American art from post–World War II to the present.

Joan T. Washburn 20 W. 57th St. (between Fifth and Sixth Aves.) (212) 397-6780. American art from World War I to the present is the territory staked out by this long-established gallery, which handles the estates of the painters Jackson Pollock and Myron Stout, Louise Nevelson's sculpture and drawings from the 1930's and 40's, and David Smith's paintings from the same period. Its contemporary stable includes the sculptors Jack Youngerman and Gwynn Murrill and the painter Richard Baker.

Kennedy Galleries 730 Fifth Ave. (at 56th St.) (212) 541-9600. Now celebrating its 127th year, Kennedy is one of the oldest dealers in American art. In its plush, carpeted quarters, it shows paintings from an inventory that runs from the 18th to the 20th century, including the Hudson River School, American Impressionism, Social Realism and Modernism. On the 20th-century side, it handles exclusively the estates of Charles Burchfield and Rockwell Kent, and regularly exhibits the work of American classics like George Bellows, John Sloan, Stuart Davis, Charles Demuth, John Marin and Walt Kuhn.

Knoedler & Company 19 E. 70th St. (between Fifth and Madison Aves.) (212) 794-0550. The oldest art gallery in New York, Knoedler goes back to 1846, when its French founder immigrated to America. It became a leading international dealer in European and American art and in 1930 scored a coup by buying 21 masterpieces from the Hermitage in St. Petersburg for the American acquisitor Andrew Mellon. Always a champion of contemporary artists as well, it shows works today by Helen Frankenthaler, Milton Avery, Adolph Gottlieb, Richard Pousette-Dart and other established talents.

Marian Goodman 24 W. 57th St. (between Fifth and Sixth Aves.) (212) 977-7160. An international repertory distinguishes this long-established gallery, a quiet but important presence on the art scene that has recently added significantly to its space. To its schedule of shows by prominent European and American Conceptual artists such as Jannis Kounellis, Rebecca Horn, members of the socially conscious Italian Arte Povera group, along with the Conceptual artists Lawrence Weiner and Dan Graham, it has been adding the work of contemporary photographers, among them large-scale prints by Germany's Thomas Struth.

Marlborough 40 W. 57th St. (between Fifth and Sixth Aves.) (212) 541-4900 and Marlborough Chelsea 211 W. 19th St. (between Seventh and Eighth Aves.) (212) 463-8634. The emphasis in the spacious uptown branch of this gallery is on contemporary artists with established reputations. Larry Rivers, Marisol, Alex Katz, Red Grooms and the Colombian sculptor-painter Fernando Botero are regular exhibitors at Marlborough's glossy uptown headquarters. A graphics division there shows 19th- through 20th-century work, with occasional historical shows; the roomy Chelsea branch specializes in the work of such contemporary sculptors as Anthony Caro, Magdalena Abakanowicz and Kenneth Snelson.

Mary Boone 745 Fifth Ave. (at 58th St.) (212) 752-2929; and in Chelsea, 541 W. 21st St. (between 10th and 11th Aves.). Not so cutting-edge as it once was, this trendy, highly publicized gallery, a launching pad for rockets like Julian Schnabel and David Salle, is still going strong. The gallery continues to represent some of the older talents from its roster in the 1970's and 80's, such as the painters Bill Jensen, Ross Bleckner, Eric Fishchl and Barbara Kruger, and it continues to be a showcase for younger artists, among them Leonardo Drew, Damian Loeb, Peter Wegner and Karin Davie. The gallery recently opened additional space in Chelsea for large-scale works and installations.

McKee Gallery 745 Fifth Ave. (at 58th St.) (212) 688-5951. Established contemporaries and an outlook independent of fashions or trends are the strengths of this gallery, opened in 1974. Among its painters are Vija Celmins, Jake Berthot, Harvey Quaytman and the estate of Philip Guston; its sculptors include William Tucker, Martin Puryear and the young Spanish maestra Susanna Solano.

Michael Rosenfeld 24 W. 57th St. (between Fifth and Sixth Aves.) (212) 247-0082. Specializing in American art from 1910 to 1970, the gallery has mounted "movement" shows of early American abstraction and Abstract Expressionism; it also handles the estates of the Surrealist Alfonso Ossorio and the abstractionist Burgoyne Diller, and the work of contemporaries such as Charles Seliger, Martha Madigan and Betye Saar. The gallery is particularly receptive to the work of minority artists, and has mounted a number of shows of African-American art.

PaceWildenstein 32 E. 57th St. (between Fifth and Sixth Aves.) (212) 421-3292 and 534 W. 25th St. (212) 929-7000; **Pace MacGill** 32 E. 57th St. (between Fifth and Sixth Aves.). Beautifully mounted shows in cool, elegant settings are the rule at PaceWildenstein, originally founded as the Pace Gallery in the 1960's. Not a hotbed of new talent, it's the place to see the work of contemporary "Old Masters," such as Mark Rothko, Ad Reinhardt, Louise Nevelson and the satirist Saul Steinberg, as well as living icons Julian Schnabel, Chuck Close and Alex Katz. Pace MacGill, in the same building, shows 20th-century American photography; the Chelsea branch of PaceWildenstein adds more space for larger-scale sculpture and installations.

Salander-O'Reilly Galleries 20 E. 79th St. (at Madison Ave.) (212) 879-6606. With one of the most ambitious rosters in the art world, this gallery in an impressive town house shows a broad range of American and European painting and sculpture from the 18th to the 20th century. It has mounted more than 300 exhibitions, from work by the 18th-century English painters John Constable and Joseph M.W. Turner to the American modernist Alfred Maurer and the late abstractionist Stanley Boxer. It represents the estates of Stuart Davis, Gaston

Lachaise, Gerald Murphy and Elaine deKooning, as well as the work of living artists such as Paul Georges, Don Gummer, Graham Nickson, Larry Poons, Katherine Porter and Michael Steiner.

Zabriskie 41 E. 57th St. (between Fifth and Sixth Aves.) (212) 752-1223. Opened in 1955, the Zabriskie Gallery is known for its strong emphasis on American Modernism, Dada and Surrealism, showing works in all media. It is also a stronghold of modern and contemporary French and American photography, from the Frenchman Eugene Atget to the American Nicholas Nixon. The gallery represents the estates of the sculptors Richard Stankiewicz and William Zorach as well as the work of contemporary painters such as Pat Adams and Katherine Schmidt. Group shows of important movements and periods are also part of the fare.

—*Grace Glueck*

PERFORMING ARTS
Theater in New York

Broadway, as a word, still has an enchanted sound to the stagestruck, summoning an impossibly glamorous neighborhood of palatial theaters, stars of incandenscent wattage and plays and musicals of unmatchable wit and polish. That, anyway, is the myth. In reality, such a Broadway—and by Broadway, one means an area of roughly 40 square blocks around Times Square in Midtown Manhattan—hasn't existed, if it ever did, for at least some 30 years and probably longer. Broadway more than ever is a state of mind, albeit a state within the city of New York. As a piece of nomenclature, it has never been exact, since most "Broadway" theaters are found on other streets. And if you can stretch your imagination—and your legs—to encompass at least a few hundred more blocks, you'll discover that something very much like the Broadway that was still exists. You just can't find it all in one place, anymore than all of the city's multistar restaurants are within an oyster shell's throw of one another.

Finding what meets your tastes may require a little more research than it might have in, say, the 1930's.

What is produced in the official Broadway area is still what gets the most attention nationally. The plays put on there have bigger budgets and usually bigger names, with ticket prices to match. What it seldom offers is much in the way of originality or daring. Investing in a Broadway production is a high-risk gamble and producers are accordingly cautious. That is why the neighborhood is dominated by revivals, shows based on successful movies and British imports perfumed with class and flowery reviews from abroad. With the cleaning up and slicking up of Times Square in the 1990's, there has also arisen a new crop of shows directly targeted at tourists, trading on brand-name familiarity, most notably those of Disney, whose *Lion King* (admittedly, a brilliantly rethought stage production of a cartoon movie) may well outlive us all.

There's still plenty to get excited about on Broadway. Revivals of dramas in recent seasons have been on an exceptionally high level. New musicals have tended to be either lost or leaden, with just a few the blessed exceptions, including the joyous stage adaptation of *The Producers*. But cutting-edge, or even nicking-edge, is definitely not an attribute of Midtown Manhattan theater. When a production with a cool quotient shows up on Broadway (*Urinetown*), you can safely assume that it started life in some other neighborhood. Indeed, since 1970 the overwhelming majority of Pulitzer Prizes for drama have gone to non-Broadway productions.

Finding what's hot **Off-Broadway** and in the increasingly less marginalized realm known as **Off-Off-Broadway** can take you as far from Midtown as Brooklyn or as close as Theater Row—the stretch of 42nd Street west of Eighth Avenue. There's no strict rule of thumb for conducting your search: a theater, after all, is judged by what is on its stage, and that changes constantly.

In the glitzy block of 42nd Street between Seventh and Eighth Avenues, there is a most charming and innovative new theater for children, the restored little jewel box called the **New Victory,** right next door to the goliath **Ford Performing Arts Center.** If you're looking for literate, polished plays in thoroughly professional productions, there are several institutional theaters that have become bywords for just that: the **Manhattan Theater Club, Lincoln Center, Playwrights Horizons** and to a lesser extent, the **Joseph Papp Public Theater.**

There are also younger, smaller and more vital companies that have already established a track record for putting on works that get people talking. These include the **Vineyard Theater,** off Union Square (birthplace of Pulitzer winner Edward Albee's *Three Tall Women* and Paula Vogel's *How I Learned to Drive*), the **New York Theater Workshop** on 4th Street in the East Village (the cradle of the now-fabled rock opera *Rent* and Claudia Shear's *Dirty Blonde*) and **MCC (the Manhattan Class Company)** on West 23rd Street, which brought Margaret Edson's brave, surprisingly popular *Wit* to New York. The **Drama Dept.** on East 9th Street, filled with some of the most vital young theater talents in the city, has in five years established itself as a company whose imaginative reinventions of classic plays are essential viewing.

If your tastes lean more toward the truly experimental—that is, without such conventions as plot and easily understood characters—there remains a host of fertile outlets for such work, mostly located south of 14th Street, from the legendary **LaMama** on 4th Street in the East Village to the more recently created **HERE** performing arts complex on Sixth Avenue in SoHo, where an underwater puppet show became the talk of the town several seasons ago. Two mighty bastions of the avant-garde remain indomitably in place and abidingly influential: Richard Foreman's **Ontological-Hysteric Theater** and the **Wooster Group,** both of which have hardcore cult followings, making tickets to their productions tough to come by.

For theatergoers with an international palate, there is the annual **Lincoln Center Festival,** which in recent years has brought major works from Ireland, South Africa and Eastern Europe. And just across the river from Manhattan is the **Brooklyn Academy of Music** (*see section* "Brooklyn" *in chapter* **Exploring**

New York), unquestionably the city's most ambitious and adventurous importer of theater, regularly bringing in productions from titanic directors like Peter Brook and Ingmar Bergman. Indeed, some of the most electric theater seen in New York of late has been at the Academy. Even those who consider Brooklyn a foreign country must concede that it's closer than Stockholm.

— Ben Brantley

Practical Matters

Broadway theater has become increasingly pricey (*The Producers* was first to break the $100 barrier), and squeezing into the cramped seats in the older the-aters is actually more uncomfortable than flying coach class—but those things cease to matter when the lights go down and the curtain goes up. You are in the right place.

There are 32 "Broadway" theaters, and even more Off-Broadway and Off-Off-Broadway. Off- and Off-Off are less expensive than Broadway, and the theatrical quality can be superior, but the comfort level is no better.

To find out what's playing and where, the fullest **listings** are in *Time Out New York*, *The New Yorker* and *The New York Times* (listings every day, but more on Friday and Sunday); **www.nytoday.com** also has everything you need.

If you want to see a popular show like *The Lion King* or *The Producers*, order your tickets by phone or online months in advance. Broadway theaters do not sell tickets over the phone, but some Off- and Off-Off-Broadway theaters do.

Tickets to most shows are available through **TicketMaster** (212-307-7171; *www.ticketmaster.com*) and **Tele-Charge** at (212-239-6200; *www.telecharge.com*). Both of these services tack on annoying service charges, but if you've got your heart set on a particular show, it may be worth it to you.

American Express Gold Club Events (800-448-TIKS; *www.americanex-press.com/gce*) is often able to offer hard-to-get tickets to cardholders at full price.

Several good Web sites offer up-to-date listings and discount offers to those who register. It's worth checking **www.playbill.com, www.broadway.com** and **www.theatermania.com.**

If you're not trying to see a specific smash hit and you're willing to wait until you arrive in New York to purchase tickets, you have several options. Before you try anything else, call the box office directly to determine availability; if there are tickets to be had, you can drop by the theater in person.

The best-known strategy for bargain hunters is standing on line at the half-price **TKTS booth** in Times Square, at Broadway and 47th Street. It's open 3 to 8 P.M. for evening shows (10 A.M.–2 P.M. for Wed. and Sat. matinees, from 11 A.M. on Sun. for all performances). Tickets for that day's performances are usu-ally offered at half price (a few are reduced only 25 percent), with a $2.50 per ticket service charge. Boards outside the ticket windows list available shows; you won't see the latest blockbuster listed, but there are plenty of Broadway and Off-Broadway options. No credit cards are accepted; bring cash or traveler's checks. Come early, and be prepared for a long wait. If you're willing to gamble, the line is relatively painless toward the end of the day, and you may even get lucky by scoring seats that have been released as curtain time approaches.

There's also a **downtown branch of TKTS** in Lower Manhattan's South Street Seaport, at the corner of John and Front Streets. It's open Mon.–Sat. 11 A.M.–6 P.M., Sun. 11 A.M.–3:30 P.M.; lines are usually much shorter here. At this location only, matinee tickets are sold the day before the show. Subway: 1, 2, 4, 5, J, Z, M to Fulton Street; A, C to Broadway/Nassau Street.

Do not buy tickets from scalpers hovering around the TKTS lines. They offer deeper discounts, but you run the risk that they are counterfeit and the theater will turn you away. (The same is true of hawkers around the theaters themselves.)

Another option is the **Hit Show Club,** 630 Ninth Ave., Rm. 808 (between 44th and 45th Sts.; 212-581-4211; *www.hitshowclub.com*; open Mon.–Fri. 9 A.M.–4 P.M.; subway: A, C, E to 42nd St.). When you walk in, you'll see a rack with discount coupons for some dozen shows. The choice is smaller than same-day tickets at TKTS, but there is a big advantage: You can use these coupons to buy tickets in advance. Another advantage: You don't have to stand on a long line outside in foul weather. (As an unexpected bonus, the lobby of the club's landmarked building is a gorgeous Art Deco interior.) Take your coupon to the theater, present it, and if the box office has what you want, they'll sell you one or two tickets at the discounted price. Most Hit Show Club discounts are about 40 percent, with no extra service charge. (You may also see Hit Show and other discount coupons in hotel lobbies and beside the cash register in some restaurants. Not all discounts are the same, so read the fine print carefully.) Hit Show coupons are also distributed at the **NYC & Company Visitors Center,** 810 Seventh Avenue at 53rd Street.

Classical Music

Musical life in New York begins but by no means ends with two big institutions. **Carnegie Hall** and **Lincoln Center** generate concerts of every size and description and have halls big and small in which to stage them. Next to these giants is a ring of smaller organizations; they organize chamber music, new music ensembles and recitals. Though traditionally the season stretches from September until well into June, it's now possible to find worthwhile events in August as well as November.

Surrounding these major islands of activity is an ocean of free enterprise, and it is this mass of self-generated events and cottage industries that gives New York its energy. Experimental music groups, amateur choirs with big agendas, small opera companies doing new or esoteric repertory, self-financed and self-promoted debut performances fill downtown lofts and uptown churches in profusion. The quality will vary as much as the material, but the level of ambition is always high.

Carnegie Hall *(see below for full listing)* has no resident orchestras or ensembles; it is a presenter, gathering the best orchestras, singers and recitalists from this country and the world and fitting them into subscription series. Sign up for a season-long list, or choose individual events. In the main hall (seating 2,800) expect the Vienna and Berlin Philharmonics every year, as well as the orchestras of Cleveland, Philadelphia, Boston and Chicago. The Pittsburgh and Montreal Symphonies and many others will drop in, too, and there will be both familiar and exotic symphonic visitors from Europe and the East.

A major renovation a decade ago turned the dreary small theater at Carnegie Hall into a little gem called Weill Recital Hall. Formerly a rental operation for almost all comers, it is now the home of chamber music series, musical theater in concert, song recitals by good artists and, very important, debut recitals by beginning professionals. Deciding which new talent is worth a trip and the price of a ticket is a less haphazard procedure today. The performers are selected by Carnegie Hall in conjunction with several European concert halls, and the young people give their recitals in all of them.

Lincoln Center's Avery Fisher Hall (soon to be renovated) is Carnegie's equivalent in size and seating capacity, if not beauty. It produces series in the same way as well, but with a difference. For Fisher is also the home of the New York Philharmonic, and the smaller Alice Tully Hall next door houses the Chamber Music Society of Lincoln Center. The Philharmonic is at work steadily through the season, either under its music director Lorin Maazel or guest conductors. Weekly programs are generally repeated three to four times, often with Friday morning performances for those less easy with nightlife in the city. (See the box "Lincoln Center" later in this chapter for full listings.)

The Chamber Music Society is a permanent ensemble of 10 to 20 performers. They mix and match their instruments and skills to make all possible combinations. Sextets with bassoon are no problem, but conventional quartets and trios turn up as well. The Society's programs are usually repeated only once.

Lincoln Center has several debut series as well, as does the **92nd Street Y.** And then there is the Young Concert Artists, which has been presenting and preparing young musicians and singers for a generation. The **Juilliard School** is eager to put its best students before the public and sponsors a number of in-house competitions with major public recitals as rewards. Go to the box office at the school in Lincoln Center for schedules and tickets. Most performances are free (see below for full listing).

Indeed, the students of Juilliard and their companion schools, **Mannes** and **Manhattan,** often blur the distinction between amateur and professional (see below). All three schools teem with concerts and operas at which the public is welcome, usually for free. Opera productions at the Juilliard Theater (one of the city's best spaces) are often on a par if not superior to the professional efforts of companies in other cities. Manhattan regularly puts on skillful versions of out-of-the-way 20th-century operas, and Mannes has recently been in the midst of an extensive Handel project.

Although New York is often criticized for having only one major orchestra, the accusation is deceptive. Floating groups like the estimable Orchestra of St. Luke's have their own seasons. The New York Chamber Symphony and the conductorless Orpheus are well rated, and the American Symphony Orchestra is making strides as well. Under Robert Spano, the Brooklyn Philharmonic is giving some of the most interesting orchestra programs in town. The group performs at the **Brooklyn Academy of Music** *(see box in the* "Brooklyn" *section of chapter* **Exploring New York***)*, a quick and easy subway ride across the East River from Manhattan.

Smaller venues are remarkably active. The **Miller Theater at Columbia University** has become the hotbed of choice for the serious new-music crowd. **Merkin Concert Hall** is plain to look at but night after night provides a place for every kind of music, new and old, provocative and conservative. The **Florence Gould Theater** and the **Kaye Playhouse** join the 92nd Street Y as East Side presenters. **The Kitchen** downtown near the Hudson River is a clearinghouse for musical and theatrical experiment where electronic instruments and new sounds are the norm. The **World Music Institute** brings in ethnic performers from Tibet, Africa or, for that matter, down the street.

Summer is becoming busy, although Carnegie Hall usually closes in August. In June and July, the **Lincoln Center Festival** brings operas, orchestra concerts and interesting exotica. It uses its own halls and a few others nearby. There's also the vastly popular **Mostly Mozart Festival,** which divides its frequent summer-long programs between Avery Fisher and Alice Tully Halls. The repertory is usually more comforting than challenging.

A lot of summer entertainment is free: the Met giving concert versions of operas in the parks of the five boroughs, the New York Philharmonic doing much the same, and then Lincoln Center's Damrosch Park offering concert brass bands, choruses and mostly lighthearted fare.

—Bernard Holland

Classical Music Centers

Below is a brief list of places that offer concerts on a regular basis. Serious music lovers should check the listings every Sunday in *The New York Times* "Arts & Leisure" section (the next-to-last page) or online at *www.nytoday.com.*

Bargemusic BROOKLYN Fulton Ferry Landing (between Water and River Sts.) (718) 624-4061 *www.bargemusic.org.* Olga Bloom, the driving force behind Bargemusic, deserves an award for creating a unique venue. Back in 1974, she purchased an old coffee barge and almost single-handedly refurbished it. It's now a floating chamber music space where artists can perform in an informal atmosphere and actually enjoy making music. Moored in the East River under the Brooklyn Bridge, with the Manhattan skyline providing a breathtaking backdrop, Bargemusic is a cozy, wood-paneled room that seats about 125 people on folding chairs. Year-round, the finest chamber music performers play concerts of the highest caliber. It's a magical spot, well worth the trip to Brooklyn Heights and the occasionally choppy waters. Advance reservations are necessary, as performances sell out. Tickets are usually $35 ($20 for students). **Subway:** A, C to High St.; 2, 3 to Clark St.

Carnegie Hall MIDTOWN WEST Seventh Ave. and 57th St. (212) 247-7800
www.carnegiehall.org. Can you imagine New York without Carnegie Hall? Probably not. But in 1960, its owners were ready to demolish Andrew Carnegie's
shrine to music to make way for a new skyscraper. Violinist Isaac Stern almost
single-handedly saved the world's most famous concert hall from becoming
merely a fond memory. From the time it opened in 1891 (with Tchaikovsky
conducting the inaugural concert), the 2,804-seat landmark has been synonymous with the greatest musicians of the 20th century, from Arturo Toscanini,
Marian Anderson and Vladimir Horowitz to Ella Fitzgerald, Frank Sinatra and
the Beatles.

Carnegie's acoustics are legendary, though some feel the sound was compro-
mised after much-needed renovations were completed in 1986. (A concrete slab
under the stage, discovered in 1995, didn't help matters and was later removed.)
Once you get past the claustrophobic lobby, you're in for a visual and sonic
treat. On the walls are photos and letters from famous composers, singers,
instrumentalists and conductors. The seats are plush and the gilded décor is rav-
ishing. Even if a performance does not live up to your expectations, a visit to
Carnegie always does.

During intermission, instead of squeezing into the lobby or the Cafe Carnegie,
stop by the Rose Museum on the First Tier level, where interesting music-
related exhibits give you a taste of the hall's illustrious history. On the same
level are another cafe, the Rohatyn Room and a gift shop. But beware: the shop
is even more claustrophobic than the lobby

In addition to the main 2,804-seat **Isaac Stern Auditorium,** there's also the
more intimate 268-seat **Weill Recital Hall.** In 2003, Carnegie Hall hopes to
inaugurate the 650-seat **Zankel Concert Hall,** an underground space that was a
movie theater for decades. **Subway:** B, N, Q, R to 57th St.

Juilliard School—Juilliard Theater UPPER WEST SIDE 60 Lincoln Center Plaza
(Broadway at 65th St.) (212) 769-7406, or (212) 721-6500 for Centercharge
www.juilliard.edu. The Juilliard School is one of the world's leading music conservatories. Indeed, some of the world's best-known performers are graduates.
The principal auditorium, the Juilliard Theater, is as impressive as the students
who regularly appear on its stage. A steeply raked 933-seat hall with extremely
comfortable seats, superior acoustics and excellent sightlines, it is most often
used for opera and orchestral concerts, although chamber music, drama and
dance are no strangers here. This is also one of the city's best bargains: many
performances are free. Others have relatively modest ticket prices, usually under
$20. Check the Web site for the frequently changing calendar of events. **Sub-
way:** 1, 9 to 66th St.

Kosciuszko Foundation UPPER EAST SIDE 15 E. 65th St. (between Madison
and Fifth Aves.) (212) 734-2130 *www.kosciuszkofoundation.org.* On the second
floor of the Kosciuszko Foundation's splendid three-story limestone town house,
just off Central Park, is one of the loveliest recital spaces in town. An elegant

wood-paneled parlor at the top of a red-carpeted spiral staircase, the room doubles as a gallery for 19th- and 20th-century Polish art. The Foundation, founded
in 1925, is a center for Polish culture and education, so naturally the focus of its
excellent concert series is on Polish music and musicians. It also sponsors films
screening, lectures and other events. **Subway:** 6 to 68th St.; N, R to Fifth Ave.

Manhattan School of Music UPPER WEST SIDE 122 Claremont Ave. (at Broadway and 122nd St.) (212) 749-2802 *www.msmnyc.org*. One of the country's premier conservatories, the Manhattan School of Music is located just a few blocks
from Grant's Tomb and Riverside Church. It's bustling with all sorts of music,
from student, faculty and professional recitals and chamber music to opera, jazz
and musical theater presentations. The quality is usually high and the price of
admission often free (or less than $15). The two principal spaces are Borden
Auditorium, a long, narrow 1,000-seat hall with decent if not wonderful sound,
and upstairs, the intimate, 380-seat Hubbard Recital Hall. **Subway:** 1, 9 to
125th St.

Mannes College of Music UPPER WEST SIDE 150 W. 85th St. (between Amsterdam and Columbus Aves.) (212) 580-0210 *www.mannes.edu*. Mannes is the
third big-name music school, along with Juilliard and the Manhattan School of
Music, on Manhattan's West Side. Like other conservatories, it has an impressive student body and faculty and presents a wide array of high-quality events,
from early music consorts to grand opera and beyond. Its two auditoriums—the
200-seat Concert Hall and the 60-seat Goldmark Auditorium, used mainly for
recitals—are adequate if not luxurious. (For larger-scale events, Mannes often
uses the nearby Symphony Space.) Tickets are usually free or very inexpensive.
Subway: 1, 9, B, C to 86th St.

Merkin Concert Hall UPPER WEST SIDE 129 W. 67th St. (between Broadway
and Amsterdam Ave.) (212) 501-3330 *www.elainekaufmancenter.org*. "Intimate"
is a word that's overused in describing mid-size concert venues. But in the case
of Merkin, it applies. The 457-seat hall is an attractive space with superior
acoustics, making it a favorite for chamber ensembles, recitalists and even mid-
size orchestras and choral groups. A number of popular series are held here,
including "Interpretations" and "New Sounds Live," both of which focus on
avant-garde, jazz or ethnic music. Merkin is part of the Elaine Kaufman Cultural
Center, which means that many programs here highlight Jewish roots and culture. **Subway:** 1, 9 to 66th St.

Metropolitan Museum of Art—Grace Rainey Rogers Auditorium
UPPER EAST SIDE 1000 Fifth Ave. (between 81st and 82nd Sts.) (212) 570-3949
www.metmuseum.org (click on "concerts and lectures"). An excellent 708-seat
hall, acoustically one of the best in town, it is particularly well suited for recitals
and chamber music. One of its secrets is the warm-toned African korina wood
paneling, a highly reflective material that helps magnify sound. Many of the
world's prominent performers appreciate the merits of this hall, which is why

Lincoln Center

Hardly beautiful, but stunning in its comprehensive cultural offerings, Lincoln Center for the Performing Arts is a great stop on any visitor's itinerary. Even if you don't take in the myriad programs, from opera to ballet to film to jazz, it's fun to sit and watch those who do. The winter season brings the fur-coat crowd to the Metropolitan Opera, its building a spectacular, glittering backdrop. In September, when the New York Film Festival is on, die-hard film fans as well as directors and stars come here for everything from the first screening of Woody Allen's latest to obscure films from Iran. The fountain, located in the center's plaza, is a great place to sit and watch people meet their dates, and try to conjure the day that ground was broken for the center—May 14, 1959, when President Dwight Eisenhower wielded the shovel and Leonard Bernstein led the Philharmonic and Juilliard chorus in the "Hallelujah Chorus." In the summer, there is outdoor dancing in that plaza, where New Yorkers swing and samba under the stars.   *—Jennifer Steinhauer*

Broadway (W. 62nd–66th St.) (212) 546-2656 *www.lincolncenter.org.*
Subway: 1, 9 to 66th St.—Lincoln Center; A, B, C, D to 59th St.

Alice Tully Hall (212) 875-5050. With 1,096 seats, this is a wonderful stage for chamber music and recitals, as well as small-scale opera and orchestral concerts. Jazz and avant-garde artists play here, and there's even an occasional appearance by a pop star or two. This is the regular stage for the **Chamber Music Society of Lincoln Center** (*www.chambermusicsociety.org*), which often performs with superstar guest artists. Alice Tully Hall is currently the home of **Jazz at Lincoln Center** (*www.jazzatlincolncenter.org*), Wynton Marsalis's world-renowned jazz ensemble (which will eventually move to a new home in the AOL Time Warner building rising at Columbus Circle).

Avery Fisher Hall (212) 875-5030. Its acoustics may not be perfect, but this 2,738-seat hall is one of the city's premier concert venues and home to the internationally acclaimed **New York Philharmonic.** Legendary conductor Kurt Masur retired at the end of the 2001-2002 season; his baton goes to Lorin Maazel in 2002-2003. Avery Fisher Hall also hosts the world's top visiting orchestras, instrumentalists and chamber groups, as well as pop and jazz performers. **Note:** Lincoln Center officials have been planning a redevelopment initiative that will include a major renovation of Avery Fisher Hall, but no definitive plan or schedule had been agreed upon at press time.

Library for the Performing Arts at Lincoln Center/Dorothy and Lewis B. Cullman Center (212) 870-1630. After a $38 million renovation, this branch of the New York Public Library reopened to the public in late 2001. It is a treasure trove of invaluable materials, boasting the largest reference, archival and circulating arts-related collection in the world.

Lincoln Center Theater (212) 362-7600. Lincoln Center also presents first-rate theater on two stages: the **Vivian Beaumont**, a large, modern Broadway stage and the more intimate **Mitzi E. Newhouse Theater,** which presents Off-Broadway productions. Check *www.lct.org* for details.

Metropolitan Opera House (212) 362-6000. Dominating Lincoln Center's plaza is the world's largest opera house. Five enormous glass arches overwhelm the eye. Behind them hang Marc Chagall's spectacular murals, "The Triumph of Music" on the south wall and "The Sources of Music" on the north.

Once inside the 3,900-seat house, the sweeping staircase ushers you into a glittering world of red velvet, gold leaf and gaudy crystal chandeliers that rise up to the ceiling at the beginning of each performance. Even in the nosebleed sections, the sound is good, so it's not necessary to spend $150 or more for orchestra seats. Standing-room tickets are about $15, but they sell out fast.

Technically, the Met is a director's dream, equipped with a slew of mechanical wonders: four huge stages with elevators and revolving platforms and a computerized lighting system. Every seat has a "Met Titles" screen, providing simultaneous translation. The orchestra pit accommodates more than 100 top-notch musicians under the artistic direction of James Levine.

In addition to hosting the world-renowned **Metropolitan Opera** (*www.metopera.org*), the opera house is also the home of **American Ballet Theater** (*www.abt.org*) in May, June and early July.

New York State Theater (212) 870-5570. It may not be as posh as its sister opera house across the plaza, but in some ways, the New York State Theater is the more interesting building. Designed by Philip Johnson, the 2,800-seat home for the **New York City Ballet** (*www.nycballet.com*) and the **New York City Opera** (*www.nycopera.com*) boasts a grand, four-story foyer, flanked by two marvelous white marble Elie Nadelman sculptures and surrounded by balconies. Hundreds of long chains serve as draperies for a glass wall that opens onto a large terrace facing Avery Fisher Hall. The seats are comfortable, the sightlines good.

Walter Reade Theater (212) 875-5600. This is Lincoln Center's venue for film, with a widely varied calendar of independent and foreign films. Check *www.film-linc.com* for schedules, including details on the **New York Film Festival.**

Seasonal Events: Lincoln Center's calendar is packed all year round. In summer, there's the **Lincoln Center Festival,** which draws an incredible array of performing artists from around the globe; the always-festive **Midsummer Night's Swing,** which brings would-be Freds and Gingers to the plaza for dancing to the sounds of big-band swing and salsa; **Mostly Mozart,** a month-long concert series of crowd pleasers, held in August; and **Lincoln Center Out-of-Doors,** which presents an array of free performances. (The Metropolitan Opera and the New York Philharmonic also stage free summer concerts in each borough's parks.) Autumn brings the **New York Film Festival.** *The Nutcracker* is a traditional holiday event; and the new year is always heralded by special gala performances on **New Year's Eve.** Check *www.lincolncenter.org* for details.

you'll find the Juilliard and Guarneri String Quartets, the Beaux Arts Trio and other big-name artists gracing the stage. There are also occasional jazz concerts, and many of the museum's popular lectures take place here. To enter the auditorium, you have to walk through the museum's spectacular Egyptian collection, which is always a thrill. Concerts are also regularly presented in other locations around the museum—check the Web site for times and locations. **Subway:** 4, 5, 6 to 86th St.

Opera

Opera in New York means, first and foremost, the **Metropolitan Opera** at Lincoln Center. Sometimes it seems that opera in the whole world means, first and foremost, the Metropolitan Opera. The company essentially deserves its iconic status. Leading international singers regularly perform there; indeed, a Metropolitan Opera debut is still a benchmark of a singer's career. In more than 25 years as artistic director, James Levine has built the Met orchestra into one of the finest anywhere. The musicians know they are good and play with palpable pride and confidence. The 3,900-seat opera house, which opened its doors in 1966, is looking a bit tattered these days, but the sound in the auditorium remains marvelous, and, if anything, the sound up in the cheaper balcony and family circle seats is better than that in the pricey orchestra section. (*See the box* "Lincoln Center" *earlier in this chapter for full listing.*)

Which brings up price. The Met is expensive (unless you catch one of the free summer performances in the city's parks). But putting on international-level opera is an expensive enterprise. It's mostly worth it. Yes, there are off-nights at the Met, and ill-conceived productions, and automatic-pilot performances of the most popular bread-and-butter operas. And sometimes second-string casts fall too far below the level of the name singers who open a run of an opera and garner the reviews. Still, company officials assert that, night for night, the Met presents opera on a more consistently high level than any other company, and they are right.

A newcomer to opera or a visitor from out of town will be tempted to go to the crowd-pleasers, like *La Boheme*, *Tosca* and *Aida*. These are good shows. But it would be wise to check out reviews and select something special, for the Met at its best is exhilarating. In recent seasons, for example, the presentations of Tchaikovsky's *Queen of Spades*, Mozart's *Marriage of Figaro*, Strauss's *Ariadne auf Naxos*, Wagner's *Meistersinger* and Berg's *Wozzeck* have been exceptionally produced and splendidly sung.

By the way, the Met's official guided tour is one of the best-kept secrets in New York. It's fascinating to go backstage and see the rotating stage, the set shops, the rehearsal spaces. The costume builders also demonstrate how they must adapt outfits to singers with enormously varying sizes and shapes.

Across the plaza from the Met, in the New York State Theater, is the **New York City Opera,** and the biggest frustration of this enterprising company is its location (there has been some talk that the company may someday move to a new downtown home as part of the redevelopment of the World Trade Center site, but any definitive plan is obviously years away). The mission of the company under its current leader, Paul Kellogg, is to create an identity that is distinct from its neighbor's. Why do what the Met can do better? So City Opera may not offer world-famous singers in the standard repertory, but it can offer young, eager artists who look and act like the characters they portray. Moreover, the City Opera tends to be more daring about repertory than the Met. The company regularly offers Baroque operas by Handel, neglected 20th-century works like Strauss's *Intermezzo*, Britten's *Paul Bunyan* (an entrancing production), and Carlisle Floyd's *Of Mice and Men* (a riveting musical and dramatic experience).

Ticket prices for City Opera are much more affordable than those at the Met, as well. All this has made the company attractive to younger, hipper audiences.

The company's goal of distinguishing itself from the Met would be easier, however, if it performed in a different facility in a different neighborhood. With over 2,700 seats, the New York State Theater is somewhat too big for the type of involving musical theater experience the City Opera works have to offer. And the acoustics of the auditorium are far from ideal, though the company is currently experimenting with an electronic sound-enhancement system for the space, a move that has agitated many traditionalists but been largely unnoticed by most attendees. All in all, City Opera is not just a cheaper alternative to the Met, but an interesting company in its own right.

There are many other smaller opera companies in the city, organizations that typically present two or three productions per season. **DiCapo Opera** is a scrappy company that performs in an appealing modest-sized theater on East 76th Street, and presents classics and occasionally contemporary works in effective productions with, by and large, talented young casts.

For 50 years the **Amato Opera** was a mom-and-pop outfit on a tight budget with a loyal following, presenting popular operas in a theater on the Bowery that gives new meaning to the term "intimate drama."

The **Bronx Opera** usually presents just two productions a years (check local listings), in English translation, on two consecutive weekends, first at the Lehman Center in the Bronx, then at John Jay College Theater in Manhattan.

The **Juilliard Opera Center** is not, as its name implies, a company of students from the Juilliard School, but a training institute that offers singers in leading roles who are on the brink of, or already engaged in, professional careers. Students fill out the smaller roles and provide the orchestra and chorus. But Juilliard students are more accomplished than many professionals, and the Opera Center productions are often excellent. The **Manhattan School of Music** also presents some worthwhile productions in its commodious theater on Broadway and 122nd Street, for example, an important recent revival of Ned Rorem's stirring operatic adaptation of Strindberg's *Miss Julie*. Opera at the **Mannes College of Music** on West 85th Street is also worth checking out.

The estimable **L'Opera Français de New York** presents stylish, semi-staged performances of French operas, often rarities, at Alice Tully Hall in Lincoln Center, although just two a year (check local listings). They are always first-rate.

If you can do without sets and costumes entirely, the **Opera Orchestra of New York,** directed by the conductor Eve Queler, is a must. Ms. Queler seeks out inexplicably neglected operas and presents them in concert performances at Carnegie Hall with strong casts, sometimes including major singers. In recent seasons Renée Fleming, Ruth Ann Swenson and Vesselina Kasarova, to cite just some illustrious artists, have scored triumphs with the Opera Orchestra. Ms. Queler's work reminds us that opera is, at its core, music, and can work quite effectively without its theatrical trimmings. *(See section "Classical Music Centers" earlier in this chapter for more information on venues.)*

—*Anthony Tommasini*

Amato Opera Theater 319 Bowery (between 2nd and Bleecker Sts.) (212) 228-8200 *www.amato.org.* Intimate venue, affordable tickets and innovative programming for children. **Subway:** F, V to Second Ave.; 6 to Bleecker St.

DiCapo Opera Theater 184 E. 76th St. (between Lexington and Third Aves.) (212) 288-9438. **Subway:** 6 to 77th St.

Juilliard Opera Center—Juilliard Theater 60 Lincoln Center Plaza (Columbus Ave. and 64th St.) (212) 799-5000 *www.juilliard.edu.* **Subway:** 1, 9 to 66th St.; A, B, C, D to 59th St.

Metropolitan Opera House—Lincoln Center Columbus Ave. and 64th St. (212) 362-6000 *www.metopera.org.* You can beat the high cost of tickets by paying for standing room. Standing room tickets are usually $12–$16; they go on sale at the box office Saturday mornings at 10 A.M. for the following week's performances. Lines start early. **Subway:** 1, 9 to 66th St.

New York State Theater—Lincoln Center 20 Lincoln Center Plaza (Columbus Ave. and 63rd St.) (212) 870-5570 *www.nycopera.com.* **Subway:** 1, 9 to 66th St.; A, B, C, D to 59th St.

Dance

Ballet, modern dance, jazz dance, tap dance and folk groups: As the dance capital of the world, New York plays host to them all. Troupes from abroad and resident companies perform throughout the year.

The New York City Ballet and American Ballet Theater, the country's top classical troupes, have regular seasons. Founded in 1948 by the Russian-born choreographer George Balanchine and his American patron, Lincoln Kirstein, the **New York City Ballet** (*www.nycballet.com*) remains faithful to Balanchine's view of dance for dance's sake. One-act plotless works, not story ballets, are the norm. The focus on the company's two late resident geniuses, Balanchine and Jerome Robbins, makes for high art. New works by Peter Martins, the current director, continue the emphasis on distinguished composers. The company has a winter season (including five weeks of *The Nutcracker*) and a spring season at Lincoln Center's **New York State Theater** (*see the box* "Lincoln Center" *earlier in this chapter*).

The Metropolitan Opera

American Ballet Theater (*www.abt.org*), founded in 1939, is more eclectic. Its reputation stems from its ballets in different styles and an ability to attract great dancers. Male virtuosity has been dazzling. The company tends to stage 19th-century classics and other three-act story ballets during its May and June stint at the **Metropolitan Opera House** (*see the box* "Lincoln Center"). In the fall, a brief season at **City Center** concentrates on one-act works, including premieres by contemporary choreographers such as Twyla Tharp.

New York has a variety of theaters and performing spaces that are hospitable to dance. For raw cutting-edge, the loftlike spaces of **The Kitchen** (*see section* "Other Arts Venues" *later in this chapter*), the **Dance Theater Workshop,** and **St. Mark's Church** are a must (*see below*). Many a newcomer, including Mark Morris, had a start in these well-attended nonproscenium theaters.

Brooklyn Academy of Museum (BAM)   BROOKLYN
30 Lafayette Ave. (off Flatbush Ave.) (718) 636-4100 *www.bam.org*. Autumn's **Next Wave Festival** makes BAM the mecca for trendy and serious audiences (sometimes the two overlap). Experimental dance is at the heart of the festival. Piña Bausch, Germany's iconoclastic choreographer, and Sankai Juku, a group working in Japan's post-Hiroshima Butoh style, are staples of the series. Leading American experimental choreographers associated with the Next Wave and BAM are more unpredictable and include Trisha Brown, Bill T. Jones, Meredith Monk, Lucinda Childs and Mark Morris. **Subway:** M, N, Q, R, W, 2, 3, 4, 5 to Atlantic Ave./Pacific St.

City Center of Music and Drama   MIDTOWN WEST
131 W. 55th St. (between Sixth and Seventh Aves.) (212) 581-1212 *www.city-center.org*. The Paul Taylor Dance Company performs in the spring and the Alvin Ailey American Dance Theater is here in December. Both are highly popular modern-dance companies with brilliant dancers. Taylor's choreography ranges in mood from light to dark and his mastery is unquestioned. Ailey died in 1989 but his troupe, inspired by African-American heritage, is directed now by Judith Jamison, who has brought the dancing to an even more exciting level. The company's signature work is *Revelations*, a masterpiece that Ailey set to spirituals.

    The Dance Theater of Harlem performs here (and other venues). It is an internationally known ballet troupe with a strong neo-Classical style. Arthur Mitchell, once a star at New York City Ballet, used the Balanchine aesthetic as a springboard for the company he founded in 1969 as an outlet for black ballet dancers.

    The **Martha Graham Dance Company** appears at City Center when not at the Joyce Theater. Often compared to Picasso and Stravinsky as one of the 20th century's groundbreaking artists, Graham died in 1991 but left extraordinary works that are powerfully danced by a dedicated company. Highly dramatic pieces inspired by Greek myth share the stage with the striking spare pieces of Graham's early years. (Recent financial problems have put the company's future in doubt.)

    As a different icon of American modern dance, Merce Cunningham changed the way audiences look at choreography. **The Merce Cunningham Dance Company's** works often resemble collages. When composing dances, Cunningham uses coin tossing or other chance procedures to decide which movement follows which; his experiments make him the pope of the avant-garde. Once a City Center regular, the company has recently appeared at Lincoln Center. **Subway:** B, D, E to Seventh Ave.; F, N, Q, R, W to 57th St.

Joyce Theater   CHELSEA
175 Eighth Ave. (between 18th and 19th Sts.) (212) 242-0800 *www.joyce.org*.
The choreographer Eliot Feld reinvented this former movie house as a theater
for dance and a home for his ballet company, now called Ballet Tech. Feld's
quirky ballets for young dancers have a loyal following and can be seen in the
spring and in August, with a brief season in December. In January, this 500-
seat Art Deco theater produces the "Altogether Different" series, featuring
small experimental troupes. A wide range of modern dance predominates during the year. The popular Pilobolus troupe appears in July. The Joyce now has a
satellite branch, the **Joyce SoHo** *(see listing below)*. **Subway:** A, C, E to 14th
St.; 1, 9 to 18th St.

Metropolitan Opera House   UPPER WEST SIDE
Lincoln Center, Columbus Ave. and 64th St. (212) 362-6000. *www.lincolncen-
ter.org*. In July, the Met is the way station for major ballet companies from
abroad. You might see Russia's Kirov Ballet and Bolshoi Ballet, the Royal Ballet
from England or the Paris Opera Ballet. Also in July, the Lincoln Center Festival stages dance performances in the Met, the New York State Theater and the
Center's smaller theaters. *(See the box* "Lincoln Center" *earlier in this chapter.)*
Subway: 1, 9 to 66th St.

—Anna Kisselgoff

Other Dance Theaters and Studios

Dance Theater Workshop—Bessie Schonberg Theater 219 W. 19th St.
(between Seventh and Eighth Aves.) (212) 924-0077 *www.dtw.org*. A couple of
flights of stairs and a few twists and turns get you to the Bessie Schonberg Theater, one of the city's best dance venues. The theater packs a lot of performances
into its season, with an array of artists from the dance and the music worlds generally performing for one to three nights. Best of all, tickets tend to range from
$8 to $15. **Subway:** A, C, E to 14th St.; 1, 9 to 18th St.; L to Eighth Ave.

Dixon Place at Vineyard 26 309 E. 26th St. (at Second Ave.) (212) 532-1546
www.dixonplace.org. Choreographers, actors, writers, performance artists and musicians can present works in progress here. It remains a playground for starry-eyed
wannabes and a refuge for the already established. Tickets prices range from free to
$12, depending on the event. **Subway:** 6 to 28th St.

Isadora Duncan Foundation Studio 141 W. 26th St., 3rd Fl. (between Sixth
and Seventh Aves.) (212) 691-5040. This small, attractive studio seats about 50
for its occasional shows of classic Duncan works and dances from contemporary
choreographers. **Subway:** F, V, 1, 9 to 23rd St.

Joyce SoHo 155 Mercer St. (between Houston and Prince Sts.) (212) 431-9233
www.joyce.org. The Joyce SoHo provides a place for new choreographers to
showcase their work before they venture onto larger performance spaces such as
the Joyce in Chelsea. With 75 freestanding seats, the comfortable loft-like space

has a very open feel. Thanks to the lack of columns, every seat in the house is a good one. **Subway:** F, S, V to Broadway–Lafayette St.; N, R to Prince St.

Movement Research at the Judson Church 55 Washington Sq. South (212) 477-0351 *www.judson.org*. Since the 1960's, this former house of worship has hosted performances of bold and eclectic new works by dance and performance artists. Movement Research continues the tradition with a free Monday-night series. **Subway:** A, C, E, F, S, V to W. 4th St.

Mulberry Street Theater 70 Mulberry St. (at Bayard St.) (212) 349-0126. Once a public school, this theater space has been transformed effectively into two dance studios and a black-box theater. It is home to H.T. Chen and Dancers, a company that infuses technically vigorous American modern dance with Chinese inflections. In addition to forging ahead with Chen's aesthetic imperative, Mulberry hosts programs that feature the work of unknown and mid-career artists, including "Moving Word," a series devoted to choreography inspired by poetry. **Subway:** J, M, N, Q, R, W, Z, 6 to Canal St.

St. Mark's Church in the Bowery 131 E. 10th St. (at Second Ave.) (212) 674-8112 *www.danspaceproject.org*. Following a devastating fire in 1978, the interior of the city's second-oldest church was restructured into a versatile open space that hosts performing arts, especially dance, and religious services. Danspace Project performances are daring and experimental. **Subway:** 6 to Astor Pl.

Other Arts Venues: A Mixed Bag

Many of New York's performance spaces host a wide variety of offerings. Although **Carnegie Hall** is listed under "Classical Music," its season might include anything from opera to jazz to stand-up comedy. And **Lincoln Center's** array of theaters and performance spaces play host to theater, opera, classical and chamber music, jazz, film—you name it. See also the **Exploring New York** chapter for details on **Radio City Music Hall,** where the offerings tend to be more pop and glitz than classical—but the Art Deco setting couldn't be more magical. Variety is the watchword at the venues listed below.

Brooklyn Academy of Music 30 Lafayette Ave. (off Flatbush Ave.) (718) 636-4100 *www.bam.org*. BAM is Brooklyn's answer to Lincoln Center, with an emphasis on the contemporary and the cutting-edge. This is one of the nation's leading arts centers, hosting innovative programming, including theater, dance, music, performance art and more, much of it with a dynamic and daring edge. Independent films are regularly screened at BAM Rose Cinemas, and BAM's **Next Wave Festival,** held in the fall, is a major event on the city's cultural calendar. **Subway:** M, N, Q, R, W, 2, 3, 4, 5 to Atlantic Ave./Pacific St.

Columbia University—Miller Theater 2960 Broadway (at 116th St.) (212) 854-7799. Columbia has a state-of-the-art theater that brings the finest opera, music and dance, as well as theater, poetry readings and lectures, to Morningside Heights. One extremely popular event is the sensational Sonic Boom Festival, a new-music series. **Subway:** 1, 9 to 116th St.

The Kitchen 512 W. 19th St. (between 10th and 11th Aves.) (212) 255-5793 www.thekitchen.org. The careers of avant-garde luminaries such as composer Philip Glass and performance artist Laurie Anderson began at The Kitchen. Today the theater continues to present emerging and innovative artists in dance, theater, film and everything in between. Tickets are quite affordable. **Subway:** A, C, E to 14th St.; L to Eighth Ave.

La MaMa ETC 74A E. 4th St. (between Second Ave. and Bowery) (212) 254-6468. La MaMa's four stages showcase a diverse and sometimes bizarre program of avant-garde dance, theater and performance art from American and international troupes. **Subway:** F, V to Second Ave.

Makor 35 W. 67th St. (between Central Park West and Broadway) (212) 601-1000 www.makor.org. Makor is a Jewish community arts center that's made a splash with its innovative and avant-garde events, whether it's acid jazz or Jewish/Latino hip-hop. A twenty- and thirtysomething crowd of hip intellectuals flocks here to take in music, film, gallery shows, comedy, lectures, literary readings, seminars and much more, all of it presented in an intimate setting. **Subway:** 1, 9 to 66th St.

92nd Street Y Tisch Center for the Arts 1395 Lexington Ave. (at E. 92nd St.) (212) 996-1100 or 212/415-5500 www.92ndsty.org. This is no ordinary YMCA—it's an extraordinary center for the performing arts, offering an array of top-flight entertainment and cultural programming. New Yorkers come here for the chance to see world-class performers in an intimate setting, or to hear leading writers and intellectuals engage in thought-provoking panel discussions. You might catch top classical and jazz performers, chamber music, an evening of cabaret, a lecture from a Nobel Prize winner, a documentary film screening, modern dance or a literary reading. Tickets are a great bargain given the quality of the offerings—usually under $30. **Subway:** 4, 5, 6 to 86th St.; 6 to 96th St.

Symphony Space 2537 Broadway (at 95th St.) (212) 864-1414 or 212/864-5400 www.symphonyspace.org. Symphony Space just emerged from a major renovation in spring 2002, with a revamped main stage hosting music and dance performances, a new cafe (which will host book club discussions), and a revitalization of the **Thalia Theater,** which screens classic and independent films and serves as a smaller auxiliary performance space. Regular events include an annual Bloomsday marathon reading of Joyce's *Ulysses,* performances by the New York Gilbert and Sullivan Players and the "Wall to Wall" series of marathon performances celebrating individual composers. **Subway:** 1, 2, 3 to 96th St.

Town Hall 123 W. 43rd St. (between Sixth and Seventh Aves.) (212) 840-2824 www.the-townhall-nyc.org. This landmark theater hosts theater, dance, music, lectures, pop and world music, comedy—you name it. The offerings range from live tapings of *A Prarie Home Companion* to performances by international symphony and chamber music companies. **Subway:** B, D, F, N, Q, R, S, V, W, 1, 2, 3, 7, 9 to 42nd St.

FILM

There is no question that New York is in love with film. No other American city can boast more cinemas consistently screening independent and foreign movies or showing revivals of old classics. A walk through Manhattan inevitably leads you to a block crowded with a film crew and actors, or a cluster of New York University film students fine-tuning their craft on a downtown street corner with an old camera.

So many movies are shown throughout the city in a single evening that it's important to learn a few essentials. For starters, tickets to most standard theaters are now around $10, and if you buy your tickets in advance through **Moviefone** at (212) 777-3456, an additional $1.50 will be charged to your credit card. There is no surcharge for online orders at *www.moviefone.com*. Moviefone and a similar service, **www.fandango.com,** handle most major theaters; their service charge is the price you have to pay to beat the crowds and get into a recent release. Local papers, including *The New York Times* and the *Village Voice*, print times and locations.

Serious movie buffs will want to visit the **American Museum of the Moving Image** (*see section* "Queens" *in chapter* **Exploring New York***)*.

Movie Theaters of Note

Angelika Film Center 18 W. Houston St. (at Mercer St.) (212) 995-2000. One of New York's favorite cinemas for independent and foreign films, this six-screen theater on the border of SoHo and Greenwich Village, offers the extra bonus of midnight screenings on weekends. In addition to the concession stand, the theater's lobby cafe serves higher than standard fare to match its higher prices. Buy tickets in advance, as shows can sell out quickly. **Subway:** F, S, V to Broadway-Laffayette St.; N, R to Prince St.

Anthology Film Archives 32 Second Ave. (at 2nd St.) (212) 505-5181. It's no surprise that this theater has a wealth of unusual material to offer, since it began in 1970 as a museum dedicated to avant-garde cinema. The films shown here are often unknown, but you're likely to find the best of the genre. Check listings for early works from better-known directors as well as the chance to catch a classic on the big screen. Tickets are available only at the box office. **Subway:** F, V to Second Ave.

Film Forum 209 W. Houston St. (between Sixth Ave. and Varick St.) (212) 727-8110 *www.filmforum.com*. Film buffs throughout the city know this charming three-screen theater consistently provides some of the best cinema New York offers, ranging from recent documentaries to silent films. Tickets often sell out quickly, especially on weekends. **Subway:** 1, 9 to Houston St.; C, E to Spring St.

Lincoln Plaza Cinemas 1886 Broadway (at 62nd St.) (212) 757-2280. This modest six-screen theater on the cusp of the Upper West Side may be the best place to see foreign and independent movies uptown. Don't expect to find Snow Caps or Raisinettes at the concession stand—you're more likely to overpay for a smoked salmon sandwich. **Subway:** A, B, C, D, 1, 9 to 59th St.–Columbus Circle.

The Quad 34 W. 13th St. (between Fifth and Sixth Aves.) (212) 225-8800. If the movies at this four-theater cinema were not some of the best independent and foreign shows in town, nobody would put up with watching movies on such tiny screens. But its charm as well as its selection of films keep people coming back to this Village standby. **Subway:** F, L, N, Q, R, V, W, 4, 5, 6 to 14th St.

The Screening Room 54 Varick St. (at Canal St.) (212) 334-2100 *www.the-screeningroom.com*. Found near the industrial entrance to the Holland Tunnel, this little theater redefines dinner and a movie. It's one part restaurant and one part cinema. The independent, foreign and classic flicks beat the fare found on the dinner menu. Although the schedule changes, you can count on a regular offering of Sunday brunch followed by a showing of *Breakfast at Tiffany's*. **Subway:** 1, 9, A, C, E to Canal St.

Sony IMAX at Lincoln Center 1992 Broadway at 68th St. (212) 336-5000. At the top of the casino-style four-story monolithic movie theater on the Upper West Side is a massive IMAX theater. The size and scope of the screen is tremendous, and the seats are arranged on an alarmingly steep angle. The films range from enhanced Discovery Channel material to animation and science fiction. **Subway:** 1, 9 to 66th St.

Walter Reade Theater 70 Lincoln Center Plaza (at Columbus Avenue) (212) 875-5600. This spacious, state-of-the-art theater located at the heart of the Lincoln Center complex screens a varied and diverse lineup of films. Recent festival themes have included Jewish cinema, films celebrating human rights, Iranian cinema and a "dance on camera" series. Also common are retrospectives of particular actors and directors, films by up-and-coming Independent American directors and silent movies accompanied by a live orchestra.

The best way to keep up with what's going on is via the **Film Society of Lincoln Center** Web site (*www.filmlinc.com*). Inside, the atmosphere is spacious and the single screen is large. The 268 plush, comfortable seats are set on a sloping floor, which ensures that there's not a bad seat in the house. Tickets sell out quickly. **Subway:** 1, 9 to 66th St.

The Ziegfeld 141 W. 54th St. (at Sixth Ave.) (212) 765-7600. One of the few older movie theaters left in New York that hasn't been renovated into a multiplex, this Midtown classic with a bright red décor boasts an enormous screen and seating for nearly 1,200 people. It's the perfect place to see the latest special-effects epic or a singalong revival of *The Sound of Music*. **Subway:** B, D, E to Seventh Ave.; F, N, R, Q, W to 57th St.

Film Festivals

The **New York Film Festival,** now starting its fifth decade, is easily the biggest and most famous of New York's film celebrations. Held annually in late September or early October, the festival screens around 20 independent, foreign and big-studio films in a two-week run at Lincoln Center. Buy tickets early—especially for the much-anticipated film that opens the event. Check *www.filmlinc.com* for schedules and ticketing details, or call (212) 875-5601.

Another festival of note, **New Directors/New Films** is held each March and co-sponsored by the Film Society of Lincoln Center and the Museum of Modern Art. For the past three decades the New Directors/New Films festival has offered first glimpses at the work of directors as talented and varied as John Sayles, Steven Spielberg, Peter Greenaway and Whit Stillman. Screenings have been held at MoMA in years past; in light of MoMA's move to Queens, it's likely that screenings will be held at the **Gramercy Theatre** on East 23rd Street in Manhattan, which is filling in as the venue for MoMA's ongoing film and media exhibitions. Check *www.filmlinc.com* for updates and firm venue announcements, and plan to buy tickets well in advance.

Conceived as a way to support the revitalization of Lower Manhattan after the September 11 attacks and to reinforce New York's image as a major filmmaking center, the **TriBeCa Film Festival** demonstrated serious star power during its inaugural festivities in May 2002. Staged by Robert De Niro and producer Jane Rosenthal, it will be an annual event.

Check *www.tribecafilmfestival.org* for the 2003 schedule.

For the latest information on restaurants, hotels, concerts, nightlife, sporting events and more, check online at New York Today, the *New York Times* Web site devoted entirely to life in New York City: www.nytoday.com.

Shopping in New York

Welcome to New York City, shoppers—you're in the big leagues now. What's most appealing about a Big Apple shopping spree is the myriad number of possibilities the city affords, from world-famous department stores to a seemingly infinite variety of boutiques. Special finds can be had at every price, whether you have $10 to spend or $10,000. Everything you've heard is true: You can buy anything here—and it's a lot more fun than surfing the Internet.

MIDTOWN & UPTOWN SHOPPING

Shopping in Manhattan above 34th Street is a little like ascending a Himalayan peak. The foot of the mountain is dense and rich with store growth, but there is a lot of undesirable vegetation. Ascend to the lofty heights of the peak and the views are spectacular, but the expenses are so steep that it might make your blood thin.

The trailhead for the expedition is **Herald Square**, home to **Macy's**, the world's largest department store, made famous by Thanksgiving parades. Navigating Macy's, which takes up an entire city block, is neither easy nor particularly satisfying. Your best bet is to stick to the subterranean floors, where bargains are most abundant.

Move up Broadway from 34th and come smack into the heart of the **Garment District**—not particularly inviting to casual shoppers, but a paradise for do-it-yourself fashionistas. Every fabric, button, feather or bit of leather trim ever imagined is available here. Shops tend to specialize in one niche or another, so if a particular shop doesn't have what you want, ask the proprietor to direct you to a store that will.

Continue walking north up Broadway and emerge at the recently cleansed and sanitized **Times Square**. The goods news is that the triple X pornography is gone; the bad news is that there is mostly schlock in its place. But for those who cannot leave the city without a Yankees baseball cap or a Statue of Liberty headpiece made of green Styrofoam, this is the place. Besides the innumerable trinket vendors, Disney, MTV and World Wrestling Entertainment have logo stores along Broadway. **Toys "R" Us** has opened a flagship store (they claim it's the world's largest toy store) at Broadway and 44th Street, complete with its own full-scale Ferris wheel. Nearby, 42nd Street between Seventh and Eighth Avenues has been transformed into a neon-bright shopping arcade, complete with such mall standards as the Museum Company and a Hello Kitty boutique.

Style mavens with something a little classier in mind should make a quick break east, and start strolling up Fifth Avenue. As the famous sites of St.

Patrick's Cathedral and Rockefeller Center loom ahead, **Saks Fifth Avenue**, the venerable clothier to the ladies who lunch, will appear on the right.

Fifth Avenue from 50th Street to Central Park is one of the richest shopping corridors in the world (surpassed only in recent years by Madison Avenue). As you parade up the designer-clad avenue—which has been democratized of late by super-boutiques from accessible retailers such as **Banana Republic** and **Liz Claiborne**—don't miss one of the more unique offerings. Whatever you think of the clothes, the **Versace** store at 52nd Street is worth a quick stop. Remodeled to look like an 18th-century palazzo, it comes complete with a marble facade, a sweeping serpentine staircase and elaborate mosaics.

As Fifth Avenue meets Central Park, it suddenly morphs from a commercial hub into a fancy residential boulevard. But right at the corner of 59th is a land-mark institution for children of all ages, **F.A.O. Schwartz**. For better or worse, every outlandish toy your child has ever dreamed of is in this huge city-block-long playland. Small people are free to mount the life-sized stuffed elephants or drive the pint-sized Porsches as they please.

Go east one block and yet another Gold Coast emerges. It seems that every upscale merchant on the planet has a store on Madison Avenue between 57th Street and 72nd. The boulevard continues its platinum march through the 70's and 80's, where it becomes a haven of luxury home décor shops.

Most shops along Madison specialize in sumptuous merchandise—every design house under the sun has a shop along this gold-plated stretch. It's all here, from the clean modern lines of **Calvin Klein** and **Donna Karan** to the sleek confidence of **Carolina Herrera**; from the preppy-luxe of **Michael Kors** to the knowing girlishness of Stella McCartney's **Chloé**; from the lush elegance of **Emanuel Ungaro** to over-the-top theatrics of **Valentino** and **Gianfranco Ferré**. It's worth strolling the blocks even if you don't intend to buy, as the windows can be particularly entertaining. Worth seeking out is U.K. import **Nicole Farhi's** showcase on 60th Street off Madison. It is a wide-open loft space, with clean lines, a muted palette and clothes ranging from simple cotton separates to orange leather shirt-coats, plus a stunning collection of distressed leather and globally influenced furniture and homewares on the subterranean level. The other must on Madison is **Barneys New York**, a dizzying display that makes a fitting conclusion to a shopping spree, Manhattan style.   —*Leslie Kaufman*

Garment District
Subway: A, B, C, D, E, F, N, R, S, Q, V, W, 1, 2, 3, 7, 9 to 42nd St.

Daytona Trimmings 251 W. 39th St. (between Seventh & Eighth Aves.) (212) 354-1713. Every possible kind of adornment, all excellently priced.

Hyman Hendler & Sons 67 W. 38th St. (at Sixth Ave.) (212) 840-8393 *www.hymanhendler.com*. The last word in ribbons; Martha Stewart's a fan.

Paron Fabrics Annex 206 W. 40th St. (between Seventh and Eighth Aves.) (212) 768-3266 *www.paronfabrics.com*. Other locations: Flagship retail store at 56 W. 57th St. (near Sixth Ave.), second floor (212) 247-6451; 855 Lexington Ave. (between 64th and 65th Sts.) (212) 772-7353. The city's best outlet for quality fabrics, often at a substantial discount.

Fifth & Madison Avenues

(See also "Jewelry" *later in this chapter.)*

Subway: E, N, R, V, W to Fifth Ave.; 4, 5, 6 to nearest cross street.

Ann Taylor 645 Madison Ave. (at 60th St.) (212) 832-2010
www.anntaylor.com. The gorgeous multistory flagship, carrying all lines, including career wear, petites, shoes, and fragrance.

Banana Republic 626 Fifth Ave. (at 50th St., Rockefeller Center) (212) 974-2350 *www.bananarepublic.com.* The elegant two-floor flagship emporium, carrying all clothing and home lines.

Boutique Georgio Armani 760 Madison Ave. (at 65th St.) (212) 988-9191
www.emporioarmani.com. **Emporio Armani** 601 Madison Ave. (at 57th St.)
(212) 317-0800.

Burberry 10 W. 57th St. (212) 371-5010 *www.burberry.com* Note: Burberry is scheduled to move into its new flagship store at 9 E. 57th St. by Nov. 2002.

Calvin Klein 654 Madison Ave. (at 60th St.) (212) 292-9000

Chanel 15 E. 57th St. (between Fifth and Madison Aves.) (212) 355-5050
www.chanel.com

Carolina Herrera 954 Madison Ave. (at 75th St.) (212) 249-6552
www.carolinaherrera.com

Chanel 15 E. 57th St. (between Fifth and Madison Aves.) (212) 355-5050
www.chanel.com

Chloé 850 Madison Ave. (at 70th St.) (212) 717-8220 *www.chloe.com*

Donna Karan 819 Madison Ave. (between 68th and 69th Sts.)
(212) 861-1001 *www.donnakaran.com.* **DKNY** 655 Madison Ave. (at 60th St.)
(212) 223-DKNY *www.dkny.com.*

Emanuel Ungaro 792 Madison Ave. (at 67th St.) (212) 249-4090
www.ungaro.com

F.A.O. Schwarz 767 Fifth Ave. (between 58th and 59th Sts.) (212) 644-9400
www.fao.com

Georgio Armani 760 Madison Ave. (at 65th St.) (212) 988-9191
www.emporioarmani.com. **Emporio Armani** 601 Madison Ave. (at 57th and 58th Sts.) (212) 317-0800.

Gianfranco Ferré 845 Madison Ave. (at 70th St.) (212) 717-5430
www.gianfrancoferre.com

Givenchy 710 Madison Ave. (at 63rd St.) (212) 688-4338 *www.givenchy.com*

Gucci 685 Fifth Ave. (at 54th St.) (212) 826-2600 *www.gucci.com*

Hermès 691 Madison Ave. (at 62nd St.) (212) 751-3181 *www.hermes.com*

Liz Claiborne 650 Fifth Ave. (at 52nd St.) (212) 956-6505
www.lizclaiborne.com. The two-story flagship featuring complete selections of all lines, including Liz Claiborne Woman and Petites.

Michael Kors 974 Madison Ave. (at 76th St.) (212) 452-4685

Nicole Farhi 10 E. 60th St. (between Fifth and Madison Aves.)
(212) 223-8811

Prada 724 Fifth Ave. (between 56th and 57th Sts.) (212) 664-0010
www.prada.com. Other location: 841 Madison Ave. (at 70th St.)
(212) 327-4200.

Ralph Lauren 867 Madison Ave. (at 72nd St.) (212) 606-2100 *www.polo.com*

Toys "R" Us 1514 Broadway (at 44th St.). (800) 869-7787 *www.toysrus.com*
Other location: 24-30 Union Sq. (212) 674-8697.

Valentino 747 Madison Ave. (at 65th St.) (212) 772-6969
www.valentino.it/main.htm

Versace 647 Fifth Ave. (between 51st and 52nd Sts.) (212) 317-0224 *www.ver-sace.com*. Other location: 815 Madison Ave. (between 68th and 69th Sts.)
(212) 744-6868.

DEPARTMENT STORES

Barneys New York 660 Madison Ave. (at 61st St.) (212) 826-8900 or
(212) 945-1600 *www.barneys.com*. **Barneys New York Co-Op**, 23 W. 18th St.
(between Seventh and Eighth Aves.) (212) 826-8900. Barneys continues to be
the purveyor of what is hip and fashion-chic. The beautiful store offers cutting-
edge fashion, accessories (including a killer shoe department), cosmetics and
wearable designs from up-and-coming visionaries, both international and home-
grown. The tabletop department is a dazzler. Fashionistas usually go straight for
the shoe section to pick up sharp, sexy heels. Barneys Co-Op, on 18th Street,
offers casual-chic fashions, from Daryl K jeans to Juicy Couture tees. Fabulous
twice-a-year warehouse sales are held at 255 West 17th Street (between Seventh and Eighth Aves.). The summer sale generally runs from late August until
Labor Day, the winter sale in February or March. **Subway:** 4, 5, 6 to 59th St.

Bergdorf Goodman 754 Fifth Ave. (at 58th St.) (212) 753-7300. **Bergdorf
Goodman Man**, 745 Fifth Ave. (at 58th St.). Visit Bergdorf's, a worthy neighbor of Tiffany & Co. and the Plaza, for a whiff of old New York glamour. This
purveyor of sophistication dresses both ladies who lunch and the Park Avenue
junior socialites following in their footsteps. An ultra-refined, almost exclusive
atmosphere sets the ideal stage for haute couture fashions of Badgley Mischka,
Carolina Herrera, Dolce and Gabbana, and other upscale designers. The elegant
emporium is particularly excellent in high-end housewares, handbags, jewelry
and shoes. **Subway:** E, N, R, V, W to Fifth Ave.

Bloomingdale's 1000 Third Ave. (at 59th St.) (212) 705-2000
www.bloomingdales.com. Many New Yorkers are devoted to "Bloomie's" for
everything from beaded cocktail dresses to bridal registries. This massive square-
block store attracts a diverse clientele, from trust-fund teens to stylish professionals and savvy tourists, all of whom exit with arms full of "big brown bags."
The upscale selection is a step above Macy's in quality and sophistication, but
more egalitarian and affordable than Saks. Great for shoes, coats, cosmetics and

homewares, the store also boasts a huge men's department for the fashion-conscious who demand a stylish cut. Men's and women's selections run the gamut from reliable basics to American classic designers Tommy Hilfiger and Ralph Lauren to sexy international couture threads. Regular weekend sales, which usually include designer labels, happen about once a month. Bloomingdale's is looking to expand its empire to 504 Broadway in SoHo, where they plan to open an apparel store geared to young shoppers. **Subway:** 4, 5, 6 to 59th St.

Century 21 22 Cortlandt St. (between Church St. and Broadway) (212) 227-9092 *www.c21stores.com*. This discount department store extraordinaire, heavily damaged in the World Trade Center attack, pulled off the Herculean feat of reopening its doors in March 2002. The legendary designer mart is back in full form; in fact, it's better than ever. Shopping pros come to sift through deeply discounted designer goods. With menswear on the first floor, the second floor is famous for the chaotic but bargain-rich shoe department, where the goods include Prada and Kenneth Cole at low, low prices. For the real shopaholic, the third floor is the place to be, with end-of-season steals on designer goods from the likes of Gucci, Urchin, Prada and Tocca. A worthwhile find is inevitable with patience—and in fashion currency, you'll be in the black. The weekday lunch hour isn't quite the frenetic crush it used to be, but choose a day other than Saturday to preserve your sanity. **Subway:** N, R to Cortlandt St.

Henri Bendel 712 Fifth Ave. (at 56th St.) (212) 247-1100. The signature brown-and-white striped Bendel bags alone are reason enough to buy something in this jewel box of a store. One of Manhattan's prettiest stores, Bendel's offers an excellent selection of both sophisticated and funky designer threads and accessories. The first floor greets you with counters of Bobbi Brown, MAC and Trish McEvoy cosmetics. A circular staircase winds up through the entire townhouse-style store, serving as its grand focal point and enabling you to spot a silk scarf on the third floor that will go perfectly with that cashmere twin set you're holding on the second. The hat department is a delight in any season. Although Bendel's does not carry menswear or shoes, it's an essential stop on any Fifth Avenue shopping jaunt. Hairstylist to the stars **Garren New York** (212-841-9400) keeps a chic salon on the third floor. **Subway:** 4, 5, 6 to 59th St.; E, N, R, V, W to Fifth Ave.

Lord & Taylor 424 Fifth Ave. (between 38th and 39th Sts.) (212) 391-3344 *www.lordandtaylor.com*. A few blocks from Macy's, Lord & Taylor offers reasonable prices, regular sales, quality mid-priced lines and some big-name designers. Although not exactly poised at the fashion forefront, Lord & Taylor holds a certain traditional charm of shopping days past. Shoppers browse mostly for dresses, bags and work suits; think conservative, tasteful American classics. Midtown workers come in droves to buy hosiery on their lunch breaks, especially during the first-rate sales. **Subway:** B, D, F, V, S to 42nd St.

Macy's 151 W. 34th St. (between Broadway and Seventh Ave.) (212) 695-4400 *www.macys.com*. The world's largest department store, and the historic heart of New York shopping, Macy's celebrated its centennial in 2002. The mammoth, always-crowded store is particularly well known for its storewide one-day sales (midweek, usually Wednesdays) and great Cellar bargains on essentials for the home. The extensive first-floor cosmetics department offers all major brands, and the coat, bathing suit, hosiery, and shoe sections are exceptionally large. The fourth floor junior department packs a dense array of trendy gear targeted at the quintessential American teen. You'll find a jewel of a Metropolitan Museum of Art gift boutique on the mezzanine level. Try to visit during the annual Flower Show, a two-week event that marks the launch of Spring. **Subway:** B, D, F, N, R, S, Q, V, W, 1, 2, 3, 9 to 34th St.

Saks Fifth Avenue 611 Fifth Ave. (between 49th and 50th Sts.) (212) 753-4000 *www.saksfifthavenue.com.* Poised in a coveted location across from Rockefeller Center, Saks is a city landmark for sophistication, style and selection. Saks has served an upscale crowd for almost a century with the best and most extensive designer shoe and cosmetics departments in the city, plus expansive, well-organized apparel and accessories departments. The lingerie department is also exquisite. Most high-end labels for both women and men are on hand—including Bagley Mischka, Gaultier, Lina Beday, TSE and Vera Wang—but you'll also find many upscale basics. If you visit during the holidays, get in line to see the exquisitely decorated store windows before sweeping indoors for an early gift to yourself (a pair of Ferragamo cashmere shoes, perhaps?). **Subway:** B, D, F, V, S to 47th-50th St.–Rockefeller Center; E, N, R, V, W to Fifth Ave.

DOWNTOWN SHOPPING

The premier shopping district of downtown Manhattan is the square mile known as **SoHo** (Houston to Grand Street, from Broadway to Sixth Avenue). This jumble of cobblestone streets and industrial-era loft buildings grew to prominence two decades ago as an artists' paradise—a place where an aspiring painter or sculptor could grab 6,000 square feet of raw space in crowded Manhattan for next to nothing. That's no longer true, of course. The artists created cachet, which in turn attracted rock stars, fashion models and then anyone with loads of cash.

The creative community has largely been driven out, but the cavernous spaces they once inhabited have been converted to galleries and lots and lots of fabulous stores, both familiar names and one-of-a-kind boutiques. Everything from vinyl platform boots to minimalist beige bed linens is available in this richly varied shopping district. But fair warning: Everything costs top dollar. In fact, like the Fifth and Madison Avenue corridors, SoHo is also couture territory, but with a downtown, left-of-center, rock-and-roll twist: Expect to find a world atlas's worth of artsy international designer names like **Anna Sui**, **Marc Jacobs**, **Vivienne Westwood**, **Helmut Lang**, **Vivienne Tam**, **Jill Stuart** and **Yohji Yamamoto**, plus an increasing number of hipped-up outlets of uptown retailers such as **Louis Vuitton** and **Prada**, including Prada's **Miu Miu** boutique, funkier and flouncier than the streamlined original, and **Philosophy di Alberta Ferretti**, featuring the Italian designer's more playful, (somewhat) less expensive line of sexy womenswear.

Other better-than-garden-variety, less-than-couture-priced merchants include **Otto Tootsie Plohound,** which offers the latest in platform footwear in a setting more like a dance club than a shoe store. **Anthropologie** has a whimsical selection of velvet slip dresses, antiqued candlesticks and wicker furniture to go with its exotic-tinged, mod-attic décor, while Italian import **Replay General Store** has managed to transform all-American work-a-day denim into a fashion-forward statement. Home design wears futuristic at **Property,** gets a sculptural modern look in the hot pottery of **Jonathan Adler,** and brings high style into the bathroom at **Waterworks.**

Just east of SoHo is **Nolita** (**N**orth **o**f **Li**ttle **Ita**ly), which has evolved into a tidy, stylish neighborhood with a chic shopping scene in the last couple of years. The unique boutiques along Mott, Mulberry and Elizabeth Streets are pricey but wonderful, leaning toward up-and-coming clothing, jewelry and accessories designers, plus modern home-design shops. If you have a passion for headwear, do not miss hat designer **Kelly Christy,** who can frequently be found outside her shop, sipping coffee with friends, while French handbag designer **Jamin Puech** is a standout for romantic French-sewn totes.

The East Village, especially along 9th Street east of Second Avenue, and the area called NoHo around Bond Street, has become another bastion of young designers styling one-of-a-kind wear, much of it quite affordable.

Above 14th Street, Broadway from Union Square north has become a corridor of home decorating stores. The essential stop here is **ABC Carpet & Home,** an eclectic, expensive bazaar of luxuriant clutter, from quality furnishings to international carpets to luxury linens.

Fashionistas looking for the newest frontier should head east to the Meatpacking District, where fabulous **Jeffrey New York** (think pony skin belts and fur-lined stiletto heels) is accompanied by a multiplying crop of modernist design boutiques, particularly along Gansevoort and Washington Streets.

—Leslie Kaufman

(See also "Specialty Stores" later in this chapter for recommendations on outstanding shops throughout the downtown area. See "Clothing" for **Jeffrey New York** *and* "Gifts & Homewares" *for* **ABC Carpet & Home.***)*

SoHo & Nolita

Subway: F, S, V to Broadway–Lafayette St.; N, R to Prince St.; 6 to Spring St; C, E to Spring St.

Anna Sui 113 Greene St. (between Prince and Spring Sts.) (212) 941-8406 *www.annasui.com* or *www.annasuibeauty.com*

Anthropologie 375 West Broadway (between Spring and Broome Sts.) (212) 343-7070 *www.anthropologie.com*

Helmut Lang 80 Greene St. (between Spring and Broome Sts.) (212) 334-1014 *www.helmutlang.com.* **Helmut Lang Parfums** 81 Greene St. (between Spring and Broome Sts.) (212) 334-3921.

Jamin Puech 252 Mott St. (between Houston and Prince Sts.) (212) 334-9730 *www.jamin-puech.com*

Jill Stuart 100 Greene St. (between Prince and Spring Sts.) (212) 343-2300

Jonathan Adler 465 Broome St. (between Greene and Mercer Sts.). (212) 941-8950 *www.jonathanadler.com*

Kelly Christy 235 Elizabeth St. (between Houston and Prince Sts.) (212) 965-0686

Louis Vuitton 116 Greene St. (between Prince and Spring Sts.) (212) 274-9090 *www.vuitton.com*

Marc Jacobs 163 Mercer St. (between Houston and Prince Sts.) (212) 343-1490 *www.marcjacobs.com*

Miu Miu 100 Prince St. (between Mercer and Greene Sts.) (212) 334-5156 *www.miumiu.it*

Otto Tootsie Plohound 431 West Broadway (between Prince and Spring Sts.) (212) 925-8931

Philosophy di Alberta Ferretti 452 West Broadway (near Prince St.) (212) 460-5500 *www.philosophy.it*

Prada 575 Broadway (at Prince St.) (212) 334-8888

Property 14 Wooster St. (between Grand and Canal Sts.) (917) 237-0123

Replay General Store 109 Prince St. (at Greene St.) (212) 673-6300 *www.replay.it*

Vivienne Tam 99 Greene St. (between Prince and Spring Sts.) (212) 966-2398 *www.viviennetam.com*

Vivienne Westwood 71 Greene St. (between Spring and Broome Sts.) (212) 334-5200 *www.viviennewestwood.com*

Waterworks 469 Broome St. (at Greene St.) (212) 966-0605 *www.waterworks.com*

Yohji Yamamoto 103 Grand St. (at Mercer St.) (212) 966-9066 *www.yohjiyamamoto.co.jp*

BARGAIN SHOPPING

Bargains, bargains, come and get your bargains! Manhattan, even these days, is full of hawkers.

The **Diamond District** (W. 47th St. between Fifth and Sixth Aves.) is the place to go for bargains on diamonds, precious gems, gold and other fine jewelry. The block is lined with dealers, most of whom are Hasidic Jews for whom diamonds are the family business. You can get an emerald ring for one-fifth the price of a similar ring at Tiffany's—but you have to know what you're doing. Your best bet is to prepare in advance by reading up on the kinds of gems or jewelry you're interested in, perhaps visiting some high-end jewelers in your area who can point out the features that speak quality in fine jewelry. You might also read up on shopping the district at *www.47th-street.com*, which has some frank and useful tips that will help you avoid pitfalls in the discount district, plus a full list of reputable dealers. Once you arrive in the Diamond District, be sure to price compare. And keep in mind that virtually all stores are open only weekdays, usually from 10 A.M. to 5 P.M. or so.

It's not as tough to find real bargains in clothes, but you still have to know where to go. Generally speaking, stay off Madison Avenue. Instead, try stores like **Daffy's** ("Clothing Bargains for Millionaires"). It's a badly organized, slightly neurotic atmosphere, but persevere.

And without doubt, take a subway (F train to Delancey St.) to **Orchard Street**, in the heart of the Lower East Side. Hipster boutiques are raiding this historic bargain district like wildfire, but there are still plenty of deals to be had. The street has a tarnished reputation. People say the bargains are only pseudo-bargains, but check out **Ben Freedman**, an old-world cheapie paradise with sidewalk racks that feature $5 leather belts and $6 ties. Don't miss the string of leather shops; **Grace Bags** for designer knockoff handbags of surprisingly decent quality, some for as little as $10; **Fine & Klein** or **Altman's Luggage** for brand-name luggage at a discount; and **Joe's Fabrics** for a kaleidoscope of linens, velvets, silks and damasks. The secret on Orchard Street is haggling: Don't be afraid. You don't have to be a pro. Just try walking out and see what happens. Think of what you want to pay, and just keep repeating it on your way to the door. It's fun, and you'll probably get what you want. But don't play the game if you're not serious, or you'll end up with some angry merchants! Stop in first at the **Lower East Side Visitor Center** (261 Broome St. between Orchard and Allen Sts., 888-825-8374 or 212-226-9010 *www.lowereastsideny.com*) to pick up a pamphlet-sized shopping guide (you can also find a full list of neighborhood shopping opportunities online).

Chinatown's **Canal Street** is a blast to stroll if you're looking for inexpensive backpacks, almost-free leather belts or exotic souvenirs. Stroll east from the intersection of Canal and Broadway for the best bounty, and bargain as you go. Skip the bootleg CDs, videos and DVDs though—you will be disappointed.

If you're in town just before—or better—just after Christmas, or in mid-summer, check out the sales in the world's best boutiques and department stores. Open the paper once you arrive and start researching; the sales in the finest stores usually appear in the first couple of pages. Even on sale, the prices won't be cheap at stores like Hermès and Henri Bendel, but you won't find merchandise of this quality anywhere else, including the so-called premium outlet malls.

The other secret of New York City bargains is the sample sale, in which last season's designer merchandise is offered at a fraction of the price. These sales go on throughout the year. To give you an idea, take the Echo Scarf sample sale: Silk scarves that normally sell for between $60 and $90 can be found in cardboard boxes labeled $5, $10 and $15. The best places to hunt them down is in the "Check Out" section of the weekly *Time Out New York*; *New York* magazine's New York Metro Web site (*www.nymetro.com*; click on "Shopping"), which updates its sale picks daily; and online at NYSale (*www.nysale.com*), your other best source to locate the hottest sales. When you hit a sample sale, avoid the lunch-hour crowds, bring cash, and don't expect much in the way of dressing rooms, so know your size or be ready to be creative (no returns).

Syms is the most famous of the men's discount clothiers, but they actually cater to women with careerwear, too. In the Flatiron District, the landmark **Ladies' Mile**, along Sixth Avenue below 21st Street, is lined with familiar discount names like **T.J. Maxx**, **Filene's Basement** and **Bed, Bath & Beyond**. Some say that the merchandise in these stores is picked especially for chic Manhattan shoppers and is better than what comes to the suburbs.

While you're in the neighborhood, check out the thrift shops just around the corner. The **Housing Works Thrift Shop** is a gem for men's and women's designer hand-me-downs, shoes and, best of all, furniture, with items like a great-looking oval Biedermaier table for $200.

And if you're in town on a weekend, don't forget the indoor and outdoor flea markets that operate all year round on and near the corner of Sixth Avenue and West 26th Street (see "Flea Markets" later in this chapter).

—*Tracie Rozhon*

(See "Vintage, Thrift & Resale" in the "Clothing" section for **Housing Works Thrift Shop**, **Salvation Army** and other stores for used clothing and housewares.)

Diamond District

Subway: B, D, F, S, V to 47th-50th St.–Rockefeller Center.

M Khordipour Enterprises 10 W. 47th St. (between Fifth and Sixth Aves.) (212) 869-2198

Peachtree Jewelers Inc. 580 Fifth Ave. (at 47th St.) (212) 398-1758

Unusual Wedding Rings in the National Jewelers Exchange, 4 W. 47th St., booth 86 (800) 877-3874 or (212) 944-1713 *www.unusualweddingrings.com*. Beautifully designed, top-quality wedding sets in gold and platinum at below-market prices.

Orchard Street Bargain District

Subway: F to Delancey St.; J, M, Z to Essex St.

Altman Luggage 125 Orchard St. (between Delancey and Rivington Sts.) (800) 372-3377 or (212) 254-7275 *www.altmanluggage.com*

Arivel Fashions 150 Orchard St. (between Rivington and Stanton Sts.) (212) 673-8992 *www.arivel.com*. For furs and leather goods.

Ben Freedman 137 Orchard St. (between Delancey and Rivington Sts.) (212) 674-0854

Fine & Klein 119 Orchard St. (near Delancey St.) (212) 674-6720

Grace Bags 190 Orchard St. (between Houston and Stanton Sts.) (212) 228-6118

Joe's Fabrics Warehouse 102 Orchard St. (at Delancey St.) (212) 674-7089

Klein's of Monticello 105 Orchard St. (at Delancey St.) (212) 966-1453. High-quality womenswear.

Rita's Leather Fair 176 Orchard St. (at Houston St.) (212) 533-2756

Discount Clothing

(For designer discounter **Century 21**, *see* "Department Stores" *earlier in this chapter.)*

Burlington Coat Factory 707 Sixth Ave. (at 23rd St.) (212) 229-1300 *www.coat.com.* Other location: 45 Park Pl. (between West Broadway and Church St.) (212) 571-2631. More than just coats—men's, women's and children's wear, plus housewares and luggage. **Subway:** F, V to 23rd St.

Canal Jean Co. 504 Broadway (between Spring and Broome Sts.) (212) 226-1130 *www.canaljean.com.* Cheapie jeans and T's for the MTV crowd. **Subway:** N, R to Prince St.; J, M, Q, W, Z, 6 to Canal St.

Daffy's 111 Fifth Ave. (at 18th St.) (212) 529-4477 *www.daffys.com.* Other location: 1311 Broadway (at 34th St.) (212) 736-4477; check for more locations. **Subway:** L, N, Q, R, W, 4, 5, 6 to 14th St.

Filene's Basement 620 Sixth Ave. (at 18th St.) (212) 620-3100 *www.filenes.com;* check for more locations. **Subway:** F, V to 14th St.

Loehmann's 101 Seventh Ave. (at 16th St.) (212) 352-0856 *www.loehmanns.com.* The place for designer fashions at a discount. **Subway:** 1, 2, 3, 9 to 14th St.

Moe Ginsburg 162 Fifth Ave. (at 21st St.) (212) 982-5254 or 242-3482. **Subway:** F, N, R, V to 23rd St.

Saint Laurie Merchant Tailors 350 Park Ave. (between 51st and 52nd Sts.) (212) 473-0100 *www.saintlaurie.com.* **Subway:** 6 to 51st St.

T.J. Maxx 620 Sixth Ave. (between 18th and 19th Sts.) (212) 229-0875 *www.tjmaxx.com.* **Subway:** F, V to 14th St.

Syms 400 Park Ave. (at 54th St.) (212) 317-8200 *www.syms.com.* **Subway:** 6 to 51st St. Other location: 42 Trinity Pl. (between Rector St. and Battery Park) (212) 797-1199. **Subway:** 1, 9, N, R to Rector St. Discount career wear for men and women.

ANTIQUES

New York is the largest center for antiques and collectibles in the world, a giant bazaar stocked with period furniture, china, glassware, textiles, books, coins, jewelry, rugs and toys from just about anywhere on earth. Collectors are either ecstatic by the sheer abundance of antiques, or frustrated by the difficulty of finding exactly what they seek—be it a 19th-century trotting-horse weather vane, a Ming vase, an 18th-century desk from Versailles, a 1930's Mickey Mouse toy or a baseball signed by Babe Ruth.

Another frustrating thing: the prices. Expect to pay top collectible dollar for any quality find. Still, the city remains an antique hound's dream come true.

Collectors with limited time, plan ahead. If you're a serious shopper, put together an itinerary, and let the dealers you're interested in know beforehand about the type of pieces you wish to see. Dealers are busy, especially such world-class dealers as **James J. Lally**, a specialist in Chinese art. They travel as much

as some of their clients do in order to present scholarly exhibitions with cata-
logues in their museum-style galleries.

Browsers who are not in the market for a specific piece but prefer to browse
can do well in a few select neighborhoods—most notably on the Upper East
Side, along East 59th, 60th and 61st Streets around Second Avenue, and along
Madison Avenue in the 70's. Lafayette Street north and south of Houston
Street is a good hunting ground for 20th-century finds.

New York is host to about 60 antiques fairs each year. Dealers come from
throughout the world to participate in fairs, the most notable of which take
place in the Park Avenue and Lexington Avenue armories. The **Asian Art Fair**,
a Spring event (*www.haughton.com*), is often described as the best of the art and
antiques shows in Manhattan. The preeminent dealer in Asian art, Robert H.
Ellsworth, explained its success, saying, "Even if you spent a year going around
the world, you would never be able to see all the fine Asian art exhibited here."
At the **Triple Pier Antiques Show**, held in the passenger ship terminals on the
Hudson River in March and November (212-255-0020 *www.stellashows.com*),
more than 600 dealers sell goods spanning the centuries and collectors' budgets.

Antiques and collectibles are also sold year-round at flea markets, the most
enduring of which is held on weekends at a parking lot on Sixth Avenue at
26th Street (*see* "Flea Markets" *later in this chapter*).   —*Rita Reif*

Barry Friedman Ltd. 32 E. 67th St. (between Park and Madison Aves.)
(212) 794-8950. Art Deco furniture and decorations by masters like Jean-Michel
Frank, Eileen Gray and Jean Dunand, plus avant garde art. **Subway:** 6 to 68th St.

Chisolm Gallery 55 W. 17th St. (at Sixth Ave.), 6th floor (212) 243-8834
www.vintagepostersnyc.com. A century of collectible-quality advertising posters
from around the globe. **Subway:** F, V to 14th St.

City Barn Antiques 269 Lafayette St. (at Prince St.) (212) 941-5757
www.citybarnantiques.com. One of the nation's premier specialists in mid-20th-
century Heywood Wakefield furnishings. **Subway:** N, R to Prince St.

Didier Aaron 32 E. 67th St. (between Park and Madison Aves.)
(212) 988-5248 *www.didieraaron.com*. Prominent Parisian dealer in French
17th- and 18th-century palace-quality furniture, objects and art.
Subway: 6 to 68th St.

Doyle & Doyle 189 Orchard St. (between Houston and Stanton Sts.)
(212) 677-9991 *www.doyledoyle.com*. Fine estate and antique jewelry, including
Georgian, Victorian, Edwardian, Art Deco and Art Nouveau pieces, in a jewel
box of a store. **Subway:** F to Delancey St.; J, M, Z to Essex St.

Evergreen Antiques 1249 Third Ave. (at 72nd St.) 212-744-5664
www.evergreenantiques.com. Mostly 19th-century Northern European furniture
in the neoclassical, Biedermaier and Empire styles. **Subway:** 6 to 68th St.

Guéridon 359 Lafayette St. (between Bleecker and Bond Sts.) (212) 677-7740.
French mid-century modern furnishings and accents. **Subway:** 6 to Bleecker
St.; F, S, V to Broadway–Lafayette St.

J.J. Lally & Co. 41 E. 57th St. (at Madison Ave.) (212) 371-3380. Chinese art and antiques. **Subway:** 4, 5, 6 to 59th St.; N, R to Fifth Ave.

Kentshire Galleries 37 E. 12th St. (between University Pl. and Broadway) (212) 673-6644. Large gallery dedicated to 18th- and 19th-century English antiques, ranging from jewelry and tabletop items to formal furnishings. **Subway:** L, N, R, Q, W, 4, 5, 6 to 14th St.

Manhattan Art & Antiques Center 1050 Second Ave. (between 55th and 56th Sts.) (212) 355-4400 *www.the-maac.com*. Three-floor antiques center housing more than 100 dealers. Genres run the gamut from antiquities to fine early 20th-century collectibles. **Subway:** 4, 5, 6 to 59th St.

R 82 Franklin St. (between Church St. and Broadway) (212)343-7979 *www.r20thcentury.com*. A premier source for mid-century modern legacy design. The emphasis is on Scandinavian furnishings and accessories, but you'll also find pieces from such wide-ranging masters as Henry Bertoia, Gio Ponti and the Eamses. **Subway:** 1, 9 to Franklin St.

Skyscraper 237 E. 60th St. (between Second and Third Aves.) (212) 588-0644 *www.skyscraperny.com*. High-quality Art Deco and streamline furniture and collectibles. **Subway:** N, R, W to Lexington Ave. Other locations: **Deco Deluxe**, 993 Lexington Ave. (between 71st and 72nd Sts.) (212) 472-2222. **Subway:** 6 to 68th St. **Deco Deluxe II**, 1038 Lexington Ave. (at 74th St.) (212) 249-5066. **Subway:** 6 to 77th St.

WaterMoon Gallery 211 West Broadway (between Franklin and White Sts.) (212) 925-5556. Fine Chinese and Tibetan antique furniture, Tibetan carpets, and Chinese porcelain and ceramics from the Neolithic era to the Ming Dynasty, plus an extensive selection of Chinese and Miao textiles and contemporary artwork by young Chinese artists, many of whom have never been shown outside of China. **Subway:** 1, 9 to Franklin Ave.

AUCTIONS

Despite recent price-fixing scandals among the world's biggest houses, Manhattan's world-renowned auction houses continue to provide lavish forums for those who can afford to indulge their passions for collecting. If you are interested in buying, be sure to attend the sale preview and study the catalogue for price estimates before you raise your paddle and bid. For those not in the market, simply watching the ceremonious sale can be a delight. Check local publications such as *The New York Times* and *Time Out New York*, as well as the auctions' own Web sites, for dates and events.

Christie's 20 Rockefeller Plaza (49th St. between Fifth and Sixth Aves.) (212) 636-2000 or (212) 636-2010 *www.christies.com*. Items that have graced the block at this two-century-old British institution include everything from Matisse and da Vinci canvases to the Academy Award Bette Davis won for *Jezebel*. Although this house is best known for headline-making sales, it also boasts departments for wine, cars, coins and sports memorabilia. **Subway:** B, D, F, S, V to 47th-50th Sts./Rockefeller Center.

Sotheby's 1334 York Ave. (at 72nd St.) (212) 606-7000 *www.sothebys.com*. From its humble beginnings in 1744 as a London book dealer, this house has grown into one of the world's most esteemed auction houses with branches all over the map. Auctions run the gamut, from the sale of van Gogh's "Irises" to Jacqueline Kennedy Onassis's estate. **Subway:** 6 to 68th St.

Guernsey's 108 1/2 E. 73rd St. (between Park and Lexington Aves.) (212) 794-2280 *www.guernseys.com*. One of New York's smaller auction houses, this institution is an esteemed source for modern collections, from artwork of the Soviet Union to rock-and-roll memorabilia. **Subway:** 6 to 77th St.

Swann Auction Galleries 104 E. 25th St. (between Park and Lexington Aves.) (212) 254-4710 *www.swanngalleries.com*. This specialized house devotes itself to rare books and the visual arts, including photos, vintage posters, autographs, maps and atlases, drawings and the like. **Subway:** 6 to 28th St.

Tepper Galleries 110 E. 25th St. (between Park and Lexington Aves.) (212) 677-5300 *www.teppergalleries.com*. To simply say that estates are sold off here doesn't do justice to the fine pieces that pass through this house. Offerings include antique furniture, fine silver, jewelry, carpets and fine artworks. **Subway:** 6 to 28th St.

SPECIALTY STORES
Beauty & Spa

Bath & Beauty

C.O. Bigelow 414 Sixth Ave. (between 8th and 9th Sts.) (212) 533-2700 *www.bigelowchemists.com*. This West Village spot offers a quirky mix of quality products, from the hard-to-find Biotherm skincare line to practical pillboxes. Perfect your hair with Knotty Girl Drama Queen Marshmallow moisture balance shampoo, get squeaky clean with a bath treat from Catherine Memmi, and give your daily regimen an international touch with a 2,000-bristle Elgydium toothbrush from France. **Subway:** A, C, E, F, S, V to W. 4th St.

Creed 9 Bond St. (between Broadway and Lafayette St.) (212) 228-1940. Other locations: 881 Madison Ave. (between 72nd and 73rd Sts.) (212) 794-4480; in Bergdorf Goodman, 754 Fifth Ave. (at 57th St.) (212) 872-2729. Much like an Hermès Kelly bag, a custom-made fragrance by this two-century-old French perfumer—which has designed signature scents for such larger-than-life ladies as Audrey Hepburn and Grace Kelly—is a grand splurge. You may have to be a real princess to afford it, but what wonderful company you'll be in. **Subway:** 6 to Bleecker St.

Face Stockholm 110 Prince St. (at Greene St.) (212) 966-9110 *www.facestockholm.com*. Other locations: 226 Columbus Ave. (at 70th St.)

(212) 769-1420; 687 Madison Ave. (at 61st St.) (212) 207-8833. As if lighting ceremonial candles, faithful customers stand before rows of lipsticks, glitter and nail polish, testing the wide array of hip shades, both glossy and matte. A perfect buy is one of FACE's sleek custom-filled compacts with miniature applicator. **Subway:** N, R to Prince St.

Fresh 57 Spring St. (between Lafayette and Mulberry Sts.) (212) 925-0099 *www.fresh.com.* Other locations: 1061 Madison Ave. (at 80th St.) (212) 396-0344; Bleecker St. (between Perry and W. 11th St.) (917) 408-1850. This Boston-based line excels at bath and body treats that come in delicious scents—cocoa, lychee, lemon, milk, honey, soy, rose—that are almost good enough to eat. Soaps are individually wrapped and tied with wire and stone, making perfect gifts to go. **Subway:** 6 to Spring St.

Helena Rubinstein Beauty Gallery 135 Spring St. (between Greene and Wooster Sts.) (877) 447-7646 or (212) 343-9966 *www.helenarubenstein.com.* This beauty oasis offers a moment of repose in the middle of a SoHo spree. The spacious white-on-white, gallery-like store promotes the experimentation of color. Helpful staff will advise you on beauty products like the popular Ritual Rouge lipstick, packaged in signature HR gold. **Subway:** N, R to Prince St.; 6 to Spring St.

Jo Malone 949 Broadway (between 22nd and 23rd Sts.) (212) 673-2220. *www.jomalone.com.* The North American flagship of London's favorite perfumery is located in the Flatiron Building. All products boast Jo Malone's gorgeous snow-white, black-trimmed packaging, a perfect statement of the line's elegant simplicity. Malone's philosophy is that one can find the perfect personal scent by experimenting with her 10 original fragrances, so enjoy the sniffing. **Subway:** N, R to 23rd St.

Kiehl's 109 Third Ave. (between 13th and 14th Sts.) (212) 677-3171 *www.kiehls.com.* Long lines at this venerable beauty landmark allow you to spot more products to add to your basket. Models and athletes alike are devotees of such classics as the Ultra Facial Moisturizer, Creme of Silk Groom for glossy hair and Lip Balm #1, a ubiquitous item in many city bags. Stay calm as the knowledgeable staff rewards you with more exceptional product samples, all in Kiehl's plain-wrap bottles. Saks boasts a well-stocked Kiehl's counter if you can't make it downtown. **Subway:** L, N, R, Q, W, 4, 5, 6 to 14th St.

Lafco New York 200 Hudson St. (between Canal and Vestry Sts.) (800)362-3677or (212) 925-0001 *www.lafcony.com.* This sleek and sprawling home-design store is the proud purveyor of the cult favorite Santa Maria Novella bath products. These beautifully packaged soaps by the famous Italian monastery are home accents in themselves. **Subway:** 1, 9 to Canal St.

L'Occitane 146 Spring St. (between West Broadway and Wooster St.) (212) 343-0109 *www.loccitane.com.* Other locations: 198 Columbus Ave. (at 69th St.) (212) 362-5146; 510 Madison Ave. (between 52nd and 53rd Sts.) (212) 826-5020; check for more locations. This Provençal import is a bath lovers' dream. The luxuriant hand cream is an epiphany. The most popular product is the 100 percent shea butter; extracted from the fruit of the African shea tree, it works wonders on skin, lips and hair and is an excellent treat for expectant mothers. Candles, shampoos, moisturizing soaps and fragrances are among the offerings. **Subway:** N, R to Prince St.; C, E to Spring St.

M.A.C. 113 Spring St. (between Mercer and Greene Sts.) (212) 334-4641 *www.maccosmetics.com*. Other locations: 14 Christopher St. (at Gay St.) (212) 243-4150; 1 E. 22nd St. (bet. Broadway and Fifth Ave.) (212)677-6611. M.A.C. cosmetics raise the roof with bold colors, sleek black packaging, and spokesdivas like Lil' Kim, k.d. lang and RuPaul. It's hard to resist sassy lipsticks; a purchase of one of M.A.C.'s signature Viva Glam lipsticks is also a donation to AIDS research. **Subway:** N, R to Prince St.; 6 to Spring St.

Sephora 636 Fifth Ave. (at 51st St.) (212) 245-1633 *www.sephora.com*. Other locations: 1500 Broadway (between 43rd and 44th Sts.) (212) 944-6789; 555 Broadway (between Prince and Spring Sts.) (212)625-1309; check for more locations. Sephora's black-and-white-striped columns support a dazzling beauty superstore. Gloved staff guide customers through aisles of Stila, Hard Candy, Clarins and other impressive international brands from A to Z, including its own bath line. You're invited to create your own scent at the perfume bar. **Subway:** E, V to Fifth Ave.

Shu Uemura 121 Greene St. (between Prince and Houston Sts.) (212) 979-5500. Well-lit workstations help customers identify a complexion-perfect hue from among the powders and blushes of this elegant Japanese line. With a selection of over 100 brushes, this is a great place to pick up basic makeup tools. For the perfect wink, buy the popular eyelash curler and a chic set of come-hither lashes. **Subway:** F, S,V to Broadway–Lafayette St.; N, R to Prince St.

Zitomer 969 Madison Ave. (at 76th St.) (888) 219-2888 or (212) 737-4480 *www.zitomer.com*. Probably the only pharmacy in town with a doorman, the five-decade-old Zitomer is the upscale bath, beauty and health resource for Upper East Siders, featuring such bare necessities as DeCleor sunscreen and Chanel moisturizers. Your source for the most elegant pet-care accessories, too. **Subway:** 6 to 77th St.

Day Spas

(**The Helena Rubenstein Beauty Gallery** *also offers first facials and massage in their own spa; see* "Bath & Beauty" *directly above.*)

Acqua Beauty Bar 7 E. 14th St. (between Fifth Ave. and Union Sq. West) (212) 620-4329 *www.acquabeautybar.com*. This newish spa draws a hipper-than-thou crowd with chic designer style and first-class treatments, including sublime pedicures. As you might expect from such a trendy place, a number of eastern facial and massage techniques are available, including invigorating Chinese Tui Na, yoga-like Thai massage, and the sensual two-hour Indonesian Ritual of Beauty body treatment. **Subway:** L, N, R, Q, W, 4, 5, 6 to 14th St./Union Sq.

Ajune 1294 Third Ave. (between 74th and 75th Sts.) (877) 99-AJUNE or (212) 628-0044 *www.ajune.com*. This Zen-elegant oasis offers first-rate facials and body treatments that balance aesthetic and clinical care. Serious gravity-defiers include botox and collagen injections, but the soothing and sweet Facial du Jour, rich with fresh fruits, grains and essential oils will be restorative enough for most. Body treatments run the gamut from hydrotherapy to endermologie; the sweet ginger massage comes out the winner. **Subway:** 6 to 77th St.

Avon Centre Salon & Spa Trump Tower, 725 Fifth Ave. (between 56th and 57th Sts.) (888) 577-AVON or (212) 755-AVON *www.avoncentre.com*. This chic uptowner is home to colorist-to-the-stars Brad Johns, king of the buttery blondes, and eyebrow doyenne Eliza Petrescu, the woman who revolutionized shaping and tweezing. Spa treatments run the gamut to cellulite-reducing endermologie to wellness counseling. Expensive, but worth the dough. **Subway:** N, R, W to Fifth Ave.

Bliss 568 Broadway (between Houston and Prince Sts.), 2nd floor (212) 219-8970 *www.blissspa.com*. Other location: 19 E. 57th St. (between Fifth and Madison Aves.), 3rd Floor (212) 219-8970. The Big Apple's favorite day spa is housed in stylish loft space with a funky downtown look and buckets of *Sex and the City* attitude. It may be a bit much for some, but there's no arguing with the top-notch facials and massages. Book as far in advance as possible. **Subway:** N, R to Prince St.

Carapan Urban Spa 5 W. 16th St. (between Fifth and Sixth Aves.) (212) 633-6220 *www.carapan.com*. This candlelit, Native American-inspired spa is an original oasis of tranquility in the urban jungle, working city tension out of stressed New Yorkers since 1988. Eastern and Western techniques are combined in the relaxing spa treatments, which run the gamut from aromatherapy facials to reiki to sports massage, and the romantic space is a true delight. Book it ahead if you want sauna time. The signature product collection Plateau is stellar. **Subway:** F, L, N, Q, R, V, W, 4, 5, 6 to 14th St.

Ella Baché Spa 8 W. 36th St. (between Fifth and Sixth Aves.) (212) 279-8562 *www.ellabache.com*. Women in the know have celebrated the arrival of this Parisian skincare haven on New World shores. The spa is intimate and delightful, the signature products are first-rate, and the noninvasive imported therapies—from massages to facials to body polishes to waxing—are administered with a supremely gentle touch. **Subway:** B, D, F, N, Q, R, S, V, W to 34th St.

Stone Spa 104 W. 14th St. (between Sixth and Seventh Aves.) (212) 741-8881 *www.stonespa.com*. This little, lovely, loft-style spa with a distinctly downtown edge isn't for everybody—but hot stone massage simply doesn't get better. All of the sublimely relaxing treatments incorporate soothing hot stones in some capacity (even the marvelous Jurlique facials), the therapists are all first-rate, and the soundtrack tends more toward ethereal world music than the new-age standard. The Gemstone Facial will have you feeling like a sparkling jewel. **Subway:** F, V to 14th St.

Bookstores

New York is Book City. While the big book chains' discount prices and huge inventories have driven some independents out of business, the Big Apple still shines with first-rate neighborhood and special-subject bookstores.

Major Chains

Barnes & Noble 33 E. 17th St. (at Union Square) (212) 253-0810 *www.bn.com*. Other locations: 105 Fifth Ave. (at 18th St.) (212) 807-0099; 1972 Broadway (at 66th St.) (212) 595-6859; 4 Astor Pl. (between Broadway and Lafayette St.) (212) 420-1322; check for more locations. Barnes & Noble is Manhattan's biggest book retailer with supersized stores located throughout the city. In addition to huge selections of current and backlist titles in every genre, you'll find extensive magazine racks, plus cafes in most locations. (The original Fifth Ave. and 18th St. store has been selling books since 1863—the pre-bookstore-cum-coffeehouse days—so you can't get a latte there. Its selection is heavy on academic texts.) A chock-full events calendar includes best-selling authors reading from their latest. Check *www.bn.com* for the author-appearances schedule (click on "Local Events" in the lower left corner of the "Bookstore" page), or call the stores directly. B&N events are also advertised in *The New York Times* and *Time Out New York* magazine. **Subway:** L, N, R, Q, W, 4, 5, 6 to 14th St.

Borders Books & Music 461 Park Ave. (at 57th St.) (212) 980-6785 *www.bordersstores.com*. Other locations: 550 Second Ave. (at 32nd St.) (212) 685-3938. New York's second-biggest book chain is this well-stocked retailer, which averages 150,000 book and titles per store. (The Park Avenue location is substantially larger than the Second Avenue one; both feature cafes.) Borders has a stronger emphasis on music and video than Barnes & Noble, which has largely backed out of these markets (videos and DVDs are carried only in the Park Avenue store). Call or check the Web site for music, book signings, author readings and other events. **Subway:** 4, 5, 6 to 59th St.

Independent Bookstores

Gotham Book Mart 41 W. 47th St. (between Fifth and Sixth Aves.) (212) 719-4448. This cramped and dusty new-and-used store has been a mecca for serious readers since it was founded in 1920 by the late Frances Steloff, who championed the works of Henry Miller, Gertrude Stein and other literary luminaries. She sold forbidden copies of James Joyce's *Ulysses*, and once hired Tennessee Williams as a clerk—then fired him for tardiness. Strong in intelligent fiction, literary criticism and poetry. It will be moving after 70-plus years sometime in 2003, so call before you go. **Subway:** B, D, F, S, V to 47th-50th St.–Rockefeller Center.

Madison Avenue Bookshop 833 Madison Ave. (between 69th and 70th Sts.) (212) 535-6130 *www.madisonavenuebookshop.com*. An excellent general-interest bookstore with a familiar air and great customer service. Authors often stop in to sign books. **Subway:** 6 to 68th St.

Posman Books 9 Grand Central Terminal (Vanderbilt Ave. and 42nd St.)
(212) 983-1111 *www.posmanbooks.com*. This pleasant shop on the main level at
Grand Central offers a high-quality selection of general-interest fiction and
nonfiction as well as gift books, making it an ideal stop for readers on the go.
Subway: S, 4, 5, 6, 7 to 42nd St.

Rizzoli 31 W. 57th St. (between Fifth and Sixth Aves.) (212) 759-2424.
This sophisticated bookstore has a strong emphasis on art books, but it also
makes a very browsable general-interest shop with an opinionated and helpful
staff. **Subway:** E, N, R, V to Fifth Ave.

Shakespeare & Co. 939 Lexington Ave. (at 69th St.) (212) 570-0201
www.shakeandco.com. Other locations: 137 E. 23rd St. (at Lexington Ave.)
(212) 505-2021; 716 Broadway (at Washington Pl.) (212) 529-1330; 1 Whitehall St. (between Bridge and Stone Sts.) (212) 742-7025; check for more locations. The emphasis at these comfortable, unpretentious neighborhood bookstores is on quality fiction, with a good selection of small-press titles in the mix.
A New York favorite. **Subway:** 6 to 68th St.

St. Marks Bookshop 31 Third Ave. (at 9th St.) (212) 260-7853
www.stmarksbookshop.com. This winning East Villager is a prime haunt for left-
of-center readers. The well-chosen and nicely displayed selection runs the
gamut from avant-garde poetry and alternative fiction to Eastern philosophy to
glossy photography books with an esoteric bent. **Subway:** 6 to Astor Pl.

Three Lives & Company 154 W. 10th St. (at Waverly Pl.) (212) 741-2069
www.threelives.com. This ultra-charming West Village landmark—*New York*
magazine's 2002 winner for Best Independent Bookstore— is a real find for
those who truly delight in reading, especially fiction, biography and memoirs.
Author readings are a big part of the mix. **Subway:** 1, 9 to Christopher St.

Out-of-Print, Used and Rare Books

Argosy Book Store 116 E. 59th St. (between Park and Lexington Aves.)
(212) 753-4455 *www.argosybooks.com*. This wonderful, wood-paneled septuage-
narian bookshop overflows with antiquarian, rare and well-cared-for used
books—77,000 of them, to be exact—plus antique prints, maps and autographs.
Prices run from $5 to $5,000, so there's something for everybody. **Subway:** 4, 5,
6 to 59th St.

Bauman Rare Books 535 Madison Ave. (between 54th and 55th Sts.)
(212) 751-0011; smaller gallery at the Waldorf=Astoria, 301 Park Ave. (at 49th
St.) (212) 759-8300 *www.baumanrarebooks.com*. Bauman, one of the most well-
respected rare-book dealers in the nation, has two Big Apple galleries rife with
museum-quality titles. The place to go if you're on the hunt for a rare first edition, be it the first English edition of Aristotle's *Politics* or Frank Herbert's *Dune*;
many are signed. Bring a well-padded wallet. **Subway:** 4, 5, 6 to 59th St.

Bookleaves 304 W. 4th St. (near Bank St.) (212) 924-5638. This cozy nook is everything a local used-book store should be. **Subway:** 1, 9 to Christopher St.

Gotham Book Mart *(See* "Independent Bookstores" *earlier in this section.)*

Gryphon Bookshop 2246 Broadway (between 80th and 81st Sts.) (212) 362-0706. This cramped store is a nightmare for some, but the wide array of used and rare editions makes this unusual collection a bibliophile's dream come true. **Subway:** 1, 9 to 79th St.

Housing Works Used Books Cafe 126 Crosby St. (at Houston St.) (212) 334-3324 *www.housingworksubc.com.* This warm and wonderful wood-paneled, library-like store sandwiched between SoHo and Nolita is the perfect antidote for chain-store rebels who nevertheless appreciate a good latte while perusing the stacks. The high-quality, all-used selection boasts upwards of 45,000 titles, and is particularly strong on coffee-table books and review copies. All profits go to not-for-profit Housing Works, which provides housing and services to homeless New Yorkers living with HIV and AIDS, so there's no better place to buy. **Subway:** F, S, V to Broadway–Lafayette St.; 6 to Bleecker St.

JN Bartfield Fine Books 30 W. 57th St. (between Fifth and Sixth Aves.) (212) 245-8890. Good, pricey selection of rare and antiquarian books, focusing on fine bindings. **Subway:** N, R, W to Fifth Ave.

Skyline Books & Records 13 W. 18th St. (near Fifth Ave.) (212) 759-5463. A well-chosen selection of used reads as well as jazz and blues records. **Subway:** F, L, N, R, Q, V, W, 4, 5, 6 to 14th St.

The Strand 828 Broadway (at 12th St.) (212) 473-1452 *www.strandbooks.com.* Annex, 95 Fulton St. (between William and Gold Sts.) (212) 732-6070. This epic used-book emporium—which claims to have "eight miles of books"—is heaven for used-book hounds. You could get lost in the monolithic stacks and omnipresent crowds, but patience and time are guaranteed to turn up a stack of must-haves in any category. A good selection of new books at greatly reduced prices is usually on hand at the smaller Fulton Street annex. **Subway:** L, N, R, Q, W, 4, 5, 6 to 14th St.

Ursus Books & Prints Carlyle Hotel, 981 Madison Ave. (at 76th St.), mezzanine (212) 772-8787 *www.ursusbooks.com.* Other location: 132 W. 21st St. (between Sixth and Seventh Aves.) (212) 627-5370. Like Bauman *(listed earlier in this section)*, another stop for well-funded collectors looking for first-rate rarities. Ursus stocks art in its print department as well. **Subway:** 6 to 77th St.

SPECIALTY BOOKSTORES

New York has dozens of specialty bookstores focusing on particular fields of interest—the arts, comics, yoga—you name it. The following list is just a sampling of stores in Manhattan. Many carry a full range of non-specialty titles as well. The Yellow Pages lists many more, including stores that concentrate on titles in French, German, Japanese, Spanish, Russian and other languages.

Art & Architecture

Archivia 1063 Madison Ave., 2nd Floor (between 80th and 81st Sts.) (212) 439-9194 *www.archivia.com*. A wonderful source for books on the decorative arts, architecture and gardening, with an eye-popping collection of coffee-table books. **Subway:** 6 to 77th St.

Hacker Art Books 45 W. 57th St. (between Fifth and Sixth Aves.), 5th floor (212) 688-7600 *www.hackerartbooks.com*. A comprehensive shop for the art lover, with new, rare and out-of-print titles. **Subway:** N, R, W to Fifth Ave.

Urban Center Books Villard Houses, 457 Madison Ave. (at 51st St.) (212) 935-3592 *www.urbancenterbooks.com*. The store for both serious students and avid fans of architecture, design and urban planning. **Subway:** 6 to 51st St.

Biography

Biography Bookshop 400 Bleecker St. (at 11th St.) (212) 807-8655. The most comprehensive selection for readers fascinated with the lives of others. A small nonbiography section has diversified the shelves in recent years. **Subway:** A, C, E to 14th St.; L to Eighth Ave.

Children

(See also "Toys" later in this chapter.)

Books of Wonder 16 W. 18th St. (west of Fifth Ave.) (212) 989-3270 *www.booksofwonder.com*. The city's oldest and largest independent children's bookstore. Book talks and readings are a regular feature; every Sunday at noon is storytime. **Subway:** F, L, N, Q, R, V, W, 4, 5, 6 to 14th St.

Scholastic Store 557 Broadway (between Prince and Spring Sts.). (212) 343-6166 *www.scholastic.com/sohostore*. This mammoth store sells the full line of products—books, toys, software and more—from children's publisher Scholastic. Your prime source for everything Harry Potter. A full calendar of in-store events keeps kids busy. **Subway:** N, R to Prince St.

Comics

Cosmic Comics 36 E. 23rd St. (between Park and Madison Aves.), 2nd floor (212) 460-5322 *www.cosmiccomics.com*. **Subway:** 6 to 23rd St.

Forbidden Planet 840 Broadway (at 13th St.) (212) 473-1576 *www.forbiddenplanetnyc.com*. The city's largest collection of science fiction, fantasy, comics and graphic-illustration books, plus games and toys. **Subway:** L, N, Q, R, W, 4, 5, 6 to 14th St.

St. Marks Comics 11 St. Marks Pl. (between Second and Third Aves.) (212) 598-9439 *www.stmarkscomics.com*. St. Marks boasts a huge merchandise collection and the city's largest back-issue archive. **Subway:** 6 to Astor Pl.

Cooking & Gourmet

Bonnie Slotnick Cookbooks 163 W. 10th St. (at Seventh Ave.)
(212) 989-8962 *www.bonnieslotnickcookbooks.com*. This cozy Village shop is the
prime source for out-of-print and antiquarian cookbooks. **Subway:** 1, 9 to
Christopher St.

Kitchen Arts & Letters 1435 Lexington Ave. (between 93rd and 94th Sts.)
(212) 876-5550 *www.kitchenartsandletters.com*. Food lovers from professional
chefs to take-out gourmets will relish the vast collection of more than 10,000
cookbooks here, including rare, hard-to-find, out-of-print and French-language
titles. A browser's delight. **Subway:** 6 to 96th St.

Gay & Lesbian/Gender Subjects

Bluestockings Women's Bookstore & Cafe 172 Allen St. (south of Houston St.) (212) 777-6028 *www.bluestockings.com*. With a wide and well-varied
selection, a friendly staff, and a busy calendar of events and workshops, this
feminist bookstore caters to the literary needs and wants of women, both
straight and gay. **Subway:** F, V to Second Ave.

Creative Visions Books 548 Hudson St. (between Charles and Perry Sts.)
(212) 645-7573 *www.creativevisionsbooks.com*. An excellent resource and meeting place for gay men. **Subway:** 1, 9 to Christopher St.

Oscar Wilde Memorial Bookshop 15 Christopher St. (at Gay St., between
Sixth and Seventh Aves.) (212) 255-8097 *www.oscarwildebooks.com*. This literary landmark was the world's very first bookstore catering to the gay and lesbian
community, and it's still going strong; the selection runs the gamut from vintage
to cutting-edge. **Subway:** 1, 9 to Christopher St.

Government

U. S. Government Bookstore 26 Federal Plaza (Broadway between Duane
and Worth Sts.), 2nd floor (212) 264-3825. Your complete source for books,
pamphlets and forms from the U.S. Government Printing Office, from the
Department of Interior's guide to Washington D.C. attractions to IRS bulletins
and U.S. Labor Code guides. **Subway:** 4, 5, 6 to Brooklyn Bridge/City Hall; N,
R to City Hall.

History

Chartwell Booksellers Park Avenue Plaza, 55 E. 52nd St. (between Park and
Madison Aves.) (212) 308-0643 *www.churchill-books.com*. Who knew an entire
store could focus solely on books by, about, and with contributions from Winston Churchill and still pay the rent? Actually, a fascinating collection for rare-
book collectors and history buffs. **Subway:** 6 to 51st. St.

The Liberation Bookstore 421 Lenox Ave. (at 131st St.) (212) 281-4615.
This legendary bookstore dedicated to Africa and the African diaspora is under
the threat of closure, so call first. **Subway:** 2, 3 to 135th St.

The Military Bookman 29 E. 93rd St. (at Madison Ave.) (212) 348-1280 *www.militarybookman.com*. The prime stop for books on military, naval and aviation history, with a focus on out-of-print and rare titles. **Subway:** 6 to 96th St.

Revolution Books 9 W. 19th St. (between Fifth and Sixth Aves.) (212) 691-3345. For the diehard Marxist who refuses to give up the fight, this utilitarian store is for you. **Subway:** F, V to 14th St.

Mystery
Armchair detectives will love these three shops, all stocked from floor to ceiling with both new and used mysteries, from the classics to out-of-print titles to rare signed editions to current releases.

Murder Ink 2486 Broadway (between 92nd and 93rd Sts.) (212) 362-8905 *www.murderink.com*. **Subway:** 1, 2, 3, 9 to 96th St.

The Mysterious Bookshop 129 W. 56th St. (between Sixth and Seventh Aves.) (212) 765-0900 *www.mysteriousbookshop.com*. **Subway:** N, R, Q, W to 57th St.; B, D, E, F, V to Seventh Ave.

Partners & Crime 44 Greenwich Ave. (between Sixth and Seventh Aves., at Charles St.) (212) 243-0440 *www.crimepays.com*. **Subway:** 1, 9 to Christopher St.

Religion
Christian Publications 315 W. 43rd St. (between Eighth and Ninth Aves.) (212) 582-4311 *www.christianpub.com*. The New York metropolitan area's largest Christian bookstore also stocks music and videos. **Subway:** A, C, E to 42nd St.

J. Levine Books and Judaica 5 W. 30th St. (at Fifth Ave.) (212) 695-6888 *www.levinejudaica.com*. More than a bookstore—a full resource center for Judaica. **Subway:** B, D, F, N, Q, R, S, V, W to 34th St.; 6 to 33rd St.

Theater
Drama Book Shop 723 Seventh Ave. (between 48th and 49th Sts.), 2nd floor (212) 944-0595 *www.dramabookshop.com*. The resource for books on the arts of stage and screen, including scripts and screenplays, scene and monologue books, biographies and more. **Subway:** 1, 9 to 50th St.

Richard Stoddard Performing Arts Books 41 Union Square West (at E. 17th St.), room 937 (212) 645-9576 *www.richardstoddard.com*. Specialists in out-of-print performing arts books. **Subway:** L, N, Q, R, W, 4, 5, 6 to 14th St.

Travel
Complete Traveller 199 Madison Ave. (at 35th St.) (212) 685-9007. As well as a good general-interest selection, the Complete Traveller features a room dedicated to antiquarian travelogues and guides. **Subway:** 6 to 33rd St.

Hagstrom Map & Travel Center 57 W. 43rd St. (between Fifth and Sixth Aves.) (212) 398-1222. Other location: 125 Maiden Lane (between Pearl and Water Sts.) (212) 785-5343. The top publisher of city maps runs two excellent shops dedicated to cartography and travel. **Subway:** B, D, F, V, S to 42nd St.

Rand McNally Travel Store 150 E. 52nd St. (btw. Lexington and Third Aves.). (212) 758-7488 *www.randmcnally.com*. Maps galore, from city fold-outs to world atlases, plus travel guides and on-the-road aids like voltage converters, GPS units and travel pillows. **Subway:** E, V to Lexington Ave.; 6 to 51st St.

Traveler's Choice 2 Wooster St. (between Grand and Canal Sts.) (212) 941-1535. This good general-interest travel store also features antiquarian travelogues and guides. **Subway:** J, M, N, R, Q, W, Z, 6 to Canal St.

Wellness & Eastern Teachings

East-West Books 78 Fifth Ave. (between 13th and 14th Sts.) (212) 243-5994. The shelves here are stocked with books that do as the name suggests: Bring Eastern philosophy, healing religion and literature to the West. **Subway:** F, L, N, R, Q, V, W, 4, 5, 6 to 14th St.

New York Open Center 83 Spring St. (at Crosby St.) (212) 219-2527 *www.opencenter.org*. This center for holistic learning also features a small but well-stocked bookshop. **Subway:** 6 to Spring St.

Quest Bookshop 240 E. 53rd St. (between Second and Third Aves.) (212) 758-5521 *www.theosophy-ny.org*. This petite shop stocks titles ranging from Astrology to Zoroastrianism. **Subway:** 6 to 51st St.

Cameras & Electronics

With the terrific buys available on the Web these days, New York isn't the discount electronics mecca it once was. Unless you've done your homework, stay out of the shady electronics stores that line Broadway near Times Square. Also avoid the stretch along Canal Street near East Broadway, where the hawkers will surely take advantage of your good nature given a chance.

If you are in the market for a cordless phone or VCR and don't feel like venturing downtown to J&R (*below*), East 86th Street between Second and Third Avenues is uptown's Electric Avenue, with **Circuit City** (232-240 E. 86th St., 212-734-1694) and **The Wiz** (1534-1536 Third Ave. at 86th St., 212-876-4400) within shouting distance.

B&H Photo-Video—Pro-Audio 420 Ninth Ave. (at 34th St.) (800) 606-6969 or (212) 444-6615 *www.bhphotovideo.com*. Many professional photographers wouldn't consider going anywhere else. This superstore sells everything an amateur or pro could want, from an impressive selection of cameras to darkroom equipment. Video equipment, lighting, pro audio and telescopes also fill the cavernous space, as does a decent selection of used merchandise. **Subway:** A, C, E to 34th St.

J&R Music/Computer World 23 Park Row (between Beekman and Ann Sts., across from City Hall Park) (800) 806-1115 or (212) 238-9000 *www.jandr.com*. New York's premier electronics store shines for both its extensive range of merchandise and its reasonable prices. Just about anything that plugs in or uses a battery can be found here, from travel irons to PDAs, cameras to iBooks. Great prices on CDs and DVDs, too. **Subway:** 4, 5, 6, N, R to Brooklyn Bridge–City Hall.

Olden Camera & Lens Co. 1265 Broadway (between 31st and 32nd Sts.) (212) 725-1234. This Herald Square standard carries a full timeline of photography equipment, from the most technologically advanced to used Super 8's. Prices are equally diverse. **Subway:** B, D, F, N, Q, R, S, V, W to 34th St.

Sony Style 550 Madison Ave. (between 55th and 56th Sts.) (212) 833-8000 *www.sonystyle.com*. Your source for the complete line of Sony products, from PlayStations and Vaios to fully integrated home entertainment systems. **Subway:** E, V to Fifth Ave.

Clothing

Below are just few particularly well-dressed standouts from a monster crop of clothing stores that blanket the Manhattan map. If you're in the market for couture wear, the big-name designers have one or more boutiques in one or more locations: On Fifth Avenue in the 50's, on Madison Avenue and/or in SoHo. (*See* "Midtown & Uptown Shopping" *and* "Downtown Shopping" *earlier in this chapter for addresses—and don't forget about the city's stellar department and discount stores, of course, also listed earlier in this chapter.*)

Men's & Women's

H&M 640 Fifth Ave. (at 51st St.) (212) 489-0390 *www.hm.com*. Other locations: 1328 Broadway (at 34th St.) (212) 564-9922; 558 Broadway (between Prince and Spring Sts.) (212) 343-8313. Fashion-forward wearables for men, women and kids at low, low prices from Swedish discounter Hennes & Mauritz. The youthful looks won't outlast the season—but when it's $7 for a tiny T, who cares? Accessories are so cheap they're almost free. **Subway:** E, V to Fifth Ave.

Jeffrey New York 449 W. 14th St. (between Ninth and Tenth Aves.) (212) 206-1272. If you consider yourself a big-league fashionista, then a trip to this cutting-edge fashion mecca in the booming Meatpacking District is sure to satisfy. Jeffrey dresses style-conscious women and men that demand de rigueur chic from the hottest designers, Michael Kors and John Bartlett to talented upstarts like Tuleh and Veronica Branquinho. The shoe department is a standout, sharpened by the likes of Jimmy Choo and Christian Louboutin, as is the tiny but selective cosmetics counter. **Subway:** A, C, E to 14th St.; L to Eighth Ave.

Kenneth Cole 610 Fifth Ave. (at 49th St.) (212) 373-5800 *www.kencole.com* This two-story flagship carries Kenneth Cole's complete lines of modern, casually glamorous clothing and footwear for men and women, including his affordable Reaction line. Stylish outerwear and accessories add the finishing touches. **Subway:** B, D, F, V to 47th-50th Sts./Rockefeller Center.

Lucky Brand Jeans 38 Greene St. (at Grand St.) (212) 625-0707 *www.lucky-brandjeans.com*. Other locations: 172 Fifth Ave. (at 22nd St.) (917) 606-1418; 151 Third Ave. (at 67th St.) (646) 422-1192; 216 Columbus Ave. (at 70th St.) (212) 579-1760. America's hippest name in denim operates four stylish and well-stocked city stores. **Subway:** A, C, E, J, M, N, R, Q, W, Z, 6 to Canal St.

Roots 270 Lafayette St. (at Prince St.). (212) 324-3333 *www.roots.com*. This Canadian sportswear company grabbed worldwide attention at the 2002 Winter Olympics for outfitting North America's teams in style. Expect top-quality fleece, Ts, sweats, and well-designed casual wear—not to mention oh-so-hip Olympic berets—at affordable prices. **Subway:** 6 to Spring St.; N, R to Prince St.

Seize sur Vingt 243 Elizabeth St. (between Houston and Prince Sts.) (212) 343-0476 *www.16sur20.com*. Made-to-measure businesswear with downtown flair is the stock in trade at this marvelous Nolita shop. Bespoke suits come in clean, slim, contemporary lines for both men and women. Divine Egyptian cotton shirts are both custom-tailored and pre-sized for men and women; sweaters and accessories are part of the picture now, too. **Subway:** F, V, S to Broadway—Lafayette St.; N, R to Prince St.

Shanghai Tang 714 Madison Ave. (btw. 63rd and 64th Sts.) (212) 888-0111 *www.shanghaitang.com*. Expect stylish, witty, and boldly hued takes on Chinese classics—Mandarin-collared shirts, form-fitting "Suzie Wong" chengosam dresses, glorious lounging pajamas—from this elegant Hong Kong clothier and imperial tailor. **Subway:** E, N, R, V, W to Fifth Ave.; 4, 5, 6 to 59th St.

Thomas Pink 520 Madison Ave. (at 53rd St.) (212) 838-1928 *www.thomaspink.co.uk*. Other location: 1155 Sixth Ave. (near 44th St.) (212) 840-9663. This legendary British shirt maker has taken the Big Apple by storm with its beautifully cut, classically crafted button-downs (all made from finest quality twofold pure cotton poplin) in bold colors and patterns that add a dramatic twist to the tradition. Men's ties come in dame-catching jewel tones. **Subway:** E, V to Fifth Ave.

Women's Only

Women looking for up-and-coming designers selling unique but wearable fashions at affordable prices will do well to browse East 9th Street between Second Avenue and Avenue A, where stars include **Jill Anderson** (331 E. 9th St., 212-253-1747, *www.jillanderson.com*), who unites a retro-reminiscent sensibility and the clean lines of modernism in her distinctly feminine, trend-proof and utterly stylish clothing; don't miss her Italian widow's dress, which can go corporate or clubhopping depending on how you accessorize. Another stunner on the block is **Selia Yang** (328 E. 9th St., 212-254-9073, *www.seliayang.com*), who specializes in breathtaking special-occasion sheath dresses, including beaded and bridal versions, while **Mark Montano** (434 E. 9th St., 212-505-0325, *www.markmontano.com*) defines retro glamour with Jackie O-inspired fashions.

Nolita is another excellent neighborhood for fresh fashion looks. Check out **Mayle** (252 Elizabeth St. between Houston and Prince Sts., 212-625-0406), whose vintage-inspired looks have even made a few famous fans; and **Tracy Feith**, 209 Mulberry St., between Spring and Kenmare Sts., 212-334-3097), for sexy, funky, fashion-forward looks.

Diane von Furstenberg—The Shop 385 W. 12th St. (near Washington St.) (646) 486-4800 *www.dvf.com*. The Me Decade's favorite designer gets serious props for understanding the fashion-forward value of a Meatpacking District location. Her slim, clingy, 70's look is back in style in a big way, and prices are reasonable considering the designer label. **Subway:** A, C, E to 14th St.

Eileen Fisher 395 West Broadway (between Spring and Broome Sts.) (212) 431-4567 *www.eileenfisher.com*. Other locations: 166 Fifth Ave. (between 21st and 22nd Sts.) (212) 924-4777; 1039 Madison Ave. (at 79th St.) (212) 879-7799; E. 9th St. (between First and Second Aves.) (212) 529-5715; check for more locations. Eileen Fisher's gorgeous clothing is for stylish, grown-up women who prefer season-transcending cuts that bespeak ease and movement over trendy look-at-me wear. The lines may be simple, but the fabrics—from crinkly silks to cashmere—rich textures and colors are stunning. The West Broadway flagship carries the full line, including petites and woman sizes, while the narrow 9th Street store is an outlet of sorts that's great for bargain hunters. **Subway:** N, R to Prince St.; C, E to Spring St.

Kirna Zabête 96 Greene St. (between Prince and Spring Sts.) (212) 941-9656 *www.kirnazabete.com*. Kirna Zabête is every stylish girl's new favorite SoHo shop, thanks to racks full of ultra-chic wearables from such hard-to-find design-ers as Alice Roi and Balenciaga; delightful accessories and home accents that surpass the SoHo standard; and fab mod décor that even includes a couple of iMacs to entertain significant others of the male persuasion who are far less enchanted than you are. **Subway:** F, S, V to Broadway–Lafayette St.; N, R to Prince St.; C, E to Spring St.

Makola 1045 Madison Ave. (between 79th and 80th Sts.) (212) 772-2272 This serene boutique specializes in classic mid-century dresses—the kind Grace Kelly wore so well—reinvented for the 21st-century woman. Jackets wear wide collars, tops are tailored, and skirts almost always flair. The fabrics—from classic florals and mini-checks to glamorous solid shantungs—are universally gorgeous. Prices are high, but so is the timeless quality. **Subway:** 6 to 77th St.

Men's Only

Saint Laurie Merchant Tailors 22 West 32nd St. (between Fifth and Sixth Aves.) (212) 643-1916 *www.saintlaurie.com*. The place to treat yourself to a made-to-measure suit or jacket. Visiting their new fifth-floor showroom is a joy; tables are lined with bolts of fine wools and tweeds to browse, each tagged with the prices for a suit or sport coat. You can choose both your fabric and your style—fitted, like an Italian count, or baggy like a Boston Brahmin. Their 3D Laser Body Scanner gets the most accurate three-dimensional image and body measurements possible, apparently, so you'll enjoy the perfect fit. Prices run $950 and up for a suit, around $700 for a blazer; they do custom shirts, too. **Subway:** B, D, F, N, Q, R, V to 34th St.

Children's

Bebe Thompson 1216 Lexington Ave. (between 82nd and 83rd Sts.) (212) 249-4740. The atmosphere here is exclusive and the prices high, but it's worth visiting for the very best in delightful, well-crafted imported European wear for infants and children up to size 16. **Subway:** 4, 5, 6 to 86th St.

Bu & the Duck 106 Franklin St. (between Church St. and West Broadway) (212) 431-9226 *www.buandtheduck.com*. Owner and designer Susan Lang really likes kids—and understands them. Gone are pastels and the cartoony farm animals; instead, Lang's vintage-inspired clothing and shoes are bold and interesting, practical and playful. A real gem. **Subway:** 1, 9 to Franklin St.

Lilliput/Lilliput SoHo Kids 240 & 265 Lafayette St. (between Spring and Prince Sts.) (212) 965-9567 or (212) 965-9567 *www.lilliputsoho.com*. These sibling shops offer an enjoyably eclectic selection of wear-a-day apparel for babies and youngsters for parents who'd rather not outfit their kids in uniform Gap or Oshkosh B'Gosh. Prices on some imported labels can soar, but most are reasonable. Shoes, accessories and toys are also in the mix. **Subway:** 6 to Spring St.; N, R to Prince St.

Peanutbutter & Jane 617 Hudson St. (between 12th and Jane Sts.) (212) 620-7952. This fun store for teenagers as well as younger kids stocks clothes and accessories that brim with the imagination of youth and funky West Village style. The eclectic mix ranges from girlish party dresses to leather skirts. **Subway:** A, C, E to 14th St.; L to Eighth Ave.

RockStarBaby 298 Elizabeth St. (between Bleecker and Houston Sts.). (212) 995-8638 *www.rockstarbaby.com*. Bon Jovi's Tico Torres and fashion designer Cinzia Spinetti have birthed a brand-new line of everyday wear for newborns and infants. The clothes and accessories are smartly styled, gorgeously made and moderately priced, with a just-right dash of rock 'n' roll attitude. **Subway:** 6 to Bleecker St.

Zitomer 969 Madison Ave. (at 76th Sts.) (212) 737-4480 *www.zitomer.com*. This chic Upper West Side apothecary (*see* "Beauty" *earlier in this chapter*) is also well known for its high-quality selection of baby and children's clothing, especially designer-label party and flower-girl dresses, plus little-man clothing from labels like Calvin Klein. **Subway:** 6 to 77th St.

Vintage, Thrift & Resale

Allan & Suzi 416 Amsterdam Ave. (at 80th St.) (212) 724-7445. This terrific boutique is often overlooked by thrifty shoppers who can't see beyond the Superfly-meets-Dance Fever windows. That's just fine—there's more one-of-a-kind finds for the rest of us. Most of the collection is a thoughtfully selected and well-organized 20th-century fashion timeline, from gently worn bell-bottoms to pristine couture gowns worn once and cast aside. **Subway:** 1, 9 to 79th St.

Foley & Corinna 108 Stanton St. (between Essex and Ludlow Sts.) (212) 529-2338. This warm and wonderful Lower East Side boutique specializes in hand-picked vintage finds, creative restructurings of vintage pieces (such as old T's wearing new beaded trim), and vintage-inspired new designs. **Subway:** F to Delancey St.; F, V to Second Ave.; J, M, Z to Essex St.

Housing Works Thrift Shop 143 W. 17th St. (between Sixth and Seventh Aves.) (212) 366-0820 *www.housingworks.org*. Other locations: 157 E. 23rd St. (between Lexington and Third Aves.) (212) 529-5955; 202 E. 77th St. (at Third Ave.) (212) 772-8461; 306 Columbus Ave. (between 74th and 75th Sts.) (212) 579-7566. Fashionable clothing, accessories, books, housewares, furniture and more. The wares are almost always excellent quality, and the proceeds benefit people living with HIV and AIDS. **Subway:** F, V, 1, 2, 3, 9 to 14th St.

Ina 21 Prince St. (between Mott and Elizabeth Sts.) (212) 334-9048. Other location: 101 Thompson St. (between Prince and Spring Sts.). A gorgeous designer consignment boutique specializing in vintage and current fashions for men and women, often from the world's top couture houses, from Halston to Prada. Shoes and accessories add to the gently worn glory. **Subway:** N, R to Prince St., 6 to Spring St.

Michael's 1041 Madison Ave. (between 79th and 80th Sts.), 2nd floor (212) 737-7273 *www.michaelsconsignment.com*. This elegant consignment boutique boasts top-shelf designer wear in like-new condition—but for a fraction of the original prices. Don't expect dated styles—society dames shed this season's Chloé, Chanel and Manolos faster than you'd think. The Bridal Salon is a savvy gal's dream come true. **Subway:** 6 to 77th St.

Resurrection 217 Mott St. (between Prince and Spring Sts.) (212) 625-1374. Other location: 123 E. 7th St. (between First Ave. and Ave. A) (212) 228-0063. Vintage wears like-new price tags here, but designer threads chosen with an artist's eye make up the coolest, most pristine collection of retro-wear in the city. Expect an emphasis on the 1960's and 70's, with such designer names as Pucci and Halston peppering the racks. **Subway:** N, R to Prince St.; 6 to Spring St.

Screaming Mimi's 382 Lafayette St. (between 4th and Great Jones Sts.) (212) 677-6464. Laura Wills's legendary store boasts a top-notch collection of vintage threads, all at reasonable prices. Every piece is something special, whether it's a vivid floral design stamped onto an A-line mini-dress or a perfect vintage suit from the 40's. Housewares, bags, shoes, lingerie, even vintage New York souvenirs are on hand, all prettily displayed. **Subway:** 6 to Bleecker St.

Tokio 7 64 E. 7th St. (between First and Second Aves.) (212) 353-8443 *www.tokio7.com*. Here's a funky designer consignment shop for the downtown set, featuring gently used couture from labels like Anna Sui, Helmut Lang and Vivienne Westwood. **Subway:** 6 to Astor Pl.

Flea Markets

Manhattan's flea markets offer wonderful opportunities for bargain hunters in
search of antiques and collectibles. Whether your grail is pristine Lustreware,
vintage velvet Elvis paintings or old opera 78's, you have a good shot at finding
what you want at the **Annex Antiques Fair and Flea Market** (212-243-5343,
www.annexantiques.citysearch.com), the city's biggest and best outdoor flea market, held in a series of adjoining parking lots on Sixth Avenue between 24th
and 27th Streets every Saturday and Sunday year-round. Some of New York's
finest retro merchants started out here, so you can expect top-quality finds in
furnishings, clothing and jewelry. Once you're done, head over to **The Garage**,
(112 W. 25th St., between Sixth and Seventh Aves., 212-647-0707), the city's
largest indoor market, also brought to life every Saturday and Sunday.

    Greenflea (212-721-0900) operates at two Upper West Side markets: on
West 84th Street between Columbus and Amsterdam avenues on Saturdays,
and at I.S. 44 on Columbus Avenue at 77th Street on Sundays. Serious flea fans
swear by these events, where you can find anything from used records and vintage jewelry to farm-fresh veggies and discount pet supplies.

Food Markets

Agata & Valentina 1505 First Ave. (at 79th St.) (212) 452-0690. Focused on
the foods of Sicily, there isn't a better selection of olives, oils, and Italian meats
and cheeses in the city, and the prepared foods surpass the gourmet-market standard. Pricey, but the quality and service are peerless. **Subway:** 6 to 77th St.

Barney Greengrass 541 Amsterdam Ave. (between 86th and 87th Sts.)
(212) 724-4707. The self-proclaimed "Sturgeon King" has been a fixture on the
Upper West Side since 1929, selling caviar, smoked fish and herring since 1908
out of the sit-down deli and shop. The sturgeon is exquisitely moist and thin, as
is the smoked salmon. The excellent whitefish salad, borscht and chicken livers
can also be carried out or eaten in the lively diner. **Subway:** 1, 9 to 86th St.

Chelsea Market 88 10th Ave. (between 15th and 16th Sts.) (212) 243-5678
www.chelseamarket.com. This huge, brick-walled ex-cracker factory overflows
with wonderful purveyors of gourmet goods, from bakers (**Amy's Bread**, 212-
462-4338; **Fat Witch Bakery**, 212-807-1335) to butchers (**Frank's Butcher
Shop**, 212-242-1234) to professional kitchenware hawkers (**Bowery Kitchen
Supplies**, 212-376-4982)—and much, much more. You can lunch at several
small restaurants inside and outside the concourse. **Subway:** A, C, E to 14th
St.; L to Eighth Ave.

Citarella 2135 Broadway (at 75th St.) (212) 874-0383 *www.citarella.com*.
Other location: 1313 Third Ave. (at 75th St.) (212) 874-0383. What was
always the city's best seafood market has expanded in recent years to excel on
all gourmet fronts. The store is bright and well organized and the prepared foods
are first-rate. Choice and service like this comes at a price, but Citarella offers
great value and service. **Citarella To Go** (Sixth Ave. at 49th St.) makes a great

lunch stop in the Rockefeller Center area; an adjacent full-service restaurant opened in mid-2001. **Subway:** 1, 9 to 79th St.

Dean & Deluca 560 Broadway (at Prince St.) (212) 431-1691 *www.dean-deluca.com*. So what if prices are stratospheric? This gorgeous SoHo grocer is New York's best. A mecca for well-heeled foodies, Dean & Deluca offers picture-perfect produce, stunning flowers by the bunch, and dazzling selections of pâtés, cheeses, meats, fish, baked goods and prepared foods, all handsomely displayed and knowledgeably attended. A small selection of fine cookware and cookbooks is nestled in back. **Subway:** N, R to Prince St.

Eli's Vinegar Factory 431 E. 91st St. (near York Ave.) (212) 987-0885 *www.elizabar.com*. **Eli's Manhattan** 1411 Third Ave. (between 80th and 81st Sts.) (212) 717-8100. To rival his uncles on Broadway (*see* **Zabar's** *below*), Eli Zabar turned an old vinegar factory into a gourmet market overflowing with top-quality produce, cheese, meat, fish, prepared foods, fresh flowers, baked goods and Eli's tasty breads, as well as wines and housewares. Prices—even for tomatoes grown in the rooftop greenhouse—are not unreasonable. Brunch is served on weekends. Eli's Manhattan offers virtually the same products and services, as well as a restaurant and cafe. **Subway:** 4, 5, 6 to 86th St.

Grace's Marketplace 1237 Third Ave. (at 71st St.) (212) 737-0600. Grace Balducci's uptown market offers fine service, stunning displays of produce, wonderful baked goods and cheeses, quality smoked and fresh meats and fish, fresh pastas, whole-bean coffee and everything else worth wanting in a gourmet grocery. Pre-made sandwiches are excellent and fairly priced. **Subway:** 6 to 68th St.

Grand Central Market Grand Central Terminal, Lexington Ave. (between 42nd and 44th Sts.) *www.grandcentralterminal.com*. The crown jewel of Grand Central's glorious renovation is this spiffy gourmet food mart, where the array of first-rate vendors include **Koglin German Hams** (212-499-0725) for quality cold cuts and meats; **Adriana's Caravan** (212-972-8804) for spices from around the world; **Pescatore Seafood Company** (212-557-4466) for a first-quality range of fresh catches; and **Li-Lac Chocolates** (212-370-4866) for old-fashioned handcrafted sweets. **Subway:** S, 4, 5, 6, 7 to 42nd St.

Kam Man Food Products 200 Canal St. (between Mott and Mulberry Sts.) (212) 571-0330. **Kam Kuo Foods** 7 Mott St. (on Chatham Square at Park Row) (212) 349-3097. These two markets are New York's largest Asian grocers. Kam Man specializes in fresh and bulk foods, including barbecued meats, fresh water chestnuts, fresh and dried fish, pickled vegetables, dozens of soy and hoisin sauces, a broad selection of fresh vegetables and specialties from Vietnam and Thailand. Smaller, with fewer cooked foods and less produce, Kam Kuo carries frozen Chinese foods, a large selection of teas and cooking utensils. The language barrier can be formidable, but English-language signs at Kam Kuo sometimes help matters. **Subway:** J, M, N, Q, R, W, Z, 6 to Canal St.

Russ & Daughters 179 E. Houston St. (between Allen and Orchard Sts.) (800) RUSS-229 or (212) 475-4880 *www.russanddaughters.com*. The Lower East

Side's premier Jewish gourmet market has been supplying smoked fish, cream cheese and sturdy, old-fashioned, bagels (made at nearby Kossar's bakery) to loyal shoppers since 1914. Schmooze with the countermen, who will tell you how to prepare the excellent herring. Prices are lower than in most uptown stores, even for the divine caviar. **Subway:** F, V to Second Ave.

Union Square Greenmarket E. 17th St. and Broadway (212) 477-3220. The city's premier greenmarket is held alfresco year-round at Union Square (Mon., Wed., Fri., Sat., 8 A.M.–6 P.M.), with the biggest markets on Saturday and Wednesday. You might discover crosnes (tiny snail-like vegetables that taste like Jerusalem artichokes but don't require peeling), diminutive Japanese turnips and baby Chinese cabbages, fresh baked goods, exotic fresh flowers and more. Everything is fresh, lots of organics are on hand, and prices tend to be low. More important, this is the real New York: diverse, friendly and enthusiastic. **Subway:** L, N, Q, R, W, 4, 5, 6 to 14th St.

Zabar's 2245 Broadway (at 80th St.) (800) 697-6301 or (212) 496-1234 *www.zabars.com*. Visiting this West Side institution is like dropping into a scene from a Woody Allen movie. It's particularly well known for its smoked fish and herring counter, where you can sample the goods before your smoked nova is sliced paper-thin. Other delights include hundreds of cheeses, condiments, breads, cold cuts and pâtés, kosher foods and an array of prepared foods, including divine rice and tapioca puddings (no greens, though). Service is fast and efficient. Bargain housewares fill the second floor, and a corner cafe features hot foods and sandwiches. **Subway:** 1, 9 to 79th St.

Ethnic Markets

With immigrants from virtually every country living in New York, intrepid foodies can really go around the world in a day. (*See also* **Kam Man Food, Agata & Valentina, Barney Greengrass** *and* **Russ & Daughters**, *above.*)

African: West African Grocery 535 Ninth Ave. (between 39th and 40th Sts.) (212) 695-6215. **Subway:** A, C, E to 42nd St.

English: Myers of Keswick 634 Hudson St. (between Jane and Horatio Sts.) (212) 691-4194 *www.myersofkeswick.com*. **Subway:** A, C, E to 14th St.; L to Eighth Ave.

German: Schaller & Weber 1654 Second Ave. (between 85th and 86th Sts.) (212) 879-3047 *www.schallerweber.com*. **Subway:** 4, 5, 6 to 86th St.

Indian: Foods of India 121 Lexington Ave. (between 28th and 29th Sts.) (212) 683-4419. **Subway:** 6 to 28th St.

Japanese: Katagiri & Co. 224 E. 59th St. (between Second and Third Aves.) (212) 755-3566 or (212) 838-5453 (gift store) *www.katagiri.com*. **Subway:** 4, 5, 6 to 59th St.

Korean: Han Arum Market 25 W. 32nd St. (between Broadway and Fifth Ave.) (212) 695-3283. **Subway:** B, D, F, N, Q, R, S, V, W to 34th St.

Latin American: Mosaico 175 Madison Ave. (between 33rd and 34th Sts.) (212) 213-4700. Restaurant and grocer. **Subway:** 6 to 33rd St.

Mexican: Kitchen Market 218 Eighth Ave. (at 21st St.) (800) HOT-4433 or (212) 243-4433 *www.kitchenmarket.com*. A prime stop for chiles, spices and hot sauces; first-rate prepared foods, too. **Subway:** C, E to 23rd St.

Middle Eastern/International: Kalustyan's 123 Lexington Ave. (between 28th and 29th Sts.) (212) 685-3451 *www.kalustyans.com*. Excellent selection of spices and beans, plus a globetrotting selection of gourmet foods, from Bangladesh to the West Indies. **Subway:** 6 to 28th St.

Polish: Kurowycky Meat Products 124 First Ave. (between 7th St. and St. Marks Pl.) (212) 477-0344. **Subway:** 6 to Astor Pl.

West African: West African Grocery 535 Ninth Ave. (between 39th and 40th Sts.) (212) 695-6215. **Subway:** A, C, E to 42nd St.

Gifts & Homewares

New York is such a home-design mecca that the list of shops below barely scratches the surface. Shoppers looking for one-of-a-kind home décor can't go wrong exploring Madison Avenue in the 80's for luxury goods with a European flair. SoHo and Nolita are best for offbeat and international looks.

The West Village is a delight for browsers. The leafy, town-house-lined streets run the style gamut. Boutiques range from **The Lively Set** (33 Bedford St., between Downing and Carmine Sts., 212-807-8417), a charming shop overflowing with collectible-quality home and garden accents from days past, to **Flight 001** (96 Greenwich Ave., near 12th St., a block west of Seventh Ave., 212-691-1001, *www.flight001.com*), for the grooviest travel-related goods, both chic and practical, around. And be sure to check out modern **Mxyplyzyk** (123-125 Greenwich Ave. at 13th St., 212-989-4300), a fun-filled shop offering high-design housewares, arty toys for grown-ups and the like, all at affordable prices.

Additionally, the far East 50's have blossomed into a home-design mecca of late, no doubt inspired by the arrival of the **Terence Conran Shop**, London's high-design twist on IKEA-style home décor, located in the **Bridgemarket complex**—worth a look in itself for its stunning architecture (407 E. 59th St. at First Ave., 212-755-9079, *www.conran.com*). Joining Sir Terence in the area are upscale boutiques such as **Extraordinary*** (251 E. 57th St. between Second and Third Aves., 212-223-9151, *www.extraordinaryny.com*), a warm and wonderful gallery that beautifully displays portable, affordable home accents handcrafted around the world, from Japanese lacquer coasters to horn-carved dishes from Madagascar, and more; and the ultra-elegant **Royal Hut** (328 E. 59th St. between First and Second Aves., 212-207-3027, *www.royalhut.com*), offering stunning cross-cultural furnishings and textiles from, or inspired by, Africa and Asia. Also consider **Bacarrat** and **Tiffany & Co.** for crystal and silver, Fifth Avenue style (*see* "Jewelry" *later in this chapter*).

ABC Carpet & Home 881 and 888 Broadway (at 19th St.) (212) 473-3000 *www.abccarpet.com*. Two landmark buildings house the city's crown jewel of home shopping, with 10 floors abundantly stocked with luxury home furnishings and wares. The first floor indulges shoppers with eclectic tastes in home accessories, from baby Tiffany lamps to bead-fringed cashmere pillows. On other floors you will find a wide-ranging mix that includes Indonesian wooden chests, flat screen TVs, mid-century modern office chairs, luxury linens, imported fabrics on the bolt and much, much more. And of course, there are the rugs—a whole building, in fact, dedicated to helping you find that perfect gabbeh to place beneath your feet. **Subway:** L, N, Q, R, W, 4, 5, 6 to 14th St.

The Apartment 101 Crosby St. (between Prince and Spring Sts.) (212) 219-3066 *www.theapt.com*. In this super-groovy shop, outfitted like a real New York apartment, you can browse and buy the clever modern goods on display in every room, from the bed to the slippers half-hidden underneath. Beyond the pop value, the goods are first-rate. **Subway:** N, R to Prince St.; 6 to Spring St.

Apartment 48 48 W. 17th St. (between Fifth and Sixth Aves.) (212) 807-1391. Apartment 48 takes The Apartment concept (*above*) one step further, expanding the design spectrum from antique to sleek—and cozying it up substantially in the process. **Subway:** F, L, N, Q, R, V, W, 4, 5, 6 to 14th St.

Avventura 463 Amsterdam Ave. (at 82nd St.) (212) 769-2510 *www.forthatspecialgift.com*. This stunning Upper West Sider is two stores in one: One side is stocked with eye-catching art glass from the best Italian artisans, while the other boasts beautifully displayed Italian table settings and serveware. The Carlo Moretti glassware alone is worth a look. Prices are high, as is the quality. **Subway:** 1, 9 to 79th St.

Breukelen 69 Gansevoort St. (between Washington and Greenwich Sts.) (212) 645-2216. Funky form tends to prevail over function in the majority of the post-modern shops that have come on strong in the Meatpacking District. Not so at Breukelen, a stunning shop overflowing with the finest in contemporary design, from furniture to lighting to tableware, much of it Scandinavian-inspired and designed by Brooklyn-based designers. **Subway:** A, C, E to 14th St.; L to Eighth Ave.

Chelsea Garden Center 435 Hudson St. (between Leroy and Morton Sts.) (212) 727-7100 *www.chelseagardencenter.com*. This loftlike space is a haven of green in the concrete jungle. The marvelous store sells everything from bonsai-scale cacti to full sets of garden furniture, plus all the essentials for city gardening and gorgeous garden-inspired gifts. **Subway:** 1, 9 to Houston St.

Dune 88 Franklin St. (between Broadway and Church Sts.) (212) 925-6171 *www.dune-ny.com*. Dune designs and manufactures (in its own Brooklyn factory) some of the most thrilling and multifunctional contemporary furniture on the market today, by some of today's most inspired designers—including Nick Dine, Michael Solis, Fabian Baron and Dune owner Richard Shemtov. Each piece is custom-built to order, so you can choose fabric and finish, and even modify measurements as you wish. Expensive, but well worth it for a destined-to-be-classic modern piece. **Subway:** 1, 9 to Franklin St.

Homer 939 Madison Ave. (between 74th and 75th Sts.) (212) 744-7705 *www.homerdesign.com* Create the perfect Hamptons-modern look at designer-to-the-stars Richard Mishaan's home design showcase. The joyous mix—of legacy pieces, Mishaan's own strong-lined furnishings, and accessories from some of today's most thrilling designers—sings with artful inspiration and vibrant color. **Subway:** 6 to 77th St.

Leekan Designs 93 Mercer St. (between Spring and Broome Sts.) (917) 226-7226. Come to this SoHo boutique for affordable gifts and housewares from Asia, Oceania, and Africa, from Morrocan table linens to handwoven sisal baskets to Japanese lanterns—and much, much more. **Subway:** N, R to Prince St.; C, E to Spring St.

MoMA Design Store 44 W. 53rd St. (between Fifth and Sixth Aves.) (212) 767-1050 *www.momastore.org.* Other location: 81 Spring St. (at Crosby St.) (646) 613-1367. The best museum shop in the city is operated by the Museum of Modern Art, and will remain open even while the museum itself is temporarily exiled to Queens. The modern goodies range from clever toys and desktop accessories to licensed reproductions of Alvar Aalto free-form vases, Eames chairs and the like. The new SoHo location is even bigger and better. **Subway:** E, V to Fifth Ave.

Moss 146-150 Greene St. (between Houston and Prince Sts.) (212) 226-2190 *www.mossonline.com.* Murray Moss has created an industrial design museum of the highest order. Homewares, mostly of European design, are displayed in glass cases as if they were priceless art; in reality, many of the items are homeware basics, like staplers, glasware and kitchen knives—albeit the most perfectly realized examples in existence. Bathroom fixtures and a contract division are part of the thoroughly modern mix. **Subway:** N, R to Prince St.

Pearl River 277 Canal St. (at Broadway) and 200 Grand St. (between Mott and Mulberry Sts.) (212) 431-4770 and (212) 966-1010 *www.pearlriver.com.* These sister department stores are Chinatown's top stops for exotic souvenirs, from paper lanterns to mandarin-collared silk pajamas to Hong Kong action videos; everything's so cheap it's almost free. The Canal Street emporium is the larger of the two; look for it to relocate one block north on Broadway in the coming year. **Subway:** J, M, N, Q, R, W, Z, 6 to Canal St.

Steuben 667 Madison Ave. (at 61st St) (212) 752-1441 *www.steuben.com.* This glittering gallery is the flagship store for America's premier manufacturer of fine glass and crystal. **Subway:** N, R, W to Fifth Ave.

Takashimaya 693 Fifth Ave. (between 54th and 55th Sts.) (212) 350-0100. This is Zen shopping, exquisite and spare. This Japan-goes-French country store beckons customers to browse with an air of tranquility after escaping the sensory overload of Fifth Avenue. Takashimaya specializes in high-end household gifts for people with an eye for design, from subtly fragranced soaps to delicate beaded floral barrettes. Exotic flowers and elegant garden essentials fill the first floor, while the upper floors offer home, bath and fashion accessories both luxe and minimalist. **Subway:** E, V to Fifth Ave.

TransLuxe 10 Greene St. (north of Canal St.) (212) 925-5863. This tiny shop is a hidden gem for anybody who ever despaired of the perfect lampshade. Sandra Santos crafts elegant one-of-a-kind shades and hanging lamps in elegant and fluid shapes using vintage and exotic fabrics. Choose from the ready-to-wear selection, or have her design and craft your own original inspiration; you can even bring her your own fabric to work with. Some gorgeous lamp bases are also on hand. **Subway:** J, M, N, Q, R, W, 6 to Canal St.

Jewelry

All of the biggest names in diamonds, gold and platinum have dazzling boutiques on Fifth Avenue in the 50's, often with a second location on Madison Avenue. Witness **Bulgari** (*www.bulgari.com*), whose bold, flashy Italian jewels can be had at 730 Fifth Avenue at 57th Street (212-315-9000), and 783 Madison Avenue between 66th and 67th Streets (212-717-2300); and **Cartier** (*www.cartier.com*), whose luxe French designs are available at 653 Fifth Avenue at 52nd Street (212-753-0111) and 828 Madison Avenue at 69th Street (212-472-6400). Fifth Avenue is also home to the timelessly glamorous wedding sets of **Harry Winston** (718 Fifth Ave. at 56th St., 212-245-2000, *www.harrywinston.com*), considered "King of the Diamonds"; and **Van Cleef & Arpels** (744 Fifth Ave. at 57th St., 212-644-9500, *www.vancleef.com*), with its movie-star glamorous jewels. The crystal, gold and silver of **Baccarat** (625 Madison Ave. at 59th St., 212-826-4100, *www.baccarat.fr*) are surprisingly modern, while the first name in estate jewelry and Oscar baubles is **Fred Leighton** (773 Madison Ave. at 66th St., 212-288-1872).

Those looking for cutting-edge styles and lower prices will do well to browse Nolita, where the fashion-forward jewelry designers include **Me & Ro** (239 Elizabeth St. between Prince and Houston Sts., 917-237-9215, *www.meandrojewelry.com*), whose beautiful contemporary designs—many with Near East inspirations that lend them a gypsy feel—appeared on Julia Roberts in *The Mexican.* **Push** (240 Mulberry St. between Prince and Spring Sts., 212-965-9699, *www.pushjewelry.com*), showcases Karen Karch's rough-hewn, nature-inspired, gem-studded jewelry; she crafted Uma Thurman's wedding band for Ethan Hawke. **Jill Platner** (113 Crosby St., between Houston and Prince Sts., 212-324-1298, *www.jillplatner.com*) showcases her own marvelous aboriginal-inspired silver collars and bracelets, many strung on brightly colored Goretex, lending her pieces a wonderfully contrary modern accent.

For antique pieces, browse the stalls at the **Manhattan Art & Antiques Center**, where a number of dealers specialize in collectible jewelry of yore, or visit **Doyle & Doyle** (*see* "Antiques" *earlier in this chapter*). Additionally, hardcore hunters might want to seek out street vendor **Olivia Garay**, who sells vintage jewelry, both cheap and couture chic, at her own open-air tables at the corner of Third Avenue and 70th Street; she's developed a loyal fan base with her constantly revolving first-class collection. And don't forget to check out the **Diamond District** if you're in the market for a nice rock or custom-designed piece at a bargain price (*see* "Bargain Shopping" *earlier in this chapter*).

Fortunoff 681 Fifth Ave. (at 54th St.) (212) 758-6660 *www.fortunoff.com*. Known for fine merchandise and competitive prices, Fortunoff boasts one of the city's largest selections of fine jewelry, and an especially impressive selection of silver and other bridal registry staples. Stone cuts and designs stick close to the classics, but the discount prices are very attractive. **Subway:** E, V to Fifth Ave.

H. Stern 645 Fifth Ave. (between 51st and 52nd Sts.) (212) 688-0300. Other location: 301 Park Ave. (at 49th St., in the Waldorf=Astoria) (212) 753-5595. This elegant Brazilian company specializes in high-end contemporary designs, with many pieces at the affordable end of the spectrum. Some of the pieces are crafted with unusual semiprecious stones. **Subway:** E, V to Fifth Ave.

Mikimoto 730 Fifth Ave. (between 56th and 57th Sts.) (888) 701-2323 or (212) 457-4600 *www.mikimotoamerica.com*. This beautiful Japanese shop is known exclusively for high-luster cultured pearls. While countless perfect strands come from Mikimoto's own farms, you can also find some of New York's most respectable South Sea and fresh-water varieties. **Subway:** E, N, R, V, W to Fifth Ave.

Reinstein/Ross 29 E. 73rd St. (between Fifth and Madison Aves.) (212) 772-1901 *www.reinsteinross.com*. Other location: 122 Prince St. (between Greene and Wooster Sts.) (212) 226-4513. This fine jeweler has been a huge hit with young brides in search of wedding sets with an exotic look. Expect matte finishes, rich-hued high-karat gold, intricate detailing and unusual gems. **Subway:** 6 to 77th St.

Stuart Moore 128 Prince St. (at Wooster St.) (212) 941-1023 *www.stuart-moore.com*. This futuristic jewel box is the place to come for the sleekest, most ultra-modern designs around in fine jewelry, including wedding sets. **Subway:** N, R to Prince St.

Tiffany & Co. 727 Fifth Ave. (at 57th St.) (212) 755-8000 *www.tiffany.com*. Long before Holly Golightly gazed into its jewel-bedecked windows, Tiffany's was firmly established as one of the world's premier jewelers. The collection is remarkable, ranging from affordable silver pieces in signature Tiffany designs to nature-inspired and jewel-studded baubles soaring into the thousands. The collection is elegantly displayed on multiple floors; don't be shy about just stopping into browse—everybody else does. The fine china, sterling silver and crystal are also magnificent. Small pieces—money clips, key chains and the like—for less than $100 let even shoppers with limited budgets depart with a signature blue box in tow. **Subway:** E, R, V, W to Fifth Ave.

Tourneau 12 E. 57th St. (between Fifth and Madison Aves.) (212) 758-7300 *www.tourneau.com*. Other locations: 500 Madison Ave. (at 52nd St.) (212) 758-6098; 200 W. 34th St. (at Seventh Ave.) (212) 563-6880. The city's finest collection of watches is available at Tourneau, particularly at the large 57th Street location, **Tourneau Time Machine**, where brands range from Swiss Army to Rolex. **Subway:** E, N, R, W to Fifth Ave.

Leather, Handbags & Luggage

(See "Midtown & Uptown Shopping" *in this chapter for details on top designers,* *many of whom*—**Gucci**, **Prada**, **Kenneth Cole** *and others*—*make gorgeous hand-* *bags and leather goods. Check out the Lower East Side for discount bags and luggage;* *see "Bargain Shopping" earlier in this chapter.*

Bottega Veneta 635 Madison Ave. (between 59th and 60th Sts.) (212) 371-5511 *www.bottegaveneta.com*. This Gucci offshoot specializes in fine woven leather and other chic handbags—with shoes and coats (and designer price tags) to match. **Subway:** 4, 5, 6 to 59th St; N, R, W to Lexington Ave.

Coach 595 Madison Ave. (at 57th St.) (212) 754-0041 *www.coach.com*. Other location: 342 Madison Ave. (at 44th St.) (212) 599-4777; check for other loca- tions. Known for butter-soft leather and classic handbag designs, Coach has hipped up its high-quality everyday lines of late, adding vivid colors, 21st-cen- tury fabrics, and fashion-forward backpacks, computer bags, shoes, and super- cool pet accessories. The two Madison branches also carry Coach's new line of footwear for men and women. **Subway:** 4, 5, 6 to 59th St.; N, R, W to Fifth Ave.

Greenwood Leather Goods & Gifts 263 Bleecker St. (between Sixth and Seventh Aves.) (212) 366-0825. While Original Leather *(below)* is your best Greenwich Village source for leather coats and pants, this tidy shop is the top stop for leather handbags, wallets, backpacks, luggage and the like from quality manufacturers like Frye and Latico. The selection is excellent, and prices are very reasonable. **Subway:** 1, 9 to Houston St.

Jutta Neumann 158 Allen St. (between Stanton and Rivington Sts.) (212) 982-7048 *www.juttaneumann-newyork.com*. German-born leather worker Jutta Neumann has crafted her own bold-lined, brightly hued line of handbags, backpacks, wallets and sandals. Her leather cobbling style may be retro, but her designs are entirely fashion-forward. The slides and strappy sandals are particu- larly stunning. **Subway:** F, V to Second Ave.

kate spade 454 Broome St. (at Mercer St.) (212) 274-1991 *www.katespade.com*. Everybody knows about handbag and accessories maven Kate Spade by now; her cute rectangular totes are carried by stylish, *Sex and the City*-watching gals around the world. Here you'll find the whole super-chic collection, which has expanded to include accessories, pajamas, shoes, stationery and a travel line large enough to justify its own store, **kate spade travel** (59 Thompson St. between Spring and Broome Sts., 212-965-8654). **Subway:** N, R to Prince St.

Louis Vuitton 116 Greene St. (between Spring and Prince Sts.) (212) 274-9090. Other location: 703 Fifth Ave. (at 55th St.) (212) 758-8877. The most instantly recognizable designer leather goods and luggage on the planet is the perpetually chic Vuitton line. The empire has expanded to include bold fashions, shoes, outerwear and even travel guides over the years, but the unmistakably monogrammed bags—from totes to steamer trunks—are the heart of the matter. **Subway:** N, R to Prince St.

Manhattan Portage Factory Store 333 E. 9th St. (between First and Second Aves.) (212) 995-5490 *www.manhattanportageltd.com*. First loved for their durable, colorful, made-in-New York messenger bags finished with a red skyline logo, Manhattan Portage is also the place to go for those hip one-shoulder backpacks and DJ bags that everybody's wearing these days. **Subway:** 6 to Astor Pl.

Original Leather Store 171 W. 4th St. (between Sixth and Seventh Aves.) (212) 675-2303 *www.originalleather.com*. Other location: 256 Columbus Ave. (at 72nd St.) (212) 595-7051; check for more locations. Greenwich Village is well known for its collection of leather houses hawking outerwear at discount prices, but Original Leather boasts the best selection, usually without the hard sell that's so common in this district. **Subway:** A, C, E, F, S, V to W. 4th St.

Rafe New York 1 Bleecker St. (at Bowery) (800) 486-9544 *www.rafe.com*. By taking classic shapes and imbuing them with color, wit and exotic twists, Rafe ("rah-fee") Totengco is crafting the most gorgeous designer handbags in the city. The collection is a thrill to browse, from smooth-finish, contrast-stiched leather to bamboo, willow, pandanus and exotic fabrics. Beading and embroidery sometimes add elegant and playful accents. Apparently, Sandra Bullock and Cameron Diaz are fans. **Subway:** 6 to Bleecker St.

T. Anthony Ltd. 445 Park Ave. (at 56th St.). (212) 750-9797 *www.tanthony.com*. This luxury luggage company crafts bold-hued, contrast-stiched leather pieces that are practical, eye-catching and classic. This is luggage built to last—and remain stylish—for a lifetime. No wonder Marilyn Monroe was a fan. Wonderful handbags and accessories, too. **Subway:** 4, 5, 6 to 59th St.

Music

Greenwich Village is a record-hunting bonanza just north of Houston Street, mainly along Bleecker and West 3rd Streets. Between Sixth and Seventh Avenues, the highlights include legendary **Bleecker Bob's Golden Oldies** (118 W. 3rd St. between Macdougal St. and Sixth Ave., 212-475-9677), a dirty hole of a store that's nevertheless a prime source for vinyl collectors; **Bleecker St. Records** (239 Bleecker St. near Carmine St., 212-255-7899), a real standout for its clean and well-organized selection of CDs and vinyl, which offers everything from blues, folk and golden oldies to 70's punk and current rock; **Vinylmania** (60 Carmine St. near Bedford St., 212-924-7223, *www.vinylmania.com*), a prime stop for DJs as well as hip-hop, classic funk and current dance music fans. East of Sixth Avenue, **Generation Records** (210 Thompson St. between Bleecker and W. 3rd Sts., 212-254-1100), is a bright and well-organized store specializing in hardcore sounds upstairs, with one of the city's best used CD departments downstairs; and **Rebel Rebel** (319 Bleecker St. between Christopher and Grove Sts., 212-989-0770), the place for U.K. imports from glam to alt-pop to techno.

In the East Village, St. Marks Place between Second and Third Avenues is another prime hunting ground, especially for used CDs; the lineup of shops seems to be ever-chaning, but you'll always find bargain-basement prices. A standout is **Mondo Kim's** (6 St. Marks Pl., 212-598-9985, *www.kimsvideo.com*), for anything weird on CD, DVD and video; and **13** (13 St. Marks Pl., 212-477-4376), an orderly shop boasting standout collections in rock, metal, country, blues, jazz and folk. Around the corner is **Wowsville** (125 Second Ave., 646-654-0935, *www.wowsville.net*), a hoot of a shop specializing in 60's psychedelia, Ramones-era punk, psychobilly and other underground sounds on vinyl, CD and video. Around the corner on Third Avenue is **Norman's Sound & Vision** (67 Cooper Sq., 212-473-6610), a tidy, well-stocked store with a straightforward selection of new and used CDs.

If you're in the market for musical instruments, West 48th Street between Sixth and Seventh Avenues is your neighborhood. The block's big kahuna is **Sam Ash** (160 W. 48th St., 212-719-2299, *www.samashmusic.com*), hawking everything from pro-DJ turntable systems to Les Pauls and Flying V's to the latest in accordions. **48th Street Custom Guitars** (170 W. 48th St., 212-764-1364) specializes in axes.

Academy Records & CDs 12 W. 18th St. (between Fifth and Sixth Aves.) (212) 242-3000 *www.academy-records.com*. Other location: 77 E. 10th St. (between Third and Fourth Aves.) (212) 780-9166. This tidy, relaxed shop is the prime city stop for used classical, opera, jazz and soundtrack LPs and CDs, plus video and DVDs. The E. 10th St. location specializes in jazz, pop vocal, and genre vinyl. **Subway:** F, L, N, Q, R, V, W, 4, 5, 6 to 14th St.

Colony\ Music Center 1619 Broadway (at 49th St.) (212) 265-2050 *www.colonymusic.com*. Housed in the legendary Brill Building—the Tin Pan Alley of the 50's and 60's, where songwriters like Neil Diamond crafted such pop classics as "I'm a Believer"—this emporium of nostalgia doesn't offer any bargains, but it does have an excellent selection of vintage vinyl and CD reissues of classic and contemporary pop and Broadway cast recordings. A wide range of sheet music is also on hand, especially for the latest top-40 hits and Broadway scores. **Subway:** N, R to 49th St.

Footlight Records 113 E. 12th St. (between Third and Fourth Aves.) (212) 533-1572 *www.footlight.com*. Serious aficionados of cast recordings, big band, pop vocalist and spoken-word collectibles should skip Colony and head straight for this collectors' favorite.**Subway:** L, N, Q, R, W, 4, 5, 6 to 14th St.

Jazz Record Center 236 W. 26th St. (between Seventh and Eighth Aves.), room 804 (212) 675-4480 *www.jazzrecordcenter.com*. Here you'll find New York's best selection of jazz on vinyl and CD, including a phenomenal choice of rare and out-of-print records. **Subway:** C, E, 1, 9 to 23rd St.

Joseph Patelson Music House 160 W. 56th St. (between Sixth and Seventh Aves.) (212) 582-5840 *www.patelson.com*. Where better to house the city's finest collection of classical sheet music—some 47,000 titles—than behind Carnegie Hall? The collection features both common and unusual scores and sheet music, as well as metronomes and pitch pipes. **Subway:** F, N, R, Q, W to 57th St.; B, D, E to Seventh Ave.

Other Music 15 E. 4th St. (between Broadway and Lafayette St.) (212) 477-8150 *www.othermusic.com*. Eclectica is treated like academia at this super-cool store, which spans the globe and expands your mind with other-worldly sounds. This is the place for the most esoteric new releases, including out-there electronica, avant-garde and Japan-only releases, plus cult classics (MC5, Holy Modal Rounders), groove and free jazz, and 70's Krautrockers who make Kraftwerk seem like a household name. **Subway:** 6 to Bleecker St.

Stern's Music 71 Warren St. (at West Broadway) (212) 964-5455 *www.sterns-music.com*. This tri-continental cubby (with outposts in London and São Paulo) is a prime source for world music, especially African and Brazilian. **Subway:** 1, 2, 3, 9 to Chambers St.

Tower Records 692 Broadway (at 4th St.) (212) 505-1500 *www.towerrecords.com*. Other location: 1961 Broadway (at 66th St.) (212) 799-2500. The nation's best chain music retailer has a veritable compound surrounding the Greenwich Village on E. 4th Street between Broadway and Lafayette, where you'll not only find the mainstream retail outlet (including Tower's first-rate classical department) but also **Tower Books and Video** (384 Lafayette St., 212-228-5100). **Subway:** 6 to Bleecker St.; F, S, V to Broadway–Lafayette St.

Virgin Megastore 1540 Broadway (at 45th St.) (212) 921-1020 *www.virginmega.com*. Other location: 52 E. 14th St. (212) 598-4666. Richard Branson's rollicking entertainment complex—complete with a huge CD collection, listening posts, an extensive video and DVD department, a small but eclectic bookstore and a cafe, as well as a travel agent and multiplex movie theater—is a Times Square attraction unto itself. The CD selection is excellent, new releases are usually on sale, and celebrity appearances are common. **Subway:** N, Q, R, S, W, 1, 2, 3, 7, 9 to 42nd St.

Shoes

New York has an endless supply of shoe retailers. Madison Avenue is the place to be if you're willing to pay top dollar for the biggest names. Look for **Timberland** (709 Madison Ave. at 63rd St., 212-754-0436, *www.timberland.com*), smart sophisticates **Cole Haan** (667 Madison Ave. at 61st St., 212-421-8440, *www.cole-haan.com*) and **Bally of Switzerland** (628 Madison Ave. at 59th St., 212-751-9082), and stiletto mavens **Stuart Weitzman** (625 Madison Ave. at 59th St., 212-750-2555, *www.stuartweitzman.com*) and **Sergio Rossi** (835 Madison Ave. near 69th St. 212-396-4814, *www.sergiorossi.it*).

SoHo and adjacent Nolita are tops for shoe fanatics looking for top quality with a twist, be it from **Camper** (125 Prince St. at Wooster St., 212-358-1842, *www.camper.com*), offering runway-hot updates on the classic bowling shoe and other smart-comfy styles; funky, punky, youth-minded **John Fluevog** (250 Mulberry St. at Prince St., 212-431-4484, *www.fluevog.ca*); **Hogan** (134 Spring St. between Greene and Wooster St., 212-343-7905), whose grown-up styles are comfortably preppy-chic; and strappy, sexy **Sigerson Morrison** (28 Prince St. between Mott and Elizabeth Sts., 212-219-3893). The stores that dot Broadway between 8th and Canal Streets tout styles that emphasize affordability and comfort.

For the latest trendy footwear at affordable prices, stroll 8th Street between Fifth and Sixth Avenues in Greenwich Village, and newly cutting-edge Orchard Street in the Lower East Side, where you'll find such outposts of hip as **alife** (178 Orchard St. south of Houston St., 646-654-0628).

The major department stores also have sizable shoe departments offering a sampling of famous labels, from casual to couture. Another great place to shop for shoes is in stylish clothing boutiques that carry their own lines, such as the **Kenneth Cole** flagship store or **Jeffrey New York** (*see* "Department Stores" *and* "Clothing.") Also see "Leather, Handbags & Luggage," as many of the retail outlets—including **Jutta Neumann, kate spade** and **Coach**—also carry their own shoe lines. For athletic shoes, you can't beat **Niketown** or **Modell's** (*see* "Sporting Goods" *later in this chapter*).

Arche 10 Astor Pl. (between Broadway and Lafayette St.). (212) 529-4808 *www.arche-shoes.com*. Other location: 128 W. 57th St. (between Sixth and Seventh Aves.) (212) 262-5488; check for more locations. Women's casual shoes don't get more comfortable than these French-made sandals and slip-ons, which come in a rainbow of soft nubucks that feel like suede but wear beautifully. **Subway:** 6 to Astor Pl.

Harry's Shoes 2299 Broadway (at 83rd St.) (866) 4-HARRYS or (212) 874-2035 *www.harrys-shoes.com*. If you prefer comfort and quality over flashy couture labels, head to Harry's for the biggest and best selection of shoes for the entire family. You name it, Harry's has it: comfort brands like Rockport, Mephisto, Ecco, Clark's and Dansko; weekend footwear by New Balance, Birkenstock and Teva; as well as kids favorites Keds and Stride Rite. You can price- and style-compare at nearby **Tip Top Shoes** (155 W. 72nd St. between Broadway and Columbus Ave., 800-WALKING, *www.tiptopshoes.com*), which carries a similar, comfort-minded selection. **Subway:** 1, 9 to 86th St.

Jimmy Choo 645 Fifth Ave. (entrance on 51st St.) (212) 593-0800 *www.jimmychoo.com*. These seductive designs unite bold finishes and come-hither allure with the very best materials and workmanship. The sexy women's line is what Jimmy Choo is about, but the eye-catching men's line is worth a look, too. **Subway:** E, V to Fifth Ave.

Manolo Blahnik 31 W. 54th St. (between Fifth and Sixth Aves.) (212) 582–3007. The first name in ultra-sexy, ultra-luxury pumps and mules for women who firmly believe that it's better to look good than to feel good. Manolo's sultry signatures are pointy toes, narrow stiletto heels and platinum-card pricing. **Subway:** E, V to Fifth Ave.

Stapleton Shoe Company 68 Trinity Place (at Rector St.). (212) 964-6329. The place for deep discounts on designer men's shoes bearing such top-quality labels as Bally, Johnston & Murphy, and Timberland. **Subway:** N, R to Rector St.

Varda 147 Spring St. (between West Broadway and Wooster St.)
(212) 941-4990. Other locations: 786 Madison Ave. (between 66th and 67th
Sts.) (212) 472-7552; 2080 Broadway (near 72nd St.) (212) 873-6910. These
gorgeous styles in soft and supple Italian leather are the Manolo equivalent for
the mid-priced and more practical woman. Varda's shoes are not only beautifully crafted, but they'll last—and remain in style—for years to come. **Subway:**
C, E to Spring St.; N, R to Prince St.

Sporting Goods

Bicycle Habitat 244 Lafayette St. (between Prince and Spring Sts.)
(212) 431-3315 *www.bicyclehabitat.com*. Downtown's most highly regarded bike
shop is this friendly SoHo cubby, featuring wheels from Trek and Specialized,
plus Mercian custom road frames, rentals and repairs. **Subway:** 6 to Spring St.;
N, R to Prince St.

Bicycle Renaissance 430 Columbus Ave. (at 81st St.) (212) 724-2350.
Selling everything from the newest mountain and racing models to custom
bikes built by in-house professionals, this friendly and well-regarded shop also
offers repair services. **Subway:** 1, 9 to 79th St.

Eastern Mountain Sports 591 Broadway (south of Houston St.) (212) 505-
9860 *www.shopems.com*. Other location: 20 W. 61st St. (at Broadway)
(212) 397-4860. If you are planning a camping trip, learning to kayak or just
want the best insect repellent for a Central Park picnic, EMS can meet your
needs. They sell several top labels as well as their own sturdy brand of outdoor
wear and gear. **Subway:** F, S, V to Broadway–Lafayette St.; 6 to Bleecker St.

Mets Clubhouse Shop 143 E. 54th St. (btw. Lexington and Third Aves.)
(212) 888-7508 *www.mets.com*. Stop in for amazin' goods galore—baseball caps,
T-shirts, posters, Piazza jerseys, '69 Miracle Mets memorabilia and much more.
Fans can also score tickets. **Subway:** E, V to Lexington Ave., 6 to 51st St.

Modell's 1293 Broadway (at 34th St.) (212) 244-4544 *www.modells.com*. Other
location: 51 E. 42nd St. (between Vanderbilt and Madison Aves.) (212) 661-
4242; check for more locations. Family owned and operated since 1889, Modell's can't be beat for one-stop athletic wear and sporting goods shopping. The
range of brand names runs the gamut and prices are fair. Great for home team
souvenirs, too. **Subway:** 1, 2, 3, 9 to 34th St.

NBA Store 666 Fifth Ave. (at 52nd St.) (212) 515-NBA1 *www.nbastore.com*
This tri-level mega-store is a high-tech multimedia celebration of pro-basket-
ball, both NBA and WNBA. Star-studded events are frequent. **Subway:** E, V to
Fifth Ave.

Niketown 6 E. 57th St. (between Fifth and Madison Aves.) (212) 891-6453
www.niketown.com. This high-design five-story advertorial for all things Nike
carries the full line, all stunningly displayed. You'll pay full retail prices, but the
shopping experience is first-class. **Subway:** N, R, W to Fifth Ave.

Paragon Sports 867 Broadway (at 18th St.) (212) 255-8036
www.paragonsports.com. This sprawling shop covers all the bases, from racquet
sports and golf to ice skating and sailing. Equipment is top of the line and prices
can be steep, but sales are gold mines. **Subway:** L, N, Q, R, W, 4, 5, 6 to 14th St.

Patagonia 101 Wooster St. (between Prince and Spring Sts.) (212) 343-1776
www.patagonia.com. Other location: 426 Columbus Ave. (between 80th and
81st Sts.) (917) 441-0011. The first name in eco-friendly fleece and other
nature-minded sports and adventure wear for men, women and kids (no gear,
though). **Subway:** N, R to Prince St.; 6 to Spring St.

Scandinavian Ski & Sports Shop 40 W. 57th St. (between Fifth and Sixth
Aves.) (212) 757-8524. Come to this cozy Midtown nook before you hit the
slopes to meet all your ski and board needs, from boots, goggles, parkas and
poles to high-end après ski wear. **Subway:** N, R, W to Fifth Ave.

Yankees Clubhouse Shop 245 W. 42nd St. (between Seventh and Eighth
Aves.) (212) 768-9555 *www.yankees.com.* Check for more locations. The Big
Apple's favorite home team has its own mini-chain of boutiques where you can
pick up everything from logo jerseys to home-game tickets. **Subway:** A, C, E,
N, Q, R, S, W, 1, 2, 3, 7, 9 to 42nd St.

Stationery & Paper Goods

Jamie Ostrow 876 Madison Ave. (between 71st and 72nd Sts.)
(212) 734-8890. There's no better stop in town for custom stationery, business
cards and invitations. The emphasis is on bold fonts and contemporary looks.
Subway: 6 to 68th St.

Kate's Paperie 561 Broadway (between Prince and Spring Sts.)
(212) 941-9816 *www.katespaperie.com.* Other locations: 8 W. 13th St. (between
Fifth and Sixth Aves.) (212) 633-0570; 1282 Third Ave. (between 73rd and
74th Sts.) (212) 396-3670.For stationery with a twist, eye-catching invitations
for your next get-together or wrap that will make your gifts really pop, come to
Kate's, the best paper store in New York. The large selection also features beautifully bound journals and albums, fountain pens, and more, including custom
stationery. **Subway:** N, R to Prince St.

Ordning & Reda 253 Columbus Ave. (between 71st and 72nd Sts.)
(212) 799-0828 *www.ordning-reda.com.* Other location: 1088 Madison Ave.
(between 81st and 82nd Sts.) (212) 439-6355. Straight angles and Mondrian-
inspired primary colors are the keynotes of this Swedish paper and designer.
Bring order to your home and office with such clever solutions as the business-
card filing book and the perfect desktop stapler. **Subway:** 1, 2, 3, 9 to 72nd St.

Papivore 233 Elizabeth St. (north of Prince St.) (212) 334-4330 *www.papi-
vore.com.* This fragrant, candlelit shop sells the simple, delicate stationery of
Parisian papermaker Marie-Papier. Think simple lines and soft sherbet hues and
you'll get the picture. Custom cards and invites, too. **Subway:** N, R to Prince
St.; 6 to Spring St.

Toys

(See "Midtown & Uptown Shopping" *for* **F.A.O Schwarz** *and the Times Square flagship of* **Toys "R" Us.***)*

Alphaville 226 W. Houston St. (east of Varick St.) (212) 675-6850 *www.alphaville.com*. Specializing in vintage toys from the 1940's to the 70's, this gallery-like shop is entirely for grown-ups—ones who may look like doctors, lawyers and investment bankers on the outside, but are nostalgic kids at heart. The collection includes items like Mr. Potato Heads and classic Paint-by-Numbers sets, and there's a strong emphasis on TV-themed and outer-space toys. **Subway:** 1, 9 to Houston St.

Big City Kites 1210 Lexington Ave. (at 82nd St.) (888) 476-KITE or (212) 472-2623 *www.bigcitykites.com*. This entire store is a loving ode to kites. Choices range from delicate, artful tissue-paper creations to utilitarian plastic varieties that can withstand the learning curve of first-time fliers. The wonderful staff also offers repair services. **Subway:** 4, 5, 6 to 86th St.

Classic Toys 218 Sullivan St. (between Bleecker and 3rd Sts.) (212) 674-4434. Both kids and collectors love this toy store for its wide range of old and new toys, from diecast trucks and Matchbox cars to the latest modern playthings. More than a century's worth of toy soldiers are on display, as is a fascinating collection of antique toys. **Subway:** A, C, E, F, S, V to W. 4th St.

Dinosaur Hill 306 E. 9th St. (east of Second Ave.) (212) 473-5850. Toys from around the world can be found in this tiny, fanciful East Village space: old-fashioned American wooden blocks, Latin American masks, marbles, puppets, crafts and much more, as well as a good selection of children's literature. **Subway:** 6 to Astor Pl.

Enchanted Forest 85 Mercer St. (between Spring and Broome Sts.) (212) 925-6677 *www.sohotoys.com*. This fantastical gallery (designed by the set designer Matthew Jacobs) is a child's dream world actualized, from its forest of fuzzy beasts to a Victorian room straight from C.S. Lewis's Narnia tales. The emphasis is on toys based on the classic model meant to stimulate the imagination, rather than video games and the like. The selection of children's books really shines. **Subway:** N, R to Prince St.; 6 to Prince St.

Wine Shops

New York has the best selection of wine shops in the world; no other city comes close. Standouts include **Sherry-Lehmann**, regularly lauded as among the best wine shops in the world; **Morrell & Company**, boasting a sumptuous wine bar and cafe in the adjacent storefront; **Chelsea Wine Vault** at Chelsea Market; and, on the Upper West Side, **67 Wines & Spirits** and **Acker, Merrall & Condit**. These are full-service shops where the clerks are knowledgeable and always ready to rescue the clueless—provided it's not during a busy Saturday morning or in the middle of the frantic holiday season.

Bargain hunters often head to **Garnet Wines & Liquors**, **Best Cellars**, **Crossroads Wine & Liquor** and **Astor Wines & Spirits**. The atmosphere in these shops, particularly Garnet, can be hectic, so savvy customers try to know what they want before they push open the doors. If business is slow, which it rarely is, the staff can be most helpful. And prices can be appealingly low.

New York has its specialists, too. When they run short on Romanee-Conti, Burgundy and Rhône lovers head for the **Burgundy Wine Company** in the West Village, where you usually have to ring the bell and wines are often selected from an order book rather than samples on the very tiny floor.

Looking for a special Barolo or a little-known Chianti? Take a trip to the **Italian Wine Merchants**. Some of New York's best-known restaurateurs, Mario Batali (Babbo, Esca, Lupa) and Lydia Bastianich (Becco, Felidia), are partners in this first-class shop. Devotees of rare old Bordeaux know they are likely to find what they want at **Royal Wine Merchants**.   —*Frank Prial*

Acker, Merrall & Condit 160 W. 72nd St. (between Broadway and Columbus Ave. (212) 787-1700 *www.ackerwines.com*. **Subway:** 1, 2, 3, 9 to 72nd St.

Astor Wines & Spirits 12 Astor Pl. (at Lafayette St.) (212) 674-7500 *www.astoruncorked.com*. **Subway:** 6 to Astor Pl.

Best Cellars 1291 Lexington Ave. (at 87th St.) (212) 426-4200 *www.best-cellars.com*. **Subway:** 4, 5, 6 to 86th St.

Burgundy Wine Company 323 W. 11th St. (between Greenwich and Washington Sts.) (212) 691-9092 *www.burgundywinecompany.com*. **Subway:** A, C, E, 1, 2,3, 9 to 14th St.; L to Eighth Ave.

Chelsea Wine Vault Chelsea Market, 75 Ninth Ave. (between 15th and 16th Sts.) (212) 462-4244 *www.chelseawinevault.com*. **Subway:** A, C, E to 14th St.; L to Eighth Ave.

Crossroads Wine & Liquor 55 W. 14th St. (between Fifth and Sixth Aves.) (212) 924-3060. **Subway:** F, V to 14th St.

Garnet Wines & Liquors 929 Lexington Ave. (between 68th and 69th Sts.) (212) 772-3211 *www.garnetwine.com*. **Subway:** 6 to 68th St.

Italian Wine Merchants 108 E. 16th St. (between Union Square East and Irving Pl.) (212) 473-2323 *www.italianwinemerchant.com*. **Subway:** L, N, Q, R, W, 4, 5, 6 to 14th St.

Morrell & Company 1 Rockefeller Plaza (at 49th St.) (212) 981-1106 *www.morrellwine.com*. **Subway:** B, D, F, S, V to 47th-50th St.–Rockefeller Center.

Royal Wine Merchants 25 Waterside Plaza (at the East River near 23rd St.) (212) 689-4855 *www.royalwinemerchants.com*. **Subway:** 6 to 23rd St.

Sherry-Lehmann 679 Madison Ave. (between 61st and 62nd Sts.) (212) 838-7500 *www.sherry-lehmann.com*. **Subway:** N, R to Fifth Ave.; 4, 5, 6 to 59th St.

67 Wines & Spirits 179 Columbus Ave. (at 67th St.) (888) 671-6767 *www.67wine.com*. **Subway:** 1, 9 to 66th St.

New York
for Children

Most adults tend to think of New York as a less-than-hospitable place for children: all concrete and steel, with a cultural life geared strictly to grown-ups. But real New Yorkers know that the city is a magical place for kids. This chapter will highlight the city's top attractions designed especially for the under-12 set, from museums to puppet shows, playgrounds and much more.

The parks system more than makes up for the lack of street-side greenery—the Urban Park Rangers' free weekend programs are living proof that peregrine falcons and raccoons as well as Wall Street moguls reside here. **Central Park,** which all Manhattan children regard as their own personal backyard, offers playgrounds, a Swedish marionette theater, free nature workshops and a charming children's zoo. (*There is more information on the park at the end of this chapter.*)

While the **Central Park Zoo** is the most accessible choice for the typical visitor, the **Bronx Zoo** is a world-class wildlife park—definitely worth the trip. Brooklyn is home to the alluring **New York Aquarium,** where children can watch dolphin and orca shows, get nose to nose with sharks and handle crabs and starfish in a "touch tank."

Moms and dads should also check out the **Exploring New York** chapter, which covers many other sights that will be a hit with kids. Look there for details on the **American Museum of Natural History,** where the magnificent hall of dinosaurs provides New York's answer to Jurassic Park. Harrison Ford narrates a blockbuster space show that will inspire budding young astronauts at the adjacent **Rose Center for Earth and Space. Times Square,** which reigned for decades as New York's center of sleaze, has been thoroughly Disney-fied in recent years, sprouting an array of family-friendly shops, arcades, theaters and gimmicks. Young visitors will also love a **Circle Line cruise** (especially the Beast speedboat tour), the **Statue of Liberty,** the **New York City Fire Museum,** the *Intrepid* **Sea-Air-Space Museum** and the **Empire State Building.**

Also covered in the **Exploring New York** chapter are outer-borough attractions that will appeal to children, including Brooklyn's **Coney Island** amusement park, beach and boardwalk; and the new Audubon Center at the Boathouse in Prospect Park. Kids may also enjoy taking the **Staten Island ferry;** from the ferry landing, you can walk to the **Staten Island Institute of Arts and Sciences,** which has an enormous insect collection.

Almost all of the major museums and cultural institutions have young people's programs (*see "Museums for Children" later in this chapter*).

For children's bookstores, clothing stores and toy stores, see chapter **Shopping in New York.** *For great places to play and burn off excess energy, see chapter* **Sports & Recreation.**

Six Great Places for Kids

New Victory Theater   MIDTOWN WEST

209 W. 42nd St. (between Seventh and Eighth Aves.) (646) 223-3020
www.newvictory.org. If you think of children's theater as marionettes, fairy tales
and clowns, you have obviously never visited the New Victory. This is not to
say that its productions never use these elements, but if they do, the marionettes are likely to be life-size, the fairy tales sometimes grim (as well as
Grimm), and the clowns more like Bill Irwin than the Three Stooges. Opened
in 1995 as part of the redevelopment of Times Square, the New Victory is
Broadway's first theater for families, and it is determined never to condescend to
its audiences. Its season (September to June) includes the best productions
worldwide, from extravaganzas like the Shanghai Circus and Australia's Circus
Oz to small, intimate productions like *Old Man River*, a one-woman play.
Among the productions scheduled for winter and spring 2003 are *Twinkle*,
Twinkle Little Fish, an Australian black-light puppetry interpretation of the sto-
rybooks of Eric Carle, and a *Snow White* that preserves that original plot but features a cast of only three (one man plays all seven dwarfs). Generally geared to
children 6 and older, the New Victory also has Vic Teens, a program in which
teenage patrons can see certain shows and then mingle with the cast and cre-
ators. This is intelligent and creative children's theater, with family-friendly
prices ($10–$40, or you can also become a member online and enjoy a 30 percent discount). The theater is right across from *The Lion King* on 42nd Street.
Subway: A, C, E, N, Q, R, S, W, 1, 2, 3, 7, 9 to 42nd St.

Theatreworks/USA   CHELSEA

787 Seventh Ave. (between 51st and 52nd Sts.) (800) 497-5007 for box office
www.theatreworksusa.org. You don't have to fork over your money to Disney to
take your children to a memorable musical that will send them (and you) home
humming. Theaterworks/USA is America's largest non-profit theater for young
audiences. The company tours throughout the nation, but its home base is in
New York, where there's a regular slate of performances at the Auditorium at
Equitable Tower. Theatreworks' musicals and drama not only provide children
ages 5 and older with an introduction to the theater—they offer insights into
history that are so entertaining that the kids may not realize how much they're
learning. In the last several years, Theaterworks has illustrated a number of
important chapters in the growth of the United States, with plays such as *Gold
Rush, Young Tom Edison, The Color of Justice* (about Thurgood Marshall and
Brown v. Topeka) and *Paul Robeson, All-American*. It has also brought literary
favorites to the stage, such as *Ramona Quimby* (based on Beverly Cleary's nov-
els), *Charlotte's Web, A Christmas Carol, Sarah, Plain and Tall, Island of the Blue
Dolphins* and *The Lion, the Witch and the Wardrobe*. The season of hour-long
shows plays on weekends, October to April. Tickets are $20 (or $16 if you buy
10 or more throughout the season); look for special free productions over the
summer. The best works are repeated season to season, but they never get old.
Subway: 1, 2, 9 to 50th St.; N, R to 49th St.

Children's Museum of Manhattan   UPPER WEST SIDE

212 W. 83rd St. (between Amsterdam Ave. and Broadway) (212) 721-1234
www.CMOM.org. Few children's museums offer what adults might consider real
art: paintings, sculptures, photographs and installations that could just as easily
be found in a SoHo gallery. The Children's Museum of Manhattan has broken
new ground with "Art Inside Out," a new exhibition on view through the end
of 2002. Three prominent artists (Elizabeth Murray, William Wegman and Fred
Wilson) have created environments and displays that introduce children to the
ways contemporary art interprets and transforms the world. Mr. Wegman's con-
tribution is a "home" in which what is usually found in the kitchen, studio, living room and bedroom has been reimagined as a work of art (including, of
course, the artist's famous Weimaraners). Children also have many opportunities to step into the artist's role themselves.

This combination of fun and learning is typical of the museum, which is
unusual for both the breadth of its offerings and the wide age range it serves.
One of its exhibitions, "Wordplay," includes places for infants to crawl, gaze at
mobiles and push buttons as their parents learn about the role of language in
their babies' lives. Literacy, in fact, is one of the museum's passions; many of its
past exhibits have been devoted to the works of beloved children's authors.

Conveniently located on the Upper West Side (just a few minutes' walk from
Central Park, and a stone's throw from an array of family-friendly restaurants),
the museum also offers the Time-Warner Media Center, an actual television
studio where visitors 6 and over can produce their own versions of a newscast or
a talk show. The Sussman Environmental Center is an outdoor oasis for learning about urban ecology, and the HP Inventor Center is a digital design workshop where children can create their own inventions with the help of computers. Currently in the midst of a major expansion, the museum will someday offer
a renovated performance theater and a glass-enclosed rooftop garden.
Admission: $6 adults and children; $3 seniors; children under age 1 free.
Hours: Wed.–Sun. 10 A.M.–5 P.M. (also open Tue. in summer). **Subway:** 1, 9
to 86th St.

Brooklyn Children's Museum   BROOKLYN

145 Brooklyn Ave. (at St. Mark's Ave.) (718) 735-4400 www.bchildmus.org.
City chauvinists wouldn't be surprised to learn that the world's first children's
museum is in New York. They might be shocked, however, to learn that it's in
Crown Heights, Brooklyn. This museum, which celebrated its centennial in 1999,
pioneered the hands-on approach characteristic of contemporary children's exhibitions as early as 1904, when it began taking the objects on display out of their
glass cases. That's still the philosophy at the museum, which invites children to
pluck at musical instruments, handle insect models or try on shoes. Distinctive
because it has a permanent collection (very few children's museums do), the
Brooklyn Children's Museum has more than 27,000 objects, ranging from an elephant skeleton to Queen Elizabeth II coronation dolls. Early in 2000, the museum
opened Totally Tots, a gallery specially geared to toddlers under age 5. The offer-

ings here include Baby Patch, a giant artificial bird's nest; Play Pond, a series of small pools for dabbling, pouring and handling marine objects; and Kids Quarry, a wall with foam rocks for building. The museum also has a greenhouse, where children can "adopt a plant" and handle earthworms, and a live animal collection whose residents range from furry to scaly. These creatures used to be taken out only for special occasions, but in 2001 the museum opened its Animal Outpost, which puts many of them on permanent display. Children can observe species like frogs and double-crested basilisks while learning about their life cycles through displays that include animal skeletons and a microscope. After all, how many museums invite you to pet a snake? **Admission:** $4. **Hours:** Sept.–Jun. Wed.–Fri. 2–5 P.M., Sat.–Sun. 10 A.M.–5 P.M. Jul.–Aug. Mon. and Wed.–Thu. noon–5 P.M., Fri. noon–6:30 P.M., Sat.–Sun. 10 A.M.–5 P.M. Additional morning hours for Totally Tots. **Subway:** 1 or C to Kingston Ave., then a 7-block walk; weekend shuttle bus from Grand Army Plaza.

Staten Island Children's Museum   STATEN ISLAND

1000 Richmond Terrace (between Tysen St. and Snug Harbor Rd.) (718) 273-2060. Nestled in the Snug Harbor Cultural Center and boasting one of the most bucolic settings a New York institution could hope for, the museum has a huge front lawn that is turned into a festival site every spring when the museum hosts its Meadowfair, an indoor-outdoor carnival. (The lawn also has a large praying mantis—or, as the museum puts it, playing mantis—sculpture for children to climb.) Indoors, there's Block Harbor, an area for preschoolers that includes a pirate ship for small swashbucklers; Portia's Playhouse, which provides budding starlets with costumes, props and a stage; and permanent exhibitions on irresistible subjects like water and bugs (there's an Arthropod Zoo), as well as traveling displays. In the fall of 2001, the museum expanded into a two-story turn-of-the-century barn. The highlight of the new space is Great Explorations, an exhibition that invites children to discover what it was like to pioneer three challenging environments: a tropical rain forest, the ocean depths and a snowy polar landscape. **Admission:** $5; children under 2 free. **Hours:** Tue.–Sun. noon–5 P.M. (opens at 11 A.M. Jul.-Aug.) **Directions:** Staten Island Ferry to S-40 bus.

New York Hall of Science   QUEENS

47–01 111th St. (at 47th Ave.), Flushing (718) 699-0005 *www.nyhallsci.org.* Any playground is potentially a lesson in physics. But only one playground in New York is especially designed to teach children the scientific concepts behind every sway of the seesaw and zoom down the slide. That is the Science Playground at the New York Hall of Science in Queens, the largest playground of its kind in the Western Hemisphere and winner of several awards since it opened in 1997. In 1999, the Hall of Science opened a companion area, the Sound Playground, which is understandably—and educationally—noisy.

Although these special playgrounds are open only to children over 6, the Hall of Science, which began as a pavilion for the 1964–65 World's Fair, offers attractions for younger adventurers, too. The Preschool Discovery Place allows them to explore sound, color, light and simple principles of construction, while permanent displays in the Exhibition Hall offer their older siblings forays into the physical world, from the atomic level on up. Major recent additions include "Marvelous Molecules," an in-depth look at the building blocks of all life. In January 2001, the hall opened the Pfizer Foundation Biochemistry Discovery Lab, which invites visitors to explore the chemistry of living things by conducting any of 12 available experiments, on subjects ranging from why roses are red and violets are blue to how bees communicate. Recommended for ages 8 and up, the lab is open to the public on Saturdays and Sundays from noon to 4:45 P.M., and Thursdays and Fridays from 2 to 4:45 P.M.

Admission: $7.50 adults; $5 children ages 4–17 and seniors over age 62; children 3 and under free. Science Playground entry $2 per person (children must be age 6 or older). Free admission for everyone Thu.–Fri. 2–5 P.M. **Hours:** Mon.–Wed. 9:30 A.M.–2 P.M. (till 5 P.M. in Jul.–Aug.); Thu.–Sun. 9:30 A.M.–5 P.M. **Subway:** 7 to 111th St. in Queens.

—Laurel Graeber

Circuses

Big Apple Circus (800) 922-3772 *www.bigapplecircus.org*. With its local roots, intimate one-ring big top and kid-friendly mission, the Big Apple Circus has staked out its own ground between the glitz of Ringling Brothers and the artistry of Cirque du Soleil. Shows are held in the circus's quaint big top in Damrosch Park at Lincoln Center, from late October to early January.

Ringling Brothers and Barnum and Bailey Circus Madison Square Garden, Seventh Ave. (at 33rd St.) (800) 755-4000 *www.ringling.com*. The classic American three-ring circus—trapeze artists, lion tamers, elephants and all—descends on Madison Square Garden every spring, running shows in March and April. Check *www.thegarden.com* for a complete schedule and ticket purchase.

Museums and Programs for Children

(See "Six Great Places for Kids" *above for* **Brooklyn Children's Museum, Children's Museum of Manhattan** *and* **Staten Island Children's Museum.** *See also* **Lefferts Homestead Children's Historic House Museum** *in Prospect Park, described in the* "Brooklyn" *section of chapter* **Exploring New York.***)*

Children's Museum of the Arts 182 Lafayette St. (between Broome and Grand Sts.) (212) 941-9198 *www.cmany.org*. This museum includes interactive installations like the ever-popular Ball Pond, a room filled with oversized rubber balls that children can crawl through, and two floors of art studios offering hands-on projects. **Admission:** $5; free for seniors and children under age 1. **Hours:** Wed.–Sun. noon–5 P.M. **Subway:** N, R to Prince St.; 6 to Spring St.

South Street Seaport Museum 207 Front St. (between South and Water Sts.) (212) 748-8600 *www.southstreetseaport.com*. There's a special children's center in the museum here, but all of the attractions in this landmark district are meant to be family-friendly. This 11-square-block development on the East River encompasses historic buildings, several piers, shops and restaurants; kids will especially like checking out the historic ships berthed at the piers. **Admission:** Museum $6 adults; $5 seniors; $4 students; $3 children. **Hours:** Apr.–Sept. daily 10 A.M.–6 P.M. Oct.–Mar. Wed.–Mon. 10 A.M.–5 P.M. **Subway:** 2, 3, 4, 5, J, M, Z to Fulton St.

Special Children's Programs at NYC's Top Museums

(For admission prices, hours and directions, see the full museum listings in chapters **Exploring New York** *and* **The Arts.***)*

American Museum of Natural History Central Park West (at 79th St.) (212) 769-5100 *www.amnh.org.* From the Dinosaur Halls to the enormous IMAX theater to the Hall of Ocean Life, with its giant blue whale hanging from the ceiling, this is a can't-miss attraction for kids. The museum's new Discovery Room, a huge, two-level space dominated by a model of an African baobab tree (with plenty of artificial creatures in its branches), offers kids the chance to play zoologist, paleontologist, geologist and anthropologist. Check the Web site for a rundown of programs geared to kids.

Brooklyn Museum 200 Eastern Parkway, Prospect Park (718) 638-5000 *www.brooklynmuseum.org.* Kids will enjoy the largest collection of mummies outside Egypt, as well as excellent children's workshops and teen programs.

Guggenheim Museum 1071 Fifth Ave. (at 88th St.) (212) 423-3500 *www.guggenheim.org.* If nothing else, kids will enjoy the fun, spiraling space (but remember, no strollers). The Web site lists special family programs, from film screenings to multimedia workshops.

The Jewish Museum 1109 Fifth Ave. (at 92nd St.) (212) 423-3200. *www.thejewishmuseum.org.* On most Sundays, the museum offers a diverse series of family programs, from sing-a-longs to storytimes to art activities to theater performances.

Lower East Side Tenement Museum 90 Orchard St. (at Broome St.) (212) 431-0233 *www.tenement.org.* On weekends, the museum offers the Confino Apartment Tour, a living history tour that allows kids to try on period clothes and talk with an actor who portrays a recent immigrant.

Metropolitan Museum of Art 1000 Fifth Ave. (at 82nd St.) (212) 535-7710. *www.metmuseum.org.* Children and adults alike will find the Met overwhelming, so come here with a game plan. The "Museum Hunt" guides, available at the Uris information desk, near the 81st Street entrance, are a good place to start: they present special and permanent collections to kids through fun activities. Most children are entertained by the Egyptian collection (spooky mummies!). There are frequent family tours, hands-on workshops, storytelling sessions, films and much more.

MoMA QNS 33rd St. and Queens Blvd., Long Island City, Queens (212) 708-9805 *www.moma.org*. In its new location, MoMA continues to offer family-oriented gallery talks (usually $5 per family) and special workshops.

P.S. 1 22-25 Jackson Ave. (at 46th Ave.), Long Island City, Queens. (718) 784-2084 *www.ps1.org*. P.S. 1, MoMA's cutting-edge affiliate, offers summer "art camps" and other programs geared to families.

The Whitney Museum 945 Madison Ave. (at 75th St.) (212) 570-7710. *www.whitney.org*. The Whitney offers activities in conjunction with current exhibitions, encouraging adults and children to learn about American art and culture together. In addition, families can attend a free guided tour featuring sketching and discussion every Saturday at 11:30 A.M. No reservations are required. Special print and audio guides for kids are available at the information desks.

Music for Children
(For more information, see chapter **The Arts.***)*

Amato Opera-in-Brief 319 Bowery (at 2nd St.) (212) 228-8200. *www.amato.org*. In addition to its standard performances, this company has been staging opera for children for over 50 years. "Opera-in-Brief" performances are fully costumed, abbreviated versions of classic operas, featuring interwoven narration so everyone can follow the story. Performances are 90 minutes long (including intermission) and should be appropriate for children 5 and up. **Prices:** $15 all seats. **Schedule:** Usually 10 performances per year, all start at 11:30 A.M. Sat, dates vary.

Carnegie Hall Family Concerts 152 W. 57th St. (at Seventh Ave.) (212) 903-9670. *www.carnegiehall.org*. At these hour-long concerts, kids ages 7 and up get an introduction to music and musical instruments and concepts through a variety of demonstrations led by well-known performers and groups. (Parents with younger children should seek out the "CarnegieKids" interactive concerts, in which little ones get to play along with musicians and a storyteller.) **Prices:** Family Concerts $5, CarnegieKids $3. **Schedule:** Selected Saturday afternoons throughout the season.

Lincoln Center Children's Programs
Many people don't know about the special kids' concerts available at Lincoln Center. Unfortunately, there are only a few each year, and schedules can vary from season to season; parents should check for tickets well in advance.

Growing Up With Opera (212) 769-7008 *www.operaed.org*. The Metropolitan Opera sponsors a few shows each year for kids ages 4–6 and 6–12, often featuring question-and-answer sessions and "cast parties" with the artists afterward. **Prices:** $7–$10.

Jazz for Young People Alice Tully Hall (212) 258-9800 *www.jazzatlincolncenter.org*. Wynton Marsalis, director of Jazz at Lincoln Center, is passionate about educating young jazz fans. He hosts and performs at educational concerts, with themes like "Who Is John Coltrane?" and "What Is Samba?" Concerts are usually held three Saturdays a year. **Prices:** $15 adults; $10 children 18 and under.

Little Orchestra Society (212) 971-9500 *www.littleorchestra.org.* Each season, the Society sponsors three classical-music concerts geared toward children ages 6–12 at Avery Fisher Hall (plus an additional series of Lolli-Pops concerts for kids ages 3–5 at the Kaye Playhouse). **Prices:** $10–$55.

New York Philharmonic Young People's Concerts (212) 721-6500 *www.nyphilharmonic.org.* The Philharmonic offers four Saturday-afternoon concerts each year, providing a fun introduction to symphonic music for 6- to 12-year-olds. Ticket holders can also attend the one-hour "Kidzone Live!" sessions before each concert, which allow children to make music. **Prices:** $6–$24.

Play Spaces

Chelsea Piers West Side Hwy. at 23rd St. (212) 336-6666 *www.chelseapiers.com.* You name it—they've got it. Families can enjoy skating, bowling, batting cages and much, much more. Facilities include a toddler gym; supervised child care for ages 18 months to 8 years (reservations required); and separate rock-climbing walls for children and teens. City kids can enroll in all kinds of classes and activities, from gymnastics to soccer to dance. Prices vary according to the activity, but it's not exactly cheap. *(See the box in chapter* **Sports & Recreation.***)* **Subway:** C, E to 23rd St.

Lazer Park 163 W. 46th St. (between Broadway and Sixth Ave.) (212) 398-3060 *www.lazerpark.com.* In addition to the 5,000-square-foot laser tag arena, meant solely for older kids and grown-ups looking to get in touch with their inner child, there's a huge array of video and virtual-reality games. **Subway:** B, D, F, N, Q, R, V, W, 1, 2, 3, 7, 9 to 42nd St.

Playspace 2473 Broadway (at 92nd St.) (212) 769-2300. This is a bright and clean operation, with a good cafe for parents. It will be crowded on rainy weekends. It also offers birthday parties and classes. **Subway:** 1, 2, 3, 9 to 96th St.

Rain or Shine 202 E. 29th St. (at Third Ave.) (212) 532-4420. *www.rainorshinekids.com.* Everything under one roof: a playhouse, art center and baby center. Some days they offer puppet shows and free playtime. **Subway:** 6 to 28th St.

Puppets

The Lenny Suib Puppet Playhouse 555 E. 90th St. (between York and East End Ave.) (212) 369-8890, ext. 159. This theater offers puppets, magicians, clowns, ventriloquists and storytellers. **Prices:** $7. **Subway:** 4, 5, 6 to 86th St.

Puppetworks 338 Sixth Ave. (at 4th St.), Park Slope, Brooklyn (718) 965-3391 *www.puppetworks.org.* This group has been performing with hand-crafted marionettes since 1938. They generally offer three or four stories per year, with two performances each Saturday and Sunday. Reservations are required. **Prices:** $7 adults; $6 children. **Subway:** F to Seventh Ave., then a six-block walk.

Swedish Cottage Marionette Theater Central Park West Drive (at 79th St.) (212) 988-9093 *www.centralparknyc.org.* Puppet shows, often such classics as *Peter Pan* or *Cinderella*, are staged at 10:30 A.M. and noon Tuesday through Friday, 1 P.M. on Saturdays (no Saturday shows in July or August). The season runs from early November through mid-August; advance reservations are required. **Prices:** $6 adults; $5 children. **Subway:** B, C to 81st St.

Science for Children

(See "Six Great Places for Kids" *earlier in this chapter for the* **New York Hall of Science***.)*

Liberty Science Center 251 Phillip St. (at Communipaw Ave.), Jersey City, New Jersey (201) 200-1000 *www.lsc.org.* Each of the center's three floors is devoted to a specific theme: environment, health and invention. Visitors of all ages can touch starfish or giant insects, crawl through a 100-foot "touch tunnel" or play virtual basketball. At Roach World, renowned entomologist Betty Faber will teach you everything there is to know about your unwelcome kitchen guests. There's also an IMAX theater, plus temporary exhibitions, such as "Kid Stuff: Great Toys from Our Childhood," which runs through January 2003. **Admission:** $10 adults; $8 children and seniors; free for children under age 2. Additional fees for IMAX and 3-D Laser Shows. **Hours:** Daily 9:30 A.M.–5:30 P.M. **Directions:** Take the NY Waterways Ferry from North End Avenue and Vesey Street in Lower Manhattan, near the World Financial Center; or take the PATH train to Pavonia/Newport and transfer to the Hudson-Bergen Light Rail.

Sony Wonder Technology Lab 550 E. 56th St. (between Madison and Fifth Aves.) (212) 833-8100 *www.sonywondertechlab.com.* No doubt about it: This is one of the city's coolest destinations for kids, and it's free. Kids can produce their own TV shows or remix a song by Celine Dion. At a command center, they can analyze weather data to avert disasters or watch HDTV. But keep in mind, this free public space dedicated to technology education just happens to be operated by Sony's retail division, and, not surprisingly, showcases only Sony products. **Admission:** Free. Reservations required. **Hours:** Tue.–Wed. and Fri.–Sat. 10 A.M.–6 P.M.; Sun. noon–6 P.M.; Thu. 10 A.M.–8 P.M. **Subway:** E, V to Fifth Ave.; 4, 5, 6 to 59th St.; N, R to Fifth Ave.

Theater for Children

(For the **New Victory Theater** *and* **Theatreworks/USA,** *see* "Six Great Places for Kids," *earlier in this chapter.)*

Arts Connection 120 W. 46th St. (between Sixth Ave. and Broadway) (212) 302-7433 *www.artsconnection.org.* Ask about the affordable "Saturdays Alive" series of performances and workshops, held from October to May. In addition to theater productions, you might catch dance performances or a special holiday show. **Subway:** B, D, F, N, Q, R, V, W, 1, 2, 3, 7, 9 to 42nd St.

Beauty and the Beast Lunt-Fontanne Theater, 205 W. 46th St. (between Eighth Ave. and Broadway) (212) 575-9200. Disney's stage adaptation of its animated classic is more pedestrian than the breathtaking film version, but little ones will love it anyway. Even adults will go home humming the catchy show-stopper "Be Our Guest." **Prices:** $60–$95. **Subway:** A, C, E, N, Q, R, S, W, 1, 2, 3, 7, 9 to 42nd St.

Grove Street Playhouse 39 Grove St. (between Bedford and Bleecker Sts.) (212) 741-6436. This group occasionally adapts classics for children with humor for adults, and presents shows in a participatory manner: kids are encouraged to talk, move, and even shout. **Subway:** 1, 9 to Christopher St.

Henry Street Settlement—Abrons Arts Theater 466 Grand St. (at Pitt St.) (212) 598-0400 *www.henrystreetarts.org.* This historic settlement house features an arts center with an array of dance, theater and music performances for the whole family, sometimes featuring mime, puppetry and magic. One recent show was Red Ridin' in the Hood, an updated retelling of the classic fairy tale set to a jazz score. Reserve for weekend shows at least a week in advance. **Prices:** $6 adults; $4 children. **Subway:** F to Delancey St.; J, M, Z to Essex St.

Kids 'N Comedy 34 W. 22nd St. (between Fifth and Sixth Aves.) (212) 877-6115 *www.kidsncomedy.com.* Monthly children's shows and comedy workshops are offered at the Gotham Comedy Club for kids ages 9 to 15. **Prices:** $15. **Subway:** F, N, R, V, 1, 9 to 23rd St.

The Lion King New Amsterdam Theater 214 W. 42nd St. (between Seventh and Eighth Aves.) (212) 282-2900. Tickets are hard to come by, but it's worth the effort. When Julie Taymor's life-size animal puppets lumber down the aisles during the opening number, it's pure enchantment. This Tony Award–winning show is a smash with kids and sophisticated adults alike. **Subway:** A, C, E, N, Q, R, S, W, 1, 2, 3, 7, 9 to 42nd St.

TADA! Youth Ensemble 120 W. 28th St. (between Sixth and Seventh Aves.) (212) 627-1733. Tada! presents one-hour original shows with a multi-ethnic perspective; they're all performed by 6-to-17-year-old actors. The schedule runs throughout the year, and frequently includes weekday and Friday night performances. Tickets sell out quickly. **Subway:** 1, 9, to 28th St.

13th Street Repertory Theater 50 W. 13th St. (between Fifth and Sixth Aves.) (212) 675-6677 *www.13thstreetrep.org.* Located in a Greenwich Village brownstone, this 72-seat theater offers weekend-afternoon children's shows, such as *Rumple Who?.* **Prices:** $7. **Subway:** L, N, Q, R, W, 4, 5, 6 to14th St.

Vital Children's Theatre 432 W. 42nd St. (212) 268-2040 *www.vitaltheatre.org.* This program of the Vital Theatre Company offers a five-

show season of high-quality children's productions from October through April.
Prices: $10. **Subway:** A, C, E to 42nd St.

Zoos & Wildlife Centers

Bronx Zoo Wildlife Conservation Park 2300 Southern Blvd. at Bronx Park
South (718) 367-1010 *www.wcs.org*. *(See section* "The Bronx" *in chapter* **Exploring New York** *for full details.)* Every kid loves to visit the zoo, and this one is
New York's best. Parents of serious young zoologists might want to sign them up
for a special educational outing, such as "Breakfast with the Butterflies." The
most popular offering is the "Family Overnight Safari," in which families camp
out overnight in the zoo and meet nocturnal animals; offered three times a year,
the program runs $240 for one adult and one child.

Central Park Zoo Fifth Ave. and 64th St. (212) 861-6030 *www.wcs.org*. *(See
section* "Central Park" *in chapter* **Exploring New York** *for full listing.)* The Tisch
Children's Zoo allows kids to get up close and personal with a menagerie of
gentle creatures. There's also a series of special children's educational programs.

New York Aquarium for Wildlife Conservation Surf Ave. and W. 8th St.,
Brooklyn (718) 265-FISH *www.wcs.org*. Located on a strip of coastline between
Coney Island and Brighton Beach, the aquarium is worth the long schlep from
Manhattan. With more than 300 species of marine life and an impressive collection of marine mammals, it features narrated feedings, underwater viewing
areas and up-close animal encounters. Check out sea lion and dolphin performances in the Aquatheater, as well as the hands-on Discovery Center. **Admission:** $11 adults; $7 children ages 2–12 and seniors; children under 2 free. Children under 18 must be accompanied by an adult. **Hours:** Mon.–Fri. 10 A.M.–6
P.M.; Sat.–Sun. and holidays 10 A.M.–7 P.M. **Subway:** F, Q to W. 8th St.; take
pedestrian bridge to aquarium.

Prospect Park Zoo 450 Flatbush Ave., Brooklyn (718) 399-7339
www.wcs.org. It isn't as comprehensive as the Bronx Zoo, but this 19-acre park
still merits a trip out of Manhattan. It's extremely kid-friendly, featuring giant
lily pads and kid-size goose eggs to play with, plus a "barnyard" with assorted
touchable animals. Kids will also enjoy the interactive Wildlife Center, which
offers lectures and workshops throughout the year. **Admission:** $2.50 adults;
$.50 children ages 3–12; $1.25 seniors; children under 3 free. **Hours:** Daily 10
A.M.–4:30 P.M. **Subway:** Q to Prospect Park.

Queens Zoo 111th St. (at 54th Ave.), Flushing, Queens (718) 271-1500
www.wcs.org. This 11-acre park, which focuses on the wildlife of the Americas,
is child-oriented and interactive. Kids will enjoy the aviary, the herd of bison,
and a variety of domesticated animals in the petting zoo. There are also seasonal
events, like an elaborate Groundhog Day "celebration of prognosticating
rodents." **Admission:** $2.50 adults; $.50 children ages 3–12; $1.25 seniors; chil-
dren under 3 free. **Hours:** Daily 10 A.M.–4:30 P.M. **Subway:** 7 to 111th St.

Staten Island Zoo 614 Broadway (at Glenwood Pl.), Staten Island (718) 442-3100 *www.statenislandzoo.org*. It may be smaller than the zoos in the other four boroughs, but the Staten Island Zoo holds its own with a menagerie of more than 400 animals on its eight acres. There's also an aquarium, a children's zoo where kids can feed the animals, a noteworthy display of reptiles, a tropical forest exhibit and a simulation of the African savannah at twilight. **Admission:** $3 adults; $2 children ages 3–11; children under 3 free. **Hours:** Daily 10 A.M.–4:45 P.M.

Outdoor Attractions and Activities for Children

(See also chapter **Sports & Recreation,** *and the section on* **Prospect Park** *near the end of chapter* **Exploring New York.***)*

Central Park *(See section "Central Park" in chapter* **Exploring New York** *for full listing. See chapter* **Sports & Recreation** *for details on renting bikes and in-line skates.)* Central Park's Children's District (mid-park, 64th–65th St.) offers a wealth of activities, from the Carousel and Wollman Skating Rink to the Heckscher Playground. A good place to start is **The Dairy** (mid-park at 64th St.)—originally a real dairy, now an information center with a variety of activities for children. It also offers an excellent map of the park.

Perhaps the most popular children's attraction in the park lies to the east, along Fifth Avenue: the **Children's Zoo,** part of the Central Park Wildlife Conservation Center, offers pint-sized displays and a petting zoo.

Around 74th Street, also on the east side of the park, lies **Conservatory Water,** a popular pond where kids and adults can rent remote-controlled boats in the afternoon. Nearby are the well-known statues of Alice in Wonderland and Hans Christian Andersen (check out the **story readings** here Wed. and Sat. at 11 A.M. in summer). Toward the center of the park, around 79th Street, is **Belvedere Castle**; kids will love this miniature storybook castle and the Nature Observatory inside. You can also see a show at the **Swedish Cottage Marionette Theater,** located just to the west of the Castle *(see "Puppets" earlier in this chapter, for details)*.

If you find yourself above the 97th Street Transverse, stop at the **North Meadow Recreation Center** (mid-park, around 98th St.) to borrow one of their "field kits" for kids, packed with toys and activities to try in the park. And if you're at the very top of the park, plan to spend some time around the body of water known as **Harlem Meer**. From the **Charles A. Dana Discovery Center** to **Conservatory Garden**, with its charming Secret Garden statue, to **Lasker Rink and Pool,** families will easily find a fun way to while away the afternoon.

New York Botanical Garden 200th St. (at Southern Blvd.), the Bronx (718) 817-8705 *www.nybg.org*. *(See the section "The Bronx" in chapter* **Exploring New York** *for full listing.)* The Everett Children's Adventure Garden provides eight acres and hours of entertainment, including a three-foot-high hedge maze that will delight small children. The Garden offers numerous workshops and activities, including a summer storytelling series.

KID-FRIENDLY RESTAURANTS

Little Italy

Lombardi's 32 Spring St. (near Mott St.) (212) 941-7994. The chefs at historic Lombardi's love to show off their pizza oven. If it's not too busy, they shepherd children to the rear, explain how the oven works and even allow them to toss in a chunk of coal. **Subway:** 6 to Spring St.; N, R to Prince St.

TriBeCa

Bubby's 120 Hudson St. (at N. Moore St.). (212) 219-0666. Here's a homey, loft-like neighborhood spot, serving up terrific versions of the comfort foods kids love: burgers, ribs, macaroni-and-cheese. But the real stars of the show here are the fresh-baked pies (the chocolate–peanut butter version is a legend in its own time). **Subway:** 1, 9 to Franklin St.

Greenwich Village

Peanut Butter & Co. 240 Sullivan St. (between Bleecker and 3rd Sts.) (212) 677-3995. What kid wouldn't love a restaurant that serves 21 different varieties of peanut butter sandwiches? Traditionalists stick to the Fluffernutter on white bread, but the most popular offering is the Elvis (grilled peanut butter, banana, honey and bacon). Finish your meal with make-your-own s'mores for the ultimate sugar buzz. **Subway:** A, C, E, F, V to W. 4th St.; 1, 9 to Houston St.

Midtown West

Carmine's 200 W. 44th St. (between Broadway and Eighth Ave.) (212) 221-3800. The giant helpings of pasta served at this rollicking restaurant are meant to be enjoyed family-style. It's a great value, so bring the whole clan and dig in. **Subway:** A, C, E, N, R, Q, S, W, 1, 2, 3, 7, 9 to 42nd St.

John's Pizzeria 260 W. 44th St. (between Seventh and Eighth Aves.) (212) 391-7560. Housed in what used to be the Christian Alliance Gospel Tabernacle Church, this is New York's largest pizzeria and its most beautiful. Service is friendly; you're likely to get a table without waiting; and the pies are some of the city's best. **Subway:** A, C, E, N, R, Q, S, W, 1, 2, 3, 7, 9 to 42nd St.

Virgil's 152 W. 44th St. (between Broadway and Sixth Ave.) (212) 921-9494. How could parents not appreciate being offered towels instead of napkins? Big and boisterous, Virgil's serves up respectable reproductions of barbecue styles from North Carolina to Texas. **Subway:** B, D, F, N, R, Q, S, V, W, 1, 2, 3, 7, 9 to 42nd St.

Upper East Side

Barking Dog Luncheonette 1678 Third Avenue (at 94th St.) (212) 831-1800. If the kids get fidgety while waiting for the All-American menu items or rich, bountiful desserts, distract them with the restaurant's dog tchotchkes. For families that can't get going in the morning, breakfast is served until 4 P.M. **Subway:** 6 to 96th St.

Serendipity 3 225 E. 60th St. (between Second and Third Aves.) (212) 838-3531. This whimsical soda fountain brings back fond memories for generations of city kids. You'll find sandwiches, hot dogs, and other diner fare on the menu, but the real point is dessert. Dig into old-fashioned favorites like lemon ice box pie, a drug-store sundae, or an outrageous banana split. Expect a long, long wait. **Subway:** N, R to Lexington Ave.; 4, 5, 6 to 59th St.

Upper West Side

EJ's Luncheonette 447 Amsterdam Ave. (at 82nd St.) (212) 873-3444. It's a retro diner, with great burgers, fries and shakes. A kids' menu offers pint-size servings, plus classics like peanut-butter-and-jelly sandwiches. **Subway:** 1, 9 to 79th St.

Gabriela's 315 Amsterdam Ave. (at 75th St.) (212) 875-8532. With a bright, colorful décor and a casual vibe, Gabriela's serves up some of Manhattan's best and most affordable Mexican fare. Mom and dad can sip margaritas while perusing the children's menu. **Subway:** 1, 2, 3, 9 to 72nd St.

Popover's 551 Amsterdam Ave. (between 86th and 87th Sts.) (212) 595-8555. The real point at this warm and welcoming cafe is the basket of warm, fluffy popovers delivered to each table. Slather them with downhome preserves or strawberry butter. Little ones are sure to be charmed by the dozens of resident teddy bears who nestle amid the country-cute décor. **Subway:** 1, 9 to 86th St.

Popular Theme Restaurants for Families

Hard Rock Café 221 W. 57th St. (at Broadway) (212) 459-9320. Once you pry your kids out of the Hard Rock souvenir store next door, service is quick and friendly, and there's an affordable kids' menu. The walls are covered with memorabilia—rock stars' guitars, platinum platters, more guitars, photos, posters. **Subway:** N, R, Q, W to 57th St.

Jekyll & Hyde Club 1409 Sixth Ave. (at 57th St.) (212) 541-9505. Jekyll & Hyde features hair-raising hourly entertainment, animated skeletons, roving actors and a conversational sphinx. The best tables for catching the action are on the first two floors of this dark old four-story mansion. Waits can be long, but children are usually enchanted. **Subway:** N, R, Q, W to 57th St.

Mars 2112 1633 Broadway (at 51st St.) (212) 582-2112. Your visit here starts with a stomach-churning mock flight to Mars, where steaming lava pools greet your arrival. At the Mars Bar, you'll find everything from planetary news and weather reports to scenic views of the planet, not to mention a large menu of "Marstinis" (which parents may need). Dig into the surprisingly decent menu items, such as Big Bang bruschetta and Ziggy Stardust spaghetti. Kids are entertained by a video arcade. **Subway:** N, R, W to 49th St.; 1, 9 to 50th St.

Nightlife

By now, most visitors (as well as the majority of residents) have grown tired of tall tales and song lyrics about "the city that never sleeps." Well, like most myths and clichés, the ones about New York at night are almost always based on truth. With the possible exception of New Orleans during Mardi Gras, New York reigns as—get ready for another cliché—the nightlife capital of the world.

All platitudes aside, bar closing time *is* at 4 A.M. Dance clubs often stay open until well into the morning, but stop serving at the bar. Music venues may close after the last set or keep jumping with a DJ or jukebox until the last customer has gone home. Whichever nighttime activities are on the agenda, chances are you will be exhausted before your options are.

The distinctions among bars, lounges, clubs and music venues are blurry at best. Expect live music at bars and clubs, dancing at lounges and music venues, and DJs everywhere. Because so many establishments feature a variety of activities, it is always important to check local listings. *The New York Times* (Friday), *www.nytoday.com* (*The New York Times's* city guide on the Web), *Time Out New York*, the *Village Voice*, *New York* magazine, *The New Yorker* and the *New York Press* all run weekly listings.

BARS & LOUNGES BY NEIGHBORHOOD

Many tourists concentrate on dance clubs and other places with music (*discussed later in this section*) when planning their evenings in the city. But while New York's clubs are essential to the city's nightlife, it's often in the pubs and lounges, the neighborhood watering holes and swank hot spots, that New York after dark can really be appreciated. From the most elegant hotel bars to the deepest of dives, New York has something for everyone—often all on one block.

The difference between bars and lounges is subtle and usually lies in the attitude—and maybe a few couches. Lounges also often have DJs, but not the cabaret license required to host legal dancing. Throughout the Giuliani administration raids were frequently conducted, but these days the requisite signs reading, "No dancing by order of law," are often disregarded by patrons and displayed with a wink from the management.

The following listings cover only a small fraction of the more than 1,000 bars in Manhattan. A handful from each neighborhood were chosen for their historical significance, popularity, location or other particular points of interest. For more listings go to *www.nytoday.com*. Also remember that many restaurants and hotels have great bar scenes. If you can't find a bar to your liking listed here, check the **Restaurants** and **Hotels** sections. (*For Brooklyn bars see separate listings in chapter* **Exploring New York**.)

TriBeCa/SoHo

Anotheroom 249 West Broadway (between White and Beach Sts.)
(212) 226-1418. The owner of Anotheroom (who also owns **The Room** in
SoHo and **The Otheroom** in the West Village), has perfected a simple formula:
Find a small pleasant space and serve only beer and wine. It works. Anotheroom
is a tiny, oblong room, decorated in the kind of warm, minimal style that manages to be both cozy and classy at the same time. **Subway:** 1, 9 to Franklin St.

Bubble Lounge 228 West Broadway (between White and Franklin Sts.)
(212) 431-3433. With over 290 types of champagne and sparkling wine, expensive cigars, caviar and clams on the half shell, there's no shortage of opportunities to splurge here. With plush red couches, seductive lounge music and dim
lighting, this sophisticated bar is a great place to take a date if you're trying to
look classier than you really are. **Subway:** 1, 9 to Franklin St.

Ear Inn 326 Spring St. (between Greenwich and Washington Sts.)
(212) 226-9060. Built in the 1830's, this landmark Federal-style house once
stood on the river's edge and was a favorite spot for sailors. Although landfill
has pushed the shoreline a few blocks westward, the bar still sports remnants of
its nautical past. In this friendly neighborhood atmosphere, you're likely to find
men in pinstripe suits sharing the bar with tattooed bikers.
Subway: C, E to Spring St.; 1, 9 to Houston St.

El Teddy's 219 West Broadway (between Franklin and White Sts.)
(212) 941-7070. Finding decent Mexican food and drink in this city is harder
than finding a good apartment. It's no wonder, then, that El Teddy's is constantly packed to the gills, combining a schmaltzy 1980's wonderland décor with
solid cocktails and dining. Its TriBeCa location means the bar is packed with
after-work Wall Streeters slamming back drinks over some seriously tasty gua-
camole and chips. **Subway:** 1, 9 to Franklin St.

Fanelli 94 Prince St. (at Mercer St.) (212) 226-9412. Fanelli, an unfussy place
with tiled floors, tin ceilings and a lot of old New York atmosphere (it opened
in 1872), is nestled among SoHo's glitzier restaurants and stores. The bar draws
a mixed clientele and can be crowded on weekends, but during the week the
place caters to locals, and is always laid-back. Basic but tasty bar food is available, and there is a back room intended for those more interested in eating than
imbibing. The bartenders are friendly, and the old-fashioned mugs are perfect
for a frosty beer. **Subway:** F, S, V to Broadway–Lafayette St.; N, R to Prince St.

Grace 114 Franklin St. (between West Broadway and Church St.)
(212) 343-4200. Grace is attractive and warm, with a narrow front area dominated by the long, deep mahogany bar, behind which friendly bartenders pour
tasty drinks from an extensive collection of liquors. Bowls of plump olives keep
the crowd fed until they order from the menu of light entrees. Classical light
fixtures and mahogany walls complete the picture. **Subway:** 1, 9 to Franklin St.

Liquor Store 235 West Broadway (at White St.) (212) 226-7121. The laid-back locals who frequent this undersized corner bar blend congenially with the more upscale crowd that takes over on the weekend. Big windows and little attitude tempt you to kick back and watch the goings-on across the street at the Bubble Lounge. Summertime means a happy clutter of plastic chairs—many without tables—are scattered outside, just waiting for you to plop down and have a cool margarita. Cash only. **Subway:** 1, 9 to Franklin St.

Puffy's Tavern 81 Hudson St. (between Harrison and Jay Sts.) (212) 766-9159. On a sleepy TriBeCa corner, Puffy's offers a low-key, scene-free, classic neighborhood bar. And it may actually stay that way because it's the kind of exceptionally unexceptional place that most people won't go out of their way to get to. If they did, they'd find a beautiful, welcoming, old-fashioned place with dark wood, sultry fans and a darts alcove, frequented by locals, old-timers and folks from the nearby financial district. **Subway:** 1, 9 to Franklin St.

Sway Lounge 305 Spring St. (between Greenwich and Hudson Sts.) (212) 620-5220. The neon sign outside may read McGoverns Bar, but this is no Hibernian homestead. Sway has the look and feel of a gigantic VIP room. Hand-picked by an oh-so-hip gatekeeper, those lucky enough to be let into this Moroccan-style lounge drink expensive cocktails and move to the beat of a different drum 'n' bass DJ. **Subway:** C, E to Spring St.

Walkers Restaurant 16 North Moore St. (at Varick St.) (212) 941-0142. Walkers' enormous mahogany bar, high tin ceilings and good, uncomplicated cuisine recall old New York—right down to the red-and-white-checked tablecloths. There's plenty of history in the walls, or you can write your own in Crayolas on the white paper table covers. This is a down-to-earth holdout in a neighborhood where prices—and attitude—snake steadily heavenward. Cash only. **Subway:** 1, 9 to Franklin St.

Lower East Side/Chinatown/Little Italy

Angel 174 Orchard St. (between Houston and Stanton Sts.) (212) 780-0313. This Lower East Side lounge is long like a swimming pool with its walls painted a vibrant aquamarine and three bubble-like mirrors above the bar that conjure up portholes on a ship. Yet though there's an underwater feel to the place, the high ceilings make a visitor feel anything but claustrophobic. At the back there's a loft where the main attraction is the DJ. **Subway:** F, V to Second Ave.

Double Happiness 173 Mott St. (at Broome St.) (212) 941-1282. It's easy to miss this Chinatown lounge: Only the line outside gives it away. Once inside, you will be surrounded by the young and fashionable nestled comfortably into various softly lit nooks. Settle into your own corner and sip the bar's delectable martinis (including the house speciality, which adds a dash of green tea to the concoction). **Subway:** F, S, V to Broadway–Lafayette St.; N, R to Prince St.; 6 to Spring St.

Happy Ending 302 Broome St. (between Forsyth and Eldridge Sts.)
(212) 334-9676. The coy name alone is enough to entice a visit to this
nightspot in a former Chinese massage parlor. There is a bar area with wood
paneled walls, concrete floors and high-backed, crescent-shaped banquettes clad
in red velvet, surrounding tables that look as if they've been dunked in red glitter. Another funky feature is the ceiling that emulates a sunset, changing colors
over the course of several hours. Expect a crowd of uptown patrons mixed in
with some locals. **Subway:** F, V to Second Ave.

Kush 183 Orchard St. (between Houston and Stanton Sts.) (212) 677-7328.
Were it not for the small blackboard on the sidewalk out front, you might walk
right past this oasis. Inside, all things Moroccan adorn the whitewashed walls,
bathed in soft, warm lighting. On weekends, a DJ spins a variety of sensuous
music for a swank crowd. The marinated olives at the bar provide a welcome
change from the traditional pretzels. **Subway:** F, V to Second Ave.

M & R Bar 264 Elizabeth St. (between Houston and Prince Sts.)
(212) 226-0559. Any evening is a good one at M & R, where the curvy bar, tin
ceilings and brick wall beckon. The bar staff is never too stuffy to chat or too
busy to keep you filled up. Friday nights the DJ, set up in one corner of the bar,
spins Latin, jazz and funk. M & R's bar area fills up fast and, unless you're eating dinner, it can be tough to get a seat. **Subway:** F, S, V to Broadway–
Lafayette St.; N, R to Prince St.

Mare Chiaro 176 1/2 Mulberry St. (between Broome and Grand Sts.)
(212) 226-9345. At first glance, Mare Chiaro seems like the ultimate in Little
Italy authenticity: old Italian men smoking cigars, a jukebox that's about 85 percent Sinatra and photos of the owner alongside Ol' Blue Eyes himself. Look
more closely and you'll notice that the crowd is largely hipsters and slumming
Ivy Leaguers. It's this crazy mix that makes Mare Chiaro such a good time. Cash
only. **Subway:** N, R to Prince St.; 6 to Spring St.

Max Fish 178 Ludlow St. (between Houston and Stanton Sts.)
(212) 529-3959. One of the first venues to attract bar-goers to the burgeoning
Lower East Side scene, Max Fish still draws its fair share of hipsters. Brightly lit
and without downtown attitude, Max Fish is both hip and casual at the same
time. Never lacking in interesting artwork, this spot also offers plenty of other
attractions, including pinball, video games, a pool table and cheap beer. Cash
only. **Subway:** F, V to Second Ave.

Puck Fair 298 Lafayette St. (between Houston and Prince Sts.)
(212) 431-1200. This inviting bar is massive, yet full of enough nooks and cran-
nies that patrons can easily find an intimate corner. A popular after-work spot,
there are three levels, usually filled with young professionals. The exposed
beams and wooden booths on the main floor and balcony, and the dungeonlike
basement effectively conjure a medieval feel.
Subway: F, S, V to Broadway–Lafayette St.; 6 to Spring St.

Welcome to the Johnsons 123 Rivington St. (between Norfolk and Essex Sts.) (212) 420-9911. Welcome to the Johnsons is a nostalgic visit to some cool kid's 70's-style basement. Everything about this bar is designed to make you feel at home (that is, someone else's retro home). The orange-and-brown furniture is covered in plastic and the place is snazzed-up with macramé curtains, trophies and houseplants. Strong mixed drinks are whipped up behind the bar, and bottles are served from a vintage, avocado-green refrigerator. Cash only. **Subway:** F, V to Delancey St.; J, M, Z to Essex St.

East Village

(See also "Dive Bars in the East Village" *later in this section.)*

Beauty Bar 231 E. 14th St. (between Second and Third Aves.) (212) 539-1389. A beauty salon for decades, it's now a bar. From the people who brought you **Barmacy** (538 E. 14th St.)—a mom-and-pop pharmacy reinvented as a hipster watering hole—comes this popular spot. You can sit beneath antique hair dryers and swill Rolling Rocks, or go whole hog and get your nails done at the bar—just don't soak 'em in your Jack Daniel's. Is it mere coincidence that many of Beauty Bar's female clientele resemble 50's pinup icon Bettie Page? **Subway:** N, Q, R, W, 4, 5, 6 to 14th St.; L to Third Ave.

d.b.a. 41 First Ave. (between 2nd and 3rd Sts.) (212) 475-5097. A chalkboard over d.b.a's long bar lists 18 draught beers, nearly 150 bottled beers, some 70 single-malt whiskies and 30 tequilas. Filled with locals and die-hard regulars, everything served here is first-rate, and the staff is usually helpful in navigating you through the choices. The interior is simple and spacious, with marble-topped tables and church pews. In warmer weather, the garden out back is the perfect place to contemplate what next to imbibe on the gargantuan menu. **Subway:** F, V to Second Ave.

McSorley's Old Ale House 15 E. 7th St. (between Second and Third Aves.) (212) 473-9148. Anybody who has ever read a book by Joseph Mitchell owes himself a visit to this historic bar, though it's not as old as it pretends. Have a beer and forget the food. Cash only. **Subway:** 6 to Astor Pl.; F, V to Second Ave.

288 Bar (a.k.a. Tom and Jerry's) 288 Elizabeth St. (at Houston St.) (212) 260-5045. This friendly neighborhood bar offers a relaxed atmosphere and more space than can normally be found in an East Village venue. There are several large tables that allow groups to sit together, and a cavernous area in the back of the bar where you can actually talk to a group of people without the feeling that you're blocking traffic. 288 features average prices for drinks (including a decent Scotch selection) and a jukebox heavy on classic-rock tunes. Cash only. **Subway:** F, S, V to Broadway–Lafayette St.; 6 to Bleecker St.

Von 3 Bleecker St. (between Elizabeth St. and Bowery) (212) 473-3039. Von is a compromise between old (Bowery grunge) and new (SoHo chic). A yuppyish crowd saunters in for after-work wines and hors d'oeuvres before giving way to a

Dive Bars in the East Village

Neighborhood bars and local holes-in-the-wall are some of the best places to see the real New York. This is particularly true in the East Village, where dives are equivalent to town hall. Hipsters, artists and colorful residents retreat to shoot pool, chat over cheap drinks or melt into a bar stool. If you find a surly bartender, the smell of stale beer, and air thick with smoke and character appealing, an East Village dive crawl is highly recommended.

Ace Bar 531 E. 5th St. (between Aves. A and B) (212) 979-8476. Ace is perfect for people with limited attention spans—pool, darts, pinball and video games are all provided for your enjoyment, as well as a virtual museum of over 100 children's lunch boxes.

Blue and Gold Tavern 79 E. 7th St. (between First and Second Aves.) (212) 473-8918. This is a no-nonsense beer and whisky kind of a place, where many a cigarette has been smoked over a Bud in the ancient booths. On weekends the pool table can see some heated action.

Cherry Tavern 441 E. 6th St. (between First Ave. and Ave. A) (212) 777-1448. One of the hippest of the East Village dives, Cherry Tavern has seen a model or two in the crowd. Though there's a pool table and a good jukebox, the drink special—a shot of tequila and a can of Tecate beer for $4—may be Cherry's biggest attraction.

Coyote Ugly Saloon 153 First Ave. (between 9th and 10th Sts.) (212) 477-4431. It's ugly, all right, but there's something truthful—even pure—about this place, with its warped floorboards, lopsided bar stools, country jukebox and buxom bartender in her half-shirt and tight jeans.

Holiday Cocktail Lounge 75 St. Marks Pl. (between First and Second Aves.) (212) 777-9637. This classic East Village hangout is famous for its never-changing aesthetic; quilted faux-leather booths, a cigarette machine, a jukebox and video games are worn and sprinkled with a palpable seediness. Be prepared for the bar to close at the bartender's whim.

International Bar 120 First Ave. (between 7th St. and St. Marks Pl.) (212) 777-9244. Much like **Johnny's S&P** in the West Village, International is very local, very casual and very cheap. Though this tiny bar can get crowded on the weekends, it remains unaffected.

Joe's 20 E. 6th St. (between Aves. A and B) (212) 473-9093. The jury's still out on whether this hole-in-the-wall is a dive or a honky-tonk bar. On the dive side it's unpretentious and homey, and on the honky-tonk side, it's known for its mostly country jukebox. It attracts a neighborhood mix of old-timers and young locals.

Marz Bar 25 E. 1st St. (at Second Ave.). This punk-art bar has been around for well over a decade, and continues to revel in its downhill slide. We're talking hardcore—yet harmless. This unpretentious little dive is a breath of fresh air for those who don't associate spending money with being cool.

neighborhood clientele later at night. With its scuffed wooden bar and tattered leather couches, Von has the air of an upper-class saloon, and its lack of pretension and quiet location foster a desire to sit and stay for a while. The wine-and-beer-only drink menu is limited but well chosen.
Subway: F, S, V to Broadway–Lafayette St.; 6 to Bleecker St.

WCOU Radio (a.k.a. Tile Bar) 115 First Ave. (at Seventh St.) (212) 254-4317. The sister bar of the lively **WXOU** in the West Village and **Magician** in the Lower East Side, WCOU has a handsome tile floor, a nice old bar and a decent blues and rock jukebox. The bartenders are sociable, and the view of the action of First Avenue can be entertaining. You can usually find a place to sit on a weekend night, and if you bring your own crowd, you can pretty much set the mood for the whole bar. **Subway:** F, V to Second Ave.; L to First Ave.

Greenwich Village/West Village

Apt. 419 W 13th St. (near 10th Ave.) (212) 414-4245. New York's latest clandestine watering hole is worth finding. Pass through the anonymous door and discover the apex of lounges: a sleek, modern living room in shades of electric orange and chocolate brown. The tone is relaxed, the staff personable and the music at a decent volume. The crowd is diverse but upscale.
Subway: A, C, E to 14th St.

Art Bar 52 Eighth Ave. (between Jane and Horatio Sts.) (212) 727-0244. Certainly more bar than gallery, the Art Bar consists of two spaces: a front barroom with large, curvy booths and a cozy back room with a working fireplace. Candles provide intimate lighting and a jukebox plays rock music, but not so loudly as to drown out conversation. The womblike back room, with its antique couches and armchairs, is a particularly good spot for couples and small groups. **Subway:** A, C, E to 14th St.; L to Eighth Ave.; 1, 2, 3, 9 to 14th St.

Blind Tiger Ale House 518 Hudson St. (between Christopher and W. 10th Sts.) (212) 675-3848. It's dark and smoky here, but in a nice, welcoming, neighborhood kind of way. The floors and furniture match the darkly paneled walls. Classic-rock bands scream out of the speakers, and drinks are reasonably priced and generously proportioned. The pleasant and unassuming crowd, including the bartenders, is a great reflection of the West Village's diversity.
Subway: 1, 9 to Christopher St.

Chumley's 86 Bedford St. (between Bleecker St. and Seventh Ave. South) (212) 675-4449. The story of Chumley's heyday as a speakeasy is as worn as its old wood tables, but it seems to keep people coming to the place in droves. The pub's three rooms are rustic, with a fireplace, sawdust on the floors and walls hung with book jackets by famous authors who used to be regulars. F. Scott Fitzgerald allegedly wrote part of *The Great Gatsby* in a corner booth, Robert Kennedy wrote a speech here, and the place is said to be haunted by the ghost of the woman who owned it in the 30's. All lore aside though, today Chumley's resembles an upscale frat house for a clientele of young professionals swilling

pints of the impressively varied beers on tap. Cash only.
Subway: 1, 9 to Christopher St.; A, C, E, F, S, V to W. 4th St.

Corner Bistro 331 W. 4th St. (at Jane St.) (212) 242-9502. If a simple, straightforward place to drink a beer (or something stiffer) and chomp on a top-notch burger is what you're after, then the Corner Bistro is a godsend. The front room has a worn, wooden bar and worn, wooden tables all on top of a worn, wooden floor. In back is more worn seating, and if you arrive after 7 P.M. any night of the week, be prepared to wait for a table. Cash only.
Subway: A, C, E, 1, 2, 3, 9 to 14th St.; L to Eighth Ave.

White Horse Tavern 567 Hudson St. (at 11th St.) (212) 989-3956. Located in one of the few remaining wood-framed buildings in Manhattan, the White Horse Tavern opened in 1880. The tavern was a speakeasy during Prohibition, and poet Dylan Thomas was a regular in the late 1940's. Legend has it that, in 1953, Thomas drank 18 shots of whisky, stepped outside onto the sidewalk and dropped dead. (The truth is it was about seven whiskies, and what really killed him was a misdiagnosis of his diabetes.) Though once considered a "writer's bar," the three darkly paneled sections are now populated with more former frat boys than literary types. Cash only.
Subway: A, C, E, 1, 2, 3, 9 to 14th St.; L to Eighth Ave.

West 425 West St. (at W. 11th St.) (212) 242-4375. As the sun sets over the Hudson, the bar at West begins to fill. With unparalleled views of the river and the twinkling lights of Jersey beyond, this bar has become a destination for those who work and live in the neighborhood. The window-lined room is sur-rounded by low-slung leather banquettes, with walls composed of black slate stacked like Lincoln logs. The smoky room has a friendly, chatty vibe, sound-tracked with old soul tunes and alternative rock. **Subway:** A, C, E to 14th St.

Flatiron/Union Square

Old Town Bar and Restaurant 45 E. 18th St. (between Broadway and Park Ave. South) (212) 529-6732. There are no gas-lit lamps or horse-drawn car-riages on the streets outside this tavern. But inside, you feel as though you have entered a bygone era from New York's history. Built in 1892, Old Town is one of the city's oldest taverns. From the 14-foot pressed-tin ceiling to the mahogany bar and huge beveled mirrors, it's filled with details from another time. Even the booths tell a story: They were specially built during Prohibition with a hidden compartment for stowing liquor. **Subway:** L, N, Q, R, W, 4, 5, 6 to 14th St.

Park Bar 15 E. 15th St. (between Union Sq. West and Fifth Ave.)
(212) 367-9085. Park Bar is a small but pleasing space designed for the area's after-work crowd. From the pressed-tin ceiling and modernist light fixtures to the slightly-older-than-average drinking crowd, Park Bar is a relaxing place to spend an evening in an area that doesn't have many.
Subway: L, N, Q, R, W, 4, 5, 6 to 14th St.

Sing, Sing a Song: Karaoke in New York

Karaoke, once considered corny by the uninitiated, has had something of a surge in popularity of late. And for good reason. There's nothing quite like belting out your favorite tune in front of a crowd, cheering you on as if you were a superstar—no matter how offensive the performance.

New York has a few karaoke options. There are karaoke lounges (often run by Japanese, Chinese or Korean Americans, but usually welcoming to all) that have karaoke every night. There are also places that rent out private rooms by the hour—a blast with a group. And then there are regular bars that have weekly or monthly karaoke nights. For more venues, check *www.murphguide.com/karaoke.htm*. If you've never done karaoke, it's about time you tried. If you have, you're probably already convinced.

Arlene Grocery 95 Stanton St. (between Ludlow and Orchard Sts.) (212) 358-1633. Come for Punk Rock/Heavy Metal Karaoke Monday nights, 10 P.M. With a live band and an enthusiastic crowd, you'll feel like a rock star, or—if you'd rather just watch—a groupie. One Monday a month it's Corporate Rock (Journey, Foreigner and the like).

Asia Roma 40 Mulberry St. (between Worth and Bayard Sts.) (212) 385-1133. This basement karaoke lounge is good for intimate groups.

Japas 55 253 W. 55th St. (between Broadway and Eighth Ave.) (212) 765-1210. At this long skinny bar with an after-work crowd of both dilettantes and hardcore crooners, the bartenders bring you a mike where you're seated for $1 per song. Private rooms are available.

Toto Music Studio 38 W. 32nd St. (between Fifth and Sixth Aves.) (212) 594-6644. Private rooms only. A good spot for groups, the bigger rooms can literally hold dozens. Bring your own alcohol.

Village Karaoke 27 Cooper Square (212) 254-0066. Private rooms, a good song list and a bring-your-own-alcohol policy make this a great place to get rowdy.

Winnie's 104 Bayard St. (bet. Mulberry and Baxter Sts.) (212) 732-2384. A regular cast of folks from Chinatown shares the space with Lower East Side hipsters, rowdily handing off the microphone for both classics and Chinese pop tunes (most nights, a bartender will step out to belt a tune herself).

Pete's Tavern 129 E. 18th St. (at Irving Pl.) (212) 473-7676. "Oldest Original Bar in New York City Opened 1864," reads the sign behind the worn, ornate bar—a claim that's debatable. With its cracked tile floor, tin ceilings and hanging brass lamps, it has certainly retained that old New York flavor. O. Henry reportedly wrote "The Gift of the Magi" at one of the tavern's dark wooden booths. A casual crowd and friendly bartenders make this a nice place for a drink and snack. In warmer weather, the sidewalk tables are particularly pleasant. **Subway:** L, N, Q, R, W, 4, 5, 6 to 14th St.

Tiki Room 4 W. 22nd St. (at Fifth Ave.) (646) 230-1444. Is it possible to take the kitsch out of Tiki culture? That is the concept behind Tiki Room, a sleekly modern lounge with abstract sunsets made of backlighted Plexiglas and plasma television screens playing surf videos. Instead of servers in Don Ho attire, the waitresses wear midriff-baring Hawaiian-print halter tops. The traditional massive Tiki head is still there, but its forbidding features have been smoothed away, leaving an 18-foot-tall modernist sculpture with a V.I.P. seating area inside. **Subway:** F, N, R, V to 23rd St.

Meatpacking District/Chelsea

(For more Chelsea venues, see "Gay & Lesbian" and "Dance Clubs.")

Hogs 'n' Heifers 859 Washington St. (at 13th St.) (212) 929-0655. Tucked away in Manhattan's meatpacking district, Hogs 'n' Heifers offers a taste of Hazard County for anyone with a hankering for Budweiser and debauchery. Here brawny bikers and yuppies ogle female bartenders dancing on the bar. If nothing else, this place is a testament to the effectiveness of hard liquor and peer pressure in convincing women to abandon their inhibitions as well as their bras. Cash only. **Subway:** A, C, E, 1, 2, 3, 9 to 14th St.; L to Eighth Ave.

Lot 61 550 W. 21st St. (between 10th and 11th Aves.) (212) 243-6555. Lot 61 is housed in a vast, converted warehouse space, cleverly divided by sliding panels and bursting with furniture straight out of Elle Décor (don't miss the rubber sofas salvaged from insane asylums). In keeping with the area's burgeoning art scene, the walls are adorned by all the right painters' works (Hirst, Landers and Salle, to name a few). And if that weren't enough eye candy, there's always the drop-dead gorgeous staff. **Subway:** C, E to 23rd St.

Lotus 409 W. 14th St. (between Ninth and 10th Aves.) (212) 243-4420. With the no-dancing lounge scene feeling more and more tired, nightlife entrepreneurs are diversifying, creating ambitious hybrids. Lotus is a fine example, fusing a restaurant, lounge and nightclub into a single, three-level space—divided, of course, by a velvet rope or three. **Subway:** A, C, E to 14th St.

Passerby 436 W. 15th St. (between Ninth and 10th Aves.) (212) 206-6847. British gallery owner Gavin Brown has taken over the space next door to his gallery and converted it into a bar. No sign marks the space as a bar, and tinted windows obscure any activity. As a result, most of the patrons are either artists and gallery owners, or friends of Brown. Though not exactly diverse , anyone wishing to rub elbows with working artists could hardly ask for a better crowd. **Subway:** A, C, E to 14th St.

Triple Crown Ale House 330 Seventh Ave. (between 28th and 29th Sts.) (212) 736-1575. A perfect mix of Irish pub and American sports bar, the Triple Crown caters to a mostly young professional crowd during the week and post-event crowds from Madison Square Garden on the weekends. Spacious with elegant, dark-wood paneled walls, the bar goes on red alert for sporting events.

Eight TVs (one of them a very, very big-screen) broadcast the action for those who care. The full menu features excellent pub fare. **Subway:** 1, 9 to 28th St.

Midtown/Murray Hill

(See also box "A Grand Oasis: New York's Hotel Bars" *in this chapter.)*

Bliss 256 E. 49th St. (at Second Ave.) (212) 644-8750. You can't miss Bliss—just look for the garish, blue-lit sign, just the first of several features that make this two-story bar a distinctive alternative to nearby bars. The first floor features a clean, sleek, metallic bar. Wade through the thick traffic to find a stairway to the candle-lit second floor, which has a separate lounge in the back and large windows overlooking Second Avenue. **Subway:** 4, 5, 6, 7 to 42nd St.

Campbell Apartment Grand Central Terminal, 15 Vanderbilt Ave. (at 42nd St.) (212) 953-0409. Between cocktails at the Campbell Apartment patrons crane their necks to take in the 30-foot wood-beam ceilings. They admire the deep blue Moroccan-inspired rug, the overstuffed couches set against stone walls and the huge steel safe installed by John Campbell, the original inhabitant of the space. Tucked away in Grand Central, it's sure to become a classic. **Subway:** 4, 5, 6, 7 to 42nd St.

Divine Bar 244 E. 51st St. (between Second and Third Aves.) (212) 319-9463. File this one under "Great First-Date Spots." Divine Bar has everything you're looking for to avoid those awkward silences: loud music, good beer and a crowd interesting enough to talk about. It might be difficult to find a quiet little corner in which to chat, but the nook you'll find will be cozy, if not downright cramped. **Subway:** 4, 5, 6, 7 to 42nd St.

Ginger Man 11 E. 36th St. (between Fifth and Madison Aves.) (212) 532-3740. Combining old-world charm with new-world overkill, the Ginger Man has the feel of a British pub—just on a larger scale, with 100 bottled beers and 66 beers on tap from around the world. A 45-foot-long oak bar dominates the spacious high-ceilinged area in the front. In the back room the atmosphere is more intimate, with comfortable couches and chairs ideal for the end-of-day unwind. The menu contains all kinds of bar food with an upscale twist. **Subway:** 6 to 33rd St.

Jimmy's Corner 140 W. 44th St. (between Sixth Ave. and Broadway) (212) 944-7819. Tucked away among big Midtown hotels, is this New York gem. Covering almost every inch of wall space at this narrow spot are posters, photos and newspaper clippings about boxing. The space at front is so small that you can barely squeeze past the regulars holding court at the bar, but that's not a problem, because everyone is friendly. The crowd is happily diverse: There are scruffy slacker types and men and women in suits, construction workers and, of course, boxing enthusiasts, all glad to have found this slice of authenticity in touristy Midtown. **Subway:** B, D, F, N, Q, R, V, W, 1, 2, 3, 7, 9 to 42nd St.

Landmark Tavern 626 11th Ave. (at 46th St.) (212) 757-8595. When it first opened in 1868, the view from the Landmark's three-story brick building was

A Grand Oasis: New York's Hotel Bars

New York City is filled with unappreciated treasures. But in the world of food and drink, none are so neglected as hotel bars. Some are new additions, but many have been here for ages, planted like pillars around the city, elegantly decorated like miniatures of the grand hotels that engulf them. Perhaps that is why they tend to be overlooked by New Yorkers. But beyond the barrier of the hotel lobbies lie some of the city's most secluded oases, where you can relax over a well-mixed drink, be treated like a king or simply be as anonymous as the bars themselves.   —*Amanda Hesser*

(See chapter **Hotels** *for addresses and phone numbers; see also* "Cabarets and Supper Clubs" *later in this chapter for more listings.)*

Cafe Pierre—Hotel Pierre
The dark and often empty Cafe Pierre could be a French Embassy tearoom. There is piano music every evening at 8:30 P.M.

Cellar Bar—Bryant Park Hotel
This vast bar with vaulted ceilings and geometric furniture bathed in orange light is a place to see, be seen and lounge with the beautiful people.

Fifty-Seven Fifty-Seven—Four Seasons Hotel
At the top of a short set of polished stone stairs on the main floor of the Four Seasons, is in an icy space with 30-foot ceilings, enormous mirrors and hardwood floors. It attracts mainly executives with a yen for heavily made-up companions and pricey drinks.

44 Bar—Royalton Hotel
A sleek, austere corridor lobby filled with chic women. If you're really ambitious, try to snag a seat in the tiny Round Bar.

Grand Bar—SoHo Grand Hotel
The polyglot crowd at this striking, plush and expensive hotel bar creates an energetic buzz that makes you feel like you're at the center of things—much like New York itself.

Journeys Bar—Essex House Hotel
This tiny bar in the Essex House hotel has an opulent, old-money feel to it, though it has occupied the space only since 1989.

King Cole Bar—St. Regis Hotel
The very essence of swank, where even the chips are served in silver-plated dishes. The King Cole Bar also claims to have invented the Bloody Mary—though they call it the Red Snapper. Whatever you order, it's bound to be well made. The friendly bartenders know a thing or two about mixing drinks.

Mark's Bar—The Mark Hotel
The Mark Hotel is known for its relaxed elegance, a reputation that rightly

extends to its gemlike bar, which draws in European tourists and Upper East Side matrons-in-training.

Mercer Kitchen—Mercer Hotel

Cool lighting and clean lines make the bar at Mercer Kitchen feel like the set for a fashion shoot. Identification is probably not necessary, but something with a Prada tag may be.

Morgans Bar—Morgans

At the cavelike bar, calling ahead for a table is a good idea. The place can get quite crowded on weekends—or, during the summer, on Thursday, when the pre-Hamptons crowd congregates.

Oak Room and Bar—Plaza Hotel

A beer hall for men in suits. The Oak Room features live cabaret nightly.

Oasis Bar—W New York Hotel

The ambiance at the Oasis Bar at the W New York Hotel is California and casual. One day it is calm and Zen-like, the next it is filled with *Friends* cast look-alikes.

Serena—Chelsea Hotel

Though almost antithetical to the Chelsea Hotel spirit, this swank lounge that opened in 1999 quickly became a major hot spot. (Think very thin people lining up in very expensive dresses to push through Serena's heavy wrought-iron door to sip cosmopolitans under tin palm trees and lounge on plush couches).

Thom's Bar—Thompson Hotel

This bar offers a quiet little sanctuary for intimate conversation and a safe haven away from the majority of the "gotta-be-seen" SoHo bars. Minimalist in design with stark white walls, dim lighting and cozy chairs, this low-key locale is a perfect spot to catch up with friends after work or meet a date for a drink without the threat of loud music or boisterous conversation.

Villard's Bar & Lounge—New York Palace Hotel

Elegant rooms that had been offices in the Villard Houses have been restored to their rouged and gilded glory in the French Empire and Victorian styles and turned into the Villard Bar & Lounge. There are four lounges on two floors, some intimate and others grand with soaring ceilings. Fancy snacks (caviar, foie gras, oysters) are available.

Whiskey Bar—Paramount Hotel

Adjacent to the hyper-swanky Paramount (a hotel so exclusive it lacks a marquee), the Whiskey is smaller than one might expect, but just as dark and well appointed as the Paramount's lobby. The bar attracts an odd mix of business types, tourists and hipsters.

of bustling piers and a neighborhood full of longshoremen. Since then, the river's edge has moved westward, pushed back by landfill and 12th Avenue, and the docks have gone quiet. But unlike the streets around it, the Landmark Tavern has hardly changed. Not that it still serves nickel beers, but the enormous bar—turned from a single mahogany tree—and the potbellied stove in the rear dining room remain. **Subway:** A, C, E to 42nd St.

P.J. Carney's 906 Seventh Ave. (between 57th and 58th Sts.) (212) 581-4138. Just a few steps from Carnegie Hall in the heart of the 57th Street tourist mecca, P.J. Carney's is an old standby for locals. The crowd fills up on shepherd's pie and 20-ounce pints of Guinness and hard cider at the bar's handful of tightly packed tables, while a grinning bartender dressed in overalls, who knows every other customer by name, glides back and forth behind a wee horseshoe-shaped bar. **Subway:** N, R, Q, W to 57th St.; B, D, E to Seventh Ave.

Revolution 611 Ninth Ave. (between 43rd and 44th Sts.) (212) 489-8451. More restaurant than bar, this spot does a terrific job of providing an inviting place to have drinks with friends. Elegantly decorated, the front of Revolution has a small lounge area with antique sofas and chairs around a fireplace. A friendly after-work crowd and weekend patrons often fill Revolution to capacity. **Subway:** A, C, E to 42nd St.

Siberia 356 W. 40th St. (between Eighth and Ninth Aves.) (212) 333-4141. Gritty and down-to-earth, Siberia is a bar-lover's bar: no pretenses, no trendsetters—just cheap drinks and good music. A group of second-hand couches are clustered together on the first floor surrounded by an old Pacman console and a pinball machine. Be sure to venture down the narrow stairs to the basement where bands play. **Subway:** A, C, E to 42nd St.

Upper East Side

Auction House 300 E. 89th St. (between First and Second Aves.) (212) 427-4458. The main room in this opulent bar has a decorative fireplace, cut-glass chandeliers, couches, Oriental rugs and window seats on either side of the front door. Gilt-framed mirrors and a few oil paintings hang on the exposed brick walls. The Auction House's patrons are drawn from the neighborhood, but they tend to be older and better dressed (no baseball hats or sneakers are permitted) than at other bars in the area. **Subway:** 4, 5, 6 to 86th St.

Dorrian's Red Hand Restaurant 1616 Second Ave. (at 84th St.) (212) 772-6660. This bar may never live down its association with Robert Chambers, who met Jennifer Levin here in 1986 and then murdered her the same night in Central Park. Despite the bad publicity, Dorrian's has recovered from the heady days of the late 80's and remains a respectable neighborhood bar and restaurant with an eclectic menu and window seating at red-checkered tables. Ask the bartender about the gory legend of the "red hand." **Subway:** 4, 5, 6 to 86th St.

Elaine's 1703 Second Ave. (between 88th and 89th Sts.) (212) 534-8103. A meeting place for the older guard of New York's celebrity elite (think Joan Collins and Ivana Trump). A collage of literati memorabilia covers the walls, and *Entertainment Weekly* has been throwing its Oscar party here for years. In addition to the famous frequenters, watch for Elaine herself, who opened these doors almost 40 years ago and routinely table-hops to schmooze with her guests. But you won't received the royal treatment if they don't know you. **Subway:** 4, 5, 6 to 86th St.

Fitzpatrick's 1641 Second Ave. (at 85th St.) (212) 988-7141. This old Irish pub—founded in 1917—came under new ownership in 1996. Completely renovated and very clean (even the bathrooms!), the pub has retained its friendly neighborhood feel, absent in many bars nowadays. From 10:30 A.M. until early evening, the older gents sitting at the mahogany bar make up a family of sorts. In the evening, and especially on weekends, Fitzpatrick's comes alive, even turning people away. **Subway:** 4, 5, 6 to 86th St.

Madison Pub 1210 Madison Ave. (between 79th and 80th Sts.). This divey little former speakeasy, surrounded by some of the city's most expensive real estate, has been in business since 1920. It's probably not much different today than it was decades ago, a fact that lends the place quite a lot of charm. The walls of the dimly lit room are painted with the names of hundreds of customers from long ago; the kitchen serves cheap burgers and cold sandwiches, as well as more expensive fare like steaks and seafood. **Subway:** 6 to 77th St.

Subway Inn 143 E. 60th St. (at Lexington Ave.) (212) 223-8929. With a worn bar, cracked red-and-white tile floor and a row of dingy, high-backed booths, the surprise in this seediest of seedy bars is a strong showing of stylishly outfitted young people found mixing with workers from the nearby hotels and stores, and students from Hunter College. Yet there's no threat of the place being overrun by beautiful people: It's still a place where they serve dollar draft beers, though only during the day. Cash only.
Subway: N, R to Lexington Ave; 4, 5, 6 to 59th St.

Upper West Side

All State Cafe 250 W. 72nd St. (between Broadway and West End Ave.) (212) 874-1883. Inside this narrow, cozy, basement-level pub, there's a small bar up front, with a fabulous selection of tunes on the jukebox and a fire crackling in the hearth in winter. In the back, you'll find simple wooden tables where you can pull up a chair and enjoy the neighborhood's best burger. Cash only. **Subway:** 1, 2, 3, 9 to 72nd St.

Dive 75 101 W. 75th St. (at Columbus Ave.) (212) 362-7518. Tucked away on a side street, Dive 75 merges the friendliness of a neighborhood bar with the atmosphere of a living room. A large blue aquarium separates the bar area from a small collection of tables; wooden bookshelves house a selection of board games. It's a nice alternative to the West Side's concentration of raucous frat bars. **Subway:** 1, 2, 3, 9 to 72nd St.

Evelyn Lounge 380 Columbus Ave. (at 78th St.) (212) 724-2363. This subterranean lounge is a swanky spot lined with velvet banquettes. It's a big pick-up scene on weekends, when a cool crowd of young professionals gathers here for cocktails from the extensive martini menu. There's occasional live jazz or blues; if not, the soundtrack tends toward electronica. **Subway:** 1, 9 to 79th St.

Hi-Life Bar and Grill 477 Amsterdam Ave. (at 83rd St.) (212) 787-7199. With its stylish retro furnishings, the Hi-Life was quite the trendy scene when it opened back in the late 80's. It has survived all these years by losing the attitude and evolving into a casual neighborhood hangout, offering sidewalk seating in summer and a decent, affordable lunch and dinner menu year-round. **Subway:** 1, 9 to 79th St.

79th Street Boat Basin Cafe In Riverside Park at the Hudson River (212) 496-5542. The food and drinks are merely passable, but that's beside the point. When it's a breezy summer evening and there's a colorful sunset behind the houseboats bobbing in the river, there's no finer place on the West Side to down a beer. Bring the kids or even Fido—everyone's welcome. **Subway:** 1, 9 to 79th St.

West Side Brewing Company 340 Amsterdam Ave. (at 76th St.) (212) 721-2161. A nice selection of beers, surprisingly good food (make sure to order sweet-potato fries along with your sandwich), and an array of TVs tuned to the big game—what more do you need for a relaxing jeans-and-sneakers night out? **Subway:** 1, 9 to 79th St.

GAY & LESBIAN

The following listings are a selection of bars that cater to the gay and lesbian communities of New York. Also, many of the city's premier dance and cabaret venues are predominately gay or gay-friendly; several have gay or lesbian parties at least one night per week. (*See* "Dance Clubs" *and* "Cabarets and Supper Clubs" *later in this chapter.*) Check *Homo Xtra (HX)*, *Next magazine*, *HX for Her*, or *Time Out New York* for weekly events at a variety of bars, lounges and clubs.

Men

Barracuda CHELSEA 275 W. 22nd St. (between Seventh and Eighth Aves.) (212) 645-8613. This popular gay bar is often described as an oasis of East Village-style nightlife in the heart of tan-and-taut Chelsea. Barracuda's décor is decidedly low-key, effecting an Alphabet City aesthetic of kitschy squalor. But don't be fooled. Despite the assumed atmosphere, aging disco-bunny muscle-queens in tank tops and skin-tight Diesel gear still abound. Cash only. **Subway:** C, E, 1, 9 to 23rd St.

Blu CHELSEA 161 W. 23rd St. (between Sixth and Seventh Aves.) (212) 633-6113. Blu is a large, comfortable spot promoting itself as a "cy-bar" for the gay Chelsea nightlife scene. With four free customer-ready computers

connected to Web-TV, Blu makes it possible for drinkers to cruise for Web sites as well as other patrons. Blu attracts a mostly down-to-earth assortment of gay men who avoid the pretensions found at nearby gay bars.
Subway: F, V, 1, 9 to 23rd St.

Chase MIDTOWN WEST 255 W. 55th St. (between Eighth Ave. and Broadway) (212) 333-3400. This attractive bar, located on the northern border of Hell's Kitchen, is a comfortable spot for locals and out-of-towners. While the actual bar can accommodate only six or seven people, there's room up front for a modest crowd, and a cozy lounge in the back. The atmosphere is best described as serene, with a tasteful array of flowers and candles, and a subdued level of background music. **Subway:** A, B, C, D, 1, 9 to 59th St.

Cleo's Ninth Ave. Saloon MIDTOWN WEST 656 Ninth Ave. (between 45th and 46th Sts.) (212) 307-1503. About the only dead giveaway to the gay and lesbian nature of this friendly, laid-back bar is the large rainbow flag that hangs on the back wall. Otherwise, distinguishing Cleo's from any other local dive would take a discerning eye. The beer is cheap (Budweiser is served in a can), the jukebox has a good selection and they serve popcorn in a basket. Cash and checks only. **Subway:** A, C, E to 42nd St.

Excelsior BROOKLYN 390 Fifth Ave. (between 6th and 7th Sts.) (718) 832-1599. This warm, inviting bar with a great garden area attracts a mellow local crowd. There's plenty of action, but it's done Brooklyn-style, without all the show. Though Excelsior is definitely for the boys, the crowd can be mixed. **Subway:** F, N, R to Fourth Ave.

G Lounge CHELSEA 223 W. 19th St. (between Seventh and Eighth Aves.) (212) 929-1085. Smart-dressed Chelsea guys line up to get into this den of chic, with a juice bar in the back and a bar in the middle of the main room to encourage smooth cruising. G also features some of the best DJs in the city. A hot spot from the day it opened. Cash only. **Subway:** C, E, 1, 9 to 23rd St.

Hell WEST VILLAGE 59 Gansevoort St. (between Washington and Greenwich Sts.) (212) 727-1666. A nice, dimly lit lounge up the street from the popular late-night diner Florent, Hell attracts a mostly gay clientele (and a classy, not overtly cruisey one at that). It's a swell place to have a cosmopolitan as long as there's a DJ spinning. Otherwise it's those same old Erasure and Everything But the Girl songs on the jukebox—always something there to remind you of an ex-boyfriend or two. **Subway:** A, C, E to 14th St.; L to Eighth Ave.

The Monster WEST VILLAGE 80 Grove St. (between W. 4th St. and Waverly Pl.) (212) 924-3557. Located on Sheridan Square (with a view of Stonewall), the Monster is one of New York's oldest gay establishments. On the main floor, there's a huge, attractive wooden bar with plenty of seating for everyone. Moving farther in, you'll hear various patrons by the piano belting out a favorite show tune (or 10). Venture downstairs and there's another large bar and a fairly spacious dance floor. Cash only. **Subway:** 1, 9 to Christopher St.

Go East, Young Man

The West Village and Chelsea have always reigned as the major centers of gay nightlife in Manhattan. While these neighborhoods still boast some of the most well-known and popular spots, the East Village is giving the West Side a run for its money. The area has become home to a slew of smaller, more casual bars for men with a downtown style and attitude. If you prefer a younger, hipper crowd, this neighborhood is probably just the scene for you. (Note: Many of these bars take cash only, so hit the ATM before you go.)

Subway: L to First Ave; F to Second Ave.

Boiler Room 86 E. 4th St. (at Second Ave.) (212) 254-7536

The Cock 188 Ave. A (at 12th St.) (212) 777-6254

Wonderbar 505 E. 6th St. (between Aves. A and B) (212) 777-9105

Dick's Bar 192 Second Ave. (at 12th St.) (212) 475-2071

Phoenix 447 E. 13th St. (at Ave. A) 212-477-9979

SBNY FLATIRON/UNION SQUARE 50 W. 17th St. (between Fifth and Sixth Aves.) (212) 691-0073. SBNY is a friendly, wholesome bar—except for the go-go boys, the cruisey atmosphere and the almost exclusively male crowd. SBNY, formerly Splash, keeps its customers coming back with cozy seating around the downstairs bar and a dance floor with music that ranges from disco classics to 90's dance favorites. **Subway:** F, L, N, Q, R, V, W, 4, 5, 6 to 14th St.

Stonewall WEST VILLAGE 53 Christopher St. (between Sixth and Seventh Aves.) (212) 463-0950. Get out your gay history books: Stonewall is the little hole in the wall where the famous riots started. (The brief version: The police raided the bar, a drag queen threw a bottle, purses flew and, over the course of a couple of days in the summer of 1969, the gay rights movement was born.) These days, the bar is a quieter, more open, less tumultuous neighborhood hangout. Cash only. **Subway:** 1, 9 to Christopher St.

Townhouse MIDTOWN EAST 206 E. 58th St. (between Second and Third Aves.) (212) 826-6241. A "gentleman's club" in the truest sense of the term, this classy gay bar has the old boys' atmosphere down pat. A dress code ensures that the clientele maintains the proper image at all times. Dark wood, tapestry carpeting and paintings of hunting scenes provide the perfect backdrop for the civilized meeting and greeting that goes on here. The crowd consists of older, well-polished men in suits lounging on couches or leaning suavely against walls. **Subway:** 4, 5, 6 to 59th St.; N, R, W to Lexington Ave.

View Bar CHELSEA 232 Eighth Ave. (at 22nd St.) (212) 929-2243. Living up to its name, this attractive addition to the Chelsea bar scene has a flirty gay clientele and much to recommend: friendly service, cheap drink options and comfortable spaces in which to sit or stand. In case you weren't sure this was a gay-friendly bar when you entered, flat-screen TVs on the wall display sexually explicit video art. Perhaps the best thing the View Bar has to offer, is the superb skyline view in the back room. **Subway:** C, E, 1, 9 to 23rd St.

The Works UPPER WEST SIDE 428 Columbus Ave. (between 80th and 81st Sts.) (212) 799-7365. An ad for The Works proclaims: "89% have jobs, 73% own their own apartments, the odds are in your favor. Find your new husband here." A hint, ladies: This ad isn't aimed at you. This bar is a neighborhood fixture, and—as the ad might indicate—attracts guppies of all ages. The crowd is friendly, and the bartender swears that the chocolate martinis are delicious. Cash only. **Subway:** B, C to 81st St.

XL CHELSEA 357 W. 16th St. (between Eighth and Ninth Aves.) (212) 995-1400. One of the newer hot spots, XL features cabaret on Monday nights and a great happy hour throughout the week. Lauded for its décor and fabulous lighting, it's a welcome addition to the Chelsea scene. **Subway:** A, C, E to 14th St.; L to Eighth Ave.

Women

Cubby Hole WEST VILLAGE. 281 W. 12th St. (at W. 4th St.) (212) 243-9041. A lack of pretension characterizes this narrow room, which lives up to its matchbook's claim of being "the friendly neighborhood bar." Although it caters predominantly to casually dressed, local lesbians in their 30's and 40's, this West Village bar welcomes all. A miscellaneous collection of genders, races, ages and styles makes up the usual crowd. Cash only. **Subway:** 1, 2, 3, 9 to 14th St.

Ginger's BROOKLYN 363 Fifth Ave. (between 5th and 6th Sts.). The owners of the **Rising Café** (listed below) have expanded their domain on Park Slope's Fifth Avenue with this casual neighborhood bar. A dimly lit space with a vaguely nautical theme, Ginger's provides just the right pub-like elements: tables for two, a long wooden bar that runs the length of the front room, a pool table, darts in the back and a greenly glowing jukebox replete with an eclectic selection. The clientele is representative of the neighborhood: racially mixed, straight and gay. **Subway:** F, N, R to Fourth Ave.

Henrietta Hudson WEST VILLAGE 438 Hudson St. (between Morton and Barrow Sts.) (212) 924-3347. A younger, less high-powered crowd than at Rubyfruit. Some nights are packed, others are dead, but the service is always pleasant and friendly. The crowd ranges from locals to bridge-and-tunnel girls, seductively (they think) grinding their hips to Madonna. **Subway:** 1, 9 to Christopher St.

Meow Mix LOWER EAST SIDE 269 E. Houston St. (between Aves. A and B) (212) 254-0688. The epicenter of the lesbian queercore scene, Meow Mix has been featured in several films including *All Over Me* and *Chasing Amy*. It's a tiny place with a rec-room-type basement where young lesbians can go and shoot pool, flirt and drop quarters in the Ms. Pac Man machine. There's a small stage upstairs where local bands perform and the bar's restrooms feature the most exciting graffiti in town. Although primarily lesbian there's almost always a handful of men in attendance, with no hostility toward them. Cash only. **Subway:** F, V to Second Ave.

Rising Café BROOKLYN 186 Fifth Ave. (at Sackett St.) (718) 622-5072. Though the clientele is mainly lesbian, all are welcome at this neighborhood cafe, which serves good coffee, beer and light food. Wood floors and art on the walls give the Rising Café an air of casual elegance. This former storefront can get quite crowded during live folk, jazz and poetry performances. **Subway:** R to Union St.

Rubyfruit Bar and Grill WEST VILLAGE 531 Hudson St. (between W. 10th and Charles Sts.) (212) 929-3343. A mature, friendly lesbian crowd gathers here to relax at the bar or on one of the richly upholstered settees. The tables are made of such artifacts as old-fashioned sewing machines, with pedals that still work. For added privacy, there is a step-up seating area at the back of the bar area, partially enclosed by lush draperies. **Subway:** 1, 9 to Christopher St.

DANCE CLUBS

More than any other nightlife activity in New York, dancing requires some research. Most of the city's dance clubs host several different parties each week. There is usually a cover charge that differs with each event and an occasional dress code. In addition, thanks to periodic raids and the economic downturn, there's always a chance that a venue will be closed. It is in any club-goer's best interest to call first and check local listings (*see* **Nightlife** *introduction for resources*). Note: Clubs usually do not accept credit cards for the cover charge.

Also very popular are roving parties that change location at will, and organizations that sponsor various events. **Organic Grooves** (212-439-1147) and **Giant Step** (*www.giantstep.net*) are among the best. In warmer months, outdoor events at venues like the **Frying Pan** at Chelsea Piers and **P.S. 1** in Queens are not to be missed. And don't ignore the outer boroughs. These days some of the best parties occur in out-of-the-way spots like **Frank's Lounge** and **The Anchorage** in Brooklyn. Events can be found by picking up a *Time Out New York* or a *Flyer* magazine.

Baktun WEST VILLAGE 418 W. 14th St. (between Ninth Ave. and Washington St.) (212) 206-1590. Take a trip way west and check out the grooves at Baktun, an up-and-coming club with a chill attitude. Though the club's art-house scene is sometimes a bit heavy-handed (let's be honest: who really enjoys listening to the recorded sounds of metal grinding and children screaming?), on a good day the club can't be beat. **Subway:** A, C, E to 14th St.

Centro-Fly FLATIRON/UNION SQUARE 51 W. 21st St. (between Fifth and Sixth Aves.) (212) 627-7770. The motif at work at Centro-Fly is futurism, which from a decorative standpoint apparently means Op Art spirals, plentiful Plexiglas and a door staff dressed in orange jumpsuits. The club, which boasts a state-of-the-art DJ booth, has been a hot spot since opening in 1999, drawing big crowds of electronic music aficionados and just plain dancing fools. **Subway:** F, V to 23rd St.

Cheetah FLATIRON/UNION SQUARE 12 W. 21st St. (between Fifth and Sixth Aves.) (212) 206-7770. The former Sound Factory space has changed clientele entirely; the gay crowd stays away, while the champagne-swilling European set flocks here on weekends. The venue's tacky décor leaves a lot to be desired, but Cheetah's a good space as far as midsized clubs go. There is also a mellower downstairs lounge. **Subway:** F, N, R, V, 1, 9 to 23rd St.

Club New York MIDTOWN WEST 252 W. 43rd St. (between Broadway and Eighth Ave.) (212) 997-9510. If you're looking for a comfortably mainstream crowd in a comfortably mainstream setting, you could hardly do better than Club New York. The Times Square club (yes, the one where the Puff Daddy scandal went down) targets the hotel and international tourist crowd. Most of the club's DJs spin a dance-friendly mix of accessible house and hip-hop. Be prepared to part with $20 at the door for men, $10 for women, and obscene sums at the bar. **Subway:** A, C, E, N, Q, R, W, 1, 2, 3, 7, 9 to 42nd St.

Don Hill's SOHO 511 Greenwich St. (at Spring St.) (212) 219-2850. This small bar on the fringes of SoHo plays host to several popular nights featuring drag queens and dominatrixes, though Squeezebox, the club's most well known party, has left the building. As popular as ever, though somewhat straighter than it once was, Don Hill's is a safe bet if you like 70's and 80's kitsch and the crowd that goes along with it. **Subway:** 1, 9 to Canal St.; C, E to Spring St.

Exit MIDTOWN WEST 610 W. 56th St. (between 11th and 12th Aves.) (212) 582-8282. Formerly Carbon (and, before that, Mirage), Exit is one of New York's largest, least subtle clubs. With four floors and room for 5,000 partiers, Exit tries to offer everything for everyone—often at the same time. **Subway:** A, B, C, D, 1, 9 to 59th St.

Filter 14 432 W. 14th St. (at Washington St.) (212) 366-5680. If you aren't choosy about wall coverings and light fixtures, and are attracted by rumors of bartenders lighting their nipples on fire, this might just be your favorite new destination. The dance floor is worked-in wood, perfect for shimmying the night away; there is a small stage for the exhibitionists in you; and there's even a cool spirograph laser-light display that's fun to stare at. Nonsmokers beware, though—ventilation, if it exists at all, is next to nil. **Subway:** A, C, E to 14th St.

Fun CHINATOWN 130 Madison St. (at Pike St.) (212) 964-0303. Nestled right under the Manhattan Bridge, Fun is one of the city's latest (and possibly greatest) super-lounge. The club's fringe location mirrors its operating philosophy, namely, unrepentant keeping a distance from the cooler-than-thou attitude that accompanies many an A-list clubbing address. Not that Fun is lacking in pretensions—$10 martinis, a VIP room and a black-clad clientele meet that demand—but the place does have a certain frivolous, fun-house appeal. **Subway:** F, V to E. Broadway.

La Nueva Escuelita MIDTOWN WEST 301 W. 39th St. (at Eighth Ave.) (212) 631-0588. Transsexuals, drag queens, gay men and the women who love them, and a progressive straight crowd mix it up on the dance floor. It's one of the cheaper dance venues in town—patrons pay $5–$15 on most nights and when you add the free condoms you can score in the back, it's clearly worth the price. Cash only. **Subway:** A, C, E, N, Q, R, W, 1, 2, 3, 7, 9 to 42nd St.

Nell's WEST VILLAGE 246 W. 14th St. (between Seventh and Eighth Aves.) (212) 675-1567. The old mainstay from the 80's is still kicking along, but you won't see any of the big names that made the scene—they've all had children and moved to Westchester. Nell's is mostly hip-hop these days. **Subway:** A, C, E, 1, 9 to 14th St.; L to Eighth Ave.

NV TRIBECA/SOHO 304 Hudson St. (between Spring and Vandam Sts.) (212) 929-6868. This hot spot on the western bounds of SoHo is a lounge palace. Heavy scarlet curtains cloak the main parlor and a brown-marble and copper bar curves along the length of the mezzanine. NV puts on its club face every night at 10 P.M., when the $20 cover charge kicks in and DJs meld dance tracks with hip-hop and R&B. A favorite among New York's professional athletes, NV has also seen Mariah Carey do some impromptu time in the DJ booth. **Subway:** 1, 9 to Houston St.; C, E to Spring St.

Ohm FLATIRON/UNION SQUARE 16 W. 22nd St. (at Sixth Ave.) (212) 229-2000. An ultra-swank dance and supper club that features an eclectic array of expensive food, a lounge area and a dance floor upstairs. A second lounge and DJ-driven dance area are downstairs. Ohm is currently undergoing renovation and is scheduled to reopen in Fall 2002. **Subway:** F, V to 23rd St.

Roxy CHELSEA 515 W. 18th St. (between 10th and 11th Aves.) (212) 645-5156. A cavernous Chelsea club that takes its weekend parties deep into the night (and early morning). The club draws a mixed crowd and music ranging from house to trance, depending on the night. Saturdays are mostly gay and on Wednesdays the place turns into a roller disco as it was originally. Cash only. **Subway:** A, C, E to 14th St.

Sapphire Lounge LOWER EAST SIDE 249 Eldridge St. (between Houston and Stanton Sts.) (212) 777-5153. On weekends, the $5 cover, velvet rope, hulking bouncers, pounding dance music and young, rowdy crowd spilling onto the grubby street outside the Sapphire Lounge suggest a large, exclusive club. In truth, Sapphire is a small, overstuffed bar, decorated in cheap, haphazard lounge style. DJs spin a range of house, funk and jazz, making Sapphire a good place for some weeknight dancing. Cash only. **Subway:** F, V to Second Ave.

Shine TRIBECA 285 West Broadway (at Canal St.) (212) 941-0900. Banquettes and booths line most of the room, creating a rather antisocial setup, and the long, well-stocked bar in the back is really too far away from the stage. Still, Shine attracts both decent musical acts (Cheryl Crow and Mono have performed here) and nightlife events, like those put on by the popular Giant Step on Thursday nights. **Subway:** A, C, E to Canal St.

Sound Factory MIDTOWN WEST 618 W. 46th St. (between 11th and 12th Aves.) (212) 489-0001. Closed for a short time by federal prosecutors, the Sound Factory re-emerged, bloodied but unbowed. It's still a hopping late-night weekend destination that keeps the deep house pumpin' until well beyond dawn. Not quite as enthralling as the original Sound Factory, its latest incarnation nevertheless boasts an impressive sound system in addition to one of the more workable dance floors in town. Cash only. **Subway:** A, C, E to 42nd St.

Spa EAST VILLAGE 76 E. 13th St. (between Broadway and Fourth Ave.) (212) 388-1062. Holistic pretensions aside, Spa is all about commotion. Visitors pack its bars three deep, and the lines to the bathrooms (decorated like saunas, get it?) snake out their doors. The club also traffics in such notions as a two-bottle minimum (at $250 a bottle) for all who wish to occupy its white leather booths. Spa also has a back room, a quieter, classier space where the minimum-bottle business is less strict and the music is devoted to rhythm and blues, trance and pop. **Subway:** L, N, Q, R, W, 4, 5, 6 to 14th St.

13 EAST VILLAGE 35 E. 13th St. (between University Pl. and Broadway) (212) 979-6677. This cozy second-story boîte below Union Square hosts a number of weekly parties, most notably Sunday night's long-running Shout!, a glamorous but young gathering of immaculately turned-out mods, skins, soulies and ska babies, all frugging away to an eclectic 60's soundtrack. It's an Anglophile's dream. Cheap drinks, comfy seating and a small dance floor help to make 13 an off-the-beaten-path downtown gem. **Subway:** L, N, Q, R, W, 4, 5, 6 to 14th St.

Twirl CHELSEA 208 W. 23rd St. (between Seventh and Eighth Aves.) (212) 691-7685. Of all the mid-size clubs to set up shop in Chelsea, Twirl may be the most high-concept. In addition to the usual squad of bouncers, visitors are greeted by an endless array of candles and a wall of televisions—a throwback to 80's-era excess. The 80's nostalgia continues throughout the club. The crowd, predictably, is young, European and energetic. DJs spin dance-friendly house and hip-hop on the main floor. In the mellow basement lounge, expect Depeche Mode and canoodling couples. **Subway:** C, E, 1, 9 to 23rd St.

Webster Hall EAST VILLAGE 125 E. 11th St. (between Third and Fourth Aves.) (212) 353-1600. A cavernous, multilevel East Village club. On weekends you can't get near the place, which may be just as well; 11th Street is closed to all through traffic. Thursday is Girls Night Out, with free admission for the ladies. Various DJs spin various sounds in various rooms.
Subway: L, N, R, 4, 5, 6 to 14th St.

POPULAR MUSIC VENUES
Rock, Folk & Country

Acme Underground EAST VILLAGE 9 Great Jones St. (between Lafayette St. and Broadway) (212) 677-6963. Located beneath Acme Bar and Grill, Acme Underground presents live rock and eclectic music most nights. (Weekend shows tend to be strictly 21 and over, while weekday age limits fluctuate.) There's room for a standing crowd of 225 and performers often mingle with the crowd as they walk to the stage, giving the place an intimate atmosphere. **Subway:** F, S, V to Broadway–Lafayette St.; 6 to Bleecker St.

Arlene Grocery LOWER EAST SIDE 95 Stanton St. (between Ludlow and Orchard Sts.) (212) 358-1633. With its stellar sound system, relaxed atmosphere, willingness to book unknown acts and free admission, Arlene Grocery (housed in an old bodega) has quickly become an integral part of Lower East Side bar circuit. Emerging stars such as Beth Orton and Ron Sexsmith, as well as older performers like Marianne Faithful, have used the 150-person-capacity club for intimate engagements. The club has the feel of a musicians' hangout, much like CBGB in its 1970's heyday. Cash only. **Subway:** F, V to Second Ave.

Baggot Inn GREENWICH VILLAGE 82 W. 3rd St. (between Thompson and Sullivan Sts.) (212) 477-0622. Formerly the Sun Mountain Cafe, the Baggot Inn continues the folk music tradition of long-gone 1960's coffeehouses on Bleecker Street. Occasionally, performers go electric among the flock of aspiring singer-songwriters. For the most part, however, the stage at the back of the club offers acoustic sounds, or poetry, comedy, open-mike nights and DJ events. **Subway:** A, C, E, F, V to W. 4th St.

Bitter End GREENWICH VILLAGE 147 Bleecker St. (between Thompson St. and La Guardia Place) (212) 673-7030. Bob Dylan, Joan Baez, Harry Chapin, Paul Simon and Patti Smith have graced this rickety wooden stage on their way to larger fame, and the promotional posters that line the walls give a sense of the venue's history. Opened in 1961 as an ice cream shop, the Bitter End has maintained its informal feel and continues to present aspiring folk and rock acts for a mix of curious tourists, N.Y.U. students and each band's contingent of fans. Cash only. **Subway:** A, C, E, F, V to W. 4th St.

The Bottom Line GREENWICH VILLAGE 15 W. 4th St. (at Mercer St.) (212) 228-7880. Since 1974, the Bottom Line has presented singer-songwriters—a young Bruce Springsteen, an older Elvis Costello, among others—in its spacious room. Patrons sit cabaret-style at tables, and though the seating is a bit cramped, it is more pleasant than standing, especially when the main musical fare is meant more for listening than dancing. The crowd varies according to the performer, but audiences tend to be slightly older than those at typical New York concerts. One of the best things about the Bottom Line is its willing-

ness to book rarely heard country and bluegrass performers. Cash only.
Subway: F, S, V to Broadway–Lafayette St.; N, R to 8th St.

CBGB LOWER EAST SIDE 315 Bowery (at Bleecker St.) (212) 982-4052. The
famed CBGB's is still an ideal place to try out unknown rock bands and catch
the occasional bigger name playing an intimate show. Since its heyday (the
Ramones, the Talking Heads and Blondie are some of the bands that got their
start here), CB's has lost some of its hold on the rock scene, but only because
other similar venues have arisen. Patrons are allowed to enter and leave the
club at will, giving CB's a neighborhood-hangout feel. Cash only.
Subway: 6 to Bleecker St.; F, S, V to Broadway–Lafayette St.

CB's 313 Gallery EAST VILLAGE 313 Bowery (at Bleecker St.) (212) 677-0455.
By presenting mellow, acoustic-based sounds and monthly art exhibits in a cafe
setting, CB's Gallery offers an entirely different experience from its legendary
progenitor, CBGB. Here you'll find tables and candles instead of a mosh pit,
spoken word and poetry instead of guitar distortion and sonic shriek. Like the
original CBGB, however, the gallery makes an effort to present new and
unknown talent. **Subway:** 6 to Bleecker St.; F, S, V to Broadway–Lafayette St.

Continental EAST VILLAGE 25 Third Ave. (between St. Marks Pl. and 9th St.)
(212) 529-6924. With a dive-bar feel, four to five aspiring rock bands nightly
and a blaring sound system, the sublimely sleazy Continental is the tongue-
pierced stud at the mouth of St. Marks Place. Formerly known as the Continental Divide, the bar has launched many a career—from jam-band success Blues
Traveler to garage-rock renovators the Pristeens. Punk legends such as Iggy Pop,
Patti Smith and the late, great Joey Ramone have been known to perform
unannounced sets. Cash only. **Subway:** 6 to Astor Pl.

Fez Under Time Cafe EAST VILLAGE 380 Lafayette St. (at Great Jones St.)
(212) 533-2680. Two floors below the trendy Time Cafe, Fez presents indie-
rockers, weekly jazz band "workshops," comedy acts and cabaret shows—all in a
swank clubhouse atmosphere. It's equal parts Moroccan hashish den (hence the
name), jazz club and gangster hideaway. Patrons, generally a bit older than your
average rock club crowd, sit at tables or in the plush leather booths that line the
back wall of the room, which accommodates about 150. **Subway:** 6 to Bleecker
St.; F, S, V to Broadway–Lafayette St.

Lakeside Lounge EAST VILLAGE 162 Ave. B (between 10th and 11th Sts.)
(212) 529-8463. Enter the Lakeside Lounge and you could be in a shack on the
edge of a pond deep in the country—it's trout fishing in Alphabet City. At first
glance, East Village hipsters appear to dominate the front-room bar, but all are
welcome. Excellent rockabilly, country and "cowpunk" bands appear most
nights. Cash only. **Subway:** L to First Ave.

The Living Room LOWER EAST SIDE 84 Stanton St. (at Allen St.)
(212) 533-7235. With its affordable but scrumptious vegetarian-leaning menu
and its intimate folk music, the Living Room lives up to its name. The décor is

Rock Alternatives: A Music Scene Migrates to Brooklyn

It's not quite the end of the city's rock world as we know it, but Manhattan's downtown music scene is shrinking again, even as Brooklyn's expands. The latest downtown casualty is Brownies, that East Village temple of alternative rock wedged into a dive of a bar. Many other downtown clubs have closed in recent years, including Wetlands, Tramps, the Cooler, Coney Island High, Nightingales and No Moore, for reasons including skyrocketing rents and low profit margins. For local musicians, the closings mean fewer places to showcase their sound, just as the city is experiencing a rock renaissance not heard since the late 1970's.

But in the last year, a musical beachhead has established itself in Williamsburg and other Brooklyn neighborhoods. New clubs like Northsix (which opened in 2001 in a former steel mill), Club Luxx, Warsaw and South Paw are starting to supplant those in Manhattan as rock hothouses.

Few musicians are complaining. What Manhattan offered in sweat-soaked stages and indiscriminate crowds, Brooklyn has replied with loft-size arenas, devoted fans and, notably, dressing-room showers. Moreover, musicians say, the young club owners are less jaded, more respectful of their craft and more generous with backstage beers.

With venerable clubs like CBGB, Bowery Ballroom, Mercury Lounge and the Knitting Factory still kicking, Lower Manhattan remains a center for indie music. But rather than mimic that scene, Brooklyn clubs are creating their own.

Luxx 256 Grand St., Williamsburg (718) 599-1000

Northsix 66 N. 6th St.,Williamsburg (718) 599-5103

Pete's Candy Store 709 Lorimer St., Williamsburg (718) 302-3770

South Paw 125 Fifth Ave., Park Slope (718) 230-0236

Warsaw 261 Driggs Ave., Williamsburg (718)387-5252

makeshift, and there are games for playing with friends or for breaking the ice. Rows of tables take up most of the floor space leading up to the stage. Fans of singer-songwriter folk music will enjoy the relaxed atmosphere, the sincere performances, and the casual, parlor-room feel. **Subway:** F, V to Second Ave.

Luna Lounge LOWER EAST SIDE 171 Ludlow St. (between Houston and Stanton Sts.) (212) 260-2323. Luna Lounge is half bar hangout, half free-music venue. Décor is minimal, but the wood bar adds a touch of elegance. The back room is an intimate space where alternative pop acts play for free each night. At the infamous Monday night comedy sessions, local pros try out their more edgy material. After the bands, a good jukebox makes Luna Lounge a quality last stop on the Ludlow Street bar circuit. Cash only. **Subway:** F, V to Second Ave.

Mercury Lounge LOWER EAST SIDE 217 E. Houston St. (between Essex and Ludlow Sts.) (212) 260-4700. The Mercury Lounge attracts a varied crowd that comes to listen to everything from singer-songwriters and alterna-rockers to the latest experimental electronic music practitioners. Since the back room holds only 200 people, buying tickets at the bar ahead of time is recommended when bigger names are on the bill. Inside the performance space, there are a few highly coveted tables, but most patrons stand. Be sure to bring ID; most shows are strictly 21 and over. **Subway:** F, V to Second Ave.

Paddy Reilly's Music Bar MURRAY HILL 519 Second Ave. (at 29th St.) (212) 686-1210. Over the last few years, this bar has become a prime spot for all things Irish. The Irish expatriate community gathers here to catch up on gossip and news and to drink and dance, but all are welcome. The décor of the long bar, the small stage and the adjoining billiard room strike a balance between dive-bar sublimity and aged-wood elegance. Of particular interest are the "sessi-uns," traditional Irish jam sessions where participants sit in a circle and play Celtic songs on guitar, hand drum and sometimes the uilleann pipes. Cash only. **Subway:** 6 to 28th St.

Rodeo Bar MURRAY HILL 375 Third Ave. (at 27th St.) (212) 683-6500. When it opened in 1987, the Rodeo Bar was one of the first places in New York to feature roots-rock made for and by local performers. Since then, it has expanded its booking policy to include touring roots-rockers as well. Long wooden railings and peanut shells on the floor add to the honky-tonk atmosphere. There is no music cover, making the Rodeo Bar a prime spot for savoring the flavor of long-time New York bar bands. **Subway:** 6 to 28th St.

Roseland Ballroom 239 W. 52nd St. (between Broadway and Eighth Ave.) (212) 247-0200 *www.roselandballroom.com*. Arena-like rock shows are the name of the game at this old converted ballroom. Opened by Louis Brecker in 1951, the Ballroom moved to its current location on 52nd Street, once occupied by the Gay Blades ice-skating rink, in 1956. Inside, the gigantic dance floor (it can hold 3,200 people) fills up for intimate rock concerts by big-name acts like No Doubt, Garbage and Oasis. Arrive early, since the line to get in, complete with friskers and multiple ticket checks, can wrap around the block. Occasional swing and salsa nights usually require formal or semi-formal attire. **Subway:** C, 1, 9 to 50th St.

Jazz, Blues & Experimental

Birdland MIDTOWN WEST 315 W. 44th St. (between Eighth and Ninth Aves.) (212) 581-3080. Birdland features some of the most thoughtfully booked jazz in the city. The club pays direct homage to its namesake, the legendary original Birdland at Broadway and 52nd Street. (The only thing missing are the caged parakeets that used to slowly asphyxiate on cigarette smoke during bebop's heyday in the 1940's and 50's.) Though it's a fully functional restaurant with a Southern-tinged menu, Birdland's main attraction is music. Reservations are recommended for the music sets ($20–$35 and a $10 food or drink minimum). **Subway:** A, C, E to 42nd St.

Blue Note GREENWICH VILLAGE 131 W. 3rd St. (between Sixth Ave. and Mac-dougal St.) (212) 475-8592. Performances by jazz heavyweights such as Tony Bennett, Oscar Peterson and Chick Corea, and exhilarating double bills are the main attractions at the Blue Note. A night at the Blue Note can easily cost you $100. Because the club's seating sometimes makes rush-hour subway trains seem cozy, reservations and early arrival are essential. Record labels use Monday nights, when it's considerably less expensive, to break in new acts—a real bargain when established musicians join in. **Subway:** A, C, E, F, S, V to W. 4th St.

Iridium Jazz Club MIDTOWN WEST 1650 Broadway (at 51st St.) (212) 582-2121. Since it opened in 1993, this tony club has become one of the top jazz venues in the city. Success has led to a recent move and a series of "Live at the Iridium" recordings on various labels. In addition to presenting legendary guitarist Les Paul every Monday night, Iridium features both established and up-and-coming jazz stars. **Subway:** 1, 9 to 66th St.

Izzy Bar EAST VILLAGE 166 First Ave. (between 10th and 11th Sts.) (212) 228-0444. Upstairs there's a bar with fashionable club music on the speakers and fashionable young Manhattanites on the comfy chairs. The bottom floor, unexpectedly, has a music space for fairly experimental jazz and dance music; center stage seats are almost right in the bandleader's face. Bookings are a mixed lot and the cover charge is usually $10 or less. **Subway:** L to First Ave.

Knitting Factory TRIBECA 74 Leonard St. (between Broadway and Church St.) (212) 219-3055. With four spaces for live music, the Knitting Factory is host to not only the avant-garde jazz that first earned this place its reputation, but also rock, spoken word, theater, film and even children's shows. So much is going on in the Knitting Factory on any given night that there's often a bottleneck at the front door. The Main Space holds 350 patrons and can get quite crowded. The Alterknit Theater presents lesser-known acts as well as spoken word, theater and films in a space that holds 90. Free performances occur in the downstairs Tap Room, which has over 15 microbrews on tap. And the newest space, the Old Office, presents up-and-coming jazz artists in a more traditional jazz-club setting. **Subway:** 1, 9 to Franklin St.; A, C, E to Canal St.

Lenox Lounge HARLEM 288 Lenox Ave. (between 124th and 125th Sts.) (212) 427-0253. This Harlem Art-Deco bar is rich with musical history, including a corner banquette where Billie Holiday liked to claim a regular table. Bandleaders are mostly drawn from New York jazz's middle-aged netherworld: Musicians like Chico Freeman and James Spaulding—too old to be lions, too young to be legends. And the management doesn't rustle you out between sets; you can settle in for the evening. That's the type of peace of mind you can't buy downtown. **Subway:** 2, 3 to 125th St.

Roulette TRIBECA 222 West Broadway (between Franklin and North Moore Sts.) (212) 219-8242. Above boisterous young professionals drinking champagne in the Bubble Lounge, serious avant-garde music takes place in Roulette. This nonprofit performance space has a mix of elegant informality and concentrated audacity, with musicians trying all sorts of new, experimental ideas. Avant-garde saxophonist John Zorn performed some of his first "game piece" compositions at Roulette, and everyone from Oliver Lake, the esteemed jazz composer, to Thurston Moore, guitarist for Sonic Youth, has appeared as part of Roulette's concert programs. Cash only. **Subway:** 1, 9 to Franklin St.

Smoke UPPER WEST SIDE 2751 Broadway (between 105th and 106th Sts.) (212) 864-6662. Smoke (formerly known as Augie's Pub) captures the spirit of legendary jazz jam joints like Minton's—where bebop was born in the 1940's. Up-and-coming jazz musicians blow and wail in the small, cozy storefront room. It can get quite packed, but the atmosphere is friendly and the music is almost always exciting. Jazz aficionados such as the authors Stanley Crouch and Albert Murray regularly show up, crowding in alongside Columbia University students. Cash only. **Subway:** 1, 9 to 103rd St.

St. Nick's Pub HARLEM 773 St. Nicholas Blvd. (at 149th St.) (212) 283-9728. A legendary Harlem jazz bar, St. Nick's still serves up live jazz six nights a week, Wednesday to Monday. Saxophonist Patience Higgins and the Sugar Hill Jazz Quartet lead a popular jam session every Monday, with musicians playing well past 1 A.M. When the band takes a booze break, the jukebox cranks up, blaring both classic jazz and R&B, as well as contemporary hip-hop. Even on a Monday, seats are difficult to come by in this tiny shoebox of a bar. Cash only. **Subway:** A, B, C, D to 145th St.

Terra Blues GREENWICH VILLAGE 149 Bleecker St. (between Thompson St. and La Guardia Pl.) (212) 777-7776. In the heart of the Village, a flight above Bleecker Street, Terra Blues is home to both local and national blues acts. Though it's named after an obscure, rural Mississippi blues genre, Terra Blues is a modern-day urban saloon with surreal sculpture and blowzy curtains framing the small stage. Musicians like playing the club and the same performers are likely to return throughout the month. **Subway:** A, C, E, F, V to W. 4th St.

Tonic LOWER EAST SIDE 107 Norfolk St. (between Delancey and Rivington Sts.) (212) 358-7503. Downtown nightlife goes synergistic in the former kosher wine market. Tonic, which opened in early 1998, used to be a hair salon, but is now a night spot with experimental jazz, comedy nights, spoken word and occasional movie screenings. Cash only. **Subway:** F to Delancey St.; J, M, Z to Essex St.

Village Vanguard WEST VILLAGE 178 Seventh Ave. South (between W. 11th St. and Waverly Pl.) (212) 255-4037. Known for its intimacy, pristine acoustics and lack of pretense, the Village Vanguard is the one of the world's finest jazz venues. Since 1935, this basement hideaway has hosted a staggering lineup— from Barbra Streisand and Woody Allen to John Coltrane and Thelonious Monk. Over 100 albums bear the imprimatur "Recorded Live at the Village Vanguard." In 1965, the Mel Lewis-Thad Jones Orchestra began a Monday night big band tradition that endures under the moniker Vanguard Jazz Orchestra. Reservations are recommended. Cash only. **Subway:** 1, 2, 3, 9 to 14th St.

World & Latin

Bistro Latino MIDTOWN WEST 1711 Broadway (at 54th St.) (212) 956-1000.
Most of the friendly, all-aged Latino crowd at the upscale Bistro Latino come for
dinner and stay for salsa on Fridays and Saturdays, featuring free dance lessons.
You can also pay a small cover to skip dinner and go straight for the music and
dancing and sip one of the Bistro's delicious, fruity cocktails made with man-
goes, passion fruit and South American specialty liquors such as Chilean Mus-
cat brandy or Brazilian sugar cane rum. **Subway:** A, B, C, D, 1, 9 to 59th St.

El Flamingo CHELSEA 547 W. 21st St. (between 10th and 11th Aves.)
(212) 243-2121. A snazzy venue that plays up the Art Deco supper-club theme
to the hilt. The main room has a good-sized dance floor that splits in half when
the club hosts live music performances; the non-rhythmically inclined can
watch from above. Various promoters use El Flamingo for shows, so keep an eye
out for upcoming gigs. **Subway:** C, E to 23rd St.

S.O.B.'s TRIBECA/SOHO 204 Varick St. (at Houston St.) (212) 243-4940. The
audience sways more than the palm fronds on the faux-tree, making S.O.B.'s
one of the city's best clubs for Latin, Caribbean and Afropop music. Decorated
in a Copacabana-hut style, but with disco lights, S.O.B.'s is a dancer's heaven.
The club even offers salsa and tango lessons before most weekend shows. In the
best New York manner, ethnic groups mix at S.O.B.'s to produce a culture
greater than that of any individual subgroup. Purchase advance tickets for popular shows. **Subway:** 1, 9 to Houston St.; C, E to Spring St.

Zinc Bar GREENWICH VILLAGE 90 W. Houston St. (between Thompson St. and
La Guardia Pl.) (212) 477-8337. The Zinc Bar is a downtown venue that manages to be sophisticated yet retain an informal atmosphere. Opened in 1993, the
Zinc presents some of the best up-and-coming jazz and world sounds—especially
Brazilian music—in the city. The Zinc Bar can get quite crowded, so arrive early
if you want to sit. Be on the lookout for two kinds of cats at the Zinc Bar:
famous jazz musicians kicking back after a gig and the two felines who fearlessly
roam through the crowd. **Subway:** F, S, V to Broadway–Lafayette St.

CABARET

One of the singular attractions of New York City is its busy cabaret scene. The
term "cabaret" applies to high-end supper clubs featuring singers who perform
popular standards from the pre-rock era on. Cabaret flourishes in New York
because of its proximity to Broadway. Theater stars often moonlight as cabaret
performers, and a nightclub act can also be a stepping-stone to Broadway.
Cabaret also intersects with the world of jazz, although these two worlds are quite
distinct.

   An evening of top-flight cabaret with an entertainment charge and a food
and drink minimum can cost quite a bit more than a Broadway show. But the
kind of magical intimacy that the best cabaret can offer is something that can

only be experienced in a nightclub where the lights are low and the champagne is flowing.

The city's leading cabarets are the chic **Café Carlyle**, the **Oak Room** at the **Algonquin Hotel** and **Feinstein's at the Regency** (named after the popular singer and pianist Michael Feinstein, who helps book the club and sometimes performs there). Make reservations well in advance, and note that the top clubs sometimes close in summer.

Café Carlyle In the Carlyle hotel, 35 E. 76th St. (at Madison Ave.) (212) 570-7189. The Café Carlyle, the Rolls-Royce of the city's cabarets (with cover charges to match), tends to book the same performers every year for extended engagements. Ruling the roost in the late spring and late fall is the singer and pianist Bobby Short, who has appeared there every year for more than three decades. Now in his 70's, Mr. Short is an effervescent musical bon vivant with exquisite taste in songs, who brings the urbane music of Cole Porter, Cy Coleman and others thrillingly to life in performances that have the feel of nightly parties. **Subway:** 6 to 77th St.

Feinstein's at the Regency In the Regency Hotel, 540 Park Ave. (at 61st St.) (212) 339-4095 *www.feinsteinsattheregency.com.* Pricey and elegant, situated in the hotel's "power breakfast" room, Feinstein's at the Regency books big-name talent that has run the gamut from comedy (the Smothers Brothers) to Las Vegas legends (Keely Smith). Performers who appear there regularly and have solid followings include jazz pianist John Pizzarelli and Michael Feinstein himself. The atmosphere might be described as "romantic library." **Subway:** N, R, W to Lexington Ave.; 4, 5, 6 to 59th St.

Firebird Café 365 W. 46th St. (between Eight and Ninth Aves.) (212) 586-0244. The cafe, an adjunct of the Firebird Restaurant (which serves Russian haute cuisine), has a high turnover of mid-level cabaret and jazz performers (some of them very promising) who are not yet well enough known to have extended engagements. Subway: A, C, E to 42nd St.

Oak Room In the Algonquin hotel, 59 W. 44th St. (between Fifth and Sixth Aves.) (212) 840-6800. The Oak Room of the Algonquin (the site of the famous literary Round Table in the 1920's and 30's) is the regular home of singer and actress Andrea Marcovicci, a diehard romantic, who appears in the late fall resurrecting the Golden Age of American popular song. **Subway:** B, D, F, S, V to 42nd St.

—by Stephen Holden

Other Cabarets and Supper Clubs
(See also "A Grand Oasis: New York's Hotel Bars," earlier in this chapter.)

Bemelmans Bar In the Carlyle Hotel, 35 E. 76th St. (at Madison Ave.) (212) 744-1600. Named after illustrator Ludwig Bemelmans, who created the beloved Madeline children's books after painting the charming murals here, Bemelmans is a sumptuous spot for a classic cocktail. For a $15 cover, you can hear jazz and cabaret, often from celebrity performers. (Tony Bennett has been known to drop in for a song or two.) Sink into a private, romantic booth or reserve a small table for two right by the piano. **Subway:** 6 to 77th St.

Danny's Skylight Room 346 W. 46th St. (between Eighth and Ninth Aves.) (212) 265-8133. This rather unadorned, crowded room in the back of Danny's Grand Sea Palace (a good Thai place on Restaurant Row) hosts some of the city's finest cabaret performers, from fresh upstarts, to great old-timers such as Blossom Dearie. As you enter Danny's, there's also a narrow piano bar, a cramped but festive spot decked out with strings of Christmas lights, where you can sing along with the theater types who've made the stools around the piano their second home. **Subway:** A, C, E to 42nd St.

Don't Tell Mama 343 W. 46th St. (between Eighth and Ninth Aves.) (212) 757-0788 *www.donttellmama.com.* This enterprising Theater District perennial is really three venues in one: two cabaret rooms and a piano bar under the same management. On weekdays, there are up to four shows a night, and on weekends, up to eight—and that's in addition to the virtually nonstop show in the bar, which features singing waiters after 9 P.M. Cover charges and minimums vary, but the piano bar has no cover. **Subway:** A, C, E to 42nd St.

The Duplex 61 Christopher St. (at Seventh Ave. South) (212) 255-5438. This casual Village bar and cabaret ought to be called Camp Duplex, given the nature of the largely gay crowd and many of the shows. It's the oldest continuously running cabaret in the city. With three levels—a festive piano bar on the first, a lounge/game room on the second and, tucked away off to the side between the two, a small cabaret/theater—the Duplex is always hopping. The cabaret has a tiny proscenium stage (an unusual feature for a cabaret) with rows of crowded cocktail tables providing the seating. Besides the standard show tunes, there's comedy, improv, theater and drag. Cash only.
Subway: 1, 9 to Christopher St.

Joe's Pub 425 Lafayette St. (between Astor Pl. and 4th St.) (212) 539-8777 www.joespub.com. A portrait of the legendary producer Joseph Papp watches over the plush banquettes, red votives and zinc balustrades at this lovely supper club and cabaret. Joe's is a friendly watering hole, serving an American menu and offering an eclectic lineup of entertainment, from top-quality jazz performers to solo shows from Broadway stars like Audra MacDonald. DJs take over after 11 P.M. on many nights. **Subway:** 6 to Astor Pl.; N, R to 8th St.

Judy's Chelsea 169 Eighth Ave.(between 18th and 19th Sts.) (212) 929-5410 www.judyschelsea.com. Judy Kreston, a singer, and her husband, David Lahm, a pianist, run this Chelsea cabaret and restaurant that hosts cabaret performances most evenings. The piano bar, which features singing waiters, stays open till 4 A.M. Cash only. **Subway:** A, C, E to 14th St.

Rose's Turn 55 Grove St. (between Bleecker St. and Seventh Ave. South) (212) 366-5438. One of the friendliest cabaret and piano bars in the West Vil-

lage, Rose's Turn attracts a mixed crowd—gay, straight, locals and tourists who hear the music and laughter and wander in off the street. Upstairs there are singers, comedy acts and musical revues (usually for a cover charge and a two-drink minimum). Downstairs you can just hang out at the bar or sit by the piano. The in-house talent varies from night to night, but expect a piano player who takes requests (anything except Barry Manilow's "Mandy") and surprisingly talented singing waiters and bartenders. It's a casual, rollicking place.
Subway: 1, 9 to Christopher St.

Torch 137 Ludlow St. (between Rivington and Stanton Sts.) (212) 228-5151. Its elegance is a little out of place in the grungy Lower East Side. The atmosphere at Torch is a throwback to lounges of the 1940's or 50's, with a long narrow bar area at the front, semicircular booths at the back and cabaret seating in front of a small stage. Expect fabulous torch singers, all glammed up, filling the air with newfangled renditions of jazz classics or Latin sounds.
Subway: F, V to Second Ave.

Triad Theater 158 W. 72nd St. (between Columbus Ave. and Broadway) (212) 362-2590. The tiny Triad Theater is usually home to a show with an open-ended run, and after 10 P.M. becomes a cabaret space. What it lacks in atmosphere it makes up in sightlines and proximity to the performers. Downstairs, in the Dark Star Lounge, an average of four performers a night keep customers satisfied. Food is served in both rooms, and downstairs, in addition to the comfortable tables near the stage, there's a friendly bar that attracts neighborhood regulars. **Subway:** 1, 2, 3, 9 to 72nd St.

COMEDY CLUBS

(Many music venues and cabarets have comedy nights, such as **Luna Lounge**, **Fez Under Time Cafe** *and* **Rose's Turn**. *Check local listings for schedules.)*

Boston Comedy Club GREENWICH VILLAGE 82 W. 3rd St. (between Sullivan and Thompson Sts.) (212) 477-1000. This lesser-known basement club features comedy nightly, often with several acts on the bill. Monday is open-mike.
Price: $8–$12 cover, two-drink minimum. **Subway:** A, C, E, F, V to W. 4th St.

Caroline's MIDTOWN WEST 1626 Broadway (at 49th St.) (212) 757-4100. Just when you were afraid fun had been banished from Times Square, Caroline's comes to the rescue. In 15 years, Caroline Hirsch's club has gone from a comedy fledgling to a block-long complex where many TV stars perform, often testing new material. Ask about the dinner-and-show packages. **Price:** $15–$35 cover, two-drink minimum. **Subway:** N, R, W to 49th St.; C, E, 1, 9 to 50th St.

Comedy Cellar WEST VILLAGE 117 Macdougal St. (between 3rd and Bleecker Sts.) (212) 254-3480. In the more than 20 years that it has been open, Robin Williams, Stephen Wright and Jerry Seinfeld have made surprise appearances at this intimate Greenwich Village club. **Price:** $10–$15 cover, two-drink minimum. **Subway:** A, C, E, F, V to W. 4th St.

Comic Strip Live UPPER EAST SIDE 1568 Second Ave. (between 81st and 82nd Sts.) (212) 861-9386. You'll find 24 years' worth of autographed photos on the wall of alums such as Eddie Murphy (one of the club's discoveries), Paul Reiser and Chris Rock. New comics are so eager to perform in the no-cover Monday Talent Spotlite that twice a year they line the streets to get a lottery number. Drinks are top-dollar, but usually so are the headliners. **Price:** $12–$15 cover, two-drink minimum. **Subway:** 4, 5, 6 to 86th St.

Dangerfield's Comedy Club MIDTOWN EAST 1118 First Ave. (between 61st and 62nd Sts.) (212) 593-1650. Rodney Dangerfield's 30-year-old club feels like it's in a 1960's time warp with its swingin' red velvet and wood paneling. There's no drink minimum (a rarity in New York), affordable parking and a large menu. The featured acts are pros from the circuit, and Rodney himself performs when in town. **Price:** $12.50–$20 cover. **Subway:** N, R, W to Lexington Ave.; 4, 5, 6 to 59th St.

Gotham Comedy Club FLATIRON/UNION SQUARE 34 W. 22nd St. (between Fifth and Sixth Aves.) (212) 367-9000. With its comfortably upscale atmosphere this Flatiron oasis beckons audiences tired of divey or over-crowded clubs. Top-notch comics who regularly emcee jokingly complain that the bathrooms here are nicer than their apartments. The room is only a few years old, but stars and TV comics perform, and there are frequent new talent nights. **Price:** $10–$15 cover, two-drink minimum. **Subway:** F, N, R, V, 1, 9 to 23rd St.

New York Comedy Club FLATIRON/UNION SQUARE 241 E. 24th St. (between Second and Third Aves.) (212) 696-5233. It's a small, divey joint that many comedians have played at least once. Despite its size, the club does pull in pros, and on a regular night, expect truly funny performances from younger comedians. **Price:** $7–$10 cover, two-drink minimum. **Subway:** 6 to 23rd St.

Stand-Up New York UPPER WEST SIDE 236 W. 78th St. (between Broadway and Amsterdam Ave.) (212) 595-0850. What do Denis Leary, Jon Stewart and Comedy Central's Dr. Katz have in common? They all started at this 10-year-old club. While short on atmosphere, it's full of comedy history. There have been surprise visits from stars like Drew Carey, Robin Williams, Dennis Miller and Al Franken. **Price:** $7–$12 cover, two-drink minimum. **Subway:** 1, 9 to 79th St.

Upright Citizens Brigade Theater CHELSEA 161 W. 22nd St. (between Sixth and Seventh Aves.) (212) 366-9176. The Upright Citizens Brigade, which had a series on Comedy Central, has its own 74-seat theater in Chelsea, where you can find some of the most talented performers around. They supplement their comedic arsenal with equally talented guests, like David Cross of Mr. *Show* and Janeane Garofalo. The Sunday 9:30 show is free. **Price:** $5–$7 cover. **Subway:** F, V, 1, 9 to 23rd St.

Whether you're looking to burn some extra calories or park yourself in the bleachers, hot dog in hand, you'll find that New York is a great sports town.

For those who want to be part of the action, there are plenty of places to play throughout the city. The Parks Department alone encompasses hundreds of playgrounds, playing fields and tennis courts; dozens of swimming pools and recreation centers; plus golf courses, ice rinks, stadiums and zoos. (The department's Web site, *www.nycparks.com*, is extremely useful, with information on facilities and activities throughout the year.)

SPORTS & ACTIVITIES
Basketball

Pick-up, playground basketball is one of New York's great traditions. NBA stars like Stephon Marbury have honed their game on the city's blacktop courts, as have legends of more local renown, such as Earl "The Goat" Manigault and Joe "The Destroyer" Hammond.

If it's sunny, you'll find pick-up games at many city parks and playgrounds. Some of the best full-court games include **Riverside Park** (courts can be found at 76th, 96th and 110th Sts.), **Central Park** (just north of the Great Lawn), **Asphalt Green** (York Ave. between 91st and 92nd Sts.), the **96th Street Playground** (96th St. between First Ave. and the FDR Dr.), and the courts at **37th Street and Second Avenue.** Just show up and ask "Who's got winners?"

The **West 4th Street courts** (at Sixth Ave.) have been seen in more basketball-related commercials than Michael Jordan. It's always a mob scene, making it all but impossible to just walk on. Nevertheless, these courts host frequent tournaments that feature some of the city's best street talent. You may get lucky and spot a former NBA star posting up hapless opponents.

In the winter or at night, it's tougher to find a pick-up game. Your best bet is **Basketball City,** which offers six hardwood courts at 24th Street and West Street (West Side Highway) and allows walk-ons (212-924-4040; *www.basketballcity.com*). It's open Mon.–Fri. 9 A.M.–3 P.M., with a changing schedule on weekends; call to check availability and rates before going. There's also the **Field House at Chelsea Piers** (*see box* "Chelsea Piers" *later in this chapter*).

Three of the city's **YMCAs** (*www.ymcanyc.org*) offer basketball, but call ahead for the schedule at each facility before showing up, as games are only scheduled on occasional nights, varying from location to location. Day passes range from $10 to $20. There's the **West Side YMCA** (5 W. 63rd St. off Central Park West; 212-787-1301), which has one of the nicest full-length floors;

the **Vanderbilt YMCA,** which has a smaller court (47th St. between Second and Third Aves.; 212-756-9600); and the **Harlem YMCA** (180 W. 135th St.; 212-281-4100).

Biking

Intrepid New Yorkers bike in city traffic all the time, but you have to be alert and daring to try. If you're visiting, and you're not used to maniacal local drivers, play it safe and stick to biking in the parks.

The **Central Park Drive loop** is 6 miles; this road is closed to cars 10 A.M.–4 P.M., and then again 7 P.M.–dusk. Even when vehicular traffic is permitted, there is a multi-use lane for runners, bikers and in-line skaters.

There's also a beautiful **paved multi-use path** that now extends along the entire west side of Manhattan along the Hudson River, from the George Washington Bridge right down to Battery Park City.

Organizations and Tours

Bike New York 891 Amsterdam Ave. (at 103rd St.) (212) 932-2300 *www.bikenewyork.org.* Bike New York is a 42-mile, five-borough tour of New York City that takes place each year in early May. The ride begins at Battery Park and then winds its way through the Bronx, Queens and Brooklyn before it ends at Fort Wadsworth in Staten Island. There are plenty of rest stops, and the route is entirely traffic-free. Register well in advance.

The Fast and Fabulous Cycling Club *www.fastnfab.org.* Fast and Fab is a lesbian and gay bike club that sponsors regular rides. Check the calendar on the amusing Web site, and call the ride leader if you'd like to join in.

Five Borough Bicycle Club (212) 932-2300 *www.5bbc.org.* For more than a decade, this friendly bike club has been organizing free day rides in the city, and excursions farther afield—cruising to nearby beaches, the Hudson River Valley, and the Berkshires. Yearly membership fees are $15, and there's a charge for longer trips.

Time's Up! (212) 802-8222 *www.times-up.org.* Activist in spirit, Time's Up! sponsors a number of free bicycle and in-line skate tours that challenge the traffic-centered nature of New York City. The monthly "Critical Mass" ride is an attempt to defy the dominance of motor vehicles and assert equal rights to the road. On the other hand, many of the club-sponsored rides have no political aim at all: they're simply fun and even educational. Check the Web site for a calendar of rides.

Bicycle Rentals

There are a number of rental shops around the city, most charging around $7.50 per hour, or $25–$30 per day for a decent set of wheels. You'll usually need to leave a credit card deposit to rent.

Among the reputable choices are **Eddie's Bicycle Shop,** 490 Amsterdam Ave. (between 83rd and 84th Sts.; 212-580-2011), conveniently located near

Central Park; **Larry and Jeff's Bicycles Plus**, 1690 Second Ave. (between 87th and 88th Sts.; 212-722-2201); and and **Toga Bike Shop**, 110 West End Ave. (at 64th St.; 212-799-9625; daily rentals only—no hourly rates). **Metro Bicycle** Stores has six locations around the city: 332 E. 14th St. (between First and Second Aves.; 212-228-4344); 546 Sixth Ave. (at 15th St.; 212-255-5100); 417 Canal St. (212-334-8000); 231 W. 96th St. (between Broadway and Amsterdam Ave.; 212-663-7531); 360 W. 47th St. (at Ninth Ave.; 212-581-4500); and 1311 Lexington Ave. (at 88th St.; 212-427-4450).

In the heart of Central Park, **Loeb Boathouse,** near 74th St. and Park Drive North (212-517-2233), offers three-speed, 10-speed and tandem bikes for rent, for $10 to $20 per hour.

Billiards/Pool

At all of the pool halls listed below, you can expect to pay about $7 to $12 per player, per hour.

Amsterdam Billiard Club 344 Amsterdam Ave. (at 77th St.; 212-496-8180); and 210 E. 86th St. (between Second and Third Aves.; 212-570-4545). Upscale but not obnoxiously so. You'll find plentiful, well-kept tables, a full bar and amiable table-to-table waitress service. **Subway:** West Side 1, 9 to 79th St.; East Side 4, 5, 6 to 86th St.

Billiard Club 220 W. 19th St. (between Seventh and Eighth Aves.) (212) 206-7665. Head here for an intimate game of pool in a somewhat clubby environment, with its polished pine floor, low-key atmosphere and dark wood paneling. The 42 tables are spread out over two levels. **Subway:** 1, 9 to 18th St.

Corner Billiards 85 Fourth Ave. (at 11th St.) (212) 995-1314. Corner Billiards is your best bet in the Village. The 28 Brunswick Gold Crown Tables, a cafe, a microbrewery and waitress service all conspire to make this a civilized experience. **Subway:** L, N, Q, R, W, 4, 5, 6 to 14th St.

Slate 54 W. 21st St. (between Fifth and Sixth Aves.) (212) 989-0096. Slate is an upscale billiards hall and restaurant with an impeccable trendy pedigree—it was featured in *Sex and the City*. Visitors can play on one of the 34 top-quality pool tables (billiards and snooker tables also available). Expect a DJ, upscale drinks, and a crowd of beautiful people. **Subway:** F, N, R, V, 1, 9 to 23rd St.

SoHo Billiard Sport Center 56 E. Houston St. (between Mulberry and Mott Sts.) (212) 925-3753. Brightly lit and pleasantly spacious, this street level pool hall has a young downtown crowd. Players shoot pool on 28 tables spread out on multiple levels. **Subway:** F, S, V to Broadway–Lafayette St.; 6 to Bleecker St.; N, R to Prince St.

Boating

Downtown Boathouse West St./Pier 26 (between Chambers and Canal Sts.); also Pier 64 (at the end of W. 24th St.) (646) 613-0375 for general info; (646) 613-0740 for daily status; *www.downtownboathouse.org*. Mid-May through mid-

October, the Downtown Boathouse offers free kayaking between two piers on the Hudson River. A staff of volunteers will outfit you with a life jacket and a boat and give you some basic instruction. Once you've got a little experience under your belt, you can join them for longer kayaking trips. All trips are free, and offered on a first-come, first-served basis. **Subway:** 1, 9 to Canal St.; A, C, E to 23rd St.

Floating the Apple Hudson River (at 44th St.) (212) 564–5412 *www.float-ingtheapple.org.* The aim of this club is to make the waters of New York City more accessible to boating enthusiasts. They offer a series of weekly events in Manhattan, Brooklyn and the Bronx that encourage use of the area's waterways and harbor by water-sports aficionados. The Manhattan activities originate at Pier 40 (Hudson River at Houston St.) and include youth and adult rowing programs. The club also sponsors various sailing and swimming events, including the Great Hudson River Swim from the Marina at 79th Street to Chelsea Piers at 23rd Street.

Loeb Boathouse Central Park Lake (near 74th St. and East Drive) (212) 517-2233. For a relaxing and romantic afternoon, rent a rowboat and ply the waters of one of Central Park's most scenic areas. Boats are available year-round, weather permitting. Rowboats rent for $10 for the first hour, $2.50 every 15 minutes thereafter. A $30 deposit is required, and reservations are accepted. You can also book gondola rides here. **Subway:** 6 to 77th St.; A, B, C, D to 72nd St.

Prospect Park Brooklyn (718) 282-7789. Get some exercise and a different view of the park by touring the Lullwater and the Lake on a pedal boat. A great way to spend a lazy summer afternoon. **Subway:** Q to Prospect Park or Parkside Ave.

Bowling

Bowlmor Lanes 110 University Pl. (between 12th and 13th Sts.) (212) 255-8188 *www.bowlmor.com.* It's disco bowling! Bowlmor is an authentically retro bowling alley that's been around since 1938. But it now draws a hipster crowd, with day-glo pins, a DJ and the occasional celebrity sighting on the lanes. Two floors of lanes and a large bar area keep the party going till 4 A.M. on weekends and Mondays. Expect to wait for a lane. Prices are $7.25 per person per game on weeknights, $7.95 on weekends. On the building's rooftop is Pressure, a chic lounge featuring a martini menu, movie screens, dozens of pool tables and a fabulous Austin Powers décor. **Subway:** L, N, Q, R, W, 4, 5, 6 to 14th St.

Chelsea Piers *(See box "Chelsea Piers" in this chapter.)*

Leisure Time Bowling 625 Eighth Ave., 2nd Fl. (at Port Authority Bus Terminal) (212) 268-6909. When Leisure Time Bowling opened its modern 30 lanes a few years ago on the second floor of the Port Authority Bus Terminal, it seemed just a wee bit out of place. Now the alley is more popular than ever, with people of all ages trying to knock down a few on the lanes. Waits can be over two hours on weekends and when the weather is bad. **Subway:** A, C, E, N, R, Q, W, 1, 2, 3, ,7 9 to 42nd St.

Golf

Surprisingly, New York City offers a number of excellent golf courses, in addition to other golf resources such as driving ranges and instruction. Listed below are some of the most noteworthy and accessible of the area links.

Greens fees vary from course to course, but here's a general guideline for weekends: $10 for nine holes of early-morning play; $19 for a full round before 1 P.M.; $18 after 1 P.M.; $10 for twilight rounds. Rates are lower by a dollar or two for weekday play; on weekdays only, there are also special discounts for senior citizens and juniors under age 18. These rates are for city residents with a resident golf permit; add $4 to each fee if you're a visitor or a resident without a permit.

Tee times for most of the New York City–area golf courses listed below can be made by calling **New York Golf** at (718) 225-4653. There's a $2 reservation fee per player.

Douglaston Golf Course 6320 Marathon Pkwy. (at Commonwealth Blvd.), Queens (718) 428-1617. This short course will challenge you with narrow fairways, and its hilly nature will often result in uneven lies. While there is only one water hazard on the course, the many blind shots required make Douglaston relatively difficult. The course's signature hole is no. 18, a 550-yard, par 5, requiring an approach shot to a large, well-bunkered green. **Reservations:** 10 days in advance. **Directions by car:** Long Island Expy. east to Douglaston Pkwy.; turn left, continue to 61st Ave. and make a left; turn right on Marathon; drive two blocks and course will be on the right. Or take the Grand Central Pkwy. to the Little Neck Pkwy., then take exit 32 to the course.

Dyker Beach Seventh Ave. and 86th St., Brooklyn (718) 836-9722. This is perhaps the ultimate inner-city golfing experience; the sounds of the city usually follow you along the fairway. The course has undergone a dramatic renaissance, and is now one of the best maintained in the city, despite the over 80,000 rounds played here each year. **Reservations:** Seven days in advance. **Subway:** R to 86th St.; walk along 86th Street to course or take B-64 bus or cab. **Directions by car:** Brooklyn-Queens Expy. (BQE) to 86th St. exit or Belt Pkwy.

Kissena Park Golf Course 164–15 Booth Memorial Ave., Flushing, Queens (718) 939-4594. This is a short course (the back tees play only 4,727 yards), but the hilly terrain makes it a rather difficult one. Built in 1934 and redesigned in 1986, the course requires a variety of shots. According to the course pro, it will require every club in your bag. **Reservations:** Seven days in advance. **Subway:** 7 to Main St.– Flushing or E to Parsons Blvd.; cab from station. **Directions by car:** Long Island Expy. east to Exit 24 (Kissena Blvd.); take the service road to 164th St., turn left, go to the traffic light (Booth Memorial Ave.); turn right, you'll see the course from there.

La Tourette Golf Course 1001 Richmond Hill Rd., Staten Island (718) 351-1889. Once a private course, this verdant oasis from the city offers open, rolling fairways, plenty of bunkers and countless trees. The 1836 Greek-revival clubhouse is a landmark itself, and this venerable course is home to the annual New

Chelsea Piers

New York boasts the mother of all sports complexes, Chelsea Piers (extending from 17th to 23rd Streets on the Hudson River). This gargantuan facility offers everything from basketball and batting cages to golf and gymnastics. Once the city's premier passenger terminal, it is a site steeped in history; this was the intended destination of the *Titanic* (instead, the *Carpathia* arrived with the "unsinkable" ship's 675 survivors on April 20, 1912). There may be more scenic playing fields in New York, but nowhere else will you find so many activities in one location. Call (212) 336-6666 for general information, or check out *www.chelseapiers.com*.

Baseball/Softball Field House (212) 336-6500. There are four batting cages (two for righties, one for lefties, and another that serves both). Try hitting major-league heat in the fast-pitch cage, where the speed is set to about 90 mph. 10 pitches for $1.

Basketball Field House (212) 336-6500. There are two hardwood courts in the Field House. Walk-ons are welcome, but call ahead for available hours, since there is frequent league play. The cost is $7 per hour. There are also three courts in the main Sports Center, where day passes are available and pick-up sessions are available.

Bowling Chelsea Piers Bowl (212) 835-BOWL. This facility has 40 high-tech lanes. Bowl a few frames anytime, or come late on a weekend night for "Extreme Bowling," complete with day-glo pins and a DJ. Prices are $7 per person per game ($8 for Extreme Bowling), $4.50 for shoe rental.

Dance Field House (212) 336-6500. The 1,400-square-foot air-conditioned dance studio hosts classes in jazz, tap and modern dance.

Golf Golf Club at Chelsea Piers (212) 336-6400. This multitiered, year-round facility has to be seen to be believed. Offering 52 heated stalls and an automatic tee-up system, the driving range is a net-enclosed, artificial turf fairway stretching 200 yards out into the Hudson River. There is also a 1,000-square-foot putting area, or call ahead to rent a sand bunker for practice. Lessons are available at the Golf Academy, where PGA pros offer video analysis of your swing. Rates are $15 minimum for 60 balls (89 in off-peak hours); club rentals are available.

Gymnastics Field House (212) 336-6500. With 23,000 square feet of floor space, Chelsea Piers Gymnastics is the city's largest and best-equipped gymnastics training center and the only one sanctioned by USA Gymnastics for competitions. Call for class schedule and walk-on hours.

Health Club Sports Center (212) 336-6000. The 150,000-square-foot Sports Center offers two fitness studios with over 150 sports and fitness classes a week; a huge indoor running track; a 200-meter banked competition track; three basketball/volleyball courts; Manhattan's only indoor sand volleyball court; one of the largest and most challenging rock climbing walls in the world; a six-lane, 25-yard swimming pool; a separate Spinning Room; two outdoor sun decks overlooking the Hudson; extensive cardio- and strength-training areas; a boxing ring and equipment circuit; personal training; and baby-sitting. Once you're spent from all that activity, relax in the café or indulge in a spa treatment (*see below*). You deserve it. Day passes for non-members are a hefty $50 per day ($25 if you're with a member).

Ice Hockey/Ice Skating Sky Rink (212) 336-6100. Sky Rink, a twin-rink facility on Pier 61, operates 24/7, welcoming skaters of all ages and ability levels for recreational skating, figure skating lessons, and pick-up and league hockey. There's a complicated daily schedule ruling ice times for each activity, so call ahead or check the Web site for details. It's $22 for 80 minutes of freestyle ice skating or pick-up ice hockey (goalies play for free).

In-line Skating/Roller Hockey/Skateboarding Roller Rink (212) 336-6200. Open skating time is available on both the outdoor (weather permitting) and indoor roller rinks. Admission for a free-skate session is $7 for adults, $6 for kids; skates and protective gear can be rented. In addition to hosting numerous leagues and clinics, Chelsea Piers also offers open roller hockey on the weekends. Cost is $15 for 1 1/2 hours of pick-up play. There's also a newly expanded outdoor **Extreme Park,** offering challenging ramps, rails and launch boxes for BMX bikers, skateboarders and daring in-line skaters. A session in Extreme Park is $12.50; protective gear rental, but no skate rental, is available.

Rock Climbing Field House (212) 336-6500. The 30-foot-high artificial rock surface offers a variety of routes that challenge climbers of all skill levels. Cost is $20 per person. Check ahead for available times. There's also a climbing wall at the Sports Center.

Soccer/Lacrosse Field House (212) 336-6500. This facility has two state-of-the-art indoor playing fields built specifically for indoor soccer and lacrosse. Measuring 55-by-110 feet, the climate-controlled, artificial turf fields are surrounded by Plexiglas boards, and equipped with goals, nets and electronic scoreboards.

Spa Origins Feel-Good Spa (212) 336-6780. Treat yourself to a massage, a facial, a manicure or a body wrap. Check *www.origins.com/spa/spa-newyork.tmpl* for a menu of treatments and prices.

General Information: Dining: There are several casual dining choices, from snack bars to the Chelsea Brewing Company (212) 336-6440. **Parking:** Available at Pier 62. **Subway:** C, E, F, V, 1, 9 to 23rd St.

York City Amateur tournament. It is the only city course that offers a driving range on the property. **Reservations:** 10 days in advance. **Directions by car:** Brooklyn-Queens Expy. (BQE) to Verrazano Bridge to the Bradley Ave. exit; at second traffic signal (Wooley Ave.), turn left and proceed past the next five traffic signals; left on Richmond Hill Rd.

Marine Park Golf Course 2880 Flatbush Ave., Brooklyn (718) 338-7149. Built in 1964, Marine Park was designed by the legendary Robert Trent Jones Sr. and its large and undulating greens are, according to regulars, the finest in the city. The signature hole is no. 15, a 467-yard, par 4, featuring a well-bunkered fairway and requiring a downhill approach shot to a sloping green. **Reservations:** Seven days in advance. **Subway:** 2, 5 to Flatbush Ave.; then Q-35 Green bus to course. **Directions by car:** Belt Pkwy. to exit 11N (Flatbush Ave.), drive to the second traffic signal; course entrance is on the left.

Mosholu Golf Course 3700 Jerome Ave., Bronx (718) 655-9164. Narrowly avoiding demolition last year, Mosholu is another classic inner-city course, with tenements rising above the many trees to provide a uniquely urban backdrop. Built in 1904, it is one of the oldest in the city. Nine holes were lost some years ago to the addition of parkways to the area, but it is a difficult course nonetheless: the tree-lined fairways are narrow, the medium-sized greens are fast, and there are several blind fairways in the design. Easy to reach via public transportation. **Reservations:** Two days in advance. **Subway:** 4 to Woodlawn (last stop). **Directions by car:** Major Deegan Expy. to exit 13.

Pelham Bay/Split Rock 870 Shore Rd., Bronx (718) 885-1258. Pelham Bay Park offers two excellent 18-hole courses in a bucolic setting, where pheasant, wild turkey and deer might cross your path. The Pelham Bay Course offers a links-style design, and it the easier of the two. Its signature hole is no. 9, a 433-yard, par 4, requiring a shot to an extremely undulating green that is well bunkered. The Split Rock Course is more difficult because it is very wooded and has tight fairways. A creek comes into play on four holes, and the terrain is rolling. The signature hole on the Split Rock Course is no. 18, a 392-yard, par 4, requiring an approach shot around what may be America's oldest living White Oak tree. **Reservations:** 10 days in advance. **Subway:** 6 to Pelham Bay Park; W-45 or M-45 bus or cab to course (as this is quite a long trip, driving is preferable). **Directions by car:** FDR Dr. to Triborough Bridge, exit toward Bronx; take 95 going North (New England Thruway); get off at Exit 8B; the course is one mile away—look for the course entrance off Shore Rd. Or take Hutchinson River Pway. to Orchard Beach/City Island.

Silver Lake Park 915 Victory Blvd. (near Forest Ave.), Staten Island (718) 447-5686. This course is well manicured and located within a tight wooded area. The design includes several sloping, tight fairways, two water hazards and many trees lining the fairways. **Reservations:** 11 days in advance. **Directions by car:** Brooklyn-Queens Expy. (BQE) to Verrazano Bridge; stay on the Staten Island Expy., get off at the Clove Rd.–Victory Blvd. exit, turn right on Clove Rd.; proceed on to Victory Blvd., travel one mile, and the course is on the left.

South Shore Golf Course 200 Huguenot Ave., Staten Island (718) 984-0101. This very scenic and picturesque course was built on hilly terrain and seems to have been cut out of the forest itself. Designed by Alfred H. Tull in 1927, the course challenges golfers with narrow fairways and large, fast greens. **Reservations:** 11 days in advance. **Directions by car:** Brooklyn-Queens Expy. (BQE) to Verrazano Bridge; stay on the Staten Island Expy., get off at exit 5–Rte. 440 South/West Shore Expy. exit; take Rte. 440 south to exit 4; make a left onto Arthur Kill Rd.; stay straight to Huguenot Ave.

Van Cortlandt Golf Course Van Cortlandt Park S. and Bailey Ave., Bronx (718) 543-4595. The granddaddy of New York City courses and the nation's oldest public course, designed by Tom Bendelow and built in 1885. Van Cortlandt is well maintained, and there is a nice mix of long par 5s and short par 4s, with a few difficult par 3s thrown in for good measure. While you might drive the green on no. 6, a 292-yard par 4, watch out for no. 2, the signature 620-yard par 5 and the par 3 no. 13 that requires a shot over water to a large, undulating green. The final four holes are extremely hilly and offer a challenging end to this scenic course. In 2001 a new irrigation system was installed, improving conditions on a course that sees over 63,000 rounds played per year. **Reservations:** 10 days in advance. **Subway:** 1, 9 to W. 241 St./Van Cortlandt Park (last stop); walk east to clubhouse. Directions by car: Major Deegan Expy. to W. 230th St.

Gyms & Health Clubs

There are hundreds of health clubs around the city, and most offer one-day passes to visitors. You'll save time and money if your bring your own lock, though most will rent you one and nearly all (even the Y's) will provide a towel. Make sure to bring a picture ID too, as most require one for their records.

Health Clubs

Asphalt Green between 90th and 92nd Sts. at York Ave. (212) 369-8890 *www.asphaltgreen.org*. This non-profit organization stands out from other gyms with its full-size Astroturf soccer field, outdoor track and Olympic-size pool. There's a full fitness center with cardio equipment and weights, plus a busy schedule of fitness classes. Day passes are $20 for the pool only, $25 for the pool and fitness center. **Subway:** 4, 5, 6 to 86th St.

Crunch Fitness *www.crunch.com*. This chain of gyms has a hip urban personality. There are 10 locations in Manhattan, well-equipped with cardio and weight-training equipment and featuring an array of classes (everything from serious yoga instruction to cardio strip-tease and karaoke spinning). A day pass at any of Crunch's gyms is $24.

New York Sports Club (800) 796-NYSC for nearest location. *www.nysc.com*. This upscale chain has 16 Manhattan locations, with high-quality equipment and a wide variety of classes. Two of the Midtown locations feature pools. Day passes are $25.

YMCAs

New York City's YMCAs offer an affordable alternative to the health club scene, though day passes tend to be comparably priced. The gyms can often be quite crowded, but equipment is usually top-of-the-line. (**Note:** The **McBurney YMCA** is undergoing a major renovation, and will move into a new state-of-the-art facility on West 14th Street sometime in 2003.) Check *www.ymcanyc.org* for details on programs, facilities and membership.

Harlem YMCA 180 W. 135th St. (between Lenox Ave. and Adam Clayton Powell Jr. Blvd.) (212) 281-4100. **Day pass:** $12. **Subway:** 2, 3 to 135th St.

Vanderbilt YMCA 224 E. 47th St. (between Second and Third Aves.) (212) 756-9600. **Day pass:** $25. **Subway:** 6 to 51st St.

West Side YMCA 5 W. 63rd St. (between Broadway and Central Park West) (212) 875-4100. **Day pass:** $25. **Subway:** A, B, C, D, 1, 9 to 59th St.; 1, 9 to 66th St.

Horseback Riding

Claremont Riding Academy 175 W. 89th St. (between Amsterdam and Columbus Aves.) (212) 724-5100. Built in 1892, Claremont is the oldest continuously operating stable in the country. Experienced equestrians (who can walk, trot and canter comfortably) can hire horses by the hour to ride on the six miles of bridle paths in nearby Central Park. Lessons are available and there is an indoor arena for beginners. **Price:** $45 per hour. **Subway:** 1, 9 to 86th St.

Kensington Stables 51 Caton Pl., Brooklyn (718) 972-4588 *www.kensingtonstables.com.* Horses can be hired here for leisurely guided rides on Prospect Park's trails. Lessons are also available. **Price:** $25 per hour. **Subway:** F to Ft. Hamilton Pkwy.

Ice Skating

Central Park—Lasker Rink Central Park at 106th St. (212) 534-7639. Located just below the scenic Harlem Meer, the Lasker Rink is open for ice skating during the winter season (it serves as Central Park's only swimming pool in the summer months). **Subway:** 6 to E. 103rd St.; B, C to W. 103rd St.

Central Park—Wollman Memorial Rink Enter park at Sixth Ave. and Central Park South (212) 439-6900 *www.wollmanskatingrink.com.* The 33,000-square-foot Wollman Rink offers a spacious skating area and an unparalleled view of the Duck Pond framed by landmark buildings like the Plaza Hotel. **Admission:** $7.50 adults ($8 on weekends); $3.75 children under 12 and seniors. Skate rental is $3.75. **Subway:** N, R, W to Fifth Ave.

Chelsea Piers (*See box* "Chelsea Piers" *in this chapter.*)

Prospect Park—Wollman Rink Near the Lincoln Rd. entrance of Prospect Park (718) 287-6431. Kate Wollman Center and Rink is open for ice skating from December until March (you can rent pedal boats here in spring and summer). An especially nice feature of this rink is the early-bird session from 8:30–10:30 A.M. on weekdays. If you're an avid skater who hates the crowds at most public rinks, this is the place for you. **Admission:** $4. Skate rental is $3.50. **Subway:** Q to Parkside Ave.

Rink at Rockefeller Plaza 601 Fifth Ave. (between 49th and 50th Sts.) (212) 332-7654 *www.rockefellercenter.com*. Throughout the holiday season, music plays as skaters waltz around the rink under the glow of the awe-inspiring Rockefeller Center Christmas tree. Sure, the rink is cramped and crowded, but the thrill of skating at the epicenter of the city's holiday spirit is unrivaled. Visit earlier or later in the season for a less crowded experience. Call ahead for available dates and times. **Admission:** $14; $10 children under 12 (admission varies, so call ahead). Skate rental is $6. **Subway:** B, D, F, S, V to 47th-50th St.–Rockefeller Center.

In-Line Skating

Popular street skating spots include "the cube" at Astor Place in the East Village, "the banks" under the Brooklyn Bridge (Manhattan side) and Union Square. Central Park is full of great places to skate in addition to Wollman Rink (listed below); try the main drives throughout the park, the open plaza at the north end of the Mall and the closed driveway west of the Mall. Skating in the Riverside Park grounds near 108th Street, which is permitted in the warmer months, requires a helmet, signing of a waiver and a $3 fee. Wrist and kneepads are essential, and elbow pads are recommended (212-408-0239 for info).

If you need to rent skates, try **Blades Board & Skate** (*www.blades.com*), with locations at 160 E. 86th St. (between Third and Lexington Aves.; 212-996-1644); 120 W. 72nd St. (between Amsterdam and Columbus Aves.; 212-787-3911); and three other outlets around town. *(See also "Chelsea Piers" in this chapter.)*

Central Park—Wollman Memorial Rink Enter park at Sixth Ave. and Central Park South (212) 439-6100. During the summer months, Rollerblades replace ice skates at Wollman Rink. The rink also offers classes and guided skating tours around the park. Compared to the skating lanes in the park, the rink is fairly uncrowded, leaving plenty of room for New Yorkers to strut their stuff. Rollerblades and safety equipment (state law requires children 14 and under to wear helmets and pads) can be rented for rink use ($6) or for park use ($15 with a $100 deposit). **Admission:** $7.50 adults; $3.75 children and seniors. **Subway:** N, R, W to Fifth Ave.

Empire Skate Club of New York (212) 774-1774 *www.empireskate.org*. The Empire Skate Club of New York is a non-profit organization of in-line skaters dedicated to having fun and improving the skating environment in New York. The Club organizes regular social skates and get-togethers in the city, trips around the eastern seaboard and farther afield, clinics, seminars, parties and skate advocacy. A year's membership is $25.

Running

While out-of-towners may think of New York City as a concrete jungle with few safe places to run, there are actually many excellent—even tree-lined and relatively bucolic—routes right in Manhattan. **East River Park** is a favorite of those living downtown, offering a scenic course that stretches along the river just across from downtown Brooklyn. The **Battery Park Promenade** offers a shady, paved path for joggers, bikers and in-line skaters, who enjoy water views while they work out. This promenade is now paved all the way **up the West Side** of Manhattan, running up through Midtown, Riverside Park and all the way up to the George Washington Bridge.

But the crown jewel of the NYC runner's kingdom is **Central Park,** unofficial home of the **New York Road Runners Club** (212-860-4455; *www.nyrrc.org*). The club sponsors many races throughout the year, usually along the Park's main Loop, the most famous race being the New York City Marathon, finishing at Tavern on the Green on the West Side. You don't have to be a member to run in club-sponsored events (though there's usually a small fee); check *www.nyrrc.org* to find out about upcoming races.

The length of the entire **Central Park Loop**—the road that follows a circular route through the interior of the park—is 6.1 miles. This road is closed to cars 10 A.M.–4 P.M., and then again 7 P.M.–dusk. During the hours when vehicular traffic is permitted, you can run in the multi-use lane for runners, bikers and in-line skaters, though it is unprotected. Good short courses include the 3.5-mile route used by Chase's Corporate Challenge race, which begins at the Puppet Theater (roughly W. 70th St.), follows the Loop to the 102nd Street transverse, rejoins the Loop on the east side, and ends at the Rumsey Playground (where SummerStage events are held) at about East 70th Street. A popular 5K course (3.1 miles) begins at the East Drive (Loop) and 86th Street, proceeds north and across the 102nd Street transverse, back onto the Drive and finishes at the Engineer's Gate (90th St. and Fifth Ave.). The **Reservoir** run is one of the most popular courses in the city. The cinder track offers a level run of 1.6 miles and offers great views of the Manhattan skyline at virtually every step. In spring it is especially pleasant as flowering trees line the eastern side of the course. Enter the park at 86th Street on the east or west side. Don't run in the park at night.

The best spot for a run in Brooklyn is definitely **Prospect Park.** There is a dirt path, roughly three miles, on the inside of the roadway (3.5 miles) circling the park grounds, along with other isolated trails. The **Prospect Park Track Club** has regular workouts (check *www.pptc.org* for schedules); nonmembers are welcome.

Swimming

(*See section* "Gyms & Health Clubs" *for YMCAs and private gyms with pools.*)

Public Pools

Asphalt Green between 90th and 92nd Sts. at York Ave. (212) 369-8890 *www.asphaltgreen.org.* Asphalt Green has one of the biggest and newest public pools in the city, complete with a hydraulic floor that adjusts the water depth for children and those learning to swim.. The 50-by-20-meter indoor pool is heated to an even 80 degrees. While nonmembers can purchase a day pass to swim, some lap swimming lanes are always reserved for members only. Day passes are $20 to use the pool only, $25 to use the pool and other facilities. **Subway:** 4, 5, 6 to 86th St.

Lasker Pool Central Park, East Drive and 106th St. During the summer months, Lasker is open for community swimming, racing and lessons. At less than four feet deep, the pool is ideal for kids. You can't beat the cost either—it's totally free. Swimmers must wear a swimsuit (no denim shorts or t-shirts). Lockers are available, but bring your own lock. **Subway:** 6 to E. 103rd St.; B, C to W. 103rd St.

Riverbank State Park Pool 679 Riverside Dr. (at 145th St.) (212) 694-3666. How's this for a funky location? Here's a pool built atop a sewage treatment center on the Hudson. It's not as grim as it sounds: the park is very attractive, perched 69 feet above the river, and offers many other sports in addition to swimming. The view along the river on a clear day is quite spectacular. There's an indoor Olympic-size pool, plus an outdoor lap pool and wading pool.

Municipal Pools

New York City's municipal pools require a year's membership, but it's only $25 and can be paid on the spot by personal check or money order. If you're planning on returning to the Big Apple in the next 12 months, this might be your best option.

East 54th St. Recreation Center 348 E. 54th St. (212) 397-3154 Midtown

59th Street Recreation Center 533 W. 59th St. (212) 397-3166 West Side

Asser Levy Park 23rd St. and Asser Levy Pl. (212) 447-2020 Gramercy Park

Carmine Street Recreation Center 1 Clarkson St. (212) 242-5228 Greenwich Village

Dry Dock Swimming Pool 408 E. 10th St. (212) 677-4481 Alphabet City

Hamilton Fish Recreation Center Pool 128 Pitt St. at Houston St. (212) 387-7687 Downtown

John Jay Swimming Pool 77th St. and Cherokee Pl., east of York Ave. (212) 794-6566 Upper East Side

Lenox Hill Neighborhood House 331 E. 70th St. (212) 744-5022 Upper East Side

Tennis

Public Courts

The 24 Har-tru public courts at **Central Park's** venerable Tennis Center (midpark, 94th-96th Sts.) are among the nicest in the city, but half are booked in advance, and the rest are usually reserved on a first-come, first-serve basis early each morning. Plus, you have to put up with a lot of attitude on the part of regulars who treat the Center as their own private club. But if you can handle these obstacles, playing amidst the trees of the park is a real treat. The Center, open April through November, also offers a pro shop, a locker room with showers, and a snack bar. Call (212) 360-8131 for information.

Other less crowded courts include those at **Riverside Park,** which boasts beautiful red-clay courts at the western end of 96th Street (no reservations) and recently restored hard-surface courts at 118th Street. East River Park (East River at Broome St.) also offers 12 hard-surface courts, perhaps the least crowded in Manhattan.

In Brooklyn, **Prospect Park Tennis Center** provides 10 Har-tru courts, located at the southwest corner of the park, near the Park Circle. From mid-October through the end of April, a bubble structure covers these courts, and a private company rents them by the hour (call one day ahead to make reservations). Also in Brooklyn are the six excellent hard-surface courts at Fort Greene Park. These are among the least used in the city, and, while there is a core group of regulars, it's relatively easy to walk on and play.

Use of all city tennis courts requires either a **season pass** ($50) or a **day pass** ($5), which can be purchased either at the Tennis Center or Paragon Sporting Goods (867 Broadway at 18th St.). Permits are less apt to be checked at the courts at Riverside and 118th and Fort Greene Park. The season is April to November, daily from 7 A.M. till 8 P.M. (light permitting).

Private Courts

Crosstown Tennis Club 14 W. 31st St. (212) 947-5780
www.crosstowntennis.com. The Crosstown facility, just steps from the Empire State Building, offers four Championship DecoTurf tennis courts, each with an 18-foot back-court area and 40-foot ceilings. **Price:** $50–$75 per hour. **Subway:** B, D, F, N, Q, R, S, V to 34th St.

Midtown Tennis Club 341 Eighth Ave. (at 27th St.) (212) 989-8572
www.midtowntennis.com. When it opened in 1965, the Midtown Tennis Club was the first indoor club in Manhattan, and it's still one of the largest and most accessible tennis sites in the city. Air-conditioned, with eight tournament Har-tru courts, and full locker-room facilities, the club offers tennis in a comfortable and relaxed atmosphere. **Price:** $45–$75 per hour indoors; $30–$40 outdoors. **Subway:** 1, 9 to 28th St.; C, E to 23rd St.

USTA National Tennis Center Flushing Meadows–Corona Park, Queens (718) 760-6200 ext. 6213, ask for the program office. *www.usopen.org.* The USTA National Tennis Center, site of the **U.S. Open,** is the largest public tennis facility in the world, offering nine indoor courts, 18 practice courts and 18 tournament courts. All are open to the public year round except for August and September, during the U.S. Open itself. They reopen for public play one week after the last day of the Open. **Price:** $32–$48 per hour indoors (with off-peak weekday junior and senior rates); $16–$24 outdoors ($8 fee for lights for night play). **Subway:** 7 to Willets Point—Shea Stadium.

BEACHES

When you're in the depths of Manhattan's concrete canyons, it's easy to forget that beyond the city's wall of skyscrapers lie miles and miles of Atlantic beaches. There are city beaches in Brooklyn, Queens and the Bronx, as well as some very accessible spots on Long Island. If the temperature hits 90 degrees on a summer weekend, expect crowds (and that's an understatement). For millions of New Yorkers, the Atlantic provides the only way to beat the heat.

Brooklyn

Coney Island at Surf and Stillwell Aves. (718) 946-1350. *(See section "Brooklyn" in chapter* **Exploring New York** *for full entry.)* Have a hot dog at Nathan's, ride the Cyclone, stroll the boardwalk and spread out your towel. Though this is by far the most famous of the Brooklyn beaches, you may also want to try Brighton Beach right next door or Manhattan Beach just beyond. **Subway:** F, N, Q to Stillwell Ave.–Coney Island.

Bronx

Orchard Beach Long Island Sound (between Park Dr. and Bartow Circle) (718) 885-2275. At the turn of the century, this was a popular bathing spot for the affluent residents of Pelham Manor. A large, luxurious stand of trees skirts the beach, creating a lovely backdrop. Standing on the patio between the two halves of the old bathhouse, you can gaze over the entire expanse of sand, as idyllic as a postcard. **Subway:** 6 to Pelham Bay Park; BX 12 bus to Orchard Beach. **By car:** Hutchinson River Pkwy.; exit at City Island–Orchard Beach.

Queens

Rockaway Beach Beach 1st and Beach 149th Sts. (718) 318-4000. "Rockapulco" has a plain plank boardwalk, a pale arc of fine sand and high-rise condos. That's not to say it's without character. The beautiful old buildings, nearby hotels and ornate subway station have a kind of wind-swept, sunburned grandeur, and the fact that it's accessible only by bridge gives it the aura of adventure and isolation. **Riis Park,** a beach that is often overcrowded in the summer, is just west; despite the crowds, the sands are gorgeous and it's surprisingly well maintained by the National Park Service. **Subway:** A to Rockaway Park. **Directions by car:** Take Rte. 278 (BQE/Gowanus Expy.) south to Shore Pkwy. (aka Belt Pkwy.) east to Marine Pkwy./Gil Hodges Bridge; then follow signs for Riis Park.

Long Island

Fire Island (516) 852-5200. Fire Island is a barefoot society, car-free and carefree. A barrier island, it stretches across 32 miles between the end of **Robert**

Moses State Park (best bet for day-trippers, since that's the only part of Fire Island that's accessible by car) and Moriches Inlet, where the Hamptons begin. Despite an influx of tourist attention, the island has changed little in the last century. Cedar-shingled cottages are hemmed in by pines and bayberry; everyone gets around by biking and walking. The beach itself, a National Seashore, is gorgeous. **Directions:** From Penn Station, take the Long Island Railroad to Bay Shore, Patchogue or Sayville. Then take a taxi to the ferry docks in any of these towns (total price, $15–$20 round trip).

Jones Beach (516) 785-1600. Jones Beach is the single most popular site in the entire state park system, averaging nearly seven million visitors a year. This is a rollicking beach party, with radios blaring. Elsewhere in the 2,413-acre park, determined joggers, bikers and skaters swoosh along their designated paths. Surf-casters think bluefish, while anglers on the four bay piers are after fluke. **Directions:** From Penn Station, take the Long Island Railroad to Freeport. Buses run every half hour from the train station to the beach ($11, includes shuttle bus). By car, take the Long Island Expy. to Meadowbrook Pkwy. south; follow signs for Jones Beach. If you drive, go early; parking lots fill quickly.

Long Beach In recent years, this seaside city has made a remarkable comeback. Smart, new high-rise oceanfront buildings have emerged, and young families, attracted by the soft sands of the Atlantic and the 53-minute commute by train to Manhattan, are moving here in droves. For the weekend visitor, the best reasons to trek to Long Beach are its wonderful sands and its boardwalk. At a little more than two miles in length, the boardwalk is Long Island's longest, featuring a block of stores and eateries. **Directions:** From Penn Station, take the Long Island Railroad to Long Beach ($11 round-trip package).

SPECTATOR SPORTS
Baseball

New York Yankees—Yankee Stadium 161st St. (at River Ave.), Bronx (718) 293-6000 *www.yankees.com*. One of the most storied venues in sports history, Yankee Stadium may be a little worn around the edges, but there's no denying its aura. The original stadium opened in 1923, as 74,200 fans packed the massive three-tiered facility and watched Babe Ruth christen his new home with a towering shot as the Yankees beat their hated rivals, the Boston Red Sox. Because Ruth was such a tremendous draw, Yankee Stadium almost immediately acquired its moniker, "The House that Ruth Built." The park was remodeled and scaled down slightly in the mid-70's, but historic touches remain, including Monument Park and the decorative white colonnade above the outfield. Some of baseball's most legendary names have played at the Stadium, including Ruth, Lou Gehrig, Joe DiMaggio, Yogi Berra and Mickey Mantle, to name but a few. It was here that Gehrig delivered his famous farewell address ("Today I consider myself the luckiest man on the face of the earth"), and here that three perfect games have been hurled (by Don Larsen, David Wells and David Cone). The

Barton Silverman/The New York Times

Yankee Stadium

current team, World Champions in 1996, 1998, 1999 and 2000, is a perennial contender to do it again—just like the "Murderer's Row" squads of the 1920's and 1930's, and the unstoppable Yankees juggernaut of the early 1960's. Buy tickets in advance, and take public transporation to the stadium (traffic is a nightmare). Don't miss the raucous chants from Bleacher Creatures—as if you could. Hardcore fans can take **stadium tours;** call (718) 579-4531 or check the Web site for details. **Tickets:** $8–$65; available through Ticketmaster, at *www.yankees.com*, at the stadium or at Yankees Clubhouse stores. **Subway:** 4, B, D to 161st St.—Yankee Stadium.

New York Mets—Shea Stadium 123–01 Roosevelt Ave. (between Grand Central Pkwy. and Van Wyck Expy.), Flushing, Queens (718) 507-6387 *www.mets.com*. While the Yankees have a certain air of invincibility and corporate efficiency, the Mets are your little brother's team. They are more colorful, more melodramatic and more unpredictable than their Bronx counterparts. The Amazin's began in 1962 as lovable losers, when the likes of Marvelous Marv Throneberry made them the most inept team in the history of the game: 40 wins and a whopping 120 losses. But things soon turned around, as the Mets completed an improbable championship run in 1969, defeating the Orioles four games to one and coining the phrase "You gotta believe!" They won their second championship in 1986, breaking hearts all over New England as the Red Sox went down in flames yet again. Though Mike Piazza & Co. have been thwarted by the Yankees and the Braves in recent years, it's always exciting to watch the ups and downs of the Mets—you gotta believe they've always got one more come-from-behind victory up their sleeves. **Tickets:** $12–$43; available at the stadium, at *www.mets.com*, over the phone from the Mets ticket office or from Mets Clubhouse stores. **Subway:** 7 to Willets Point—Shea Stadium. **Long**

Island Railroad: Stops at stadium on game days (from Penn Station, peak $5.50, off-peak $3.75, one way).

Brooklyn Cyclones—Keyspan Park 1904 Surf Ave. (between W. 17th and W. 19th Sts.), Coney Island, Brooklyn (718) 449-8497 *www.brooklyncyclones.net.* "Baseball returns to Brooklyn!" So read many of the tabloid headlines when the first pitch was thrown at Keyspan Park in 2001. The Cyclones, a Mets minor league affiliate, are the first professional team to play in Brooklyn since the departure of the Dodgers for Los Angeles in 1958, and base-ball couldn't ask for a better venue. This gorgeous 7,500-seat ballpark is located on Surf Avenue in legendary Coney Island, offering fans an ocean view and the chance to ride the famed Cyclone roller coaster after the game. Buy tickets way in advance; 2002 tickets sold out months before the season started. **Tickets:** Under $10. **Subway:** F, N, Q to Stillwell Ave.–Coney Island.

Staten Island Yankees—Richmond County Bank Ballpark 75 Richmond Terrace (718) 720-9265 *www.siyanks.com.* While the Cyclones may get all the press, a Yankees minor league squad has landed in New York City, too, and a new Big Apple rivalry has been born. Also new in 2001, their appealing 6,500-seat stadium offers views of New York Harbor and the Statue of Liberty. **Tick-ets:** Under $10. **Directions:** 4, 5 subway to Bowling Green, or N, R to White-hall (as of this writing, 1, 9 service to South Ferry has not been restored); take the Staten Island Ferry across the harbor and exit from the lower deck; the ball-park is on the right.

Basketball

New York Knicks—Madison Square Garden 2 Penn Plaza (at 33rd St. and Seventh Ave.) (212) 465-6727 *www.nba.com/knicks.* Madison Square Garden is home to the Knicks, who were largely defined as Patrick Ewing's team through-out the 1990's. Though they were contenders through much of the last decade, the most vivid memories in recent years have been of playoff defeats. The Knicks have recently become a high-payroll disappointment. Major retooling is needed before the franchise can make another serious run; trading away Marcus Camby signals a sea change. Tickets are obscenely expensive, but with the team's declining fortunes, they've become easier to obtain. **Tickets:** $26.50–$1,500; available through Ticketmaster at (212) 307-7171 or at the Garden box office; for ticket info call (212) 465-JUMP. **Subway:** A, C, E, 1, 2, 3, 9 to 34th St.

New Jersey Nets—Continental Airlines Arena (Meadowlands) 50 Rte. 120 (at Rte. 3), East Rutherford, NJ (201) 935-3900 *www.nba.com/nets.* After grinding away in mediocrity for more than two decades, the Nets came out of nowhere and made it all the way to the NBA finals in 2002, powered by the dazzling play of gritty point guard Jason Kidd. Since the Nets' ascendancy coin-cided with the Knicks' decline, the team has won thousands of new fans. **Tick-**

ets: $10-$600; available through Ticketmaster online or at (201) 507-8900; for info, call (800) 7NJ-NETS or check the Web site. **Directions:** Bus service for all events at the Meadowlands Sports Complex from Manhattan's Port Authority ($6.50 round trip). By car, take the New Jersey Turnpike to exit 16W to Complex. Or take the Garden State Pkwy. south to exit 153 (153N if you're northbound), Rte. 3 east.

New York Liberty—Madison Square Garden 2 Penn Plaza (at 33rd St. and Seventh Ave.) (212) 564-WNBA *www.wnba/liberty.* The Liberty squad is a bona fide power in the WNBA. And they've built quite a fan base, one that Liberty die-hards proudly describe as noncorporate, unlike the clientele of their male counterparts. Also unlike Knicks games, it's easy to get good seats that won't cost you a second mortgage. **Tickets:** $8–$225; available through Ticketmaster at (212) 307-7171 or at the Garden box office. **Subway:** A, C, E, 1, 2, 3, 9 to 34th St.

Boxing

Madison Square Garden 2 Penn Plaza (at 33rd St. and Seventh Ave.) (212) 465-6727 *www.thegarden.com* Madison Square Garden has a long and storied history of boxing, a tradition that began inside its original 19th-century building in Madison Square at 23rd Street (built in 1879, this roofless arena was also the site of chariot races) and continuing through to its present and fourth location. On March 8, 1971, one of the most anticipated sporting events of the 20th century took place when Joe Frazier defeated Muhammad Ali in a 15-round decision for the heavyweight title. In a pale imitation of that bout in March 1999, Evander Holyfield battled Lennox Lewis to a draw in a 15-round fight. Your best hope for exciting (and affordable) boxing is the annual **Golden Gloves** tournament (April), in which kids from around the city battle for top honors in all weight divisions. **Tickets:** Available through Ticketmaster at (212) 307-7171, or at the Garden box office. **Subway:** A, C, E, 1, 2, 3, 9 to 34th St.

Church Street Boxing Gym 25 Park Pl. (between Church St. and Broadway) (212) 571-1333 *www.nyboxinggym.com.* This is New York City's premier boxing training facility, with over 10,000 square feet of gym space located in the heart of downtown Manhattan. The well-known gym has showcased many up-and-coming professional boxers, kickboxers and Thai-boxers and has worked on-site with such marquee names as Evander Holyfield, Larry Holmes and Mike Tyson. Call for a fight schedule. **Subway:** 4, 5, 6 to Brooklyn Bridge; 2, 3 to Park Pl.

Cricket

Because of the concentration of recent immigrants from cricket-playing countries (mainly from India, Pakistan and the West Indies), it's not surprising that the New York metropolitan area is considered the mecca of cricket in North

America. There are 12 leagues comprising over 200 clubs, and play can be watched in a number of area parks. **Bronx:** Van Cortlandt Park, Ferry Point Park, Randall's Island, Soundview. **Queens:** Flushing Meadow Park, Baisley Park, Kissena Park, Edgemere. **Brooklyn:** Marine Park, Seaview.

Football

New York Giants—Giants Stadium (Meadowlands) 59 Rte 120 (at Rte. 3), East Rutherford, NJ (201) 935-3900 *www.giants.com*. "Big Blue" moved to its 77,716-seat New Jersey home in 1976. Tickets are available by subscription only. If you get yourself on the waiting list soon, perhaps your grandchildren will get a seat one day. **Directions:** See New Jersey Nets entry.

New York Jets—Giants Stadium 59 Rte 120 (at Rte. 3), East Rutherford, NJ (201) 935-3900 *www.newyorkjets.com*. "Gang Green" was lured to the Meadowlands after the 1983 season, so both metropolitan-area NFL franchises are actually New Jersey teams, despite what it says on their helmets. It's almost as hard to get a ticket for a Jets game as it is for those of their co-tenants: the waiting list for season tickets is currently 12 years. **Directions:** See New Jersey Nets entry.

Hockey

New York Rangers—Madison Square Garden 2 Penn Plaza (at 33rd St. and Seventh Ave.) (212) 465-6471 *www.newyorkrangers.com*. One of the "Original Six" NHL teams, the Rangers have a long tradition, although their fortunes have dimmed since winning the Stanley Cup in 1994. But win or lose, the Rangers have some of the most loyal—and vociferous—fans in the league, and games at the Garden are rowdy fun. **Tickets:** $22–$675; available through Ticketmaster at (212) 307-7171, or at the Garden box office. **Subway:** A, C, E, 1, 2, 3, 9 to 34th St.

New York Islanders—Nassau Veterans Memorial Coliseum 1255 Hempstead Tpke., Uniondale, Long Island (516) 794-9300 *www.newyorkislanders.com*. The Islanders won four successive Stanley Cups in the early 80's. Fans think back fondly on those years: the team hasn't qualified for the playoffs since, although it is steadily improving. **Tickets:** $14–$85; available at the box office or through Ticketmaster. **Directions:** Long Island Railroad to Hempstead; walk one block to the Hempstead Bus Terminal and take N 70, N 71 or N 72 bus to Coliseum. By car, take the Midtown Tunnel to Long Island Expy. (495) east to exit 38; Northern State Pkwy. to exit 31A; Meadowbrook Pkwy. south to exit M4, Nassau Coliseum. Parking is $6.

New Jersey Devils—Continental Airlines Arena 50 Rte. 120 (at Rte. 3), East Rutherford, NJ (201) 935-3900 *www.newjerseydevils.com*. Transplanted from Colorado in 1982, the Devils have risen from depths of their division to become one of the better teams in the NHL and a perennial playoff contender.

The Devils took the Cup in 2000, but lost hard-fought playoff series in 2001
and 2002. **Tickets:** $20–$150; available at the box office, or through Ticketmaster online or at (201) 507-8900. **Directions:** See New Jersey Nets entry.

Horse Racing

Aqueduct Racetrack 110th St. (at Rockaway Blvd.), Ozone Park, Queens
(718) 641-4700 *www.nyra.com/Acqueduct*. The old Aqueduct, which opened in
1894, was replaced by the new "Big A" in 1959. In 1975 the inner track was
constructed, allowing for winter racing. On July 4, 1972, Aqueduct was the
scene of Secretariat's first event, a 5.5 furlong maiden race. **Hours:** Gates open
at 11 A.M. **Admission:** Grandstand $1; Clubhouse $3; Skyline Club $4; chil-
dren under 12 free. **Subway:** A to Aqueduct Racetrack; courtesy bus service to
admission gate. **By car:** Midtown Tunnel to Long Island Expy. east, to Van
Wyck Expy. south to exit 3, Linden Blvd.; right on Linden to track. Parking
$1–$5.

Belmont Park 2150 Hempstead Tpke. (at Plainfield Ave), Elmont, Long
Island (718) 488-6000 *www.nyra.com/Belmont*. In addition to hosting the Belmont Stakes each year, the final leg of the Triple Crown, Belmont Park has
been the scene of many other historic events. One of America's oldest and most
beautiful tracks, Belmont opened on May 4, 1905; it was here that the Wright
brothers supervised an international aerial tournament before 150,000 spectators in 1910. But most important, of course, is its glorious racing past. It was
here in 1973 that Secretariat won the Triple Crown, winning the race by an
astonishing 31 lengths and becoming a racing legend. **Hours:** Gates open at 11
A.M. Closed Mon.–Tue. except holiday weekends (closed Wed.). Season is generally May–Jul. and Sept. to mid-Oct. **Admission:** Grandstand $2; Clubhouse
$4; children under 12 free. **Directions:** Long Island Railroad; round-trip pack-
age from Penn Station includes $1 off admission. By car, take the Cross Island
Pkwy. to exit 26D. Parking $2–$6.

Meadowlands Racetrack Rte. 3, East Rutherford, NJ (201) THE-BIGM
www.thebigm.com. Harness and thoroughbred horse racing are the staples at this
one-mile oval track next to Giants Stadium. The 40,000-person-capacity racetrack was built in 1976 and christened in high style when horseman Anthony
Abbatiello rode across the George Washington Bridge to the Meadowlands.
Admission: Grandstand $1–$1.50; Clubhouse, $3; Pegasus (Dining Floor) $5.
Directions: See New Jersey Nets entry. General parking free; Clubhouse and
valet parking $5.

Yonkers Raceway Central Ave., Yonkers (914) 968-4200 *www.yonkersrace-
way.com*. Although the history of the modern Yonkers Raceway dates from only
1950, the Westchester oval's impressive past actually dates back to the 19th
century, when it was founded as a replacement for Fleetwood Park, a Grand Circuit stop in the Bronx. The facility reopened as Yonkers Raceway and had its
inaugural meet on April 27, 1950. **Hours:** Post time 7:40 P.M. Mon.–Tues. and

Fri.–Sat. **Admission:** Grandstand $2.25; Empire Terrace $4.25. **Subway:** 4 to
Woodlawn; B, D to Bedford Park Blvd.; 5 to 238th St.; 1, 9 to 242nd St. Take
express buses from stations to track. **By car:** New York Thruway I-87 to exit 2
North, exit 4 South; Bronx River Pkwy. to Oak St., Mt. Vernon exit; Saw Mill
River Pkwy. to Cross County Pkwy. to Yonkers or Central Ave. exit). Parking $2.

Soccer

New York/New Jersey MetroStars—Continental Airlines Arena 50 Rte.
120 (at Rte. 3), East Rutherford, NJ (201) 935-3900 *www.metrostars.com*.
Major League Soccer began in 1996 amidst the enthusiasm generated by the
World Cup. Certainly the best soccer in America is being played in MLS
venues, and with the recent ban of the game-deciding shootout in favor of over-
time, league officials are trying to make this a more exciting game for purists.
The season runs April through September. **Tickets:** $18– $60; available
through Ticketmaster online or by calling (888) 4METROTIX. **Directions:** See
New Jersey Nets entry.

Tennis

Chase Championships—Madison Square Garden *www.thegarden.com* Taking place in Madison Square Garden every November, the Chase Championships is one of the WTA's top tournaments, featuring a singles field limited to
the top 16 point-earners on the tour, and a similar field of eight doubles teams.
The tennis is top-notch, and the Garden ambiance is electric. **Tickets:**
$20–$150; available through Ticketmaster at (212) 307-7171, or at the Garden
box office. **Subway:** A, C, E, 1, 2, 3, 9 to 34th St.

U.S. Open—USTA National Tennis Center Flushing Meadows—Corona
Park, Queens (718) 760–6200 *www.usopen.org*. The most prestigious American
tournament, a Grand Slam event, is held in late August and early September at
the National Tennis Center. The world's best tennis players converge on the
city, hoping to vie for the championship in the spacious Arthur Ashe Stadium.
Fans can pay top dollar for a seat at the showcased matches, or purchase
grounds admission, which entitles them to wander from one early-round match
to another; prices go up as the tournament progresses. Buy tickets well in
advance; they go on sale in June. **Tickets:** Grounds admission $40–$44; showcase match at Arthur Ashe Stadium $44–$89. Available at the box office or
through Ticketmaster online or at (866) OPEN-TIX. **Subway:** 7 to Willets
Point—Shea Stadium. **Long Island Railroad:** Trains from Penn Station stop at
the stadium during the Open.

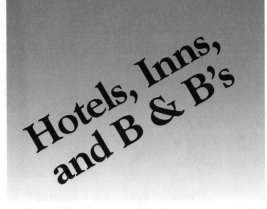

Hotels, Inns, and B & B's

While New York remains one of the most expensive hotel cities in the country, there's good news for price-watchers. The intersection of the economic downturn (and a commensurate decrease in expense-account travel), slowing tourism numbers, and a glut of new hotel development in 2000 and 2001 has created a buyer's market out of a seller's one. While the average city room rate was a sky-high $227 in 2001, it has declined to a far more reasonable $168 in 2002.

What does that mean for a visitor? More bargaining power. Don't expect a bargain anytime soon—hoteliers are keeping rack rates high in the name of "rate integrity," but they do exhibit far more flexibility these days. Resurrect your negotiating skills, especially if you'll be visiting between January and August, when hotels compete hardest for visitors. During autumn and holiday time, you may still have to reconcile yourself to paying closer to full price, but there are some insider tips worth noting even in these seasons. For instance, hotels in Midtown West charge higher-than-usual rates for Thanksgiving, especially along the Macy's parade route; however, deals can often be had on the east side of town and downtown. And bargains abound in Financial District hotels during the holiday season, and over just about any weekend.

One more important thing you need to know: Room size is almost invariably smaller here than in most other cities. Sure, more money will usually buy you more space, but not always. Bathrooms and closets tend to be on the small side even at the luxury level. Space limitations (as well as hotels that are generous with space) are noted in the reviews, but if you require extra space, be sure to make specific inquiries when you book.

It is easy to spend a fortune for the privilege to a sleep in Manhattan, but it's not necessary to do so. The city boasts many great places to stay for (relatively) reasonable rates. The best way to find them is to forsake a prime Midtown location for another part of the city. Consider staying in one of Manhattan's hip downtown neighborhoods, or in quiet Murray Hill, or in the family-friendly Upper West Side instead, where you'll almost always get more hotel room for your money. And don't worry about convenience. Each of these neighborhoods is well connected to Midtown by mass transit, which can have you to the Theater District inside 15 minutes—and with more money to spend on yourself.

Getting the Best Rate

All hotels have official "rack rates"—sometimes published, sometimes unpublished—which they'll often discount to get you in the door. Each listing in this section includes dollar signs that reflect the average daily rate for a double room at each given hotel:

$ under $150
$$ $150–$249
$$$ $250–$375
$$$$ $375 and over

However, keep in mind that rates vary dramatically depending on dates and availability. Also remember that every hotel room is subject to a hotel tax of 13.25 percent plus $2 per night.

Don't accept the first rate you're quoted; always see if they can do better. Ask about special packages, discounts for seniors or AAA members, or whatever else might score you a savings.

You might also check with the following hotel reservation agencies, which buy up blocks of rooms in advance and offer them to buyers at discounted rates. Among the most reliable agencies are:

Quikbook (800) 789-9887, (212) 779-7666 *www.quikbook.com*

Hotel ConXions (800) 522-9991 or (212) 840-8686 *www.hotelconxions.com*

HotelDiscount!com (800) 364-0801 *www.hoteldiscount.com* or *www.180096hotel.com*

Accommodations Express (800) 277-1064 *www.accommodationsexpress.com*

You might also try such online booking sites as **Expedia.com, Travelocity.com** and **Orbitz.com,** which can often score you excellent discounted rates that aren't accompanied by the heavy cancellation and change restrictions that bookings through reservations are. (Always check the individual cancellation and change policies that accompany any reservation you make, as they can vary from booking to booking—and you'll want to avoid any unwanted surprises.) Members of the American Automobile Association should also try the **AAA Travel Agency,** which often can reward members with seriously discounted rates (*www.aaa.com*, or dial the number listed on the back of your AAA card).

Never just book a room through a reservation agency without shopping around; otherwise, you may end up paying more, not less. Compare the rate to what your travel agent can do, or what you can get by booking directly through the hotel; often, you can score a better rate by calling or surfing the hotel's own Web site.

DOWNTOWN

Abingdon Guest House   VERY GOOD $$

13 Eighth Ave. (between W. 12th and Jane Sts.), West Village
www.abingdonguesthouse.com   Phone: (212) 243-5384   Fax: (212) 807-7473

Two historic town homes and two professional owners, both with creative
vision and unimpeachable taste, add up to one of New York's most charming
guest houses. Located in the brownstone-lined, boutique-dotted West Village,
the Abingdon boasts an inviting residential ambiance that combines an authentic neighborhood vibe with all the modern comforts. Since there's no resident
innkeeper, the house is best for independent-minded guests who prefer artistically outfitted, one-of-a-kind accommodations and genuine New York
ambiance over a generic Midtown hotel.

Each room has a private bath, cable TV, a private phone with answering
machine and bold, beautiful décor. Walls are painted in deep, vibrant hues and
furnishings are well chosen for both beauty and comfort. The best of a very
attractive bunch is the Ambassador Room, which boasts a grand four-poster
king, a sitting area that can sleep a third person, a wet-bar-style kitchenette and
a VCR. Maid service is a daily feature on all but major holidays. On the downside, there's no elevator, so overpackers and travelers with mobility issues should
stay elsewhere. Eighth Avenue can be noisy; choose a back room if you want
maximum quiet (located at patio level, the Garden Room is a good choice).

Rooms: Nine; four floors; all nonsmoking rooms. **Hotel amenities:** None. **Food
services:** Coffee bar at street level. **Cancellation:** Four days prior to arrival (10
days during holiday season). **Wheelchair access:** None. **Note:** Not for children.
Subway: A, C, E, 1, 2, 3, 9 to 14th St.

Best Western Seaport Inn   GOOD $$

33 Peck Slip (at Front St., two blocks north of Fulton St.), South Street Seaport
www.bestwestern.com/seaportinn
Phone: (212) 766-6600, (800) 468-3569   Fax: (212) 766-6615

Behind a beautifully restored red-brick 1852 facade lies a perfectly unremarkable but comfortable hotel. Outfitted in green and beige, the motel-goes-tradi-
tional rooms are generic but do the trick; all have VCRs and work desks, and
some have sleeper sofas and/or dining tables, others steam or jetted baths. Corner rooms are largest; ask for one with a terrace and a harbor view. Experienced
with visiting Wall Streeters who consider this their home away from home, the
staff is quite attentive, and rooms are kept consistently fresh and appealing. The
historic seaport is steps away.

Rooms: 72; seven floors; designated nonsmoking rooms. **Hotel amenities:** Dry-
cleaning and laundry service, exercise room, video library. **Food services:** Rates
include continental breakfast. **Cancellation:** 4 P.M. day of arrival. **Wheelchair
access:** ADA compliant. **Subway:** J, M, Z, 2, 3, 4, 5 to Fulton St.; A, C to
Broadway–Nassau St.

Cosmopolitan Hotel—TriBeCa   GOOD $

95 West Broadway (at Chambers St.), TriBeCa   *www.cosmohotel.com*
Phone: (212) 566-1900, (888) 895-9400   Fax: (212) 566-6909

In the heart of hip TriBeCa is one of Manhattan's best cheap hotels. Make no mistake—rooms are little and appointments are strictly budget, but everything is very nice. A pleasant lobby area and elevator leads to well-maintained rooms furnished in a pleasant modern IKEA-ish style, and each has its own tiny but pristine black-and-white-tiled bathroom. Linens and towels are of good quality, and mattresses are firm. All rooms have a work desk and TV, and most have an armoire (a few have wall racks instead). For a few extra dollars, you can have a sitting area with a love seat, or a two-level mini-loft.

The neighborhood is one of city's hippest, offering a wealth of first-rate restaurants at every price. With the Chambers Street subway stop out the front door ready to whisk you to Times Square in five minutes, the TriBeCa location is a practical choice. Services are nonexistent—but at these prices, who cares?

Rooms: 113; seven floors; designated nonsmoking rooms. **Hotel amenities:** None. **Food services:** None. **Cancellation:** 24 hours prior to day of arrival. **Wheelchair access:** Not accessible. **Subway:** A, C, 1, 2, 3, 9 to Chambers St.

Embassy Suites New York   EXCELLENT $$$

102 North End Ave. (between Vesey and Murray Sts.), Battery Park City
www.embassysuites.com
Phone: (212) 945-0100, (800) 362-2779 (EMBASSY)   Fax: (212) 945-3012

This new-in-2000 all-suite hotel has emerged from the World Trade Center disaster in top form—and as a veritable hero. Located next to the World Financial Center, the relatively unscathed hotel served as a 24-hour triage and rest area for rescue and recovery workers for months. It's now back to serving its original purpose, and it's looking terrific. Other than a dynamic new restaurant, Unity, serving upscale American cuisine, everything else about the hotel is as it was.

The hotel is ideally suited to business travelers, of course-—but the Embassy Suites goes a step further by mixing leisure, fun and families with the world of finance. There is magnificent modern art throughout. Curated by the Public Art Fund, the collection includes works by such notables as Claes Oldenburg, Ellsworth Kelly and Julian Schnabel. Hudson River views, proximity to waterside parks and Statue of Liberty ferries, and a wealth of open space lend the hotel a relaxed, artistic air that elevates it well above the business standard. While the warm, contemporary décor isn't exactly cutting edge, the hotel has substantially more panache than most of its peers—without sacrificing comfort.

Best of all is the wealth of space. Open hallways overlook a soaring, light-filled atrium and lead to extra-large, all-new suites, which range from a whopping 450 to a cavernous 850 square feet. Each has a living room with dining area and pullout sofa; a wet-bar kitchenette with microwave and coffee maker; two TVs with on-screen Web access; high-speed Internet access for laptop toters; and nice bathrooms with generous counter space. (Executive suites also have fax, VCR, CD player and an extra-large dining/meeting table.) Rates are expense-account-targeted on weekdays, but substantial weekend discounts and slow-season packages are a steal for families.

Rooms: 463; 14 floors; designated nonsmoking floors. **Hotel amenities:** Concierge, dry-cleaning and laundry service, coin-operated laundry, health club, business center, full conference center, executive suites for small meetings, adjacent 16-screen movie theater. **Food services:** Two restaurants; room service; rates include full breakfast. **Cancellation:** 24 hours prior to arrival. **Wheelchair access:** Fully accessible. **Subway:** E to World Trade Center; A, C, 1, 2, 3, 9 to Chambers St.

Holiday Inn Downtown/SoHo   BASIC $$

138 Lafayette St. (between Canal and Howard Sts.), Chinatown
www.holidayinn-nyc.com or *www.holiday-inn.com*
Phone: (212) 966-8898, (800) 465-4329 (HOLIDAY)   Fax: (212) 941-5832

This chain-standard hotel overlooking Chinatown is nothing to write home about. However, shoppers in search of a SoHo location for half of what the luxury hotels charge will consider this a find, since the boutique-lined streets of SoHo and Nolita are just a stroll away. Rooms are utterly unremarkable, and many are quite small, but they're clean and comfortable in a completely reliable Holiday Inn way. A good number of government contractors are among the guests, so the place feels like a business hotel, but Asian decorative accents and a good Cantonese restaurant add neighborhood flair. Chinatown is fun for those who enjoy the exotica and bustle (not to mention the food), but ask for a room at the back of the hotel if you're a light sleeper.

Rooms: 227; 14 floors; designated nonsmoking floors. **Hotel amenities:** Concierge, dry cleaning and laundry service, meeting room. **Food services:** Chinese restaurant, bar, room service. **Cancellation:** 24 hours before arrival. **Wheelchair access:** Accessible. **Subway:** J, M, N, Q, R, W, Z, 6 to Canal St.

Holiday Inn Wall Street   EXCELLENT $$$

15 Gold St. (at Platt St.), Lower Manhattan   *www.holidayinnwsd.com*
Phone: (212) 232-7800, (800) 465-4329 (HOLIDAY)   Fax: (212) 425-0330

Forget your motel expectations—this new-in-1999 Holiday Inn is a first-rate hotel. In fact, it's Manhattan's most technologically advanced hotel. The high-tech toys greet you in the small but pleasant lobby, where you can choose to bypass the professionally staffed front desk in favor of an ATM-style machine where you can check in with one touch; you can also download city information to your PDA at the mobile concierge or print out city info from a PC.

Rooms are very comfortable and boast conveniences galore for the traveling executive, or anybody who just likes toys. The eight-foot L-shaped workstation boasts desk-level "Plug and Play" high-speed ethernet input for laptop toters; an ergonomic chair; dual-line cordless phone with direct-dial number; and the kind of supplies you never bring but always need, like paper clips, Liquid Paper, and a Webster's thesaurus. Cellular connection services let you forward calls to your cell when you're away from your room. About half of the rooms feature their own T1-connected PC with a 14-inch flat-screen monitor, MS Word and Office applications, and full Internet access. For after-work time, there's always a CD player, TV with on-screen Internet access and Nintendo. SMART rooms feature laptop computers with carrying cases and wireless ethernet cards for mobile Internet access, Canon fax/copier/printers and other upgraded amenities, like turndown and complimentary buffet breakfast.

Furnishings are surprisingly nice, if not particularly stylish, and everything is like new. The staff prides itself on service, and there is an amenity station on each floor stocked with everything from toothpaste to extra blankets.

Rooms: 138; 18 floors; designated nonsmoking floors. **Hotel amenities:** Concierge, dry cleaning and laundry service, coin-operated laundry, exercise room, business center, state-of-the-art executive boardroom, CD library. **Food services:** Italian restaurant, bar, 24-hour room service, plated delivery from a range of restaurants. **Cancellation:** 48 hours before arrival. **Wheelchair access:** Fully accessible. **Subway:** 2, 3 to Wall St.

Larchmont Hotel   GOOD $

27 W. 11th St.(between Fifth and Sixth Aves.), West Village
www.larchmonthotel.com   Phone: (212) 989-9333   Fax: (212) 989-9496

New York could use a dozen more Larchmonts. This cheerful European-style hotel is an excellent value for those who don't mind sharing hall bathrooms with fellow guests in exchange for a very low rate. You'll feel the warm and welcoming vibe the instant you enter the butter-yellow lobby, where you'll be greeted by the professional staff. Each bright room is prettily furnished in rattan, with a writing desk and a wash basin, plus a TV and telephone (not a given in this price range), a ceiling fan, a library of books and a nice cotton robe and slippers that allow you to comfortably pad down the hall to the older but spotless shared bathrooms. The hotel's leafy brownstone-lined street brims with old New York charm, and a wealth of subway lines are a short walk away. Loyal guests keep this jewel booked, so reserve as far in advance as possible.

Rooms: 58 (all with shared bathrooms); six floors; smoking allowed. **Hotel amenities:** Fax service, common kitchens. **Food services:** Rates include continental breakfast. **Cancellation:** Two days prior to arrival. **Wheelchair access:** Not accessible. **Subway:** A, C, E, F, S, V to W. 4th St. (use 8th St. exit).

The Mercer   EXCELLENT $$$$

147 Mercer St. (at Prince St.), SoHo   *www.mercerhotel.com*
Phone: (212) 966-6060, (888) 918-6060   Fax: (212) 965-3838

The Mercer is so cool that it's downright frosty. Still, modern design buffs will love the stunning Christian Liagre–designed interiors, which are brazenly angular but comfortable nonetheless; gorgeous textured fabrics and rich African woods soften the look and add character. The high-ceilinged guest rooms are spacious and practical with extra-large work desks that double as generous dining tables. Steel carts add extra storage in the big and beautiful architecturally impressive bathrooms, which boast either an oversized shower or a tub for two.

TVs with on-screen Web access and VCRs, plus CD players, are on hand to keep you entertained (if the beautiful-people clientele isn't enough).

No other chic SoHo hotel is so well located, and no other hotelier knows how to run a luxury boutique hotel like Andre Balazs (also the power behind L.A.'s legendary Chateau Marmont). Despite the requisite chic lobby lounge scene, the air is more regal and exclusive than that at party scenes like Schrager's Royalton or the W hotels. The chic restaurant is the domain of superstar chef Jean-Georges Vongerichten (of four-star Jean Georges).

Rooms: 75; six floors; smoking allowed. **Hotel amenities:** 24-hour concierge, laundry and dry-cleaning service, business services, video and CD libraries. **Food services:** Restaurant and bar (The Mercer Kitchen), lobby cafe and bar, 24-hour room service. **Cancellation:** 48 hours prior to arrival. **Wheelchair access:** Fully accessible. **Subway:** N, R to Prince St.

New York City Howard Johnson Express Inn   GOOD $
135 E. Houston St. (at Forsyth St.), Lower East Side   *www.hojo.com*
Phone: (212) 358-8844, (800) 406-1411   Fax: (212) 473-3500

This brand-new budget hotel is a welcome addition to the rapidly gentrifying Lower East Side. It sits on a pleasing Houston Street block, shoulder-to-shoulder with both the best of the old Jewish-immigrant enclave and the newly hip 'hood: Next door are Yoneh Shimmel's Knish Shop (same as it ever was) and Sunshine Cinemas, a state-of-the-art art-house movie complex contained in a beautifully renovated Yiddish vaudeville house. The hotel itself offers similarly cross-pollinated appeal: It's ideal for any traveler in search of high-quality comforts or a trendy location at a low price——or both.

Management deserves kudos for outfitting a budget hotel so very well. Sure, rooms are petite——don't expect much spreading-out room. But furnishings and textiles are well made and attractive, beds are pleasingly firm, work desks boast desk-level inputs and an ergonomic chair, and the granite bathrooms are nicer than many you'll find in $300-a-night hotels; some even have whirlpool tubs. (Hint: You'll get the most square footage for your money if you request a room number ending in 01, 02 or 03.) The staff is professional and friendly, and free continental breakfast heightens the already great value. Dense with bars, live-music clubs, and affordable restaurants, the neighborhood can hop well into the wee hours, so request a room in the back of the building if you're a light sleeper.

Rooms: 46; six floors; designated non-smoking rooms. **Hotel amenities:** Laundry and dry-cleaning service. **Food services:** Rates include continental breakfast. **Cancellation:** 48 hours prior to arrival. **Wheelchair access:** ADA compliant. **Subway:** F, V to Second Ave.

New York Marriott Financial Center   GOOD $$$
85 West St. (at Carlisle St.), Financial District   *www.marriott.com*
Phone: (212) 385-4900, (888) 236-2427   Fax: (212) 227-8136

Rooms are utterly unremarkable but just fine at this nondescript but perfectly comfortable business hotel, which deserves kudos for serving as a home base for rescue workers in the months following the World Trade Center attacks. It's fully open once again, and just steps from Wall Street. Some rooms have appealing views of the southern tip of the island. On site is good, tropical-accented Roy's New York, the first eastern U.S. restaurant from venerable Hawaiian chef Roy Yamaguchi. Weekend rates drop substantially, and all of Lower Manhattan's attractions are just a walk away.

Rooms: 507; 38 floors; designated nonsmoking rooms. **Hotel amenities:** Concierge, laundry and dry-cleaning service, health club with sauna and swimming pool, good business center, meeting rooms, valet parking. **Food services:** Roy's New York restaurant and bar, casual tavern-style restaurant, room service, complimentary coffee in lobby. **Cancellation:** Before 6 P.M. day of arrival. **Wheelchair access:** Fully accessible. **Subway:** N, R, 1, 9 to Rector St.

Pioneer of SoHotel   BASIC $

341 Broome St. (east of Elizabeth St.), Nolita   *www.pioneerhotel.com*
Phone: (212) 226-1482   Fax: (212) 226-3525

This older, European-style hotel is as simple and spare as they come. But if you're a budget traveler in search of a clean, quiet, friendly accommodation with a private bathroom for less than $100 per night, the Pioneer is an excellent option. Both the hotel itself and the surrounding neighborhood have seen steady improvements over the last few years, and things just keep getting better.

The Pioneer is housed in a four-story walkup just off the Bowery's light fixture/restaurant supply district, which has grown into a safe and convenient hub near SoHo, Chinatown and the Lower East Side. You'll climb one level from the street to the lobby, which is older but bright and agreeable, with a pleasantly professional staff and morning coffee. Decorative painting—stippling, colorful murals, and the like—lends an attractive accent to guest rooms that would otherwise be institutional, and hanging plants add color in the halls. Rooms have black linoleum floors, mix-and-match lamps and chairs, ceiling fans (in addition to air-conditioning), and fresh and firm platform beds (which may be a bit too firm for some). Some have simple armoires, others a rack on the wall instead of a closet. Most rooms have a minuscule but spotless bathroom with a shower stall. A few rooms have no windows, but they're blissfully silent and will even save you a few dollars. Ask for a renovated room (most are). Bring your own alarm, hair dryer, and cell phone, as amenities don't go beyond the basics.

Rooms: 125 (about 35 with with shared bathroom), 4 floors, smoking allowed. **Hotel amenities:** None. **Food service:** Morning coffee in lobby. **Cancellation:** Before 6 P.M. day of arrival. **Wheelchair access:** Not accessible. **Subway:** F, V to Second Ave.; 6 to Spring St.

Regent Wall Street   EXTRAORDINARY $$$$

55 Wall St. (at William St.), Financial District   *www.regenthotels.com*
Phone: (212) 845-8600, (800) 545-4000   Fax: (212) 845-8601

The Regent isn't just the Financial District's finest hotel—it's one of the finest hotels in the city. The stunning 1842 Greek Revival building originally served as the New York Mercantile Exchange, then the U.S. Customs House; the legendary architectural firm of McKim, Mead and White remade the grand interiors in Italian Renaissance style in 1907. Its overarching neo-classical grandeur has been both beautifully preserved and smartly updated to meet its new purpose as a grand luxury hotel for a discerning expense-account audience.

Averaging a massive 600 square feet—larger than many Manhattan apartments—the guest rooms are done in an elegant style and muted palette that bespeaks refinement and tranquility, yet isn't too stiff or formal. The décor seamlessly fuses neoclassical details and contemporary luxury. First-class appointments include monster marble bathrooms with his-and-hers vanities and extra-large soaking tubs, 34-inch TVs, CD and DVD players, executive-size work desks with printer/fax/copier and cordless phones. Facilities include an intimate but excellent full-service spa. There's simply no better choice for visiting CEOs. Visit over a weekend or holiday, when promotional and special deals cut rates by half or more—sometimes as low as $245—and you don't have to be a platinum-card-toting executive to bask in the luxury of the Regent.

Rooms: 144; nine floors; designated nonsmoking floors. **Hotel amenities:** 24-hour concierge, excellent full-service health club and full-service spa, business center, laundry and dry-cleaning service, spectacular Wedgwood-ceilinged ballroom, meeting rooms, DVD and CD libraries, valet parking. **Food services:** Two restaurants (one with open-air terrace); lounge for afternoon tea, cocktails and light meals; 24-hour room service. **Cancellation:** 24 hours prior to arrival. **Wheelchair access:** Fully accessible. **Subway:** 2, 3 to Wall St.

Ritz-Carlton New York, Battery Park   EXCELLENT $$$$

2 West St., Battery Park City   www.ritzcarlton.com
Phone: (212) 344-0800, (800) 241-3333   Fax: (212) 877-6465

The reliably refined Ritz-Carlton chain unveiled Manhattan's first-ever waterside luxury hotel in early 2002, and it's a winner. The shiny new glass-and-brick Battery Park City tower stands like a modern sentry over the Hudson River, overlooking waterfront Robert Wagner Park and just a shout from the World Financial Center and Wall Street, so it's no surprise that the hotel is geared toward high-level business travelers. Due to a happy accident of architecture that no one could have foreseen in the planning stage, two-thirds of the guest rooms face away from the World Trade Center site, toward the water instead; even those with city views are far enough away from the construction to avoid the noise and dust.

You don't have to be a CEO or senior VP to appreciate the amenity-laden rooms, which combine Ritz-Carlton's classic European style with Art-Deco-goes-contemporary style, with rich marquetry wood finishes and luxurious fabrics. Appointments emphasize luxury (think Frette linens, feather beds, the works), cutting-edge technology (including CD players, cordless phones, high-speed Internet access and technology butler service), and sweeping views; harbor-view rooms even feature telescopes so you can enjoy close-ups of Lady Liberty. In consistent Ritz-Carlton fashion, the ultimate in luxury is reserved for the club-level floors, where additional perks include DVD/CD players with surround sound, dedicated concierge and private lounge with complimentary food service all day and evening. Expect impeccable service throughout.

Rooms: 298; 39 floors (hotel occupies first 14 floors); designated nonsmoking floors. **Hotel amenities:** Concierge, fitness center, full-service spa, state-of-the-art business center with secretarial services, laundry and dry-cleaning service, conference and meeting/function rooms. **Food services:** Elegant fine-dining restaurant; lobby lounge with afternoon tea service; 14th-floor lounge with alfresco deck, Statue of Liberty views, and light meals; 24-hour room service. **Cancellation:** 24 hours prior to arrival. **Wheelchair access:** Fully accessible. **Subway:** 4, 5 to Bowling Green.

Second Home on Second Ave.   GOOD $–$$

221 Second Ave. (between 13th and 14th Sts.), East Village
www.secondhome.citysearch.com   Phone/Fax: (212) 677-3161

The exterior of this comfortable guest house promises little—but as soon as you walk up the flight of stairs to the first level of guest rooms, you'll know that you have stumbled onto a nifty secret. The pleasant rooms are large enough to accommodate two double beds in most, and the terrific suite has a pullout sofa as well. Each is tastefully outfitted, usually on a loose theme (tribal, modern, Caribbean and so on). Each room has its own phone, and big TV with VCR and CD player, both uncommon extras in this price category. The two priciest rooms have private baths, while the others share.

It wouldn't be a second home without a kitchen; this one is clean, modern and well stocked with the basics: pots, pans, dishes and silverware. There's no elevator and no resident innkeeper, so the guest house isn't suitable for heavy packers, those with limited mobility or travelers who need personal guidance. But if you're an intrepid type who will like easy access to the East Village's hip restaurants, bars and clubs, Second Home is a good choice.

If you're in need of even cheaper shoestring accommodations, inquire with the owner about his fun and funky Alphabet City guest house, **East Village Bed & Coffee**—another great value.

Rooms: Six (four with shared bathroom); four floors (guest house is on third and fourth floors); smoking allowed. **Hotel amenities:** Common kitchen. **Food services:** None. **Cancellation:** One week prior to arrival. **Wheelchair access:** Not accessible. **Subway:** L to First or Third Ave.; N, Q, R, W, 4, 5, 6 to 14th St.

60 Thompson   VERY GOOD $$$$

60 Thompson St. (between Spring and Broome Sts.), SoHo
www.60thompson.com   Phone: (212) 431-0400, (877) 431-0400
Fax: (212) 431-0200

Despite its chic modernist lines and sky-high hip factor, this super-cool SoHo hotel gets the restful residential mood just right. The entrance alone sets the tone: The facade is set back from the street, behind a courtyard of birch trees and blending easily with the surrounding cast-iron buildings and brownstones.

Thomas O'Brien of Aero Studios hit all the right notes with the modernism-goes-domestic interiors. Public spaces are designed for easy lounging, and guest rooms, done in a soothing celadon-and-mahogany palette, are plush, comfortable and sexy without feeling faddish. While not large, they are well equipped, with DVD and CD players, high-speed Internet access, comfortable seating areas and marble baths that are the most beautiful in town. O'Brien's signature low-slung, wing-backed Thompson chair makes the perfect reading cradle, while the abstract photography of Laura Resen adds artistic accents. Suites add VCRs, fax machines and Bose stereos to the amenity list.

The restaurant, Thom (from the folks behind Indochine, Republic and Bond Street), has made a splash among the beautiful-people crowd thanks to its stylish indoor-outdoor setting and edgy Asian fusion fare. One of the best things about 60 Thompson is its wealth of alfresco spaces, which also include a patio off the clubby, intimate Thom's Bar and a beautifully landscaped rooftop garden. Check online for special rates, which can be as low as $159.

Rooms: 100; 10 floors; designated nonsmoking floors. **Hotel amenities:** 24-hour concierge, dry-cleaning and laundry service, CD and DVD libraries. **Food services:** Thom restaurant, Thom Bar/breakfast room with terrace, room service. **Cancellation:** 24 hours prior to arrival. **Wheelchair access:** Fully accessible. **Subway:** C, E to Spring St.

SoHo Grand Hotel   EXCELLENT $$$$
310 West Broadway (between Grand and Canal Sts.), SoHo *www.sohogrand.com*
Phone: (212) 965-3000, (800) 965-3000   Fax: (212) 965-3200

Although built less than a decade ago, this designer hotel harkens back to SoHo's 19th-century cast-iron past with Industrial Age details (including Edison light bulbs), retro-minded furnishings with a strong Arts-and-Crafts influence, and gorgeous William Morris fabrics. Still, the overall effect is wholly modern, and comforts are 21st-century luxurious. The grand staircase that ascends from the ground floor to the lobby sets the tone from the start, as urban-industrial hardware gives way to 24-foot ceilings and two-story windows.

The understated but lovely guest rooms boast a studied Arts-and-Crafts ambiance with an Asian slant. Custom furnishings include saddle-stitched leather headboards, large, functional desks that resemble artists' drafting tables and side tables fashioned after potters' stands. The natural tones are warm and soothing, textiles are plush, and soft lighting abounds. CD players and VCRs add to the luxury, while minibars stocked by Dean & Deluca and Kiehl's toiletries in the bathrooms accent the Big Apple vibe. The building's T shape gives many rooms entrancing views (including one north to Midtown that is worth the price of admission), but bathrooms are generally small. The chic clientele includes more than a few celebrities, who prefer the slightly more relaxed vibe of this hotel over the party scene at sister hotel the TriBeCa Grand *(below)*. The comfortable Grand Bar and Lounge remains a stylish hangout, while Chef John Delucie brings a global spin to the renowned comfort food served in the recently reinvented restaurant. Owned by Hartz Mountain, the hotel welcomes pets, who even have their own room-service menu.

Rooms: 369; 17 floors; designated nonsmoking floors. **Hotel amenities:** Concierge, fitness center, laundry and dry cleaning, meeting and function rooms, stylish Privé salon at street level. **Food services:** Restaurant, bar, lounge, 24-hour room service, butler's pantry with coffee, tea and hot chocolate on every floor. **Cancellation:** Before 3 P.M. the day prior to arrival. **Wheelchair access:** Fully accessible. **Subway:** A, C, E, 1, 9 to Canal St.

St. Mark's Hotel   BASIC $

2 St. Marks Pl. (at Third Ave.), East Village   www.stmarkshotel.qpg.com
Phone: (212) 674-0100, (212) 674-2192   Fax: (212) 420-0854

In a city where ancient carpet and dingy walls are the norm in budget hotels, this bright and clean hotel offers welcome relief. It is housed in a freshly renovated four-story walkup on St. Marks Place, the heart of the rock-and-roll East Village, lined with used record stores, cheap-eats restaurants and bars, and a never-ending parade of pierced, tattooed youth. Travelers in search of silent nights or grown-up pursuits will hate the location, but those attracted to New York's funky side will love it.

From the second-floor reception area, bright oak-and-marble hallways lead to sparsely furnished but relatively spacious guest rooms (most painted a pretty butter yellow) with tiny, freshly tiled bathrooms. Everything is strictly budget-basic, but even the smallest room features like-new kelly-green carpet, a firm bed, a new TV and a phone (with voice mail); nicely framed prints brighten things up a bit. Expect nothing in the way of service or amenities, but there's just about anything you could want within blocks.

Rooms: 67; four floors; smoking allowed. **Hotel amenities:** None. **Food services:** None. **Cancellation:** No charge. **Wheelchair access:** None. **Note:** No credit cards accepted. **Subway:** 6 to Astor Pl.; N, R to Eighth St.

TriBeCa Grand Hotel   EXCELLENT $$$$

2 Sixth Ave. (at White and Church Sts.), TriBeCa   www.tribecagrand.com
Phone: (212) 519-6600, (877) 519-6600   Fax: (212) 519-6700

This chic sister to the highly successful SoHo Grand (reviewed above) is another winner in the downtown luxury category. The brick-and-cast-iron exterior is right at home in the historic neighborhood—but inside, an unabashedly modern world awaits. Designer Larry Bogdanow has styled a dramatic eight-story atrium lobby—which gives the hotel an air of luxury that only open space can bestow—in one of the best public areas that any city hotel has to offer. The Church Lounge, with luxurious leather-and-velvet seating nooks, is a hugely popular hangout with a designer-clad downtown crowd.

Set along open, atrium-facing corridors, the guest rooms feature similar smart-meets-luxe modern design, although they've been deservedly criticized for emphasizing utilitarianism over leisure. An extra-long, built-in, L-shaped work desk with an ergonomically correct Herman Miller chair dominates the room, as does cutting-edge technology that includes a TV with wireless Internet access and VCR, a CD player, high-speed Internet access, fax/printer/copier and a cordless phone, plus a second TV in the gorgeous bath. A warm gold-and-red palette, sumptuous velvet, and soft, glowing light soften the look and add luxury-level comfort. The most beautiful staff in town adds to the downtown appeal, and their professionalism is welcome relief from the chic-boutique standard. Pets are warmly welcomed by owner Hartz Mountain.

Rooms: 203; eight floors; designated nonsmoking floors. **Hotel amenities:** 24-hour concierge, fitness center, business center with PC workstations, laundry and dry-cleaning service, video and CD libraries, screening room, function rooms, coffee/tea/cocoa bar on each floor. **Food services:** Restaurant, lounge, 24-hour room service. **Cancellation:** Before 3 P.M. the day prior to arrival. **Wheelchair access:** Fully accessible. **Subway:** 1, 9 to Franklin St.

Union Square Inn   GOOD $

209 East 14th St. (between Second and Third Aves.), East Village
www.unionsquareinn.com   Phone: (212) 614-0500   Fax: (212) 614-0512

This newish budget hotel excellently located a few blocks east of Union Square is a first-rate find for discerning travelers who want standard comforts at an affordable rate. There's no elevator, no facilities, no services to speak of, and rooms are small and lack anything resembling a view. But pillow-top mattresses, good-quality linens, contemporary redwood furniture, cheery autumn-hued prints and art, and brand-new bathrooms tiled in pretty Italian ceramic add up to comforts that are far superior to most hotels in this price category.

Rooms: 40; five floors; designated nonsmoking rooms. **Hotel amenities:** None. **Food services:** Rates include a basic continental breakfast; cafe serving light lunches. **Cancellation:** 48 hours prior to arrival. **Wheelchair access:** Not accessible. **Subway:** L, N, Q, R, W, 4, 5, 6 to 14th St.

Wall Street Inn   VERY GOOD $$$

9 South William St. (at Broad St.), Financial District *www.thewallstreetinn.com*
Phone: (212) 747-1500   Fax: (212) 747-1900

This serene and welcoming small hotel offers an excellent alternative for business travelers (and leisure visitors looking for a downtown perch) who prefer intimate inns over anonymous corporate hotels. This is a boutique hotel in the true rather than trendy sense; management has done everything right here, paying close attention to the fundamentals and staying away from showy gimmicks. The plush Americana-style interiors are the perfect match for the historic building. Rooms are not overly large, but the décor is extremely attractive, the bedding is very high quality, and marble bathrooms are spacious and pretty. Nice extras include two-line phones, mini-refrigerators and VCRs. Windows are double-paned and filled with argon gas for extra noise abatement. Seventh-floor rooms are best, as the bathrooms have extra counter space and jetted tubs. The staff excels at offering individualized service and a personal touch. A terrific choice on every front—and heavily discounted weekend rates make it a veritable steal for weekenders.

Rooms: 46; seven floors; designated nonsmoking floors. **Hotel amenities:** Concierge, fitness room with steam and sauna, business center, meeting room, laundry and dry-cleaning service, video library. **Food services:** Rates include continental breakfast. **Cancellation:** 24 hours prior to arrival. **Wheelchair access:** Accessible. **Subway:** 2, 3 to Wall St.; J, M, Z to Broad St.; N, R to Whitehall St.

Washington Square Hotel   BASIC $–$$

103 Waverly Pl. (between Macdougal and Waverly Sts.), West Village
www.wshotel.com
Phone: (212) 777-9515, (800) 222-0418   Fax: (212) 979-8373

This budget-minded hotel overlooking Washington Square Park, in the heart of N.Y.U. territory, has been in the Paul family for more than two decades. A surprisingly luxurious marble-and-brass lobby leads to teensy rooms that are little more than budget-basic, but each is clean and has a private bathroom. A recent upgrade in décor added sponged sea-green walls, firm mattresses and new furniture. Ceilings are high, but closet space is nil. Still, the Washington Square is a perfectly good choice if you'd rather take a pass on space or first-class service in favor of a bustling Village location convenient to good restaurants, bars and live music venues. You don't even have to leave the building for a good meal or a martini, since the hotel's own North Square bistro and lounge attracts locals in its own right, especially for Sunday jazz brunch (*www.northsquarejazz.com*). Jazz fans can also benefit from value-added packages that include tickets to the Blue Note or the Village Vanguard; both legendary clubs are nearby.

Rooms: 170; nine floors; smoking allowed. **Hotel amenities:** Exercise room, laundry and dry-cleaning service. **Food services:** Restaurant and lounge; lobby cafe; rates include continental breakfast. **Cancellation:** 48 hours prior to arrival. **Wheelchair access:** Not accessible.

CHELSEA/FLATIRON/
GRAMERCY PARK

Chelsea Inn   BASIC $–$$

46 W. 17th St. (between Fifth and Sixth Aves.)   *www.chelseainn.com*
Phone: (212) 645-8989, (800) 640-6469   Fax: (212) 645-1903

A hotel with a lot of heart and a lot of stairs, the Chelsea Inn offers friendly, simple and spotlessly clean lodging. Two 19th-century brownstones have been merged to form an eclectic mix of rooms and suites. Don't expect much in the way of décor; the rule of thumb is mix-and-match thrift-store furnishings, faded textiles, and mattresses that range from decent to mushy, all of which make the place feel more like a genuine New York City tenement than a hotel. Still, everything is neat as a pin. The ceilings are remarkably high, which adds to the feeling of space. Closets are big, bathrooms are fine and all rooms feature a hot plate, minifridge, coffee maker, a cheap set of cups and utensils, a safe and free coffee; those without private bathroom have their own sink, and you'll only have to share with one other room. The shared baths are pleasingly painted by art students from the nearby Parsons School. If there's more than two of you, you can pair up two doubles that share a bathroom, creating a family-sized unit, and usually negotiate a discount on it. In fact, Internet specials are a regular feature, and the reservations staff is usually willing to negotiate in all but the busiest seasons, so be sure to give it a shot; also inquire about specially discounted weekly rates (currently as low as $350). The front desk isn't staffed 24 hours, but guests are given keys to the front door, and phones have voice mail.

Rooms: 26 (eight with shared bathrooms); five floors; smoking allowed. **Hotel amenities:** None. **Food services:** None. **Cancellation:** 48 hours prior to arrival. **Wheelchair access:** Not accessible. **Subway:** F, L, N, Q, R, V, W, 4, 5, 6 to 14th St.

Chelsea Lodge/Chelsea Lodge Suites   VERY GOOD $–$$
318 W. 20th St. (between Eighth and Ninth Aves.)
www.chelsealodge.com, www.chelsealodgesuites.com
Phone: (212) 243-4499, (800) 373-1116   Fax: (212) 243-7852

This absolute gem of a hotel offers two kinds of lodging for discriminating budget travelers who want spotless accommodations, a dash of style and a location in the heart of the Chelsea Historic District surrounded by excellent restaurants and night spots. All rooms in the original walk-up brownstone are petite yet delightful doubles with a unique semi-private bath situation: Each room has a sink and a stall shower, so guests only have to share toilets. The entire building has been gorgeously renovated, and both public spaces and guest rooms overflow with country-in-the-city charm. Rooms are small but superior comforts include high-quality bedding, smartly refinished vintage furniture, TVs and lovely little touches like Hershey's Kisses on the fluffy pillows. Everything is like new and impeccably kept, and the staff is friendly. High ceilings make the first-floor rooms feel a bit larger.

The lodge has been such a success that the innkeepers now let four additional studio-style suites in a nearby brownstone. Each features a queen bed, a brand-new marble bathroom, a fully outfitted kitchenette and a sitting area with TV/VCR and pullout sleeper sofa that allows the suites to accommodate up to four. Two suites share a private garden.

Rooms: 22 doubles with semiprivate bathrooms, four studios; three floors; all nonsmoking. **Hotel amenities:** None. **Food services:** None. **Cancellation:** 72 hours prior to arrival. **Wheelchair access:** Not accessible. **Subway:** C, E, 1, 9 to 23rd St.

Chelsea Pines Inn   VERY GOOD $–$$
317 W. 14th St. (between Eighth and Ninth Aves.)   *www.chelseapinesinn.com*
Phone: (212) 929-1023, (888) 546-2700   Fax: (212) 620-5646

This delightful walk-up on a very busy street in the heart of gay New York is targeted at gay and lesbian travelers, but all are welcome. The spotlessly kept rooms are attractively and wittily appointed. Each is named for a Golden Age film star—Susan Hayward, Rock Hudson, Paul Newman and so on—and fea-

tures vintage poster art from the star's classic filmography (hence the groovy kit-
ten-with-a-whip poster in the Ann-Margret room). Otherwise, décor is very
comfortable, everything is like new, and floral-print textiles create a pleasant
homey feeling. All rooms have minifridges and a phone with voice mail; most
have queen beds and daybeds for extra seating/sleeping. A half-dozen deluxe
rooms have breakfast areas with cafe tables and microwaves, plus a mini sound
system with CD player, for just a few extra dollars. Private bathrooms are bright
and freshly renovated; rooms that share baths have private showers and sinks, so
budget-minded guests only have to share a hall toilet. Service is professional
and friendly, and the generous breakfast spread includes fresh Krispy Kreme
doughnuts. Ask about special multinight packages and discounted weekly rates.

Rooms: 24 (9 with shared bathroom); 5 floors; smoking allowed. **Hotel amenities:** Fax service, greenhouse-style breakfast/sitting room, back garden. **Food
services:** Rates include continental breakfast. **Cancellation:** 7 days prior to
arrival; $50 cancellation fee. **Wheelchair access:** Not accessible. **Note:** Not for
children. **Subway:** A, C, E to 14th St.

Chelsea Savoy Hotel   GOOD $–$$
204 W. 23rd St. (at Seventh Ave.)
www.chelseasavoynyc.com, www.chelseasavoy.qpg.com
Phone: (212) 929-9353   Fax: 212-741-6309

This modern hotel has won a committed clientele with generic but consistent
comforts. Locals love to hate the boxy modern structure, but it's blessedly free of
the quirks that most mid-priced hotels shoulder: Hallways are wide, elevators
swift and quiet, rooms are pleasant and good-sized, and bathrooms are spacious
and well endowed with counter space. Those with two doubles are big enough
for small families and budget-minded shares. This isn't Chelsea's prettiest corner, but the neighborhood has definitely arrived; restaurants and nightlife
abound in the surrounding blocks and the city's best weekend flea markets are a
block over on Sixth Avenue. Front rooms are brightest but overlook either 23rd
Street or Seventh Avenue, both of which can be noisy; ask for a darker back-
facing room if you need total quiet. The hotel's restaurant, the Bull Run Grill,
offers reasonable prices, a nice wine cellar and unlimited mimosas at brunch.

Rooms: 90; six floors; designated nonsmoking floors. **Hotel amenities:** None.
Food services: Restaurant. **Cancellation:** 24 hours prior to arrival. **Wheelchair
access:** Fully accessible. **Subway:** 1, 9 to 23rd St.

Colonial House Inn   GOOD $
318 W. 22nd St. (between Eighth and Ninth Aves.)   *www.colonialhouseinn.com*
Phone: (212) 243-9669, (800) 689-3779   Fax: (212) 633-1612

This lovely brownstone on a leafy Chelsea block was the first permanent home
of the Gay Men's Health Crisis (GMHC). It's now an attractive and comfortable bed-and-breakfast that caters largely to a gay crowd but welcomes everybody. Rooms are small and simple but very nice. Almost half have private baths,
and a few in the deluxe category have refrigerators and working fireplaces

(Duraflame logs are supplied). All have TV, phone, radio and a comfortable bed, and everything is well tended. A surprisingly terrific collection of original abstract art (the work of owner and activist Mel Cheren) fills the public spaces, breakfast room and guest rooms, adding a thoughtful, creative air to the place. The staff is professional and friendly, and the expanded continental breakfast is bounteous with fresh baked goods. There's also a clothing-optional rooftop sun deck. All in all, an excellent choice. Book well in advance, especially for weekend stays. Inquire about discounted weekly rates.

Rooms: 20 (12 with shared bathrooms); 4 floors; smoking allowed. **Hotel amenities:** None. **Food services:** Rates include continental breakfast. **Cancellation:** Two weeks prior to arrival. **Wheelchair access:** None. **Subway:** C, E to 23rd St.

Gramercy Park Hotel GOOD $$

2 Lexington Ave. (at 21st St.)   *www.gramercyparkhotel.com*
Phone: (212) 475-4320, (800) 221-4083   Fax: (212) 505-0535

This old-world hotel overlooking the lovely square-block that is Gramercy Park boasts mammoth rooms and an appealing well-worn Luddite charm from the pre-card-key days. With a thrillingly noirish New York vibe, famous-name guests have run the gamut from Babe Ruth and Humphrey Bogart to the Rolling Stones, Blondie and Jewel. (The Gramercy was such a 70's rock-and-roll haven that Cameron Crowe filmed scenes for *Almost Famous* here).

In 2002, hotel scion David Weissberg mysteriously leaped to his death from the rooftop garden. Solely owned for decades by the Weissberg clan—it's now under the guiding hand of David's brother Steven Weissberg, the current CEO—this grand dowager has been going strong since 1924, and continues to stick firmly to its roots. The interiors tout history over high design, but space makes up for a lot: With a king or two double beds, even standard doubles are large enough for families. Suites are mammoth, with a sleeper sofa in the living room. Furnishings are older but everything is traditionally styled, relatively attractive and comfortable. Bathrooms are dated, but they're universally large, too. Every room has a fridge, while park-view doubles and suites also have small kitchenettes. Management is currently undergoing a modest upgrade that will replace the *Starsky & Hutch*–era TVs alongside additional improvements.

One of the best things about staying at this hotel is that guests have access to gated Gramercy Park, which feels like an elite London square. The park is off-limits to almost everyone (area residents must have windows that overlook the park to qualify for a key), so hotel guests beat out locals on this score. The long-employed staff is attentive in the old-world way. The shabby-chic cocktail lounge and adjacent continental restaurant have closed, but a new restaurant and bar are on the drawing board.

Rooms: 509; 18 floors; designated nonsmoking rooms. **Hotel amenities:** Laundry and dry-cleaning service, meeting and function rooms (including roof deck), access to gated Gramercy Park. **Food services:** Restaurant and lounge scheduled to reopen in late 2002. **Cancellation:** 72 hours prior to arrival. **Wheelchair access:** Fully accessible. **Subway:** 6 to 23rd St.

Hotel Chelsea   GOOD $$

222 West 23rd St. (between Seventh and Eighth Aves.)   *www.hotelchelsea.com*
Phone: (212) 243-3700   Fax: (212) 675-5531

Dozens of legendary writers, artists, actors and other creative types, ranging from William Burroughs to Sid Vicious, have stayed at or lived in this hotel since it opened in 1884. Artwork from tenants (often offered in lieu of rent in decades past) fills the lobby, enlivening every available space. The hotel is still largely occupied by residents with an artistic bent, but about 100 rooms are available to short-term visitors with a bohemian spirit. Rooms are large and eccentrically outfitted with generally older fixtures and furnishings, but usually comfortably so. The hotel is generally well kept, but the ghosts hovering in every corner of this landmark see to it that nothing is obsessively clean. Travelers in search of predictable comforts should stay elsewhere. Still, you get more space than in most New York hotels; most rooms have good light, many have kitchenettes, some have hand-carved marble fireplaces, and walls are famously thick. The staff is offbeat but friendly, attentive and used to meeting requests that range from the mundane to the extraordinary.

Rooms: 400 (usually about 100 available to travelers, some with shared bathroom); 12 floors; smoking allowed. **Hotel amenities:** Bell service (will send out dry-cleaning, pick up take-out food and so on). **Food services:** El Quijote restaurant, hip bar Serena. **Cancellation:** 48 hours prior to arrival. **Wheelchair access:** ADA compliant. **Subway:** C, E, 1, 9 to 23rd St.

Hotel Giraffe   VERY GOOD $$$–$$$$

365 Park Ave. South (at 26th St.)   *www.hotelgiraffe.com*
Phone: (212) 685-7700, (877) 296-0009   Fax: 212-685-7701

Designed from the ground up by supremely talented husband-and-wife team Stephen B. Jacobs (the architect) and Andi Pepper (the designer), this Flatiron District boutique beauty brims with Art Moderne–inspired elegance. Rooms aren't huge, but 10-foot ceilings create an open feeling, and honey-hued built-ins that include generous granite-topped work desks use the available space beautifully, giving both business and leisure travelers the necessary room to move in, spread out and reside in real comfort. Amenities include VCRs, CD players, cordless phones, high-speed Internet access and windows that shut out virtually all street noise, plus gorgeous granite bathrooms. Deluxe rooms have French doors opening onto a juliet balcony, while suites add a separate living room with a long-legged coffee table that doubles beautifully for dining.

Rooms: 73; 12 floors; dedicated nonsmoking floors. **Hotel amenities:** Concierge, business services, laundry and dry-cleaning service, video and CD libraries, rooftop garden, 1,000-square-foot penthouse suite with terrace for events. **Food services:** Rates include continental breakfast, all-day cappuccino and snacks, and wine and cheese during the cocktail hour; room servce; restaurant and bar scheduled to reopen in late 2002. **Cancellation:** 24 hours prior to arrival. **Wheelchair access:** Fully accessible. **Subway:** 6 to 28th St.

The Inn at Irving Place   EXCELLENT $$$–$$$$

56 Irving Pl. (between 17th and 18th Sts.)   *www.innatirving.com*
Phone: (212) 533-4600, (800) 685-1447   Fax: (212) 533-4611

Romance is the rule at this impeccably run, supremely elegant bed-and-break-fast inn, housed in adjoining 1834 Greek Revival brownstones on a lovely cafe-dotted Gramercy Park block. Each stunning guest room has its own layout, design and theme, usually a literary allusion (the Madame Olenska room, the Else deWolf suite, and so on). No matter which one you choose, you can expect lavish high Victorian appointments that include well-chosen antiques and art, a grand nonworking fireplace, Oriental rugs, luxurious fabrics and a supremely comfortable Frette-made queen bed. The cream-and-white-tiled bathrooms are brand-new and beautiful. Modern-day luxuries include a TV with VCR (hidden in an armoire so as not to disturb the mood) and a CD player. Deluxe rooms feature a small seating area, and the ultra-luxurious suites are larger than most Manhattan apartments, but standard rooms are sufficiently conducive to romance. The elegant staff is trained not to say no, and they usually don't. Lady Mendl's Tea Salon is a dream come true for those who like high tea—it doesn't get any better than this. Avoid rooms that overlook the basement-level restaurant's back-garden patio. And beware—there's no elevator. Otherwise, B & B fans looking for a special-occasion splurge should be thrilled; only Inn New York City comes close *(see section "Uptown" later in this chapter)*.

Rooms: 12; three floors; no smoking. **Hotel amenities:** Business services, laundry and dry-cleaning service, light shopping service. **Food services:** American bistro (Irving on Irving), elegant tearoom (Lady Mendl's), cocktail lounge (Cibar), 24-hour room service; rates include continental breakfast. **Cancellation:** 48 hours prior to arrival. **Wheelchair access:** Not accessible. **Note:** Not appropriate for children under 12. **Subway:** L, N, Q, R, W, 4, 5, 6 to 14th St.

The Inn on 23rd St.   VERY GOOD $$

131 W. 23rd St. (between Sixth and Seventh Aves.)
www.innon23rd.com, www.bbonline.com/ny/innon23rd
Phone: (212) 463-0330, (877) 387-2323   Fax: (212) 463-0302

This marvelous full-service bed-and-breakfast in the heart of Chelsea offers a perfect blend of genuine B & B charm and real-hotel amenities. Friendly innkeepers Annette and Barry Fisherman renovated this spacious 19th-century town house in the heart of Chelsea, and got everything exactly right in the process. The beautifully outfitted rooms and one suite have been outfitted by Annette with an eye to both style and function. Every room is themed, but in a classy, not kitschy, way: The 40's room is outfitted in Heywood-Wakefield and vintage bark cloth, while the Bamboo Room is elegantly Zen. The Loft Room has a loft bed at skylight level that the sleeper reaches via a ship's ladder, and Ken's Cabin is a large, lodgey brick-walled room outfitted in wonderfully worn leather and delightful Americana accents, from Navajo rugs to vintage license plates. Appointments are first-class all the way. One of the great things about the Inn on 23rd is that it's child-friendly, and a number of rooms feature pullout sofas or Murphy beds for extra travelers. A real charmer and an excellent value.

Rooms: 11; five floors; no smoking allowed. **Hotel amenities:** Business services, living room-style library. **Food services:** Rates include expanded continental breakfast (prepared by the culinary department at the New School for Social Research). **Cancellation:** One week prior to arrival. **Wheelchair access:** Fully accessible.**Subway:** 1, 9 to 23rd St.

The Marcel   VERY GOOD $–$$
201 E. 24th St. (at Third Ave.)   *www.nychotels.com*
Phone: (212) 696-3800, (888) 66-HOTEL (664-6835)   Fax: (212) 696-0077

Generally the Amsterdam Hospitality Group's hotels are nothing to rave about, but this one is a standout for budget-minded travelers who like a strong dash of style. This Gramercy Park hotel brings high design to the people, with fabulous faux 60's Scandinavian stylings and bold geometric patterns. A teak lobby with abstract murals, mod leather furniture and a surprisingly beautiful powder blue and chocolate color scheme gives way to guest rooms where smart blond-wood built-ins make terrific use of space. Extras include writing desks, marble baths, VCRs and CD players. Considering that it's often possible to score a rate that's barely over the $100 mark, it's easy to overlook the just-okay beds.

One of the strongest appeals of the Marcel is Spread, a stylish hybrid restaurant/lounge. Chef Michael Navarro's innovative small-plates and sushi menu is so terrific that it's drawing in throngs of locals. Low-slung interiors, inspired cocktails and a savvy DJ add to the lounge-style allure. Even more coolly chic is Coal, Spread's star-studded subterranean cocktail hideaway.

Rooms: 97; eight floors; two designated smoking floors. **Hotel amenities:** Laundry and dry-cleaning service, meeting room. **Food services:** Spread restaurant and lounge, 24-hour cappuccino bar, room service; rates include continental breakfast. **Cancellation:** Before 3 P.M. day prior to arrival. **Wheelchair access:** ADA compliant. **Subway:** 6 to 23rd St.

W Union Square   VERY GOOD $$$–$$$$
201 Park Ave. South (at 17th St. and Union Sq. East)   *www.whotels.com*
Phone: (212) 253-9119, (877) 946-8357 (W-HOTELS)   Fax: 212-253-9229

The magnificent 1911 Beaux-Arts Guardian Life building boasts great bones and a terrific location, overlooking leafy, lively Union Square. Architect David Rockwell has done an excellent job of shepherding the transformation from office building to a luxury boutique-chic hotel, successfully fusing original architectural details with clean-lined modernism. Because it's smaller, the bright, comfortable, high-ceilinged lounge-like lobby isn't quite the frenzied scene that the original W New York is—which many will consider a benefit. It's also cozier and warmer, with the W chain's signature wheat grass in planters used to great effect. Off the lobby is celebrity chef Todd English's Olives, which serves up very good Mediterranean-inspired nouveau fare, while sultry subterranean lounge Underbar is the domain of nightlife impresario Rande Gerber (Mr. Cindy Crawford).

Guest rooms are done in dark, angular woods and gorgeous muted tones, with plush fabrics and aubergine-purple accents, divinely inspired beds with leather-cushioned headboards, large worktables, full-length mirrors and excellent bathrooms with luminous mother-of-pearl countertops, plus technological perks like high-speed Internet access and CD players. Suites also have fax machines and corner views overlooking Union Square Park. Service is a beneficial fusion of boutique intimacy and chain-standard reliability. Weekend and Internet-only rates are a great way to score high W style at a reasonable price.

Rooms: 286; 21 floors; designated nonsmoking floors. **Hotel amenities:** Concierge with W's signature "Whatever/Whenever" service, laundry and dry-cleaning service, exercise room, stunning ballroom, state-of-the-art meeting space. **Food services:** Noted restaurant, living room-style lounge, stylish subterranean Underbar, 24-hour room service. **Cancellation:** 4 P.M. day before arrival. **Wheelchair access:** Fully accessible. **Subway:** L, N, Q, R, W, 4, 5, 6 to 14th St.

MIDTOWN EAST & MURRAY HILL

The Benjamin   EXTRAORDINARY **$$$**
125 E. 50th St. (at Lexington Ave.)   *www.thebenjamin.com*
Phone: (212) 715-2500, (888) 4-BENJAMIN (423-6526) Fax: (212) 715-2525

The gorgeous, low-key Benjamin is the flagship of the Manhattan East Suites group, and it's a real winner. Housed within a stunning 1927 Emery Roth–designed building, the Benjamin boasts all the hallmarks of a boutique hotel, including a gracious staff. The magnificent lobby sets the tone with a tranquil silver-and-taupe palette, beautifully preserved architectural details, Venetian mirrors and a sweeping staircase leading to the mezzanine-level lounge.

The beautifully outfitted guest rooms are some of the best in town, especially for the money. They're gorgeously decorated in a sophisticated neoclassical-meets-modern style, wearing rich textiles (chenille, mohair, linen) and champagne hues. But the real story is the appointments—the custom-designed Serta mattresses dressed in Frette linens and down-filled duvets, with cushioned headboards and a choice of 11 pillow types; the best kitchenettes in town, featuring microwaves and coffee makers, and stocked with china and gourmet goodies; oversized work desks wired for high-tech travelers, with fax/printer/copiers, high-speed Internet access and outlets at desk level, ergonomic executive chairs, task lighting, two-line cordless phones and pullout undertables that are ideal for in-room dining; and Web TV and video games on 27-inch TVs. Service is excellent, and rooms are blissfully free of street noise. The white marble bathrooms are on the small side, but use space beautifully. Suites add a divine sitting room with a full sofa, a super-cozy wingback mohair chair and a CD player, plus terraces in some. The full-service spa is an attraction in its own right, as is Larry Forgione's stellar restaurant, An American Place.

Rooms: 209; 26 floors; dedicated nonsmoking floors. **Hotel amenities:** Concierge, full-service Woodstock Spa & Wellness Center with gym, laundry and dry-cleaning service, business services, executive boardroom and function rooms. **Food services:** Restaurant, An American Place; lounge; 24-hour room service. **Cancellation:** 3 P.M. day of arrival. **Wheelchair access:** Fully accessible. **Subway:** 6 to 51st St.

Crowne Plaza at the United Nations   VERY GOOD $$$

304 E. 42nd St. (east of Second Ave.)   www.united-nations.crowneplaza.com
Phone: (212) 986-8800, (800) 879-8836   Fax: (212) 297-3440

A striking 1931 neo-Tudor building houses one of Manhattan's best chain hotels, located and designed to appeal to discerning diplomats. It also makes sense for visitors who want to be near Midtown, but not in the thick of it. Rooms are outfitted in a very comfortable and surprisingly high-quality traditional style. Italian marble baths and bedside controls for climate and lighting, a coffee maker, and well-chosen belle époque poster art and vintage black-and-white New York scenes add to the feeling of luxury; select rooms and suites also have whirlpool tubs and pullout sofas or love seats. Triple-paned windows shut out street noise entirely. High-speed Internet access is a plus for laptop toters. Dining and service surpass chain expectations, as they should in a hotel that caters to the U.N. clientele. Weekend, holiday and promotional rates can often score bargain hunters an excellent value.

Rooms: 300; 20 floors; designated nonsmoking rooms. **Hotel amenities:** Concierge, fitness center with sauna, business center, laundry and dry-cleaning service, meeting and function rooms. **Food services:** Restaurant and bar, lounge for light dining, room service. **Cancellation:** 6 P.M. day of arrival. **Wheelchair access:** Fully accessible. **Subway:** S, 4, 5, 6, 7 to 42nd St.

Fitzpatrick Grand Central Hotel   VERY GOOD $$-$$$

141 E. 44th St. (at Lexington Ave.)   www.fitzpatrickhotels.com
Phone: (212) 351-6800, (800) 367-7701   Fax: (212) 818-1747

This lovely hotel from the Dublin-based Fitzpatrick hotel group is notable for its distinctive Emerald Isle personality, its warm hospitality and its excellent location, just steps from Grand Central Terminal. Kelly-green-carpeted hallways lead from the small but welcoming lobby to elegant guest rooms that far surpass the business-hotel standard with elegant half-canopied beds, luxury fabrics and colors, very pleasing and spacious navy-and-white baths, a fridge stocked with complimentary Irish spring water, a coffee maker, two-line phones, fax machine, high-speed Internet access and plush terry robes. The junior suites also have VCRs, CD players and extra TVs (including one in the giant bathroom), but they're not particularly suitable for families, since the sitting-room sofa isn't a sleeper model. The Liam Neeson penthouse offers Waterford-and-marble-adorned ultra-luxury, including many imported-from-Ireland amenities. The Garden Suites are not quite as luxurious, but outdoor patios and big, beautiful baths make them a worthwhile splurge. Check for special packages and heavily discounted Internet rates, especially for weekend stays (as low as $139 at times).

Rooms: 155; 10 floors; designated nonsmoking rooms. **Hotel amenities:** Concierge, exercise room, laundry and dry-cleaning service, small meeting room, car service. **Food services:** Wheeltapper Irish pub, 24-hour room service. **Cancellation:** Before 3 P.M. day prior to arrival. **Wheelchair access:** Fully accessible. **Subway:** S, 4, 5, 6, 7 to 42nd St.

Four Seasons Hotel New York

EXCELLENT $$$$

57 E. 57th St. (between Park and Madison Aves.)   www.fourseasons.com
Phone: (212) 758-5700, (800) 819-5053   Fax: (212) 758-5711

This ultra-modern, I.M. Pei-designed hotel is a haven of ultra-luxury for international CEOs and superstars. Pei's sleek 52-story limestone tower is the tallest hotel in Manhattan and rife with 1930's-meets-21st-century glamour. The combination of stunning spaces, first-class amenities and impeccable Four Seasons service makes this one of the city's most outstanding places to stay. Come with your platinum card in hand, though. It is shockingly expensive.

The money-is-no-object ostentation begins the moment you step into the soaring, streamlined lobby with its reflective marble floors and backlit onyx ceiling. All but the cheapest rooms are large—500 to 600 square feet, 800 in suites—and sumptuously designed in a lovely cream-on-white style that harkens back to the Golden Age of Hollywood. Standout features include lustrous silks, warm English sycamore furnishings that include an oversized dining/work table, spacious dressing areas, massive Florentine marble baths with soaking tubs that fill in 60 seconds, fax/printer/copiers and high-speed Internet access, and floor-to-ceiling windows framing breathtaking views (plus bedside controlled window treatments if you prefer to shut them out); a lucky handful of rooms have balconies, too. VCRs and CD players are available upon request. The custom Frette-dressed, Sealy PostureLux mattresses offer a night's sleep so legendary that many guests purchase them as a big-ticket souvenirs for back home.

Rooms: 368; 52 floors; designated nonsmoking floors. **Hotel amenities:** 24-hour concierge; full-service spa and fitness center with steam, whirlpool and sauna; full-service business center; laundry and dry-cleaning service; health club; extensive meeting and conference space. **Food services:** *New York Times* three-star Fifty Seven Fifty Seven restaurant and martini bar, Lobby Lounge for afternoon high tea, light fare and cocktails; 24-hour room service. **Cancellation:** 24 hours prior to arrival. **Wheelchair access:** Fully accessible. **Subway:** 4, 5, 6 to 59th St.; E, V to Fifth Ave.

The Helmsley Middletowne

GOOD $$

148 E. 48th St. (between Lexington and Third Aves.)   www.helmsleyhotels.com
Phone: (212) 755-3000, (212) 888-1624, (800) 221-4982   Fax: (212) 832-0261

A converted apartment building that still feels like one, the Middletowne doesn't have room service, an exercise room or even much of a lobby. What it does have are large, relatively affordable rooms and suites (both junior suites and full one- and two-bedrooms). Every room has a refrigerator (most have wet bars, too), two-line phones, older but nice bathrooms and generous closet space. Furnishings are older and lack anything called style, but mattresses are fresh and firm, and carpets, textiles and linens are like-new. The one- and two-bedroom suites are big enough to call home, and full galley kitchenettes make it so (some cabinets are without dishware, though); some also have terraces and/or fireplaces. The location is pleasant and convenient, and the long-employed staff is friendly and strives to meet your needs.

Rooms: 192 (includes 42 suites); 18 floors; designated nonsmoking floors. **Hotel amenities:** Laundry and dry-cleaning service, meeting room. **Food services:** Rates include a basic continental breakfast. **Cancellation:** Before 4 P.M. day prior to arrival. **Wheelchair access:** Fully accessible. **Subway:** 6 to 51st St.

Hotel Bedford   BASIC $$
118 E. 40th St. (between Park and Lexington Aves.)   *www.bedfordhotel.com*
Phone: (212) 697-4800, (800) 221-6881   Fax: (212) 697-1093

The Bedford offers comfortable, no-style lodging in a great location, just two blocks from Grand Central Terminal. Owner Hy Arbesfeld really cares about giving guests a good experience and value for their dollar. There are generously sized studios and suites with generic Levitz-style furnishings, serving pantries with microwaves and coffee makers, trouser presses (a quaint retro touch), hair dryers in the standard bathrooms and little else, but everything is neat and clean. The good space and safe neighborhood makes this a reasonable choice for wallet-watching families. Check for Internet discounts and value-added packages.

Rooms: 136; 17 floors; designated nonsmoking rooms. **Hotel amenities:** Laundry and dry-cleaning service, coin-op laundry. **Food services:** Restaurant, room service; rates include continental breakfast. **Cancellation:** 24 hours prior to arrival. **Wheelchair access:** Not accessible. **Subway:** S, 4, 5, 6, 7 to 42nd St.

Hotel Elysée   VERY GOOD $$$
60 E. 54th St. (between Park and Madison Aves.)   *www.elyseehotel.com*
Phone: (212) 753-1066, (800) 535-9733   Fax: (212) 980-9278

Built in 1926, this charming and intimate hotel makes a lovely choice for travelers who want a boutique hotel without pretensions. Styled like a small European hotel, rooms and suites are generously sized and traditionally decorated in dark woods and soft, pretty pastels. Entry halls and vestibules make the rooms feel more residential and buffer guests from hallway noise (as do the thick walls). All accommodations have nice, firm beds, well-maintained marble baths, good closet space, VCRs and high-speed Internet access. A handful of junior suites have nonworking fireplaces, while two deluxe rooms and a suite have much coveted terraces. Rooms with two doubles are especially large and suitable for families and shares; suites also have sleeper sofas. Complimentary breakfast, all-day coffee and cookies, and weekday afternoon wine and cheese is served in the supremely comfortable, Euro-elegant sitting room, which recalls the French Empire with its rich velvets and reds and golds. The service is intimate and attentive, and the location is the very best part of Midtown. The legendary Monkey Bar is hip again thanks to an appearance on *Sex and the City*.

Rooms: 101; 15 floors; designated nonsmoking rooms. **Hotel amenities:** Laundry and dry-cleaning service, sitting room, clubby library with flat-screen PC with free Internet access, free access to nearby health club, video library. **Food services:** Monkey Bar restaurant and bar, room service; rates include continental breakfast and daytime snacks. **Cancellation:** 24 hours prior to arrival. **Wheelchair access:** ADA compliant. **Subway:** E, V to Lexington Ave.

Kimberly Hotel
VERY GOOD $$$

145 E. 50th St. (between Lexington and Third Aves.) *www.kimberlyhotel.com*
Phone: (212) 755-0400, (800) 683-0400   Fax: (212) 486-6915

This low-profile hotel was conceived in the mid-1980's as an apartment building but, during construction, was reconceived as a hotel. The practical effect of this quick change is plenty of room for guests. The very pleasing hotel boasts mostly apartment-style one-bedroom and two-bedroom/two-bath suites featuring all the comforts of home, including a fully outfitted kitchen with full-size appliances; a fully furnished living room with a dining area and Oriental rugs; marble bathrooms; and large, well-appointed rooms. One-bedroom suites run about 600 square feet, two-bedroom suites a whopping 1,200 square feet, making them perfect for families and business travelers looking to stay awhile. Video games are on hand to please the kids and fax machines and two-line phones are en suite for business travelers. A number of attractive and comfortable standard doubles with especially nice bathrooms and deep soaking tubs are also available, but the best values are clearly the suites. The generally traditional décor isn't what you'd call stylish, but the comfort level is very high. Service is refined and attentive. On site is Olica, the stylish French-Mediterranean domain of Michelin two-star chef Jean-Yves Schillinger, as is chic nightclub One51. The Kimberly's ongoing promotions and package rates are excellent; almost no one pays full rack rate here, so be sure to mine for discounts.

Rooms: 186 (mostly suites); 30 floors; designated nonsmoking floors. **Hotel amenities:** Concierge, laundry and dry-cleaning service, business center, penthouse meeting suite, free access to nearby health club with swimming pool, complimentary sunset cruises in spring, summer and autumn. **Food services:** Two restaurants, two bars, room service. **Cancellation:** Usually 6 P.M. day of arrival (varies by reservation). **Wheelchair access:** Fully accessible. **Subway:** 6 to 51st St.

The Kitano New York
EXCELLENT $$$$

66 Park Ave. (at 38th St.)   *www.kitano.com, www.summithotels.com*
Phone: (212) 885-7000, (800) KITANO-NY (548-2666)   Fax: (212) 885-7100

This elegant Japanese-owned hotel is a sea of tranquility in the bustle and chaos of New York City. Botero's voluptuous bronze sculpture "Dog" greets you at the entrance—and the art collection only gets better from there. The clean-lined lobby exudes luxury in the high quality of the materials—deep-grained mahogany, rich suede-upholstered sofas and fabulous, mostly modern art. The overall feeling is one of warmth, sophistication and Zen-like repose.

The modern guest rooms and suites are clean-lined, natural-hued havens of Japanese luxury and practicality. The building's corner location grants impressive cityscape views to most. Though the windows do open, they seem to hermetically seal each room from street noise. Other luxury extras include large work desks with fax machines, heated towel racks, bathrobes and umbrellas for borrowing. If you're the adventurous sort in the mood for something special, book New York's only authentic Tatami Suite, which boasts its own Japanese tea ceremony room. Nadaman Hakubai, the hotel's elegant kaiseki restaurant, is exceptional, and the largely Japanese staff specializes in flawless service. Weekend packages and special Internet rates (as low as $199 at times) are the way to go for vacationers in search of a Far Eastern-flavored getaway.

Rooms: 149; 19 floors; designated nonsmoking rooms. **Hotel amenities:** Concierge, business services, laundry and dry-cleaning service, boardroom, meeting space, free access to nearby health club. **Food services:** Nadaman Hakubai restaurant, continental cafe, lounge, room service. **Cancellation:** 24 hours prior to arrival. **Wheelchair access:** Fully accessible. **Subway:** S, 4, 5, 6, 7 to 42nd St.

Le Marquis   VERY GOOD $$$

12 East 31st St. (between Fifth and Madison Aves.)   *www.lemarquisny.com*
Phone: (212) 889-6363, (866) MARQUIS (627-7847)   Fax: (212) 889-6699

This lovely all-new boutique hotel is the creative brainchild of interior designer George Patero, who really knows how to unite style and comfort to make the most of space-challenged city hotel rooms. The comfortably elegant tone is set in the gorgeous classic-goes-contemporary lobby, dressed in the warm cherry woods and deep blues that pervade the hotel. In the back is a delightful living room-style lounge where you're invited to pull a book off the shelf, check your e-mail on a PC with free high-speed Internet access, or sink into a sofa, put your feet up and watch a classic flick on the 40-inch flat-screen TV.

Patero has outfitted the smallish guest rooms beautifully with custom furnishings that include armoires, efficient work desks and platform beds wearing goosedown and Frette. Further in-room luxuries include DVD/CD players, Nintendo, two-line phones, high-speed Internet access and mini-bars (a vanishing breed in this price category). The sparkling white, cobalt-accented bathrooms boast double-wide glassed-in shower stalls with rainshower heads (a few have standard tub/shower combos) and Aveda toiletries. Management is attentive to every detail, so this newbie will only improve with time. Internet rates and seasonal specials (as low as $149) can make this hidden gem an excellent value.

Rooms: 123; 14 floors; designated nonsmoking rooms. **Hotel amenities:** 24-hour concierge, laundry and dry-cleaning service, exercise room with Finnish sauna, conference room, DVD and CD libraries. **Food services:** Breakfast buffet (for a charge) and all-day coffee bar in library lounge, chic Bar 12:31 serving light Thai fare, room service. **Cancellation:** Before 3 P.M. day prior to arrival. **Wheelchair access:** ADA compliant. **Subway:** N, R to 28th St., 6 to 33rd St.

Library Hotel

VERY GOOD $$$

299 Madison Ave. (at 41st St.)

www.libraryhotel.com

Phone: (212) 983-4500, (877) 793-7323

Fax: (212) 499-9099

One of the best among the bevy of turn-of-the-21st-century boutique hotels is this biblio-themed charmer, located just a stone's throw from the New York Public Library, the hotel's inspiration. The Library Hotel is intimate and beautifully outfitted in a classic-goes-contemporary style; the clear and consistent unifying theme establishes a tone of both residential-tinged luxury and joyful discovery. The floors are categorized by the Dewey Decimal system, with each room's "subject" reflected in the framed photography and books within: Romance Languages, Ethics, Botany, Fairy Tales, Erotic Literature, African Religion and so on. Would-be astronauts might like the Astronomy room (Neil Armstrong did), while those with a penchant for the past might prefer the Twentieth Century room (on the History floor) or the Dinosaurs room (Math and Science). The Love room (on the Philosophy floor) is a must for romancing couples, who can read Shakespeare's sonnets to each other. Fiction and nonfiction books covering a range of subjects also fill the cozy penthouse-level library; overall, the hotel's collection numbers more than 6,000 titles.

The guest rooms themselves are an understated but beautiful haven of smart design dressed in a rich and restful natural palette. Mahogany built-ins provide a wealth of work and storage space; bathrooms aren't very big, but they're beautifully and smartly designed. Amenities include VCRs and CD players (the full library of the American Film Institute's top 100 films is on hand for you to borrow, as is a music library), cordless phones and high speed Internet access. Considering the quality, prices are reasonable.

Rooms: 60; 14 floors; designated nonsmoking rooms. **Hotel amenities:** Laundry and dry-cleaning service, business center, penthouse-level conference room, library lounge with fireplace, penthouse-level terrace, free access to New York Sports Club. **Food services:** Northern Italian restaurant Vigneti with sidewalk dining, room service; rates include continental breakfast, all-day cappuccino and cookies, weekday wine and cheese. **Cancellation:** 24 hours prior to arrival. **Wheelchair access:** ADA compliant. **Subway:** S, 4, 5, 6, 7 to 42nd St.

The Lombardy

EXCELLENT $$$–$$$$

111 E. 56th St. (between Park and Lexington Aves.)

www.lombardyhotel.com

Phone: (212) 753-8600, (800) 223-5254

Fax: (212) 754-5683

Built in 1926 by William Randolph Hearst for his mistress, silent film star Marion Davies, the Lombardy is a marvelous vestige of old New York, one of its last genuine apartment hotels. The Lombardy is a co-op residence made up of individually owned apartments—75 one-bedrooms and 40 studios—that are let as hotel rooms, along with a full spectrum of hotel services. The superior products here are the huge one-bedroom suites, which average 850 square feet. Décor varies dramatically since they're individually owned, but almost all have been beautifully renovated, some remarkably so. Studios, which average about 450 square feet, are a bit of a crapshoot décor-wise, but owners are held to a high standard, and you still get a lot for your money. All units have fully equipped kitchenettes in separate rooms; all have fridges and microwaves, most have coffee makers, and many have stovetops and/or dishwashers. Bathrooms are usually marble and always pleasant, but not large; on the other hand, most New Yorkers would kill to have this much closet space. Other common features include dining areas and work desks; maid service is also a part of the package. A standout is no. 402, a glorious one-bedroom outfitted with marble floors, two glorious marble baths, a new kitchen and a museum-worthy collection of mid-century and modern furnishings and art.

The hotel runs like a well-oiled machine: The entire place is immaculately kept, the fiercely loyal staff is equally solicitous to residents and hotel guests alike, and management is striving to always improve an already-stellar property. Smoking is allowed in all rooms (unless the owner prohibits it), but the hotel is so well maintained that it's hard to smell a whiff anywhere in the hotel.

Rooms: 115 (mostly suites); 14 floors; smoking allowed. **Hotel amenities:** Concierge, day spa and salon, laundry and dry-cleaning service, exercise room, business center, meeting and function space. **Food services:** Restaurant and lounge, room service. **Cancellation:** 24–48 hours prior to arrival, depending on season. **Wheelchair access:** Fully accessible. **Note:** Children under 12 not accepted. **Subway:** 4, 5, 6 to 59th St.

Metropolitan Hotel   GOOD $$–$$$
569 Lexington Ave. (at 51st St.)   *www.metropolitanhotelnyc.com*
Phone: (212) 752-7000, (800) 836-6471   Fax: (212) 758-6311

The formerly staid but completely reliable Loews New York has undergone a transformation into the moderately stylish Metropolitan Hotel. The redesigned public spaces take cues from the Morris Lapidus's curvilinear 1961 architecture. Pottery Barn–style furnishings, good lighting and a stylish contemporary palette (sand, ochre, olive, cardamom) replace a dark and dated corporate look. The rooms are both comfortable and a good value, though they haven't been remodelled as of yet. Large rooms with two double beds and junior suites with queen sleeper sofas and bathroom access from both bedroom and living area are a big hit with families, as is the Loews chain's corporate-wide warm welcome for kids and pets.

Rooms: 722; 20 floors; designated nonsmoking floors. **Hotel amenities:** Concierge, business center, exercise room, laundry and dry-cleaning service, hair and nail salons, concierge-level lounge with open-air desk for "M Club" members, meeting and function rooms. **Food services:** Restaurant, elegant cocktail lounge, room service. **Cancellation:** 24 hours prior to arrival. **Wheelchair access:** Fully accessible. **Subway:** 6 to 51st St.

Morgans   VERY GOOD $$$
237 Madison Ave. (between 37th and 38th Sts.)   *www.ianschragerhotels.com*
Phone: (212) 686-0300, (800) 334-3408   Fax: (212) 779-8352

Ian Schrager's first boutique hotel opened in 1984 as a low-profile "anti-hotel" without a sign or a staff member experienced in hotel management. There's still little to give away its quiet Murray Hill location except for the limos occasionally dropping off some high-profile type, but today the staff is experienced and competent. Andrée Putman's interiors eschew the over-the-top, hotel-as-theater elements of Schrager's other Philippe Starck-designed hotels in favor of a low-key, grown-up sensibility. Hotel restaurants don't get more popular than the perennially hot Asia de Cuba, but tucked away with a separate entrance, the scene doesn't intrude on the hotel's tranquil domestic tone.

Rooms are not huge, but low-to-the-ground furnishings and beautiful maple-eye built-ins—including cushioned window seats for both lounging and out-of-sight luggage storage—make them feel spacious, and the taupe-and-black colors are serene and restful. The beds are luxuriously comfy, with 300-thread-count Egyptian cotton sheets, down comforters, Scottish wool blankets and suede headboards. Other extras include VCRs, CD players, spacious work desks and two-line phones with direct-dial numbers. The small bathrooms are a Putman signature, with black-and-white checkered tile and stainless-steel sinks; most have double-wide stall showers, so request a tub when booking if you want one.

Rooms: 154; 19 floors; designated nonsmoking rooms. **Hotel amenities:** 24-hour concierge, business services, dry-cleaning and laundry service, state-of-the-art meeting space. **Food services:** Asia de Cuba restaurant, Morgans Bar, 24-hour room service; rates include continental breakfast served in the cozy Living Room. **Cancellation:** 24 hours prior to arrival. **Wheelchair access:** ADA compliant. **Subway:** S, 4, 5, 6, 7 to 42nd St.

Murray Hill Inn   BASIC $
143 E. 30th St. (between Lexington and Third Aves.)   *www.murrayhillinn.com*
Phone: (212) 683-6900   Fax: (212) 545-0103

Rooms are small, spare and as stylish as your great-aunt Erma's house. But this well-managed walk-up hotel, sister to the Union Square Inn (*see* "Downtown") and the Amsterdam Inn (*see* "Uptown"), makes an excellent choice for travelers on a strict, less-than-$100-per-night budget. Most rooms are tiny, outfitted with a single bed, bunks or a double bed; a TV; a phone; a wall rack for hanging clothes; and a cheap set of drawers. Guests share like-new bathrooms that are substantially nicer than those in most shared-bath budget hotels. Those rooms with private bathrooms are quite nice, and most have sleeper sofas. Facilities and services are virtually nonexistent, as is standard for New York's cheapest hotels. Always ask for a better rate; management is usually willing to negotiate.

Rooms: 50 (39 with shared bathrooms); five floors; designated nonsmoking rooms. **Hotel amenities:** None. **Food services:** None. **Cancellation:** 48 hours prior to arrival. **Wheelchair access:** Not accessible. **Subway:** 6 to 33rd St.

Omni Berkshire Place   EXCELLENT $$$–$$$$
21 E. 52nd St. (at Madison Ave.)   *www.omnihotels.com*
Phone: (212) 753-5800, (800) THE-OMNI (843-6664)   Fax: (212) 754-5018

Omni may not have as high a profile as some hotels in the city, but this tranquil and refined luxury hotel is first-rate on all fronts, from the comfortably traditional décor to the impeccable service. Built by internationally renowned architectural firm Warren & Wetmore in 1926, the hotel underwent a complete $70 million renovation in 1995 that went so far as to redesign floor plans. Thus, the guest rooms are freshly appointed from top to bottom, and the rose-hued marble-and-granite bathrooms are substantially larger than those in most other historic luxury hotels. Even standard rooms are large, and luxury appointments include silken grosgrain duvets, TVs with Internet access and Nintendo, CD players, fax machines, robes and umbrellas, plus a bedside superphone that controls the lights, TV, music and more. A serene air pervades all of the public spaces and guest floors, and double-glazed windows mean that even the second-floor meeting rooms on the Madison Avenue side are ultra-quiet.

Management is first-class and Omni corporate (which manages just 38 hotels) keeps a tight rein, so service is first-rate. Extensive business services are available for corporate travelers, and the neighborhood is prime hunting ground for shoppers. Discounts and special packages abound for savvy travelers.

Rooms: 396; 21 floors; one designated smoking floor. **Hotel amenities:** Clef d'Or concierge, full-service business center, good fitness center with sun deck, laundry and dry-cleaning service, extensive meeting and function space (including executive boardroom), Omni Kids program, CD library. **Food services:** Restaurant, bar, lounge for afternoon tea and light fare, 24-hour room service. **Cancellation:** Before noon day prior to arrival. **Wheelchair access:** Fully accessible. **Subway:** 6 to 51st St.; E, V to Fifth Ave.

The Roger Smith   GOOD $$$
501 Lexington Ave. (at 47th St.)   *www.rogersmith.com*
Phone: (212) 755-1400, (800) 445-0277   Fax: (212) 758-4061

The Roger Smith manages to be frumpy, eccentric, hip and reliable, all at the same time. Owner/sculptor James Knowles has infused his hotel with a wide-ranging art collection and a truly independent spirit; frankly, it's a welcome relief from the standard East Side stuffiness. Knowles's own bronzes stand sentry at the entrance, for which he hand-casted the main door pulls. The art collection that fills the hotel stands in amusingly quirky contrast to the grandma-reminiscent Americana-style décor. Appointments aren't perfect, street noise can be an issue, and most bathrooms are older, but rooms are quite large and amenities include fridges, coffee makers and writing desks, plus sleeper sofas and pantries with microwaves in suites; VIP rooms have newish granite bathrooms with whirlpool tubs. The regular client base consists of Swedish businessmen, European honeymooners, tennis pros and low-key touring rockers who like the easygoing vibe and midline rates. There's nothing offbeat about the terrific location, however. Definitely not for everybody, but a good choice for travelers who delight in a few funky twists. Check for seriously discounted off-season rates.

Rooms: 130; 16 floors; designated nonsmoking rooms. **Hotel amenities:** Laundry and dry-cleaning service, iMac for e-mail access, rooftop garden, meeting and function rooms, car service, video library, art gallery. **Food services:** Restaurant, bar, 24-hour room service from surrounding restaurants; rates include expanded continental breakfast. **Cancellation:** 24 hours prior to arrival. **Wheelchair access:** ADA compliant. **Subway:** S, 4, 5, 6, 7 to 42nd St.

The Roger Williams

VERY GOOD $$$

131 Madison Ave. (at 31st St.) *www.rogerwilliamshotel.com*

Phone: (212) 448-7000, (888) 448-7788, (877) 847-4444 Fax: (212) 448-7007

This pleasing hotel presides over lower Madison Avenue like a temple of sleek modern design. The two-story lobby sets a tranquil tone that's carried into the compact but smartly designed guest rooms. Architect Rafael Viñoly has used space very well, with blond built-ins that include platform beds, entertainment centers, and user-friendly worktables; task lighting, shoji-like window coverings and white-on-white Belgian linens. Many guests prefer the hunter green-and-white-tiled baths with the double shower stalls over the tub/shower combos. Additional perks include VCRs, CD players and complimentary bottled water; in addition, kings and penthouse-level rooms have "sound therapy" machines that set an ocean, rainforest or babbling-brook mood. Penthouse rooms also have semi-private terraces with memorable views of Midtown.

Rates are slashed during slow periods, and some type of discount or value-added theater or dining package is almost always available (deals were as low as $169), so be sure to ask.

Rooms: 183; 16 floors; designated nonsmoking rooms. **Hotel amenities:** Concierge, laundry and dry-cleaning service, exercise room, business center, mezzanine-level guest lounge, CD and video libraries. **Food services:** Cookies and 24-hour self-serve cappuccino bar; room service at lunch and dinner; rates include continental breakfast. **Cancellation:** 24 hours prior to arrival. **Wheelchair access:** Fully accessible; ADA compliant. **Subway:** 6 to 33rd St.

The St. Regis, New York

EXTRAORDINARY $$$$

2 E. 55th St. (at Fifth Ave.) *www.stregis.com*

Phone: (212) 753-4500, (877) 787-3447 Fax: (212) 787-3447

Commissioned by industrialist John Jacob Astor and opened in 1904 when 55th Street was still considered the suburbs, the St. Regis still reigns supreme as the pinnacle of Gilded Age wealth, grace and civility. This Beaux Arts landmark is a monument to Industrial Age conspicuous consumption with 22K gold leaf, Italian marble, Louis XVI antiques and Waterford crystal covering every square inch (apparently, even the walls of the boiler room are marble). A complete restoration in 1991 ensured thoroughly modern conveniences, but the style remains unabashedly, ostentatiously Old World.

After checking in, guests are escorted to their floor, where they are greeted by a butler who will see to every need during the course of the stay. Even the smallest guest room is at least 430 square feet, and brims with luxury features: high ceilings, silk wall coverings, king beds dressed in 300-thread-count Egyptian cotton sheets, bedside controls, VCRs, high-speed Internet access (in most rooms), executive work desks with fax machines, and glamorous bathrooms with double sinks and ultra-plush bathrobes. Formal French dining doesn't get any better than Lespinasse, one of only a fistful of *New York Times* four-star winners. With its Maxfield Parrish mural and legendary bar nuts, the King Cole Bar is the most well-heeled of Midtown watering holes, and the St. Regis Rooftop is one of New York's most sought-after spaces for society weddings and other once-in-a-lifetime events.

Rooms: 315; 18 floors; designated nonsmoking rooms. **Hotel amenities:** Concierge, Maitre d'Etage butler service, business center, fitness center with saunas, barber shop/salon, laundry and dry-cleaning service, extensive meeting and function space. **Food services:** Lespinasse restaurant, King Cole Bar, Astor Court tea lounge, 24-hour room service. **Cancellation:** 24 hours prior to arrival. **Wheelchair access:** Fully accessible. **Subway:** E, V to Fifth Ave.

Sheraton Russell Hotel

VERY GOOD $$$–$$$$

45 Park Ave. (at 37th St.)   *www.sheraton.com*
Phone: (212) 685-7676, (800) 325-3535   Fax: (212) 889-3193

This serene and intimate hotel is richly residential in feeling and exceptionally well run. Don't let the chain-hotel name fool you: Offering accommodations under the Sheraton brand since the 1940's, the Russell is intertwined with New York history (in fact, the property originally belonged to the family for which the surrounding Murray Hill neighborhood is named) and has its own independent spirit—not to mention a comforting sense of permanence in a city where hotels change owners and names like hats.

    The civilized tone is set in the mahogany-paneled lobby, off which sits a gorgeous living room with cozy sofas, shelves of books for borrowing and a gas fireplace. The spacious, high-ceilinged rooms are comfortably and traditionally decorated, with swagged drapes and dark furnishings, but the tones are light and the atmosphere inviting. Features include coffee makers, decent closet space and soundproofing that successfully banishes street noise. Nearly half of the rooms are designated as club-level "Smart" rooms, equipped as virtual offices; they boast some of the best work desks in the city with a leaf that pulls out for more workspace or in-room dining, a swiveling ergonomic chair, fax/printer/copier, desk-level inputs and Bose Wave radios. Suites also have queen sleeper sofas, cordless phones and second TVs.

Rooms: 146; 10 floors; designated nonsmoking floors. **Hotel amenities:** Clefs d'Or concierge, living room-style lounge, fitness room, business center, laundry and dry-cleaning service, boardroom. **Food services:** Breakfast room, bar and cocktail lounge serving complimentary hors d'oeuvres (weekdays 5-7 P.M.) and a light fare, 24-hour room service; continental buffet breakfast included in some rates (otherwise for a charge). **Cancellation:** 24 hours prior to arrival. **Wheelchair access:** Fully accessible. **Subway:** 6 to 33rd St.

Swissôtel New York—The Drake

EXTRAORDINARY $$$–$$$$

440 Park Ave. (at. 56th St.)   *www.swissotel.com*
Phone: (212) 421-0900, (888) 737-9477 (73-SWISS)   Fax: (212) 752-4593

A new-in-2001 lobby wearing a gorgeous contemporary European look completed a total facelift that transformed the 1929-vintage Drake from Depression-era dowager into the most stylish roost on Park Avenue. The high-ceilinged guest rooms wear a similarly warm and elegant Regency-goes-modern style, with bold-lined furnishings and art, plus textiles in rich coffee tones, ethnic-inspired patterns and splashes of vibrant color. Amenities include triple-paned windows, two-line phones, high-speed Internet access, an oversized work desk with fax machine and desk-level inputs, a club chair or other seating area, coffee maker, bathrobes and an umbrella for rainy days. More than 100 rooms are one- or two-bedroom suites with wet bar and fridge; larger ones have VCRs and CD players, and some Park Avenue suites feature terraces.

Terrific accommodations aside, the Drake is worth a stay for its superior facilities alone. Q56 restaurant attracts a stylish foodie crowd with a smart contemporary interior and a first-rate global seafood menu from chef Rhys Rosenblum. Ditto for Parisian chocolatier Fauchon, which operates a gorgeous retail boutique featuring sweets flown in daily, plus a dainty salon serving afternoon tea. The spa and fitness center is also a standout, featuring an extensive workout facility and one of New York's few hydrotherapy rooms. All and all, an extraordinary hotel—and destined to get even better now that stellar Singapore hotelier Raffles is in charge. Pets are welcomed.

Rooms: 495; 21 floors; designated nonsmoking floors. **Hotel amenities:** Clefs d'Or concierge; full-service Park Avenue Spa & Fitness Center; salon; laundry and dry-cleaning service; full-service, state-of-the-art business and conference center with full secretarial support; extensive meeting and function space. **Food services:** Q56 restaurant and bar, Fauchon Salon de The for afternoon tea, 24-hour room service. **Cancellation:** 4 P.M. day prior to arrival. **Wheelchair access:** Fully accessible. **Subway:** 4, 5, 6 to 59th St.

Thirty Thirty   VERY GOOD $–$$
30 E. 30th St. (between Park and Madison Aves.)   www.thirtythirty-nyc.com
Phone: (212) 689-1900, (800) 804-4480   Fax: (212) 689-0023

The former home of the Martha Washington women's hotel (model for the Tom Hanks and Peter Scolari roost in vintage sitcom *Bosom Buddies*) and legendary nightclub Danceteria (where Madonna launched her career), has been transformed into a sleek modern hotel that is ideal for budget travelers who want a great value and a dash of panache. An industrial-chic lobby leads to smallish but quite comfortable rooms that boast a hip khaki look and brand-new everything; even the hallways have a smart modern look. Nice features include cushioned headboards, firm mattresses, good bedside lighting, roman shades on the windows, built-in wardrobes and nicely tiled baths that are pretty spacious considering the low price tag. Most rooms are either queens or twin-bedded rooms, and a few larger rooms have kitchenettes. A brand-new executive level features extra-spacious rooms with either one or two queen beds, a sleeper sofa, CD player, coffeemaker and a gorgeous granite bath.

Rooms: 240; 12 floors; one designated smoking floor. **Hotel amenities:** Concierge, dry-cleaning and laundry service. **Food services:** Restaurant under construction. **Cancellation:** 24 hours prior to arrival. **Wheelchair access:** Fully accessible. **Subway:** 6 to 33rd St.

W New York—The Court   VERY GOOD $$$–$$$$
130 E. 39th St. (at Lexington Ave.)   *www.whotels.com*
Phone: (212) 685-1100, (877) W-HOTELS (946-8357)   Fax: (212) 889-0287

W New York—The Tuscany   VERY GOOD $$$–$$$$
120 E. 39th St. (between Lexington and Park Aves.)   *www.whotels.com*
Phone: (212) 686-1600, (877) W-HOTELS (946-8357)   Fax: (212) 779-7822

Like the new W Union Square, these side-by-side sister hotels are superior to their uptown counterpart, the original W New York on Lexington Avenue. The beautifully designed rooms are both substantially larger and significantly improved in both form and function. The cosmopolitan-chic look features sumptuous textiles in a restful taupe palette interrupted by just a few sexy red accents; pillowtop mattresses dressed in gorgeous linens with a cozy thermal throw; a plush chaise for before-bed lounging; and big, bold, angular furnishings that include an oversized worktable. Rooms look the same at both properties, but the Tuscany gives you a bit more space in both bedroom and bath. In-room luxuries include CD players, cordless phones and high-speed Internet access.

It used to be that the Court was the trendy crowd's activity hub, with the highly praised restaurant Icon and the hot Wetbar in residence. But the recent addition of the W Cafe in the Tuscany's living room-style lobby as well as Cherry, a bar that serves food from nightlife impresario Rande Gerber, has upped the volume of the scene at the Tuscany, too. Come to these hotels if you want a party scene; for a more restful ambiance, try the W Union Square.

Rooms: 198 rooms, 16 floors at the Court, 122 rooms, 17 floors at the Tuscany; designated nonsmoking rooms. **Hotel amenities:** 24-hour concierge with W's signature "Whatever/Whenever" service, stylish fitness center SWEAT, laundry and dry-cleaning service, meeting and function rooms. **Food services:** Icon restaurant, Wetbar at the Court; W Cafe, Cherry bar at the Tuscany; 24-hour room service. **Cancellation:** 4 P.M. day prior to arrival. **Wheelchair access:** Fully accessible. **Subway:** S, 4, 5, 6, 7 to 42nd St.

Waldorf=Astoria, A Hilton Hotel   EXCELLENT $$$–$$$$
301 Park Ave. (between 49th and 50th sts.)   *www.waldorfastoria.com*
Phone: (212) 355-3000, (800) WALDORF (925-3673), (800) 445-8667
Fax: (212) 872-7272

Waldorf Towers, A Conrad Hotel   EXCELLENT $$$$
100 E. 50th St. (at Park Ave.)   *www.waldorf-towers.com, www.conradhotels.com*
Phone: (212) 355-3100, (888) WA-TOWER (928-6937), (800) 445-8667
Fax: (212) 872-7272

Sure, everybody loves to experience the legend that is the Plaza—but many pre-fer this grande dame over that tourist magnet any day of the week. This mammoth block-square hotel is now in the capable hands of the Hilton Hotels group, and it is as glamorous as ever. Rates are actually rather reasonable in the main hotel, considering the old New York pedigree, well-appointed rooms, and first-class dining and amenities. No two rooms are alike, but you can expect a high-ceilinged room or suite that's extra-large by city standards, outfitted in a hybrid Deco-traditional style and very comfortable. Marble bathrooms are the norm, and 21st-century touches include two-line phones and fax/printer/copiers for laptop toters. Don't expect anything resembling personal attention in a hotel of this size, but the place runs remarkably smoothly considering that it's practically big enough to occupy its own ZIP code.

Operated under the Conrad Hotels flag (Hilton's new ultra-luxury brand), the exclusive Waldorf Towers occupies floors 28 through 42. This is where globe-trotting celebrities and world leaders stay (including every president from Herbert Hoover to Bill Clinton), ushered in through a separate entrance and attended by butlers around the clock. With themes ranging from French Provincial to opulent Asian, these elegant rooms and suites boast original art and antiques, crystal chandeliers and the like, plus full dining rooms, kitchens and maid's quarters in many. The ultimate in residential hotel living—which is why legends ranging from the Duke of Windsor and wife, Wallis Simpson, to Frank Sinatra called the Towers home for so many years.

Rooms: 1,246 in the Astoria, 181 in the Towers; 42 floors; designated non-smoking floors. **Hotel amenities:** Concierge, theater desk, Plus One fitness center with massage services, laundry and dry-cleaning service, legendary Starlight Ballroom and extensive meeting space; butler service and Clefs d'Or concierge in Towers. **Food services:** Bull & Bear for steaks, chops and classic cocktails; Oscar's for American brasserie food; Inagiku for nouveau Japanese; Peacock Alley for Sunday Brunch; Cocktail Terrace for afternoon tea and cocktails; Sir Harry's Bar; 24-hour room service. **Cancellation:** 24 hours prior to arrival. **Wheelchair access:** Fully accessible. **Subway:** 6 to 51st St.

MIDTOWN WEST

The Algonquin   EXCELLENT $$$

59 W. 44th St. (between Fifth and Sixth Aves.)   www.algonquinhotel.com
Phone: (212) 840-6800, (888) 304-2047   Fax: (212) 944-1419

Birthplace of *The New Yorker* and *My Fair Lady*, home to Dorothy Parker's literary "Round Table" of the 1920's, this legendary hotel has been stunningly restored to its full glory, making it one of Midtown's most evocative and enjoyable hotels. The oak-paneled lobby is as splendid as ever, and the perfect place to linger over afternoon tea or a cocktail. Hallways delightfully wallpapered with a century's worth of *New Yorker* cartoons lead to guest rooms that are not large, but fresh-feeling and exceedingly comfortable; leisure travelers out on the town all day will like them better than business travelers who need space to spread out. Boasting short but deep soaking tubs, bathrooms have been beautifully updated without losing their period vibe. Terry robes are another nice touch, and rooms with window seats set into bay windows are especially charming. Another one-of-a-kind whimsy: The hotel's own closed-circuit TV network broadcasts film versions of Broadway musicals. For the ultimate in historic appeal, book one of the delightfully and individually outfitted literary-themed suites, which also boast VCRs and CD players. Off the glorious mahogany-paneled lobby is the Oak Room, still one of the city's premier cabaret rooms. Be sure to check out the rotating collection of Hirschfield drawings in the equally atmospheric Blue Bar with its clubby, pubby appeal.

Rooms: 174; 12 floors; designated nonsmoking floors. **Hotel amenities:** Concierge, exercise room, business services, laundry and dry-cleaning service, five meeting and function rooms. **Food services:** American/Continental restaurant, lobby lounge for light meals and cocktails, Blue Bar pub, room service. **Cancellation:** 24 hours prior to arrival, September-December three days prior to arrival. **Wheelchair access:** ADA compliant. **Subway:** B, D, F, S, V to 42nd St.

Americana Inn   BASIC $
69 W. 38th St. (at Sixth Ave.)   *www.newyorkhotel.com*
Phone: (212) 840-6700, (888) HOTEL-58 (468-3558)   Fax: (212) 840-1830

Shoestring accommodations convenient to the Theater District don't get better than the Americana, run by the same reliable hotel group behind Midtown's Travel Inn and the Belvedere as well as the Upper West Side's Lucerne (all highly recommended in this chapter). Linoleum floors and fluorescent lighting lend the small property an institutional feel, but rooms and shared bathrooms are bright and spotless, beds wear nice spreads and are are quite comfortable, service is professional and an elevator (uncommon in many budget-basic hotels) makes luggage-toting easy. Every room has bulk-purchased but like-new furniture, a TV, telephone and a sink. The Garment District location is central, but ask for in the back to avoid street noise.

Rooms: 50 (all with shared bathroom); 5 floors; designated nonsmoking rooms. **Hotel amenities:** None. **Food services:** Common kitchen with fridge and microwave on each floor. **Cancellation:** 24 hours prior to arrival. **Wheelchair access:** Wheelchair accessible. **Subway:** B, D, F, N, Q, R V, W, S to 34th St.

Belvedere Hotel   GOOD $$
319 W. 48th St. (between Eighth and Ninth Aves.)   *www.newyorkhotel.com*
Phone: (212) 245-7000, (888) HOTEL-58 (468-3558)   Fax: (212) 245-4455

Here's a very nice mid-priced hotel in the heart of the Theater District, just steps away from the Broadway theaters and hip Ninth Avenue, Manhattan's newest Restaurant Row.

A Deco-inspired lobby that's more beautiful that most (even in more expensive hotels) leads to rooms that are good-sized, cheerfully decorated and very comfortable. Beds (either a queen or two doubles) are nice and firm, the cherrywood furnishings are better than average, linens are of good quality and towels are fluffy, and the smallish bathrooms are well maintained. A small kitchenette with a minirefrigerator, a microwave, coffeemaker and a few dishes adds to the appeal, as do the video games and on-screen Internet access on the TV. Execcutive-level rooms and suites also feature luxurious king beds dressed in fluffy down comforters, a work desk with an ergonomic chair and CD player. The staff is efficient and meets every request with a smile. Many guests are European leisure travelers, which adds an exotic edge to almost any elevator ride.

Rooms: 400; 17 floors; designated nonsmoking floors. **Hotel amenities:** Concierge, self-serve business center, laundry and dry-cleaning service, self-serve laundromat. **Food services:** Brazilian restaurant Churrascaria Plataforma; cafe and lounge. **Cancellation:** 5 P.M. day prior to arrival. **Wheelchair access:** Fully accessible. **Subway:** C, E to 50th St.

Big Apple Hostel BASIC $

119 W. 45th St. (between Sixth and Seventh Aves.)   *www.bigapplehostel.com*
Phone: (212) 302-2603   Fax: (212) 302-2605.

Manhattan's best hostel is budget-basic all the way, but it's spotlessly clean, well managed, as cheap as can be (usually around $30 per person in a dorm room, less than $80 for a private single or double) and fabulously located, just steps from Times Square in the heart of the Theater District. Dorm rooms feature four metal bunks and little else; linens are provided, but plan to bring your own towels. The tiny private doubles are not quite so spartan; you can expect a full-size bed, a phone, an alarm-clock radio and a small TV with cable. Shared bathrooms are better than average, as are the common spaces, which include a well-equipped kitchen and a small furnished patio with a barbecue grill. Increasingly popular with families, who like the dorm-style accommodations and central-to-everything location, as well as international tourists who can afford better but prefer spending their money in more lasting ways, so book well in advance. Beware of the dog days of summer, because there's no air conditioning; rooms are equipped with fans only. And there's no elevator for guest use, so be prepared to haul your luggage.

Rooms/beds: 112 dorm beds, 11 private rooms (all with shared bathrooms); 7 floors; no smoking allowed. **Hotel amenities:** Luggage storage. **Food services:** Common kitchen. **Cancellation:** One day prior to arrival (all cancellations subject to a $5 fee). **Wheelchair access:** Not accessible. **Subway:** 1, 2, 3, 9, N, R, S to 42nd St.

Broadway Inn VERY GOOD $$

264 W. 46th St. (at Eighth Ave.)   *www.broadwayinn.com*
Phone: (212) 997-9200, (800) 826-6300   Fax: (212) 768-2807

Here's a find for folks who want bed-and-breakfast comforts and charm without sacrificing a Theater District location. Part full-service hotel, the Broadway Inn is a haven of tranquility and good taste just off garish, neon-lit Times Square. The big draw is the phenomenal service—some of the best the city has to offer in this price range—and the charming ambiance. The simple rooms are impeccably maintained and tastefully decorated with an Art Deco flair. Beds are firm, linens are of good quality, and bathrooms are pleasant and spotless. With a sleeper sofa, microwave, minifridge and lots of closet space, the suites are a good bet for longer stays or shares. Continental breakfast is served in the charming sitting room/lobby, where brick walls, book-lined shelves, an overstuffed sofa and classical music set a restful, homey tone. Children are welcome (a nice change from the B & B norm). Rates are a bit high in fall, but reasonable the rest of the year, especially considering the quality and location. An A+ for cleanliness, reliability and service. This is a walk-up, however, so stay elsewhere if you require an elevator. And while rooms are relatively quiet, this is a noisy corner of the city; ask for a back-facing room if you want to ensure quiet.

Rooms: 41; four floors; designated nonsmoking rooms. **Hotel amenities:** Concierge, fax and copy services. **Food services:** Rates include continental breakfast; guest discounts at two nearby restaurants. **Cancellation:** 48 hours prior to arrival. **Wheelchair access:** Not accessible. **Subway:** A, C, E to 42nd St.

Bryant Park Hotel   VERY GOOD $$$$

40 W. 40th St. (between Fifth and Sixth Aves.)   *www.thebryantpark.net*
Phone: (212) 869-0100, (877) 640-9300   Fax: (212) 869-4446

Directly across from Bryant Park, one of the city's most civilized squares, this new-in-2001 boutique hotel is housed in the majestic 1924 American Radiator Building (immortalized by Georgia O'Keeffe during her New York years), whose breathtaking gilt-edged facade has been impeccably restored. The unapologetically modern-minimalist lobby comes as something of a shock, but a pleasant one.

The hotel was conceived as a high-ticket ultra-luxury palace; after the economy downturn, the hotel couldn't score those $400-plus reservations, so value-minded luxury travelers will get a lot for their money here (often for less than $300). Extra-high ceilings, super-white walls and blond-wood floors give the large, airy rooms and suites the look of finished luxury lofts. Furnishings are bold and angular, softened by ultra-luxury textiles—cashmere-covered goose-down, Tibetan rugs, phenomenal 400-thread-count Egyptian linen—and bold, autumn accent colors. Bathrooms are luxurious in an equally clean-lined, high-quality way, with a beautiful blend of travertine, stainless steel and teak furnishings, plus the most beautiful sinks to occupy any hotel bathroom. Amenities include high-speed Internet access, VCRs, Bose CD players, digitally downloadable movies, cordless phones and fax machines. Sexy subterranean Cellar Bar and chef Rick Laakkonen's delightfully innovative restaurant, Ilo—justifiably one of the hottest tables in town—multiply Bryant Park's appeal. Expect your fellow guests to be a well-heeled mix of fashion and media folks.

Rooms: 129; 22 floors; designated nonsmoking floors. **Hotel amenities:** Concierge, state-of-the-art fitness center, laundry and dry-cleaning service, boardroom, 70-seat screening room. **Food services:** Ilo restaurant, Lobby Bar, Cellar Bar, 24-hour room service. **Cancellation:** 48 hours prior to arrival. **Wheelchair access:** Fully accessible. **Subway:** B, D, F, S, V to 42nd St.

Chambers
VERY GOOD $$$$

15 W. 56th St. (between Fifth and Sixth Aves.)
www.chambers-ahotel.com, www.designhotels.com
Phone: (212) 974-5656, (800) 337-4685 · Fax: (212) 974-5657

Celebrity architect David Rockwell envisioned this boutique hotel as an uptown version of a downtown loft—and he largely succeeded. Unfinished concrete and a phenomenal (and somewhat controversial) modern art collection set a SoHo tone, while luxe fabrics and furniture, and faultless service, add Fifth Avenue polish. The hotel has made such an impression that comedian Chris Rock quipped, "The Four Seasons is a nice place to stay if Chambers is booked."

The lobby is streamlined and fairly straightforward; the magnificent art collection starts on the mezzanine-level lounge. Each guest-floor hallway wears a specially commissioned artwork or installation by a noted contemporary artist, including Katerina Grosse, Sheila Pepe and filmmaker John Waters; some simply installed a piece, while others actually used the entire hallway as their tableau. Modeled after an artist's loft, each guest room has carefully chosen furniture and objects that emphasize the cutting edge, plus at least four original artworks. The result is a stimulating combination of rough-hewn and luxurious. Turkish rugs, mohair, faux furs and hand-painted velvet soften the look, but some may consider the concrete slabs, hand-troweled walls and unfinished base moldings a bit much. Iridescent tiles, rainwater showerheads and deep tubs add luxury to the monolithic concrete bathrooms. Technology includes high-speed Internet access, cordless phones and CD/DVD players. Service has been known to be somewhat snooty, but word is that early indiscretions are on the mend.

Another notable feature is Geoffrey Zakarian's exciting restaurant Town, already a *New York Times* three-star winner.

Rooms: 77; 15 floors; two designated smoking floors. **Hotel amenities:** Concierge, fitness room (plus free access to New York Sports Club), laundry and dry-cleaning service, CD and DVD libraries, in-room spa services and yoga instruction. **Food services:** Town restaurant with bar, 24-hour room service. **Cancellation:** 24 hours prior to arrival. **Wheelchair access:** Fully accessible. **Subway:** B, D, E to Seventh Ave. St.; F, N, R, Q, W to 57th St.

City Club Hotel
EXCELLENT $$$-$$$$

55 W. 44th St. (between Fifth and Sixth Aves.) · *www.cityclubhotel.com*
Phone: (212) 921-5500, (888) 256-4100 · Fax: (212) 944-5544

Hotelier Jeff Klein has created a boutique hotel for the new millennium. It's housed behind a discreet 1904 facade on Hotel/Club Row, directly across the street from Ian Schrager's Royalton. In some ways, this delightfully antisocial hotel is the anti-Royalton: The City Club is all about solitude rather than scene, about private spaces rather than public ones. Guests are greeted with a small, simple lobby where the adornments are limited to a floor-to-ceiling painting by modern master Richard Giglio and a beautiful but well-trained staff. A skylight peeks through to a mezzanine-level lounge, a space more suited to waiting for your driver than cocooning over cocktails.

The spacious guest rooms, on the other hand, are all about cocooning. Interior designer-to-the-stars Jeffrey Bilhuber has created a residential-restful look that beautifully blends traditional furnishings and textiles with midcentury-modern lines and finishes. A gorgeous palette—soft browns, creams, light blues—adds to the serene ambiance. Custom furnishings include a marvelous window seat, cushioned from floor to ceiling and overflowing with fluffy pillows, plus a movable table for working or dining. Plump feather beds are dressed in Frette linens in a lovely blue check. High-tech luxuries include DVD and CD players, two-line cordless phones and free high-speed Internet access. Dressed in chocolate marble and chrome, bathrooms are outfitted with a double-wide shower or a tub; the larger ones have bidets, too. The art is an appealingly eclectic mix of original modern art, old New York photos, Broadway playbills from the 50's, and framed LPs from the 80's.

The restaurant is a coup for Mr. Klein: On site is *New York Times* two-star winner DB Bistro Moderne from Daniel Boulud.

Rooms: 65; seven floors; designated nonsmoking rooms. **Hotel amenities:** 24-hour concierge, complimentary access to nearby health club, laundry and dry-cleaning service, CD and DVD libraries. **Food services:** DB Bistro Moderne restaurant, room service. **Cancellation:** 24 hours prior to arrival. **Wheelchair access:** ADA compliant. **Subway:** B, D, F, V, 7 to 42nd St.

Comfort Inn Midtown   GOOD $–$$

129 W. 46th St. (between Sixth Ave. and Broadway)
www.comfortinn.com, www.applecorehotels.com
Phone: (212) 221-2600, (800) 567-7720   Fax: (212) 790-2760, (212) 764-7481

This modest but comfortable hotel, underwent a $2 million renovation a few years back. A marble-and-mahogany lobby leads to petite but pleasant guest rooms that wear cheerful Shaker-style décor and boast coffee makers, video games and TV Internet access, nice marble-and-tile bathrooms (some of which only have showers). Facilities are better than most in this price category. Rates can soar on occasion, but rooms are usually value priced in the low $100s. Complimentary continental breakfast adds to the Midtown bargain.

Rooms: 79; nine floors; no smoking allowed. **Hotel amenities:** Fitness room, business room, laundry and dry-cleaning service, meeting room. **Food services:** Rates include continental breakfast. **Cancellation:** 24 hours prior to arrival. **Wheelchair access:** Not accessible. **Subway:** B, D, F, N, Q, R, S, V, W, 1, 2, 3, 7, 9 to 42nd St.

Crowne Plaza Manhattan   GOOD $$$

1605 Broadway (between 48th and 49th Sts.)   *www.crowneplaza.com*
Phone: (212) 977-4000, (800) 243-6969   Fax: (212) 333-7393

Towering over Times Square is the international flagship of Holiday Inn's upscale brand. Style-setting designer Adam Tihany infused the public spaces with new zest in 1999, but they're still more chain-generic than boutique-stylish. Expect anonymous but comfortable accommodations outfitted with standard comforts like coffee makers and work desks. Sightlines are one of the towering glass monolith's best assets; no guest rooms are located below the 16th floor, so most are well endowed with views and quiet. There's no better perch for watching the Thanksgiving Day parade float by or the New Year's Eve ball drop. Another excellent attraction is the massive 29,000-square-foot New York Sports Club fitness center, which features a 50-foot skylit lap pool. On the downside, the hotel always bustles with convention and group business, and its huge size can make the service slow and chaotic at times.

Rooms: 770; 46 floors; designated nonsmoking floors. **Hotel amenities:** Concierge, tour desk, business center, secretarial services, New York Sports Club, laundry and dry cleaning, 29,000 square feet of meeting and function space. **Food services:** Two restaurant/bars, 24-hour room service. **Cancellation:** 24 hours prior to arrival. **Wheelchair access:** Fully accessible. **Subway:** 1, 9 to 50th St.; N, R, W to 49th St.

Doubletree Guest Suites Times Square VERY GOOD $$$

1568 Broadway (at 47th St. and Seventh Ave.) *www.nyc.doubletreehotels.com*
Phone: (212) 719-1600, (800) 222-TREE (222-8733) Fax: (212) 921-5212

This all-suite hotel's central location at the neon heart of Times Square and its extensive amenities make it a good choice for families, business travelers and theater lovers alike. Don't expect much in the way of personality, of course, but suites are spacious, attractive and contemporary. The suites are remarkably quiet, given the location, and the ceilings are low but you don't feel cramped. Each suite has a separate bedroom, a living room with a sleeper sofa (great for the kids), a table that does double duty for dining and working, a wet bar with microwave and coffee maker, and two TVs with Sony Playstation and high-speed Internet access. For business travelers, a dozen conference suites are set up for small meetings (for up to eight) and feature good workstations. A floor of childproof suites cater to families, as do a range of special amenities, including a well-outfitted playroom, a children's room-service menu, and a staff well-practiced in catering to the needs of families. Theatergoers will appreciate the connected concierge; those who want half-price tickets need only step out the front door to reach the TKTS discount ticket booth. All in all, a terrific choice, especially for those who want their space and a heart-of-it-all location.

Rooms: 460 (all suites); 43 floors; designated nonsmoking floors. **Hotel amenities:** Concierge, tour desk, business center, secretarial services, fitness center, laundry and dry-cleaning service, coin-operated laundry, meeting and function rooms. **Food services:** Broadway-theme restaurant and lounge, room service. **Cancellation:** 24 hours prior to arrival. **Wheelchair access:** Fully accessible. **Subway:** 1, 9 to 50th St.; N, R, W to 49th St.

Essex House, A Westin Hotel EXCELLENT $$$$

160 Central Park South (between Sixth and Seventh Aves.)
www.stregis.com, www.westin.com
Phone: (212) 247-0300, (800) 937-8461 (WESTIN-1) Fax: (212) 315-1839

Now operated under the Westin flag, the ornate and legendary Essex House is as glamorous as ever. The splendid Art Deco lobby gives way to two hotels in one: the main hotel, whose rooms are situated on the lower floors and wear a blue-and-silver palette; and the tony, exclusive St. Regis Club, offering an extra layer of luxury that includes private check-in, concierge-style butler service and more opulent gold-toned rooms that feature Bose CD stereos and cordless phones. Frankly, unless you feel you must, there's no need to splurge on the pricier level. The reason to stay (besides the old New York ambiance, of course, and easy access to Central Park) is the Westin Heavenly Bed, touted as "ten layers of heaven" and offering a genuinely celestial sleeping experience in every room. Otherwise, rooms vary in size from small to spacious, but they're generally well outfitted in period style and have decent-sized bathrooms (the chain's signature Heavenly showerheads are now in place) and fax/printer/copiers.

Top-quality dining is another advantage to this glamorous address. Celebrated chef Alain Ducasse keeps his phenomenally pricey, *New York Times* four-star-winning French restaurant here; those unwilling to foot the bill can enjoy a fabulous brunch at elegant, garden-like Café Botanica.

Rooms: 501, plus 104 St. Regis Club rooms; 40 floors; designated nonsmoking floors. **Hotel amenities:** Clef d'Or concierge, full-service, business center, fitness center with spa services and steam, laundry and dry-cleaning service (overnight service available), extensive meeting and function space (including Grand Salon ballroom), Westin Kids' Club (with welcome basket upon arrival); English-style butler service at St. Regis Club. **Food services:** Alain Ducasse restaurant; Café Botanica; Journeys lounge; lobby lounge for high tea; 24-hour room service. **Cancellation:** 24 hours prior to arrival. **Wheelchair access:** ADA compliant. **Subway:** F, N, R, Q, W to 57th St.

Flatotel International

135 W. 52nd St. (between Sixth and Seventh Aves.)
Phone: (212) 887-9400, (800) 352-8683

VERY GOOD $$$$
www.flatotel.com
Fax: (212) 887-9442

The recently renovated Flatotel was born as a condo development, so many rooms and suites are extra-large. A stylish lobby made for chic cocktail lounging in cowhide-covered modular chairs leads to deluxe renovated rooms outfitted in a modern Scandinavian-reminiscent style in soothing grays and naturals. Each features beautifully designed walnut furnishings (including a cushioned bench with under-drawers for storage, an extremely clever piece of hotel furniture), a gorgeous duvet-dressed platform bed, a comfortable lounging area with a Sony flat-screen TV and VCR, a CD player, cordless phone, a desk with a stylishly ergonomic Aeron chair, high-speed Internet access, an oversized full-length mirror, and a wet bar with fridge, microwave and coffee maker. The spacious bathrooms wear beautiful Bulgarian limestone and opalescent glass tiles. Unrenovated "standard" rooms and suites won't get you nearly as much in the style or amenities departments, but furnishings are decent and spaces are huge; monthly rates are available. Unfortunately, service can fall short, and some walls are paper-thin—you can likely hear the conversations of your next-door neighbors word-for-word. Another attraction is Moda restaurant, the winner of two coveted *New York Times* stars for its robust regional Mediterranean cooking.

Rooms: 268; 46 floors; designated nonsmoking floors. **Hotel amenities:** Concierge, staffed business center, fitness room, laundry and dry-cleaning service. **Food services:** Moda restaurant (with outdoor dining) and lobby bar. **Cancellation:** Before 4 P.M. day prior to arrival. **Wheelchair access:** ADA compliant. **Subway:** B, D, E to Seventh Ave.

The Gorham   VERY GOOD $$–$$$

136 W. 55th St. (between Sixth and Seventh Aves.)   *www.gorhamhotel.com*
Phone: (212) 245-1800, (800) 735-0710   Fax: (212) 582-8332

The Gorham is far from the sexiest hotel in Midtown. But its top-notch location, impeccable maintenance and service, and first-rate package deals—which can often save you big bucks and/or score you hard-to-get Broadway tickets—make it very appealing. The spacious rooms recently underwent a freshening—new textiles, new furniture and the like. Every one has a king or two doubles, plus a fully outfitted kitchenette with microwave and coffee maker, a work desk, two-line phones, free high-speed Internet access and a roomy marble bath.

The hotel prides itself on catering to families with kids. Management is happy to supply strollers and the like. Forty parlor (junior-style) suites also have "mother-in-law" den—an alcove-style additional room with a pullout sofa and a second TV. If you're traveling with a little one, the "Baby Concierge" will supply you with a crib, a stroller and a welcome diaper bag filled with practical goodies like no-tears shampoo and baby wipes. Kids will love the video games and the "Pillow Fight" menu from which they can order up themed cases, from Winnie the Pooh to Pokemon, at no charge to Mom and Dad. Toys, stuffed animals and board games are also available.

The simple but pleasant lobby is most notable for its terrific concierge, who regularly scores hard-to-get theater tickets to shows like *The Producers* and *The Lion King*.

Rooms: 115; 17 floors; designated nonsmoking floors. **Hotel amenities:** Concierge, business services, PC in lobby with free Internet access, fitness room, laundry and dry-cleaning service, meeting room. **Food services:** Breakfast room with buffet spread ($8.50-$11.50 per person), Northern Italian restaurant, room service. **Cancellation:** 24 hours prior to arrival. **Wheelchair access:** ADA compliant. **Subway:** B, D, E to Seventh Ave.; F, N, R, Q, W to 57th St.

Hilton New York   GOOD $$$

1335 Sixth Ave. (between 53rd and 54th Sts.   *www.newyorktowers.hilton.com*
Phone: (212) 586-7000, (800) HILTONS (445-8667)   Fax: (212) 315-1374

The largest hotel in New York is a virtual city unto itself, with traffic congestion in the lobby, guests from all over the globe, a staff that speaks 30 languages, even a 24-hour foreign currency exchange office. Rooms are small, as are bathrooms, but wall-to-wall windows bring in pleasing city views, especially on the upper floors, and you'll find all the reliable mid-level comforts that the Hilton name guarantees. A recent $90 million renovation has left things feeling fresh and sophisticated, and the Rockefeller Center location suits business and leisure travelers alike. The new Times Square sister hotel (*below*) is preferable, but this is by no means a bad choice—as long as you don't mind crowds and conventioneers. The hotel plays host to countless business and society functions in its whopping four floors of ballroom and meeting space.

Hallways are incredibly long, so expect a hike from your room to the nearest elevator. Standard rooms come with either a queen, a king or two double beds. You may find it worthwhile to spend a few dollars extra on an Executive-Floor room, which allows you to bypass the throngs with private check-in and awards you with a dedicated concierge, complimentary breakfast, and all-day snacks and evening hors d'oeuvres in the Executive Lounge.

Rooms: 2,041; 46 floors; designated nonsmoking rooms. **Hotel amenities:** Concierge, theater and tour desks, full-service business center with high-speed Internet access (also available on seven guest floors), fitness center and full-service day spa, laundry and dry-cleaning service, kid's "Vacation Station" in summer, meeting and function rooms. **Food Services:** Two restaurants (one Italian, one American), two bars, room service. **Cancellation:** 24 hours prior to arrival. **Wheelchair access:** Fully accessible. **Subway:** B, D, E to Seventh Ave.

Hilton Times Square   EXCELLENT $$$

234 W. 42nd St. (between Broadway and Eighth Ave.)
www.timessquare.hilton.com
Phone: (212) 840-8222, (800) HILTONS (445-8667)   Fax: (212) 840-5516

This new-in-2000 Hilton gracefully rises above the clamor of Times Square, thanks to clever design that puts all guest rooms above the 22nd floor. As a result, even the cheapest room is peacefully quiet and with a great view. As soon as you enter the 21st-story Sky Lobby, you'll realize that this isn't just another Hilton. Co-opted from the pervasive boutique-hotel movement is a living-room-style lobby with extra-high ceilings, cozy seating nooks, original contemporary art, a chic open bar, a stylish restaurant from celebrity chef Larry Forgione and a pervasive air of sophistication. Guest accommodations surpass their chain-hotel status with larger-than-standard rooms that host a king or two double beds, smart décor featuring blond wood furnishings and an attractive natural palette, original art on the walls, an easy chair with ottoman, a generous work desk, expansive marble counters in the spacious bathrooms, and technology that includes high-speed Internet access, desk-level inputs and CD players. Suites are especially comfortable and stylish, and make a worthy splurge.

Rooms: 444; 44 floors (hotel on floors 21-44); designated nonsmoking floors. **Hotel amenities:** Concierge, business center, secretarial services, fitness room, laundry and dry-cleaning service, kid's "Vacation Station," meeting and function space. **Food services:** Above restaurant, Pinnacle lobby bar, 24-hour room service. **Cancellation:** 24 hours prior to arrival. **Wheelchair access:** Fully accessible. **Subway:** A, C, E, N, Q, R, S, W, 1, 2, 3, 7, 9 to 42nd St.

Hotel Casablanca

EXCELLENT $$–$$$

147 W. 43rd St. (east of Broadway) *www.casablancahotel.com*
Phone: (212) 869-1212, (888) 922-7225 Fax: (212) 391-7585

Thanks to a designer with a deft touch and an eye for style, this Moroccan-spiced hotel avoids the kitsch in favor of a sexy, exotic look that's downright enchanting. The Casablanca is so welcoming and tranquil that it's hard to believe you're in the eye of the Times Square storm. Rooms are not large, but high-quality details—including polished rattan furnishings, Murano glass light fixtures, gorgeous Andalusian tile in the bathrooms (which have either a tub or an oversized shower), North African art, two-line phones, VCRs, CD players and ceiling fans—speak to the care that has gone into this place. While spaces are small, they're just fine for two—and the Casablanca suits a romantic mood.

The second floor is home to Rick's Cafe, an extremely inviting lounge with a serve-yourself cappuccino machine, a roaring fireplace in winter and a small alfresco patio in warmer months. You also won't encounter many warmer hotel staffs, and there's no better perch from which to watch the ball drop on New Year's Eve. Check for weekend, seasonal and Internet specials (as low as $149).

Rooms: 48; six floors; designated nonsmoking floors. **Hotel amenities:** Business center, free use of nearby New York Sports Club, laundry and dry-cleaning service, state-of-the-art conference room, video library. **Food services:** Rates include continental breakfast, all-day cappuccino at Rick's Cafe, and weekday wine and cheese. **Cancellation:** 24 hours prior to arrival. **Wheelchair access:** ADA compliant. **Subway:** B, D, F, N, Q, R, S, V, W, 1, 2, 3, 7, 9 to 42nd St.

Hotel Edison

BASIC $$

228 W. 47th St. (between Broadway and Eighth Ave.) *www.edisonhotelnyc.com*
Phone: (212) 840-5000, (800) 637-7070 Fax: (212) 596-6850

Located in the heart of the Theater District since it opened in 1931, the Edison has long been a beacon for budget-minded travelers looking for a central location. Unfortunately, popularity seems to have gone to its head—this mammoth hotel has raised its rates substantially in the last few years. Still, it continues to be a good choice for travelers who want to be in the heart of it all. Rooms don't even register on the personality meter—think run-of-the-mill motor lodge and you'll get the picture—but they're reasonably comfortable and very well kept. Most double rooms feature two twins or a full bed, but there are some queens; request one at booking and show up early in the day for your best shot at one. Quad rooms suit families well. Off the grand, block-long, Art Deco–muraled lobby is the perennially popular—and perennially cheap—Cafe Edison, a Polish deli and de facto canteen for up-and-coming theater types. Service is virtually nonexistent, so don't expect much.

Rooms: 850; 22 floors; designated nonsmoking rooms. **Hotel amenities:** Theater/transportation desk, salon, laundry and dry-cleaning service, exercise room. **Food services:** Two restaurants (one Polish deli, one continental), bar. **Cancella-**

tion: 24 hours prior to arrival. **Wheelchair access:** Fully accessible. **Subway:** A, C, E, N, Q, R, S, W, 1, 2, 3, 7, 9 to 42nd St.

Hotel Metro   VERY GOOD $$

45 W. 35th St. (between Fifth and Sixth Aves.)   *www.hotelmetronyc.com*
Phone: (212) 947-2500, (800) 356-3870   Fax: (212) 279-1310

The Metro is Midtown's best affordable hotel, period. The entire hotel brims with bright and jaunty Art Deco style, and rooms are larger and better-outfitted than others at this price. First-quality comforts include attractive neo-Deco furniture, fluffy pillows and towels, and small but beautifully appointed marble bathrooms, most with an oversized shower stall (junior suites have whirlpool tubs). Everything is spotless, and beautifully framed black-and-white photos add a touch of glamour. The Metro comes to the rescue of moderate-income families with the clever family room, a two-room suite that has a second bedroom in lieu of a sitting area. Rooms with two doubles do the trick for families on a budget.

The lobby lounge is especially comfortable and inviting, as is the library-style back lounge. Be sure to head up to the rooftop terrace on pleasant days, where you can enjoy one of the most breathtaking perspectives of the Empire State Building. The Metro Grill restaurant is surprisingly stylish and good. Despite the low rates, the hotel is very popular with the fashion and media crowds, who know a good value when they see one.

Rooms: 179; 13 floors; designated nonsmoking rooms. **Hotel amenities:** Fitness room, laundry and dry-cleaning service, meeting room. **Food services:** Restaurant and bar, alfresco rooftop bar weekdays in summer, room service; rates include continental breakfast. **Cancellation:** 4 P.M. day prior to arrival. **Wheelchair access:** Accessible. **Subway:** B, D, F, N, Q, R, S, V, W to 34th St.

Hudson   VERY GOOD $$

356 W. 58th St. (between Eighth and Ninth Aves.)
www.hudsonhotel.com, www.ianschragerhotels.com
Phone: (212) 554-6000 (800) 444-4786   Fax: (212) 554-6054

Many love the Hudson, but it is not for everybody. The newest creation from the team of Ian Schrager (owner, and the man behind the entire boutique hotel movement) and designer Philippe Starck is less about service than scene.

With the Hudson, Schrager has transformed an unhip block of 58th Street into Scene Central, attracting star-studded events and premier parties to its wealth of riotously designed public spaces, including the ivy-draped lobby, the second-level Private Park deck and the 15th-floor Sky Terrace (two of the best alfresco spaces in the city), and the white-hot Hudson Bar with its glowing floor and Francesco Clemente-frescoed ceiling. These spaces often overflow with revelers, so you must love a party to enjoy the Hudson.

Schrager made big news by pricing the smallest guest rooms at just $95. These tiny doubles are so small that they look like they could've been airlifted from a cruise ship, or Tokyo. In fact, even the pricier doubles are small, so if you're a heavy packer or need space to spread out, stay elsewhere. But style hounds will prize the beauty and efficiency of Starck's design. Rooms were modeled on the retro-romantic idea of the early 20th-century ocean liner, with rich detailing that includes African Makore paneling, hardwood floors, white-leather steamer trunk upholstery, and white-on-white beds dressed in down and 300-count Egyptian cotton, plus tiny but gorgeous white-marble baths. Technology includes a CD player, satellite radio, two-line phones and high-speed Internet access. Expect zero in the way of personal attention.

Rooms: 1,000; 24 floors; designated nonsmoking rooms. **Hotel amenities:** 24-hour concierge, fitness center, business center, laundry and dry-cleaning service, indoor and outdoor event space, state-of-the-art conference center, welcome gift for kids, in-room spa services. **Food services:** Hudson Cafeteria restaurant, Hudson Bar, library lounge with cognac/brandy bar, 24-hour room service. **Cancellation:** Before 3 P.M. day prior to arrival. **Wheelchair access:** Not accessible. **Subway:** A, B, C, D, 1, 9 to 59th St.

The Iroquois New York   GOOD $$$–$$$$

49 W. 44th St. (between Fifth and Sixth Aves.)   *www.iroquoisny.com*
Phone: (212) 840-3080, (800) 332-7220   Fax: (212) 398-1754, (212) 719-0006

For those of you who like the intimacy a boutique hotel can offer but prefer to pass on the highbrow modernism that seems to go hand-in-hand with the concept these days, there's the Iroquois. This understated hotel is a favorite among business and leisure travelers beccause of its domestic, clubby ambiance.

The Iroquois's rooms and suites are outfitted in a traditional French townhouse style, in a soft color scheme of celadon, taupe, rose and cream. Nice touches include jacquard textiles, 300-count Frette linens and robes, CD player, TV with VCR and video games, two-line phones and Italian marble bath. Rooms are too small for the money, though, even in the deluxe category. About half of the rooms have an executive-size work desk with desk-level jacks, so request one when booking. Rack rates are ridiculously high, but Internet and seasonal specials can lower rates appreciably (as low as $189).

The cozy James Dean Lounge, named for the hotel's most famous resident (1950-53) makes a great place to kick back with a cocktail. Dinner at intimate, elegant Triomphe, chef Steven Zobel's *New York Times* two-star winner, is a must.

Rooms: 114; 12 floors; designated nonsmoking floors. **Hotel amenities:** 24-hour concierge, fitness room with Finnish sauna, business center, two library-style lounges (one with PC with free Internet access), laundry and dry-cleaning service, meeting and function rooms, video library. **Food services:** Triomphe restaurant, James Dean Lounge, 24-hour room service. **Cancellation:** Before 3 P.M. day prior to arrival. **Wheelchair access:** ADA compliant. **Subway:** B, D, F, S, V to 42nd St.

Le Parker Meridien   EXTRAORDINARY $$$$

118 W. 57th St. (between Sixth and Seventh Aves.)   *www.parkermeridien.com*
Phone: (212) 245-5000, (800) 543-4300   Fax: (212) 307-1776

The Parker may be the most successful hotel in New York at fusing chic modern style with classic, full-service functionality. The attitude embodied in their tagline—"Uptown. Not Uptight"—immediately apparent in the soaring neo-classical lobby, a stage set for classic modern furnishings, pinwheel art from Brit bad-boy Damien Hirst and a hip staff all dressed in one color. The hotel over-flows with top-notch facilities, including a massive 17,000-square-foot health club and spa, a glass-enclosed penthouse-level swimming pool, two terrific restaurants—high-design Norma's for all-day gourmet breakfast and charming Seppi's for Alsatian French—and a Jetsons-inspired cocktail lounge. Two concierges on staff have Clef d'Or designation, so service is first-rate, and the Parker is legendary for being the most pet-friendly hotel in town.

Rooms are spacious and outfitted in chic Scandinavian-modern style, in blond woods and warm blue and ecru textiles. Features include comfy platform feather beds, extra-large worktables with ergonomically correct (and beautiful) Aeron chairs and desk-level inputs, plus a wealth of technology that includes a 32-inch TV with video games, DVD/CD player and VCR, cordless phones and high-speed Internet access. Bathrooms wear warm slate-gray tile and good mir-rors. Junior suites are beautifully configured for work and play, with a cozy seat-ing area with pullout sofa, extra work space and a swivel entertainment center that caters to both living area and bedroom. Specials abound (as low as $169).

Rooms: 730; 41 floors; designated nonsmoking floors. **Hotel amenities:** Clefs d'Or concierge, full-service business center, 15,000-square-foot Gravity fitness center and spa, penthouse-level pool, laundry and dry-cleaning service, meeting and function rooms, complimentary weekday transportation to Wall St. **Food services:** Two restaurants, Jack's cocktail lounge, 24-hour room service. **Cancel-lation:** Before 3 P.M. day before arrival. **Wheelchair access:** Fully accessible. **Subway:** F, N, R, Q, W to 57th St.

The Mansfield   GOOD $$–$$$

12 W. 44th St. (between Fifth and Sixth Aves.)   *www.mansfieldhotel.com*
Phone: (212) 944-6050, (877) 847-4444, (800) 255-5167
Fax: (212) 894-5220, (212) 764-4477

The Mansfield exemplifies how distinctive a small hotel can be. This 1905 hotel beautifully fuses romance and modernism in rooms that are very inviting despite their small size. The public spaces are dressed mainly in period style, with their original terrazzo floors and mahogany balustrades beautifully main-tained. A more heavily modern fusion look takes over in the rooms, where nat-ural-fiber rugs cover ebony-stained floors, contemporary metal-mesh sleigh beds wear gorgeous Belgian linens, and bathrooms are stylishly updated with lime-stone and stainless steel, while framed prints and wood Venetian blinds keep a nostalgic cast. Nice plusses include VCRs and CD players.

A lovely fireplace-lit library doubles as a breakfast room and all-day lounge for serve-yourself cappuccino and tea. Stylish M Bar makes a romantic cocktail spot. Management is thoughtful and keeps the place in excellent shape. Rack rates are too high, but discounts are often available, so always ask.

Rooms: 124; 12 floors; designated nonsmoking floors. **Hotel amenities:** Fax ser-vice, laundry and dry cleaning, small meeting room, video and CD libraries. **Food services:** M Bar with light menu, lounge with continental or full breakfast (for a charge) and complimentary cappuccino, tea and cookies; 24-hour room service. **Cancellation:** Before 3 P.M. day prior to arrival. **Wheelchair access:** Not accessible. **Subway:** B, D, F, S, V to 42nd St.

Millennium Broadway
VERY GOOD $$$$

145 W. 44th St. (between Broadway and Sixth Ave.) *www.millennium-hotels.com*
Phone: (212) 768-4400, (800) 622-5569   Fax: (212) 768-0847

The Millennium is built for business, but it's ideal for any visitor who wants an attractive, well-mannered hotel in the heart of the Theater District. A vast, mahogany-and-marble lobby leads to the original Millennium rooms, in the main building. They are large and attractively outfitted in a smart Art Deco style, with rich red mahogany and black lacquer furnishings; good-quality mattresses, comforters and textiles; comfy streamlined club chairs; two-line phones and spacious marble baths. But the real perks come in the Premier tower, built from scratch in 1999. These designer rooms manage to combine sleek design, coziness and 21st-century technology in one beautiful package. White sycamore predominates, giving the rooms a feeling of openness and light, accented by green glass and natural-fiber textiles (such as a sumptuous merino wool throw). The Premier tower is not as tall as the Millennium, so the views are not as good, and some of the closets are small—but bathrooms are big and beautiful, and the custom bedding is heaven-sent. Premier guests also have access to their own lounge with 24-hour dedicated concierge and food service, plus a flat-screen TV.

Rack rates are high at the Millennium, but one of its greatest appeals are terrific package rates—especially on weekends—so be sure to inquire.

Rooms: 750; 52 floors (22 floors in Premier tower); designated nonsmoking floors. **Hotel amenities:** Concierge, fitness center with sauna, full-service business center with secretarial services, laundry and dry-cleaning service, 110,000-square-foot Millennium Conference Center with meeting and function rooms, restored 1903 Hudson Theatre for presentations and events. **Food services:** Charlotte restaurant (celebrated for its weekend brunch), cocktail lounge, room service. **Cancellation:** 24 hours prior to arrival. **Wheelchair access:** ADA compliant. **Subway:** B, D, F, N, Q, R, S, V, W, 1, 2, 3, 7, 9 to 42nd St.

The Muse
EXCELLENT $$$

130 W. 46th St. (between Fifth and Sixth Aves.)   *www.themusehotel.com*
Phone: (212) 485-2400, (877) NYC-MUSE (692-6873)   Fax: (212) 485-2900

With its emphasis on both comfort and functionality, the Muse is ideal for travelers who want the tone and service boutique hotels can offer but find no appeal in their often steely and unwelcoming modern design (and attitude). A modern sculptural exterior gives way to a warm, wood-paneled lobby where management has done away with the traditional front desk in favor of full concierge service that makes everyone feel like a VIP. After a welcoming hassle-free check-in, you'll be led to your inviting room, which features modern furnishings in warm woods with classic lines. Bathrooms are handsome and well outfitted. Perks include plump feather beds and duvets (hand-screened by a contemporary artist in warm colors), CD players, high-speed Internet access, cordless phones, coffee makers and business cards personalized with your in-house direct-dial number; select rooms also have DVD players, wide-screen TVs, exercise equipment and desktop computers. Service is excellent. Pets are warmly welcomed.

Don't miss the gorgeous David Rockwell-designed District, a stellar New American brasserie. All in all, a hidden gem that's well worth seeking out; value-added packages are usually available.

Rooms: 200; 19 floors; three designated smoking floors. **Hotel amenities:** Concierge, business services, fitness room, in-room spa services, laundry and dry-cleaning service, meeting rooms. **Food services:** District restaurant and bar, room service. **Cancellation:** 24 hours prior to arrival. **Wheelchair access:** ADA compliant. **Subway:** B, D, F, V to 47th-50th Sts.

New York Marriott Marquis   VERY GOOD $$$

1535 Broadway (between 45th and 46th Sts.)   *www.marriott.com*
Phone: (212) 398-1900, (800) 843-4898   Fax: (212) 704-8930

This hulking monolith has a look somewhere between a convention hall and a parking garage. It takes a good 10 minutes to ascend a variety of escalators and always-packed elevators from street level to your room. But once you get there, your room will be surprisingly spacious (by New York standards, anyway) and decently outfitted. Rooms are especially well designed for business travelers, with good work space, two-line phones and high-speed Internet access; an executive floor is available for those who need extra attention. Generic is the overarching theme—and service is less than attentive at a hotel of this size, of course—but the location couldn't be better for theatergoers. Skyline views are stellar from the revolving rooftop lounge, even if service isn't.

Rooms: 2,002; 49 floors; designated nonsmoking floors. **Hotel amenities:** Concierge, tour desk, full-service business center, health club with sauna, laundry and dry-cleaning service, guest laundry, salon, extensive meeting and function space. **Food services:** Four restaurants (one American buffet, one steakhouse, one sushi bar, one rooftop revolving restaurant and lounge), two additional bars, coffee bar, room service. **Cancellation:** 6 P.M. day of arrival. **Wheelchair access:** Fully accessible. **Subway:** N, Q, R, S, W, 1, 2, 3, 7, 9 to 42nd St.

Paramount   GOOD $$$

235 W. 46th St. (between Broadway and Eighth Ave.)
www.ianschragerhotels.com
Phone: (212) 764-5500, (800) 225-7474   Fax: (212) 354-5237

Style over square footage is the mantra at Ian Schrager and Philippe Starck's first entry into the high design/low price hotel market, a decade before the now stylish Hudson (*see above*). The minuscule rooms are all whites and grays, with compact stainless-steel bath, a cartoonish cafe table and chairs, a swiveling armoire hiding a small TV and VCR, two-line phones, and a low-slung platform bed dressed in 300-count Egyptian cotton and lorded over by a silk-screen version of Vermeer's "The Lacemaker" or another classic work doubling as art and headboard. Be prepared, because it's a tight fit—you'll need an extra room if there's more than two of you, or a suite if you can't manage to pack light. These rooms are only for visitors who really value style over space; otherwise, you're much better off elsewhere. The Art-Deco-meets-industrial lobby isn't the scene that the Royalton or Hudson's lobby is, but it's still a good perch for people watching. Check for Web-only and seasonal rates (as low as $135 at times).

Rooms: 610; 19 floors; designated nonsmoking floors. **Hotel amenities:** 24-hour concierge, business center, fitness room, laundry and dry-cleaning service, meeting room, welcome gift for kids, video library. **Food services:** Restaurant, two bars, Dean & Deluca coffee bar, 24-hour room service. **Cancellation:** 24 hours prior to arrival. **Wheelchair access:** Not accessible. **Subway:** A, C, E, N, Q, R, S, W, 1, 2, 3, 7, 9 to 42nd St.

The Peninsula New York

EXTRAORDINARY **$$$$**

700 Fifth Ave. (at 55th St.)
Phone: (212) 956-2888, (800) 262-9467

www.peninsula.com
Fax: (212) 903-3949

In a stunning neoclassical building, renovated to the tune of $45 million in 1998, is one of New York's best ultra-luxury hotels. The lobby largely retained its longstanding Beaux Arts grandeur, but guest rooms were completely gutted and laid out afresh to allow for extra-large room configurations, monster-size marble bathrooms and state-of-the-art wiring. No other hotel so successfully fuses old New York style with 21st-century luxury.

The décor is exquisite, a dramatic but sublimely comfortable fusion of Art Nouveau lines, elegant Asian accents and contemporary art. Mahogany is polished to a high sheen and silks are lustrous. A wealth of beautifully designed storage space and a CEO-sized work desk with desk-level outlets and T1 connectivity, a leather executive chair and fax/printer/copier adds a practical edge to the elegance. But the technology isn't limited to business travelers: In the bathroom, a tub-level panel lets you to control the room-wide sound system, answer the phone and even watch TV (in all but the cheapest rooms). A bedside console controls the mood lighting, climate, TV, "Do Not Disturb" sign— in short, does everything but tuck you in. There's even an outside climate display next to the door so you know if you need to take an umbrella.

The spectacular tri-level spa is a big asset, offering a full range of services, a complete health club and a swimming pool with panoramic skyline views. Service is flawless, and small pets are welcome.

Rooms: 239; 23 floors; designated nonsmoking rooms. **Hotel amenities:** 24-hour concierge; complete fitness center, full-service spa and sun deck; business center; laundry and dry-cleaning service; meeting and function rooms. **Food services:** Two excellent restaurants, library-style lounge, indoor/outdoor rooftop bar with Fifth Avenue views, 24-hour room service. **Cancellation:** 24 hours prior to arrival (48 hours prior for suites). **Wheelchair access:** Fully accessible. **Subway:** E, V to Fifth Ave.

The Plaza
VERY GOOD $$$$

768 Fifth Ave. (at Central Park South and 59th St.)   *www.fairmont.com*
Phone: (212) 759-3000, (800) 441-1414   Fax: (212) 759-3167

If ever a hotel has earned the right to be officially declared a landmark, it is the
Plaza. Designed and built by Henry J. Hardenbergh, the stately French Renaissance hotel—which sits at one of the world's most glamorous intersections—has
hosted countless famous names and events since 1907, from the visits of Mark
Twain and "Diamond" Jim Brady to the recent nuptials of Michael Douglas and
Catherine Zeta-Jones. No doubt you already know what the Plaza looks like,
thanks to films such as *North by Northwest*, *Funny Girl* and *Home Alone 2*.

Now under the guiding hand of the Fairmont hotels group, the Plaza is looking pretty fabulous these days. While some suites still wear a garish red and gold,
most accommodations have been redone in soft and sophisticated corals, yel-
lows and blues, with luxury touches like pillowtop mattresses and big leather-
top desks with fax machines and high-speed Internet access, plus two-line
phones and TVs with video games. Even the smallest room is a reasonable size,
and the building's U-shape means that every one gets a measure of fresh air and
sunlight. After a stylish culinary and design reinvention, the dated Edwardian
Room has been reinvented as OneCPS, but other dining-and-cocktail options,
including the gilded Palm Court for tea and the justifiably legendary Oak Room
and Oak Bar, remain pleasingly old world. A new-in-2000 spa—with a full-service menu, a state-of-the-art gym and his-and-hers tiled Jacuzzis—is a marvelous addition. Unfortunately, hordes of tourists in the public spaces often
undermine the elegance. Small pets are welcome.

Rooms: 805; 19 floors; designated nonsmoking rooms. **Hotel amenities:**
Concierge, theater desk, 8,000- square-foot full-service spa and fitness center,
full-service business center, laundry and dry-cleaning service, extensive meeting
and function space, including the Grand Ballroom. **Food services:** OneCPS
restaurant, Oyster Bar English-style pub, Palm Court restaurant, Oak Room,
Oak Bar, 24-hour room service. **Cancellation:** 24 hours prior to arrival. **Wheelchair access:** Fully accessible. **Subway:** N, R, W to Fifth Ave.; 4, 5, 6 to 59th St.

Red Roof Inn
VERY GOOD $–$$

6 W. 32nd St. (between Fifth and Sixth Aves.)
www.redroof.com, *www.applecorehotels.com*
Phone: (212) 643-7100, (800) 567-7720, (800) RED-ROOF (733-7663)
Fax: (212) 790-2760, (212) 643-7101

The first Big Apple outpost of one of Middle America's favorite motel chains
has been a red-hot success thanks to comfortable, freshly outfitted rooms, a bet-
ter-than-budget lobby and amenities, and professional service. Don't expect
anything in the way of style or luxury comforts; Red Roof earns its "Very Good"
rating with reliable middle-of-the-road comforts, including relatively spacious
bedroom and bathroom configurations; in-room features—including coffee
makers and Web TV—that emphasize comfort and convenience; and pleasant
public spaces that include a mezzanine-level lounge, a business center and an

exercise room. Lined with affordable Korean restaurants and other mid-priced hotels, the bright, safe and bustling block is also well located, just a stone's throw from Macy's, the Empire State Building and a clutch of subway lines. Rates have been known to swing wildly by season, but you can usually score one in the low $100s; your best bet is to price-compare by calling both toll-free numbers and checking the Web sites.

Rooms: 172; 17 floors; designated nonsmoking floors. **Hotel amenities:** Concierge, mezzanine-level lounge, exercise room, business center, laundry and dry-cleaning service, meeting room. **Food services:** Rates include continental breakfast. **Cancellation:** Before 3 P.M. day prior to arrival. **Wheelchair access:** Accessible. **Subway:** B, D, F, N, Q, R, S, V, W to 34th St.

Ritz-Carlton New York, Central Park   EXCELLENT $$$$

50 Central Park South (at Sixth Ave.)   *www.ritzcarlton.com*
Phone: (212) 308-9100, (800) 241-3333   Fax: (212) 207-8331

The former St. Moritz was reborn in mid-2002 as Ritz-Carlton's glamorous uptown root, and it's a star. This is not the place to parade through the lobby in your faded jeans and flip-flops; unlike its sister hotel in Battery Park *(reviewed earlier in this chapter)*, which wears a contemporary sheen, this hotel bespeaks opulent, old money formality from the doorman-attended gilded front doors through the glittering lobby (often filled with the sweet sounds of a harpist). Even standard guest rooms are a sizeable 425 square feet and boast just about every imaginable luxury: Feather beds wear custom-designed 300-count Frette linens; minibars come stocked with Dean & Deluca gourmet munching and Opus One wine for private-label quaffing. State-of-the-art technology includes a 27-inch flat screen TV, a DVD player, high-speed Internet access and multi-line cordless phones. The marble baths feature a deep tub, separate shower and Frederic Fekkai bath products. If you can afford to score a park-facing room, you'll be rewarded with majestic views. The Ritz-Carlton's faultless service is in full swing; you can even call on the Bath Butler to draw you a custom soak. The Ritz's Club Level is always worth the price of admission, since you'll enjoy dedicated concierge service and an elegant park-view lounge with five complimentary food presentations a day, including an expanded continental breakfast.

Rooms: 277; 33 floors; designated nonsmoking floors. **Hotel amenities:** Concierge, 24-hour technology butler, full-service business center, fitness center, full-service La Prairie spa, laundry and dry-cleaning service, conference and meeting/function rooms, car service, meeting space, DVD library of Academy Award–winning films. **Food services:** Atelier restaurant; Star Lounge for the legendary afternoon tea service, cocktails and light meals; 24-hour room service. **Cancellation:** 24 hours prior to arrival. **Wheelchair access:** Fully accessible. **Subway:** F to 57th St.

Royalton   VERY GOOD $$$–$$$$

44 W. 44th St. (between Fifth and Sixth Aves.)   *www.ianschragerhotels.com*
Phone: (212) 869-4400, (800) 635-9013   Fax: (212) 869-8965

This super-stylish, spectacularly social hotel may be the best effort from bad-boy boutique-hotel pioneers Ian Schrager and Philippe Starck. Rooms are gorgeously designed after ocean-liner cabins, with rich mahogany, low-slung furniture covered in white cotton duck, dove gray carpet, porthole-like windows and slate floors in the exceptionally appealing slate-tiled bathrooms, which feature either a five-foot round tub or an oversize shower. With fluffy down and all-white 300-count Egyptian cotton, the bedding is simple but luxurious. The overall effect is cool and uncluttered. All rooms feature CD players, VCRs and two-line phones; some have working fireplaces. A perennially popular and relentlessly fashionable lounge scene occupies the lobby and restaurant; don't miss the tucked-away Round Bar, one of the coolest hangouts in the city.

The hotel was set to begin a major renovation in autumn 2002, which should only improve matters. However, it will remain open throughout the process (which has earned it a downgrade from "excellent" to merely "very good"), so inquire about the current status when booking, and make sure your room is away from the fray.

Rooms: 205; 12 floors; designated nonsmoking rooms. **Hotel amenities:** 24-hour concierge, exercise room, laundry and dry-cleaning service, boardroom and penthouse suites for meetings and events, welcome gift for kids, video library. **Food services:** Restaurant, two bars, 24-hour room service. **Cancellation:** 24 hours prior to arrival. **Wheelchair access:** Accessible. **Subway:** B, D, F, V, 7 to 42nd St.

Sofitel New York

EXCELLENT $$$$

45 W. 44th St. (between Fifth and Sixth Aves.)
Phone: (212) 354-8844, (800) SOFITEL (763-4835)

www.sofitel.com
Fax: (212) 354-2480

This sophisticated French import is the best among a large crop of new luxury hotels. The good impressions begin with the brand-new curvilinear tower, which occupies a narrow but block-deep lot on Hotel Row (the block is home to the Algonquin, the Royalton, and the chic new City Club, among others). Once you enter the stunning lobby, with its soaring ceilings, fluted columns and streamlined Art Moderne club chairs, its clear that this is one handsome hotel.

The Sofitel is beautifully run, too. The front desk is at the far end of the ballroom-sized lobby, tucked away to the side, which gives the entrance a wonderfully serene quality. The bilingual staff (they are required to speak both English and French, at minimum) is thoughtful, efficient and attentive. Filled with well-chosen and beautifully displayed Parisian- or New York-themed gifts—Guy Buffet china, Lenôtre chocolates, coffee-table books on the Big Apple—even the boutique is something special.

Sofitel's thoroughly French perspective also adds a fashionable flair to the guest rooms, where dramatic design seamlessly blends Art Deco and contemporary elements. Amenities include first-rate soundproofing, desk-level inputs with high-speed Internet access, CD players, Web TV and plush robes. The spacious bathrooms are done in honey-hued marble with separate tub and shower, plus a beautifully lit beveled mirror. All standard rooms have queen-sized beds; king beds are available only in suites.

Rooms: 398; 30 floors; designated nonsmoking floors. **Hotel amenities:** Concierge, business center, laundry and dry-cleaning service, ballroom, state-of-the-art meeting and function space, including a grand ballroom. **Food services:** Stylish French brasserie and piano bar, 24-hour room service. **Cancellation:** 24 hours prior to arrival. **Wheelchair access:** Fully accessible. **Subway:** B, D, F, S, V, 7 to 42nd St.

Super 8 Hotel Times Square   VERY GOOD $-$$

59 W. 46th St. (between Fifth and Sixth Aves.)

www.super8.com, www.applecorehotels.com

Phone: (212) 719-2300, (800) 567-7720   Fax: (212) 790-2760, (212) 921-8929

This smart new addition to the Theater District hotel scene is a joint venture between Apple Core hotels (the company behind a few value-priced midtowners, including the Comfort Inn Midtown and the Red Roof Inn, also recommended in this chapter) and the Super 8 chain, best known for its reliable highway motor lodges and making its first foray into the Big Apple. The partnership really pays off for budget-minded travelers, who can enjoy reliable comforts and a central-to-everything location for a terrific price (usually in the low to mid $100s, sometimes even less). The spacious rooms boast a king bed or two doubles, all-new furnishings, brand-new bathrooms, coffee makers, and Web TVs with video games. The décor won't win any awards from Metropolitan Home, but it's fresh and pleasant. Value-minded families will love the family suite, which features a king bed in one room and two twins in an adjacent room, so there's no fussing with a pullout sofa. Service is professional, and free continental breakfasts adds to an already excellent value.

Rooms: 206; 12 floors; designated nonsmoking rooms. **Hotel amenities:** Exercise room, business center, laundry and dry-cleaning service, meeting room. **Food services:** Rates include continental breakfast. **Cancellation:** Before 3 P.M. of the day prior to arrival. **Wheelchair access:** Accessible. **Subway:** B, D, F, S, V, 7 to 42nd St.

The Time   GOOD $$$

224 W. 49th St. (between Broadway and Eighth Ave.)   *www.thetimeny.com*
Phone: (212) 320-2900, (877) TIME-NYC (846-3692)   Fax: (212) 320-2926

This fashion-forward hotel, the first to be designed by Adam Tihany (most famous for colorful, big-ticket restaurant design), is a study in Mondrian-like modernism. All clean lines and straight angles, the guest rooms are decorated in white, black and gray with vivid accents of primary color in either fire-engine red, canary yellow or electric blue. Appointments are attractive and remarkably efficient—big worktables, soft backlighting, coffee maker caddies, custom valets and cubbies in the bathrooms—but some rooms (and bathrooms) remain uncomfortably petite nonetheless. VCRs, Bose radios and fax/printer/copiers are nice additions, but closets are small and sometimes enclosed only by a drape rather than a door. Coco Pazzo Teatro is an excellent choice for Tuscan-style dining, but the ultra-modern cocktail lounge has more style than substance. Rates are too high (rooms don't warrant a $250-plus rate); look for discounts.

Rooms: 200; 16 floors; designated nonsmoking rooms. **Hotel amenities:** Concierge, exercise room, laundry and dry-cleaning service, meeting room, video library. **Food services:** Coco Pazzo Teatro restaurant, Time Lounge, room service. **Cancellation:** Before 3 P.M. day prior to arrival. **Wheelchair access:** Not accessible. **Subway:** N, R, W to 49th St.; C, E to 50th St.

Travel Inn   GOOD $–$$

515 W. 42nd St. (between 10th and 11th Aves.)   *www.newyorkhotel.com*
Phone: (212) 695-7171, (800) 869-4630, (888) HOTEL58 (468-3558)
Fax: (212) 967-5025

Now that far-west Midtown is rife with chic restaurants and resident yuppies, this agreeable motor inn isn't so far removed anymore. The recently renovated rooms are universally large, clean, bright and comfortable, if nondescript. Even the smallest room is spacious and has a good-sized bathroom; those with two double beds make well-priced shares for families. In-room perks include Web TVs with video games. But the best reason to stay here is the free parking— with in and out privileges—since virtually every other hotel in town charges anywhere from $20 to $45 a day. The rooftop outdoor pool and well-furnished sun deck—another otherwise-nonexistent perk in the Big Apple—is a refreshing summertime treat that makes the Travel Inn a worthwhile choice even for those who don't have their own wheels. The Javits Convention Center is just three blocks away. What's more, Internet and other specials often drop prices.

Rooms: 160; seven floors; designated nonsmoking rooms. **Hotel amenities:** Exercise room, rooftop swimming pool and sun deck, laundry and dry-cleaning service, meeting room, Gray Line tour desk. **Food services:** Coffee shop, 24-hour room service. **Cancellation:** 24 hours prior to arrival. **Wheelchair access:** Not accessible. **Subway:** A, C, E to 42nd St.

The Warwick   GOOD $$$

65 W. 54th St. (at Sixth Ave.)   *www.warwickhotelny.com*
Phone: (212) 247-2700, (800) 223-4099   Fax: (212) 247-2725

The formerly dowdy Warwick was reinvented in the late 1990's, given renovated rooms, marble and palms in the lobby, and the overarching air of a smallish European hotel despite its rather large size. This hotel always had good bones, not to mention a few celebrity associations: It was built in 1927 by William Randolph Hearst for his mistress Marion Davies, the Beatles often stayed here when they were in the Big Apple, and Cary Grant lived in one of the apartment-style suites (no. 2706, to be exact) for 12 years.

You're less likely to find a star in residence these days, but you will find liberally sized rooms decorated in a light and pleasant traditional English country style. Features include mahogany furnishings, large marble bathrooms, good closet space, multilined phones and double-glazed windows to restrict street noise. Suites, some of which have wraparound terraces, are downright massive. Randolph's Bar is ideal for a sophisticated tipple.

Rooms: 495; 33 floors; designated nonsmoking floors. **Hotel amenities:** Clef d'Or concierge, business center, renovated exercise room, laundry and dry-cleaning service, freshly renovated meeting and function rooms. **Food services:** Randolph's Bar and Restaurant, room service. **Cancellation:** 24 hours before arrival. **Wheelchair access:** Fully accessible. **Subway:** B, D, E to Seventh Ave.

W Times Square   EXCELLENT $$$-$$$$
1567 Broadway (at 47th St.)   *www.whotels.com*
Phone: (212) 930-7400, (877) 946-8357 (W-HOTELS)   Fax: (212) 930-7500

Conceived as the flagship hotel for Starwood's designer-label chain, the newest W hotel is also the hippest of a very sleek bunch. A sleek, mod-inspired lobby— think Mod Squad era with a 21st-century twist and Zen-like water features for an air of groovy tranquility—leads to guest rooms that unite modern linearity with luxury-level comfort. Perks include cloud-fluffy pillowtop beds (an equally fabulous version of sister brand Westin's divinely inspired Heavenly Bed) with luminous resin cubes serving as nightstands; Web TVs with, VCR and DVD; CD stereo; a coffee maker and joyfully stocked minibar (with such goodies as gummi bears and Slinkys); high-speed Internet access, two-line cordless phones and a large worktable; sexy bathrooms with circular sinks, suspended as if in midair, and lightweight cotton pique bathrobes; and lighting that makes everybody look great. Supermod seafooder Blue Fin won two precious *New York Times* stars out of the gate, and the Whiskey Bar is an even better realization than nightlife impresario Rande Gerber's original hotspot. You can bring the W lifestyle home by flexing your credit card at W The Store, on the lobby level. Destined to be a favorite among the style-conscious entertainment crowd whose offices fill the surrounding blocks.

Rooms: 509; 57 floors; designated non-smoking floors. **Hotel amenities:** Concierge with W's signature "Whatever/Whenever" service, business center, exercise room, laundry and dry-cleaning service, meeting rooms. **Food services:** Blue Fin restaurant, Whiskey Bar, 24-hour room service. **Cancellation:** 24 hours prior to arrival. **Wheelchair access:** Fully accessible. **Subway:** N, R to 49th St.

UPTOWN

Amsterdam Inn   BASIC $
340 Amsterdam Ave. (at 76th St.)   *www.amsterdaminn.com*
Phone: (212) 579-7500   Fax: (212) 579-6127

This sister property to the Murray Hill Inn (*earlier in this chapter*) is a similarly wallet-friendly choice for budget travelers. The narrow rooms are outfitted with little more than a bed, a wall rack for hanging clothes and a cheap set of drawers; only a small TV and a telephone make them more luxurious than monk's quarters. About half the rooms have private baths, and the rest share; all of the like-new bathrooms are the nicest available in this under-$100 price range. Visitors opting for a double with private bathroom will find slightly nicer rooms at the Murray Hill Inn (where they take credit cards), but the Amsterdam is a fine option, too, and the upscale residential neighborhood is terrific. Note, however, that some "doubles" have single beds with a pull-out trundle rather than a real bed for two, so find out exactly what you're reserving. Facilities and service are virtually nonexistent, as in most of New York's cheapest hotels.

Rooms: 25 (12 with shared bathrooms); four floors; smoking allowed. **Hotel amenities:** None. **Food services:** None. **Cancellation:** 48 hours prior to arrival. **Wheelchair access:** Not accessible. **Note:** Cash and traveler's checks only. **Subway:** 1, 9 to 79nd St.

The Bentley

VERY GOOD $$

500 E. 62nd St. (at York Ave.)
Phone: (212) 644-6000, (888) 66-HOTEL (664-6835)

www.nychotels.com
Fax: (212) 207-4800

There's no denying the Bentley's out-of-the-way location on the far East Side, but it has three main selling points: great East River views from three sides; cheap on-site valet parking for visitors with cars ($20 a night); and low rates, considering the space and stylishness of the accommodations. From the outside, the Bentley still looks like an office building; in fact, it was once the NAACP headquarters. Inside, the corporate look gives way to fluid modern style that stars warm khaki tones and natural elements (including fresh flowers in wall-mounted bud vases in the halls and river-rock wall accents in the rooms); the look is attractive and contemporary rather than coldly modern. Good room layouts accommodate two doubles or a king. The platform beds fall short of ideally comfortable, but they're not bad. Nice amenities include decent work desks, marble baths, good bedside lighting, CD players, two-line phones, comfortable chenille chairs for reading and pullout sofas in the suites. Corner rooms are most spacious, and views of the 59th Street Bridge are spectacular.

Rooms: 208; 21 floors; designated nonsmoking floor. **Hotel amenities:** Laundry and dry-cleaning service. **Food services:** Rooftop restaurant and bar; room service; sitting room with self-serve 24-hour cappuccino bar, tea and cookies. **Cancellation:** 24 hours prior to arrival. **Wheelchair access:** Accessible. **Subway:** N, R, W to Lexington Ave.; 4, 5, 6 to 59th St.

The Carlyle

EXTRAORDINARY $$$$

35 E. 76th St. (at Madison Ave.)
Phone: (212) 744-1600, (800) 227-5737

www.thecarlyle.com
Fax: (212) 717-4682

The discreet and elegant Carlyle epitomizes Upper East Side glamour. About half of the hotel is occupied by permanent residents, while the other half is made up of rooms and multibedroom suites available to short-term guests with deep pockets. The softly lit lobby is distinctly un-public, which heightens the exclusive residential feel. Generations of famous faces and power brokers have been attracted by this low-profile ambiance, as well as the impeccable attention to detail and the unmatched service.

Individually decorated rooms and suites are luxuriously appointed, but not in the gilded, big-money way of luxury palaces like the St. Regis. Think understated, traditional, rare, and you'll get the picture: Chintz, satin, antiques, original Audubon prints and oils depicting English country scenes on the walls, Oriental rugs over gleaming wood floors. There is a full roster of amenities you have every right to expect at this price level, including jetted tubs, plus many less common luxuries, such as terraces, grand pianos and/or full kitchens. Many regulars prefer the high-floor tower rooms; they're not large, but the light and the views—particularly those overlooking Central Park—are enthralling.

Cafe Carlyle is New York's premier cabaret room, and still the domain of the legendary Bobby Short and other big-ticket song stylists; Woody Allen is usually in the house on Monday, swinging on clarinet with the Eddy Davis New Orleans Jazz Band. Jazz vocalists entertain a well-heeled crowd at the recently renovated but still utterly glamorous Bemelmans Bar. The elegant lobby is undergoing a redressing in summer 2002. Pets are welcome; in fact, the staff will even walk Bowser for you.

Rooms: 180; 33 floors; designated nonsmoking rooms. **Hotel amenities:** Concierge; attractive fitness center with whirlpool, sauna and spa services; business services; laundry and dry-cleaning service; high-end retail shops, meeting and function rooms. **Food services:** Elegant French restaurant, Bemelmans Bar, Café Carlyle supper club, Gallery for afternoon tea and light fare, 24-hour room service. **Cancellation:** 24 hours prior to arrival. **Wheelchair access:** Fully accessible. **Subway:** 6 to 77th St.

Country Inn the City   VERY GOOD $$

270 W. 77th St. (between Broadway and West End Ave.)
www.countryinnthecity.com   Phone: (212) 580-4183   Fax: (212) 874-3981

This beautifully outfitted guest house is a true delight, offering both amenity-laden accommodations and a true taste of New York living to discerning visitors who want more personality than your average hotel offers. Tucked away on a leafy block just off Broadway, this 1891 limestone town house features four spacious and impeccable studio suites, each outfitted by innkeepers with an eye for design and a nose for practicality. Apartments are bright and elegant, and homey features include wood floors covered with Oriental rugs, a beautifully dressed queen bed (two are four-posters, one a romantic canopy bed) with a high-quality mattress, a cozy sitting area facing a nonworking fireplace, and bright colors, original art and well-chosen collectibles that heighten the domestic air. Modern appointments include a fully equipped galley kitchen, a cafe-style dining table for two and a private phone with answering machine.

There are a few downsides that you should be aware of before you book. There is no resident innkeeper, so the inn is best for independent types who don't need anything in the way of personal service. As in most New York brownstones, there's no elevator, either. And while each kitchen comes stocked with coffee and basic breakfast fixings, you're likely to have to stock up on your own if you're staying beyond the three-night minimum. Lastly, maid service is offered only every three or four days for long-term stays, so be prepared to pick up after yourself and make your own bed. Last-minute travelers should be sure to check online or inquire about late-booking specials (as low as $110).

Rooms: Four; five floors; smoking not allowed. **Hotel amenities:** None. **Food services:** Stocked breakfast pantry. **Cancellation:** 30 days prior to arrival; $30 cancellation fee if apartment is not rebooked. **Wheelchair access:** Not accessible. **Note:** Limit two per apartment; no children under 12; credit cards not accepted. **Subway:** 1, 9 to 79th St.

Excelsior Hotel   VERY GOOD $–$$

45 W. 81st St. (between Columbus Ave. and Central Park West)
www.excelsiorhotelny.com
Phone: (212) 362-9200, (800) 368-4575   Fax: (212) 580-3972

This recently renovated hotel has a lot going for it, most notably an amazing location: It sits across the street from the American Museum of Natural History's new Rose Center for Earth & Space, on a block of regal apartment buildings, with a prime entrance to Central Park in one direction, boutique- and restaurant-lined Columbus Avenue in the other. This is the very best residential territory the Upper West Side has to offer.

But the appeal doesn't end with the address. A richly wood-paneled lobby that looks like it belongs in a far more expensive hotel leads to freshly outfitted, traditionally styled guest rooms and suites that are good-sized, comfortable and well outfitted with good-quality bedding and textiles, white-tiled bathrooms with floral accents and a fax/copier/printer on the work desk. The plush library-style lounge—with gorgeous leather seating nooks, fireplace, books and games, and a large flat-screen TV with VCR and DVD player—is additional value-added attraction. Service isn't faultless, but it's perfectly acceptable considering the intersection of quality amenities and low rates.

Rooms: 196; 16 floors; designated nonsmoking rooms. **Hotel amenities:** Concierge, exercise room, entertainment room/library, laundry and dry-cleaning service, conference room. **Food services:** Breakfast buffet served in library (full or continental, for a charge). **Cancellation:** Before 4 P.M. day prior to arrival. **Wheelchair access:** Not accessible. **Subway:** 1, 9 to 79th St.

Holmes Bed & Breakfast   VERY GOOD $

W. 91st St. (off Amsterdam Ave.)   *www.holmesnyc.com*
Phone: (917) 838-480   Fax: (212) 769-2348

A nicely maintained traditional brownstone on a pretty tree-lined residential block houses this little-known but excellent-quality budget B & B. Four guest rooms are available on two floors, two with private bath and two that share a bath, all value priced. Owner Marguerite Holmes is an accomplished artist; not only do her terrific multigenre paintings (which run the gamut from pastoral scenes to impressive abstracts) fill the hallways and guest rooms, but her creative eye has turned what could be very basic accommodations into something really special. Each clean and well-maintained room has a TV with cable (some have VCRs); a direct-dial phone; a fridge, coffee maker, microwave and toaster oven (the shared-bath rooms also share a pantry kitchenette); a well-chosen mix of vintage furnishings and original art; and good-quality bedding. The Cranberry Room is the best of the bunch, with its own very nice marble bath with shower, generous closet space, and terrace.

There's no formal breakfast serving, but a cupboard is stocked with morning foodstuffs. As with most B & B's, Holmes is best for independent-minded travelers, but the young and friendly resident innkeeper (also an artist) is on hand and glad to help if you need advice or assistance. All in all, an excellent choice for budget travelers who prefer offbeat, home-style accommodations.

Rooms: Four (two with shared bathroom); three floors; smoking not allowed. **Hotel amenities:** None. **Food services:** Cupboard with breakfast items. **Cancellation:** 14 days prior to arrival; $50 processing fee. **Wheelchair access:** None. **Subway:** 1, 2, 3, 9 to 96th St.

Hotel Beacon   VERY GOOD $$

2130 Broadway (at 75th St.)   www.beaconhotel.com
Phone: (212) 787-1100, (800) 572-4969   Fax: (212) 724-0839

The focus at the Beacon isn't on amenities or service but on room size and value for dollar—and on those counts, it scores extremely well. Built in 1929 for permanent residents, the Beacon has grown into an Upper West Side staple since becoming a full-fledged hotel a dozen or so years ago. Almost half of the rooms are apartment-sized suites, but even the standard configurations can easily accommodate four in two double beds. Every room and suite features a modern kitchenette with cooktop, coffee maker, minifridge (a full-size fridge in suites), microwave (plus a stove in suites) and a full complement of cookware and dishes; and a new marble bathroom; plus a pullout sleeper sofa in suites. The gargantuan two-bedroom/two-bath suites are value-priced for larger families. The generic décor isn't likely to win any ardent fans, but there's no arguing with the comfort level. The location, at the heart of one of Manhattan's most desirable and family-friendly neighborhoods, and just a stone's throw from some of New York's finest gourmet markets, is first-rate. Front, Broadway-facing rooms can't avoid street noise, so ask for a back unit or a high floor.

Rooms: 236; 25 floors; designated nonsmoking rooms. **Hotel amenities:** Concierge, laundry and dry-cleaning service, coin-operated laundry, meeting room. **Food services:** 24-hour coffee shop. **Cancellation:** Before 6 P.M. day prior to arrival. **Wheelchair access:** Fully accessible. **Subway:** 1, 2, 3, 9 to 72nd St.

Hotel Olcott   BASIC $

27 W. 72nd St. (between Central Park West and Columbus Ave.)
www.hotelolcott.com   Phone: (212) 877-4200   Fax: (212) 580-0511

This old-world apartment house is spectacularly located in first-class Upper West Side residential territory, just steps from the legendary Dakota (where John Lennon once lived, and Yoko still does), as well as the absolute best part of Central Park. The cheaply appointed apartments—more than half of which are one- and two-bedroom suites—are as stylish as a discount furniture store in the Nixon era, but they're clean, monster-sized and bargain-priced. Each has a kitchenette, a large bathroom, roomy closets, a dining table and double-paned windows for noise reduction; otherwise, expect low tech and you won't be disappointed. Most kitchenettes and bathrooms have been recently renovated with all-new, bright-white tile and modern fixtures. Sofas aren't sleepers, but most bedrooms are so enormous that they hold two queens, and the friendly management will be happy to lend you a cot. Discounts on weekly stays make the already-attractive rates an even better bargain. The hotel's affordable barbecue restaurant serves decent ribs and bathtub margaritas.

Rooms: 150; 16 floors; smoking allowed. **Hotel amenities:** None. **Food services:** Dallas BBQ restaurant and bar. **Cancellation:** Seven days prior to arrival. **Wheelchair access:** Fully accessible. **Subway:** 1, 2, 3, 9 to 72nd St.

Hotel Wales   GOOD $$–$$$

1295 Madison Ave. (between 92nd and 93rd Sts.)   www.waleshotel.com
Phone: (212) 876-6000, (877) 847-4444   Fax: (212) 894-5220, (212) 860-7000

Built in 1901, this freshly renovated but still-quirky Victorian-style hotel offers relatively affordable accommodations in a shopping and museum-convenient corner of the extremely civilized Upper East Side called Carnegie Hill. Most guest rooms are not large; luckily, almost half are suites and ample amenities—including pillowy beds beautifully dressed in Belgian linens, VCRs and CD players—up the appeal substantially. The new look mixes contemporary touches with turn-of-the-century Victorian details for a pleasing look. Original woodwork is beautifully refinished, walls wear warm and pretty cream and mint hues, furnishing accents the heritage without adding frill. In addition, the Victorian lobby, a generous breakfast buffet and all-day snacks laid out in a sunny lounge and wonderful home-style-chic Sarabeth's restaurant contribute a lot to making the Wales a pleasing place to stay. Be aware, however, that the nearest subway stop is a good 10-minute hike from the hotel.

Rooms: 87; 10 floors; one designated smoking floor. **Hotel amenities:** Lounge, rooftop terrace, exercise room, in-room spa treatments, laundry and dry-cleaning service, fax service, video and CD libraries. **Food services:** Sarabeth's restaurant, room service; rates include help-yourself cappuccino, tea and cookies. **Cancellation:** 24 hours prior to arrival. **Wheelchair access:** Not accessible. **Subway:** 6 to 96th St.

Inn New York City   EXCELLENT $$$$

266 W. 71st St. (between Broadway and West End Ave.)
www.innewyorkcity.com   Phone: (212) 580-1900   Fax: (212) 580-4437

This one-of-a-kind, four-suite luxury inn just may be the most romantic place to stay in the city. Its only peer is the Inn on Irving Place, but this place has an air of private luxury and personalized hospitality that's unparalleled. There are no public spaces whatsoever—no front desk, no concierge, no lobby—so upon entering the beautifully restored brownstone you'll feel like you're the treasured guest of a doting, and very rich, friend with impeccable taste. Each of the four suites takes up an entire floor, and you may not even ever see your fellow guests.

Each suite has a unique theme and tailored amenities, plus 12-foot ceilings, a fully equipped gourmet kitchenette, sumptuously outfitted sleeping quarters, a terrific bathroom, beautifully chosen antiques and only the plushest textiles, CD players and VCRs. On the grand parlor-floor the Opera Suite has a baby grand piano, a working fireplace in the bedroom, a Jacuzzi tub in the bath and French doors leading to a private terrace. One entire room of the ultra-romantic, Victorian-style spa suite is dedicated to the art of bathing, with a monster Jacuzzi tub (big enough for a party), a fireplace, a glass-block shower and a cedar-lined sauna, plus a vintage barber chair for character. The skylit, somewhat masculine and extremely handsome Library Suite is ideal for small families or shares, since pocket doors can convert the mammoth living room into a second bedroom. The duplex Vermont Suite is also available for month-long stays.

The discreet service is impeccable; the innkeepers will leave you entirely alone if you prefer, or will be at your service with the push of a button. The Inn is very expensive, but simply stunning—you will get your money's worth.

Rooms: Four suites; four floors; smoking not allowed. **Hotel amenities:** Copy and fax services, dry-cleaning service, washer/dryers in three suites (maid will do laundry for Opera Suite guests). **Food services:** Stocked breakfast cupboard in each suite. **Cancellation:** 14 days prior to arrival, $50 cancellation fee. **Wheelchair access:** Not accessible. **Note:** Best for children over 12. **Subway:** 1, 2, 3, 9 to 72nd St.

The Lowell   EXCELLENT $$$$
28 E. 63rd St. (between Madison and Park Aves.)   *www.lhw.com*
Phone: (212) 838-1400, (800) 221-4444   Fax: (212) 319-4230

The low-profile Lowell is the hidden jewel of the Upper East Side—small, quiet, private, residential, elegant and service-oriented. Even though it's at the Midtown end of the Upper East Side, it feels like a secret hideaway from the moment you enter the intimate, Deco-influenced French Empire lobby. Two-thirds of the accommodations are suites; each has a well-equipped kitchenette but is otherwise unique, with individual appointments ranging from wood-burning fireplaces to an in-suite gym (a result of a request from Madonna while in residence some years ago). Chintzed to the max, the Lowell suites are just right for honeymoons and other special occasions. The Hollywood Suite has a 41-inch TV, a full selection of Hollywood classics on video and a delightful collection of movie paraphernalia, while the Garden Suite boasts not one but two ultra-romantic terraces. Expect a full slate of luxuries in any accommodation. Warmth is the order of the day from the first-rate staff, who leave Bulgari chocolates and complimentary Fiji water as bedtime treats at turndown.

Rooms: 68; 17 floors; designated nonsmoking rooms. **Hotel amenities:** 24-hour concierge, good fitness center, secretarial services, laundry and dry-cleaning service, limousine service, meeting and function rooms, video library. **Food services:** Post House steakhouse, Pembroke Room for continental cuisine and afternoon tea, 24-hour room service. **Cancellation:** 48 hours prior to arrival. **Wheelchair access:** Accessible. **Subway:** N, R, W to Lexington Ave.; 4, 5, 6 to 59th St.

The Lucerne

EXCELLENT $$–$$$

201 W. 79th St. (at Amsterdam Ave.)

www.newyorkhotel.com

Phone: (212) 875-1000, (800) 492-8122

Fax: (212) 579-2408

A landmark 1903 terra-cotta building houses one of the city's best mid-priced hotels. The bright and comfortably furnished marble lobby leads to extremely well-maintained rooms that are generally spacious; even the standards are large enough to accommodate a king or queen bed, or two doubles for shares or small families. Outfitted in an attractive and comfortable Americana style, all rooms have TVs with Nintendo and Web TV, coffee maker and an attractive bathroom with spacious travertine counters. One-bedroom suites have granite-counter wet-bar kitchenettes with microwave, plus sleeper sofas, extra sitting room and TVs; the deluxe king suite also has a Jacuzzi tub. Corner units are especially light and bright. Management is fanatical about excellent service, so you can count on it; in fact, the service is otherwise unrivaled in this price range. The upscale residential neighborhood is excellent, and the subway is less than a block away, ready to whisk you to Midtown in minutes.

Rooms: 250; 14 floors; designated nonsmoking floors. **Hotel amenities:** Laundry and dry-cleaning service, fitness room, penthouse meeting space. **Food services:** Bar and grill, room service; expanded buffet continental breakfast served in the penthouse-level breakfast/meeting room (included in some rate packages). **Cancellation:** 24 hours prior to arrival. **Wheelchair access:** Fully accessible. **Subway:** 1, 9 to 79th St.

The Mark

EXCELLENT $$$$

25 E. 77th St. (at Madison Ave.)

www.mandarinoriental.com

Phone: (212) 744-4300, (800) THE-MARK (843-6275)   Fax: (212) 744-2749

This Big Apple representative of the world-renowned Mandarin Oriental hotel group is the Carlyle's chief neighborhood rival for the deepest-pocketed travelers. Boasting an intricate Art Deco facade and outfitted in an elegant English-Italian neoclassical style, the Mark is nevertheless lighter and more contemporary in feeling than the Carlyle and most other hotels in the super-luxury category. Rooms are a comfortable mix of classic and contemporary design, with luxuriant textiles; pillowy king-sized beds dressed in Belgian and Frette linens; a stylish, oversized and well-lit bathroom, most with separate tub and shower; plus modern features like VCRs, fax machines and two-line phones with cordless handsets. About three-quarters of the rooms and suites have full kitchens or kitchenettes. Service is beyond reproach, and Mark's is one of the city's best hotel restaurants. An excellent choice on all counts. Prime your plastic, shoppers, because the location is in prime platinum-card spending territory.

Rooms: 180; 15 floors; designated nonsmoking floors. **Hotel amenities:** Clefs d'Or concierge, fitness center with sauna and steam, full-service business center, laundry and dry-cleaning service, meeting and function rooms, complimentary weekday-morning shuttle to Wall Street. **Food services:** Mark's Restaurant, which serves a memorable Asian afternoon tea; intimate and romantic Mark's Bar; 24-hour room service. **Cancellation:** 4 P.M. day prior to arrival. **Wheelchair access:** Fully accessible. **Subway:** 6 to 77th St.

The Melrose Hotel, New York

VERY GOOD $$$

140 E. 63rd St. (at Lexington Ave.)
Phone: (212) 838-5700, (800) 223-1020

www.melrosehotel.com
Fax: (212) 753-0360

A literary landmark thanks to poet Sylvia Plath's memoir of tormented youth, *The Bell Jar*, the former Barbizon is now under the guiding hand of the Dallas-based Melrose Hotel group. At the southern end of the residential Upper East Side, just three blocks from Bloomingdale's, location is a prime asset. The hotel was refurbished to the tune of $40 million just a few years ago, so it's in very good shape. Rooms are undistinctive but comfortably outfitted with firm beds, soft pastels (mostly blues and greens), and attractive wrought-iron furnishings, nice baths, two-line phones and CD players. On the downside, many are small. Still, rooms are light and bright, and housekeeping is immaculate. Deluxe rooms buy you more space and a foldout love seat.

In the top-of-the-line Tower Suites, located on the 18th and 19th floors, the hotel's Moorish architecture is in evidence, particularly the intricate detailing and Romanesque arches of the nicely furnished terraces attached to about half of these rooms. Views are stunning, décor is slightly more luxurious, and Jacuzzi tubs and Dolby surround-sound stereos are among the extras.

Rooms: 306; 22 floors; designated nonsmoking floors. **Hotel amenities:** Concierge, 34,000-square-foot Equinox Fitness Club and Spa with pool on site (use fee charged; included in some rate plans), salon, laundry and dry-cleaning service, CD and video libraries. **Food services:** Restaurant, lobby bar, "sign and dine" program with nearby restaurants, room service. **Cancellation:** 24 hours prior to arrival. **Wheelchair access:** Fully accessible. **Subway:** F, N, R, W to Lexington Ave.; 4, 5, 6 to 59th St.

On The Ave

GOOD $$–$$$

2178 Broadway (at 77th St.)
Phone: (212) 362-1100, (800) 497-6028

www.ontheave-nyc.com
Fax: (212) 787-9521

Travelers with mid-range budgets and an eye for modern design will appreciate this sleekly styled hotel, a recent reinvention of a down-at-the-heels residence hotel. Rooms feature Scandinavian-style modular furniture, earth tones and attractive modern art specially commissioned for the hotel. Bathrooms are marble, with slate floors and custom-designed stainless sinks; some have showers only, so request one with a tub if it matters to you. Spaces are not huge, especially at the cheapest price point, furnishings should be a bit more practical and beds a bit more comfortable, but rooms are rather comfortable overall. Those in the deluxe category offer the best space-for-money ratio. Penthouse rooms and suites are an incredible bargain considering their large alfresco terraces and terrific views. Request a nonsmoking room if you want one, because rooms seem to hold onto the cigarette smell. Services are minimal, but the terrific residential neighborhood abounds with good restaurants, and slow-season pricing can be a phenomenal deal (as low as $115 at times).

Rooms: 251; 15 floors; designated nonsmoking rooms. **Hotel amenities:** Concierge, laundry and dry-cleaning service. **Food services:** 24-hour room service available from nearby restaurants. **Cancellation:** 24 hours prior to arrival. **Wheelchair access:** ADA compliant. **Subway:** 1, 2, 3, 9 to 72nd St.

The Pierre   EXCELLENT $$$$

2 E. 61st St. (at Fifth Ave.)   *www.fourseasons.com/pierre*
Phone: (212) 838-8000, (800) 332-3442   Fax: (212) 940-8109

This old-world, well-mannered, very European-style residential hotel is enormously appealing. A stay in the beautifully restored 1930's Georgian-style building will make you feel regal. The old-world ambiance is extremely formal—with doormen worthy of the Queen's Guard and white-gloved elevator operators—but not uninvitingly so. Opulent, almost museum-like public spaces give way to guest rooms that are individually appointed in a supremely elegant classical style featuring English chintzes, Oriental toiles and dark woods polished to a high sheen. Ceilings are high, so even the smaller rooms feel light, airy and spacious. The rooms are less about business and technology (rooms are wired for high-speed Internet access, but amenities like VCRs and fax machines are mostly on request) and more about supreme comforts and superbly fluid service—the staff will graciously fulfill any request. Services include elevators staffed around the clock; anytime laundry, dry cleaning and pressing; packing and unpacking service; even special menus and amenities for well-heeled kids. Grand suites are apartment-like and uniquely appointed; many include full dining rooms, park views and/or terraces. The most thrilling rooms are those with views over Central Park, which is just across the street. For a memorable experience, take traditional high tea in the distinctive Rotunda Room, with its trompe l'oeil murals by Edward Melcarth. Keep in mind, though, that this is the kind of hotel where you must be willing to dress the well-heeled part, or you will feel out of place.

Rooms: 201; 41 floors; designated nonsmoking rooms. **Hotel amenities:** Concierge and theater desk, 24-hour elevator operator, full-service business center, fitness center, Dominique Salon (with spa services), laundry and dry-cleaning service, two grand ballrooms and extensive meeting and function space, courtesy car to Theater District. **Food services:** Cafe Pierre for elegant continental dining; Rotunda for breakfast, light fare and afternoon tea; 24-hour room service. **Cancellation:** 24 hours prior to arrival. **Wheelchair access:** ADA compliant. **Subway:** N, R, W to Fifth Ave.

The Regency Hotel   EXCELLENT $$$$

540 Park Ave. (at 61st St.)   *www.loewshotels.com*
Phone: (212) 759-4100, (800) 23-LOEWS (235-6397)
Fax: (212) 688-2898, (212) 826-5674

A favorite among visiting Hollywood elite for decades—including Audrey Hepburn, Elizabeth Taylor and Princess Grace—the Regency has new polish, grace and energy following a major $35 million remake in 1999 under the direction of designer Connie Beale. She has done fine work infusing ornate spaces both public and private with warmth and a comfortable feeling of contemporary luxury; this is a Park Avenue address where you can feel comfortable putting your feet up. Plush materials—rich mahogany, deep-hued leather, silks and velvets—do much of the work. A strong lineup of amenities helps, too. The rooms have large granite-top work desks with ergonomic chairs and fax/printer/copiers, digital two-line phones, high-speed Internet access, CD and video players, beds dressed in Frette linens and goose-down duvets and extra TVs in the bathrooms. About half of the rooms have microwaves, and fridges can be supplied. Though well equipped, the bathrooms are quite small.

Under the guiding hand of the Loews hotel chain, the Regency just may be the best choice in the luxury category for visiting families. Extensive children's services and amenities include a dedicated "kid concierge," who will do everything from play soccer in the hallways on rainy days to read bedtime stories. Dog-walking and other pet-friendly services also make the Regency ideal for travelers with Rover in tow. The 540 Park restaurant is considered to be the original New York home of the power breakfast, while Feinstein's at the Regency has evolved into one of the city's top cabaret rooms.

Rooms: 351; 21 floors; designated nonsmoking floors. **Hotel amenities:** Concierge, full-service fitness center (personal training and massage available), salon, full-service business center, laundry and dry-cleaning service (including overnight service), meeting and function rooms, limousine service; in-room fitness equipment available. **Food services:** 540 Park restaurant, Feinstein's at the Regency supper club, Library lounge, 24-hour room service. **Cancellation:** 24 hours prior to arrival. **Wheelchair access:** Fully accessible. **Subway:** N, R, W to Lexington Ave.; 4, 5, 6 to 59th St.

The Stanhope, Park Hyatt New York

VERY GOOD $$$$

995 Fifth Ave. (at 81st St.)   www.parkhyatt.com
Phone: (212) 774-1234, (888) 591-1234   Fax: (212) 517-0888

This bright and elegant member of the posh Park Hyatt chain is ideal for museum lovers, since the Metropolitan Museum of Art is just across tony Fifth Avenue, and the Frick, the Guggenheim, the Whitney and other Museum Mile institutions are within easy walking distance. That's enough reason to stay, but the Stanhope offers many additional incentives, too—most notably, a feeling of privacy and accessible Old World luxury. The Versailles-inspired lobby displays Louis XIV antiques and museum-quality tapestries, while the rooms are done in a very pleasing peach-and-gold-tone French Empire style with Chinoiserie accents. The impressive list of amenities include CD players, VCRs and fax machines, plus small but well-outfitted bathrooms. The location keeps the clientele pleasantly mixed between business travelers and vacationers. Sidewalk cafe seating in warm weather is another appeal.

Rooms: 185; 17 floors; designated nonsmoking floors. **Hotel amenities:** Concierge, fitness room, business center, laundry and dry-cleaning service, meeting and function rooms, personal shopping service, complimentary car service to Midtown Tuesday through Friday. **Food services:** Restaurant, bar serving light meals, 24-hour room service. **Cancellation:** Before 3 P.M. on the day prior to arrival. **Wheelchair access:** Fully accessible. **Subway:** 6 to 77th St.

Surrey Hotel   VERY GOOD $$$–$$$$

20 E. 76th St. (at Madison Ave.)   *www.mesuite.com*
Phone: (212) 288-3700, (800) ME-SUITE (637-8483)   Fax: (212) 628-1549

This all-suite hotel has two prime draws: a tony Upper East Side address for less
than most neighborhood hotels charge and room service from Daniel Boulud's
Cafe Boulud, a *New York Times* three-star restaurant. Done in 18th-century
English parlor style, the lobby has an unmemorable old world air, and the hallways could do with some gentler lighting. But spacious suites—studios, one- and
two-bedrooms—offer solidly reliable accommodations. Rooms and closets are
large, black-and-white-tiled bathrooms are spacious and pleasant (the two-bedrooms have two full baths), and thick walls keep things quiet. Every one has a
fully equipped kitchen and a dining area—and the staff will even do your shopping for you. Other perks include Web TVs and two-line phones.

Rooms: 130 (all suites); 17 floors; designated nonsmoking floors. **Hotel amenities:** Concierge, exercise room, secretarial services, fitness room, laundry and
dry-cleaning service, guest laundry, small meeting room, grocery shopping service. **Food services:** Cafe Boulud, bar, room service. **Cancellation:** 6 P.M. day of
arrival. **Wheelchair access:** Fully accessible. **Subway:** 6 to 77th St.

Trump International Hotel & Tower   EXTRAORDINARY $$$$

1 Central Park West (at Columbus Circle)   *www.trumpintl.com*
Phone: (212) 299-1000, (888) 44-TRUMP (448-7867)   Fax: (212) 299-1150

Controversial real-estate developer and Page Six favorite Donald Trump is
something less than universally beloved by New Yorkers. Even so, it is hard to
imagine anybody finding fault with the jewel of a hotel that bears his name. It is
simply spectacular.

The hotel is housed in a mirrored tower at Columbus Circle, overlooking
Central Park; park views are most prized, of course, but the tower's freestanding
situation awards all rooms with light, and three sides offer at least a glimpse of
the green. Rooms with city views over Broadway lose a bit of the magic but
retain their status as an unreserved cocoon of contemporary luxury.

About three-quarters of the accommodations are suites. High ceilings, floor-
to-ceiling windows, and smart design maximize space. The look is definitely
sumptuous, but in a restrained, meditative way with warm beiges and honey
hues predominating. Appointments include TV with VCR and video games,
CD stereo, two-line phones, high-speed Internet access and fax (PCs and print-
ers on request), a Jacuzzi tub in the marble bath and a telescope for taking in the
thrilling views. Most rooms and all suites also have top-of-the-line Euro-style
kitchens stocked with Limoges china and crystal. If you don't feel like relying
on run-of-the-mill room service or hiking all the way down to the lobby level to
dine at glorious *New York Times* four-star winner Jean Georges, one of Jean-
Georges's sous-chefs will prepare your meal en suite. What's more, guests are
assigned a personal concierge for the course of their stay.

Rooms: 167; 52 floors (hotel rooms housed on floors 3 through 17); designated
nonsmoking rooms. **Hotel amenities:** Concierge; Trump Attaché butler service;

6,000-square-foot health club with spa services, swimming pool, steam and sauna; full-service business center; laundry and dry cleaning; meeting and function rooms; CD library. **Food services:** Jean Georges restaurant, 24-hour room service. **Cancellation:** 24 hours prior to arrival. **Wheelchair access:** Fully accessible. **Subway:** A, B, C, D, 1, 9 to 59th St.

B & B BOOKING AGENTS AND SHORT-TERM APARTMENT RENTALS

Independent-minded travelers who are looking for home-style accommodations and a high value-to-dollar ratio can often do well by booking a bed-and-breakfast room (either hosted or unhosted) or a private apartment through a rental agency. Accommodations can run the gamut from spartan to splendid, from studios to multibedroom homes (which makes this a great option for families), and always come fully equipped. You don't have to be coming to the city for the long term to take advantage of these kinds of accommodations; many agencies require just a two-, three- or four-night minimum, and rates on full studio apartments can start as cheaply as $90 or $100 a night.

Another advantage to booking an accommodation through a booking agency rather than a formal hotel is that taxes are often lower, usually just 8.25 percent, instead of the standard 13.25 percent plus $2 per night hotel tax. Sometimes, tax is eliminated altogether on longer stays, thanks to a loophole in the tax laws; ask for the details on sales tax when you book.

If you opt to book an accommodation in this manner, be prepared to be largely on your own. You won't have the services that a hotel offers, like maid service. In fact, many accommodations that call themselves bed-and-breakfasts don't even offer breakfast as part of the package ("guest house" would be a better term), so ask. In fact, get all promises in writing and an exact total up front to avoid any misunderstandings. And try to pay by credit card if you can, so you can dispute payment if the agency fails to live up to its promises.

You'll probably have the best luck with Judith Glynn's Manhattan Getaways (212-956-2010, *www.manhattangetaways.com*), which offers consistently reliable apartments and service. The following agencies are also usually reliable bets:

Abode Apartment Rentals (212) 472-2000, (800) 835-8880, *www.abodenyc.com*

A Hospitality Company (212) 965-1102, (800) 987-1235, *www.hospitalityco.com*

City Sonnet (212) 614-3034, *www.citysonnet.com*

Homestay New York (718) 434-2071, *www.homestayny.com*

Manhattan Lodgings (212) 677-7616, *www.manhattanlodgings.com*

New York Habitat (212) 255-8018, *www.nyhabitat.com*

If you're an independent-minded traveler interested in arranging an apartment swap with a New Yorker, your best source is *www.newyork.craigslist.org*.

BEYOND MANHATTAN
THE BRONX

Le Refuge Inn   GOOD $
620 City Island Ave. (between Sutherland and Cross Sts.), City Island
www.lerefugeinn.com   Phone: (718) 885-2478   Fax: (718) 885-1519

This pleasant old 19th-century sea captain's house on the main strip of enjoyably funky City Island in the far reaches of the Bronx, makes for a pleasant country-in-the-city-style getaway. The warmth of the welcome, the delightful French meals prepared by Normandy-born innkeeper and chef Pierre Saint-Denis (who also presides over Le Refuge Restaurant on the Upper East Side), and the chamber concerts on Sunday afternoons are the best reasons to visit the inn. M. Saint-Denis imbues the inn with the genuine ambiance of his homeland. The backyard faces the water, offering delightful views.

Rooms: Nine (some with shared bathrooms); three floors; no smoking allowed. **Hotel amenities:** None. **Food services:** Rates include continental breakfast; prix-fixe dinner $45, Sunday brunch $19.50. **Cancellation:** One week prior to arrival. **Wheelchair access:** Not accessible. **Directions:** 6 to Pelham Bay Park; then transfer to City Island Bus No. 29 toward City Island (third stop).

BROOKLYN

Bed & Breakfast on the Park   VERY GOOD $$–$$$
113 Prospect Park West (between 6th and 7th Sts.), Park Slope *www.bbnyc.com*
Phone: (718) 499-6115   Fax: (718) 499-1385

A beautifully restored town house built in 1895 situated right across the street from Prospect Park now houses Brooklyn's best bed-and-breakfast inn, and one of the finest in the entire city. The house is enchantingly and lavishly outfitted with antiques, oriental rugs, fine oil paintings and stained glass. The rooms are individually appointed, but each is ultra-romantic in its own way; the most sumptuously outfitted suites stumble into the $$$ price category. Breakfast is vast and satisfying. A real jewel. Be prepared when you pay your bill: A 10 percent staff gratuity is requested.

Rooms: Eight (two with shared bathroom); four floors; no smoking allowed. **Hotel amenities:** None. **Food services:** Rates include full breakfast. **Cancellation:** 10 days prior to arrival, subject to cancellation fee. **Wheelchair access:** Not accessible. **Subway:** F to Seventh Ave.

New York Marriott Brooklyn   VERY GOOD $$
333 Adams St. (between Tillary and Willoughby Sts.), Downtown Brooklyn
www.marriott.com
Phone: (718) 246-7000, (888) 436-3759   Fax: (718) 246-0563

Unveiled in the heart of Brooklyn in 1998, this Marriott, which occupies seven floors of a big office tower, is the first full-service hotel Brooklyn has had in over 50 years, and a prime symbol of the booming gentrification of downtown Brooklyn. It's an attractive and well-outfitted hotel with nods to its home borough that pulls it out of the chain-generic doldrums. Behind the front desk is a mural of the Brooklyn Bridge, and artwork and photos of Brooklyn or by Brooklyn artists adorn the walls throughout the hotel.

Once you reach your room, it's strictly Marriott, but all the bases are well covered. Even though the hotel is built over busy Adams Street, the rooms are tranquil. Quite a few subway lines converge in this area, so citywide access is easy, and you can be in Manhattan inside 10 minutes.

Rooms: 376; seven floors; designated nonsmoking floors. **Hotel amenities:** Concierge, business center, health club with lap pool, laundry and dry-cleaning service, meeting and function rooms, valet parking. **Food services:** Restaurant, cocktail lounge, room service. **Cancellation:** 6 P.M. day of arrival (may vary with some rate plans). **Wheelchair access:** Fully accessible.
Subway: M, N, R to Court St.; 2, 3, 4, 5 to Borough Hall; A, C, F to Jay St.–Borough Hall.

STATEN ISLAND

Harbor House GOOD **$**
1 Hylan Blvd.(at Edgewater St.) *www.nyharborhouse.com*
Phone: (718) 876-0056 Fax: (718) 420-9940

Built in 1890, the Harbor House is not luxurious in any way, but it does have wonderful views over the harbor to Manhattan, taking in the Verrazano Bridge and Lady Liberty as well. One smart man rented the whole place for the Fourth of July and had his family there to watch the fireworks. The house feels more like a beach house than anything else, and you can lie in bed and look out to the water. Rooms tend to be large, with a TV, dresser, armoire and ceiling fan, but no phone.

Rooms: 11 (six with shared bathroom); three floors; no smoking allowed. **Hotel amenities:** None. **Food services:** Rates include continental breakfast. **Cancellation:** 10 days prior to arrival, $20 cancellation fee. **Wheelchair access:** Not accessible. **Directions:** Staten Island Ferry to S-51 bus to Hylan and Bay Street; walk across Bay Street and down one block.

AIRPORTS
*(For directions to airports see chapter **Visiting New York**.)*

La Guardia Airport

Crowne Plaza Hotel La Guardia GOOD **$$–$$$**
104-04 Ditmars Blvd. (at 23rd Ave.), East Elmhurst
www.crowneplaza.com, www.crowneplazalaguardia.com
Phone: (718) 457-6300, (800) 692-5429 Fax: (718) 899-9768

This recently renovated airport hotel features classic-contemporary rooms that have ample amenities. Closets aren't large and ceilings are low but the soundproofing is very good; rooms feature coffee makers (ideal for that early morning flight) and Nintendo on the TV. A few dollars extra will garner you a club-level room, which comes with access to a complimentary full American breakfast buffet, evening hors d'oeuvres and slightly improved accommodations. An airline screen shows up-to-date flight information.

Rooms: 370; seven floors; designated nonsmoking rooms. **Hotel amenities:** Concierge; full-service business center; fitness center with swimming pool, sauna and whirlpool; laundry and dry-cleaning service, guest laundry; meeting space, including conference theater with high-speed Internet access, complimentary airport shuttle. **Food services:** Restaurant, bar, room service. **Cancellation:** 6 P.M. day of arrival. **Wheelchair access:** Fully accessible.

La Guardia Marriott
GOOD $$

102-05 Ditmars Blvd. (at 23rd Ave.), East Elmhurst   *www.marriott.com*
Phone: (718) 565-8900, (800) 228-9290   Fax: (718) 898-4955

Here's a competent and comfortable, if not particularly colorful, hotel near La Guardia's terminal, which keeps the noise-level down (runway-close hotels are much noisier). All of the familiar Marriott and airport-hotel trappings are here, including a executive concierge level and an airline monitor.

Rooms: 439; nine floors; designated nonsmoking floors. **Hotel amenities:** Concierge; business center; fitness center with swimming pool, sauna and whirlpool; laundry and dry-cleaning service; extensive meeting and function space. **Food services:** Restaurant, sports bar, room service; complimentary coffee in lobby, complimentary airport shuttle. **Cancellation:** 6 P.M. day of arrival. **Wheelchair access:** Fully accessible.

J.F.K. Airport

Holiday Inn New York—J.F.K. Airport
GOOD $$

144-02 135th Ave. (Van Wyck Expressway, exit 2), Jamaica
www.holidayinnjfk.com, www.sixcontinentshotels.com
Phone: (718) 659-0200, (800) 692-5350   Fax: (718) 322-2533

Situated on the airport's periphery, this Holiday Inn offers some serenity. It has quiet rooms, a pleasant pool area and even a Japanese garden. In fact, if you have a room facing away from the airport, you'd hardly know you were there. Rooms aren't exactly charming, but they are clean, comfortable and decently sized; bedding is quite comfortable, and bathrooms are plain but adequate.

Rooms: 360; 12 floors; designated nonsmoking rooms. **Hotel amenities:** Concierge, business center, fitness center; indoor/outdoor pool with sauna and whirlpool; laundry and dry-cleaning service, guest laundry, meeting and function rooms, 24-hour courtesy airport transportation. **Food services:** Restaurant, sports bar, room service. **Cancellation:** 6 P.M. day of arrival. **Wheelchair access:** Fully accessible.

Radisson Hotel J.F.K. Airport   GOOD $$
135-30 140th St., Jamaica   *www.radisson.com*
Phone: (718) 322-2300, (800) 333-3333   Fax: (718) 322-5569

Opened in 1998, this Radisson is the newest of J.F.K.'s airport hotels. Rooms are traditionally decorated and moderately attractive; mattresses are good, but your sleep may be undermined by noise from the Belt Parkway just outside. Other in-room perks include high-speed Internet access, on-demand video games and a coffee maker; junior suites add a pullout sofa and a spacious work desk. The hotel's biggest selling point is that it's the only area hotel to have a 24-hour restaurant.

Rooms: 386; 12 floors; designated nonsmoking floors. **Hotel amenities:** Business center, fitness room, laundry and dry-cleaning service, meeting and function rooms. **Food services:** 24-hour restaurant, bar with large-screen TV, 24-hour room service, complimentary airport transportation. **Cancellation:** 24 hours prior to arrival. **Wheelchair access:** Fully accessible.

Newark International Airport, Newark NJ

Newark Airport Marriott   GOOD $$$
Newark International Airport   *www.marriotthotels.com/ewrap*
Phone: (973) 623-0006, (800) 882-1037   Fax: (973) 623-7618

The only hotel on Newark Airport property, this Marriott has the company's familiar combination of comforts and corporate-traveler-friendly amenities. Most important, the windows offer virtually complete soundproofing against airplane noise. Rooms aren't particularly spacious, but they're perfectly adequate and feature in-room coffee makers.

Concierge-level rooms have additional amenities and use of a separate lounge serving complimentary continental breakfast and evening hors d'oeuvres. A telescope helps you keep track of the air traffic, and an airline monitor in the lobby helps you keep track of flight schedules.

Rooms: 597; 10 floors; designated nonsmoking floors. **Hotel amenities:** Concierge; business center; health club with swimming pool, sauna and whirlpool; laundry and dry-cleaning service, and guest laundry facilities; extensive meeting and function space, complimentary airport shuttle. **Food services:** Restaurant, lounge, cigar bar, 24-hour room service. **Cancellation:** 6 P.M. day of arrival. **Wheelchair access:** Fully accessible.

HOTELS BY PRICE

$$$$ Very Expensive

Bryant Park Hotel	Midtown West	VERY GOOD
The Carlyle	Upper East Side	EXTRAORDINARY
Chambers	Midtown West	VERY GOOD
Essex House, A Westin Hotel	Midtown West	EXCELLENT

Four Seasons Hotel New York	Midtown East	EXCELLENT
Inn New York City	Upper West Side	EXCELLENT
The Kitano New York	Murray Hill	EXCELLENT
Le Parker Meridien	Midtown West	EXTRAORDINARY
The Lowell	Upper East Side	EXCELLENT
The Mercer	SoHo	EXCELLENT
Millennium Broadway	Times Square	VERY GOOD
The Mark	Upper East Side	EXCELLENT
The Peninsula New York	Midtown West	EXTRAORDINARY
The Pierre	Upper East Side	EXCELLENT
The Plaza	Midtown West	VERY GOOD
The Regency Hotel	Upper East Side	EXCELLENT
Regent Wall Street	Financial District	EXTRAORDINARY
Ritz-Carlton New York, Battery Park	Battery Park	EXCELLENT
60 Thompson	SoHo	VERY GOOD
Sofitel New York	Midtown West	EXCELLENT
SoHo Grand Hotel	SoHo	EXCELLENT
The Stanhope, Park Hyatt New York	Upper East Side	VERY GOOD
The St. Regis New York	Midtown East	EXTRAORDINARY
Tribeca Grand Hotel	TriBeCa	EXCELLENT
Trump International Hotel & Tower	Upper West Side	EXTRAORDINARY
Waldorf Towers, A Conrad Hotel	Midtown East	EXCELLENT

$$$–$$$$

City Club Hotel	Midtown West	EXCELLENT
Hotel Giraffe	Flatiron District	VERY GOOD
The Inn at Irving Place	Gramercy Park	EXCELLENT
The Iroquois New York	Midtown West	GOOD
The Lombardy	Midtown East	EXCELLENT
Omni Berkshire Place	Midtown East	EXCELLENT
Royalton	Midtown West	VERY GOOD
Sheraton Russell Hotel	Murray Hill	VERY GOOD
Swissôtel New York-The Drake	Midtown East	EXTRAORDINARY
Waldorf=Astoria, A Hilton Hotel	Midtown East	EXCELLENT
W New York—The Court	Midtown East	VERY GOOD
W New York—The Tuscany	Midtown East	VERY GOOD
W Times Square	Times Square	EXCELLENT
W Union Square	Union Square	VERY GOOD

$$$ Expensive

The Algonquin	Times Square	EXCELLENT
The Melrose Hotel, New York	Upper East Side	VERY GOOD
The Benjamin	Midtown East	EXTRAORDINARY
Crowne Plaza at the United Nations	Midtown East	VERY GOOD
Doubletree Guest Suites	Times Square	VERY GOOD
Embassy Suites New York	Battery Park City	EXCELLENT

Flatotel International	Midtown West	GOOD
Hilton New York	Midtown West	GOOD
Hilton Times Square	Times Square	EXCELLENT
Holiday Inn Wall Street	Financial District	EXCELLENT
Hotel Elysée	Midtown East	VERY GOOD
Kimberly Hotel	Midtown East	VERY GOOD
Le Marquis New York	Murray Hill	VERY GOOD
Library Hotel	Midtown East	VERY GOOD
Morgans	Murray Hill	VERY GOOD
The Muse	Midtown West	EXCELLENT
New York Marriott Brooklyn	Brooklyn	GOOD
New York Marriott Financial Center	Financial District	GOOD
New York Marriott Marquis	Times Square	GOOD
The Roger Smith	Midtown East	GOOD
The Roger Williams	Midtown East	GOOD
Surrey Hotel	Upper East Side	VERY GOOD
The Time	Times Square	GOOD
Wall Street Inn	Financial District	VERY GOOD
The Warwick	Midtown West	GOOD

$$–$$$

Crowne Plaza Hotel La Guardia	Queens	GOOD
Fitzpatrick Grand Central Hotel	Midtown East	VERY GOOD
The Gorham	Midtown West	VERY GOOD
Hotel Casablanca	Times Square	EXCELLENT
Hotel Wales	Upper East Side	GOOD
The Mansfield	Midtown West	GOOD
Metropolitan Hotel	Midtown East	GOOD

$$ Moderate

Abingdon Guest House	West Village	VERY GOOD
Bed & Breakfast on the Park	Brooklyn	VERY GOOD
The Belvedere	Midtown West	GOOD
The Bentley	Upper East Side	GOOD
Best Western Seaport Inn	Lower Manhattan	GOOD
Broadway Inn	Midtown West	VERY GOOD
Chelsea Lodge Suites	Chelsea	VERY GOOD
Country Inn the City	Upper West Side	VERY GOOD
Gramercy Park Hotel	Gramercy Park	GOOD
The Helmsley Middletowne	Midtown East	GOOD
Holiday Inn Downtown/Soho	Chinatown	BASIC
Holiday Inn New York—J.F.K. Airport	Queens	GOOD
Hotel Beacon	Upper West Side	VERY GOOD
Hotel Bedford	Midtown East	BASIC
Hotel Chelsea	Chelsea	GOOD
Hotel Edison	Times Square	BASIC

Hotel Metro	Midtown West	VERY GOOD
Hudson	Midtown West	VERY GOOD
The Inn on 23rd St.	Chelsea	VERY GOOD
La Guardia Marriott	Queens	GOOD
The Lucerne	Upper West Side	EXCELLENT
Newark Airport Marriott	Newark	GOOD
On the Ave	Upper West Side	GOOD
Paramount	Times Square	GOOD
Radisson Hotel J.F.K. Airport	Queens	GOOD

$–$$

Chelsea Inn	Flatiron District	BASIC
Chelsea Pines Inn	Chelsea	VERY GOOD
Chelsea Savoy Hotel	Chelsea	GOOD
Comfort Inn Midtown	Midtown West	GOOD
Excelsior Hotel	Upper West Side	GOOD
The Marcel	Gramercy Park	VERY GOOD
Red Roof Inn	Midtown West	VERY GOOD
Super 8 Hotel Times Square	Midtown West	VERY GOOD
Thirty Thirty	Murray Hill	VERY GOOD
Travel Inn	Midtown West	GOOD
Washington Square Hotel	East Village	BASIC

$ Inexpensive

Americana Inn	Midtown West	BASIC
Amsterdam Inn	Upper West Side	BASIC
Chelsea Lodge	Chelsea	VERY GOOD
Colonial House Inn	Chelsea	GOOD
Cosmopolitan Hotel—Tribeca	Tribeca	GOOD
Harbor House	Staten Island	GOOD
Holmes Bed & Breakfast	Upper West Side	GOOD
Hotel Olcott	Upper West Side	GOOD
Larchmont Hotel	West Village	GOOD
Le Refuge Inn	The Bronx	GOOD
New York City Howard Johnson Express	Lower East Side	GOOD
Pioneer of SoHotel	Nolita	BASIC
Murray Hill Inn	Murray Hill	BASIC
Second Home on Second Ave.	East Village	GOOD
St. Mark's Hotel	East Village	BASIC
Union Square Inn	East Village	GOOD

Restaurants in New York City

According to *New York Times* food critic, William Grimes, "The quality, range and sheer number of the city's restaurants has made New York the world's most exciting place to eat. Paris may have more French restaurants, and Rome more trattorias, but no city on earth offers the adventurous eater more variety and depth than New York at the present moment," says *New York Times* food critic William Grimes.

For more than 30 years, New Yorkers have been relying on restaurant reviews in the *Times* for the most trustworthy advice about where to eat in their hometown. The 300 or so restaurants included here have all been reviewed by the major food critics of the *Times*: William Grimes, Eric Asimov and Ruth Reichl. Since 1992 Eric Asimov has been responsible for finding those quintessential New York restaurants that serve high quality food at reasonable prices (his reviews are clearly identified by the term **"$25 & Under"** which appears at the top of the review). Restaurants with stars have been reviewed by Mr. Grimes since 1999 and by Ms. Reichl before then. Her original reviews have been updated in the "Eating Out" and "Good Eating" columns that appear weekly in the newspaper and those changes are reflected here. In addition, Mr. Grimes and Mr. Asimov have done recent updates for this *Guide*.

(Note: The best restaurants in Brooklyn, Queens and the other boroughs can be found in the appropriate sections.)

Using This Guide

What the Stars Mean:

☆ ☆ ☆ ☆	Extraordinary
☆ ☆ ☆	Excellent
☆ ☆	Very Good
☆	Good

Price Range: The dollar signs that appear at the top of each review are based on the cost of a three-course dinner and a 15 percent tip (but not drinks).

$	$25 and under
$$	$25 to $40
$$$	$40 to $55
$$$$	$55 and over

$25 & Under: At these restaurants you can get a complete meal, exclusive of drinks and tip, for $25 or less; recently, as a concession to inflation, some restaurants have been included where only an appetizer and main course total $25.

Abbreviations: Meals: B = Breakfast, Br = Brunch, L = Lunch, D = Dinner. LN = Late Night (restaurants open till midnight or later). Credit cards: AE = American Express; DC = Diner's Club; D = Discover; MC = Master Card; V = Visa; if there is no credit card information it means that at least three of these cards are accepted.

The Best Restaurants in New York City

☆ ☆ ☆ ☆—EXTRAORDINARY

Alain Ducasse
Bouley

Daniel
Jean Georges

Le Bernardin
Lespinasse

☆ ☆ ☆—EXCELLENT

Aquavit
AZ
Babbo
Café Boulud
Chanterelle
Craft
Danube
Felidia
Fiamma Osteria
Fifty Seven Fifty Seven
The Four Seasons
Gotham Bar and Grill
Gramercy Tavern

Honmura An
Ilo
JoJo
Judson Grill
Kuruma Zushi
La Caravelle
La Côte Basque
La Grenouille
Le Cirque 2000
March
Next Door Nobu
Nobu
Oceana

Olica
Park Bistro
Patria
Periyali
Picholine
Pico
San Domenico
Sushi Yasuda
Tabla
Town
Union Pacific
Veritas

☆ ☆—VERY GOOD

Ada
An American Place
Aquagrill
Arqua
Artisanal
Atelier
Balthazar
Bambou
Bayard's
Beacon
Beppe
Bice
Blue Fin
Blue Hill

Blue Ribbon Sushi
Brasserie
Cafe Sabarsky
Campagna
Centoline
Chelsea Bistro & Bar
Chez Josephine
Chicama
Cho Dang Gol
Chola
Christer's
Churrascaria Plataforma
Circus
Citarella the Restaurant

City Hall
Compass
D'Artagnan
DB Bistro Moderne
The Dining Room
Eight Mile Creek
Eleven Madison Park
Esca
Estiatorio Milos
Etats-Unis
F.Illi Ponte
Firebird
Fleur de Sel
Gabriel's

Guastavino's
Hangawi
The Harrison
Hatsuhana
Heartbeat
Icon
Il Valentino
I Trulli
Joe's Shanghai
Kai
Kang Suh
Le Colonial
Le Perigord
Little Dove
Lutèce
Manhattan Ocean Club
Marseille
Maya
Meigas
Mercer Kitchen
Mesa Grill
Mi

Michael Jordan's
Michael's
Mi Cocina
Moda
Molyvos
Nadaman Hakubai
New York Noodle Town
Nick & Toni's Cafe
Nicole's
Odeon
Orsay
Otabe
Ouest
Paola's
Papillon
Parioli Romanissimo
Park Avenue Cafe
Park View at the
  Boathouse
Payard Patisserie
Petrossian
Ping's Seafood

Remi
Ruby Foo's
Salaam Bombay
Savoy
Screening Room
Sea Grill
71 Clinton Fresh Food
Shun Lee Palace
Smith & Wollensky
Solera
Sono
Surya
Tamarind
Thalia
Tocqueville
The Tonic
Tribeca Grill
Triomphe
21 Club
Union Square Café
Zarela

☆—GOOD

Arezzo
Asia de Cuba
Atlantic Grill
Avra
Baldoria
Barrio
Blue Smoke
Blue Water Grill
Bouterin
Brasserie 8 1/2
Butter
Calle Ocho
Commissary
Coup
Dawat
Della Femina
Delmonico's
Dim Sum Go Go
District
Dock's Oyster Bar

Frank's
Goody's
Jack Rose
Jane
Jarnac
Jean-Luc
La Nonna
Lentini
Les Halles Downtown
Le Zinc
Lotus
Man Ray
Maritime
Medi
Meet
92
NL
Olives
Osteria Del Circo
Pastis

Patroon
Peasant
Pop
Provence
Red Bar Restaurant
The Red Cat
Redeye Grill
Scalini Fedeli
Strip House
Suba
TanDa
Tappo
The Tasting Room
Tavern on the Green
Théo
Thom
Verbena
Viceversa
Zipangu
Zitoune

Quick Guide to the
Best Inexpensive Manhattan Restaurants

Selected by Eric Asimov

aKa Café
Alias
Bar Pitti
Beyoglu
Bread Bar at Tabla
Bright Food Shop
Bukhara Grill
Congee Village
Cooke's Corner
Craftbar
Dakshin
El Presidente
Euzkadi
Funky Broome
Grand Sichuan Int'l
Holy Basil
'ino
Katsu-Hama
Katz's Deli
Komodo
Kori
La Palapa
Le Zie 2000
Lombardi's
Luca

Lupa
Mama's Food Shop
Mavalli Palace
Mexicana Mama
Mirchi
Moustache
Nam
National Cafe
Nha Trang
Our Place Shanghai
    Tea Garden
Pao
Pearl Oyster Bar
Pepolino
Po
Pongal
Prune
Sabor
Snack
Soba-Ya
Supper
Taco Taco
Turkuaz
Vatan
Wu Liang Ye

MANHATTAN RESTAURANTS, A-Z

Acquario $25 & Under   MEDITERRANEAN
5 Bleecker St. (near Bowery)   (212) 260-4666
With its candles, brick walls and casual service, Acquario is a small, warm place straight out of the Village's bohemian past. A couple of Acquario's large appetizers can easily make a light meal. Try the fresh sardines, which have a strong, briny aroma but a mild, wonderfully nutty flavor and are served with a small green salad. Fennel salad is also wonderful, though it's hard to find a more alluring dish than the Portuguese fish stew. **Price range:** Entrees, $12–$18. Cash only. **Meals:** D. Closed Sun. **Subway:** 6 to Bleecker St.

Ada   ☆☆   **$$$$**   INDIAN
208 E. 58th St. (between Second and Third Aves.)   (212) 371-6060
Ada aims to elevate the status of Indian cuisine in New York. The décor steers clear of Indian fabrics, ornate brass plates and beaded curtains; the owner is intent on giving the food an upgrade as well. One of the best appetizers is a slow-grilled white-pea and potato cake accented with garam masala, fennel and cilantro, and surrounded by caramelized bananas coated with crème fraîche. Spices are used with great delicacy in most dishes, and they penetrate every fiber of tandoori-cooked meats, which arrive in a state of melting tenderness. The dessert menu uses a few Indian ingredients strategically, with some success. **Price range:** Prix fixe, $55 or $65. **Meals:** L, D. **Subway:** 4, 5, 6 to 59th St.

aKa Café $25 & Under   FUSION
49 Clinton St. (near Rivington St.)   (212) 979-6096
This storefront offshoot of 71 Clinton Fresh Food offers food that takes the familiar downtown sandwich-and-wine bar into a stratosphere of unexpected flavor combinations. The signature lamb tongue sandwich is the oddest offering, but it's one of the most successful, a balance of savory, sweet and rich on spongy Italian bread. The back-lighted bar is the central feature of an otherwise minimally decorated room. Yet the menu grabs the attention right away, even though it offers no more than soups, salads and sandwiches. **Price range:** Everything is $5–$7. **Meals:** D. Closed Sun. **Subway:** F, J, M to Delancey St.

Alain Ducasse at the Essex House   ☆☆☆☆   **$$$$**   FRENCH
155 W. 58th St.   (212) 265-7300
When it opened a few years ago, Alain Ducasse at the Essex House was more expensive, more sumptuous, more ritualized — more everything — than any other restaurant in Manhattan. But the food, although very good, did not measure up to expectations, and certainly not to the prices on the menu. The kinks have been worked out of the service, which now has a polish and grace befitting the jewel box of a dining room. The easier, happier atmosphere emanates, ultimately, from the kitchen. Mr. Ducasse has always sworn allegiance to the philosophy that ingredients should rule the kitchen and his menu abounds in simple classic preparations. The payoff is evident every night at the Essex House,

where Mr. Ducasse now offers, with much less fanfare, the kind of food that
brings diners to their knees. **Price range**: Prix-fixe and tasting menus, $145-160
(lunch "menu salad," $65; truffle menu, $300). **Meals:** L (Thu. & Fri.), D.
Closed Sun. **Subway:** F, N, Q, R, W to 57th St.

Alias $25 & Under   NEW AMERICAN
76 Clinton St. (at Rivington St.)   (212) 505-5011
Alias serves conventional appetizer-main course meals but in jaunty bistro style.
The small, boxy dining room shows a clean, modern design. Tables are close
together but it's comfortable unless you are stuck in the low-ceilinged alcove
near the restroom, which is loud and claustrophobic. The menu is small and
predictably eccentric, but you'll love the silken-textured, melt-in-your-mouth
house-cured sable and the precise flavors of the fluke ceviche, too, with its Mexican accent courtesy of the chili-spiked pumpkin-seed oil. **Price range:** Entrees,
$15-$18. **Meals:** D. Closed Sun. **Subway:** F, J, M to Delancey St.

Alley's End $25 & Under   BISTRO/NEW AMERICAN
311 W. 17th St. (between Eighth and Ninth Aves.)   (212) 627-8899
Enter a portal and traverse a passageway, and you leave the workaday Chelsea
world for Alley's End, a lovely network of dining rooms and gardens that feels as
pastoral and isolated as an oasis. The brief menu manages to match the romantic draw of the interior. **Price range:** Entrees, $14–$22. **Meals:** D. **Subway:** A,
C, E to 14th St.; L to Eighth Ave.

Alouette $25 & Under   BISTRO/FRENCH
2588 Broadway (near 97th St.)   (212) 222-6808
Dishes at Alouette are cleverly conceived, beautifully presented and moderately
priced; each item promises excitement. Service has its ups and downs, and the
second floor is rather warm and stuffy. **Price range:** Entrees, $15–$18.50. **Meals:**
Br, D. **Subway:** 1, 2, 3, 9 to 96th St.

Amy Ruth's $25 & Under   SOUTHERN
113 W. 116th St. (between Lenox and Seventh Aves.)   (212) 280-8779
Amy Ruth's presents Southern food that is up-to-date without sacrificing time-
honored traditions. Chicken is served with crisp yet fluffy waffles, a common
pairing, but you can order whole-grain waffles, and they're all served with real
maple syrup. The stars of the menu include short ribs that are falling-off-the-
bone tender in an earthy, oniony brown gravy, and baked spareribs served in a
sweet barbecue sauce. Side dishes shine, like buttery string beans and eggy
potato salad. Deep-dish sweet potato pie and pineapple-coconut cake are terrific.
Price range: Dinner, $7.95–$17.95. **Meals:** B, L, D. **Subway:** 2, 3 to 116th St.

An American Place   ☆☆ $$$$ NEW AMERICAN
565 Lexington Ave. (between 50th and 51st Sts.)   (212) 888-5650
The name is as simple as Main Street, and like Main Street it has been around
long enough that it seems almost timeless, expressing a vision of American cui-

sine as an infinitely renewable resource. The food has the right blend of bold-
ness and subtlety. The pot-roasted short ribs do not require a lot of fuss and
bother; this signature dish is served with whipped potatoes that cut the richness of the meat with a sharp horseradish edge and fresh herbs. The cedar-
planked salmon has a nice, crisp char, and the rich, pillow-soft dollop of corn
pudding on the side cannot be beat. The wisest course for dessert is to order
the double chocolate pudding, a satisfyingly regressive treat served with
Schrafft's sugar cookies. **Price range:** Entrees, $26–$32. **Meals:** B, Br, L, D.
Subway: 6 to 51st St.

Aquagrill ☆☆ $$$ SEAFOOD
210 Spring St. (at Sixth Ave.) (212) 274-0505
Aquagrill has the comfortable air of a neighborhood place, the sort of restaurant
that ought to be serving burgers and beer. Instead there's an oyster bar in front
and the menu is refreshingly original. Devoted almost entirely to fish, it offers
unusual dishes like "snail-snaps" (bite-size popovers with a single snail) and
salmon in falafel crust. Soups are also satisfying. All the fish is well prepared and
some with imagination. **Price range:** Entrees, $18.50–$26. **Meals:** Br, L, D.
Closed Mon. **Subway:** C, E to Spring St.

Aquavit ☆☆☆ $$$$ SWEDISH
13 W. 54th St. (between Fifth and Sixth Aves.) (212) 307-7311
Marcus Samuelsson, Aquavit's restlessly inventive executive chef, is not the for-
mula type. He is a fully mature artist with a distinctive style in which precisely
defined flavors talk back and forth to each other rather than blending into a
single smooth harmonic effect. The menu sparkles with bright thoughts. Her-
ring, of course, remains on the menu, a reminder that, to the Swedes, this fish is
a form of cultural expression that is part of the genetic code. Mr. Samuelsson's
pièce de résistance is his pellucid arctic char, pinkish orange and delicately
smoked. A waiter pours a steaming mushroom consommé, or possibly a spring-
onion broth, over the fish. **Price range:** Pre-theater menu, $39; prix fixe and
tasting menus, $67–$110. **Meals:** L, D. **Subway:** B, D, E to Seventh Ave.

Arqua ☆☆ $$ ITALIAN
281 Church St. (at White St.) (212) 334-1888
The setting of this restaurant named for a village in northern Italy, is alluring,
but the noise can be deafening when all the chairs are occupied at night. Lunch
is a more tranquil time, and the rustic fare is unfailingly good. Starters include
grilled chicken and mushroom sausage on a warm lentil salad; fresh pickled sardines with sweet and sour onions; a soup of the day; and several homemade pastas. Some recommended main dishes are pan-seared tuna loin with ginger sauce;
baked duck breast with a sauce of black currant and cassis; and braised rabbit
with white wine and herbs. Before the espresso, try a ricotta cheesecake or a
poached pear with caramel sauce and ice cream. **Price range:** Entrees, $16–$22.
Meals: L, D. **Subway:** 1, 9 to Franklin St.

Arezzo ☆ $$$ ITALIAN
46 W. 22nd St. (bet. Fifth & Sixth Aves.)   (212) 206-0555
Arezzo, a modest low-ceiling dining room with a coal-burning oven, is the setting for Tuscan and Piedmontese cuisine, with some modernizing. The oven,
source of the more traditional dishes, produces what may be the best appetizer
on the menu, a focaccina, a flatter relative of the famed focaccia, split in half
and spread with a mixture of robiola cheese, potato and spinach, then drizzled
with truffle oil. The pastas are good, not great. Pea-flavored cavatelli with a
sauce of hot and sweet sausages is among the best on the list. Arezzo has a lot of
desserts. The pastry chef outdoes himself with a very dense, intensely flavored
bitter-chocolate panna cotta. **Price range:** Lunch: apps., $7–$12; entrees,
$14–$22. Dinner: apps., $9–$18; entrees, $17–$35; desserts, $8.50. **Meals:** L, D.
Closed Sun. **Subway:** N, R to 23rd St.

Artisanal ☆☆ $$$$ BISTRO
2 Park Ave. (at 32nd St.)   (212) 725-8585
Artisanal is a big, very good-looking brasserie with more varieties of cheese
(nearly 200) than most human beings will encounter in a lifetime. About half
the menu at Artisanal is honest bistro cooking. The other half shows some genuinely inspired flashes, like rabbit in riesling sauce. After the entrees comes the
moment of truth. You will have plenty of help putting together a good cheese
plate, and Artisanal makes all of its 140 or so wines available by the glass, so no
cheese need be eaten without the mathematically precise wine pairing.
Price range: Entrees, $16–$36. **Meals:** L, D, LN. **Subway:** 6 to 33rd St.

Asia de Cuba ☆ $$$ ASIAN/LATIN AMERICAN
237 Madison Ave. (near 37th St.)   (212) 726-7755
You won't eat very well at Asia de Cuba. But the manic energy of the place
makes every night feel like a party. There aren't many main dishes to recommend. But who can think about all that when desserts are exploding all over the
room? Guava Dynamite is just guava mousse wrapped in a chocolate tuile, but
the sparkler on top is seductive. **Price range:** Entrees, $22–$34.
Meals: L, D, LN. **Subway:** 6 to 33rd St.

Atelier ☆☆ $$$$ FRENCH
Ritz-Carlton Hotel, 50 Central Park S. (at Sixth Ave.)   (212) 521-6125
Atelier serves refined modern French cuisine in a cool, elegant, L-shaped hotel
dining room decorated with fine art. Gabriel Kreuther, formerly the chef de cuisine at Jean Georges, has an elegant touch and a distinctive way of deploying
herbs and vegetables, treating them almost as co-stars instead of supporting
players. **Price range:** Entrees, $22–$40; prix fixe and tasting menus, $32–$95.
Meals: L, D. **Subway:** N, Q, R, W to 5th Ave.

Atlantic Grill ☆ $$ SEAFOOD
1341 Third Ave. (near 77th St.)   (212) 988-9200
This appealing, affordable restaurant with its bustling but surprisingly quiet
dining room and attentive service will rarely let you down. The cold seafood

platter with four sauces, which serves four, is fresh and tasty; a better appetizer is the sweet, smoky, hickory-roasted sea bass with cucumber and ginger salsa. Simplicity is the key to the best main dishes: fish served with rice and vegetables is perfectly grilled to order and makes a satisfying meal. And the red Thai curry is an absolute delight. **Price range:** Entrees, $14.50–$19.95. **Meals:** Br, L, D. **Subway:** 6 to 77th St.

Avenue $25 & Under
520 Columbus Ave. (at 85th St.)   BISTRO/FRENCH
                                                                   (212) 579-3194
This informal corner restaurant (with an unexpectedly French atmosphere and efficient service) serves breakfasts and light meals by day and full dinners at night. Smoked pork loin, sliced lamb and sliced steak are excellent. At brunch, try the hot chocolate, which is thick as pudding and rich as a chocolate truffle. From the terrific food to the daylong service and the good values, Avenue is a formula that works. **Price range:** Entrees, $13.95–$16.95. **Meals:** B, Br, L, D, LN. **Subway:** 4, 5, 6 to 86th St.

Avra ☆ $$$
141 E. 48th St. (between Third and Lexington Aves.)   GREEK/SEAFOOD
                                                                   (212) 759-8550
Greek cuisine is a modest thing, a fairly limited catalog of simple pleasures, and Avra gives it honest, honorable representation. Fresh fish, barely touched, is the selling point here. In the open kitchen, a ball of fire blasts each side of a sea bass or red snapper imprisoned in a grilling basket; the fish gets a squirt of lemon, a drizzling of olive oil and a sprinkling of herbs, then heads to the table. The seafood counter offers about a dozen fish. Lamb loin chops, served with lemon potatoes and okra, are tender and flavorful, and grilled chicken is served with string beans, in a zesty stewed tomato sauce. Avra's spanakopita is a flawless layering of good feta, firm spinach and leeks, with crackling-fresh leaves of phyllo dough. **Price range:** Entrees, $18.50–$26. **Meals:** L, D. **Subway:** S, 4, 5, 6, 7 to 42nd St.

AZ ☆☆☆ $$$$
21 W. 17th St. (between Fifth and Sixth Aves.)   FUSION
                                                                   (212) 691-8888
AZ is gorgeous, an improbable but enchanting blend of strict Asian geometry, Western Art Nouveau and turn-of-the century Viennese craft influences. The décor, in other words, matches the menu. When the food arrives, however, Patricia Yeo's highly inventive, extroverted and wildly successful brand of fusion cooking holds center stage. Duck schnitzel sounds like a joke. The laughter stops when the rich duck meat, wrapped in a paper-thin crunchy layer of breading, makes contact with brown butter, specks of hazelnut and an intervention of sweet and bitter flavors provided by sliced golden beets. Ms. Yeo also works wonders with Asian teas. Chicken smoked in Lapsang souchong leaves absorbs the dusky perfume of the tea, which is nicely offset by a scallion pancake and a thick fig chutney. Two non-Asian desserts make the strongest impression, a fig tarte Tatin with fromage blanc ice cream, and a small coconut financier. **Price range:** Three-course prix fixe, $52; six-course tasting menu, $75. **Meals:** Br, L, D. **Subway:** F to 14th St.

Babbo ☆☆☆ $$$$ ITALIAN
110 Waverly Pl. (bet.. Sixth Ave. and Washington Sq. Park)   (212) 777-0303
The menu here is loaded with dishes Americans are not supposed to like: fresh
anchovies and warm testa (head cheese) are among the appetizers, and pastas
include bucatini with octopus, and ravioli filled with beef cheeks and topped
with crushed squab livers. One of the best pastas is made with calf's brains
wrapped in tender sheets and sprinkled with fragrant sage and thyme flowers;
there is also a pasta tasting menu: five different pastas followed by two desserts.
But a meal at Babbo is not complete without spicy, robust calamari. Wine is
served by quartinos (250 milliliters, or a third of a bottle); if you don't like one,
the kitchen will take it back. The best ending to a meal here is saffron panna
cotta with poached peaches. The upstairs room is small, spare and intimate with
warm golden light. Downstairs the bar is crowded and lively but the tables are
uncomfortable. **Price range:** entrees, $15–$35; tasting menus, $59–$65.
Meals: D. **Subway:** A, C, E, F, S to W. 4th St.

Baldoria ☆ $$$ ITALIAN
249 W. 49th St. (between Seventh and Eighth Aves.)   (212) 582-0460
Baldoria (meaning "rollicking good time") is a big slice of neighborhood Italian,
New York style. They serve feel-good food in a feel-good atmosphere that
inclines diners to overlook shortcomings. When it's good, Baldoria is quite good.
The greens and the tomatoes are always fresh and flavorful. Pastas, too, perform
strongly, especially trenette with prosciutto, peas and onions in a light cream
sauce. Standard appetizers are respectable, as are main courses like sweet sausages
with pepper and onions. Get the costata di manzo, a thuggish-looking hunk of
charred rib chop, weighing in at 54 ounces; it's an incredibly flavorful piece of
beef, juicy, tender and perfectly cooked. **Price range:** Entrees, $18–$32.
Meals: D. Closed Sun. **Subway:** C, E, 1, 9 to 50th St.

Bali Nusa Indah $25 & Under   INDONESIAN
651 Ninth Ave. (near 45th St.)   (212) 765-6500
Bali Nusa Indah offers fresh and lively Indonesian dishes in a tranquil and
pretty setting. Most of the food is forcefully spiced, yet respectful of the flavors
of each dish. Among the dishes worth trying are Javanese fisherman's soup; corn
fritters gently flavored with shrimp; nasi goreng, the wonderful Indonesian version of fried rice; and sea bass broiled in a banana leaf. There are exceptional
desserts as well. **Price range:** Entrees, $6–$13.50. **Meals:** L, D. **Subway:** A, C, E
to 42nd St.

Balthazar ☆☆ $$$ BISTRO, FRENCH
80 Spring St. (between Lafayette St. and Broadway)   (212) 965-1785
Dinner at midnight? If you don't have the private number for this oh-so-trendy
SoHo French brasserie, that is probably what you'll be offered, so book weeks in
advance. Try going for breakfast or lunch; the room is still beautiful, the affordable food still delicious. The Balthazar salad is a fine mix of asparagus, haricots
verts, fennel and ricotta salata in a truffle vinaigrette. Sautéed foie gras is excel-

lent, as is an appetizer of grilled mackerel with a warm potato salad. The short ribs are awesome: rich and meaty, they are accompanied by fat-soaked carrots and buttery mashed potatoes. Lighter dishes are also attractive, like seared salmon served over soft polenta. **Price range:** Entrees, $16–32. **Meals:** B, L, D, LN. **Subway:** 6 to Spring St.; N, R to Prince St.

Bambou ☆☆ $$$ CARIBBEAN

243 E. 14th St. (between Second and Third Aves.) (212) 505-1180
The best Caribbean food in the city is served in a room with such cozy elegance, it feels as if a warm breeze is blowing through it. There is no better way to begin a meal here than with the eggplant soup, a thick dark liquid with the scent of curry and the deep, intoxicating taste of coconut. Bambou shrimp, each encrusted in coconut, are sweet and tasty, an appetizer that could almost be a dessert. The tropical fruit plate glows with color and the coconut crème brûlée is fabulous. **Price range:** Entrees, $18–$26. **Meals:** D. **Subway:** L to Third Ave.; N, Q, R, W, 4, 5, 6 to 14th St.

Bandol $25 & Under FRENCH

181 E. 78th St. (between Third and Lexington Aves.) (212) 744-1800
Bandol, named for a fine Provençal wine, offers dreamy Mediterranean flavors. The food is very good, the atmosphere warm and neighborly. Even the overly familiar dishes like lamb shank, salmon and scallops have clear, direct flavors that convey their appeal rather than their popularity. Among the appetizers, the pissaladiére, a tart of onions, olives and anchovies, is so good that you could eat two and call it a meal. While the main courses don't have the consistency of the appetizers, they are still satisfying. Coq au vin is lighter than usual, grilled steak is juicy and flavorful, and the tender lamb shank offers primal enjoyment. The mostly French wine list is long but not very exciting. **Price range:** Entrees, $16–$22. AE only. **Meals:** Br, L, D. **Subway:** 6 to 77th St.

Barking Dog Luncheonette $25 & Under DINER

1678 Third Ave. (at 94th St.) (212) 831-1800
1453 York Ave. (between 77th and 78th Sts.) (212) 861-3600
With its dark wood paneling, comfortable booths, bookshelves and low-key lighting, the Barking Dog looks more like a library than a luncheonette. That, in part, explains its appeal to adults, along with its up-to-date American menu, which ranges from hamburgers, fried chicken and meatloaf to leg of lamb and roasted trout. If the children begin to fidget while waiting for the rich, bountiful desserts, distract them with the restaurant's dog tchotchkes, which can be a parent's best friend. **Price range:** Entrees, $11. Cash only. **Meals:** B, Br, L, D, LN. **Subway:** Third Ave.: 6 to 96th St. York Ave.: 6 to 77th St.

Bar Pitti $25 & Under ITALIAN

268 Sixth Ave. (near Houston St.) (212) 982-3300
This casual cafe offers superbly simple Tuscan fare and draws a fashion-conscious crowd. Bar Pitti's ease with people and with food is what makes it seem

so Italian; its atmosphere of jangly controlled frenzy makes it a wonderful New York experience. Outdoor seating on Sixth Avenue is remarkably pleasant. The menu is small and familiar, and almost all the main courses are superb. **Price range:** Entrees, $10.50–$19. Cash only. **Meals:** L, D, LN. **Subway:** A, C, E, F, S to W. 4th St.

Barrio   ☆ $$$ BISTRO
99 Stanton St. (at Ludlow St.)   (212) 533-9212

Barrio's round-the-clock, seven-day schedule makes it a cross between a diner and a bistro. That means the food needs to be sharp and hip, but not so clever that it scares away local residents hankering for a quick bite. The lunch menu is mostly given over to soup, sandwiches and salads. But the soup could be a thick, silken blend of rutabaga and parsley root, sneakily spiced with cayenne and ginger, and the sandwiches outperform their bargain price. The prix-fixe makes it possible to enjoy lunch with substantial main courses like braised veal cheeks on a sweet-sour bed of marinated beet greens. **Price range:** Entrees, $13–$27. **Meals:** Open 24 hours. **Subway:** F to Second Ave.

Bayard's   ☆ ☆ $$$$ FRENCH
1 Hanover Sq. (between Pearl and Stone Sts.)   (212) 514-9454

Bayard's may be the most distinctive, romantic dining room in Manhattan, and the food suits the surroundings. Chef Eberhard Müller grows his own produce, and it features prominently on the menu. When this approach works, it works spectacularly. Steamed savoy cabbage encases a breast of chicken folded over a slice of foie gras, sitting in a shallow pool of chicken-vegetable broth; you would have to search far and wide for a better chicken dish. The knockout wine list is a lengthy document, peppered with bargains, that many restaurants would kill for. The solid dessert list offers classics as well as highly inventive desserts like a Moroccan citrus soup with Lillet granite. **Price range:** Entrees, $29–$38. **Meals:** D. Closed Sun. **Subway:** 2, 3 to Wall St.

Bayou $25 & Under   CAJUN/SOUTHERN
308 Lenox Ave. (between 125th and 126th Sts.)   (212) 426-3800

Bayou, a handsome Creole restaurant in Harlem, would do any New Orleans native proud. With its brick walls, retro brass lamps and woody touches, Bayou looks like countless other neighborhood bars and grills, but its big picture windows and second-floor setting offer an unusual New York panorama, unimpeded by tall buildings. The menu is short, but includes standout appetizers like earthy chicken livers in a rich port wine sauce, and shrimp rémoulade, piquant with mustard and hot pepper and served with deviled eggs. The rich turtle soup is thick with bits of turtle meat and smoky andouille sausage, spiked with sherry and lemon. The sautéed snapper Alexandria, sprinkled with roasted pecans and drenched with lemon butter, is moist and altogether delicious. For dessert, both a bread pudding with a vanilla-whiskey sauce and a fudgy, wedge-shaped pecan brownie topped with peppermint ice cream and chocolate sauce are excellent. **Price range:** Entrees, $12.95–$21.95. **Meals:** L, D. **Subway:** 2, 3 to 125th St.

Beacon ☆☆ **$$$**   NEW AMERICAN
25 W. 56th St. (between Fifth and Sixth Aves.)   (212) 332-0500
This classy looking midtown restaurant offers civilized dining in a beautiful set-
ting. Organized around an open kitchen and a huge wood-burning oven, it deliv-
ers uncomplicated big-flavored food emphasizing fresh, seasonal ingredients.
Meat and fish pick up a smoky tang from the oven, roasted vegetables are served
with entrees and even desserts feature roasted fruits. Two of the best entrees are
triple lamb chops, rubbed with cumin and pureed picholine olives, and a plain
trout roasted with a bright vinaigrette of chervil, parsley, cilantro and shallots.
For dessert, a carmelized apple pancake grabs the brass ring. **Price range:**
Entrees, $19–$32. **Meals:** L, D. Closed Sun. **Subway:** N, R, W to Fifth Ave.

Beppe ☆☆ **$$$**   ITALIAN
45 E. 22nd St. (between Broadway and Park Ave. South)   (212) 982-8422
Beppe, named for Chef Cesare Casella's grandfather, is worth a detour. The
comfortable rustic Tuscan room has exposed brick walls, wood beams, antique
wooden floors and a wood-burning fireplace that is damped down in the summer. Mr. Casella is at his very best with the Tuscan dishes: Order anything made
with farro, the nutty whole grain, which is served in soup and a risotto-style
dish. The fried chicken would make a cook of the Deep South proud, and the
11-herb pasta is filled with flavor. For dessert, try a Tuscan riff on ice cream
sandwiches, made with toasted buccellati, the Tuscan version of panettone.
(*Marian Burros*) **Price range:** Pasta, $16–$20; Entrees, $23–$29. **Meals:** L, D.
Closed Sun. **Subway:** 6 to 23rd St.

Beyoglu **$25 & Under**   TURKISH
1431 Third Ave. (at 81st St.) `   (212) 570-5666
The owner is adamant: Beyoglu (pronounced BAY-oh-loo) is not a Turkish
restaurant, he insists. It is a meze house, a meyhane. The menu consists of 20 or
so mezes, or little tastes, a snacking tradition in Turkey, Greece, the Balkans and
parts of the Middle East and North Africa. Many of the selections are familiar,
yet deliciously executed, like creamy hummus, which balances its chickpea and
tahini flavors. As good as these dishes are, the highlights are a lovely, pastoral
soup of creamy yogurt, rice and mint and crisp little cubes of pan-fried calf's liver,
served with red onions dusted with cumin. **Price range:** Mezes, $3.50–$14.50.
Meals: D. **Subway:** 4, 5, 6 to 86th St.

Bice ☆☆ **$$$**   ITALIAN
7 E. 54th St. (between Fifth and Madison Aves.)   (212) 688-1999
With a main dining room done in beige and wood with brass sconces and indi-
rect lighting, Bice is the handsomest Italian restaurant in town. If you have lots
of money, good ears and a desire to see the fast and the fashionable, this off-
shoot of a Milanese restaurant is for you. Fresh pastas, risotto, and uncompli-
cated main courses—veal chop, chicken paillard and duck breast with mango—
are all recommended. The mostly Italian wine list is well chosen. **Price range:**
Avg. Entree, $24–$31. **Meals:** L, D, LN. **Subway:** E, F to Fifth Ave.

Bistro le Steak $25 & Under   BISTRO/STEAK

1309 Third Ave. (at 75th St.)   (212) 517-3800

Bistro le Steak hardly strikes a false note. It does look Parisian. The friendly staff conveys warmth and informality, and the food is both good and an excellent value. Steak is the specialty, but other simple bistro specialties are consistently satisfying and desserts are terrific. **Price range:** Entrees, $15–$30. **Meals:** L, D. **Subway:** 6 to 77th St.

Blue Fin   ☆ ☆ $$$ SEAFOOD

W Times Square Hotel , 1567 Broadway (at 47th St.)   (212) 918-1400

At Blue Fin, from the operation that runs Blue Water Grill, Isabella's and Ruby Foo's, the theme is fish. And because it's part of an empire that buys a lot of fish, it gets first dibs. The quality is unmistakable. There are 20 varieties of sushi and sashimi, but the main menu is where Blue Fin impresses the most. The chef does not overload the plate or step on the fish. The most impressive entree is a crisply sautéed fillet of Atlantic black bass served on a creamy shrimp and asparagus risotto. The genius touch is a shallow pool of chive nage. Desserts are first-class, especially the coconut-milk panna cotta and the sour-cherry toasted almond cake. **Price range:** Entrees, $11–$38; desserts, $8–$9. **Meals:** L, D, LN. **Subway:** N, Q, R, W to 49th St.; B, D, F, V to 47th St.

Blue Hill   ☆ ☆ $$ FRENCH

75 Washington Pl. (at Sixth Ave.)   (212) 539-1776

A few steps below sidewalk level, Blue Hill almost shrinks from notice. But the quiet, adult setting admirably suits a style of cooking that is both inventive and highly assured. There are dull spots on the menu, but the overall standard is high enough to make up for the excruciating banquette seating. Poached duck deserves to be the restaurant's signature: a skinned duck breast, poached in beurre blanc and duck stock, is paired with leg meat done as a confit, then crisped at the last minute and placed over pureéd artichokes. For dessert, chocolate bread pudding is a conversation-stopper. **Price range:** Entrees, $18–$23. **Meals:** D / Closed Sun. **Subway:** A, C, E, F, S to W. 4th St.

Blue Ribbon Sushi   ☆ ☆ $$$ JAPANESE/SUSHI

119 Sullivan St. (between Prince and Spring Sts.)   (212) 343-0404

Blue Ribbon Sushi has good fish and an awesome list of sakes, but beyond that it has very little in common with a classic Japanese sushi bar. If you have ever felt like a clumsy foreigner and worried about doing the wrong thing, this is the sushi bar for you. The menu is enormous, and almost everything is good, from a pretty seaweed salad to broiled yellowtail collar. But the high point of the meal is always sushi and sashimi. The sushi chefs are at their best when inventing interesting specials. Unfettered by tradition, they create unusual special platters filled with whatever happens to be best that day. Just name the price you are willing to pay and let them amaze you. **Price range:** Entrees, $11.75–$27.50. **Meals:** D, LN. Closed Mon. **Subway:** C, E to Spring St.; N, R to Prince St.

Blue Smoke ☆ $$ BARBECUE

116 E. 27th St. (bet. Park & Lexington Aves.) (212) 447-7733

In this rustic dining room, Danny Meyer has taken on the quixotic quest of building a fine barbecue emporium in Manhattan. Unfortunately, the barbecue is inconsistent. The beef ribs are among the best you'll find anywhere, but the brisket, the staple dish of Texas barbecue, is texturally more reminiscent of corned beef than fine Texas brisket. Desserts are direct, uncomplicated, huge. **Price range:** Entrees, $12–$23. **Meals:** D, LN. **Subway:** 6 to 28th St.

Blue Water Grill ☆ $$ SEAFOOD

31 Union Sq. W. (at 16th St.) (212) 675-9500

Built as a bank in 1904, this is a big, breezy room with a sidewalk cafe and a casual air. Along with pleasant service, large portions and reasonable prices can come large crowds and long waits. Shrimp and oysters are good choices; so is the grilled fish. Desserts are not among the happy surprises, but the brownie sundae would make most people very happy. **Price range:** Entrees, $18–28. **Meals:** Br, L, D, LN. **Subway:** L, N, Q, R, W, 4, 5, 6 to 14th St.

Boca Chica Restaurant $25 & Under LATIN AMERICAN

13 First Ave. (at 1st St.) (212) 473-0108

Many cuisines are juxtaposed on the enticing menu of this little pan-Latin restaurant. Top choices include camarones chipotle, shrimp in a tomato, chili and cilantro sauce; crisp, tangy chicharrones de pollo, the classic Dominican dish of chicken pieces marinated in lime, soy and spices; and pinones, sweet plantains stuffed with ground beef and pork. **Price range:** Entrees, $6.50–$15.95. **Meals:** L, D. **Subway:** F to Second Ave.

Bongo $25 & Under SEAFOOD

299 10th Ave. (near 28th St.) (212) 947-3654.

On any given day, Bongo serves half a dozen kinds of oysters, from Fanny Bays, which have a flavor shockingly like cucumbers, to Pemaquids, which are impressively salty, to Wellfleets, which have a pronounced mineral tang. With no more than a squirt of lemon, and they are always impeccably fresh and gloriously sensual. The decadent allure of the oysters makes an amusing contrast to the style of the room, a quirky replica of 1950's living rooms. The limited menu has a few other highlights, like wonderful, meaty lobster rolls and an excellent smoked trout salad **Price range:** Oysters, $1.50–$2.25 each. MC/V only. **Meals:** D, LN

Bouley ☆☆☆☆ $$$$ FRENCH

120 West Broadway (at Duane St.) (212) 964-2525

This restaurant crackles with energy, and Mr. Bouley turns out food that is nothing less than inspired. It is stunningly good, and consistently ascends to the highest level. As a chef, Mr. Bouley has it all—elegance, finesse and flair. His flavors are extraordinarily clear and exquisitely balanced; his use of seasoning is so deft as to be insidious. Even his most complex creations have a classical simplicity to them. Despite the fireworks in the kitchen, Bouley retains the feel of a small neighborhood restaurant. Diners feel comfortable showing up in shirt-sleeves, and the staff shrewdly maintains a delicate balance between informality and the more disciplined level of service implicit in the food and décor. The intensity of the service at Bouley is also remarkable in New York. The waiters seem passionate about the food and deeply concerned that diners enjoy it to the full. **Price range:** Entrees, $27–$38. **Meals:** L, D. **Subway:** A, C, 1, 2, 3, 9 to Chambers St.

Bouterin   ☆   **$$$$**   FRENCH
420 E. 59th St. (between First Ave. and Sutton Pl.)   (212) 758-0323
Serving Provençal food in a Provençal atmosphere, this restaurant can be charming. The best dishes are the chef's old family recipes, like the hearty vegetable soupe au pistou, which tastes the way it might if had been made on a wood-burning oven on a Provençal farm, the tarte a la Provençale, the rack of lamb wrapped in a herbal crust, and sea bass in a bold bouillabaisse sauce. The daube of beef, too, is delicious, the beef slowly stewed in red wine and garlic. **Price range:** Entrees, $20–$32. **Meals:** D. **Subway:** 4, 5, 6 to 59th St.; N, R to Lexington Ave.

Brasserie   ☆☆   **$$$**   BISTRO/FRENCH
100 E. 53rd St. (at Lexington Ave.)   (212) 751-4840
The old Brasserie (which closed in 1995 after a kitchen fire) was a part of the city's fabric. When patrons enter the newly-renovated restaurant, their jaws drop. The staircase down to the dining room has been transformed into a gentle slope of translucent steps. In futuristic booths along the side of the room, the tables are slabs of translucent lime-green acrylic. The Brasserie is ready for a new life, and Chef Luc Dimnet delivers sensible, well-executed food with up-to-date touches but not too many neurotic kinks. For dessert try the chocolate beignets: each powdered morsel, oozing with a perfectly measured mouthful of molten chocolate, reaffirms the genius of the doughnut concept. **Price range:** Entrees, $14–$28. **Meals:** B, Br, L, D, LN. **Subway:** 6 to 51st St.

Brasserie 8 1/2   ☆   **$$$**   BRASSERIE/FRENCH
9 W. 57th St. (between Fifth & Sixth Aves.)   (212) 829-0812
Visually, Brasserie 8 1/2 is a knockout. The dining room could be a galactic mess hall, with a white terrazzo tile floor and black leather booths. The traditional brasserie menu can be seen in a mostly standard raw bar selection, an iced seafood platter and a weekly rotation of specials like bouillabaisse on Fridays and confit of suckling pig on Thursdays. For dessert try the arresting milk–chocolate crème brûlée, iced with a rose marmalade and surrounded by candied rose petals. **Price range:** Entrees, $18–$30. **Meals:** B, Br, L, D, LN. **Subway:** N, R to Fifth Ave.

Bread $25 & Under   SANDWICHES
20 Spring St. (near Elizabeth St.)   (212) 334-1015
It's hard to imagine a simpler place than Bread, where the most complex piece
of equipment is probably the espresso maker. When a restaurant specializes in
sandwiches and salads, ingredients are the most important thing. There, Bread
succeeds marvelously. Sandwiches are carefully constructed and manageable,
each a well-designed combination of complementary flavors and textures, like
Gorgonzola with apple slices and honey on dense cranberry-raisin bread.
Heartier pressed sandwiches include speck, an Alpine ham, with sharp Brie and
asparagus on ciabatta. **Price range:** Sandwiches, $7–$9; other dishes, $4–$16.
Meals: L, D. **Subway:** 6 th Spring St.; N, R to Prince St.

Bread Bar at Tabla $25 & Under   NEW AMERICAN/FUSION
11 Madison Ave. (at 25th St.)   (212) 889-0667
Bread Bar, Tabla's less formal, less expensive cousin, radiates a beauty of its own
that shines right through its dim and noisy dining room. Bread Bar serves home-
style dishes and street snacks full of authentic flavors, with the occasional Western element thrown in. Bread Bar operates family style, with dishes arriving as
they are ready. Lamb shank is great balancing act between the lush sweetness of
apricots and the tender meat's spicy coating of mace, cardamom and chili, while
chicken tikka is a dream, moist and full of gingery, peppery flavor. For dessert,
the coffee kulfi pop is a triumph. **Price range:** Small dishes, $6–$9; large dishes,
$10–$18. **Meals:** L, D. **Subway:** 6, N, Q, R, W to 23rd St.

Bright Food Shop $25 & Under   NEW AMERICAN
216 Eighth Ave. (at 21st St.)   (212) 243-4433
This spare, minimalist former luncheonette serves an exciting blend of Asian
and Southwestern ingredients. The menu changes frequently and may include
dishes like a tart green chili pozole; smoked trout and red peppers wrapped in
rice and seaweed; or bluefish salpicon, in which the fish is chopped and pickled
with vinegar and chilies and served in corn tortillas. **Price range:** Entrees,
$11.75–$17.25. Cash only. **Meals:** Br, D. **Subway:** C, E to 23rd St.

Bukhara Grill $25 & Under   INDIAN
230 E. 58th St. (bet. Second & Third Aves.)   (212) 339-0090
217 E. 49th St. (bet. Second & Third Aves.)   (212) 888-2839
The northern Indian cooking here is mostly superb, with the sort of precise, res-
onant, yet subtle spicing that is all too rare in Indian restaurants. Bukhara's
extensive, fairly priced wine list also stands out. Try the slender, lively kebabs
made entirely of minced vegetables, and excellent curries like pepper chicken, a
rich dish with distinct layers of black pepper, ginger and chili flavors. **Price
range:** Entrees, $12–$28. **Meals:** L, D. **Subway:** 49th St.: E, F, 6 to 51st St.
58th St.: 4, 5, 6, N, Q, R, W to Lexington Ave.–59th St.

Butter   ☆ $$$
NEW AMERICAN

415 Lafayette St. (near Astor Pl.)   (212) 253-2828

Upstairs at Butter is a professionally run vaulted dining room that looks like a
cross between a chalet and a sauna. Downstairs is a dim and smoky lounge. The
chef has put together a serious contemporary American menu with all the requisite high-end ingredients and global touches. Appetizers struggle to hold up
the food end. Main courses, especially fish dishes, are more sure-footed. A lamb
chop and loin are juicy enough, and a beef fillet will do the job of placating beef
lovers. The amiable list of desserts does not break new ground, though some
offer appealing architecture. **Price range:** Entrees, $27–$30. **Meals:** D, LN.
Subway: 6 to Astor Pl.; N, R, to 8th St.

Café Boulud   ☆ ☆ ☆ $$$$
FRENCH

20 E. 76th St. (near Madison Ave.)   (212) 772-2600

Café Boulud is sleek and easy; this is your opportunity to find out what
happens when a great chef at the top of his form stretches out and takes
chances. The menu, which changes frequently, is divided into four sections:
La Tradition (classic country cooking), La Saison (seasonal dishes), Le
Potager (vegetarian choices), and Le Voyage (world cuisine). What that
really means is, anything goes. Most days there are 30 or more dishes, and
none are ordinary. Soup is a sure thing, and the wine list explores little-
known vineyards. **Price range:** Entrees, $24–$32. **Meals:** L, D. **Subway:** 6 to
77th St.

Café de Bruxelles $$
BELGIAN

118 Greenwich Ave. (between Seventh and Eighth Aves.)   (212) 206-1830

The little zinc-topped bar at this cozy Belgian café is a warm and welcoming stop.
The frites, served in silver cones with dishes of mayonnaise, go beautifully with
the unusual Belgian beers, while mussel dishes and heartier Belgian stews are all
very good. The small tables near the battered zinc bar are good for solo diners.
Price range: $13.75–$19.50. **Meals:** Br, L, D. **Subway:** A, C, E, 1, 2, 3, 9 to
14th St.; L to Eighth Ave.

Café des Artistes $$$
CONTINENTAL

1 W. 67th St. (between Central Park W. and Columbus Ave.)   (212) 877-3500

Its signature murals, leaded-glass windows and paneled wood walls contribute to
the genteel impression at this grand cafe. The main room is more neighborly
and louder than the intimate tables that ring the bar on the second level. The
continental food, however, is surprisingly old-fashioned. Best for grazing before
or after a concert. **Price range:** Entrees, $22–$40. **Meals:** Br, L, D. **Subway:** 1, 9
to 66th St.

Cafe La Grolla $25 & Under
ITALIAN

411A Amsterdam Ave. (near 80th St.)   (212) 579-9200

This cafe is tiny, holding no more than 30 people. The lighting is a little too
bright, the walls a little too plain, but almost everything on the menu is deli-

cious and it is anything but generic Italian. Salads are excellent and individual pizzas are superb. Agnolotti is rich and warming, delicate ravioli squares filled with veal in a velvety sage-scented reduction of beef broth. Fish are treated with the utmost respect at Cafe La Grolla, and meat dishes like calf's liver and roasted pork tenderloin have a nice vinegary edge. Even desserts are very good, especially a carefully constructed berry tart in a light marzipan crust. **Price range:** Entrees, $9–$20. **Meals:** D. **Subway:** 1, 9 to 79th St.

Café Loup $$ BISTRO
105 W. 13th St. (between Sixth and Seventh Aves.) (212) 255-4746
Every neighborhood should have a place like easy, comfortable Café Loup, where you can effortlessly feel like a regular. The menu of traditional bistro favorites doesn't challenge, but the restaurant does well by the standards, and that's really the point. **Price range:** Entrees, $13.50. **Meals:** Br, L, D. **Subway:** F, 1, 2, 3, 9 to 14th St.

Cafe Sabarsky ☆☆ $$ AUSTRO-HUNGARIAN
Neue Gallerie, 1048 Fifth Ave. (near 86th St.) (212) 288-0665
At this authentic Viennese cafe, the end of the meal is the beginning, really. The rest of the menu presents some tried and true Austro-Hungarian staples, but the goulash, herring sandwiches and boiled beef are merely a warm-up to the desserts. The house specialty is a Klimt torte, neatly stacked layers of hazelnut cake alternating with firm, bittersweet chocolate. It deserves classic status, along with the linzer torte and the Sacher torte, both flawless. The coffee at Cafe Sabarsky comes from Meinl's in Vienna, and I'm prepared to state that it's the best coffee in the city: rich, robust and deep. **Price range:** Entrees, $10–$25. **Meals:** L, D. **Subway:** 4, 5, 6 to 86th St.

Calle Ocho ☆ $$ SPANISH/DINER
446 Columbus Ave. (between 81st and 82nd Sts.) (212) 873-5025
At this homage to South American cooking, the kitchen makes food with authority, like complicated ceviches and seductive shrimp chowders. It is hard to resist the beauty of camarones, big shrimp brushed with rum and beautifully arranged around a heap of fried seaweed, or crisp chicken cooked in lime. The dining room is handsomely decorated, and the big, separate bar in front has turned into a singles scene where people sip rum, lime juice and mint mojitos while they listen to soft mambo music. **Price range:** Entrees, $16–$24. **Meals:** Br, D. **Subway:** B, C to 81st St.; 1, 9 to 79th St.

Campagna ☆☆ $$$ ITALIAN
24 E. 21st St. (between Broadway and Park Ave. South) (212) 460-0900
The rustic charm of the setting befits the bold, alluring cooking at this popular restaurant. It's an unbeatable combination: big portions and a big scene. To begin there is grilled sausage (made on premises), and grilled calamari adorned with arugula and marinated tomatoes. Pastas include spaghetti in white baby clam sauce and goat cheese tortellini mixed with fava beans, asparagus, peas and pro-

sciutto. For main courses, try grilled pork chop, aromatic of lemon and thyme, served with roasted fennel; and salmon baked with olives, capers and sun-dried tomatoes. **Price range:** Entrees, $17–$35. **Meals:** L, D. **Subway:** 6 to 23rd St.

Carne $25 & Under   STEAKHOUSE
2737 Broadway (at 105th St.)   (212) 663-7010

Carne, a small steakhouse-style restaurant near Columbia University, draws a steady stream of diners from the neighborhood. The appeal is clear. In an area with plenty of inexpensive restaurants, one option was lacking: a grown-up place for a well-made cocktail, a thick steak and a good bottle of wine. The appetizers are a plain but satisfying prelude to the main courses, like strip steak, a thick, charred cut of meat. If it doesn't quite have the tang of aged prime beef, it still beats most other similarly priced steaks out there. **Price range:** Entrees, $9–$19. **Meals:** Br, D. **Subway:** 1 to 103rd St.

Carnegie Deli $$ DELI
854 Seventh Ave. (at 55th St.)   (212) 757-2245

A quintessential New York City experience, from pickles to pastrami. Carnegie's sandwiches are legendarily enormous, big enough to feed you and a friend and still provide lunch for tomorrow. That doesn't stop people from try-ing to eat the whole thing, a sight that must gratify the notoriously crabby wait-ers. The pastrami is wonderful, of course, but so are the cheese blintzes with sour cream, which are only slightly more modest. **Price range:** Entrees, $10–$20. Cash only. **Meals:** B, L, D, LN. **Subway:** N, R, Q, W to 57th St.

Caribbean Spice $25 & Under   CARIBBEAN
402 W. 44th St. (between Ninth and 10th Aves.)   (212) 765-1737

This little storefront offers refined Caribbean cooking to a steady stream of show business types. Little beef patties, gently spiced bits of ground beef encased in half-moons of flaky dough, are a savory way to begin, and earthy red bean soup has a long, lingering, slightly smoky flavor. Island Spice's jerk barbecue (pork or chicken) is excellent. Island Spice serves beer and wine as well as Caribbean concoctions like sorrell, a tart, refreshing deep-red beverage made from hibiscus. **Price range:** Entrees, $8.95–$21.95. **Meals:** L, D. **Subway:** A, C, E to 42nd St.

Centolire   ☆☆ $$$ ITALIAN
1167 Madison Ave. (near 86th St.)   (212) 734-7711

Centolire is a large, good-looking trattoria with a warm, beating heart. The food, doled out in substantial portions, is honest, well executed and deeply satis-fying. One of Centolire's gimmicks is the coccio, or crock, that appears as a lit-tle symbol next to several dishes. It's shorthand for rustic, and most of the dishes cooked in the coccio are also covered in a thick bread dough, crosta di pane, that transforms them into an Italian potpie. The golden-brown dough lid cre-ates an aromatic sauna for a baby chicken and artichokes in a thick, marjoram-suffused sauce. The menu divides appetizers, pastas and entrees into two cate-gories, Old World and New World. The pastas, old or new, have a rough-hewn integrity that makes them impossible not to order. Pappardelle with porcini cream sauce and walnuts should immediately claim top honors as New York's official cold-weather pasta. **Price range:** Entrees, $12–$34. **Meals:** Br, L, D. **Subway:** 4, 5, 6 to 86th St.

Chanterelle ☆☆☆ $$$$ FRENCH
2 Harrison St. (at Hudson St.) (212) 966-6960

Few restaurants are as welcoming or comfortable to enter as Chanterelle, and there's a soft, casual edge to the atmosphere and the service. Chef David Waltuck favors an opulent style. His strong suits are depth and intensity of flavor, and he doesn't shy away from thick, rich sauces in his quest to ravish the palate. The menu changes every four weeks and includes splendid dishes like a simple, pristine beef fillet, drenched in a red wine and shallot sauce with more layers of flavor than a complex Burgundy. There are always some thrilling desserts like a courageously bitter chocolate tart, served with a pastry ice-cream cone filled with banana malt ice cream. The room itself looks as though it should be serene and hushed, but the acoustics are poor. **Price range:** Three-course prix-fixe, $75; five-course tasting menu, $89 or $139 with matching wines. **Meals:** L, D. Closed Sun. **Subway:** 1, 9 to Franklin St.

Chat 'n Chew $25 & Under NEW AMERICAN
10 E. 16th St. (between Fifth Ave. and Union Sq. West) (212) 243-1616

Middle American farm dishes and homespun décor set the tone at this restaurant, which could lead you to believe it was off a small-town courthouse square rather than off Union Square. Portions are huge, desserts are luscious and the place is particularly appealing to children. **Price range:** Entrees, $7–$14. **Meals:** Br, L, D. **Subway:** L, N, Q, R, W, 4, 5, 6 to 14th St.

Chelsea Bistro & Bar ☆☆ $$$ BISTRO/FRENCH
358 W. 23rd St. (between Eighth and Ninth Aves.) (212) 727-2026

With a cozy fireplace, a great wine list and really good French bistro food, this is a find in the neighborhood. If the first thing you eat here is the fabulous mussel and clam soup, you will be hooked forever. The fricassee of lobster and sea scallops is almost as good. The hanger steak is fine and rare, with a dense red-wine sauce. The restaurant serves predictable and good classic New York bistro desserts. The bread pudding is slightly less conventional, if only because it is enlivened with a shot of rum. **Price range:** entrees, $17.95–$27; pre-theater prix-fixe, $28.50. **Meals:** D, LN. **Subway:** C, E to 23rd St.

Chez Josephine ☆☆ $$$ BISTRO/FRENCH
414 W. 42nd St. (between Ninth and 10th Aves.) (212) 594-1925

This Theater Row pioneer has been entertaining us with its colorful parade of musicians, singers and dancers for more than a decade and is still going strong. Its reliably pleasing bistro fare and attentive service add to the charm. Highlights among starters include the endive salad topped with crumbled Roquefort and crushed walnuts and the subtle goat-cheese ravioli in a delicate veal broth scented with fresh dill. Favorite entrees include lobster cassoulet; sautéed calf's liver with honey mustard sauce and grilled onions; and grilled salmon with a coulis of fine herbs. **Price range:** Avg. entree, $19. **Meals:** D, LN. Closed Sun. **Subway:** A, C, E to 42nd St.

Chicama ☆☆ $$$ LATIN AMERICAN
35 E. 18th St. (at Broadway)   (212) 505-2233
Hung with Peruvian rugs and decorated with Peruvian religious statues, this restaurant has a eucalyptus-burning wood oven and a big ceviche bar. The chef generates a special brand of excitement that somehow becomes part of the food, cooking in an exuberant, often flashy style that can be overwhelming, with plate-filling dishes that seem like the culinary equivalent of a carnival float. Alio chicken is a half chicken, smoky tasting after roasting over eucalyptus wood, served on a hash made from malanga root and suffused with a truffle mushroom mojo. Supporting the ceviche menu is a long list of serious beers, but the dessert list is short and almost chaste. Vanilla flan infused with bay leaf may be, in a mild way, the most striking dessert on the menu. **Price range:** Entrees, $19–$39. **Meals:** L, D, LN. **Subway:** L, N, Q, R, W, 4, 5, 6 to 14th St.

Chimichurri Grill $$ LATIN AMERICAN/ARGENTINE
606 Ninth Ave. (between 43rd and 44th St.)   (212) 586-8655
This is a good, casual place for dinner before or after the theater. Simultane-ously sophisticated and homelike, it combines all the elements that make the food of Argentina so appealing: great grilled beef, a few Italian pasta dishes and some pure home cooking, like the tortilla, a frittata filled with potatoes, chorizo and onions. The empanadas are excellent, crisp little turnovers filled with a mixture of ground beef and olives. **Price range:** Entrees, $14–$24. **Meals:** L, D. Closed Mon. **Subway:** A, C, E to 42nd St.

Cho Dang Gol ☆☆ $$ KOREAN
55 W. 35th St. (between Fifth and Sixth Aves.)   (212) 695-8222
Cho Dang Gol serves uniquely rustic food that is very different from what is available at other Korean restaurants in the surrounding blocks. The specialty here is fresh soybean curd, made daily at the restaurant. The kitchen makes each dish with extreme care, but for the uninitiated, searching out the best dishes is not easy. Try cho-dang-gol jung-sik. It arrives in three bowls: one with rice dotted with beans, another with "bean-curd dregs" (which hardly conveys its utter deliciousness) and the third with a pungent soup-stew containing pork, seafood, onions and chilies. Also excellent is chung-kook-jang, soybean-paste stew with an elemental flavor, and doo-boo doo-roo-chi-gi, a combination of pork, pan-fried kimchi, clear vermicelli and big triangles of bean curd.
Price range: Entrees, $6.95–$17.95. **Meals:** L, D, LN. **Subway:** B, D, F, N, Q, R, S, W to 34th St.

Chola   ☆☆ $$ INDIAN

232 E. 58th St. (between Second and Third Aves.)   (212) 688-4619

The menu at this modest, crowded restaurant roams across the Subcontinent, offering special dishes from the Jews of Calcutta, fiery dishes beloved by the English and wonderful vegetarian dishes like dosa from South India. Start with Mysore masala dosa, a thin, crisp, lacy crepe stuffed with a hot and fragrant potato mixture. Uthappam is a scallion-laced vegetable pancake that is among the great pancakes of the world. Having started in southern India, continue with a fine dish from Kerala, konju pappas, shrimp in a chili-laden sauce. Among the excellent desserts are kulfi, a grainy frozen dessert flavored with nuts and saffron, and rasmalai, an addictive, sweet sort of homemade cheese. Best of all is the extraordinary Indian coffee: strong, milky and sweet. **Price range:** Entrees, $10.95–$24.95. **Meals:** L, D. **Subway:** 4, 5, 6 to 59th St.; N, R, W to Lexington Ave.

Christer's   ☆☆ $$$$ SCANDINAVIAN

145 W. 55th St. (between Sixth and Seventh Aves.)   (212) 974-7224

This relaxed, upscale Scandinavian restaurant shows how a fine chef translates his love for American ingredients and ideas into traditional dishes. The chef and owner specializes in seafood, salmon in particular. Everything he makes from salmon is good, from seared smoked salmon with black beans, corn, avocado and tomatillo salsa—more Southwestern than Scandinavian—to gentle citrus-glazed salmon. His smorgasbord is wonderful, while his fricadelles, Swedish meatballs made of veal, are hearty and comforting. Desserts like Pavlova, an airy confection of ice cream, fruit and meringue, and a tart of poached apples are perfect endings. **Price range:** Entrees, $18–$26. **Meals:** L, D. **Subway:** B, D, E to Seventh Ave.; N, R, Q, W to 57th St.

Churrascaria Plataforma ☆☆ $$$ LATIN AMERICAN/STEAKHOUSE

316 W. 49th St. (between Eighth and Ninth Aves.)   (212) 245-0505

Two things are required to truly appreciate this all-you-can-eat Brazilian restaurant: a large appetite to keep you eating and a large group to cheer you on. The salad bar is extraordinary, a long two-sided affair anchored at the corners by four hot casseroles. Go easy: This is only the appetizer. The waiters will entice you with ham, sausage, lamb, wonderfully crisp and juicy chicken legs, pork ribs, even the occasional side of salmon, which is delicious in its caper sauce. But it is beef that has pride of place: sirloin, baby beef, top round, skirt steak, brisket, short ribs, special top round. **Price range:** All-you-can-eat rodizio meal, $38.95; children under 10, $19.50. **Meals:** L, D, LN. **Subway:** C, E to 50th St.

Circus Restaurant   ☆☆ $$$ BRAZILIAN

808 Lexington Ave. (near 62nd St.)   (212) 223-2965

An upscale Brazilian restaurant that turns into a party every night. Circus serves the food your mother might cook if you were raised in São Paulo or Bahia. It is a warm and cozy place, usually packed with Brazilians eager for a taste of home. The camarao na moranga is excellent, a heap of tiny, tender rock shrimp sautéed with fresh corn, hearts of palm, shallots, peas and coconut milk, mixed with cheese and baked in an acorn squash. Another satisfying dish is an appetizer, bolo de milho e rabada, little polenta cakes baked with Manchego cheese and served with a robust oxtail sauce. Among the sweet, tropical desserts, the best is caramelized bananas with ice cream. **Price range:** Entrees, $15–$23. **Meals:** L, D, LN. **Subway:** N, R, W to Lexington Ave.; 4, 5, 6 to 59th St.

Citarella the Restaurant ☆☆ $$$$ SEAFOOD/FUSION
1240 Sixth Ave. (near 49th St.)　　　　　　　　　　　　(212) 332-1515
At this offshoot of the famous food store, the theme is fish, fresh from the market. In the cozy second-floor dining room, with wraparound views of 49th Street and the Exxon Building fountain across the avenue, the subtly sparkling wall panels are dotted with little underwater dioramas. On balance, dishes are fresh, exciting and in every way worthy of the top-quality ingredients. Even the bad ideas are bad in an interesting way. The presentation of sushi is simple, the fish pristine. Citarella's dessert menu ratchets the entire operation up at least one notch. The warm vanilla cake with vanilla ice cream is already gaining cult status. **Price range:** Entrees, $21–$37. **Meals:** L, D. Closed Sun. **Subway:** B, D, F, V to 47th St.; N, Q, R, W to 49th St.

City Hall ☆☆ $$$ AMERICAN
131 Duane St. (near Church St.)　　　　　　　　　　　　(212) 227-7777
The cavernous dining room has the spare quality of an old steakhouse; the clean details, loud music and hip clientele give it an up-to-date air. The menu includes all the old classics, from iceberg lettuce to baked Alaska, but there is more to City Hall than old-fashioned fare. The plateau de fruits de mer, which feeds six to eight, is a behemoth so impressive that people invariably gasp as it is carried across the room. You also can't go wrong with oysters at City Hall, raw or cooked. Among the meat dishes there is a huge double steak, still on the bone and served for two. For dessert, the apple bread pudding made with brioche is very, very good. **Price range:** Entrees, $18–$32. **Meals:** L, D. Closed Sun. **Subway:** A, C, 1, 2, 3, 9 to Chambers St.

Cocina Cuzco $25 & Under PERUVIAN
55 Ave. A (at 4th St.)　　　　　　　　　　　　　　　　(212) 529-3469
Cocina's Peruvian cuisine is a melting pot of Asian, European, African and ancient American influences. There are half a dozen ceviches, including some excellent choices like ceviche de concha, clams marinated in lime and served on the half shell, covered with cilantro and tiny cubes of pickled onions and peppers. Main courses demonstrate many sides of Peruvian cuisine. Lomo saltado is stir-fried beef flavored with soy and onions and served over rice and French fries, and red snapper is crusted in thin slices of sweet potatoes, making it crisp on the outside and moist within. Other fine main courses include juicy chicken and chewy, flavorful skirt steak. Desserts are delicious, like bread pudding flavored with dulce de leche. **Price range:** Entrees, $8.95–$13.95. Cash only. **Meals:** L, D, LN. **Subway:** F to Second Ave.

Commissary ☆ $$$ MEDITERRANEAN/NEW AMERICAN
1030 Third Ave. (at 61st St.)   (212) 339-9955

Commissary makes a cold first impression, figuratively and literally: the design is minimal to the point of severity. But like many difficult personalities, Commissary is worth getting to know. The well-known chef, Matthew Kenney, draws on his extensive Mediterranean vocabulary and brings a little sparkle to standard bistro dishes like roast chicken, crab cakes, seared scallops and grilled duck, often spinning them just a half turn. One of his most successful pan-Mediterranean ventures is a full-flavored loin of lamb wrapped around a filling of goat cheese, mint, dates and almonds. The most successful dessert is a straightforward chocolate soufflé cake. **Price range:** Entrees, $15–$26. **Meals:** Br, L, D. **Subway:** 4, 5, 6 to 59th St.; F, N, R to Lexington Ave.

Compass ☆☆ $$$ NEW AMERICAN
208 W. 70th St. (bet. Amsterdam & West End Aves.)   (212) 875-8600

The main dining room here is striking, with slate-covered pillars and a long abstract painting in red along the rear wall, but formality is not enforced. The menu is simultaneously simple yet sneakily sophisticated in the contemporary American vein, and the ingredients are superb. A sturdy cylinder of pork loin, juicy and full of flavor, arrives towering over a gorgeous sliced heirloom tomato, sweet and tangy as an apple, and a sweet charred Vidalia onion. Compass also offers an attractive lounge menu, with dishes like crunchy saffron-risotto fritters and a grilled lamb burger. **Price range:** Entrees, $22–$32. **Meals:** Br, D. **Subway:** 1, 2, 3 to 72nd St.

Congee Village $25 & Under   CHINESE
100 Orchard St. (between Delancey and Broome Sts.)   (212) 941-1818
1848 Second Ave. (near 95th St.)

The best congee in New York is in these friendly restaurants. Congee, also known as jook, is nothing more than Chinese hot cereal, a milky rice porridge. More than two dozen versions of congee are served here, some with additions as exotic as fish maws or frog. At the uptown location, most of the rest of the menu is devoted to generic sweet and crispy Chinese-American dishes and a selection of surf-and-turf meals. The downtown restaurant offers excellent Cantonese and Hong Kong dishes. **Price range:** Congee, $2.50–$4.75; entrees, $5.50–$16.95. **Meals:** L, D, LN. **Subway:** Downtown: F to Second Ave. Uptown: 6 to 96th St.

Cooke's Corner $25 & Under   EUROPEAN/AMERICAN
618 Amsterdam Ave. (at 90th St.)   (212) 712-2872

This charmingly subdued little restaurant, with its small, well-designed menu and intelligent wine list, caters to grown-ups and makes no apologies for it. The menu is quietly satisfying with attention to details. Mixed field greens is a superb selection of gently dressed lettuces, accented with sweet grape tomatoes and stuffed grape leaves. Main courses include a juicy, flavorful roast chicken served over polenta with a mushroom stew. Beef, braised for four hours until remarkably tender, has a lively Eastern European scent of caraway and coriander seeds and comes with buttery spaetzle. **Note:** Some daily specials are priced at $25, far more than the regular menu items. **Price range:** Entrees, $12–$25. AE only. **Meals:** D. Closed Mon. **Subway:** 1, 9 to 86th St.

Cookies and Couscous   **$25 & Under**   MOROCCAN
230 Thompson St. (at 3rd St.)   (212) 477-6562

This small, bright restaurant has more going for it than the peculiar name might suggest. The short menu emphasizes flavorful seasonal ingredients. Soups and salads are all tasty but almost unnecessary because all the main courses are so big. Most are made with couscous and they too are excellent, whether served with vegetables alone or with meat as well. As for the cookies, they are all very good but not as interesting as the house-made sorbets and ice creams in subtle flavors like tart plum-anise, and soothing cinnamon-apple. **Price range:** Entrees, $10–$19. Cash only. **Meals:** L, D. **Subway:** A, C, E, F, S to W. 4th St.

Coup   ☆   **$$**   FRENCH/NEW AMERICAN
509 E. 6th St. (between Aves. A and B)   (212) 979-2815

Like the rest of the East Village, Coup takes an ascetic stand on visual stimulation. Somehow, this sensory deprivation induces a feeling of tranquility. Beneath the cloak of mystery lies a deceptively normal neighborhood restaurant, one that fits stylistically with the blocks around it. The food does not aim too high, but what it aims at, it hits. It's the kind of place that always seems like a good idea. The roast Cornish hen takes some beating. Brown as a berry and pleasingly plump, it's packed with chunks of coarse-grained sourdough bread and Michigan cherries. The stuffing is beyond praise. Coup also has a deeply limey Key lime pie and an honest, homey pineapple upside-down cake. **Price range:** Entrees, $16–$21. **Meals:** D. **Subway:** F to Second Ave.; L to First Ave.

Craft   ☆ ☆ ☆   **$$$$**   NEW AMERICAN
43 E. 19th St. (between Broadway and Park Ave. South)   (212) 780-0880

This is a handsome restaurant, with a clean, vaguely Mission-influenced look that supports the culinary theme. Craft offers a vision of food heaven, a land of strong, pure flavors and back-to-basics cooking techniques. But Craft is also one of the most baroque dining experiences in New York: diners build their own meals here, with side dishes and even sauces presented as options. The saving grace is the high quality of the ingredients and their masterly handling by the kitchen. Nothing at the restaurant sounds like much, but every bite is a revelation. The oysters sparkle. The veal, a humble cut of meat wrapped around some simple roast vegetables, has an honesty and a depth of flavor that will stop you cold. And in a city famous for steak worship, the frighteningly large porterhouse ranks as one of the finest large-scale hunks of beef you'll encounter. For dessert, try a light, chiffonlike steamed lemon pudding or the custardy pain perdu, which can easily handle anything thrown at it. **Price range:** Entrees, $22–$36. **Meals:** L, D. **Subway:** L, N, Q, R, W, 4, 5, 6 to 14th St.

Craftbar $25 & Under NEW AMERICAN

47 E. 19th St. (bet. Park Ave. S. & Broadway) (212) 780-0880

In looks and service alone, Craftbar sets itself leagues beyond the typical low-rent sandwich shop. And yet, its snacks, soups, salads and sandwiches, supplemented each day by a meat, a fish and a pasta dish, exude the simplicity of a wine bar, where needs are joyfully met rather than challenged. Sandwiches are uniformly excellent; warm pressed sandwiches rely on blends of flavors, as with earthy duck ham, hen of the woods mushrooms and mild taleggio cheese. For dessert, coconut panna cotta is light and flavorful. **Price range:** Entrees, $14–$18. **Meals:** L, D, LN. **Subway:** 4, 5, 6, L, N, Q, R, W to Union Sq.

Cyclo $25 & Under VIETNAMESE

203 First Ave. (at 12th St.) (212) 673-3957

This stylish little East Village restaurant serves some of the best Vietnamese food in New York City: It is inventive, impeccably fresh and meticulously prepared, while service is friendly and informative. Try cha gio, crisp and delicate spring rolls, and chao tom, grilled shrimp paste wrapped around sugar cane. Don't hesitate to order fruit for dessert, like cubes of wonderfully fresh mango that are the perfect end to a stellar meal. **Price range:** Entrees, $10–$15. **Meals:** D, LN. **Subway:** L to First Ave.

Da Ciro $25 & Under ITALIAN

229 Lexington Ave. (near 33rd St.) (212) 532-1636

An excellent, often overlooked little Italian restaurant. Specialties, cooked in a wood-burning oven, include terrific pizzas. Also excellent is a casserole of wild mushrooms baked in a crock with arugula, goat cheese, olives, tomatoes and mozzarella. The pastas are simple but lively, and full-flavored desserts like bitter chocolate mousse cake and hazelnut semifreddo more than hold their own. **Price range:** Entrees, $15.50–$28. **Meals:** L, D. **Subway:** 6 to 33rd St.

Dakshin $25 & Under INDIAN

1713 First Ave. (near 89th St.) (212) 987-9839

Much Indian food in Manhattan is bland, so it is a great pleasure to find lively spicing in more than a few dishes at Dakshin, like jhinga jal toori, small but flavorful shrimp in a sauce of tomatoes and onions made tangy by mustard greens and enhanced by the nutty, slightly bitter aroma of curry leaves. Dakshin's breads are excellent, especially mint paratha and garlic nan, made smoky in the clay oven. Among the meat main courses, try the chicken Chettinad, with the chicken in a thick sauce made lively by black pepper and curry leaves. Dakshin's vegetable dishes also excel. **Price range:** Entrees, $7–$17. **Meals:** L, D. **Subway:** 4, 5, 6 to 86th St.

Daniel ☆☆☆☆ $$$$ FRENCH

Mayfair Hotel, 60 E. 65th St. (between Madison and Park Aves.)

(212) 288-0033

This is a top-flight French restaurant, sumptuous and rather grand, but still very much the personal expression of its chef and owner, Daniel Boulud. His menu is overwhelming, with a dozen appetizers and ten main courses supplemented by a daily list of specials and assorted tasting menus. The influences come from all over the Mediterranean, and as far afield as Japan and India, pulled in and made French with total assurance. There are lots of pleasant surprises at Daniel, culminating in a dessert menu remarkable for its elegance and restraint. It is also highly advisable to study the cheese trolley when it rolls around. The selection is well organized, the cheeses superb. It is possible to spend lavishly on wine, but there is also a strong selection of half bottles, wines by the glass and modestly priced bottles. Service, confident and expert, goes a long way to explain the neighborhood's love affair with Daniel. Diners feel well cared for. The tone is pitch-perfect, and as a result, patrons feel at ease. **Price range:** Prix-fixe and tasting menus, $78–$140. **Meals:** L, D / Closed Sun. **Subway:** 6 to 68th St.

Danube ☆☆☆ $$$$ AUSTRIAN

30 Hudson St. (at Duane St.) (212) 791-3771

David Bouley does not do things in a small way. Using fin-de-siécle Vienna as a culinary source, and a repository of romantic images, he has created Danube, the most enchanting restaurant New York has seen in decades. This is an opiate dream of lush fabrics, deeply saturated decadent colors and lustrous glazed surfaces. If ever a restaurant was made for a four-hour meal, Danube is it. After anchoring the menu with a handful of classics, he has conjured up his own private Austria or, in some cases, taken leave of the country altogether with impressive appetizers like a delicate, complexly orchestrated dish of raw tuna and shrimp. More typically, Mr. Bouley has lightened, modernized and personalized traditional dishes, or invented new ones using traditional ingredients, often with stunning results. Two traditional desserts are both impeccable: a Czech palacsintak, or crêpe, and a Salzburger nockerl, a mound-shaped soufflé dusted in confectioners' sugar and served with raspberries. **Price range:** Entrees, $29–$35. **Meals:** L, D. **Subway:** A, C, 1, 2, 3, 9 to Chambers St.

D'Artagnan ☆☆ $$$$ FRENCH

152 E. 46th St. (between Lexington and Third Aves.) (212) 687-0300

D'Artagnan has so much personality it could sell it by the pound. The food is Gascon, from France's legendary region of foie gras, duck, Armagnac and prunes, and owner Ariane Daguin has turned D'Artagnan into a "Three Musketeers" theme park. The food is authentic, robust, earthy and powerfully flavored, enlivened by a whimsical sense of humor. Foie gras appears in many guises, the most seductive of which is the simple foie gras terrine, with a deep, dark, gamy tinge. Cassoulet is a religion in Gascony, and the one served at D'Artagnan is excellent. Fish, however, doesn't have a chance. The cheese course is small but pleasing, but for the most part, the desserts seem like a distraction before the important business of pouring the aged Armagnac. **Price range:** Entrees, $19–$26. **Meals:** L, D. Closed Sun. **Subway:** S, 4, 5, 6, 7 to 42nd St.

Dawat ☆ $$$ INDIAN
210 E. 58th St. (between Second and Third Aves.)   (212) 355-7555
Most of the vegetable dishes here—the small baked eggplant with tamarind sauce, the potatoes mixed with ginger and tomatoes, the homemade cheese in spinach sauce—are excellent. The set lunches are a bargain. Cornish hen with green chilies offers heat balanced by the sweet and sour flavor of tamarind. And sarson ka sag, a sour, spicy, buttery purée of mustard greens, is extremely flavorful. Bhaja are also impressive: Whole leaves of spinach, battered so lightly that the green glows through the coating, are paired with light little potato-skin fritters. **Price range:** Entrees, $15.95–$23.95. **Meals:** L, D. **Subway:** 4, 5, 6 to 59th St.; N, R to Lexington Ave.

DB Bistro Moderne ☆☆ $$$$ BISTRO
55 W. 44th St. (between Fifth and Sixth Aves.)   (212) 391-2400
Daniel Boulud's newest venture is a lively, even raucous restaurant that tries to pass for a bistro but can't quite disguise its high-class leanings. The cooking, although simplified to suit the bistro concept and even countrified on occasion, plays to Mr. Boulud's strength, his refined rusticity. He simply shows that rock-solid technique, good ingredients and a sound idea translate into gustatory bliss. There's nothing fancy about his tarte Tatin, but a perfect buttery crust and flavorful tomatoes make it a little miracle. Gazpacho is clean, crisp and clear, and roasted duck breast has great depth of flavor. Years of catering to an Upper East Side clientele have also given Mr. Boulud a supernatural hand with salads and spa fare. Cristina Aliberti makes excellent light desserts, as well as richer ones like her clafoutis tout chocolat, a small round chocolate cake, runny in the center, that could win over the most hardened chocolate skeptic. **Price range:** Entrees, $28–$32. **Meals:** L, D. Closed Sun. **Subway:** B, D, F, S to 42nd St.

Della Femina ☆ $$$$ NEW AMERICAN
131 E. 54th St. (between Madison and Lexington Aves.)   (212) 752-0111
Della Femina attracts a tony Upper East Side clientele. With its cool, restrained, Yankeefied setting straight out of Martha Stewart, it looks like a television commercial for the good life, late 1990's style. The cooking is usually described as American with international accents: perfectly poached, unusually flavorful chunks of lobster stand out in a cool salad of young greens, herbs and mango, dressed with a basil-caviar vinaigrette. Roasted turbot, rich and firm, gets just the right support from spring-fresh green peas, morels and a tomato-tarragon essence. There can be inconsistencies but when the kitchen is on its game, Della Femina is very good indeed. Desserts, however, are consistently outstanding, especially the steamed lemon pudding. **Price range:** Entrees, $26–$42. **Meals:** L, D. Closed Sun. **Subway:** 6 to 51st St.; E, F to Lexington Ave.

Delmonico's ☆ $$$ ITALIAN/NEW AMERICAN
56 Beaver St. (at Williams St.)   (212) 509-1144
Opulent, old-fashioned and dignified, the huge rooms at this American icon are
rich with stained wood and soft upholstery, and the tables are swathed in oceans
of white linen. The best dishes are in the section headed "Pasta, Risotti." Lin-
guine with clams is a classic that is very well done. Ricotta and spinach ravioli
may lack delicacy, but they are generous little pockets topped with clarified butter and fresh sage, and they make a satisfying meal. The rib-eye may not have
the pedigree of a porterhouse or Delmonico, but it is big, tasty and perfectly
cooked. **Price range:** Entrees, $21–$34. **Meals:** L, D. **Subway:** 2, 3 to Wall St.;
4, 5 to Bowling Green; J, M, Z to Broad St.

Dim Sum Go Go ☆ $$ CHINESE
5 E. Broadway (at Chatham Sq.)   (212) 732-0797
Dim Sum Go Go is a bright, happy extrovert clinging to the edge of Chinatown
like a goofy sidekick. There's a sameness to the dim sum lineup that's hard to
ignore; the better, more inventive food can be found on a larger menu abound-
ing in pleasant surprises. Bean curd skin is one of them, stuffed with bits of
black mushroom and chopped spinach, then folded like a crepe and fried. In
another, swiss chard is used to wrap crunchy julienned vegetables, arranged
around a tangle of frilly white fungus, supple yet crunchy, which the Chinese
often use in medicinal soups. The restaurant's interior design has a clean,
streamlined look, with perforated steel chairs, bright red screens and a clever
wall pattern taken from medieval scrolls with dining scenes. **Price range:**
Entrees $8.95–$16.95. **Meals:** L, D. **Subway:** J, M, N, R, Q, W, 6 to Canal St.

The Dining Room ☆☆ $$$ NEW AMERICAN
154 E. 79th St. (at Lexington Ave.)   (212) 327-2500
The Dining Room is sincere and unassuming, an attractive setting for attractive, intelligently conceived food. The menu, like the restaurant, is small, but it
works some intriguing variations on familiar ingredients. Good ingredients carry
most of the load, notably in the powerfully flavored lamb and a he-man portion
of prime rib. Two desserts fly right off the charts: a column of bread pudding,
soaked in coconut milk, and a chocolate caramel icebox cake. **Price range:**
Entrees, $19–$28. **Meals:** D. **Subway:** 6 to 77th St.

District ☆ $$$$ NEW AMERICAN
130 W. 46th St. (between Sixth and Seventh Aves.)   (212) 485-2999
There's a theatrical aspect to dining at District. The walls look like flats, and
ropes behind the banquettes create the illusion that the scenery might be raised
at any moment. It is witty, sophisticated and surprisingly cozy, especially if you
land one of the wraparound booths. When the kitchen hits the marks, it's worth
the ticket. The food is over the top and, when it works, irresistible in a way that
makes you feel vaguely guilty. The main courses sing at top volume, especially
the fearsome chicken cannelloni, two buckwheat-pasta wrappers the size of
Christmas crackers that are filled with ricotta and chicken, balanced atop a

crisped chicken leg done as a confit, outfitted with a hefty serving of roasted squash and surrounded by a sage and brown butter sauce. For dessert, a tall, fluffy cheesecake with huckleberry compote scores a direct hit. **Price range:** Entrees, $21–$37.50. **Meals:** B, L, D. **Subway:** B, D, F, N, Q, R, S, W, 1, 2, 3, 7, 9 to 42nd St.

Dock's Oyster Bar ☆ $$$ SEAFOOD
633 Third Ave. (at 40th St.) (212) 986-8080
2427 Broadway (at 89th St.) (212) 724-5588
These bustling fish houses are crowded fish emporiums that give you your money's worth, with sparkling shellfish bars from which to choose shrimp or lobster cocktails or oysters and clams on the half shell. Favorites among starters are the Docks clam chowder, Maryland crab cakes and steamers in beer broth. Engaging entrees include grilled red snapper with coleslaw and rice, grilled salmon steak with coleslaw and steamed potatoes and Caesar salad with grilled tuna. Steamed lobsters come in one- to two-pound sizes, and there is a New England clambake on Sunday and Monday nights. **Price range:** Entrees, $15–$29. **Meals:** Br, L, D, LN. **Subway:** Midtown: 4, 5, 6, 7, S to 42nd St. Uptown: 1, 9 to 86th St.

Do Hwa $$ KOREAN
55 Carmine St. (at Bedford St.) (212) 414-2815.
Do Hwa is one of a new breed of Korean restaurants trying to win converts by making their food more understandable to curious Americans. Entrees include kalbi jiim (stewed chunks of beef rib and potatoes) and kimchi chigae (pork and kimchi soup). All entrees come with panchan, the traditional palate-provoking condiments like kimchi, pickled radish or salted shrimp. It sounds like home cooking, and it is. The executive chef is the owner's mother. With a lively bar scene, Do Hwa is also a great place in the area for a drink. **Price range:** $12–$21. **Meals:** L, D. Closed Sun. **Subway:** 1, 9 to Houston St.; A, C, E, F, S to W. 4th St.

Eight Mile Creek ☆☆ $$$ AUSTRALIAN
240 Mulberry St. (at Prince St.) (212) 431-4635
When a restaurant announces that it will be serving Australian cuisine, you expect good comic material, not good food. The joke stops when the kangaroo salad arrives: large cubes of the tender, richly flavored loin languish in a marinade flavored with coriander seed, smoked paprika and poached garlic, and then are seared and served on lettuce-leaf wrappers. The menu is short, but the chef makes every dish count. Oyster pie is a pastry-wrapped stew of precisely cooked oysters, still plump and juicy, suspended in a cream sauce chunky with salsify and leeks. Australia without lamb is an impossibility, and the chef merely braises a whopping big shank and surrounding it with parsnips, chanterelles and roasted apple. **Price range:** Entrees, $17–$23. **Meals:** D. **Subway:** N, R to Prince St.

El Cid   **$25 & Under**   SPANISH
322 W. 15th St. (between Eighth and Ninth Aves.)   (212) 929-9332
El Cid is delightful, with delicious food and a professional staff that handles any
problem with élan. Tapas are a highlight, and you can make a meal of dishes
like grilled shrimp that are still freshly briny; tender white asparagus served cool
in a delicate vinaigrette; robustly flavorful peppers; tiny smelt fillets marinated
in vinegar and spices; and chunks of savory marinated pork with french fries.
The paella is exceptional. This is not a restaurant for quiet heart-to-heart talks.
The simple décor features hard surfaces that amplify noise, producing a rollicking party atmosphere as the room gets crowded. And it does get crowded. **Price
range:** Entrees, $14.95–$27.95. AE/D only. **Meals:** L, D. Closed Mon. **Subway:**
A, C, E to 14th St.; L to Eighth Ave.

Eleven Madison Park   ☆☆   **$$$$**   CONTINENTAL
11 Madison Ave. (at 24th St.)   (212) 889-0905
Eleven Madison Park occupies the stately ground floor of a grand Art Deco building near the Flatiron building. The restaurant is an homage to the area's past, and
the menu is a thoughtful return to Continental cuisine. The best main courses are
skate grenobloise and the choucroute of salmon and trout. Sweetbreads are spectacular, too. Desserts are irresistible. **Price range:** Entrees, $19–$32. **Meals:** L, D.
Subway: 6 to 23rd St.

El Fogon   **$25 & Under**   SPANISH/PUERTO RICAN
183 E. 111th St. (between Lexington and Third Aves.)   (212) 426-4844
The Puerto Rican specialties are fabulous at this friendly neighborhood hangout, which generally offers two interesting main courses each day. Corned beef
is ground fine and served in a rich sauce with olives, squash, peppers and
onions, enhancing its briny, smoky flavor. Roasted pork is moist and garlicky
and chicken fricassee is a beautifully flavored stew. Each dish comes with white
rice and plump red beans; for an extra $1, try a remarkably flaky and crisp
pastelillo, the Puerto Rican version of empanadas. **Price range:** Avg. entree, $6.
Cash only. **Meals:** L, D. Closed Sun. **Subway:** 6 to 110th St.

El Presidente   **$25 & Under**   CARIBBEAN/PAN-LATIN
3938 Broadway (between 164th and 165th Sts.)   (212) 927-7011
This small, bright restaurant specializes in the foods of the Hispanic Caribbean
—Cuba, Puerto Rico and the Dominican Republic — where flavors are powered by garlic, bell peppers and annatto rather than the heat of chilies. Pernil,
or roast pork, is simple but wonderfully satisfying. El Presidente also serves an
excellent charcoal-broiled skirt steak, with grilled onions and peppers, well-
charred around the edges yet still juicy. **Price range:** Entrees, $5.50–$14.75.
Meals: B, L, D, LN. **Subway:** A, C, 1, 9 to 168th St.–Washington Heights.

Emily's   **$25 & Under**   SOUTHERN
1325 Fifth Ave. (at 111th St.)   (212) 996-1212
This pleasant but institutional restaurant offers a diverse Southern menu and
draws an integrated crowd. If you go, go for the meaty, tender baby back pork ribs,

subtly smoky and bathed in tangy barbecue sauce, or the big plate of chopped pork barbecue. The best sides include savory rice and peas (actually red beans) and peppery stuffing, and all dishes come with a basket of fine corn bread. Sweet potato pie is the traditional dessert, and Emily's version is nice and nutmeggy. **Price range:** Entrees, $10–$25. **Meals:** Br, L, D, LN. **Subway:** 6 to 110th St.

Emo's $25 & Under KOREAN
1564 Second Ave. (near 81st St.) (212) 628-8699

Emo's pulls few punches, offering robust, spicy, authentic fare that is full of flavor. The highlights here are the superb main courses, like oh jing uh gui, wonderfully tender cylinders of barbecued squid scored to resemble pale pine cones and touched with hot sauce. A variation of this is jae yook gui, barbecued pork in a delectable smoky, spicy sauce. An American-style bar lines the entryway to the spare, narrow but airy dining room. **Price range:** Entrees, $11–$18. **Meals:** L, D. **Subway:** 6 to 77th St.

Empire Diner $$ DINER
210 10th Ave. (at 22nd St.) (212) 243-2736

One of the early entries in the modern revival of America's love affair with diners was this campy Art Deco gem that attracted a hip late-night crowd in the 1980's. Nowadays, the Empire is a tourist destination. The up-to-date diner basics with some Mediterranean touches are not bad at all—better than at most diners, in fact—which is reflected in the prices. **Price range:** Entrees, $10–$17. **Meals:** B, Br, L, D, LN. **Subway:** C, E to 23rd St.

Esca ☆☆ $$$ ITALIAN/SEAFOOD
402 W. 43rd St. (at Ninth Ave.) (212) 564-7272

At Esca—the name means "bait"—the most important word in the Italian language is *crudo*. It means raw, and that's the way the fish comes to the table in a dazzling array of appetizers that could be thought of as Italian sushi. The *crudo* appetizers at Esca are the freshest, most exciting thing to happen to Italian food in recent memory. By changing olive oils, adding a bitter green, or throwing in a scattering of minced chilies, the chef works thrilling variations on a very simple theme. The menu changes daily depending on what comes out of the sea. Look hard enough, and you can find a dish like guinea hen or roast chicken, but it seems perverse to order anything but seafood. The lemon-yellow walls and sea-green tiles give it a bright, cool look, and the solid wooden table in the center of the dining room, loaded down with vegetable side dishes, strikes a rustic note while communicating the food philosophy: fresh from the market, and prepared without fuss. **Price range:** Entrees, $17—$26. **Meals:** L, D / Closed Sun. **Subway:** A, C, E to 42nd St.

Esperanto $25 & Under PAN-LATIN
145 Ave. C (at 9th St.) (212) 505-6559

This is a warm and welcoming place with Latin food that can be surprisingly subtle and delicate. Bolinho de peixe, deep-fried balls of codfish, are exceptionally light, crisp and flavorful, with a terrific dipping sauce galvanized by spicy mustard. Esperanto's main courses are sturdy and hard to mess up, like a good and beefy steak bathed in chimichurri, the Argentine condiment of garlic and parsley. Esperanto serves potent caipirinhas or mojitos, a sort of Cuban mint julep—and don't miss the stellar coconut flan. **Price range:** Entrees, $9 to $14. AE only. **Meals:** D, LN. **Subway:** L to First Ave.

Estiatorio Milos   ☆☆ $$$$ GREEK/SEAFOOD
125 W. 55th St. (between Sixth and Seventh Aves.)   (212) 245-7400
The restaurant is clean, spare, blindingly white, and the entire focus is on the display of gorgeous fish by the open kitchen. Choose one and it is grilled simply and brought to the table. All the fish are cooked whole. And the lamb chops, a concession to meat eaters, are excellent. Appetizers are wonderful, too. The octopus, charred and sliced, mixed with onions, capers and peppers, is truly delicious. Thick homemade yogurt is the ideal way to end these meals. **Price range:** fish for main courses is sold whole and by weight, from $25–$34 a pound. **Meals:** L, D, LN. Closed Sun. **Subway:** B, D, E to Seventh Ave.; N, Q, R, W to 57th St.

Etats-Unis   ☆☆ $$$ NEW AMERICAN
242 E. 81st St. (between Second and Third Aves.)   (212) 517-8826
This once intimate, clubby restaurant has taken on a snazzy bistro look. It is still tiny, and still a bright spot in the neighborhood, but the kitchen has lost some of the excitement of its early years. The eclectic menu, a little French and a little American (braised pork shoulder in a spicy barbecue sauce is typical), pleases well enough, but the overall average is, well, pretty average. An exception must be noted: the signature date pudding, a dessert that must never be allowed to leave the menu. **Price range:** Entrees, $24–34. **Meals:** D. **Subway:** 6 to 77th St.

Euzkadi $25 & Under   BASQUE
108 E. 4th St. (bet. First & Second Aves.)   (212) 982-9788
Euzkadi reflects the East Village far more than the Pyrenees. No traditional Basque outfits or sheep-herding scenes here, just a small, brick-walled dining room with comfortable Mission-style banquettes and a young, cigarette-loving clientele. The menu is not so much unusual as subtly different. Dishes served á la plancha, or sizzling on a cast-iron skillet, like shrimp, which arrive with heads still on, are first-rate. Seafood dominates the menu, but also try the pork paillard, served over a delicious ragout of escarole, sausage and white beans, and tender braised rabbit in a slightly sweet wine and prune sauce. **Price range:** Entrees, $13–$15. American Express only **Meals:** D. Closed Sun. **Subway:** F, V to Second Ave.

Evergreen Shanghai $25 & Under   CHINESE
63 Mott St. (near Bayard St.)   (212) 571-3339
10 E. 38th St. (between Fifth and Madison Aves.)   (212) 448-1199
Concentrate on the long menu's Shanghai specialties, like cold appetizers of aromatic beef, a Chinese version of barbecued brisket, and smoked fish, sweet with

light, smoky notes and hints of star anise. Great main courses include bean curd with crab sauce and yellowfish with seaweed. The staff is friendly, with enough English speakers to help with the selections. **Price range:** Entrees, $5.95–$24. Cash only at Mott St. **Meals:** L, D, LN. **Subway:** Downtown: J, M, N, Q, R, W, Z, 6 to Canal St.; Midtown: 6 to 33rd St.; 7 to Fifth Ave.

Felidia ☆☆☆ $$$$ NORTHERN ITALIAN
243 E. 58th St. (between Second and Third Aves.)   (212) 758-1479
Felidia offers itself in the guise of an old-fashioned restaurant, comfortable and rustic, but there's a professional polish in the dining room and high ambition in the kitchen. The seasonal menu concentrates on the foods of Italy's northeast: Friuli, the Veneto as well as Istria, now part of Croatia, and the home of owners Felice and Lidia Bastinich. This is robust food served in generous portions, revolving around game, organ meats, and slow-cooked sauces. This is not to say you can't eat lightly. Felidia serves lots of seafood, including lobster and crab-meat salad, and an impressive spiced monkfish in clam broth. Despite her expanding career as a television chef and cookbook writer, Ms. Bastianich has managed to keep standards admirably high at Felidia. **Price range:** Entrees, $27–$35. **Meals:** L, D. Closed Sun. **Subway:** 4, 5, 6 to 59th St.; N, R to Lexington Ave.

Fiamma Osteria ☆☆☆ $$$ ITALIAN
206 Spring St. (near Sullivan St.)   (212) 653-0100
Fiamma Osteria is a beautifully realized restaurant, highly satisfying in every way. The upstairs dining room has a subdued atmosphere with rich, saturated reds and browns; the downstairs room is lighter, brighter and louder, more brasserie than restaurant. The food lives up to the setting. The chef stays firmly rooted in the core principles of Italian cooking, putting prime ingredients on a sparely designed stage and letting them speak with minimum interference. The pastas at Fiamma are exceptional, especially the raviolini stuffed with braised veal shank in a potent, highly reduced veal sauce enriched with formaggio de fossa. The dessert rotation changes, but the showstopper is a layered hazelnut chocolate torte on a crackling pastry base, served with gianduja gelato and chocolate sauce. **Price range:** Entrees, $21–$32. **Meals:** L, D. **Subway:** C, E to Spring St.

Fifty Seven Fifty Seven ☆☆☆ $$$$ AMERICAN
Four Seasons Hotel, 57 E. 57th St. (between Park and Madison Aves.)
        (212) 758-5757
With its solicitous service in a memorable public space, Fifty Seven Fifty Seven sets a new standard for an old tradition. The menu changes frequently, but it still offers something for absolutely every taste. The food is decidedly American with a modern bent. Vegetarians will find many choices; dieters will find starred offerings low in fat and salt. And those with an appetite for meat and potatoes have many options, from rack of veal in a red wine sauce to grilled beef tenderloin with rose-

mary cream potato pie. One of the finest dishes, offered on occasion, is cured swordfish, sliced very thin and served with asparagus, greens and cherries. The visually restrained desserts are rich in flavor and texture, but the chocolate desserts are the greatest triumph. **Price range:** Entrees, $25–32. **Meals:** B, L, D. **Subway:** 4, 5, 6 to 59th St.; N, R to Lexington Ave.

F.Illi Ponte   ☆☆ $$$$ ITALIAN
39 Desbrosses St. (between Washington St. and West Side Hwy.)

(212) 226-4621

This is a great, rustic room with bare brick walls, beamed ceilings and a fabulous view of the Hudson. The menu features admirable Italian fare and fine spicy lobster. The porchetta, spit-roasted baby pig, is superb. Fried calamari are sweet, crisp, irresistible. Shrimp cocktail is just about perfect. There is an excellent veal chop and good (if expensive) broccoli rape. Even if the menu were not filled with excellent dishes, it would be worth going to F.illi Ponte for the sheer pleasure of sitting in that beautiful old room watching the light fade over the Hudson River and to bask in the extraordinary service. **Price range:** Entrees, $17–$35. **Meals:** L, D. Closed Sun. **Subway:** 1, 9 to Canal St.

Firebird   ☆☆ $$$ RUSSIAN
365 W. 46th St. (between Eighth and Ninth Aves.)   (212) 586-0244
This jewel box of a restaurant boasts a dining room as ornate and luxurious as a Fabergé egg, and a staff so polished, it really does seem that you have entered some more serene and lavish era. The caviar arrives with its own private waiter who turns the service into a performance, pouring hot butter onto the plate, spooning on the caviar and then delicately twirling the blini around the roe. Firebird continues to offer imaginatively updated Russian classics, like chicken tabaka with plum sauce, and grilled sturgeon with sorrel-potato purée. Desserts, once a weak point, have improved greatly . **Price range:** Entrees, $26–$38. **Meals:** L, D. **Subway:** A, C, E to 42nd St.

First $25 & Under   NEW AMERICAN
87 First Ave. (between 5th and 6th Sts.)   (212) 674-3823
Ambitious, creative contemporary American fare at relatively modest prices, served late into the night. First also offers an intelligently chosen list of wines and beers and worthwhile weekly specials, like its Sunday night pig roast. **Price range:** Avg. entree, $17. **Meals:** D, LN. **Subway:** F to Second Ave.

Fleur de Sel   ☆☆ $$$$ FRENCH
5 E. 20th St. (between Fifth Ave. and Broadway)   (212) 460-9100
Who doesn't pine for that little neighborhood restaurant, tucked away on a side street, where the lighting is subdued, the chef is French and the food is terrific? Well, here it is. The fixed-price menu is perfectly calibrated to the small room, and the chef knows in a quiet sort of way how to create excitement on the plate. It might be an unfamiliar ingredient, or an unexpected flavor combina-tion, like a purée of rose water and apricots which seems to coax extra richness

and depth from seared foie gras. Large ravioli stuffed with bits of sweetbread and cepes also do the trick, each package containing a rich, meaty ooze. The raspberry feuillete is a disarmingly simple-looking thing, two rectangular pastry leaves, some fat fruit and a blob of white-chocolate caramel ganache, but the pastry melts on the tongue, and the ganache is almost criminally delicious. **Price range:** Three courses, $52. **Meals:** L, D. **Subway:** N, R to 23rd St.

Flor's Kitchen $25 & Under   VENEZUELAN
149 First Ave. (near 9th St.)   (212) 387-8949
Tiny, bright and colorful, this new Venezuelan restaurant offers many snacking foods like empanadas criollas, smooth, crisp pastries with fillings like savory shredded beef or pureed chicken. The arepas—corncakes with varied fillings—include a wonderful chicken and avocado salada. Two sauces—one made with avocado, lemon juice and oil; the second, a hot sauce—make dishes like chachapas (corn pancakes with ham and cheese) taste even better. Soups are superb, and desserts are rich and homespun. **Price range:** Entrees, $4–$9. **Meals:** L, D, LN. **Subway:** F to Second Ave.; L to First Ave.

The Four Seasons   ☆☆☆ $$$$ NEW AMERICAN
99 E. 52nd St. (between Park and Lexington Aves.)   (212) 754-9494
Designed by legendary architect Philip Johnson, The Four Seasons is a gracious reminder that restaurants can still be comfortable and relaxing. The Grill room is still the power lunch place for those who count in fashion, finance and publishing. At lunch the menu is straightforward: begin with a big baked potato, served with its own bottle of olive oil, followed by meaty crab cakes or the bunless burger with creamed spinach and crisp onions. The Pool Room is at its best with unfussy food like broiled dover sole or rack of lamb and the perfect steak tartare. Wherever you are seated, it is hard to eat at the Four Seasons without luxuriating in an extraordinary sense of privilege. **Price range:** Entrees, $34–$55. **Meals:** L, D. Closed Sun. **Subway:** E, F to Lexington Ave.; 6 to 51st St.

Frank $25 &   Under   ITALIAN
88 Second Ave. (near 5th St.)   (212) 420-0202
This sweet, unpretentious restaurant, with its crowded, ragtag dining room, has been packed from the moment it opened. Start with an order of insalata Caprese, ripe tomatoes and mozzarella di bufala; among the entrees, try the polpettone, a savory meatloaf, with a classic, slow-cooked gravy, and orecchiette with fennel and pecorino Toscano. If you go early, you can expect special touches, like a free plate of tiny potato croquettes, or a dish of olive oil flavored with orange rind with your bread. **Price range:** Entrees, $6.95–$14.95.Cash only. **Meals:** Br, L, D, LN. **Subway:** F to Second Ave.

Frank's   ☆ $$$ STEAKHOUSE
85 10th Ave. (at 15th St.)   (212) 243-1349
A paradise for carnivores and smokers. The bare brick walls and long bar announce this as a restaurant whose only desire is to serve big portions to hun-

gry people. Three or four shrimp in a cocktail would probably provide enough protein for an average person: they are giant creatures of the sea, and absolutely delicious. The T-bone steak has the fine, funky flavor of meat that has been dry-aged for a long time and the steak fries are long and thick. The same family has been running Frank's since 1912; they will make you feel at home. **Price range:** Entrees, $18–$30. **Meals:** L, D. **Subway:** A, C, E to 14th St.; L to Eighth Ave.

Funky Broome $25 & Under   CHINESE
176 Mott St. (between Broome and Kenmare Sts.)   (212) 941-8628
From its odd name to its brightly colored interior, Funky Broome suggests youth and energy rather than conformity. Though the menu is largely Cantonese and Hong Kong, Funky Broome has stirred it up a bit with some Thai touches and by making mini-woks centerpieces. Some of the dishes are unusual and good, like plump and flavorful oysters stuffed with green onions and steamed in a red wine sauce. Seafood dishes are excellent, and Funky Broome can breathe new life into hoary old dishes like crisp and tender beef with broccoli. **Price range:** Entrees, $6.95-$15.95. **Meals:** L, D, LN. **Subway:** 6 to Spring St.

Gabriela's $25 & Under   MEXICAN
685 Amsterdam Ave. (at 93rd St.)   (212) 961-0574
311 Amsterdam Ave. (at 75th St.)
There really is a Gabriela, and she makes terrific, authentic Mexican dishes. Taquitos al pastor, tiny corn tortillas topped with vinegary roast pork, pineapple salsa and cilantro, are a wonderful Mexican street dish. Gabriela's pozole, the traditional Mexican soup made with hominy, is an entire meal in itself, served in a huge bowl with chunks of tender pork or chicken. Entrees all come with tortillas so fragrant that the aroma of corn rises with the steam. Gabriela's also offers superb desserts, including capirotada, a buttery bread pudding with lots of honey. **Price range:** Entrees, $5.95–$14.95. **Meals:** B, L, D. **Subway:** 93rd St.: 1, 2, 3, 9 to 96th St.; 75th St.: 1, 2, 3, 9 to 72nd St.

Gabriel's ☆☆ $$$ ITALIAN
11 W. 60th St. (between Broadway and Columbus Ave.)   (212) 956-4600
This clubby and comfortable restaurant offers great big portions and fabulous friendly service. Although the food is called Tuscan, it is far too American for that, too original. The dish on almost every table is an earthy and seductive buckwheat polenta. None of the pastas are ordinary, either. The real winner here is homemade gnocchi, little dumplings so light they float into your mouth and down your throat. Among the entrees, the best dish is the sea bass cooked in a terra cotta casserole. Desserts, with the exception of the wonderful sorbets and gelatos, are not very exciting. **Price range:** Entrees, $18–$32. **Meals:** L, D. Closed Sun. **Subway:** A, B, C, D, E, 1, 9 to 59th St.

Gennaro $25 & Under   ITALIAN/MEDITERRANEAN
665 Amsterdam Ave. (near 93rd St.)   (212) 665-5348
This tiny, simply decorated Italian restaurant is one of the best things to happen

to the Upper West Side in years, serving wonderful dishes like an awesome osso bucco and terrific pastas. Appetizer specials are satisfying, like ribbolita, the classic Tuscan vegetable and bean soup. Cornish hen roasted with lemon is also excellent. Gennaro serves its own pear tart, flaky and delicious, and a rich flourless chocolate cake. **Price range:** Entrees, $8.50–$14.95. Cash only. **Meals:** D. **Subway:** 1, 2, 3, 9 to 96th St.

Good $25 & Under   LATIN AMERICAN
89 Greenwich Ave. (at Bank St.)   (212) 691-8080

It's possible to eat unusually, eclectically and very well here. Crisp peanut chicken is a welcome old dish, while grilled calamari, a newcomer, takes its cue from Asia, arriving in a lime-and-mint dressing. Also good are the grilled flank steak with parsley-garlic sauce and sauteed rock shrimp, flavored with garlic and served over gloriously mushy grits with corn relish. The service is warm and professional. The signature dessert, house-made doughnuts, are rather dry and tasteless, although the demitasse of Oaxacan chocolate served with them is delicious. **Price range:** Entrees, $10–$17. **Meals:** L, D. Closed Mon. **Subway:** 1, 2, 3, 9 to 14th St.

Good World Bar and Grill $25 & Under   SCANDINAVIAN
3 Orchard St. (at Division St.)   (212) 925-9975

Good World Bar and Grill beckons because it's a bar in an old barbershop near Chinatown that serves Scandinavian food. It offers a spirit of adventure, a departure from the routine, that makes Good World's world a good world indeed. Basic dishes like Swedish meatballs and potato pancakes can be unpredictable; Good World is on far firmer ground with seafood. Skagen is shrimp with créme fraîche and dill, served on toast. It's a nice prelude for the tender and tasty sautéed squid, or the fabulous fish soup, a bisque that tastes like the essence of the sea. **Price range:** Medium and large plates, $8 to $16. **Meals:** D, LN. **Subway:** F to East Broadway.

Goody's   ☆ $ CHINESE
1 East Broadway (at Chatham Sq.)   (212) 577-2922

Goody's pride is the crab meat version of soup dumplings, xiao long bao, tinted pink by the seafood that glows through the sheer, silky skin. But there are other unusual dishes, like fabulous turnip pastries, yellowfish fingers in seaweed batter, and braised pork shoulder, a kind of candied meat. This dish is so rich that it must be eaten in small bites. Goody's kitchen also works magic with bean curd, mixed with crab meat so it becomes rich and delicious. **Price range:** $15–$20. **Meals:** L, D. **Subway:** J, M, N, Q, R, W, Z, 6 to Canal St.

Gotham Bar and Grill   ☆ ☆ ☆ $$$$ NEW AMERICAN
12 E. 12th St. (between Fifth and University Pl.)   (212) 620-4020

Gotham Bar and Grill is a cheerful, welcoming restaurant in an open, high-ceilinged room with a lively bar along one side. Waiters take their cues from the customer—anticipating their every wish and making diners feel remarkably well cared for. And then there's the food, which seems modern but is almost classic in its balance. The signature dish is seafood salad, a spiral of scallops, squid, octopus, lobster and avocado that swirls onto the plate like a mini-tornado. Main courses are more straightforward, like rosy slices of duck breast set off by a single caramelized endive and a sweet potato purée. Desserts, like the wonderful chocolate cake, are intense and very American. **Price range:** Entrees, $28–$38. **Meals:** L, D.l **Subway:** F, L, N, Q, R, W, 4, 5, 6 to 14th St.

Gradisca $25 & Under   ITALIAN
126 W. 13th St. (between Sixth and Seventh Aves.)   (212) 691-4886
Gradisca epitomizes the local trattoria, downtown style. The dining room is rustic, but the waiters conform to a more modern stereotype: young, hip and lanky in tight black T-shirts. The menu offers simple, delicious flavors, like piadinas, round, unleavened flatbreads, cooked on a griddle and then stuffed with things like prosciutto and fresh mozzarella (a marvelously nutty combination), or spinach and pecorino. There are two superb main courses: sliced leg of lamb in a red wine sauce, and a big pork chop under a cloud of crisp leeks. Dessert standouts include a deliciously dense, bittersweet chocolate torte and a satisfying amaretto semifreddo. **Price range:** Entrees, $12–$20. Cash only. **Meals:** D. **Subway:** F, 1, 2, 3, 9 to 14th St.

Gramercy Tavern   ☆☆☆ $$$$ NEW AMERICAN
42 E. 20th St. (between Broadway and Park Ave. South)   (212) 477-0777
The large and lively tavern has redefined grand dining in New York. Chef Tom Colicchio cooks with extraordinary confidence, creating dishes characterized by bold flavors and unusual harmonies. To experience Mr. Colicchio's cooking at its best, consider the chef's extraordinary market menu. It is expensive, but perfect for special occasions. For a less expensive alternative, the handsome bar in front offers a casual but excellent menu. On a recent visit, the restaurant lived up to its three stars, with consistently fresh, inventive new American dishes; desserts also remain a highlight. **Price range:** Prix-fixe and tasting menus, $65–$90. **Meals:** L, D. **Subway:** N, R, 6 to 23rd St.

Grand Sichuan $25 & Under   CHINESE
229 Ninth Ave. (at 24th St.)   (212) 620-5200
The owner of this terrific restaurant hands out a 27-page pamphlet that explains five Chinese regional cuisines and describes dozens of dishes the restaurant serves. The eating is as interesting as the reading, with wonderful dishes like sour stringbeans with minced pork and tea-smoked duck. While Sichuan food is indeed spicy, that is only part of the story, as you see when you taste a fabulous cold dish like sliced conch with wild pepper sauce, coated with ground Sichuan peppercorns, which are not hot but bright, effervescent and almost refreshing. **Price range:** Entrees, $5.95–$16.95. **Meals:** L, D. **Subway:** C, E to 23rd St.

Grange Hall $25 & Under   AMERICAN
50 Commerce St. (at Barrow St.)   (212) 924-5246
Grange Hall celebrates Depression-era American food of the Midwest with flair, from fat little loaves of white bread to succotash, pork chops and lake fish. The food is usually pretty good, the décor is inspiring and the all-American wine and beer list is appealing. **Price range:** Entrees, $10.50–$21. AE only.
Meals: Br, L, D. **Subway:** A, C, E, F, S to W. 4th St.

Guastavino's   ☆☆ $$$$ ENGLISH/FRENCH
409 E. 59th St. (between First and York Aves.)   (212) 980-2455
This dazzling transformation of the Queensboro Bridge vaults gives New Yorkers a glimpse of a swaggering international restaurant style where the scenes are loud, lively and up to the minute, and the food often runs second to the design. Guastavino's fits the pattern. The raw, almost brutal granite blocks that make up the caissons of the bridge have been left exposed. But the overall design is as sleek and international the Concorde. It's not so much a restaurant as an opportunity to live, for two or three hours, a certain mood, and a certain sense of style, that suits every time zone and speaks every language. A long, low-slung bar on the main level pulls a large Upper East Side crowd. Guastavino Restaurant, on the first floor, is a 300-seat brasserie, clamorous and casual, with a glorious brasserie-style shellfish display in front of the kitchen. Up a curved marble staircase, the more formal and intimate Club Guastavino, which seats 100, hangs over the first floor like a giant balcony. Guastavino's two kitchens feed a lot of people out there, and they do a more than respectable job. At its best, these are well-conceived, well-executed dishes that really can compete with the surroundings. **Price range:** Guastavino Restaurant: $14–$30. Club Guastavino: Dinner, three courses, $65.
Meals: L, D. **Subway:** 4, 5, 6 to 59th St.; N, R to Lexington Ave.

Gus's Figs Bistro and Bar $25 & Under   MEDITERRANEAN
250 W. 27th St. (between Seventh and Eighth Aves.) (212) 352-8822
This restaurant captures the dreamy, generous, sun-soaked aura that makes the Mediterranean so endlessly appealing. The chef excels at blending flavors and textures in main courses like moist, flavorful chicken, braised in a clay pot and served over creamy polenta. Top dishes include tender pieces of lamb served over a soft bread pudding made savory with goat cheese and pine nuts and sweetened with figs; and pan-roasted cod with grilled leeks, orange sections and pomegranate vinaigrette. **Price range:** Entrees, $13–$19.50.
Meals: L, D, LN. **Subway:** C, E, 1, 9 to 28th St.

The Half King $25 & Under   PUB/AMERICAN
505 W. 23rd St. (between 10th and 11th Aves.)   (212) 462-4300
Owned by Sebastian Junger, author of *The Perfect Storm*, this unconventional writers' bar serves Irish pub grub, skillfully elevated from its proletarian moorings while retaining its heartiness and simplicity. Excellent starters include a light cake constructed of potatoes and goat cheese, wrapped in excellent

smoked salmon. Main courses include a superbly flavorful pork roast and a surprisingly delicate fillet of sole. The shepherd's pie, made with chopped beef, is
ample and excellent. Desserts are good and rustic, like a rough-hewn berry,
peach and apple crumble. A small garden in the rear is pleasant at lunch or at
breakfast. **Price range:** Entrees, $9–$16. **Meals:** B, L, D.
Subway: C, E to 23rd St.

Han Bat $25 & Under   KOREAN
53 W. 35th St. (between Fifth and Sixth Aves.)   (212) 629-5588
This spare, clean, round-the-clock restaurant specializes in the country dishes of
southern Korea. Typical Korean dishes, like scallion and seafood pancakes, fiery
stir-fried baby octopus and bibimbab, are all excellent. Meals here are served
family style and include several little appetizers; almost all dishes are served
with rice and crocks of the rich beef soup, full of noodles and scallions.
Price range: Entrees, $6.95–$15.95. **Meals:** L, D. Open 24 hours.
Subway: B, D, F, N, Q, R, S, W to 34th St.

Hangawi ☆☆ $$ KOREAN/VEGETARIAN
12 E. 32nd St. (between Fifth and Madison Aves.)   (212) 213-0077
Hangawi leaves you feeling cleansed and refreshed, as if you had come from a
spa instead of a vegetarian Korean restaurant. Diners remove their shoes on
entering and sit at low tables with their feet dangling comfortably into the
sunken space beneath them. They are surrounded by unearthly Korean music,
wonderful objects and people who move with deliberate grace. Many of the
exotic greens, porridges and mountain roots on the menu can be sampled by
ordering the emperor's meal, which includes a tray of nine kinds of mountain
greens surrounded by 10 side dishes. **Price range:** Entrees, $14.95–$24.95.
Meals: L, D. **Subway:** 6 to 33rd St.

The Harrison   ☆☆ $$$ NEW AMERICAN
355 Greenwich St. (at Harrison St.)   (212) 274-9319
With a clean, all-American look for the interior, the Harrison offers a modestly
priced menu poised carefully between new American and fusion cooking. The
food may speak with an accent, but it's American food. Shell steak gets some
inspired Italian tailoring, a rich, crunchy topping of crisped pancetta with bitter
radicchio and balsamic vinegar. Likewise, chicken crisped in the pan with
lemon-mustard sauce has the immediacy of a slap in the face. For desserts, the
quince and apple crisp is a rip-roaring mainstream pleaser. **Price range:** Entrees,
$9–$28. **Meals:** L, D. Closed Sun. **Subway:** 1, 2 to Franklin St.

Hatsuhana   ☆☆ $$$ JAPANESE/SUSHI
17 E. 48th St. (between Fifth and Madison Aves.)   (212) 355-3345
237 Park Ave. (at 46th St.)   (212) 661-3400
Of all the city's sushi bars, Hatsuhana is the one that best bridges the gap
between East and West. It is a comfortable and welcoming restaurant where you

can depend on being served high-quality sushi whether you speak Japanese or not. Real connoisseurs sit at the downstairs sushi bar and enjoy extraordinary chu toro, tuna that is richer than maguro but less rich than toro, and ika uni, pure white squid cut into long strips as thin as spaghetti. The quality of the cooked food is excellent, too. The Park Avenue location is not nearly as good as the 48th Street location. **Price range:** Avg. entree, $30. **Meals:** L, D. Closed Sun. **Subway:** S, 4, 5, 6, 7 to 42nd St.

Havana NY $25 & Under
LATIN AMERICAN

27 W. 38th St. (between Fifth and Sixth Aves.)   (212) 944-0990

There's little not to like about this bustling Cuban restaurant, a lunchtime hot spot serving tasty, inexpensive food in pleasant surroundings. The food is typically robust, flavored with lusty doses of garlic and lime, yet it can be delicate, too, as in an octopus salad, which is marinated in citrus until tender like a ceviche. Chilean sea bass, is moist and subtly flavored, not the sort of dish that would succeed in an assembly-line kitchen, and grilled skirt steak is excellent. All the main courses are enormous, served with rice, beans and sweet plantains—so appetizers are usually unnecessary. Service is swift and likable. **Price range:** Entrees, $8.95–$12.95. **Meals:** L, D. Closed Sat., Sun. **Subway:** B, D, F, N, Q, R, S, W to 34th St.

Heartbeat   ☆☆ $$$
NEW AMERICAN

149 E. 49th St. (at Lexington Ave.)   (212) 407-2900

New York's hippest spa food brings models to mingle with moguls in a slick setting. You could describe Heartbeat that way, but it would be doing the restaurant a disservice; this is a very comfortable, crowded and surprisingly quiet room with good service and good food. This approach works best when the food is simply left alone. Try the simple grills, the good meats and the Japanese-accented dishes. **Price range:** Entrees, $18–$30. **Meals:** B, Br, L, D. **Subway:** 6 to 51st St.; E, F to Lexington Ave.

Hell's Kitchen $25 & Under
MEXICAN

679 Ninth Ave. (near 47th St.)   (212) 977-1588

This restaurant makes creative use of Mexican flavorings and cooking techniques, adding ingredients and dishes from the global palette of contemporary American cooking. Head directly for the interpretations of Mexican dishes. The appetizer of tuna tostadas is brilliant. Part of the menu is devoted to quesadillas; in size, they are like small main courses; in spirit, they succeed because they retain their Mexican identity even with creative enhancements. The best main course is a pork loin flavored with chili. For dessert try the intense fruit sorbets, served over fruit with a surprising touch of chili. The loud music and hopping bar suggest that conversations will be difficult, but once you sit down the acoustics are surprisingly good. **Price range:** Entrees, $13—$18. **Meals:** D, LN. **Subway:** C, E to 50th St.

Henry's Evergreen $25 & Under   CHINESE
1288 First Ave. (near 70th St.)   (212) 744-3266
This bright and appealing restaurant follows the decorating scheme of many
other Chinese restaurants, but adds a surprising wine list strong in California
reds, midlevel zinfandels, pinot noirs and whites that go brilliantly with the
food. For the most part, the menu will not surprise you but many of the dishes
are fresh and appealing. The real excitement is discovering how good the wine
and food combinations can be. Dim sum and appetizers tend to be the best part
of Henry's menu; main courses are much less consistent.
Price range: Entrees, $7.95–$27.50. **Meals:** L, D. **Subway:** 6 to 68th St.

Holy Basil $25 & Under   THAI
149 Second Ave. (between 9th and 10th Sts.)   (212) 460-5557
This is one of the best Thai restaurants in the city, turning out highly spiced,
beautifully balanced dishes like green papaya salad, elegant curries and delicious noodles. The dining room looks more like a beautiful church than a
restaurant, jazz usually plays in the background and the wine list offers terrific
choices. **Price range:** Entrees, $8–$16. **Meals:** D, LN. **Subway:** F to Second
Ave.; L to First or Third Ave.

Honmura An   ☆☆☆ $$$ JAPANESE/NOODLES
170 Mercer St. (between Houston and Prince Sts.)   (212) 334-5253
Making the buckwheat noodles known as soba is not easy, but the soba chefs at
Honmura An have clearly put in their time—the soba in this spare, soothing
space is wonderful and worth the high price. Many appetizers, as well as good
tempura, are worth trying here, but nothing is remotely on a par with the noodles. To appreciate how fine they are, you must eat them cold. The noodles are
earthy and elastic, and when you dip them into the briny bowl of dashi (dipping
sauce), land and sea come, briefly, together. Honmura An also makes excellent
udon, fat wheat noodles. Served hot, in the dish called nabeyaki, they virtually
redefine the dish. **Price range:** entrees, $13–$22. **Meals:** L, D. Closed Mon.
Subway: N, R to Prince St.; F, S to Broadway–Lafayette St.

Icon   ☆☆ $$ NEW AMERICAN
130 E. 39th St. (between Lexington and Park Aves.)   (212) 592-8888
Icon has a mildly lurid décor and a lighting philosophy perfectly designed for
illegal trysts and furtive meetings. It is attached to the W Court Hotel, ensuring
a steady flow of youngish, stylish diners. Visually, it is soothing to the nerves.
Aurally, it's touch and go. As the evening progresses, a thumping rock soundtrack forces diners to shout across the table, and the noise from Wet Bar across
the lobby becomes intrusive. The food at Icon is better than the setting might
suggest. Desserts are not flashy; quiet good taste is more the style. **Price range:**
Entrees, $19–$25. **Meals:** B, Br, L, D. **Subway:** S, 4, 5, 6, 7 to 42nd St.

Il Mulino $ $ $ $ ITALIAN
86 W. 3rd St. (between Sullivan and Thompson Sts.)   (212) 673-3783
Big portions, long waits, a halcyon atmosphere. No wonder New Yorkers are so
enthralled with this garlic haven. While the portions are large, so are the prices.
Dinner might begin with a dish of shrimp fricassee with garlic; bresaola of beef
served over mixed greens tossed in a well-seasoned vinaigrette, or aromatic
baked clams oreganato. The pasta roster includes fettuccine Alfredo; spaghet-
tini in a robust Bolognese sauce; trenette tossed in pesto sauce; and capellini
all'arrabbiata, or in a spicy tomato sauce. The menu carries a dozen veal preparations, along with beef tenderloin in a shallot, white wine and sage sauce; and
broiled sirloin. **Price range:** Entrees, $24 and up. **Meals:** L, D, LN. Closed Sun.
Subway: A, C, E, F, S to W. 4th St.

Ilo   ☆ ☆ ☆ $ $ $ $ NEW AMERICAN
Bryant Park Hotel, 40 W. 40th St. (bet. Fifth and Sixth Aves.)   (212) 642-2255
At Ilo, a Finnish word meaning something like "bliss," Chef Rick Laakkonen
creates complex dishes that seem simple. He knows how to coax pure flavors
from his ingredients, and how to keep those flavors clear and distinct. Grilled
quail, as meaty and tender as any in recent memory, stand out heroically from
their busy tableau, where a feather-light cheese flan is surrounded by spicy
minced peppers, chilies, coriander and lime. Ilo's rabbit is done country style,
pan-roasted with olives and accented with oregano and preserved lemon. Tasting menu portions are mercifully calibrated to a normal appetite. Don't miss
the chilled apricot soup, a regular on the dessert menu. And it's worth waving
over the sommelier, because the 250 or so wines on the list include many
unusual grapes and lesser known regions. **Price range:** Entrees $26–$38; beef
tasting menu, $85 ($120 with wines); seven-course vegetarian tasting menu,
$65; eight-course chef's tasting menu, $110 ($165 with wines). **Meals:** L, D.
Subway: B, D, F, S to 42nd St.

Il Valentino   ☆ ☆ $ $ ITALIAN
Sutton Hotel, 330 E. 56th St. (between First and Second Aves.) (212) 355-0001
In a city where purely pleasant restaurants have become increasingly rare, Il
Valentino feels like an oasis. The food is reliable, you don't have to wait for
your table and you know you will be able to hear your friends when they talk.
The timbered ceiling and terra cotta floor give the room a cool rustic feeling,
and the food is simple, tasty Tuscan fare. The artichoke salad is delicious, and
the Caesar salad impressive. But it is the pastas that really shine. Marinated
grilled lamb chops in a mustard seed sauce and osso buco are also excellent.
Price range: entrees, $16–$25. **Meals:** L, D. **Subway:** 4, 5, 6 to 59th St.; N, R
to Lexington Ave.

'ino $25 & Under   ITALIAN/SANDWICHES
21 Bedford St. (between Sixth Ave. and Downing St.)   (212) 989-5769
This inviting little Italian sandwich shop and wine bar offers intensely satisfying
variations on three types of sandwich: panini, sandwiches made with crusty
toasted ciabatta; tramezzini, made with untoasted white bread, crusts removed
and cut into triangles, and bruschetta, in which ingredients are simply placed
atop a slice of toasted bread. One dish that doesn't fall into any category but is
nonetheless wonderful is truffled egg toast, a soft cooked egg served on top of
toasted ciabatta with sliced asparagus and drizzled with truffle oil. It's like warm,
delicious baby food. **Price range:** Entrees, $2–$10. Cash only. **Meals:** B, Br, L, D.
Subway: 1, 9 to Houston St.

Inside $25 & Under   NEW AMERICAN
9 Jones St. (between 4th and Bleecker Sts.)   (212) 229-9999
The handsome wood bar in front and the professional greeting bespeak the
comfort of a more expensive restaurant, yet the almost bare white walls make
the dining room feel airy and streamlined. With dishes based on no more than
three seasonal and simple ingredients, Inside can keep prices gentle. The best
appetizer is a handful of shrimp with a light, crisp salt-and-pepper crust, topped
with a tangy grapefruit confit. Almost as good is a salad of cubed beets, endive
and peanuts, a perfect blend of sweet, bitter and crunchy. Main courses are similarly streamlined. Newport steak is thick and beefy, and tender braised lamb
with cinnamon and olives achieves an almost Moroccan balance of savory and
sweet. For dessert, try the panna cotta or a steamed chocolate pudding with
rhubarb. **Price range:** Entrees, $13–$18. **Meals:** Br, D. **Subway:** 6 to Bleecker St.

Irving on Irving $25 & Under   NEW AMERICAN
52 Irving Pl. (at 17th St.)   (212) 358-1300
This plainly-named little corner restaurant offers counter service for breakfast
and lunch. By night, waiters and waitresses come out, and it becomes a real
restaurant. The chef has put together a menu of uncomplicated ingredients, prepared simply. Appetizers show off their humble origins, like garlicky peasant
sausage on a bed of warm, vinegary lentils, and excellent codfish cakes, savory,
meaty and crisp outside. While main courses are not exactly made of humble
ingredients, they are resolutely plain, with the possible exception of the peppery
grilled swordfish, which is finely textured and full of flavor. The best dessert is
the cinnamon doughnuts, made to order and served hot and airy in a brown
lunch bag.   **Price range:** Entrees, $10.50–$16.75. **Meals:** B, L, D. **Subway:** L,
N, Q, R, W, 4, 5, 6 to 14th St.

Isola $25 & Under   ITALIAN
485 Columbus Ave. (between 83rd and 84th Sts.)   (212) 362-7400
When Isola is crowded, its dining room, full of hard surfaces, can be unbearably
loud, but the restaurant offers some of the best Italian food on the Upper West
Side, with lively pastas like spaghetti in a purée of black olives and oregano, and

fettuccine with crumbled sausages and porcini mushrooms. The wine list is nicely chosen. **Price range:** Entrees, $9.95–$18. **Meals:** Br, L, D. **Subway:** B, C to 81st St.

I Trulli   ☆☆ $$$ ITALIAN
122 E. 27th St. (between Lexington Ave. and Park Ave. South)   (212) 481-7372
This is New York City's best and most attractive restaurant dedicated to the cooking of Apulia. It serves interesting, unusual food in an understated room that is both elegant and warm; there is also a beautiful garden for outdoor dining. The rustic food from Italy's heel does not have the subtle charm of northern Italian food or the tomato-and-garlic heartiness of Neapolitan cuisine. The menu relies on bitter greens (arugula, dandelions, broccoli rape) and many foods that Americans rarely eat. The pastas have a basic earthy quality; orechiette are a house staple made by the owner. **Price range:** Entrees, $18–$32. **Meals:** L, D. Closed Sun. **Subway:** 6 to 28th St.

Jack Rose   ☆ $$$ NEW AMERICAN/STEAKHOUSE
771 Eighth Ave. (at 47th St.)   (212) 247-7518
Jack Rose is an artful exercise in nostalgia, an all-American joint that specializes in seafood, steaks, chops and no funny stuff. Although Jack Rose reserves a lot of room on the menu for steaks, they make a pretty feeble impression on the palate. But the kitchen can still win you over. It might be the oysters Rockefeller, topped with lovely fresh cress and piqued with just the right touch of Pernod, or it could be a plump, moist roasted chicken. The best desserts are bread pudding and crème brûlée. **Price range:** Entrees, $10.95—$28.50. **Meals:** L, D. **Subway:** C, E to 50th St.

Jane   ☆ $$ NEW AMERICAN/BISTRO
100 W. Houston St. (at Thompson St.)   (212) 254-7000
Jane is a restaurant with the soul of a cafe. It sets itself modest goals, and for the most part it delivers, at a fair price. Grease-free fried clams come with a hot-cold accompaniment of sweet-corn "dip," a cool, creamy slush that nicely offsets a pungent rice-wine vinegar dipping sauce steeped in habañero peppers. Entrees do not, on balance, live up to the appetizers. An exception is the dark, richly gamy hanger steak, swimming in a red wine sauce and onion marmalade. At dessert time the bias is toward American flavors, but with a little twist here and there, like the lemon-thyme sauce that brightens a dense cylinder-shaped cheesecake. **Price range:** Entrees, $17–$21. **Meals:** D. **Subway:** C, E to Spring St.; N, R to Prince St.; F, S to Broadway–Lafayette St.

Jarnac   ☆ $$$ FRENCH
328 W. 12th St. (near Greenwich St.)   (212) 924-3413
Jarnac is in many ways a dream bistro. A small and attractive restaurant, it sits on a tranquil corner of the far West Village, with windows that open out and offer prime viewing of dog-walkers, or chic couples striding briskly toward the

restaurants and clubs of the meatpacking district. The menu is short, sweet and French. The wine list has personality. At its best, Jarnac offers nicely executed food with an original twist. One of the best dishes is roasted poussin with butter walnut sauce that looks grim. Don't look, eat. The rich interplay of sweetish poussin with nuts and butter is a guilty pleasure. For dessert, the big, highly disorganized strawberry and blueberry shortcake is excellent.
Price range: Entrees, $20–$24. **Meals:** Br, D. Closed Mon., Sun. brunch only. **Subway:** A, C, E to 14th St.

Jean Claude $25 & Under   BISTRO/FRENCH
137 Sullivan St. (between Prince and Houston Sts.)   (212) 475-9232
The dining room is authentically Parisian, with the scent of Gitanes and the sound of French in the air. For these low prices you don't expect to find appetizers like seared sea scallops with roasted beets or main courses like roasted monkfish with savoy cabbage, olives and onions. **Price range:** Entrees, $12–$16. Cash only. **Meals:** D. **Subway:** C, E to Spring St.; N, R to Prince St.; F, to Broadway–Lafayette St.

Jean Georges   ☆☆☆☆ $$$$ NEW AMERICAN
Trump Hotel, 1 Central Park West (at 60th St.)   (212) 299-3900
Chef and co-owner Jean-Georges Vongerichten has created an entirely new kind of four-star restaurant. He has examined all the details that make dining luxurious, and refined them for an American audience. Most important, he has returned the focus to the food, although there are signs, recently, that his daring experiments in French-Asian fusion may be becoming a bit mannered. Still, even if the restaurant has become as much a meeting place for the rich and powerful as a culinary showcase, Jean Georges remains deeply impressive. And while some restaurants are more concerned with who is in the room than what is on the plate, the people at Jean Georges neither fawn nor intimidate; all over the dining room, waiters bend over the food, carving or pouring, intent only on their guests' pleasure. **Price range:** Prix-fixe and tasting menus, $45-$115. **Meals:** L, D. Closed Sun. **Subway:** A, B, C, D, 1, 9 to 59th St.

Jean-Luc   ☆ $$ BISTRO/FRENCH
507 Columbus Ave. (near 84th St.)   (212) 712-1700
New York has lots of technically correct bistros, but they often lack a certain something — something that Jean-Luc indisputably has. Something that emanates from Edmond Kleefield, better known as Jean-Luc. It is called personality. Night after night, Mr. Kleefield meets and greets, circulates from table to table, and holds forth on any topic that comes into his head. The noise level can be deafening. The menu includes some strange, not very successful dishes, as well as completely enthralling inventions. The "mouthwatering" tournedos of beef really does deserve special billing. Pan-seared magret of duck carries a recommendation, as does the poussin with candied root vegetables. **Price range:** Entrees, $17–$25. **Meals:** D. Closed Mon. **Subway:** 1, 2, B, C to 86th St.

Jewel Bako $25 & Under   SUSHI
239 E. 5th St. (between Second and Third Aves.)   (212) 979-1012
The first taste at Jewel Bako, a sparkling new Japanese restaurant in the East
Village, will leave no doubt that here is great sushi. Add the welcoming charm
of the owners and the warmth of the chef, and you come close to the ideal for a
neighborhood sushi bar. The chef focuses on the freshest and best ingredients;
order à la carte, allowing him to guide you. Each piece of sushi seems an almost
perfect unit of rice and fish, often with a dot of complementary flavoring, like
an almost smoky vinegar jelly, a touch of hot chili or a breezy hint of shiso.
There is a refreshing dessert of stewed mission figs, served cool in a sweetened
white wine and shiso broth. **Price range:** Sushi and sashimi selections,
$12–$29; à la carte, $3–$4.50 a piece; some specials higher. **Meals:** D. Closed
Sun. **Subway:** F to Second Ave.

Joe Allen $$ NEW AMERICAN
326 W. 46th St. (between Eighth and Ninth Aves.)   (212) 581-6464
Chili and celebrities in the heart of Broadway. The food's not great, but it's not
expensive either. If you're looking for safe, unpretentious American food in the
high-rent Restaurant Row, this is the place. You need to reserve both before and
after the theater. **Price range:** Entrees, $9–$24. **Meals:** Br, L, D. **Subway:** A, C,
E to 42nd St.

Joe's Shanghai   ☆☆ $ CHINESE
24 W. 56th St. (between Fifth and Sixth Aves.)   (212) 333-3868
9 Pell St. (between Mott St. and Bowery)   (212) 233-8888
These spartan restaurants serve awesome xiao lung bao—Shanghai soup
dumplings, modestly listed on the menu as "steamed buns". The chef has perfected the art of wrapping hot liquid in pastry: the filling is rich, light and swimming in hot soup. Everybody orders them, but there are many other wonderful
dishes, including smoked fish, strongly flavored with star anise, vegetarian
duck, thin sheets of braised tofu folded like skin over mushrooms, and drunken
crabs, raw marinated blue crabs with a musty, fruity flavor that is powerful and
unforgettable. **Price range:** A la carte $9.50 and up. **Meals:** L, D. **Subway:**
Downtown: J, M, N, Q, R, Z, 6 to Canal St. Midtown: N, R, W to Fifth Ave.

Jo Jo   ☆☆☆ $$$$ NEW AMERICAN
160 E. 64th St. (bet. Lexington & Third Aves.)   (212) 223-5656
After an extensive renovation, Jo Jo has shown, with extraordinary grace, how a
restaurant can age without looking old. The place looks sumptuous now. At the
same time, it still has the heart of a bistro. The style of service is not overformal.
The menu is a fairly short read, and the wine list makes a serious effort to please
the $50 customer. The food at Jo Jo never clamors for attention. A few signa-
ture dishes remain, including the renowned roast chicken with chickpea fries.
In a bold but entirely successful move, Mr. Vongerichten conjures up a light,
bright and fruity sauce for black sea bass, with sweet shreds of carrot "confit"

suspended in orange juice and olive oil accented with cumin. For dessert, straw-
berries and rhubarb find shared bliss on clouds of mascarpone sandwiched
between thin sheets of pastry.
Price range: Entrees, $18–$35; prix fixe and tasting menus, $20–$65. **Meals:**
L,D. **Subway:** 6 to 68th St.; N, R to Lexington Ave.

Josie's $25 & Under   NEW AMERICAN
300 Amsterdam Ave. (at 74th St.)   (212) 769-1212
565 Third Ave. (at 37th St.)   (212) 490-1558
Much of the food at Josie's is billed as organically raised; the surprise is that so
much of the food is so good, with highlights like light potato dumplings served in a
lively tomato coulis spiked with chipotle pepper, ravioli stuffed with sweet potato
purée, superb grilled tuna with a wasabi glaze and wonderful gazpacho. Josie's offers
many reasonably priced wines, some organic beers and freshly squeezed juices,
including tart blueberry lemonade. Even the organic hot dogs are good. **Price
range:** Entrees, $9.50–$16. **Meals:** L, D, LN. **Subway:** 1, 2, 3, 9 to 72nd St.; 6
to 33rd St., 4, 5, 6, 7 to 42nd St.

Jubilee $25 & Under   FRENCH
347 E. 54th St. (between First and Second Aves.)   (212) 888-3569
Small, crowded and exuberant, this is a great East Side find. It offers simple and
good bistro food, like steak frites and roast chicken. The restaurant makes something of a specialty of mussels, offering them in five guises with terrific french
fries or a green salad, all for reasonable prices. **Price range:** Entrees, $13.50–$24.
Meals: L, D. **Subway:** E, F to Lexington Ave.; 6 to 51st St.

Judson Grill   ☆☆☆ $$$$ NEW AMERICAN
152 W. 52nd St. (bet Sixth and Seventh Aves.)   (212) 582-5252
Judson Grill is big, bright and utterly urban, a mature restaurant with none of the
irritating glitches of a new establishment. Its lighting is right, they've got the service down pat, and the wine list has had time to develop its own quirky personality. In the skillful hands of the chef, Bill Telepan, the food is unassuming but
extremely eloquent, so roaring with flavor that the minute you finish one bite you
instantly want another. The organically grown meats are especially impressive.
Desserts include the restaurant's Jack Daniel's ice cream soda and its chocolate
sampler. **Price range:** Entrees, $22–$35. **Meals:** L, D. Closed Sun.
Subway: 1, 9 to 50th St.; N, R to 49th St.

Kai   ☆☆ $$$$ JAPANESE
822 Madison Ave. (at 69th St.)   (212) 988-7277
Kai is short for kaiseki, the traditional meal of refined little bites that grew up
around the tea ceremony. The simplest of the three prix fixe formulas here
includes a cup of fragrant, floral jasmine tea, a small plate of tiny bites (deai)
that might include rich slices of duck or sliced bamboo shoots, soup, and a small
plate of sashimi with freshly grated wasabi. The executive chef has grafted

French ideas onto kaiseki cuisine, and he has done so with an elegant hand. Yogan yaki, small, dice-size cubes of aged prime beef, bears a family resemblance to filet mignon with béarnaise sauce. Chilled soba noodles, made at the restaurant, always round out the meal, followed by desserts and green tea. **Price range:** Prix fixe $55-$85. **Meals:** L, D. Closed Sun. **Subway:** 6 to 68th St.

Kang Suh   ☆ ☆   **$$**   KOREAN
1250 Broadway (at 32nd St.)   (212) 564-6845
This is the most accessible of the Korean restaurants in the small Koreatown locally known as Sam Ship Iga (32nd St.). Downstairs is a sushi bar, upstairs a huge menu of Korean dishes. Two things make this special: it's open 24 hours and you can grill your own food over live charcoal at the table. **Price range:** Entrees, $6.99–$30. **Meals:** Open 24 hours. **Subway:** B, D, F, N, Q, S, R to 34th St.

Katsu-Hama   **$25 & Under**   JAPANESE
11 E. 47th St. (between Madison and Fifth Aves.)   (212) 758-5909
Katsu-Hama doesn't offer much in the way of atmosphere or creature comforts, but it is an authentic Japanese experience. To enter it, you need to walk through a takeout sushi restaurant (Sushi-Tei) and pass through a curtain divider; there, you encounter an almost entirely Japanese crowd who've come for the restaurant's specialty: tonkatsu, or deep-fried pork cutlets. The best variation is unadorned, dipped into a special condiment that resembles freshly made Worcestershire sauce blended with sesame seeds. **Price range:** $8.95–$13.95, including soup and rice. **Meals:** L, D. **Subway:** S, 4, 5, 6, 7 to 42nd St.

Katz's Deli   **$**   DELI
205 E. Houston St. (at Ludlow St.)   (212) 254-2246
A wonderful Lower East Side artifact, originator of the World War II slogan, "Send a salami to your boy in the Army," and one of the few delis that still carves pastrami and corned beef by hand, which makes for delicious sandwiches. **Price range:** Entrees, $5–$10.95. **Meals:** B, Br, L, D, LN. **Subway:** F to Second Ave.

Komodo   **$25 & Under**   JAPANESE/LATIN AMERICAN
186 Ave. A (between 11th and 12th Sts.)   (212) 529-2658
With a shared taste for ingredients like cilantro, chilies and rice, Mexico and Asia have more grounds for compatibility than most. Komodo's small storefront dining room is clean, simple and cool; the food never seems forced or needlessly flamboyant. A simple appetizer like beef satay is rubbed with ground ancho chilies and served with peanut sauce, a combination that seems effortlessly natural. Even better are Asian guacamole rolls, flavored with ginger and wasabi and combined with sweet potato and cumin. Grilled sirloin topped with oysters tempura and crisp fried leeks is excellent, and good dessert choices include a rich chocolate pot de créme flavored with black litchi tea, and an apple empanada. **Price range:** Entrees, $10–$16. **Meals:** D. Closed Mon. **Subway:** L to First Ave.

Kori $25 & Under   KOREAN
253 Church St. (near Leonard St.)   (212) 334-0908
Kori succeeds in merging East and West, old and new. It seems a wholly personal expression of its owner and chef, Kori Kim: up-to-date and appealing to
Americans but tied to Korean traditions. She learned to cook in a big, traditional Korean family in Seoul, but it is hard to imagine Ms. Kim serving food at
home as polished as her dubu sobegi, a tofu croquette stuffed with savory ground
Asian mushrooms and beautifully presented like a rectangular gift box. Galbi
jim is a wonderful stew of short ribs with sweet dates, chestnuts and turnips.
Price range: Entrees, $12.95–$21. **Meals:** L, D, LN. **Subway:** 1, 9 to Franklin St.

Kuruma Zushi   ☆☆☆ $$$$ SUSHI
7 E. 47th St. (between Fifth and Madison Aves.)   (212) 317-2802
Few restaurants are more welcoming to diners who do not speak Japanese, and
few chefs are better at introducing people to sushi than Toshiro Uezu, proprietor
of Kuruma Zushi. One of New York City's most venerable sushi bars, it serves
only sushi and sashimi and is, admittedly, expensive. But after eating at Kuruma
Zushi it is very hard to go back to ordinary fish. **Price range:** Entrees, $25–$100.
Meals: L, D. Closed Sun. **Subway:** S, 4, 5, 6, 7 to 42nd St.

La Caravelle   ☆☆☆ $$$$ FRENCH
33 W. 55th St (between Fifth and Sixth Aves.)   (212) 586-4252
La Caravelle is a French restaurant of the old school, a great social stage
where people go to look at one another. The pretty murals and flattering
lighting make everyone look good, and the captains are skilled at making
their customers feel as good as they look. No restaurant in New York does a
better job at guarding tradition while honoring the present. If you are searching for solid French cooking, you will find it here. Current chef Troy Dupuy
has a delicate hand, especially with seafood. Little Asian aromas and textures
seem exactly right in La Caravelle's thoughtfully conservative approach to modern French cooking; black seas bass, for example, is lovely with accents of
cilantro and ginger. **Price range:** Prix-fixe and tasting menus, $68–110. **Meals:**
L, D. Closed Sun. **Subway:** E, F, N, R to Fifth Ave.

La Côte Basque   ☆☆☆ $$$$ FRENCH
60 W. 55th St. (between Fifth and Sixth Aves.)   (212) 688-6525
For 36 years La Côte Basque was a bastion of civility on East 55th Street. After
settling gracefully into intimate new quarters, the food is still well-prepared and
well-presented, but rarely so unmannerly as to call undue attention to itself.
Similarly, the menu is smaller, more modern and easier to read than the one in
the old restaurant. The most exciting entree is cassoulet, a splendid pile of
white beans cooked with pork loin, duck confit and fat chunks of garlic sausage
until each bean bursts with fat and flavor. Dover sole, a frequent special, is the
best of the fish. The fillet of black bass is a close second. These dishes are
extremely well executed, and each plate is piled with food. **Price range:** Prix-
fixe dinner $68, with supplements. **Meals:** L, D. **Subway:** E, F, N, R to Fifth Ave.

La Fonda Boricua $25 & Under   LATIN AMERICAN
169 E. 106th St. (between Third and Lexington Aves.)   (212) 410-7292
This handsome little place in East Harlem offers big helpings of excellent
Puerto Rican home cooking. Chicharrones of chicken is Caribbean fried
chicken, crisp and greaseless. Pork dishes include roast pork shoulder, full of garlic and pepper, satisfying baked pork chops smothered in onions. Steak, marinated in tangy citrus juice is remarkably tender and also comes covered in
onions. **Price range:** Entrees, $4.50–$9. Cash only. **Meals:** B, L, D.
Subway: 6 to 103rd St.

La Grenouille   ☆☆☆ $$$$ FRENCH
3 E. 52nd St. (near Fifth Ave.)   (212) 752-1495
La Grenouille is the most frustrating restaurant in New York. This is not
because the food is bad or the service unpleasant. Just the opposite, in fact,
the restaurant displays such flashes of brilliance that each failure is a deep disappointment. It is also one of the few New York restaurants that still serves
many of the French classics, including quenelles de brochette, perfectly grilled
Dover sole and the best souffles in New York. La Grenouille could so easily be
a four-star establishment with its golden light, magnificent floral displays and
professional and caring staff. Each meal offers moments of joyful excellence,
but many dishes are entirely forgettable. You can count on a good meal at La
Grenouille. If you're lucky, however, you may get a great one. **Price range:**
Three course prix-fixe dinner $80; lunch $45, Tasting menu $100. **Meals:** L,
D. Closed Sun., Mon. **Subway:** E, F to Fifth Ave.

La Locanda dei Vini $25 & Under   ITALIAN
737 Ninth Ave. (near 50th St.)   (212) 258-2900
La Locanda serves pastas and meat dishes that stand out for their simplicity and
flavor, and offers an enticing and unusually arranged wine list. Start with the
basket of freshly baked bread and focaccia. Second, try one of the large and
alluring salads, like insalata rifredda, essentially an Italian version of the frisée
salad. Pastas can be excellent, either as a shared appetizer or as a main course.
Sliced leg of lamb, served like all the main courses with roasted potatoes and
sauted broccoli rape, is past the point of pink, but the sauce imbues the meat
with flavor. The same is true of veal shoulder. La Locanda also makes its own
desserts, some of which are quite good, especially the rustic blueberry tart or the
compact French-style strawberry tart. **Price range:** Pastas and entrees,
$11–$21.50. **Meals:** L, D. **Subway:** C, E to 50th St.

La Nonna   ☆ $$$ ITALIAN
133 W. 13th St. (between Sixth and Seventh Aves.)   (212) 741-3663
La Nonna is a warm, inviting place with a no-nonsense menu of thoroughly traditional Tuscan dishes, with an emphasis on meat and fish roasted or grilled in a
wood-burning oven. A moist and tender marinated Cornish hen makes the best
advertisement for the oven, but pasta turns out to be the most dependable category on the menu. A standout is strozzapreti, slightly sticky dumplings of Swiss

chard and spinach firmed up with ricotta and Parmesan cheese, then doused
with butter and sage. **Price range:** Entrees, $16.50–$24.50. **Meals:** L, D.
Subway: F, 1, 2, 3, 9 to 14th St.

La Palapa $25 & Under   MEXICAN
77 St. Marks Pl. (at First Ave.)   (212) 777-2537
This bright and cheerful restaurant shows off the regional glories of Mexico
rather than the familiar one-dimensional margarita-fueled Tex-Mex dishes. A
moist cod fillet is served in pipian verde, a sauce based on ground pumpkin
seeds, given its color by cilantro and extra taste by a mild chili. Tacos are
authentically Mexican, made with soft corn tortillas, and are also artful, with
fillings like chili-rubbed chicken, shrimp in adobo sauce or mild poblano chili
with epazote and onions. The real excitement comes with the main courses, like
thin slices of duck breast, fanned out in a wonderful sesame mole, or chicken
enchiladas in a soupy tomatillo sauce that is very spicy. For dessert, try rich
Mexican chocolate ice cream and a spicy chili-laced peach sorbet. **Price range:**
Entrees, $11.95–$18.95. **Meals:** L, D, LN. **Subway:** 6 to Astor Pl.

Lavagna $25 & Under   MEDITERRANEAN
545 E. 5th St. (at Ave. B)   (212) 979-1005
Lavagna's food is fresh and generous, with honest, straightforward flavors. The
simple rectangular dining room is casual and inviting, but can get loud when it's
crowded. Pastas are best, both simple dishes like rigatoni with crumbled fennel
sausage, peas, tomatoes and cream, and more complicated ones like fresh pappardelle with rabbit stew. Cacciucco, the Tuscan fish soup scented with saffron
and anise, and served with mussels, cockles and chunks of fish, is a great value.
Price range: Entrees, $11–$16.50. Cash only. **Meals:** D, LN. Closed Sun.
Subway: F to Second Ave.

Layla $$$ MEDITERRANEAN/MIDDLE EASTERN
211 West Broadway (at Franklin St.)   (212) 431-0700
For months after Sept. 11, Layla remained closed, but finally reopened in the
spring with a new chef and a new menu. Now the attitude of the Middle East is
conveyed more through spices and flavorings than the usual repertory of
regional dishes. Alongside the chunky hummus and earthy merguez, served with
slivers of dates, are appetizers like pistou, the Provencal vegetable soup, and
fried sardines. Among the main courses, dishes that you would have expected to
find at the old Layla, like a Moroccan tagine of duck with couscous and toasted
pistachios, are supplemented by scallop-size cylinders of monkfish, wrapped in
prosciutto, with pesto-flavored risotto. **Price range:** Entrees, $20–$29. **Meals:** L,
D. **Subway:** 1, 9 to Franklin St.

Le Bernardin   ☆☆☆☆ $$$$ FRENCH/SEAFOOD
155 W. 51st St. (between Sixth and Seventh Aves.)   (212) 489-1515
Most restaurants grow into their stars. Not Le Bernardin: at the ripe old age of
three months, it had all four stars bestowed upon it. The restaurant has been in

the spotlight ever since. Its hallmark is impeccably fresh fish cooked with respect and simplicity. Most of the problems that plague other great establishments are solved here: there are no rude reservations takers, no endless waits for tables, no overcrowding in the dining room. The waiters know their jobs and keep their distance. Dinners are appropriately paced. When you reserve a table at Le Bernardin, you can count on being seated promptly, served beautifully and fed fabulously. A subtle face lift in the summer of 2001 has freshened the dining room without changing the character of the place. As for the food, it only seems to improve; the subtlety and finesse of Mr. Ripert's cooking is a marvel. Le Bernardin once showed New York how to eat fish; now it is showing the city how a four-star restaurant should behave. **Price range:** Dinner prix-fixe, $77; tasting menu, $95–$125. **Meals:** L, D. Closed Sun. **Subway:** B, D, F, S to 42nd St. **Meals:** L, D. **Subway:** N, R to 49th St.; 1, 9 to 50th St.

Le Cirque 2000   ☆ ☆ ☆   **$$$$**   FRENCH/ITALIAN
New York Palace Hotel, 455 Madison Ave. (between 50th and 51st Sts.)
                                                            (212) 303-7788
As pure spectacle, there is nothing in New York like Le Cirque. It is more and less than a restaurant. First and foremost, it is a social institution and an emblem of status. Diners check in, have their self-esteem validated by Sirio Maccioni and settle in for a sumptuous evening surrounded by their own kind. More than any restaurant, Le Cirque is a one-man show. Diners put themselves in Mr. Maccioni's practiced hands, not the kitchen's. But food was never the most important thing about Le Cirque, and at the moment, it may not even be the second or third thing. The menu moves back and forth between two poles: an almost rustic simplicity and sometimes heavy, lavishly presented fancy food. One of Le Cirque's signature dishes, black sea bass wrapped in sheets of crisp, paper-thin potato and lavished with Barolo sauce, is still excellent, and simpler dishes deliver, like beef short ribs, a mighty cube of savory meat in a rich reduction sauce. At dessert time, ridiculous sugar sculptures and chocolate trees make their way to tables where diners grin like kids at a birthday party. **Price range:** Entrees, $28–$39. **Meals:** L, D. **Subway:** 6 to 51st St.; E, F to Lexington Ave.

Le Colonial   ☆ ☆   **$$**   VIETNAMESE
149 E. 57th St. (between Lexington and Third Aves.)   (212) 752-0808.
Vietnamese cuisine, as interpreted here, is sedate Asian fare that is more delicate than Chinese food, less spicy than Thai and notable mostly for its abundance of vegetables and its absence of grease. Spring rolls at Le Colonial are so delicate you tend to forget that they are fried. The beef salad, the only really spicy dish here, is excellent. **Price range:** Entrees, $14–$23. **Meals:** L, D. **Subway:** 4, 5, 6 to 59th St.; N, R, W to Lexington Ave.

Le Gigot   **$25 & Under**   FRENCH
18 Cornelia St. (between 4th and Bleecker Sts.)   (212) 627-3737
This little restaurant pulses with the welcoming spirit of a Parisian hangout. The Provence-inflected food adds to the illusion, with excellent bistro fare like

leg of lamb in a red wine reduction; lamb stew; endive salad with apples, walnuts and Roquefort, and rounds of baguette smeared with goat cheese and
smoky tapenade. The best desserts are the sweet, moist, caramelized tarte Tatin,
the excellent bananas flambé, and the great little cheese course, not usually
available in a restaurant like this. **Price range:** Entrees, $12–$17. AE only.
Meals: Br, L, D. Closed Mon. **Subway:** A, C, E, F, S to W. 4th St.

Lentini ☆ $$$ ITALIAN
1562 Second Avenue (81st Street)   (212) 628-3131
Location and atmosphere make this a neighborhood restaurant. Some of the
dishes do, too. But look more closely at the menu, scan the ambitious wine list
and its equally ambitious prices, and it becomes clear that Chef Giuseppe
Lentini wants to be more than a nice little local standby. Pastas are a very good
bet. Tomato sauces can be light or so concentrated that you can almost slice
them like terrine. The comma-shaped gramegna has a medium weight to suit a
light tomato sauce with little cubes of swordfish and eggplant. The swordfish,
miraculously, comes out perfectly moist. For dessert, try cassata, a dense, even
sludgy mass of sweetened ricotta and spongecake topped with loose marzipan,
then iced and festively decorated with candied fruit.
Price range: Entrees, $18–$30. **Meals:** D. **Subway:** 4, 5, 6 to 86th St.

Le Périgord ☆☆ $$$$ FRENCH
405 E. 52nd St. (at First Ave.)   (212) 755-6244
Le Perigord is a French restaurant the way French restaurants used to be. The
waiters, well on in years, wear white jackets. The even more senior captains
wear tuxedos. On the dessert trolley you know that you will find floating island,
chocolate mousse and tarte Tatin. A new chef brought a new spark to the
kitchen, most notably in a stunning turbot with a crust of bread crumbs and
Comte cheese, and a glorious overlay of pungent, hazel-nutty flavor sharpened
with the faintest possible touch of mustard. If only the chef could remake the
staff. Some nights, the restaurant can seem like a cross between Fawlty Towers
and Katz's Delicatessen. The diners do not seem to mind. Inside Le Perigord,
they can swaddle themselves in a quietly civilized atmosphere, a million miles
removed from the tumult of the city outside. **Price range:** Three-course prix-
fixe, $57. **Meals:** L, D. **Subway:** 6 to 51st St.; E, F to Lexington Ave.

Les Halles Downtown ☆ $$$ FRENCH
15 John St. (near Broadway)   (212) 285-8585
The small white floor tiles and the stamped-tin ceiling feel as New York as the
Bowery, and a long mahogany bar along one wall, with smokers hunched over
their beers and aperitifs, seems in keeping with the true brasserie spirit The
benchmark dishes, the ones that would be criminal to botch, come through
with flying colors. The côte de boeuf is the king of meats at Les Halles. It is
intended for two, and it may be the most impressively succulent slab of beef on
the menu. Mussels are also a feature, and fish and chips, somewhat surprisingly,
score high. **Price range:** Entrees, $10–$26. **Meals:** L, D. **Subway:**

Lespinasse   ☆☆☆☆ $$$$ FRENCH

St. Regis Hotel, 2 E. 55th St. (near Fifth Ave.)   (212) 339-6719

Open the door and be dazzled by the golden light of chandeliers and intoxicated by the aroma of white truffles. Flowers from lavish bouquets bend to caress your shoulders as you pass. Numerous servers hover nearby, eager to anticipate every wish. In this rarefied atmosphere, the butter never gets warm and no glass is ever empty. As you might expect, the menu descriptions are elaborate, the prices stratospheric. The only strategy is to abandon yourself to the experience and pretend, if only for a few hours, that money has no meaning. The combination of the food, the quiet setting and the solicitous service create an experience so opulent and old-fashioned that it can be a serious shock to walk outside and find no coach waiting to take you home. **Price range:** entrees, $34–$46. **Meals:** D. Closed Sun., Mon. **Subway:** E, F, N, R to Fifth Ave.

Le Tableau $25 & Under   MEDITERRANEAN

511 E. 5th St. (between Aves. A and B)   (212) 260-1333

This simple storefront restaurant turns out superb Mediterranean fare. Unconventional dishes stimulate the mouth with new flavors and textures, like a spicy calamari tagine that incorporates anchovies, hummus and olive purée. Main courses are familiar, yet they are presented in inventive ways. Desserts can be excellent, like a mellow pumpkin bread pudding, a honey-nut tart and an apple tajine. The dining room is dimly lighted with candles and can become noisy, especially when a jazz trio begins playing in the late evening. **Price range:** Entrees, $9.50–$14.75. Cash only. **Meals:** Br, D. Closed Mon. **Subway:** F to Second Ave.

Le Zie 2000 $25 & Under   ITALIAN

172 Seventh Ave. (at 20th St.)   (212) 206-8686

This modest, often crowded little trattoria offers some terrific Venetian dishes, like an inspired salad that features pliant octopus and soft potatoes acting in precise textural counterpoint. The chef has a sure hand with pastas like rigatoni with rosemary, served al dente in a perfectly proportioned sauce. Risotto with squid is also superbly cooked. Striped bass fillet with fennel and white beans is moist and wonderfully flavorful. Desserts are a weak point. **Price range:** Entrees, $8.50–$16.95. Cash only. **Meals:** L, D. **Subway:** 1, 9 to 23rd St.

Le Zinc   ☆ $$ BISTRO

139 Duane St. (between Church St. and West Broadway)   (212) 513-0001

The low-key bistro menu, with an Asian accent here and a down-home touch there, qualifies as upmarket Manhattan comfort food. It's solid, reliable and reassuring, served in portions so abundant that appetizers often seem like entrees in training. And the price is right. Le Zinc offers a menu-within-a-menu of charcuterie, and there's no doubt about it, the terrines here are superior. Main courses make the usual bistro stops, with competently executed dishes like skirt steak in a red wine reduction and skate with brown butter and capers. **Note well:** Le Zinc takes no reservations. **Price range:** Entrees, $12–$19. **Meals:** Br, L, D, LN. **Subway:** 1, 9 to Franklin St.

Le Zoo $25 & Under   BISTRO/FRENCH
314 W. 11th St. (at Greenwich St.)   (212) 620-0393

This popular little restaurant can get crowded, loud and zoolike, but the food is good and often creative. Where you might reasonably expect to find steak frites, roast chicken and pâté de campagne, there are instead such combinations as monkfish with honey and lime sauce. The dessert selection is small and classically French, offering satisfying choices. The restaurant does not take reservations. **Price range:** Entrees, $12.50–$16. **Meals:** D, LN. **Subway:** 1, 9 to Christopher St.

Little Basil $25 & Under   THAI
39 Greenwich Ave. (at Charles St.)   (212) 645-8965

Little Basil serves dishes with exquisite balance, Western touches and a beautiful presentation. Dishes like lamb shank draped in herbs and delicate steamed dumplings strewn with dried shrimp are not exactly Thai home cooking, yet the food remains true to the essence of Thai cuisine. **Price range:** Entrees, $9–$16. **Meals:** D. **Subway:** 1, 9 to Christopher St.

Little Dove   ☆☆ $$$ NEW AMERICAN
200 E. 60th St. (at Third Ave.)   (212) 751-8616

The tiny dining room here looks like a cross between an antiques store and the drawing room of a dotty old aunt, but it has a civilized charm and genuine character. The menu is a brief document but each dish counts. It stresses high-quality ingredients and simple, strong, clearly defined flavors. The crust on an unassuming lemon tart with pineapple meringue is thick and flaky, the filling tartly voluptuous, the meringue lighter than air. **Price range:** Entrees, $22–$32. **Meals:** L, D. **Subway:** N, R, W to Lexington Ave.; 4, 5, 6 to 59th St.

Lombardi's $25 & Under   PIZZA
32 Spring St. (between Mulberry and Mott Sts.)   (212) 941-7994

The dining room reeks of history at this reincarnation of the original Lombardi's, which is often credited with introducing pizza to New York City. The old-fashioned coal-oven pizza is terrific, with a light, thin, crisp and gloriously smoky crust topped with fine mozzarella and tomatoes. The garlicky clam pizza is exceptional. **Price range:** Pizzas, $10.50–$20. Cash only. **Meals:** L, D, LN. **Subway:** 6 to Spring St.

Los Dos Rancheros $25 & Under   MEXICAN
507 Ninth Ave. (at 38th St.)   (212) 868-7780

The dining room may be bare-bones (unpretentious is an understatement), but the restaurant serves authentic, delicious Mexican fare, like pollo con pipián, chicken with a fiery green sauce made of ground pumpkin seeds, and excellent soft tacos with fillings ranging from chicken to braised pork to tongue and goat. **Price range:** Entrees, $2–$7.50. Cash only. **Meals:** B, L, D. **Subway:** A, C, E to 42nd St.

Lotus   ☆ $$$$ NEW AMERICAN

409 W. 14th St. (near Ninth Ave.)   (212) 243-4420

Lotus serves New American cuisine with global accents in a coolly styled dining room that feels more like a bar and lounge than a restaurant. The menu is small but very busy. The chef puts a lot of notes into every phrase. It makes for energetic food. For dessert try the cannelloni filled with crème brûlée ice cream and topped with caramel sauce. This all-out sugar assault scores a direct hit, shamelessly. **Price range:** Prix fixe and tasting menus, $55–$100. **Meals:** D. Closed Sun. & Mon. **Subway:** .A, C, E to 14th St.; L to Eighth Ave.

Luca $25 & Under   ITALIAN

1712 First Ave. (near 89th St.)   (212) 987-9260

This superb neighborhood Italian restaurant is spare but good-looking, with beige walls and rustic floor tiles. The menu offers dishes skillfully cooked to order that emphasize lusty flavors. The antipasto for two is very generous and very good. Pastas, like bigoli with a buttery shrimp-and-radicchio sauce, are terrific, as are main courses like grilled calamari and crisp grilled Cornish hen. **Price range:** Entrees, $8.50–$19.95. **Meals:** D. **Subway:** 4, 5, 6 to 86th St.

Lupa $25 & Under   ITALIAN

170 Thompson St. (near Houston St.)   (212) 982-5089.

Crowded and clamorous, Lupa serves intensely delicious Roman trattoria food. Appetizers range from the classic to the bizarre: Prosciutto di Parma arrives in thin, nutty slices, a reminder of why this combination became popular in the first place. Pastas are simple and tasty, and saltimbocca, thin slices of veal layered with prosciutto, is good and juicy. The resident wine expert takes great delight in directing you to the perfect choice on Lupa's 130-bottle wine list, and the best dessert choice is something from the cheese tray. **Price range:** Entrees, $9–$15. **Meals:** L, D. Closed Mon. **Subway:** F, S to Broadway–Lafayette St.

Lutèce   ☆☆ $$$$ FRENCH

249 E. 50th St. (between Second and Third Aves.)   (212) 752-2225

Lutèce tries to project a fresh, contemporary image while retaining an old-fashioned sense of luxury and formality. The service remains an anachronism, but chef David Féau brings a youthful touch to a classic French style, with respectful innovations that never violate good taste. Certain dishes convince you that Lutèce has found the right chef to bring it back to the first rank, especially a gently cooked John Dory with a subtle peppermint jus and pommes soufflées, and sautéed black bass with a rich vanilla jus and wilted spinach. Mr. Féau also integrates Asian spices and ingredients with a fine hand. Among the desserts, a superior pistachio soufflé with sour cherries and a tart cherry sorbet stands head and shoulders above its confrères.   **Price range:** Three-course prix fixe, $72. **Meals:** L, D. **Subway:** 6 to 51st St.; E, F to Lexington Ave.

Luzia's $25 & Under   PORTUGUESE
429 Amsterdam Ave. (between 80th and 81st Sts.)   (212) 595-2000
Luzia's began life as a takeout place. Then the neighborhood fell in love with
the cozy restaurant and started staying for dinner. Luzia's serves wonderful Portuguese comfort food, like caldo verde, shrimp pie and cataplana, the soupy stew
of pork and clams. It also produces remarkably delicious non-Portuguese dishes,
like beef brisket that is tender and peppery. Luzia's has a great flan, and a nice
list of Portuguese wines. **Price range:** $20–$25. **Meals:** Br, L, D. Closed Mon.
Subway: 1, 9 to 79th St.

Mama's Food Shop $25 & Under   AMERICAN
200 E. 3rd St. (between Aves. A and B)   (212) 777-4425
A simple takeout shop and restaurant where you point at what you want and
they dish it up. But the food is outstanding: grilled salmon, fried chicken and
meatloaf. Vegetable side dishes are especially good, like brussels sprouts, carrots,
beets and mashed potatoes. **Price range:** Entrees, $7–$8.50. Cash only.
Meals: L, D. Closed Sun. **Subway:** F to Second Ave.

Mandoo Bar $25 & Under   KOREAN
2 W. 32nd St. (near Fifth Ave.)   (212) 279-3075
Mandoo (pronounced MAHN-do) is the Korean word for dumplings, the specialty of the house. Start with a platter of baby mandoo, stuffed with beef, pork
and leeks in a wrapper so sheer that it is almost transparent. Boiled and steamed
dumplings are very good, but some of the best selections are not dumplings at
all. Slender rectangles of fried tofu make an excellent appetizer, and bibimbop, a
casserole of rice, vegetables and ground beef served in a stone crock, is fresh,
light and delicate. The dining room is spare and handsome, service is swift and
courteous, and food arrives quickly. **Price range:** Entrees, $6–$24. **Meals:** L, D.
Subway: 6 to 33rd St.; B, D, F, N, Q, R, S, W to 34th St.

Manhattan Ocean Club   ☆☆ $$$$ SEAFOOD
57 W. 58th St. (between Fifth and Sixth Aves.)   (212) 371-7777
Tony, comfortable and trim as a luxury yacht, this is the steakhouse of fish restaurants. Eating here is an indulgence, and the prices are high. Soups like the
creamy clam chowder are less expensive but no less delicious. Simple preparations are the most appealing but one of the best dishes is the oysters buried in
tiny morels covered with cream and baked in the shell. The dish is an edible def-
inition of luxury. Desserts are almost all big and sweet. **Price range:** Entrees,
$22.50–$31. **Meals:** L, D. **Subway:** N, R, W to Fifth Ave.

Man Ray   ☆ $$$ NEW AMERICAN
147 W. 15th St. (between Sixth and Seventh Aves.)   (212) 929-5000
Man Ray ought to have the DNA of a velvet-rope restaurant. The Parisian original is a celebrity magnet, the kind of loud and large New York-style dining spot
that younger French diners adore. Man Ray is not like that, though. The wel-

come at the door is warm. The servers talk like ordinary people and seem eager to please. The louche stage-set interior, with its ruby reds and jade greens, almost demands a little theatricality on the menu. But the sushi menu plays it perfectly straight. The quality is good, too. Two fish entrees stand out: turbot with a crust of goat-cheese Gouda, and Arctic char, slow-baked to a pinkish-orange pearlescence. **Price range:** Entrees, $19–$29. **Meals:** D. **Subway:** 1, 2, 3 to 14th St.

March   ☆☆☆ $$$$ NEW AMERICAN
405 E. 58th St. (near First Ave.)   (212) 754-6272
When everything is clicking, there are few places better than this cozy, antique-filled town house. The usual three-course restaurant menu is replaced with one that allows you to choose either four or seven smaller courses. At March, no dish is more than a few bites, but those are so pretty and powerful that you are almost always satisfied. The most popular items are Beggars' purses, diminutive dumplings filled with caviar, truffles or foie gras. **Price range:** Prix-fixe, $72–126 (with specially selected wines, $116–203). **Meals:** D. **Subway:** 4, 5, 6 to 59th St.; N, R to Lexington Ave.

Maritime   ☆ $$$ SEAFOOD
1251 Sixth Ave. (at W. 49th St.)   (212) 354-1717
As a piece of design, Maritime is one slippery fish: gleaming white wall tiles suggest an urban fish market, but the dark, solid wood wainscoting and cabinets feel more like a men's club. The menu is not easy to get a handle on, either. A fair number of the dishes are overthought and overwrought, but some results can be terrific. The oysters are straightforward enough; so is a crowd-pleasing shrimp cocktail. Lobster in a Portuguese tomato sauce is plump and flavorful. Two desserts break out of the pack: the Southwestern banana split and a florid apple crisp. **Price range:** Entrees, $16–$25. **Meals:** L, D. **Subway:** B, D, F, S to 47th-50th St.–Rockefeller Center.

Marseille   ☆☆ $$$ FRENCH/MEDITERRANEAN
630 Ninth Ave. (near 44th St.)   (212) 333-3410
Marseille, named for France's most Arab-influenced city, is a spacious, confident-feeling brasserie on the western edge of the theater district, with blue Moroccan floor tiles and apricot-colored walls. The chef has a fondness for couscous, preserved lemon, dates and lamb, ingredients that he uses for local color rather than in any systematic way. An ideal way to start a meal is to order a meze plate and a glass of rosé. The chef goes flat out in a very rich seafood lasagna layered with crab meat, cockles and mussels in a buttery mussel sauce; also excellent is roasted chicken, marinated in olive oil, garlic and smoked paprika. For dessert, try the renowned, or notorious, crunchy peanut butter tart. **Price range:** Entrees, $16–$24; tasting menu, $65. **Meals:** D. **Subway:** A, C, E to 42nd St.

Marumi $25 & Under   JAPANESE/SUSHI
546 La Guardia Pl. (between 3rd and Bleecker Sts.)   (212) 979-7055
This versatile, reliable Japanese restaurant near N.Y.U. offers a cross-section of
casual Japanese dining. The service is swift, efficient and charming and will
even go the extra mile in preventing bad choices. It's rare that you get such an
interesting assortment of sushi at an inexpensive restaurant, like mirugai, or
geoduck clam. Other worthwhile dishes are broiled eel, noodle soups and the
economic bento box meals. **Price range:** Entrees, $9–$15. **Meals:** L, D.
Subway: A, C, E, F, S to W. 4th St.

Mavalli Palace $25 & Under   INDIAN/VEGETARIAN
46 E. 29th St. (between Park and Madison Aves.)   (212) 679-5535
This low-key Indian restaurant turns out terrific vegetarian fare that is exciting
and full of flavor, like rasa vada, savory lentil doughnuts in a spicy broth, and
baingan bharta, a fiery blend of eggplant and peas. Mavalli means mother goddess,
and the restaurant's symbol is a goddess figure, hand out, waiting to serve. The
staff, though merely mortal, takes orders efficiently and brings food out swiftly.
Price range: $4.25–$16.75. **Meals:** L, D. Closed Mon. **Subway:** 6 to 28th St.

Max $25 & Under   ITALIAN
51 Ave. B (near 4th St.)   (212) 539-0111
Max's draw is exactly what has always attracted people to neighborhood Italian
restaurants: well-prepared food, served with warmth. Best of all, Max is cheap.
Fettuccine al sugo Toscano has a wonderfully mellow meat sauce with layers of
flavor that unfold in the mouth, while rigatoni Napoletano is served southern
Italian style, with meatballs and sausages left intact in the sauce. Order the
sauce on the side of the Neopolitan-style meatloaf, because the meatloaf is fascinating, stuffed with mozzarella, hard-boiled egg and prosciutto, making for a
savory, moist and delicious combination. **Price range:** Entrees, $8.95–$14.95.
Cash only. **Meals:** L, D, LN. **Subway:** F to Second Ave.

Max SoHa $25 & Under   ITALIAN/AMERICAN
1274 Amsterdam Ave. (at 123rd St.)   (212) 531-2221
Max SoHa offers home-style dishes with few frills and no luxuries, other than a
superior list of moderately priced Italian wines. It does not break culinary
ground, but what it does, it does very well. Each of its three salads is a good
choice, as is Max's fresh buffalo mozzarella. Pastas are basic and served in the
American fashion, under a deluge of sauce. They can be excellent, though. Specials change nightly, and may include sliced skirt steak, deliciously beefy and
redolent of rosemary, or a flawless breaded pork chop. **Price range:** Entrees,
$9–$15. **Meals:** L, D. **Subway:** 1, A, B, C, D to 125th St.

Maya   ☆☆ $$$ MEXICAN/TEX-MEX
1191 First Ave. (between 64th and 65th Sts.)   (212) 585-1818
Some of New York's most interesting Mexican food is served in this bright, fes-
tive but often noisy room. Try some of the more unusual dishes, like rock shrimp

ceviche, seafood salad, and roasted corn soup with huitlacoche dumpling. The most impressive main courses are chicken mole (the dark sauce is truly complex) and pipian de puerco, grilled pork marinated in tamarind and served on a bed of puréed roasted corn. Desserts are not impressive. **Price range:** Entrees, $18.50–$24.50. **Meals:** D. **Subway:** 6 to 68th St.

McHale's $$ BAR SNACKS/HAMBURGERS
750 Eighth Ave. (at 46th St.) (212) 246-8948

This neighborhood bar has a single specialty: great hamburgers that are big and juicy. There's really no point in ordering anything else, except maybe a beer or two. A nice place in which to be a regular. **Price range:** Entrees, $10–$18. Cash only. **Meals:** L, D, LN. **Subway:** A, C, E to 42nd St.

Medi   ☆ $$$ ITALIAN/FRENCH
45 Rockefeller Plaza (at 50th St.) (212) 399-8888

Medi looks terrific. Huge displays of massed sunflowers and small Provençal landscapes, painted in rich, saturated colors, light up the room. The window banquettes, in Provençal fabrics, are especially inviting. But this is actually a pretty ordinary Italian restaurant with some French touches and very pleasing interior decoration. The one real standout dish on the menu is the lobster Moulin de Mougins style. The pastas also score high and potato and cod tortelli in a sauce of tomato, butter and sage stands as a model. **Price range:** Entrees, $20–$37. **Meals:** L, D. **Subway:** B, D, F, V to 47–50th Sts./Rockefeller Ctr.

Mee Noodle Shop $25 & Under CHINESE
219 First Ave. (at 13th St.) (212) 995-0333
547 Second Ave. (between 30th and 31st Sts.) (212) 779-1596
922 Second Ave. (at 49th St.) (212) 888-0027
795 Ninth Ave. (at 53rd St.) (212) 765-2929

A little chain of Chinese restaurants that is a cut above takeout, with huge portions of cheap, tasty noodles. Ingredients are fresh, and dishes like lo mein with roast pork and mee fun with chicken are carefully prepared. Mee offers seven kinds of noodles. The portions are huge—complete meals in themselves—and delicious. **Price range:** $3.75–$12. AE only. **Meals:** L, D.

Meet   ☆ $$$ NEW AMERICAN
71-73 Gansevoort St. (at Washington St.) (212) 242-0990

As its name suggests, Meet wants to be a place where people meet. Ideally, these would be young, good-looking people. In an effort to attract this crowd, the owners have fashioned a visually arresting dining room. Diners who keep their attention riveted on the plate will find honest bistro fare with a contemporary spin. The kitchen is the conscience of Meet. The best desserts on the menu are also the plainest-sounding, like rice pudding fritters or ice cream sandwiches. If you like to eat, come before 8, when the waiters still control the operation. If you like to meet, come later. **Price range:** Entrees, $16–$24. **Meals:** D, LN. **Subway:** A, C, E to 14th St.

Meigas ☆☆ $$$ SPANISH
350 Hudson St. (between King and Charlton Sts.) (212) 627-5800
Meigas (may-EEH-gus) is Galician for sorceresses, and one appears in a mural at the back of this large restaurant, a spooky figure who conjures from the sea an enormous table, laden with savory dishes. Chef Luis Bollo, a Basque, cultivates homey virtues here, with judiciously applied modern touches. It's possible to order something as simple as baby squid cooked in its own ink, a traditional Basque specialty, or giant prawns grilled on a wood plank and served with lemon and olive oil. An exceptionally fruity Caroliva olive oil transforms humble fillets of grilled mackerel into a memorable, two-fisted dish, enlivened with garlic and a sharp, tingling dose of chili and Rioja vinegar. The pastry chef does some brilliant work, especially with his bread pudding, crunchy at the edges with baked sugar, and topped with a wonderfully dense, sourish ice cream. **Price range:** Entrees, $17–$27. **Meals:** L, D. Closed Sat., Sun. **Subway:** 1, 9 to Houston St.

Meltemi $25 & Under GREEK/SEAFOOD
905 First Ave. (at 51st St.) (212) 355-4040
This attractive neighborhood Greek restaurant offers big portions of simply pre- pared seafood, like grilled octopus with oil and lemon, and typical Greek offer- ings like grilled whole porgy and red mullet. Appetizers are generous, and two portions can easily feed four people. Grilled seafood is the centerpiece here. The enthusiastic staff adds to Meltemi's enjoyable atmosphere. **Price range:** Entrees, $14.95–$28.95. **Meals:** L, D. **Subway:** 6 to 51st St.; E, F to Lexington Ave.

Mercer Kitchen ☆☆ $$$$ FRENCH
Mercer Hotel, 99 Prince St. (at Mercer St.) (212) 966-5454
Jean-Georges Vongerichten strikes again in this chic SoHo restaurant filled with models and movie stars. The space is so mysteriously beautiful it makes each vegetable shimmer like a jewel in the dark. The food is equally innovative. The kitchen occasionally spins out of control, but desserts are simple and appealing, especially the fruit terrines and the rich and fascinating custard with a slice of carmelized pineapple. **Price range:** Entrees, $19–$35. **Meals:** Br, L, D, LN. **Subway:** N, R to Prince St.

Merge $25 & Under NEW AMERICAN
142 W. 10th St. (between Greenwich St. and Waverly Pl.) (212) 691-7757
The music here is too loud and the dining area close to the bar is too smoky, but the service is friendly and efficient, and the food is not only delicious but also a great value. Sushi fruit salad, a combination of coconut and mango with Asian coleslaw and thin slices of tuna and salmon, is an extraordinary blend of flavors and textures. A grilled paillard of guinea hen is given an earthy boost by a plum and foie gras sauce, and hanger steak is juicy and beefy. Desserts also include some winners, like a sweet potato panna cotta with a caramel sauce. **Price range:** Entrees, $15–$20. AE only. **Meals:** D. **Subway:** 1, 9 to Christopher St.

Mesa Grill ☆☆ $$$$ SOUTHWESTERN

102 Fifth Ave. (between 15th and 16th Sts.)   (212) 807-7400

Mesa Grill is a downtown favorite, crowded and clamorous at lunch, and even more crowded and clamorous at night. Two things set chef-owner Bobby Flay apart. First, he goes after big flavors and he knows how to get them. Second, he uses chilies and spices for flavor, not for heat. Sixteen-spice chicken sounds like a tongue-scorcher. It turns out to be a subtly handled, tingling orchestration of flavors, with an off-sweet sauce of caramelized mangos and garlic. New arrivals keep the menu fresh. The margarita list is an inspirational document, with a list of fine tequilas that can either be sipped on their own or used to upgrade a standard margarita. **Price range:** Entrees, $24–$39. **Meals:** Br, L, D. **Subway:** F, L, N, Q, R, W, 4, 5, 6 to 14th St.

Metsovo $25 & Under GREEK

65 W. 70th St. (near Columbus Ave.)   (212) 873-2300

Instead of seafood, this romantic restaurant, named after a town in northwestern Greece, specializes in hearty stews, roasts and savory pies from the hills that form a spine through the region. Try the Epirus mountain pies, which are offered with different fillings each day. Tender chunks of baby lamb and a mellow stew of robust goat blended with thick yogurt and rice are also good. Once you get through the house specialties, though, you're back in familiar territory. You may never receive the same selection of desserts twice, so hope for the luscious fig compote, or the wonderfully thick and fresh yogurt. **Price range:** Entrees, $10.50–$23.95. **Meals:** D. **Subway:** 1, 2, 3, 9 to 72nd St.

Mexicana Mama $25 & Under MEXICAN

525 Hudson St. (at W. 10th St.)   (212) 924-4119

While this colorful restaurant's small menu doesn't register high on a scale of authenticity, the food succeeds in a more important measure: it tastes good. Rather than using the traditional mutton or goat, for example, a dish like barbacoa is made with beef, braised and then cooked slowly in a corn husk until it is fall-away tender, like pot roast. Authentic? No. Tasty? Definitely. Other worthy dishes include pollo con mole, a boneless chicken breast that is surprisingly juicy, with a terrific reddish-brown mole. **Price range:** Entrees, $8–$17. Cash only. **Meals:** L, D. **Subway:** 1, 9 to Christopher St.

Mi ☆☆ $$$ ASIAN FUSION

66 Madison Ave. (near 27th St.)   (212) 252-8888

When people talk about the richness and diversity of New York dining, Mi should be Exhibit A. The small sushi bar in the main dining room says Japan. Korean vases say something else. The daring Modernist curves of the ceiling panels and the exposed industrial ducts suggest downtown. Mi draws on flavors and spices from Goa to Japan to Mexico, woven into Western dishes and ingredients. Ceviche of seared hamachi reads initially like a cross-cultural joke. Thick slices of fish, lightly seared around the edges, rest on crunchy slivers of

jicama, fennel and jalapeño, with a bright scoop of yuzu-watermelon sorbet balanced on top. But it all works, especially the sweet-tart sorbet. The quality of the fish is very good, and an absolutely stunning entree is roast rack of lamb smeared with Goan spices and surrounded with artichokes and chanterelles with mustard whipped potatoes and masala-spiced golden raisins.
Price range: Entrees, $14–$29. **Meals:** L, D. Closed Sun. **Subway:** 6 to 28th St.; N, R to 23rd St.

Michael Jordan's Steak House   ☆☆ $$$$ STEAKHOUSE
23 Vanderbilt Ave. (in Grand Central Terminal)   (212) 655-2300
Despite a celebrity owner and a big-deal designer (David Rockwell), the real star of this place is Grand Central Terminal. You sit in comfort on the balcony gazing at the starry ceiling while harried commuters dash madly through the marble halls below. The menu is what you would expect, but the food, for the most part, is equal to the space. Shrimp cocktail is excellent, the meat robust, prime, aged and old-fashioned. All the standard cuts are available, but the flavorful rib eye steak is best. The hamburger is absurd; it's so enormous it looks more like an inflated basketball. Desserts are not inspiring.
Price range: Entrees, $18–$34. **Meals:** L, D. **Subway:** S, 4, 5, 6, 7 to 42nd St.

Michael's   ☆☆ $$$$ NEW AMERICAN
24 W. 55th St. (between Fifth and Sixth Aves.)   (212) 767-0555
Home of the power lunch. All of publishing goes to Michael's because the room is attractive and filled with good art. The menu offers one of the city's finest selections of fancy salads (some large enough to feed a small nation). The best food on the menu is unabashedly American, including grilled chicken, grilled lobster, good steaks and chops, and California cuisine. There are several daily fish selections. For dessert, the classic collection of tarts and cakes is very enticing. **Price range:** Entrees, $22–$34. **Meals:** B, L, D. Closed Sun. **Subway:** N, R, W to Fifth Ave.

Mirchi $25 & Under   INDIAN
29 Seventh Ave. (near Morton St.)   (212) 414-0931
A vast majority of Indian restaurants in Manhattan settle for a dreary sameness; Mirchi tries to break the imprisoning mold, and it succeeds often enough for its failures to be forgiven. The clean and simple design, casual service and loud music suggest other youth-oriented restaurants with bar crowds, yet the food is strictly Indian, with not even a hint of fusion. Portions are quite large and spicing is forceful, with occasionally very high heat (the word mirchi means hot, as in chilies). Chicken tak-a-tak, shredded chicken essentially stir-fried, is exceptional. Among the main courses jaipuri lal maas is a fabulous and subtle lamb dish, made, the menu says, with 30 red chilies.
Price range: Entrees, $9–$19. **Meals:** L, D. **Subway:** 1, 9 to Houston St.

Miss Maude's Spoonbread Too $25 & Under   SOUTHERN

547 Lenox Ave. (near 137th St.)   (212) 690-3100

This bright restaurant celebrates the virtues of family meals without childish nostalgia. Meals begin with a basket of mildly spicy corn bread and are served Southern style, with large portions of two sides. The smothered pork chops are thin but flavorful enough to stand up to the peppery brown gravy. Close behind are the excellent fried shrimp with traces of cornmeal in the delectable crust. Side dishes are all excellent. **Price range:** Dinners, $9.95–$12.95. **Meals:** Br, L, D. **Subway:** 2, 3 to 135th St.

Moda   ☆☆ $$$ ITALIAN

Flatotel, 135 W. 52nd St. (between Sixth Ave. and Broadway)   (212) 887-9880

Moda's coolly stylish dining room has a subtly minimalist look with warm touches. Moda's executive chef is much-traveled and it shows in his intelligent rethinking of Italian cuisine. The menu reflects a commitment to prime ingredients and a quiet determination not to let style overrule substance. The menu format is flexible, with dishes categorized as small plates and big plates; diners can make a meal of small plates, or a combination of small and large, with side dishes like whipped Parmesan potatoes or polenta with truffle oil and Gorgonzola. A simple roast chicken, plump and succulent, breaks through the boredom barrier, and grilled quail with polenta takes off with the addition of a concentrated jam heated with cracked black pepper. The easy dessert choice is a modest-looking bittersweet chocolate cake that's halfway toward being a pudding. **Price range:** Entrees, $14–$28. **Meals:** L, D.
Subway: 1, 2 to 50th St.;N, R, W to 49th St.; B, D, E to Seventh Ave.

Molyvos   ☆☆ $$$ GREEK

871 Seventh Ave. (near 55th St.)   (212) 582-7500

Molyvos is pleasingly informal, and spacious enough to cross your legs or freely throw your arm over the back of a booth without fear of catastrophe. While familiar Greek dishes dominate the menu, it's worth trying some of the more recent additions, like one called Greek fava, yellow split peas, mashed and whipped to a froth and served as an almost lighter-than-air flan. The best main courses tend to be the most straightforward. The kitchen gives special care to fresh fish grilled simply over wood, like a light, lemony branzino and the slightly richer, more strongly flavored dorade royale. Baby lamb chops are perfect with no more than a sprinkling of salt and pepper. **Price range:** Entrees, $19–$35. **Meals:** L, D. **Subway:** N, R, Q, W to 57th St.; B, D, E to Seventh Ave.

Moustache $25 & Under   MIDDLE EASTERN

90 Bedford St. (between Grove and Barrow Sts.)   (212) 229-2220
265 E. 10th St. (between First Ave. and Ave. A)   (212) 228-2022

These small, excellent Middle Eastern restaurants specialize in "pitzas," exceptional pizzalike dishes made with pita dough, including lahmajun, the Turkish specialty with a savory layer of ground lamb on crisp crust, and zaatar, a crisp individual pizza topped with a smoky, aromatic combination of olive oil, thyme, sesame seeds and sumac. A sandwich of sliced lamb in pita bread with onion and tomato is brought to life by a minty lemon mayonnaise. **Price range:** $3–$12. Cash only. **Meals:** L, D, LN. **Subway:** Bedford St.: 1, 9 to Houston St. E. 10th St.: L to First Ave.

Mughlai $25 & Under   INDIAN
320 Columbus Ave. (at 71st St.)   (212) 724-6363

Mughlai offers tantalizing glimpses of the pleasures of Indian food. Its menu offers the litany of familiar dishes, yet it also invites diners to try uncommon regional dishes, which are almost always better. Dal papri, potatoes and chickpeas blended in a tangy tamarind-and-yogurt sauce and served cool, is a superb appetizer. Pepper chicken, a dish from the southwestern state of Kerala, is another adventure. Also excellent are baghare baigan, small eggplants in an aromatic sauce of ground peanuts, sesame, tamarind and coconut. **Price range:** Entrees, $6.95–$18.95. **Meals:** L, D. **Subway:** 1, 2, 3, 9 to 72nd St.

Muzy $25 & Under   KOREAN
81 St. Marks Pl. (near First Ave.)   (212) 533-6876

Muzy practically disappears into the streetscape, yet it is pleasingly sleek and minimalist, with contoured walls made from what appear to be silver and gray industrial tiles. Though the emphasis seems to be on light dishes, Muzy's food can't help offering the robust, lusty flavors that characterize Korean cuisine. Noodle dishes occupy central stage, and giant casseroles of curly egg noodles, filled with hot chili-spiked broth, arrive boiling at the table. **Price range:** Entrees, $8–$15. **Meals:** D, LN. **Subway:** L to First Ave.

Nadaman Hakubai   ☆☆ $$$$ JAPANESE
Kitano Hotel, 66 Park Ave. (at 38th St.)   (212) 885-7111

A visit to this restaurant is like a quick trip to Japan. Kaiseki cuisine, associated with the tea ceremony, is food for the soul as well as the body, meant to feed the eye with its beauty and the spirit with its meaning. The courses follow a strict order and each is intended to introduce the coming season. The way to enjoy this is to abandon yourself to the experience, appreciating the peace, the subtlety of the flavors and the sense that you are being pampered as never before. Unless you are an extremely adventurous eater, you will probably not like every dish, but an evening in one of the private tatami rooms can be immensely rewarding. Kaiseki dinners in the main restaurant are not particularly recommended. **Price range:** $100 minimum per person, for a minimum of four people. **Meals:** B, L, D. **Subway:** S, 4, 5, 6, 7 to 42nd St.

Nam $25 & Under   VIETNAMESE
110 Reade St. (at W. Broadway)   (212) 267-1777

Nam's high ceiling, stylishly draped chairs, candles and cleverly backlighted old pictures of Vietnam make it feel almost Parisian. The menu offers some seldom-seen recipes like banh la, fragile rectangular noodles stuffed with minced shrimp, wrapped in banana leaves and steamed, giving them a deliciously cheeselike richness. More familiar dishes are also well rendered, like goi du du, or green papaya salad, which is pungent and refreshing, augmented by paper-thin slices of salty dried beef. **Price range:** Entrees, $9–$16. **Meals:** L, D. **Subway:** 1, 2 to Chambers St.

National Cafe $25 & Under   CUBAN/LATIN AMERICAN
210 First Ave. (near 13th St.)   (212) 473-9354
If you order a roast pork sandwich at this tiny Cuban restaurant, you can watch its construction. The server picks up a leg of pork and carefully carves pieces of the tender meat, piling them high on a hero roll. Then she places a chicharrón (a crisp piece of fried pork skin) on top. The result is delicious and filling, like almost everything else on the menu. **Price range:** Entrees, $6.50–$9. **Meals:** L, D. **Subway:** L to First Ave.

New Green Bo $ CHINESE
66 Bayard St., Chinatown   (212) 625-2359
This bright, plain restaurant in Chinatown looks like many other bright, plain restaurants in the neighborhood, except that it offers delicious Shanghai specialties like soup dumplings, smoked fish and eel with chives. **Price range:** Entrees, $2.75–$24. Cash only. **Meals:** L, D, LN. **Subway:** J, M, N, Q, R, W, Z, 6 to Canal St.

New York Noodle Town   ☆☆ $ CHINESE
28 1/2 Bowery (near Bayard St.), Chinatown   (212) 349-0923
With its bustle and clatter, its shared tables and its chefs wreathed in billows of steam rising from the cauldrons of soup in the front of the restaurant, New York Noodle Town is as close as you can get to Hong Kong without leaving Manhattan. It serves Chinatown's most delicious food. Everything is good, from the superb roast suckling pig to the superlative deep-fried soft-shell crabs. All the noodle dishes are wonderful, and the roasted meats are also amazing. No meal at Noodle Town is complete without one of the salt-baked specialties. **Price range:** Entrees, $4–$20. Cash only. **Meals:** B, L, D, LN. **Subway:** J, M, N, Q, R, W, Z, 6 to Canal St.

Next Door Nobu   ☆☆☆ $$$$ JAPANESE
105 Hudson St. (near Franklin St.)   (212) 334-4445
Slightly more casual than Nobu, Next Door Nobu takes no reservations and does not serve lunch. But the food is as accomplished (and as expensive) as Nobu's. It strives for its own identity, with an emphasis on raw shellfish, whole fish served for an entire table, noodles, and texture. The few meat dishes on the menu are memorable. Mochi ice cream balls are the most appealing way to end a meal. Mochi, the pounded rice candy of Japan, is stretchy and sticky when warm, but hardens into a cold tackiness when frozen. **Price range:** Noodle dishes, $10–$15; hot dishes, $8–$32; sushi and sashimi, $3–$8 a piece. **Meals:** D, LN. **Subway:** 1, 9 to Franklin St.

Nha Trang $25 & Under   VIETNAMESE
87 Baxter St. (between Canal and Bayard Sts.)   (212) 233-5948
148 Centre St. (at Walker St.)   (212) 941-9292
Nha Trang was one of the pioneering Vietnamese restaurants in Chinatown, and
it's still one of the best. Spring rolls are perfectly fried, while steamed ravioli, glistening paper-thin rice noodle crepes wrapped around minced pork and ground
mushrooms and served with slices of smooth, mild Vietnamese pork sausage, is
another excellent appetizer. Vietnamese rice noodle soups like pho tai, a huge
bowl of noodles and tender slices of beef in a coriander-scented broth, are big
enough to be an entire meal. **Price range:** Entrees, $5–$11. Cash only. **Meals:** B,
Br, L, D. **Subway:** J, M, N, Q, R, W, Z, 6 to Canal St. (for both locations).

Nick & Toni's   ☆☆ $$$ MEDITERRANEAN
100 W. 67th St. (between Broadway and Columbus)   (212) 496-4000
Nick & Toni's is a lot like the neighborhood it serves: casual, crowded and
noisy. But there is one thing that sets it apart from most of the neighborhood's
restaurants: the food is really delicious. Nick & Toni's starts with good ingredients and leaves them alone. The menu changes constantly, but there are a few
perennials, like the mussels and the impeccable Caesar salad. Often there is a
fine pasta with just the right number of baby clams. Desserts are simple and seasonal. **Price range:** Entrees, $11–$28. **Meals:** L, D. **Subway:** 1, 9 to 66th St.

Nicole's   ☆☆ $$$ ENGLISH
10 E. 60th St. (near Fifth Ave., in the Nicole Farhi store)   (212) 223-2288
At lunch Nicole's hums and buzzes. It's filled with stylish, well-heeled diners, nearly
all of them women. At night, the store closes, shadows descend, and Nicole's light
and airy downstairs dining room takes on a somber tinge. The chef has developed a
bright, appealing menu with a shrewd minimalist touch and just the right English
notes. Nicole's does not go in for big, flashy effects. It's happy with clever little
touches. The Moroccan cumin and lemon chicken is also irresistible. Nicole's also
wisely steers toward simple, homey sweets like lemon pudding, and also offers
cheeses from Neal's Yard Dairy in London. **Price range:** Entrees, $20 to $32.
Meals: L, D. **Subway:** N, R, W to Fifth Ave.

92   ☆ $$ NEW AMERICAN
45 E. 92nd St. (between Fifth and Madison Aves.)   (212) 828-5300
Ninety-two, named for its location on 92nd Street, is to all intents and purposes
a diner. The place has fat leather banquettes that look as if they might have
been taken from a 1930's train station, cozy booths and dark wooden tables.
One virtue of 92 is that it fulfills the diner role without overthinking it. There's
onion soup, along with cheeseburgers, and the fried onion rings have a sweet-
hot Thai dipping sauce. Macaroni and cheese deserves applause, and the fine-
grained meatloaf is dense and flavorful. The daily specials shine, especially the
expertly handled fish and chips and the generous slab of pork ribs. The best of
the desserts is the classic chocolate sundae and a firm, unctuous chocolate-pud-

ding cake, the sort of dessert that almost demands that you remove the spoon very slowly from your mouth after each bite. **Price range:** Entrees, $19–$29. **Meals:** Br, L, D. **Subway:** 6 to 96th St.

NL ☆ **$$$**   DUTCH/INDONESIAN
169 Sullivan St. (near Houston St.)   (212) 387-8801
A Dutch restaurant seems like an inside joke. But NL, which is short for Netherlands, has the last laugh, serving a clever mix of beloved Dutch standbys, Indonesian dishes that have gained honorary Dutch citizenship and invented dishes that use homey Dutch ingredients like herring, potatoes, cheese and the yogurt cream known as hangop. Sauerkraut risotto sounds forbidding, but it turns out to be one of the best things on the menu: the sauerkraut, distributed in fine threads, adds piquancy without bullying the dish. For dessert, try poffert-jes, soft, puffy mini-pancakes sprinkled with powdered anise and served with a scoop of vanilla butter. **Price range:** Entrees, $18–$25. **Meals:** D. **Subway:** 1, 9 to Houston St.

Nobu ☆☆☆ **$$$$**   JAPANESE
105 Hudson St. (at Franklin St.)   (212) 219-0500
Chic, casual and pulsing with energy, Nobu cannot be compared with any other restaurant. The kitchen incorporates new ingredients into old dishes and retools traditional recipes; the result is something that seems like a Japanese dish but is not. The best time to eat at Nobu is lunchtime. Order an Omakase meal and let the chefs choose your meal for you. If dishes like Funazushi, a freshwater trout buried in rice for a year, do not appeal to you, just tell the waiter the foods you do not eat. A finicky child could eat happily at Nobu, munching skewers of grilled chicken, beautifully rendered fried tempura and toro, the richest of tuna. No kitchen turns out a more spectacular plate of sushi. Desserts include a warm chocolate soufflé cake with siso syrup and green tea ice cream that comes in a bento box. **Price range:** Avg. $60–$75 per person. **Meals:** L, D. **Subway:** 1, 9 to Franklin St.

Oceana ☆☆☆ **$$$$**   SEAFOOD
55 E. 54th St. (between Park and Madison Aves.)   (212) 759-5941
Oceana's downstairs dining room is small and pretty, with an old-fashioned air. The intimate upstairs dining room is as handsome and luxurious as the dining room on a private yacht. Service is excellent, and you feel that you are about to set sail on a special voyage. Oceana's viewpoint is global—dishes are inspired by a wide variety of cuisines—while firmly rooted in an American idiom. What's more, the menu changes daily as the chef continues to experiment with new combinations. His careful spicing and the extremely intelligent use of ethnic accents brings out the essential nature of the fish. In summer, there is a huge variety of fruit desserts, and in the winter, sticky toffee pudding with vanilla ice cream. **Price range:** Prix-fixe-and tasting menus, $65–$105 ($170 with wines). **Meals:** L, D. Closed Sun. **Subway:** E, F to Lexington Ave.; 6 to 51st St.

Odeon   ☆☆   **$$**   BISTRO/NEW AMERICAN
145 West Broadway (at Thomas St.)   (212) 233-0507
TriBeCa's first great American bistro is still cooking after all these years. The
neighborhood has certainly changed, but time has stood still in the dining room.
It is still unpretentious and comfortable, and it still feels as if it is filled with
artists. It's great for burgers, omelets, pasta and roast chicken in a slightly funky
setting; it's even greater for a martini. And it's still a destination until 3 A.M.
Price range: Avg. entree, $18. **Meals:** Br, L, D, LN.
Subway: A, C, 1, 2, 3, 9 to Chambers St.

Olica   ☆☆☆   **$$$**   FRENCH/NEW AMERICAN
145 E. 50th St.   (212) 583-0001
Olica, formerly L'Actuel, is an even better restaurant than its predecessor. The
new restaurant has gotten a style upgrade that includes Oriental rugs, velvet
upholstery, and a lush green lawn of wheat grass that diners cannot resist comb-
ing with their fingers. The best dishes have the simplicity and clarity that only a
complex culinary tradition can produce. In a very strong lineup of appetizers,
top honors may go to a fresh lobster salad served with paper-thin crabmeat
crackers. In the classic Alsatian tarte flambée, the crust crackles, the bacon is
chewy and smoky, the crème fraîche richly tangy, the threads of onion oozingly
sweet. For dessert, the molten chocolate cake is a pleasant surprise. **Price range:**
Entrees, $18–$25. **Meals:** L, D. Closed Sun. **Subway:** 6, E, F to 51st St.

Olives   ☆   **$$$**   MEDITERRANEAN
281 Park Ave. S., in the W Union Square Hotel (at 17th St.)   (212) 353-8345
The food here is easy to like but hard to respect. Do not look for light, because
you won't find it, not even hidden under a cheese shaving. But it's hard to beat
chef Todd English for sheer palate-engulfing flavor. Both venison and veal fea-
ture prominently in two of the better pastas, chestnut ravioli in a venison
Bolognese sauce with creamy spinach, and mezzaluna, or pasta half-moons,
stuffed with artichokes and blanketed under a ragu of braised veal breast and
roasted tomatoes. Desserts are the kind that make diners feel pleasantly guilty.
The Napoleon, filled with layers of caramel and loaded up with hazelnuts,
banana cream and a scoop of chocolate sorbet, seems halfway between a French
pastry and an old-fashioned banana split. **Price range:** Entrees,$18–$30.
Meals: B, Br, L, D. **Subway:** L, N, Q, R, W, 4, 5, 6 to 14th St.

One If By Land, Two If By Sea   **$$$$**   CONTINENTAL
17 Barrow St. (between W. 4th St. and Seventh Ave. South)   (212) 255-8649
Considered by many to be the most romantic restaurant in New York, it is
almost always booked. The lights are low, the gas fireplaces burn even in the
summer and a pianist serenades you with music. Known mainly for the 1950's
specialty Beef Wellington, the food has grown more ambitious of late. The
seared tuna is fresh and rosy, and the lightly smoked and roasted rack of lamb is
a fine piece of meat. **Price range:** Prix-fixe, $64–75. **Meals:** D.
Subway: 1, 9 to Christopher St.

Orsay ☆☆ **$$$**   FRENCH/BRASSERIE
1057 Lexington Ave. (at 75th St.)   (212) 517-6400
Orsay looks as if it was ordered from a kit, with a lot of shiny brass, pristine
leather banquettes and authentic French waiter costumes. But the cuisine has a
fresh, wayward bent and an international style. Orsay's hickory-chip smoker
gives a dark, woodsy bite to salmon and to a dense, deeply flavored duck
sausage. Oddly enough in this traditional setting, it's the traditional brasserie
and bistro dishes that disappoint, but the restrained raspberry napoleon, with
just a few pastry layers defining the form, is a perfectly executed classic. **Price
range:** Entrees, $15–$26. **Meals:** Br, L, D. **Subway:** 6 to 77th St.

Osteria del Circo ☆ **$$$**   ITALIAN
120 W. 55th St.   (212) 265-3636
Osteria del Circo is a younger, more casual offshoot of the very grand Le Cirque
2000. It has new harlequin-pattern fabric on the chairs, circus-theme midnight-
blue banquettes, lots of trapezes hung from the ceiling, and a big metal lion
draped over the coat-check concession. The restaurant has lots of visual pizazz,
and enough Italian warmth to fire the ovens. Simple is best. Appetizers and pastas, on balance, outperform the entrees, but roasted rabbit loin stuffed with fennel sausage acquits itself with honor, and cacciucco del Circo, a rustic fish stew,
helps redeem the fish category. Desserts are often very pleasing. The zuccotto al
cioccolato looks fearsome — a dark, glistening dome that seems like a piece of
expensive candy inflated to giant size. It is a suave, velvety dessert, intensely
chocolaty without being cloying. **Price range:** Entrees, $14–$30. **Meals:** L, D.
Subway: N, R, Q, W to 57th St.; B, D, E to Seventh Ave.

Otabe ☆☆ **$$$**   JAPANESE
68 E. 56th St. (between Park and Madison Aves.)   (212) 223-7575
In the back room this is a very upscale Benihana; the elegant front dining
room serves kaiseki-like cuisine. The kaiseki dinner is a lovely and accessible
introduction to a ceremonial Japanese cuisine that is traditionally served in
many small courses meant to reflect the season. Less ambitious eaters might
want to sample fewer dishes. Desserts are the big surprise at Otabe; more
French than Japanese, they are original, beautiful and very delicious. The tep-
pan room has a separate menu, and each course is cooked before your eyes by
your personal chef. **Price range:** Entrees, $14.50–$65. **Meals:** L, D. **Subway:**
4, 5, 6 to 59th St.; E, F, N, R to Lexington Ave.

Ouest ☆☆ **$$$**   NEW AMERICAN/BISTRO
2315 Broadway (at 84th St.)   (212) 580-8700
This place looks good and it feels good. Long before the food arrives, Ouest
(pronounced WEST), with disarming confidence, has most diners eating out of
the palm of its hand. Pray for a booth, however, because the upstairs balcony
seating is dark, cramped and loud. The cooking has a sane, rooted quality that
makes it appropriate for what is, when all is said and done, a neighborhood
restaurant. Main courses drift toward the comfort zone. Roast halibut with fava

bean purée and mushroom broth has a solid, uncomplicated appeal, and the same can be said of the special section of the menu devoted to simple grilled meats. For dessert try the rhubarb crisp with strawberry juice, classic and all-American. **Price range:** Entrees, $16–$27. **Meals:** D. **Subway:** 1, 9 to 86th St.

Our Place Shanghai Tea Garden   **$25 & Under**   CHINESE
141 E. 55th St. (at Third Ave.)   (212) 753-3900
With its elevated service and thick linens, Our Place has the feel of a fine yet informal banquet. The Shanghai dishes are rich and satisfying, beautifully rendered, yet accessible to Americans, who make up most of the clientele. The waiters are supremely attentive, dividing portions onto plates, putting umbrellas into drinks for young children and generally offering to do anything short of feeding you. Silver-dollar-size steamed soup dumplings are well-seasoned and nicely textured. The kitchen excels at tofu dishes, and noodle dishes are superb. **Price range:** Entrees, $9.95–$24.95. **Meals:** L, D. **Subway:** E, F to Lexington Ave.; 6 to 51st St.

Paladar   **$25 & Under**   CARIBBEAN/MEXICAN
161 Ludlow St. (near Stanton St.)   (212) 473-3535
Paladar's menu hews closely to Mexican and Caribbean dishes. Standout appetizers include sopes,thick but delicate corn tortillas covered in avocado salsa and a fragrant sauce of fermented black beans, and a savory quesadilla with chorizo and roasted tomatoes, flavored with a smoky chipotle salsa.Seafood is a highlight, with excellent choices like roasted mahi-mahi in an orange-chili vinaigrette over coconut-flavored rice. **Price range:** Entrees, $9–$14. **Meals:** D, LN. **Subway:** F, J, M, Z to Delancey St.–Essex St.

Palm   **$$$$**   STEAKHOUSE
837 Second Ave. (between 44th and 45th Sts.)   (212) 687-2953
250 W. 50th St. (between Broadway and Eighth Ave.)   (212) 333-7256
Great steak, rude waiters, high prices and the world's best hash brown potatoes. The walls are covered with caricatures, the floor is covered with sawdust and if you want to experience what people think is the real New York rush, this is the place for you. **Price range:** Entrees, $16–$35. **Meals:** L, D. **Subway:** Second Ave.: S, 4, 5, 6, 7 to 42nd St. W. 50th St: C, E, 1, 9 to 50th St.

Pam Real Thai Food   **$25 & Under**   THAI
404 W. 49th St. (at Ninth Ave.)   (212) 333-7500
At this sweet little restaurant, your palate will revel in the kitchen's sure-handed spicing. Shredded green papaya salad, for instance, is not only both tangy and sweet but fiery as well, strewn with chewy dried shrimp and tiny red chilies, with a faint sense of pungent fish sauce in the background. Pam's curries are superb: try chu chee curry with pork, with its underlying flavor of coconut milk laced with chili heat. **Price range:** Entrees, $7–$14. Cash only. **Meals:** L, D. **Subway:** C, E to 50th St.

Pão $25 & Under   PORTUGUESE
322 Spring St. (at Greenwich St.)   (212) 334-5464

The small menu in this small restaurant offers traditional Portuguese cuisine
with a contemporary touch. To begin, try roasted quail on cabbage braised with
mild Portuguese sausage and black grapes. Main dishes include pork and clams
in a roasted-red-pepper sauce, and grilled shrimp served with a clam-and-
shrimp-studded lemony bread pudding. Desserts are not to be missed, particularly the pudding with port-and-prune sauce and the rice pudding with citrus,
nutmeg and cinnamon. **Price range:** Entrees, $13.95–$16.95. **Meals:** L, D, LN.
Subway: C, E to Spring St.

Paola's   ☆☆ $$ ITALIAN
245 E. 84th St. (between Second and Third Aves.)   (212) 794-1890

Everybody in New York seems to be looking for the perfect neighborhood
restaurant. This may be it. Paola's is one of the city's best and least-known Italian restaurants. It makes some of the city's finest pasta, and the wine list is wonderful. No regular would even consider starting a meal here without an order of
carciofi alla giudea, a fine version of baby artichokes fried in the style of the
Roman ghetto. But pastas are the soul of the menu. Filled pastas such as cazun-
zei and pansotti are wonderful. Desserts, except the ricotta cake, seem like an
afterthought. **Price range:** Pastas, $12.95–$14.95; entrees, $16.95–$26.95.
Meals: L, D. **Subway:** 4, 5, 6 to 86th St.

Papillon   ☆☆ $$$ FRENCH/NEW AMERICAN
575 Hudson St. (Bank St.)   (646) 638-2900

At Papillon, a friendly bistro in the West Village attached to a neighborhood
saloon, the menu is short. But dinner begins with as many as three palate-
teasers, small exuberant warm-ups. Plan on encountering highly unusual flavors
and ingredients in close proximity on the same plate. But above all, have faith.
The côte de boeuf, for example, is slowly cooked over hay, an old, half-forgotten
country method that adds aroma and sweetness to the meat and blends nicely
with a spicy coffee-cardamom jus, with its bitter edge. The desserts are only for
the brave. **Price range:** Dinner, $35-$45. **Meals:** Br, D.
Subway: 1, 2 to Christopher St.

Paradou $25 & Under   FRENCH/SANDWICHES
8 Little W. 12th St. (near Ninth Ave.)   (212) 463-8345

The full-scale arrival of Italian wine-and-panini shops in the last few years has
been a great thing. Paradou is a panini shop born of a different Mediterranean
coast where the specialty is "sandwichs grillés," as they would say in Provence.
Named for a Provençal bistro, Paradou excels where it counts, with a delicious
range of sandwiches, some distinctly French, and some Mediterranean. The
sampler of five tartines for $10 is the best deal. The larger grilled sandwiches,
served on pressed, toasted baguettes with a small green salad, make surprisingly
substantial meals. **Price range:** Tartines, salads and sandwiches, $5–$15; larger
plates, $12–$20. **Meals:** D, LN. **Subway:** A, C, E to 14th St.

Park Avenue Cafe ☆☆ $$$$ NEW AMERICAN
100 E. 63rd St. (near Park Ave.)   (212) 644-1900
After a decade, the restaurant feels a little past its prime. But Upper East Siders
still treat it as a beloved neighborhood fixture where they can relax and eat
sanely reinterpreted, high-spirited American food. Pastas are among the best
dishes on the menu, but the most sinfully indulgent experience is the formidable terrine of foie gras, served folksy style in a glass jar with fig jam smeared on
the hinged lid. The signature "swordchop" still holds its place on the menu, a
mighty slab of swordfish attached to the collarbone. It is juicy and big-flavored.
For dessert, try the cherry tart or the beautifully realized chocolate cube.
Price range: Entrees, $19.50–$42. **Meals:** L, D. **Subway:** N, R, W to Lexington
Ave.; 4, 5, 6 to 59th St.

Park Bistro ☆☆☆ $$$ BISTRO/FRENCH
414 Park Ave. South (between 28th and 29th Sts.)   (212) 689-1360
A classic French bistro, this restaurant offers seductive Gallic fare, good wines
at reasonable prices and a cozy setting. Among the entrees are grilled escalope
of salmon, veal medallion, roasted and caramelized shoulder of pork with carrots
and fennel, and a daube of beef with potato gnocchi. There is a daily selection
of imported cheeses, and to top off the meal, thin warm apple tart with Armagnac and vanilla ice cream; fresh roasted fig tart, or the ubiquitous crème brûlée.
There is a large and interesting selection of tea in addition to several coffees.
Price range: Avg. entree, $16–$30. **Meals:** L, D. **Subway:** 6 to 28th St.

Park View at the Boathouse ☆☆ $$$ NEW AMERICAN
Loeb Boathouse, Central Park, E. 72nd St. entrance   (212) 517-2233
Is this Manhattan's most romantic spot? Very possibly. Situated in the Loeb
Boathouse next to Central Park's prettiest lake, it combines country charm with
views of skyscrapers peeking over the trees. There is interesting, eclectic food
and a good wine list here. The setting is so swell that you feel lucky to be there.
Live jazz at the adjacent café is a real bonus. **Price range:** Entrees, $18–$30.
Meals: Br, L, D. **Subway:** B, C, 1, 2, 7, 9 to 72nd St.

Pastis ☆ $$$ BISTRO/FRENCH
9 Ninth Ave. (at Little W. 12th St.)   (212) 929-4844
Virtually every dish here could qualify for protection by the French Ministry of
Culture. And all are good. It's a deliberate invitation to simple pleasures. Pastis
needs to work on its steak frites, but rabbit pappardelle is a pleasant surprise, a
superior plate of firm pasta with a sweetly meaty sauce. For dessert, the crêpes
suzette rise up in glory, and the floating island floats, a cloud with just enough
substance to support its light custardy sauce. **Price range:** Entrees, $14–$17.
Meals: L, D, LN. **Subway:** A, C, E to 14th St.; L to Eighth Ave.

Patria ☆☆☆ **$$$$** NUEVO LATINO

250 Park Ave. S. (20th St.) (212) 777-6211

The tone here is a little quieter than it used to be, a little less like a big, nonstop party. The service is more dignified. And the food is superb. The menu is fun, high flying and inventive, but the ideas never spin out of control. Colombian pan de bono, chewy round rolls made from cornmeal, are flavored very mildly with Colombian queso fresco, but they assume lethal power when a waiter brings over a crock filled with nata, a potent mixture of butter, sour cream and roasted garlic. Ceviche maintains a delicate balance between acid, spice and fruit. An excellent entree is roast chicken in a smoky chipotle sauce flavored with huitlacoche, or corn fungus. For dessert, the honors go to three little flans, vanilla, corn and pineapple. **Price range:** Entrees, $10–$32; prix-fixe and tasting menus, $20–$79. **Meals:** L, D. **Subway:** 6, N, Q, R, W to 23rd St.

Patroon ☆ **$$$** NEW AMERICAN

160 E. 46th St. (between Lexington and Third Aves.) (212) 883-7373

The new Patroon, done up in contrasting shades of brown and beige, looks more like the dining room of an airport hotel than an up-to-date "21" Club. This is not to suggest that Patroon has become inexpensive. It's a steakhouse with steakhouse prices, but the menu has been pruned of almost all excess and, for that matter, individuality. As you might expect, simplicity now rules. Oysters on the half shell are superb, although the selection is slim. But a jumbo crab cake is practically all meat, a thoroughly satisfying mouthful of pure flavor. As far as beef goes, little things tend to go wrong, although fish dishes are excellent. **Price range:** Entrees, $20–$42. **Meals:** L, D. **Subway:** S, 4, 5, 6, 7 to 42nd St.

Payard Pâtisserie ☆☆ **$$$** BISTRO/FRENCH

1032 Lexington Ave. (at 73rd St.) (212) 717-5252

This is the ultimate Upper East Side bistro, a whimsical cafe and pastry shop, complete with mirrors, mahogany and hand-blown lamps. A recent visit showed that chef Philippe Bertineau is still going strong, with inventive, impeccably executed dishes like a twice baked cheese soufflé with Parmesan cream sauce, sardines stuffed with quince chutney, and a simple sirloin steak with four-peppercorn sauce. **Price range:** Entrees, $17–$25. **Meals:** Br, L, D. Closed Sun. **Subway:** 6 to 77th St.

Pearl Oyster Bar **$25 & Under** SEAFOOD

18 Cornelia St. (between Bleecker and W. 4th St.) (212) 691-8211

It's just a marble counter with a few small tables, but Pearl has won over its neighborhood with its casual charm and Maine-inspired seafood. The restaurant is modeled on the Swan Oyster Depot in San Francisco, and when packed exudes a Barbary Coast rakishness. The menu changes seasonally, but grilled pompano was sweet and delicious, while scallop chowder was unusual and satisfying. Lobster rolls are big and delicious, and blueberry pie is sensational. Don't forget the oysters. **Price range:** Entrees, $17–$25. MC/V only. **Meals:** L, D. Closed Sun. **Subway:** A, C, E, F, S to W. 4th St.

Peasant   ☆ $$$ ITALIAN
194 Elizabeth St. (between Prince and Spring Sts.)   (212) 965-9511
Peasant has built a following by sticking to some very simple premises. Keep the food simple, rustic and Italian. Cook it over a wood fire. Serve abundant portions. Be nice. That's about it. When the formula works, Peasant sends out highly satisfying food, with the rich tanginess that wood smoke imparts. It adds a sublime crunch to the excellent crust of Peasant's little pizzas. The pasta at Peasant is good, not great. The desserts include a few surprises. The best choices are vanilla-soaked bread pudding and a heroically proportioned peach pie with a rough lattice crust. **Price range:** Dinner, Entrees, $19–$24.
Meals: D. Closed Mon. **Subway:** N, R to Prince St.; 6 to Spring St.

Pepe Verde $25 & Under   ITALIAN
559 Hudson St. (near Perry St.)   (212) 255-2221
Pepe Verde is a slightly larger version of Pepe Rosso to Go, the excellent takeout shop in SoHo. It has tables where you can sit comfortably, but the idea is the same: freshly prepared Italian food several notches above the typical takeout fare, including excellent boneless chicken breasts, marinated in lemon and grilled; rigatoni with deliciously earthy meat sauce, and a rustic, enjoyable pear tart. **Price range:** Entrees, $4.95–$10.95. Cash only. **Meals:** L, D.
Subway: 1, 9 to Christopher St.

Pepolino $25 & Under   ITALIAN
281 West Broadway (near Lispenard St.)   (212) 966-9983
The small, cheerful dining room seems to glow with warmth, the greeting is friendly, and the service is good-natured. The gnocchi at Pepolino are ethereal, as light as miniature clouds, making up with intense flavor what they lack in mass. Whether as malfatti, gnocchi made with spinach and served in a simple sauce of butter and sage, or in their more common potato incarnation, they are meltingly good. The chef also makes a glorious pappa al pomodoro, the Tuscan specialty of ripe tomatoes, shreds of stale bread and fragrant olive oil, cooked into a delicious mush. Pastas are marvelous, and one dessert stands out: a dense chocolate cake, intensely flavored with coffee. **Price range:** Entrees, $11–$19.
AE only. **Meals:** L, D, LN. **Subway:** 1, 9 to Franklin St.; A, C, E to Canal St.

Periyali   ☆ ☆ ☆ $$$ GREEK
35 W. 20th St. (between Fifth and Sixth Aves.)   (212) 463-7890
Periyali used to be the best Greek restaurant in the city, and even now with so much new competition it is still a great place to go. The atmosphere is rustic, and the food is made with good ingredients. Recommended starters are the avgolemono soup (a rich chicken soup smoothed with lemon, egg and

semolina), and especially the tender and fresh octopus marinated in red wine
and grilled over charcoal. Grilled lamb chops with fresh rosemary and garides
Santorini—baked shrimp with tomato, scallions, brandy and feta cheese—are
some of the entrees. For dessert, try the creamy, lemon-scented rice pudding,
the moist orange semolina cake, walnut cake, or the deep-fried pastry twists
called thiples. **Price range:** Entrees, $17–$25. **Meals:** L, D. Closed Sun.
Subway: F, N, R to 23rd St.

Petrossian ☆☆ $$$$ NEW AMERICAN/RUSSIAN
182 W. 58th St. (at Seventh Ave.) (212) 245-2214
Nobody in New York City serves better caviar, and nobody does it with more
style. The dark room is covered with Art Deco splendor, the waiters wear blue
blazers and an obsequious air, and the caviar arrives with warm toast, blini and
beautiful little spoons. Vodka is served in icy little flutes that make it taste
somehow better. Should you desire something else, the food is good and surprisingly affordable. **Price range:** Entrees, $24–$34. **Meals:** Br, L, D.
Subway: N, R, Q, W to 57th St.

Picholine ☆☆☆ $$$$ MEDITERRANEAN/FRENCH
35 W. 64th St. (between Broadway and Central Park West) (212) 724-8585
Picholine, named after a Mediterranean olive, focuses on the food of southern
France, Italy, Greece and Morocco. Meals begin with good house-made breads,
bowls of the tiny olives and olive oil. Salmon in horseradish crust is a signature
dish and it is excellent. But there are also robust dishes from the north, like
daube of beef short ribs with a horseradish potato purée, and a hearty cassoulet.
The kitchen also has a way with game. Homey dishes—chestnut and fennel
soup dotted with sausage, cassoulet rich with duck confit—are all wonderful.
Don't miss the wonderfully extravagant cheese cart, worth considering if only to
hear the lovingly detailed descriptions of each cheese. **Price range:** Entrees,
$26–$36; prix-fixe, $58; four-course tasting menu, $70 ($90 for seven courses).
Meals: L, D. Closed Sun. **Subway:** 6 to 66th St.

Pico ☆☆☆ $$$ PORTUGUESE
349 Greenwich St. (at Harrison St.) (212) 343-0700
Pico is named after an island in the Azores, but it's a romantic reference, rather
than a specific culinary source. Salt cod, or bacalhau, is to Portugal what the
potato is to Ireland, the hero with a thousand faces. The chef whips up a bran-
dade of cod, potato and olive oil gently sparked with piri-piri, shaping it into a
cake and frying it until it's crisp outside, creamy inside. Suckling pig can be
almost cloyingly rich, but Mr. Villa knows how to handle this Portuguese
favorite, applying a honey-citrus glaze that leaves the skin crunchier than the
surface of a good crème brûlée. The star dessert at Pico is a heaped plate of
cinnamon-dusted puffs of dough meant to be dipped in molten bittersweet
chocolate or warm raspberry jam. **Price range:** Entrees, $24–$34.
Meals: L, D. Closed Sun. **Subway:** A, C, 1, 2, 3, 9 to Chambers St.

Pig Heaven $25 & Under   CHINESE

1540 Second Ave. (near 80th St.)   (212) 744-4333

Pig Heaven has a new, sleekly modern look, with a handsome bar, almond-shaped hanging lamps and a table of ceramic and carved decorative pigs. Its terrific Chinese-American food is spiced and presented in ways that please westerners, yet it is fresh and prepared with finesse. The best place to start is the pork selection, particularly roasted Cantonese dishes like suckling pig, strips of juicy meat under a layer of moist fat and wafer-thin, deliciously crisp skin. Most of the supposedly spicy Sichuan dishes here are good, but actually quite mild, and dumplings are excellent. **Price range:** Entrees, $7.95 to $18.95.
Meals: L, D. **Subway:** 6 to 77th St.

Ping's Seafood   ☆☆ $$ CHINESE

22 Mott St. (between Worth and Mosco Sts.)   (212) 602-9988

Near the door, a high-rise of stacked fish tanks offers the menu headliners, a stellar cast that includes but is by no means limited to lobsters, eels, scallops, sea bass and shrimp. The preparations are minimal and the results are maximal. Shrimp in the shell, crackling crisp and salty, come to the table piping hot, exhaling a delicate, fragrant steam. For the adventurous eater, the quirky and often experimental food of Hong Kong always stands as a welcome challenge. One of the house signatures, a rather simple stir-fry of squid cut into long strands woven together with dried fish and crunchy matchsticks of jicama and celery is a winner. One of the more appealing rituals at Ping's is winter melon soup. You must call a day ahead, since the melon, which flourishes in the summer despite its name, has to steam for six hours. It is the perfect emblem for Ping's, an exotic package with thrilling secrets inside. **Price range:** Entrees, $6.95-$30.
Meals: Br, L, D. **Subway:** J, M, N, Q, R, W, Z, 6 to Canal St.

Po $25 & Under   ITALIAN

31 Cornelia St. (near Bleecker St.)   (212) 645-2189

At this small, vivacious, reasonably priced trattoria, the parade of lush flavors begins with the bruschetta offered at the start of each meal, a slice of toasted Italian bread piled high with tender Tuscan white beans. Appetizers are a strong point, with unusual combinations like delicate marinated anchovies draped over a delicious heap of faro, a barleylike grain. Salads, too, are exceptional. Pasta standouts include rigatoni with cauliflower, cooked in white wine until soft, and seasoned with Parmesan, mint, sage and parsley. A paillard of lamb, as long as a skirt steak, is almost beefy, daubed with aioli and served over sweet grape tomatoes. Desserts include a sublimely dense terrine of dark chocolate with a core of rich marzipan.   **Price range:** Entrees, $12.50–$16. AE only.
Meals: L, D / Closed Mon. **Subway:** A, C, E, F, S to W. 4th St.

Pongal $25 & Under   INDIAN/KOSHER/VEGETARIAN
110 Lexington Ave. (near 27th St.)   (212) 696-9458

The delectable vegetarian cuisine of South India is the specialty at Pongal, where the food is kosher as well. The centerpiece dishes are the daunting dosai, huge crepes made of various fermented batters that are stuffed and rolled into cylinders that can stretch two-and-a-half feet. But they are light and delicious, filled with spiced mixtures of potatoes and onions. Pongal also serves a wonderful shrikhand, a dessert made of yogurt custard flavored with nutmeg, cardamom and saffron. **Price range:** Entrees, $7.95–$13.95. **Meals:** L, D. **Subway:** 6 to 28th St.

Pop   ☆ $$$ PAN-ASIAN/BISTRO
127 Fourth Ave. (near 12th St.)   (212) 767-1800

Pop is a bright, happy place with a noncommittal, nonemotive décor and a crowd-pleasing menu that hips and hops from one culinary source to another. The result is toe-tapping food. Pop feels just right, within fairly narrow limits, like an episode of "Friends." Chef Brian Young sprinkles his plates with little surprises—fun, palate-pleasing footnotes like the ingenious slaw of fine-shaved brussels sprouts that comes with a thick, juicy veal chop in quince and pomegranate sauce. For dessert, try the caramel bread pudding and the strawberry cream cake, an all-out assault on the pleasure zones. **Price range:** Entrees, $24 to $36. **Meals:** D. **Subway:** L, N, Q, R, W, 4, 5, 6 to 14th St.

Provence   ☆ $$$ FRENCH
38 Macdougal St. (near Prince St.)   (212) 475-7500

A crowded French café straight out of the French countryside, but while the atmosphere is charming and rustic, the food feels tired. Mussels gratinées, baked on the half shell and sprinkled with almonds and garlic, are very tasty. Bourride, a pale fish soup, is thickened with aioli; don't miss it. Pot au feu, a sometime special, is also a fine example of hearty country cooking, and the bouillabaisse, served only on Fridays, is superb. **Price range:** Entrees, $15.50–$26. AE only. **Meals:** L, D. **Subway:** N, R to Prince St.

Prune $25 & Under   ECLECTIC
54 E. 1st St. (near First Ave.)   (212) 677-6221.

The idiosyncratic name (the chef and owner's childhood nickname) is perfect for this unconventional little place. You could describe the food as homey, or as faintly European. Thin slices of duck breast taste deliciously of smoke, vinegar and black pepper, and are served with a small omelet flavored with rye. Roasted capon is as conventional a dish as Prune offers, yet it is marvelously juicy, served over a slice of toast imbued with garlic. Desserts are terrific, like cornmeal poundcake drenched in a rosemary syrup, with a poached pear. **Price range:** Entrees, $10–$17. **Meals:** D. Closed Mon. **Subway:** F to Second Ave.

Red Bar Restaurant   ☆ $$$

AMERICAN/BISTRO

339 E. 75th St. (between First and Second Aves.)   (212) 472-7577

In an area aswarm with taco and sushi take-away joints, Red Bar offers warmth, style and good, unpretentious food. It has limited aims, and a menu that refuses to strain for effect. Much of the menu is devoted to bistro standards, some presented very straightforwardly, others with a grace note or two. Good ingredients make the simpler dishes shine in a modest way and lend support to more adventurous excursions. For dessert, try a dense frozen parfait made with three chocolates. **Price range:** Entrees, $19–$29. **Meals:** D. **Subway:** 6 to 77th St.

The Red Cat   ☆ $$

BISTRO/AMERICAN

227 10th Ave. (near 23rd St.)   (212) 242-1122

A lot of restaurants make a big noise about being warm, welcoming and accessible. The Red Cat, with little ado, manages to be all three. It is stylish, but not snooty, cool but relaxed. The menu reflects the spirit of the place with a lineup of solid, well-executed American bistro dishes, with a little trick or twist on each plate. The obligatory steak dish comes with a ragout of roasted shallots, tomatoes and cracked olives. The short dessert list does not disappoint. **Price range:** entrees, $15–$24. **Meals:** D, LN. **Subway:** C, E to 23rd St.

Redeye Grill   ☆ $$$

NEW AMERICAN

890 Seventh Ave. (at 56th St.)   (212) 541-9000

The boisterous room seems as big as Grand Central Terminal and is lively at almost any hour. There's something for everyone on the vast menu, from smoked fish to raw clams, Chinese chicken, pasta, even a hamburger—late into the night. The small grilled lobster, served with a little potato cake and pristine haricots verts, is lovely. The steak of choice here would be the hanger steak, tender slices piled onto a biscuit. The plain Jane cream-cheese bundt cake is usually the best of the desserts. **Price range:** Entrees, $18–$29. **Meals:** Br, L, D, LN. **Subway:** N, R, Q, W to 57th St.

Remi   ☆ ☆ $$$

ITALIAN

145 W. 53rd St. (between Sixth and Seventh Aves.)   (212) 581-4242

Remi's stunning Gothic interior and the kitchen's enticing and inventive Northern Italian fare make it easy to understand its continued popularity. The diverse menu includes excellent pastas and main courses like garganelli blended with Coho salmon in balsamic sauce; veal-and-spinach-filled cannelloni in rosemary sauce; and salmon in a horseradish crust, finished with red wine sauce. **Price range:** Entrees, $16–$28. **Meals:** L, D. **Subway:** B, D, E to Seventh Ave.

Rinconcito Mexicano $

MEXICAN/TEX-MEX

307 W. 39th St. (between Eighth and Ninth Aves.)   (212) 268-1704

This tiny restaurant is little more than a smoky aisle in the garment center. English is barely spoken, but the food needs no translation: soft tacos with the freshest and most authentic ingredients, like sautéed pork, calf's tongue, goat, chorizo and pork skin. The aroma of corn rises from the steamed tacos, and the refried beans are still pleasantly grainy. **Price range:** Avg. entree, $8. **Meals:** L, D. Closed Sat., Sun. **Subway:** A, C, E to 42nd St.

Risa   **$25 & Under**   PIZZA/ITALIAN
47 E. Houston St. (near Mulberry St.)   (212) 625-1712
Risa's pizzas taste as good as they look. The crust is thin and light, with a gentle, crisp snap. The cheese and tomato pie is impeccably fresh, and other toppings only enhance. Designer pies, like one made with speck (a smoked ham), arugula and mascarpone, are notable for their subtlety. Even truffle oil, a domineering ingredient that often crowds out other flavors, is used lightly. Beyond pizzas, Risa offers pastas that are fine if not especially unusual. Appetizers are a weak link, although calamari is full of flavor and texture, and an arugula and fennel salad is appropriately refreshing. **Price range:** Pizzas, $9–$12; entrees, $8.50–$19.50. **Meals:** L, D, LN. **Subway:** F, S to Broadway–Lafayette St.

Rocking Horse   **$25 & Under**   MEXICAN
182 Eighth Ave. (near 19th St.)   (212) 463-9511
A renovation has expanded and brightened the dining room, but while the food is still inspired by Mexico, the careful and complex seasonings are now muffled. Occasionally, a dish's Mexican identity manages to peek out. Well-charred yet flavorful chicken enchiladas are the best main course, and skewers of grilled shrimp are first-rate. Desserts are highlights, with winners like a tart and refreshing Key lime custard and a dense, fudgy tart with bananas and cherimoya sorbet. Rocking Horse offers an excellent lineup of tequilas and cocktails, and an inspired list of wines that prove how well wine can go with Mexican flavors. **Price range:** Entrees, $14.95–$21.95. **Meals:** L, D. **Subway:** C, E to 23rd St.

Royal Siam   **$25 & Under**   THAI
240 Eighth Ave. (between 22nd and 23rd Sts.)   (212) 741-1732
Royal Siam's generic décor of mirrored walls, Thai posters and glass-topped tables belie some of the most flavorful and attractively prepared Thai cooking around. Dishes to look for include tom yum koong, or shrimp and mushroom soup in a lemony seafood broth; tod mun pla, fish cakes paired with a bright peanut sauce; and nuur yunk namtok, or grilled steak served sliced on a bed of mixed greens with cucumber and tomato. **Price range:** Entrees, $8.95–$14.95. **Subway:** C, E to 23rd St.

Ruby Foo's   ☆☆ $ $ PAN-ASIAN
1626 Broadway (between 49th and 50th Sts.)   (212) 489-5600
2182 Broadway (at 77th St.)   (212) 724-6700
The Upper West Side branch has everything it takes to make the neighborhood happy: fabulous décor, interesting pan-Asian food and the sort of atmosphere that appeals to families with children as well as singles on the prowl. The new location in Times Square, cheek by jowl with cartoon operations like the World

Wrestling Federation restaurant, fits right into the area, with a décor that suggests the mysterious East as imagined by a 1940's B-movie producer. The menu offers everything from dim sum to sushi with side trips through Thailand, tailored to American tastes. A memorable Japanese dish is the miso-glazed black cod. But it is the Southeast Asian dishes that really sing. The green curry chicken has a fiery coconut-based sauce that is irresistible. Desserts are purely American and purely wonderful, especially the raspberry-passion fruit parfait. **Price range:** Entrees, $9.50–$19.50. **Meals:** Br, L, D, LN. **Subway:** Midtown: 1, 9 to 50th St. Uptown: 1, 9 to 79th St.

Sabor $25 & Under   TAPAS/PAN-LATIN
462 Amsterdam Ave. (near 82nd St.)   (212) 579-2929

The menu here has enough subdivisions to keep a law student busy for hours, including ceviches, empanadas, cheeses, charcuterie, skewers, salads, a raw bar, side dishes and tapas grandes, mercifully translated as "main courses." Certain things stand out immediately among the main courses, like a fine, beefy grilled skirt steak or an impressive braised lamb shank, served off the bone over mildly sweet mashed boniato with a luscious red-wine sauce. Sabor's paella takes liberties but is delicious and beautifully presented. Also try the delightful tapas. The standout dessert is a creamy dulce de leche cheesecake.   **Price range:** Tapas, $4.50–$9.95; entrees, $10.95–$15.95. **Meals:** L (weekends only), D. **Subway:** 1, 9 to 79th St.

Salaam Bombay Indian Cuisine   ☆☆ $$ INDIAN
317 Greenwich St. (near Duane St.)   (212) 226-9400

Salaam Bombay looks much like every other upscale Indian restaurant in New York City, large and pleasant. But it departs from tradition and showcases the richness of regional Indian cooking. At lunch there's a big, affordable buffet. At dinner an interesting assortment of vegetable dishes is where this kitchen really shines. The best is ringna bataka nu shaak, a Gujarati eggplant and potato dish cooked with curry leaves and lots of spices. Also try kadhai jhinge, shrimp stir-fried with tomatoes, onions and lots of fresh and fragrant spices. For dessert, shrikhand, a dreamy, custardlike dessert, has a mysterious flavor that imparts a certain sense of wonder. **Price range:** entrees, $9.95–$19.95. **Meals:** L, D. **Subway:** A, C, 1, 2, 3, 9 to Chambers St.

San Domenico   ☆☆☆ $$$$ ITALIAN
240 Central Park South (between Broadway and Seventh Ave.) (212) 265-5959

This dignified and comfortable spot is one of a handful of American restaurants trying to showcase the cooking of the aristocratic northern Italian kitchen, the cuisine known as alta cucina. Give this staid restaurant a chance and it will manage to capture your heart. Most of the appetizers are so seductive that you will eat every meal in a flush of joyful anticipation. The restaurant's signature dish is uovo in ravioli con burro nocciola tartufato: a single large puff filled with ricotta and spinach perfumed with truffle butter. Snuggled inside is an egg that spurts golden yolk as you begin to eat. But the kitchen does not need luxury ingredients to show

its stuff. You could come to San Domenico and treat it like a trattoria, choosing only simple dishes and enjoying the care with which they are cooked.
Meals: L, D. **Subway:** A, B, C, D, 1, 9 to 59th St.

Savoy ☆☆ $$$ NEW AMERICAN
70 Prince St. (at Crosby St.)   (212) 219-8570
Savoy looks like a funky old aluminum-sided diner. But the upstairs dining room, where cooking is done right in the fireplace, is one of the city's coziest rooms. The menu dances around the globe, borrowing where it will. The results can be wildly uneven but are usually charming. If you are unlucky you may end up with one of the occasionally gummy risottos or doughy pastas. Order a salad, however, and you will instantly be seduced. Desserts are excellent and change with the market. If you have an adventurous spirit, you will discover a sense of fun that is missing in most modern restaurants. **Price range:** Entrees, $19–$26. **Meals:** L, D.
Subway: N, R to Prince St.; F, S to Broadway–Lafayette St.

Scalini Fedeli ☆ $$$$ ITALIAN
165 Duane St. (Hudson St.)   (212) 528-0400
Scalini Fedeli (which means "steps of faith") has no edge. What it has, instead, is old-fashioned grace. The dining room is as soothing as a massage. The pleasing food rarely takes flight, and when it does, the dish is likely to be disarmingly simple. The pappardelle with a sauce of Scottish hare and venison is a small feast of gloriously rich, dark meats finished off with cream and truffles. The main courses are satisfying, decorous and rather unassuming. A good-size fillet of roasted Chilean sea bass, for example, finds an ideal matchup in a sauce of sun-dried tomatoes and Sicilian and Greek olives, and saddle of rabbit, swaddled in pancetta and served with a black olive sauce, makes a simple, pleasing entrée. For dessert, the panna cotta takes a back seat to the dense chocolate tart. **Price range:** Dinner, three courses, $60. **Meals:** L, D.
Subway: A, C, 1, 2, 3, 9 to Chambers St.

Screening Room ☆☆ $$$ NEW AMERICAN
54 Varick St. (below Canal St.)   (212) 334-2100
It's a bar. It's a restaurant. It's a movie theater. The slightly funky bar serves appealing snacks like lobster rolls, onion rings and Philadelphia cheese steaks. The restaurant offers serious American food on the order of grilled duck and spectacular desserts. The best appetizer is the pan-fried artichokes, served on lemony greens topped with shavings of Parmesan cheese. The simplest entrees are the most impressive. The pastry chef does not have a loser on the list, but the best desserts are lemon icebox cake and toasted angel food cake. **Price range:** Entrees, $13–$22. **Meals:** Br, L, D. **Subway:** A, C, E, 1, 9 to Canal St.

Sea Grill ☆☆ $$$ SEAFOOD
19 W. 49th St. (in Rockefeller Center)   (212) 332-7610
During the winter the main draw here is a view of the Rockefeller Center skating rink. In warm weather, the skating rink becomes an outdoor extension of

the restaurant, with canvas umbrellas and potted shrubs. Much of the menu has a brasserie feel to it, with a changing daily menu of day-boat fish that are simply grilled, sauteed or seared. A fresh breeze blows over the rest of the menu as well, with the accent on vibrant flavors and simple preparations. The crab cake is justly renowned: a lumpy-looking thing, more ball than patty, displaying the rough-hewn virtues that distinguish a real crab cake from a thousand prettified pretenders. **Price range:** Entrees, $21–$29. **Meals:** L, D. Closed Sun. **Subway:** B, D, F, S to 47th-50th St.–Rockefeller Center.

71 Clinton Fresh Food ☆☆ $$ BISTRO/NEW AMERICAN
71 Clinton St. (near Rivington St.) (212) 614-6960
New chef Matt Reguin has wisely chosen not to venture far from the sort of elegantly composed contemporary American dishes that won Wylie Dufresne so much applause. A fat square of Arctic char is lacquered with a glaze just sweet enough to bring out the sweetness of the fish itself, which is offset by salty, spicy rounds of chorizo and slivers of green onion, a graceful and delicious combination of flavors and textures. Mr. Reguin also likes to add fruit to the mix, serving a sour cherry chutney with wonderfully tender slices of venison, creamy lentils and sublimely smoky mushrooms. The restaurant remains as crowded as ever, and its appeal is undimmed. **Price range:** Entrees, $15–$22. **Meals:** D. Closed Sun. **Subway:** F to Delancey St.; J, M, Z to Essex St.

Shun Lee Palace ☆☆ $$$ CHINESE
155 E. 55th St. (between Lexington and Third Aves.) (212) 371-8844
No restaurant in New York City can produce better Chinese food. And no restaurant in New York City does it so rarely. Shun Lee is a New York institution, with a cool opulence that is almost a caricature of a Chinese-American palace. The spareribs are long, meaty, almost fat-free and perfectly cooked. The chefs do impressive things with whole fish, and the owner likes to appear with live fish and suggest various ways the kitchen might prepare them. A recent visit served as a reminder that no one quite matches Shun Lee for its blend of showmanship and culinary quality. The menu ranges roo far and wide, but dishes like prawns on banana leaf with curry sauce could hardly be better. **Price range:** Entrees, $9–$30. **Meals:** L, D. **Subway:** E, F to Lexington Ave.; 6 to 51st St.

Shun Lee West $$$ CHINESE
43 W. 65th St. (at Columbus Ave.) (212) 595-8895
A cavernous Chinese restaurant near Lincoln Center that is always packed. The kitchen can do great things, but they are rarely produced for a clientele that sticks mostly to the familiar. If you want the best food, call ahead and discuss the menu. Good Peking duck. **Price range:** Avg. entree, $19. **Meals:** Br, L, D, LN. **Subway:** 1, 9 to 66th St.

Silver Swan   **$25 & Under**   GERMAN
41 E. 20th St. (between Broadway and Park Ave. South)   (212) 254-3611
The excellent selection of more than 75 beers and ales is reason enough to
enjoy Silver Swan's solid German fare in a friendly atmosphere. Rauchbier,
or smoked beer, made with smoked malt, goes perfectly with kassler rip-
pchen, smoked pork chops served with vinegary sauerkraut, while any of
more than a dozen Bavarian wheat beers are just right with weisswurst, mild
veal sausage, or bratwurst, juicy pork sausage. This is not the place to eat if
you are longing for vegetables; meat is another matter, however, starting with
five varieties of schnitzel and ending with a satisfying sauerbraten.
Price range: Entrees, $14–$27. **Meals:** L, D, LN. **Subway:** 6 to 23rd St.

Smith & Wollensky   ☆☆   **$$$$**   STEAKHOUSE
797 Third Ave. (at 49th St.)   (212) 753-1530
This is a place for two-fisted eating. It is also one of the few steakhouses that
never lets you down: the service is swell, the steaks are consistently very, very
good (if rarely great) and the portions are huge. The sirloins are aged for around
two weeks to intensify the flavor and give the meat a dry edge. Beyond that, if
you have noncarnivores to feed, the restaurant knows how to do it. The lobsters, clams, oysters and chicken are excellent too. Desserts, unfortunately, leave
a great deal to be desired. **Price range:** Entrees, $18.50–$65. **Meals:** L, D, LN.
Subway: 6 to 51st St.; E, F to Lexington Ave.

Snack   **$25 & Under**   GREEK
105 Thompson St. (at Prince St.)   (212) 925-1040
This is one of Manhattan's smallest restaurants. But taste the stifado, a delicately spiced stew of braised lamb, and you know right away that Snack is worth
squeezing into. Start with the impeccable cold appetizers: hummus, melitzanes
salata, taramosalata, tzatziki and skordalia. Other gems among the small selection of main courses include keftedes, or savory veal meatballs, and juicy roast
chicken. Desserts are simple and satisfying. **Price range:** Entrees, $8–$13. Cash
only. **Meals:** L, D. **Subway:** N, R to Prince St.

Soba Nippon   **$25 & Under**   JAPANESE/SUSHI
19 W. 52nd St. (between Fifth and Sixth Aves.)   (212) 489-2525
Few places make better noodles than Soba Nippon. The owner has his own
buckwheat farm and soba noodles are made daily at the restaurant. Try the cold
soba noodles served plain, on a flat basket with a dipping sauce of fish stock and
soy. Eventually, a small, simmering pot of liquid is placed on the table: this is
the broth in which the noodles were boiled. Pour the broth into the dipping
sauce, add the scallions and wasabi, and drink. It's marvelous. One fine alternative to soba is cold inaniwa udon noodles, as thin as spaghetti, with a pure,
clean flavor. Soba Nippon's hot soba soups are excellent as well.
Price range: Entrees, $8–$17. **Meals:** L, D. **Subway:** E, F to Fifth Ave.

Soba-Ya $25 & Under   JAPANESE/NOODLES

229 E. 9th St. (between Second and Third Aves.)   (212) 533-6966

Noodles are the focus at this bright, handsome little Japanese restaurant. The soba noodles — buckwheat, pale tan and smooth — are served hot in soups or cold, a better bet for appreciating their lightness and clear flavors. Appetizers are excellent, differing night to night but sometimes including cooked marinated spinach, rice with shreds of marinated sardines and fried squares of marvelously fresh tofu. **Price range:** Noodles and rice bowls, $6.50–$14. **Meals:** L, D. **Subway:** 6 to Astor Pl.; N, R to 8th St.

Soho Steak $25 & Under   BISTRO/FRENCH

90 Thompson St. (near Spring St.)   (212) 226-0602

This thoroughly French little restaurant, drawing a young, good-looking crowd, emphasizes meat but is no simple steakhouse. It is a cleverly conceived, bustling bistro that serves creative dishes for lower prices than you might imagine. Steak frites, of course, is top-notch. Few places offer this much value for this kind of money. **Price range:** Entrees, $14–$16. Cash only. **Meals:** Br, D. **Subway:** C, E to Spring St.

Solera   ☆☆ $$$ TAPAS/SPANISH

216 E. 53rd St. (between Second and Third Aves.)   (212) 644-1166

Solera looks so cozy it is almost impossible not to be drawn into the long room, with its terra-cotta tiles and romantic lighting. Pull up a chair and prepare to be seduced by the food and wine of Spain. The appetizers are all fine, but octopus with paprika and olive oil is consistently amazing. There are several versions of paella, all delicious but the seafood is the most impressive. Best of all are the crisp little lamb chops served with a ragout of beans and polenta laced with cheese. **Price range:** Entrees, $25–$35; tapas, $3–$9.50. **Meals:** L, D, LN. Closed Sun. **Subway:** E, F to Lexington Ave.; 6 to 51st St.

Sono   ☆☆ $$$$ JAPANESE/FRENCH

106 E. 57th St. (at Lexington Ave.)   (212) 752-4411

Sono—which means "garden enhanced by man"—is a showcase for Tadashi Ono's idiosyncratic, very persuasive blend of French and Japanese cooking. There is a disarming simplicity to the menu. The excitement comes from unexpected pairings, or the sheer, inexhaustible pleasure of directly communicated taste sensations, or arresting visual presentations. The chef's assortment, an appetizer, offers a whirlwind tour through Mr. Ono's mind. The lineup varies from day to day, but it's always a carousel of tastes and textures. It's enough that Mr. Ono has given the world his roasted squab smeared with a paste of kaffir lime, a kind of hollandaise made with sake and white miso. It has a counterpart on the dessert menu, an impressively tall cheesecake made with kabocha squash (Japan's favorite pumpkin) and coconut.
Price range: Dinner, three courses, $52; seven course tasting menu, $78.
Meals: L, D. **Subway:** 4, 5, 6 to 59th St.; N, R, W to Lexington Ave.

Strip House ☆ **$$$**   STEAKHOUSE
13 E. 12th St. (between Fifth Ave. and University Pl.)   (212) 328-0000
Strip House is not so much a steakhouse as a catalog of hip references to the
idea of a steakhouse. It has a cheery, comfortable atmosphere, with none of the
backslapping locker-room style of the old-line steakhouses. The filet mignon
and New York strip steaks are perfectly acceptable, but the swaggering porter-
house comes through in a big way, seared aggressively to achieve a deep crunch,
all rubescent tender meat within. For dessert, the caramelized apple tart with
mascarpone ice cream and brown sugar hard sauce is as good as it sounds.
Price range: Entrees, $22–$32. **Meals:** D. **Subway:** F, L, N, Q, R, W, 4, 5, 6 to
14th St.

Suba ☆ **$$**   SPANISH/ECLECTIC
109 Ludlow St. (near Delancey St.)   (212) 982-5714
The descent to the dining room at Suba is a series of twists and turns along a
staircase made from industrial grating. In this twilight environment, diners will
encounter food as lurid as the setting. The chef takes Spain as a departure point
but quickly speeds off to points unknown. Some of this is wildly misconceived.
Some of it is wonderful. None of it is boring. Goat cheese is everywhere on the
menu, most successfully, or at least intriguingly, in a kind of napoleon consisting
of thin black-pepper tuiles, serrano ham, quince paste and cheese. Try the flourless chocolate cake served with a coffee-avocado shake. It's a minor triumph,
and the right kind of weird. **Price range:** Entrees, $18–$25. **Meals:** D.
Subway: F, J, M, Z to Delancey St.–Essex St.

The Sultan **$25 & Under**   TURKISH
1435 Second Ave. (near 74th St.)   (212) 861-2828
This friendly storefront restaurant offers mainstream Turkish dishes that are
notable for their fresh, lively flavors. Meals begin with a basket of puffy house-
made bread studded with tiny black sesame seeds, and a dish of tahini blended
with pekmez, a thick grape syrup. Kebabs are universally good here, especially
the lamb yogurt kebab, and whole trout is grilled perfectly, then filleted at the
table. The dessert menu is predictable yet well prepared.
Price range: Entrees, $11.95–$16.95. **Meals:** L, D. **Subway:** 6 to 77th St.

Supper **$25 & Under**   ITALIAN
156 E. 2nd St. (near Ave. A)   212) 477-7600
Decorated in standard-issue mismatched tables and chairs with brick walls, tile
flooring and antique chandeliers, Supper is divided into a sidewalk area, a rear
dining room, and a front dining room centered on an open kitchen. Consider
sharing a pasta as an appetizer, especially tajarin d'ortice, the Piedmontese name
for tagliatelle prepared simply with mint and butter. On weekends, Supper
serves bollito misto, the Northern Italian feast of boiled meats. For dessert, light
and sumptuous hazelnut panna cotta, served with a pitcher of dense chocolate
sauce, is the clear highlight. **Price range:** Entrees, $7–$14. Cash only. **Meals:** D,
LN. **Subway:** F, V to Delancey St.

Surya ☆☆ $$ INDIAN

302 Bleecker St. (between Seventh Ave. South and Grove St.) (212) 807-7770
The restaurant named for the sun (in Tamil) actually has a small garden in
the back along with a sleek interior. Its menu features mostly south Indian
dishes, often filtered through the technique of France. The main courses
have a bold freshness. But what is most splendid about Surya is the entirely
meatless side of the menu. It is, in fact, difficult to come up with a more
exciting place to eat vegetables in New York City. Don't eat a meal at Surya
without ordering the okra, sautéed in a thick mixture of tomatoes, onion,
garlic and kokum (a sour Indian fruit). Try the dosai, too, and the exceptional desserts. **Price range:** Entrees, $11–$24. **Meals:** Br, D.
Subway: 1, 9 to Christopher St.

Sushi Yasuda ☆☆☆ $$$ JAPANESE/SUSHI

204 E. 43rd St. (between Second and Third Aves.)   (212) 972-1001
In one of the city's dreariest restaurant neighborhoods, Sushi Yasuda glows like a
strange mineral, with a cool, celery-green façade. Inside, the mood is quiet, con-
templative, austere. But Sushi Yasuda has a lot of downtown in its soul. The
manager and the waitresses are young. The exemplary service has an open,
friendly quality to it. At the same time, the menu is dead serious, a purist's paradise of multiple choices among fish species—nearly 30, a startling number for a
small restaurant—and elegantly presented appetizers and side dishes. But sushi
is only half the story. The daily menu includes a small sheet of special appetizers, and they are worth jumping for. **Price range:** Sushi, $3–$6.50 a piece.
Meals: L, D. Closed Sun. **Subway:** S, 4, 5, 6, 7 to 42nd St.

Sylvia's $ SOUTHERN

328 Lenox Ave. (between 126th and 127th Sts.)   (212) 996-0660.
Tour buses pull up in front for a sanitized taste of Harlem. The food's not
fabulous, but it offers everything you expect: fried chicken, collard greens and
sweet potato pie. Best for the gospel brunch on Sunday. **Price range:** Entrees,
$8.95–$13; gospel brunch: $15.95. **Meals:** Br, L, D. **Subway:** 2, 3 to 125th St.

Tabla ☆☆☆ $$$$ AMERICAN-ASIAN FUSION

11 Madison Ave. (near 25th St.)   (212) 889-0667
The newest of Danny Meyer's restaurants, Tabla vibrates with sound and sizzles
with color. At the bar downstairs, cooks grill roti and naan in odd and interesting flavors. Upstairs, the dining room is darkly sensuous with walls stained in
shades of jade and coral. Then the food arrives—American food, viewed
through a kaleidoscope of Indian spices. The powerful, original and unexpected
flavors evoke intense emotions. Those who do not like Tabla tend to dislike it
with a passion. Ignore them and abandon yourself to the joys of a fine restaurant. **Price range:** Three-course prix-fixe dinner, $52 (plus a few supplements).
Meals: L, D. Closed Sun. **Subway:** 6 to 23rd St.

Taco Taco   **$**   MEXICAN/TEX-MEX
1726 Second Ave. (between 89th and 90th Sts.)   (212) 289-8226
Every neighborhood should have a Mexican restaurant like this where the
atmosphere is casual and pleasant but the food is serious. Tacos, naturally, are
the mainstay, with fillings like pork with sautéed cabbage, tongue and crumbled
chorizo. More ambitious dishes include tender pork marinated with smoky
chipotle chilies and grilled. Even nachos are made with unusual care.
Price range: Entrees, $9–$12. Cash only. **Meals:** L, D. **Subway:** 4, 5, 6 to 86th St.

Tagine   **$25 & Under**   MOROCCAN
537 Ninth Ave. (near 40th St.)   (212) 564-7292
Tagine is, in the true bohemian spirit, a low-budget operation. The dim, alluring
dining room seems a blizzard of colors and styles and the languorous service may
lead you to believe that food is not the focus here, but you'll relax when the
food arrives. Zaalouk, an eggplant purée rich with the dusky aroma of cumin, is
wonderful on freshly baked bread. The restaurant's signature tagines, fragrant
stews served in traditional earthenware vessels with conical lids, are the least
satisfying of the main courses, though the chicken tagine and lamb shank are
quite good. Desserts can be excellent, like semolina cake soaked in orange blossom water. **Price range:** Entrees, $13–$19.50. **Meals:** L, D, LN.
Subway: A, C, E to 42nd St.

Tamarind   ☆☆   **$$**   INDIAN
41-43 E. 22nd St. (between Broadway and Park Ave. South)   (212) 674-7400
Tamarind, named for the sweet-and-sour fruit, looks and feels fresh. It is styl-
ishly decorated, and the menu treats Indian cuisine as a genuine culinary lan-
guage, like French, able to assimilate nontraditional ingredients and techniques.
Quality varies on the extensive dinner menu, but on balance, the winners out-
number the losers by about 3 to 1. For whatever reason, anything involving
shrimp succeeds wildly, like shrimp balchau, an exotic shrimp cocktail with a
smoothly fiery chili-masala sauce wrapped around tiny chunks of firm tomato.
Vegetarian dishes also seem to bring out the best at Tamarind. The tandoor does
not perform flawlessly, though some dishes emerge moist and succulent from the
oven, like noorani kebab, chunks of spiced chicken flavored with saffron. The
lunch menu at Tamarind is ingenious, with five set menus, each representing a
coherent Indian meal. **Price range:** Entrees, $15–$26. **Meals:** L, D.
Subway: 6 to 23rd St.

TanDa   ☆   **$$$**   ASIAN FUSION
331 Park Ave. S. (24th St.)   (212) 253-8400
TanDa is a swanky bistro and lounge serving modernized Southeast Asian cuisine with a strong Vietnamese bent. The Balinese roasted duck is a heady,
voluptuous experience, and the green chicken curry and the roast chicken with
cardamom foam and sour mango are both very good. Some of the more traditional dishes, like beef pho, are treated conservatively. The oddly named rice-

noodle tian, a multilevel Asian lasagna, is a triumph. For dessert, a very light hand with star anise brings crème brûlée subtly into the magic circle of Southeast Asian flavors. **Price range:** Entrees, $12–$28. **Meals:** L, D. **Subway:**

Tappo   ☆ $$ MEDITERRANEAN
403 E. 12th St. (at First Ave.)   (212) 505-0001

A really good neighborhood restaurant can be hard to find, but Tappo hits the mark. The food is simple and fresh; the setting feels like a farmhouse kitchen. The menu has a long, unchanging list of appetizers that mixes traditional Italian starters with less predictable Spanish and Middle Eastern dishes, but the best of them have the sparkle that can only come from fresh ingredients. Baby chicken sautéed in herbs and white wine is a fine, unpretentious dish, and the kitchen turns out a superior roasted branzino, firm-fleshed and moist, The pastas can be excellent, and the standout dessert is a dense panna cotta drizzled with sweetly pungent 25-year-old balsamic vinegar.
Price range: Entrees, $15–$26. **Meals:** D, LN. **Subway:** L to First Ave.

The Tasting Room   ☆ $$$ NEW AMERICAN
72 E. 1st St. (between First and Second Aves.)   (212) 358-7831

When the Tasting Room is not caught up in its own spell, it does the honorable work of serving good food at a moderate price in a pleasant atmosphere, with a clever format. What sets the restaurant apart is its ferociously ambitious, nicely-priced wine list. The menu allows diners to combine several tasting portions into a meal or to order the usual appetizer and main course. At the Tasting Room, bolder is better. Try rabbit or a simple pan-roasted sea bass. For dessert, Renée's Mother's Cheesecake is a cheesecake to die for; in comparison, the menu is a mere footnote. **Price range:** Entrees, $13–$29. **Meals:** D. Closed Sun. **Subway:** F to Second Ave.

Tavern on the Green   ☆ $$$$ NEW AMERICAN
Central Park West (at 67th St.)   (212) 873-3200

This is America's largest-grossing restaurant, a wonderland of lights, flowers, chandeliers and balloons that can make a child out of the most cynical adult. Patrick Clark, who died in February 1998, was a terrific chef, and he's left a culinary legacy for his successors to follow. But even he was not able to overcome the tavern's unaccountably rude and lax service. Even so, the people keep coming for the glittery setting. **Price range:** Entrees, $21.75–$34. **Meals:** Br, L, D. **Subway:** 6 to 66th St.

Thalia   ☆☆ $$$ NEW AMERICAN
828 Eighth Ave. (at 50th St.)   (212) 399-4444

Thalia is the Muse of comedy, and also a confusing name for a serious restaurant. Executive chef Michael Otsuka practices an intelligent form of fusion cooking, with a strong Asian influence. He has faith in the power of simple ingredients and flavors, and the wit to use them in inventive ways. A spoonful of wasabi granita, cold and crunchy, with a piercing heat, sets off Kumamoto oysters brilliantly. Foie gras fatigue disappears the moment you lay eyes on foie gras mousse, sprinkled with chopped pistachio and accompanied by figs drenched in port. It looks like dessert but it's twice as rich—damnation on a small plate. **Price range:** Entrees, $17–$29. **Meals:** L, D. **Subway:** C, E to 50th St.

Théo   ☆ $$ NEW AMERICAN
325 Spring St. (near Greenwich St.)   (212) 414-1344
Restaurants like Théo serve food, but food is not uppermost on the agenda. The upstairs lounge, with its small glass-tiled bar, inviting couches and slick cocktail list, fills up early in the evening. The dining room, on street level, is cool in a different way. The menu is an easygoing blend of bistro and diner, with some very bright spots more or less canceled out by dull ones. The most appealing dish on the menu is also the most improbable, ravioli stuffed with baked macaroni and cheese. The chef works best in a lighter vein, the prime evidence being a pristine slab of cod so lightly breaded that it would be more accurate to say it was dusted. **Price range:** Entrees, $18–$25. **Meals:** D, LN. **Subway:** 1, 2 to Canal St.

Thom   ☆ $$$ FUSION/NEW AMERICAN
Thompson Hotel, 60 Thompson St. (near Broome St.)   (212) 219-2000
In a stylishly designed boutique hotel, Thom is the place. Thom looks good. The chef, Jonathan Eismann, a model in his spare time, cooks with undeniable panache. The menu is certainly not boring, although Mr. Eismann seems to have a weakness for sweets. Pan-broiled beef fillet, with short ribs braised in cabernet, meets the sweetness challenge and emerges triumphant. When Mr. Eismann hits it, the results can be exciting. Fermented chilies added a subtle fire to shrimp in a thick curry sauce. The pastry chef also comes up with a few winning combinations, like toasted almond anglaise served with a warm plum cake, which is rich and light at the same time. **Price range:** Entrees, $19–$29. **Meals:** D. **Subway:** A, C, E to Canal St.

Tocqueville   ☆☆ $$$$ FRENCH
15 E. 15th St. (between Fifth Ave. and Union Sq. West)   (212) 647-1515
Tocqueville is a quiet haven of good taste, good food and good service. Although tiny, Tocqueville never feels cramped. The spacing between tables is generous, given the floor space, and the service, which could easily feel intrusive and hovering, achieves a laudable transparency. Billy Bi soup, the oddly named classic from France's Atlantic coast, is beyond praise. Desserts do honor to the menu, especially the upside-down banana tart, a small palisade of fat banana chunks encircling a disk of almond shortbread, teamed up with a ball of brown-sugar ice cream. **Price range:** Entrees, $22–$28. **Meals:** L, D. Closed Sun. **Subway:** L, N, Q, R, W, 4, 5, 6 to 14th St.

The Tonic   ☆☆ $$$ NEW AMERICAN
108 W. 18th St. (at Sixth Ave.)   (212) 929-9755
The Tonic serves modern American cuisine in a spacious former saloon with a
dining room on one side and a bar and lounge on the other. The food is appeal-
ing and skillfully executed. The big meat flavor is on display in the Tonic's surf
and turf, a hefty cylinder of roast filet mignon in red wine sauce accompanied
by whipped potatoes swaddling large, very tender pieces of lobster. Duck is
another attractive option. Desserts are hit or miss, but warm banana tarte Tatin
with dark-rum ice cream is simple but beautifully realized. **Price range:** Entrees,
$13–$29. **Meals:** L, D. Closed Sun. **Subway:** 1, 2 to 18th St.

Topaz Thai $25 & Under   THAI
127 W. 56th St. (between Sixth and Seventh Aves.)   (212) 957-8020
This restaurant offers fine Thai cooking. Soups, like the delicious tom kha gai,
made with chicken stock, coconut milk, chili peppers and lime, are particularly
good, as are spicy dishes like the soupy jungle curry made with scallops and
green beans. The restaurant has a peculiar nautical theme courtesy of a previous
tenant—Art Deco paneling, triangular sconces and wooden captain's chairs.
Price range: Entrees, $8–$18. **Meals:** L, D. **Subway:** N, R, Q, W to 57th St.

Town   ☆☆☆ $$$ NEW AMERICAN
Chambers Hotel, 15 W. 56th St. (between. Fifth and Sixth Aves.)
                                                     (212) 582-4445
Town has an unmistakable sense of style. It's a civilized, very adult setting that
suits the chef's elegant, clean cooking. He manages to enliven his dishes with
just the half twist that makes them distinctive, as in a simple roasted skate
served with three sorbet-shaped quenelles: pea-peppermint, apple-miso, and
eggplant with hazelnut oil and quatre-épices. Some dishes are simplicity itself.
A risotto of escargots doused with black truffle broth seems unfair. How can it
fail? It's like having the chef write you a large check. The dessert list is strong,
and one is a showstopper: it starts with a basket of sugar-powdered beignets filled
with molten chocolate. Then comes a perfect frozen dome with a matte-brown
cocoa surface, a chilled version of café brûlot, a flaming liqueur-laced coffee.
Price range: Entrees, $21–$29. **Meals:** L, D. **Subway:** N, R, Q, W to 57th St.

Tribeca Grill   ☆☆ $$$ NEW AMERICAN
375 Greenwich St. (at Franklin St.)   (212) 941-3900
Robert De Niro's first venture into the restaurant business in what the
neighbors sometimes call Bob Row is a cool, casual outpost of modern
American cuisine with an almost constant flow of celebrity guests. And the
food's good. The big, airy space with exposed bricks, colorful banquettes and
comfortable tables centers on a massive handsome mahogany bar. The
beguiling fare remains a steady lure. **Price range:** Entrees, $12–$29.
Meals: Br, L, D. **Subway:** 1, 9 to Franklin St.

Triomphe   ☆☆   **$$$**   FRENCH/NEW AMERICAN
Iroquois Hotel, 49 W. 44th St. (between Fifth and Sixth Aves.) (212) 453-4233
In a city with flash to spare, this restaurant has a rare commodity: charm. And
the food, simple and understated, matches the room. Again and again, Triom-
phe quietly strikes the right note, as with a subtle herb broth that nicely under-
lines the natural sweetness of acorn-squash wontons covered in shavings of
Parmesan cheese. When the main ingredient calls for more, the chef opens up
the flavors. A hefty rib-eye steak comes with fat grilled cepes and a muscular
brandy demi-glace, and a thick slab of salmon gets the works: a caviar-dotted
beurre blanc, a scattering of grilled shrimp and parsnip whipped potatoes.
Price range: Entrees, $23–$32. **Meals:** B, L, D. **Subway:** B, D, F, to 42nd St.

Turkuaz   **$25 & Under**   TURKISH
2637 Broadway (at 100th St.)   (212) 665-9541
The dining room here is draped in billowy fabric so that it resembles an
Ottoman tent. Seat covers give standard restaurant chairs a lush appearance,
and the staff is adorned in traditional Turkish costumes. Cold appetizers are
excellent, and main courses tend to be simple and elementally satisfying, like
beyti kebab, spicy chopped lamb charcoal-grilled with herbs and garlic. Desserts
include a neat variation on rice pudding, served with the top caramelized like
crème brûlée. **Price range:** Entrees, $8.50–$18.50. **Meals:** D.
Subway: 1, 9 to 103rd St.

"21" Club   ☆☆   **$$$$**   AMERICAN
21 W. 52nd St. (between Fifth and Sixth Aves.)   (212) 582-7200
Of all the restaurants in New York City, none has a richer history. American
royalty has been entertaining at "21" for most of this century. The restaurant
continues to be operated like a club where unknowns are led to the farthest din-
ing room as the more favored clients are pampered and petted. Nothing much
else has changed either: the tablecloths are still red and white checked, the toys
are still hanging from the ceiling, and it still looks like the speak-easy it once
was. The menu has been modernized but with mixed results. The basics are still
superb, however. Great steak, rack of lamb, Dover sole, and the "21" burger, and
several traditional desserts such as rice pudding and crème brûlée are all worth-
while. **Price range:** Entrees, $24–$39. **Meals:** L, D. Closed Sun.
Subway: E, F to Fifth Ave.

26 Seats   **$25 & Under**   FRENCH
168 Ave. B. (11th St.)   (212) 677-4787
This sweet little French restaurant is intimate yet relatively comfortable, and
the waitresses are friendly and kind to children. The menu's French country
offerings are both satisfying and a good value, like the pissaladière, a flat, wafer-
thin crusted tart of caramelized onions, made pungent with anchovy fillets and
olives, or the savory garlic sausage paired with boiled potato and hard-boiled

eggs, all dressed in a balsamic vinaigrette. The main courses are well-executed versions of familiar recipes, with the occasional pleasing twist. For dessert, a wedge of apple tart is the best choice. **Price range:** Entrees, $11–$16.50. AE only **Meals:** D. Closed Mon. **Subway:** L to First Ave.

Union Pacific ☆☆☆ $$$$ FRENCH/ASIAN
111 E. 22nd St. (near Park Ave. South)   (212) 995-8500
This is one of the most beautiful, comfortable and soothing environments in Manhattan. A curtain of falling water at the entrance has the cool, calm look of Japan. Service is professional and enthusiastic, and the chef has invented an exciting menu. Despite Asian touches in the main part of the menu, the focus here is largely French. The unusual wine list adds another dimension. Desserts are as interesting as entrees. **Price range:** Prix-fixe and tasting menus, $65–$135, with supplements. **Meals:** L, D. Closed Sun. **Subway:** 6 to 23rd St.

Union Square Café ☆☆ $$$ NEW AMERICAN
21 E. 16th St. (between Fifth Ave. and Union Sq. West)   (212) 243-4020
Union Square's pioneering fusion of fine food and wine, casual atmosphere and stellar service has made it the most influential restaurant of its time in the city, certainly one of the most popular, and a top destination for tourists. The wine list is still outstanding and still full of bargains. Don't miss the signature fried calamari, golden brown, perfectly cooked outside and inside, and nicely comple-mented with an incisive, creamy anchovy mayonnaise. Although there are sev-eral foreign accents heard on the menu, Italian dominates, especially in the pasta dishes, which put many Italian restaurants to shame. Desserts aim for an artful blend of homey and exotic, most memorably in the banana tart with a caramel shellac, a Union Square standby. **Price range:** Entrees, $18.50–$28. **Meals:** L, D. **Subway:** L, N, Q, R, W, 4, 5, 6 to 14th St.

Uskudar $25 & Under TURKISH
1405 Second Ave. (near 73rd St.)   (212) 988-2641
This restaurant is the very model of a successful neighborhood institution, and it has achieved that status without the burgers, pastas and steaks that form the default menu of most local hangouts. The selection of appetizers includes two excellent Middle Eastern spreads: patlican, smoky eggplant mashed with garlic, sesame paste and herbs; and ezme, a blend of tomatoes, onions, parsley and wal-nuts. Uskudar's kebabs are uncommonly juicy, but the best dishes are the stews, like hunkar begendi, a hearty lamb stew. Uskudar makes excellent desserts, especially kadayif, shredded wheat crowned with ground walnuts and drenched in honey. **Price range:** Entrees, $12.95–$15.95. **Meals:** L, D. **Subway:** 6 to 77th St.

Vatan $25 & Under INDIAN/VEGETARIAN
409 Third Ave. (at 29th St.)   (212) 689-5666
This astounding Indian restaurant transports you to a bright, animated Indian village with thatched roofs and artificial banyan trees. Vatan specializes in the

rich, spicy yet subtle vegetarian cuisine of Gujarat. For one price, a parade of little dishes is served, which might include khaman, a delicious fluffy steamed cake of lentil flour with black mustard seeds; delicate little samosas; patrel, taro leaves layered with spicy chickpea paste and steamed, and much more. **Price range:** $19.95. **Meals:** D, LN. Closed Mon. **Subway:** 6 to 28th St.

Verbena ☆ $$$ NEW AMERICAN
54 Irving Pl. (near 17th St.)   (212) 260-5454

The newly remodeled Verbena looks attractive. The tight dining room retains its very adult sense of calm and style, and a cool, breezy and secluded courtyard garden has been created in the back. But dishes take a long time to arrive at the table, and what arrives does not always thrill. The bolder dishes sometimes hit and sometimes miss. The sirloin steak is a remarkably rich, tender cut, beautifully charred outside. Your waiter will ask if you are interested in the baked-to-order Bing cherry upside-down cake. Say yes. **Price range:** Entrees, $14.50–$28. **Meals:** Br, D. **Subway:** L, N, Q, R, W, 4, 5, 6 to 14th St.

Veritas ☆☆☆ $$$$ NEW AMERICAN
43 E. 20th St. (near Park Ave. South)   (212) 353-3700

Small, spare and elegant, Veritas could be called a wine cellar with a restaurant attached, because at Veritas, the wine is more important than the food. The 1,300 entries on its wine list include many rarities at extremely reasonable prices. The room often seems overcrowded, but Veritas offers clean and unfussy food that works well with its wine. Main courses, to suit the powerful wines, are robust, powerful and simple—with surprisingly little red meat on the menu. The intensity does not abate with desserts. Try a startlingly delicious praline parfait with a polished reduction of clementines. **Price range:** Prix-fixe dinner, $62. **Meals:** L, D. Closed Sun. **Subway:** 6 to 23rd St.

Viceversa ☆ $$ ITALIAN
325 W. 51st St. (Between Eighth and Ninth Aves.)   (212) 399-9265

With its crisp earth-colored awnings and gleaming façade, Viceversa (pronounced VEE-chey-VAIR-suh) stands out on one of Manhattan's grungier blocks like a Versace suit. The menu is honest and unpretentious, a solid lineup of mostly northern Italian dishes presented in a perfectly straightforward manner. Casoncelli alla bergamasca deserves star billing in Viceversa's strong ensemble cast of pastas: it is a ravioli filled with chopped veal, crushed amaretti, raisins and Parmesan, then topped with butter, crisped sage leaves and crunchy bits of fried pancetta. **Price range:** Entrees, $16.50–$22.50. **Meals:** L, D. **Subway:** C, E to 50th St.

Virgil's Real BBQ $25 & Under   BARBECUE
152 W. 44th St. (between Broadway and Sixth Ave.)   (212) 921-9494

Virgil's is a wildly popular shrine to barbecue joints around the country. If the food isn't quite authentic, the formula comes close enough and it works. And the place smells great, as any barbecue place should. Highlights on the menu include hush puppies served with a maple syrup butter; smoked Texas links with mustard slaw; barbecued shrimp and Texas red chili with corn bread. For main fare, big barbecue platters carry enticing selections of Owensboro lamb, Maryland ham, Carolina pork shoulder, Texas beef brisket and more. **Price range:** Entrees, $10.95–$18.95. **Meals:** L, D, LN. **Subway:** B, D, F, N, Q, R, S, W, 1, 2, 3, 7, 9 to 42nd St.

Washington Park   ☆☆   **$$$$**   NEW AMERICAN

24 Fifth Ave. (at 9th St.)   (212) 529-4400

Washington Park, with its pale lemon walls, straw-seat bistro chairs and waiters in Thomas Pink checked shirts, takes its casualness very seriously. The sunny, airy surroundings seem perfectly suited to the simple market-inspired cooking. The seasons and the Greenmarket dictate the menu, which changes almost nightly. When things click, they achieve the small-scale perfection that can make minor art seem more satisfying than major art. When the equation doesn't quite work out, the food can seem unremarkable. The dessert menu changes frequently, but brioche pudding with lemon curd and blueberries sails right off the charts. **Price range:** Entrees, $24–$32; tasting menu, $59. **Meals:** D. **Subway:** N, Q, R, W to 8th St.

Wu Liang Ye   **$25 & Under**   CHINESE

338 Lexington Ave. (between 39th and 40th Sts.)   (212) 370-9647
215 E. 86th St. (at Third Ave.)   (212) 534-8899
36 W. 48th St. (between Fifth and Sixth Aves.)   (212) 398-2308

Though each of these branches of a Chinese restaurant chain differs slightly in menu and atmosphere, they all specialize in lively, robust Sichuan dishes, notable for their meticulous preparation. Sliced conch is one of their more unusual dishes, firm, chewy and nutty, served with spicy red oil. Four kinds of dumplings are all delicate and flavorful. **Price range:** $7.50–$20. **Meals:** L, D, LN. **Subway:** Call for directions to each location.

Xunta   **$25 & Under**   SPANISH/TAPAS

174 First Ave. (near 11th St.)   (212) 614-0620

Xunta (pronounced SHOON-tuh) has the authentic feeling of a Spanish tapas bar. It's informal, crowded, smoky and loud, with dozens of tapas. The selection of Spanish wines and sherries is just right. **Price range:** Tapas, $2.75–$16.25. **Meals:** D, LN. **Subway:** L to First Ave.

Yakiniku JuJu   **$25 & Under**   JAPANESE

157 E. 28th St. (between Third and Lexington Aves.)   (212) 684-7830

This small and friendly restaurant specializes in cook-it-yourself shabu-shabu, sukiyaki and Japanese barbecue. Try an appetizer of "salted squid guts," chewy and salty squid cut into cylinders the size of small anchovies and immersed in a pasty liquid; or takoyaki, croquettes stuffed with pieces of octopus and flavored with dried seaweed, ginger and a fruity sauce. The large main courses include yakiniku, in which you cook pieces of meat and vegetables directly on the grill; shabu-shabu, in which you swish the meat and vegetables through boiling broth; and sukiyaki, the traditional Japanese stew. **Price range:** Dinner for two, $30–$46; for four, up to $80. **Meals:** D. **Subway:** 6 to 28th St.

Zarela ☆☆ $$$ MEXICAN/TEX-MEX

953 Second Ave. (between 50th and 51st Sts.)   (212) 644-6740

Bright, bold and raucous as a party, the sort of place that looks like a typical Mexican taquería. Happily, it is not. Zarela Martinez has written several excellent Mexican cookbooks, and she serves some of the city's most exciting and authentic Mexican food. Among the best dishes are a fiery snapper hash, crisp flautas, tamales and fajitas. Good side dishes include creamy rice baked with sour cream, cheddar cheese, corn and poblano chilies, and pozole guisado, in which hominy kernels are sautéed with tomatoes, onions, garlic and jalapeño peppers. **Price range:** Avg. entree, $24. **Meals:** L, D. **Subway:** 6 to 51st St.; E, F to Lexington Ave.

Zipangu ☆ $$$ JAPANESE

71 University Pl. (bet. 10th & 11th Sts.)   (212) 673-0634

Zipangu is an idiosyncratic, even eccentric, modern Japanese restaurant. Zipangu was Marco Polo's name for the mysterious islands we now know as Japan. It has an otherworldly ring to it that suits the restaurant, which has a bar on the street level and two weirdly decorated dining rooms down a steep, narrow flight of stairs. The menu, which straddles at least two styles, is bold, inventive and, in some cases, quite strange. It demands attention, and it gets it with a startling appetizer, monkfish liver worked into a kind of dense custard with tofu, then pressed into a martini glass and topped with a slick of tart ponzu sauce. The rib-eye steak, fork-tender, is outfitted in a ceremonial robe of onion purée mixed with karashi, a hot Japanese mustard. The dessert menu includes unexpected choices like a bracing, ice-cold gelée of ruby red grapefruit and cranberry with a swirl of brandy cream sauce, and coffee is made at the table in what looks like a giant beaker and test tube heated by a Bunsen burner. **Price range:** Entrees, $14–$22; tasting menus, $40–$50. **Meals:** D. Closed Sun. **Subway:** N, R to 8th St.; 6 to Astor Pl.; L, N, Q, R, W, 4, 5, 6 to 14th St.–Union Sq.

Zitoune ☆ $$ MOROCCAN

46 Gansevoort St. (at Greenwich St.)   (212) 675-5224

Zitoune, which is Arabic for olive, is a lively bistro serving updated Moroccan cuisine. The chef may be English, but you'd never guess from the subtle touch he brings to traditional Moroccan tagines, briks, briwats and bsteeyas. Lamb tagine, one of those dishes that simply must be done right at a restaurant like this, is excellent, complexly spiced and cooked nearly to the melting point. Zitoune's best dessert, a made-to-order bsteeya packed with dried fruit and nuts, is worth the extra 20 minutes it requires. **Price range:** Entrees, $8–$20.50. **Meals:** L, D. **Subway:** A, C, E to 14th St.

Zum Schneider $25 & Under   GERMAN
107 Ave. C (at 7th St.)   (212) 598-1098
Essentially an indoor beer garden, Zum Schneider packs young people in
nightly. The simple menu hews closely to the Bavarian formula of wurst, pork
and cabbage, but it has accomplished the unlikely feat of making a German
place cool. Try the pfannkuchen soup, literally pancake soup, a mild beef broth
seasoned only with parsley and a bit of salt and containing slender strips of egg
pancakes, the equivalent of light dumplings. The best of the main courses is a
plump, rosy smoked pork chop. The bar offers a dozen excellent seasonal draft
beers, all German, and 10 more in bottles.
Price range: Entrees, $7–$12, with $3 and $6 appetizer portions.

Zuni $25 & Under   SOUTHWESTERN
598 Ninth Ave. (at 43rd St.)   (212) 765-7626
The original focus at this appealing little restaurant was Southwestern, and the
atmosphere still reflects this, but the current menu is all over the map, with
Southwestern dishes like chili-rubbed rib-eye steak, New Orleans specialties
like jambalaya and geographically indecipherable offerings like sesame-crusted
salmon with mango-and-black-bean salsa and basmati rice. If it's too confusing,
settle for meatloaf and garlic mashed potatoes. It's usually all pretty good.
Price range: Entrees, $7.50–$14.95.

A Guide to Restaurants by Cuisine

AMERICAN
An American
   Place   ☆☆
City Hall ☆☆
Fifty Seven
   Fifty Seven   ☆☆☆
Grange Hall
The Half King
Max SoHa
"21" Club ☆☆

ARGENTINE
Chimichurri Grill

AUSTRALIAN
Eight Mile Creek ☆☆

AUSTRIAN
Cafe Sabarsky ☆☆
Danube   ☆☆☆

BARBECUE
Blue Smoke ☆
Virgil's Real BBQ

BASQUE
Euzkadi

BELGIAN
Cafe de Bruxelles

CAJUN
Bayou

CARIBBEAN
Bambou   ☆☆
Caribbean Spice
Paladar

CHINESE
Big Wong
Congee Village
Dim Sum Go Go   ☆
Evergreen Shanghai
Funky Broome
Goody's
Grand Sichuan
Henry's Evergreen
Joe's Shanghai ☆☆
Mee Noodle Shop

Note: Restaurants in **boldface italics** are Eric Asimov's choices for the best inexpensive
restaurants in New York.

New Green Bo
New York Noodle
    Town ☆☆
Our Place
Pig Heaven
Ping's Seafood ☆☆
Shun Lee Palace ☆☆
Shun Lee West
Wu Liang Ye

CONTINENTAL
Cafe des Artistes
Eleven Madison
    Park ☆☆
One if By Land

DELI
Carnegie Deli
Katz's Deli

DINER
Barking Dog
Empire Diner

DUTCH
NL ☆

EAST EUROPEAN
Danube ☆☆☆

FRENCH
Alain Ducasse ☆☆☆
Alley's End
Alouette
Artisanal ☆☆
Atelier ☆☆
Balthazar ☆☆
Bandol
Barrio ☆
Bayard's ☆☆
Blue Hill ☆☆
Bouley ☆☆☆☆
Bouterin ☆
Brasserie ☆☆
Café Boulud ☆☆☆

Café Loup
Chanterelle ☆☆☆
Chelsea Bistro
    & Bar ☆☆
Chez Josephine ☆☆
Coup ☆
Daniel ☆☆☆☆
D'Artagnan ☆☆
DB Bistro Moderne ☆☆
Fleur de Sel ☆☆
Guastavino's ☆☆
Jarnac ☆
Jean Claude
Jean Georges ☆☆☆☆
Jean-Luc ☆
JoJo ☆☆☆
Jubilee
La Caravelle ☆☆☆
La Côte Basque ☆☆☆
La Grenouille ☆☆☆
Le Bernardin ☆☆☆☆
Le Cirque 2000 ☆☆☆
Le Gigot
Le Périgord
Les Halles Downtown ☆
Lespinasse ☆☆☆☆
Le Tableau
Le Zinc ☆
Le Zoo
Lutèce ☆☆
Marseille ☆☆
Medi ☆
Mercer Kitchen ☆☆
Olica ☆☆☆
Orsay ☆☆
Panaché
Papillon ☆
Paradou
Park Bistro ☆☆☆
Pastis ☆
Payard Pâtisserie ☆☆
Picholine ☆☆☆
Provence ☆
Sono ☆☆

Tocqueville ☆☆
Triomphe ☆☆
Union Pacific ☆☆☆
Virot ☆

GERMAN
Silver Swan

GREEK
Avra ☆
Estiatorio Milos ☆☆
Meltemi
Metsovo
Molyvos ☆☆
Periyali ☆☆☆
Snack

HAMBURGERS
McHale's

INDIAN
Ada ☆☆
Bread Bar at Tabla
Bukhara Grill
Chola ☆☆
Dakshin
Dawat ☆
Mavalli Palace
Mirchi
Mughlai
Pongal
Salaam Bombay ☆☆
Surya ☆☆
Tabla ☆☆☆
Tamarind ☆☆
Vatan

INDONESIAN
Bali Nusa Indah
NL ☆

ITALIAN
Arezzo ☆
Arqua ☆☆

Babbo ☆☆☆
Baldoria ☆
Bar Pitti
Beppe ☆☆
Bice ☆☆
Cafe La Grolla
Campagna ☆☆
Centolire ☆☆
Delmonico's ☆
Esca ☆☆
Fiamma Osteria ☆☆☆
F.Illi Ponte ☆☆
Felidia ☆☆☆
Frank
Gabriel's ☆☆
Gradisca
Il Valentino ☆☆
Il Mulino
'ino
Isola
I Trulli ☆☆
La Locanda
La Nonna ☆
Lentini ☆
Le Cirque 2000 ☆☆☆
Le Zie
Lupa
Max
Max SoHa
Medi ☆
Moda ☆☆
Osteria Del Circo ☆☆
Paola's ☆☆
Peasant ☆
Pepe Verde
Pepolino
Po
Remi ☆☆
Risa
San Domenico
    ☆☆☆

Scalini Fedeli ☆
Supper
Viceversa ☆

JAPANESE
Blue Ribbon Sushi
    ☆☆
Hatsuhana ☆☆
Honmura An ☆☆☆
Jewel Bako
Kai ☆☆
Katsu-Hama
Komodo
Kuruma Zushi ☆☆☆
Marumi
Nadaman
    Hakubai ☆☆
Next Door Nobu
    ☆☆☆
Nobu ☆☆☆
Otabe ☆☆
Soba Nippon
Sono ☆☆
Sushi Yasuda ☆☆☆
Yakiniku JuJu
Zipangu ☆

KOREAN
Cho Dang Gol ☆☆
Do Hwa
Emo's
Han Bat
Han Sung Garden
Hangawi ☆☆
Kang Suh ☆☆
Kori
Mandoo Bar
Muzy

LATIN AMERICAN
Asia de Cuba ☆

Boca Chica
Calle Ocho ☆
Chicama ☆☆
Chimichurri Grill
Churrascaria
    Plataforma ☆☆
Circus ☆☆
Cocina Cuzco
Cuba Libre
El Fogon
Esperanto
Flor's Kitchen
Good
Havana NY
Komodo
La Fonda Boricua
National Cafe
Patria ☆☆☆

MEDITERRANEAN
Acquario
Commissary ☆
Gus's Figs Bistro
    & Bar
Lavagna
Layla
Marseille ☆☆
Nick & Toni's ☆☆
Olives ☆
Picholine ☆☆☆
Savoy ☆☆
Tappo ☆

MEXICAN/TEX-MEX
Café Frida
Casa Mexicana
Gabriela's
Hell's Kitchen
Los Dos Rancheros
La Palapa
Maya ☆☆

Note: Restaurants in **boldface italics** are Eric Asimov's choices for the best inexpensive restaurants in New York.

Mesa Grill ☆☆
Mexicana Mama
Paladar
Rinconcito Mexicano
Rocking Horse
Rosa Mexicano ☆☆
Taco Taco
Zarela ☆☆

MIDDLE EASTERN
Cookies and Couscous
Layla
Moustache
Tagine
Turkuaz
Zitoune ☆

NEW AMERICAN
Alias
Alley's End
An American Place
   ☆☆
Aureole ☆☆
Beacon ☆☆
Bread Bar at Tabla
Bright Food Shop
Butter ☆
Chat 'n Chew
City Hall ☆☆
Commissary ☆
Compass ☆☆
Cooke's Corner
Coup ☆
Craft ☆☆☆
Craftbar
Della Femina ☆
Delmonico's ☆
The Dining Room
   ☆☆
District ☆
Etats-Unis ☆☆
First
The Four
   Seasons ☆☆☆

Gotham Bar
   and Grill ☆☆☆
Gramercy
   Tavern ☆☆☆
Heartbeat ☆☆
Icon ☆☆
Ilo ☆☆☆
Inside
Irving on Irving
Jack Rose ☆
Jane ☆
Jean Georges ☆☆☆☆
Joe Allen
Josie's
Judson Grill ☆☆☆
Little Dove ☆☆
Lotus ☆
Man Ray ☆
March ☆☆☆
Meet ☆
Merge
Michael's ☆☆
92 ☆
Odeon ☆☆
Olica ☆☆☆
Ouest ☆☆
Park Ave. Cafe ☆☆
Park View ☆☆
Patroon ☆
Red Bar Restaurant ☆
The Red Cat ☆
Redeye Grill ☆
Savoy ☆☆
Screening Room ☆☆
71 Clinton Fresh
   Food ☆☆
The Tasting Room ☆
Tavern on the Green ☆
Thalia ☆☆
Théo
The Tonic ☆☆
Thom
Town ☆☆☆
Tribeca Grill ☆☆

Triomphe ☆☆
21 Club ☆☆
Union Square
   Cafe ☆☆
Verbena ☆
Veritas ☆☆☆
Washington Park

PAN-ASIAN
Asia de Cuba ☆
Mi ☆☆
Pop ☆
Ruby Foo's ☆☆
Tabla ☆☆☆
TanDa ☆

PAN-LATIN
Boca Chica
Bolivar ☆☆
Calle Ocho ☆
Esperanto
Patria ☆☆☆
Sabor
Suba ☆

PORTUGUESE
Luzia's
Pao
Pico ☆☆☆

RUSSIAN
Firebird ☆☆
Petrossian ☆☆

SANDWICHES
aKa Café
Bread
Paradou

SCANDINAVIAN
Aquavit ☆☆☆
Christer's ☆☆
Good World Bar
   & Grill

SEAFOOD
Aquagrill ☆☆
Atlantic Grill ☆
Avra ☆
Blue Water Grill ☆
Bongo
Dock's ☆
Esca ☆☆
Estiatorio Milos ☆☆
Le Bernardin ☆☆☆☆
Manhattan Ocean
   Club ☆☆
Maritime ☆
Meltemi
Oceana ☆☆☆
Sea Grill ☆☆

SOUTHERN
Amy Ruth's
Bayou
Emily's
Hog Pit
Miss Maude's
Sylvia's

SOUTHWESTERN
Mesa Grill ☆☆

SPANISH
El Cid
Euzkadi
El Fogon
Meigas ☆☆
Solera ☆☆
Suba ☆
Xunta

STEAKHOUSE
Bistro Le Steak
Carne
Churrascaria
   Plataforma ☆☆
Frank's ☆
Jack Rose ☆
Michael Jordan's ☆☆
Palm
Smith &
   Wollensky ☆☆
Soho Steak
Strip House ☆

SUSHI
Blue Ribbon Sushi ☆☆
Hatsuhana ☆☆
Jewel Bako

Kuruma Zushi ☆☆☆
Marumi
Sugiyama ☆☆
Sushi Yasuda ☆☆☆

THAI
Holy Basil
Little Basil
Pam Real Thai Food
Royal Siam
Topaz Thai

TURKISH
The Sultan
Turkuaz
Uskudar

VEGETARIAN
Hangawi ☆☆
Mavalli Palace
Pongal

VIETNAMESE
Cyclo
Le Colonial ☆☆
Nam
Nha Trang

Index